# The Legal Relationship between Present and Future Generations

Ammar Bustami

# The Legal Relationship between Present and Future Generations

## An Intertemporal Perspective on Intergenerational Equity

Springer

Ammar Bustami
Tostedt, Niedersachsen, Germany

ISBN 978-3-032-03344-4 ISBN 978-3-032-03345-1 (eBook)
https://doi.org/10.1007/978-3-032-03345-1

This work was supported by the University of Hamburg by means of the Open Access Funds.



This Springer imprint is published by the registered company Springer Nature Switzerland AG
The registered company address is: Gewerbestrasse 11, 6330 Cham, Switzerland

*For Present and Future Generations of the Palestinian People*

# Preface

When the first idea of this book was developed in 2018, as an exposé to my underlying PhD thesis, some members of the present generation have not yet been born. Other members of the present generation have died in the meantime. The "present generation" and "future generations", however, as I understand these terms in this book, have not (essentially) changed in these seven years. It is still the (overall) same present generation that owes certain duties to the (overall) same future generations. Despite this continuity, the subject matter of the book and its respective object of research *have* further developed between 2018 and 2025.

On the one hand, there have been developments in the realm of (international) environmental law. In order to name but a few: New assessments of climate scientists render the achievement of the Paris emission targets (Article 2(1): "to limit the temperature increase to 1.5 °C above pre-industrial level") most improbable. Several Conferences of the Parties of the UN climate protection regime have taken place—most of them have disappointed proponents of the climate justice movement. And maybe most importantly for this book: More and more climate litigation proceedings have been initiated before several courts and human rights bodies on the national, regional and international level—many of them also in the name of future generations.

It has been particularly challenging to stay ahead of these ongoing developments in today's climate litigation. Many of the proceedings that I analysed in my PhD thesis have now reached next process stages, which I had to update for the publication of this book. Nonetheless, every book has a specific editorial deadline or date of last update—so has this one: in January 2025. Consequently, there will naturally be further and newer developments after this deadline that I could not take into account. Most importantly, two major international courts—the International Court of Justice and the Inter-American Court of Human Rights—will render their long-awaited advisory opinions on questions of climate protection in the course of this year. While these advisory proceedings are addressed in this book, the actual findings of the courts will have to be analysed and discussed on another occasion and in another place.

On the other hand, my personal perspective on the future of international law has drastically changed during these seven years. I am hopefully not spoiling too much of the book by foreshadowing that I attempt to take a glance at the future development of international law in the book second part. While writing the book, this perspective was still largely positive. I saw the progressive developments international law and international institutions have made in the last decades and I thought—in application of my modified doctrine of intertemporal law—that these progressive developments of substance and structures of international law will continue. I thought that these developments will also have a corresponding positive impact on the future evolution of intergenerational equity.

In the meantime, between the finalisation of my underlying PhD project in 2022 and the publication of this book, it seems that the world has changed, potentially with important impacts on the international legal order as a whole. Some of the underlying events challenged my perspective on present international law and its potential futures. In the following, I would like to illustrate some of these developments. I leave it to the readers' interpretation whether I was too optimistic or just naïve at the time of writing the book, or whether the world *has* actually changed this fast in the last years.

Russia's invasion in Ukraine in 2022 was one such disruption of the international legal order with repercussions until today. Russia's violation of the prohibition of the use of force has been perceived in Europe as a shocking event. For the Eurocentric perspective on the world—which I also had unconsciously taken before—the Russian aggression came as a breach of a taboo. This perception is regularly emphasised—notwithstanding the day-to-day reality of wars and armed conflicts world-wide, and even the considerable track record of *ius ad bellum* violations by European States and the US in the past decades. The immense repercussions of this war include, *inter alia*, a massive return to military build-up worldwide, at least in European States, and a resurgence of the old idea of deterrence through armament. This goes hand in hand with a militarisation of public discourse in many societies and a ridiculing of peace and cooperation approaches in diplomacy and foreign policy. Beyond this hardening of the front lines between Ukraine, the USA, Europe and their allies on the one hand, and Russia, China and their allies on the other hand, there is a more complex multipolarisation of international relations with more and more States of the Global South that become self-confident as independent players. These new actors do not want to ally themselves to one side, and they are more and more demanding an actual application of equality of States without the hegemony of but a few actors.

This complex situation was further met with developments in 2023 and 2024 that profoundly damaged the reputation and credibility of international law in general and the proclaimed universality of human rights law in particular: Following the attacks of Hamas and other armed groups from the Gaza strip on Israel's south, the latter reacted with a massive military invasion in the Gaza strip and a disproportionate warfare, not only against armed groups but against the whole civilian population in Gaza. The accusations against Israel and its military range from war crimes and crimes against humanity to the crime of genocide committed against the Palestinian people in Gaza. The accusation of a genocide is currently heard before the International Court of Justice since January 2024, and the Court considers this accusation in its provisional measures decisions to be plausible. Despite the most probable violations of international humanitarian and human rights law, Israel's allies have proclaimed their mostly unconditional support for Israel in its alleged ongoing self-defence for more than a year now. Although a vast majority of UN member States has repeatedly voiced strong concerns with Israel's war in Gaza in resolutions in the UN General Assembly and the Security Council, the unwavering support of Israel by States like the US and Germany contributes to the ongoing suffering and death of the Palestinian civilian population. All this has led to increasing reproaches by States in the Global South vis-à-vis the apparent double standards in the application of human rights and international law, particularly by States in the Global North.

These examples of a continuous weakening of international law and its structures are certainly not an exhaustive list, as other events could certainly be added. Also, some overall tendencies seem to point into a general return to nationalism and isolationism. Extremist parties and politicians are on the rise in many democratic States and a backlash on multilateralism and universal human rights standards can be observed world-wide—the second Trump presidency being just the most recent example.

The foregoing developments paint a bleak picture of the future of international law and international cooperation. Of course, it is possible that humanity and its institutions will still find means to overcome the aforementioned damages to the international system. And certainly, it also depends on the perspective one takes on certain developments: Others may have a much more optimistic look at the world and its future or at least remain hopeful for positive change despite such disturbing developments. Possibly, the recent backlashes are not more than a temporary low point of international cooperation. Again others might not perceive the aforementioned events as *particularly* disturbing, as they suffered from oppression and double standards of international law for a long time. Perhaps, in a few years or decades from today, historians might give an analysis why the current crisis was a logical interim phase before a return to a system of cooperation.

I take certain hope from these alternative points of view. I take this hope also from the sheer necessities the world community faces with view to global catastrophes and challenges—such as climate change, biodiversity loss and massive consumption, but also immense poverty, the oppression of vulnerable groups and the torture, rape and killing of civilians in wars and conflicts.

Eventually, it is no actual alternative for me to fall into despair or become indifferent to the injustices of the world. It would be even more unjust with view to the many living beings on Earth who did not contribute to the disastrous state of our world today. Particularly these vulnerable beings merit hope and action for a better future—be it today's children, many people living in the Global South, all animals of the world or all future generations of people and animals alike. Beyond this, it is certainly easier to stay hopeful, if one attempts to contribute to a positive change of one's own society, the relationship with other living beings and a more solidary treatment of the particularly vulnerable all over the world and all over different species.

For these reasons, I hope that this book will at least be a small contribution to a future positive change of international law that takes into account the perspective of future generations when deciding about their future present.

Tostedt, Germany
Ammar Bustami

# Acknowledgements

This book is based on a PhD project that started in 2018 in Trier (Germany). It is probably just as clichéd as it is true that this PhD journey would not have been possible without many companions on the way who helped me through the different phases of writing a PhD—from the initial enthusiasm over the interim despair and almost-resignation up to the final sprint when the journey's end seemed near. I would like to thank all of these important persons, my supervisors, colleagues, friends and family, for their support on this way.

I have the impression that it is usual to *end* the acknowledgements with a listing of the persons in one's private life, including one's parents. I would, however, like to speak of these two in the *beginning*, as I am aware of the gratitude I owe them for their irreplaceable support in my life. My parents, Eman and Hatem, have enabled my journey in many ways. On the one hand, they have supported and encouraged me during this long time, often asking how my work was going and even taking some substantive interest in the theoretical mind games of intergenerational scenarios. On the other hand, I am fully aware of the fact that educational and academic success is still dependent to a large degree on the financial, cultural and academic background of one's parents—at least in Germany. I am therefore very grateful and I try to remain humble with view to my own success. I would probably not have been able to begin or finish my journey if it were not for my parents who always had my academic and professional success in mind.

Notwithstanding this, there have been many other persons who particularly supported me in the years between 2018 and 2022. Above all, I would like to express my gratitude for this time to my PhD supervisor, Prof. Dr. Alexander Proelß, who always was approachable for scholarly exchange and any concerns during the PhD project. As my superior at the university, both in Trier and Hamburg, he always treated his research associates fairly and gave them the necessary leeway to realise their own projects, be it other publications or passionate teaching and qualification at the university. Last but not least, I am very grateful for the opportunity he offered me and my colleagues to follow him as research associates when he changed universities from Trier to Hamburg in 2018.

Getting back to this beginning of the journey in Trier, I thus only stayed a short time for my PhD project at my alma mater after finishing my studies there. Yet, this time, as well as my studies, was an essential step on the journey, as I was able to start it surrounded by my best friends in a beautiful and ancient city close to nature. I would thus like to thank my Trier flat mates and my friends, particularly my friend Tina and my initial PhD colleagues Alexander and Matthias who I had the pleasure to work with at the University of Trier during these first months and who have remained an important source of support during my further journey.

After moving to Hamburg, I had the chance to work and write my thesis in a great and supportive team at our chair of international law of the sea and international environmental law. I much enjoyed the fruitful teamwork in our many chair tasks—from teaching students to qualifying our own teaching skills, from preparing lectures to organising and attending conferences. But beyond these work-related issues, I am very grateful to my colleagues for a supportive and open-minded environment for our respective PhD projects. This also includes very helpful proof-readings and comments of parts of the thesis in the final phase before its submission. Thank you, Valentin, Julian, Alina, Felix, Nassim, Rob, Anita and Deborah as well as my PhD and teaching colleagues from other chairs. Particularly, Prof. Dr. Valentin Schatz was always a reliable and supportive source of institutional knowledge as he finished his PhD journey a year before me.

Some of the other colleagues include our student assistants at the chair, some of whom have been just as supportive: for instance, Rahel and Emma who helped me with some smaller or bigger research issues; Torben and Daniel who helped me with some structural issues in my Citavi project. Most of all, I would however like to express my gratitude to Hanna who not only developed our chair-intern Citavi citation style, but who also emerged to an absolute Citavi professional in the meantime, able to help with all complicated questions in order to bring order to some footnote chaos. Thank you that I was even able to contact you for the most recent adaptations of my citation style to Springer requirements!

Another source of support during my PhD journey have been the many occasions on scholarly exchange about the topic—from the regular chair PhD seminars to external conferences and workshops. A few months before the submission of the thesis, I had the opportunity to participate in a very fruitful workshop on "Longtermism and the Law" in Hamburg, in which I was able to present and discuss my research results with an international audience. This helped a lot shaping the final chapters and it broadened my horizon on future food for thought and necessary further research. I would therefore also like to thank the conveners and participants of this workshop. To briefly name just two examples: After another input on longtermism and animal law, I came to the conclusion that the interspecies perspective on rights and environmental degradation still requires further consideration in the future. Second, an interesting exchange with another presenter, Daniel Bertram, triggered some additional thoughts and words on intergenerational litigation and extratemporal jurisdiction, mentioned in the book.

Getting to the actual end of my PhD journey, my gratitude of course also goes to the members of my examination committee in November 2023 for their very helpful remarks and the most interesting and thought-provoking discussion during the oral defence of my thesis—Prof. Dr. Armin Hatje, Prof. Dr. Markus Kotzur and Prof. Dr. Alexander Proelß.

With regard to the present open access publication of my revised and updated work, I would also like to thank the University of Hamburg for its financial support by means of the Open Access Funds.

Last, but not (at all!) least, I would like to express my deepest and most cordial gratitude to my PhD tandem partner and friend, Verena Kahl. Without Verena and her continuous and ongoing support, I would probably have abandoned the project during the most difficult hours. Verena always offered me helpful advice and profound substantive feedback and criticism on most of my chapters. I could not have matched with a more qualified, sensitive and supportive tandem partner than with her. This also follows from her own professional and academic background, having herself recently submitted her PhD thesis on the right to a safe climate, in which she takes a holistic approach to climate justice that includes, *inter alia*, "present and future generations of allkind". Thank you, Verena—and I am looking forward to browse your very own published book soon!

Finally, I would like to extend my thanks to all of the other important persons in my life. They have spent me comfort in difficult phases of the journey, including the many years of pandemic lockdown and isolation. Particularly, Patrick has challenged my perspective on academic scholarship and privileges but also intensely supported my further path until the finalisation of "that weird long essay". I am furthermore grateful for the support of my still unmentioned friends and family members—for instance: my sisters and brothers Zina, Dina, Nadia, Susanne, Christian and Hussam (some of whom regularly asking me when there will finally be a "lawyer in the family"), my French host-family, particularly Aurora (who often discussed the rights of future generations from a philosophical perspective with me), my friends Tessa and Yasmin (who share my concern for victims of environmental degradation, human rights oppression and war) and Jonas (my longest friend and co-author of another—even more fantasy-like—book project than this one).

Thank you to all of you!

**Competing Interests** The author has no competing interests to declare that are relevant to the content of this manuscript.

# Contents

# List of Abbreviations

| | |
|---|---|
| 1975 Statute of the River Uruguay | Statute of the River Uruguay between the Government of the Eastern Republic of Uruguay and the Government of the Argentine Republic |
| 1977 Treaty concerning the Gabčíkovo-Nagymaros System | Treaty between the Hungarian People's Republic and the Czechoslovak Socialist Republic concerning the Construction and Operation of the Gabčíkovo-Nagymaros System of Locks |
| Aarhus Convention | Convention on Access to Information, Public Participation in Decision-making and Access to Justice in Environmental Matters |
| ACHPR | African Commission on Human and Peoples' Rights |
| ACHR | American Convention on Human Rights |
| AI | Artificial Intelligence |
| ARSIWA = Articles on State Responsibility | Draft Articles on the Responsibility of States for Internationally Wrongful Acts |
| Banjul Charter | African Charter on Human and Peoples' Rights |
| Basic Law of Germany | Constitution of the Federal Republic of Germany |
| Brundtland Report | Report of the World Commission on Environment and Development |
| CBD | Convention on Biological Diversity |
| CBDR | Common But Differentiated Responsibilities |
| CCLD | Climate Change Litigation Databases |
| CESCR | Committee on Economic, Social and Cultural Rights |
| CITES | Convention on International Trade in Endangered Species of Wild Fauna and Flora |
| CJEU | Court of Justice of the European Union |
| Constitution of Norway | Constitution of the Kingdom of Norway |
| COP | Conference of the Parties |

| | |
|---|---|
| CRC | Committee on the Rights of the Child |
| CSD | Commission on Sustainable Development |
| ECHR | (European) Convention for the Protection of Human Rights and Fundamental Freedoms |
| ECOSOC | United Nations Economic and Social Council |
| ECtHR | European Court of Human Rights |
| EIA | Environmental impact assessment |
| Escazú Agreement | Regional Agreement on Access to Information, Public Participation and Justice in Environmental Matters in Latin America and the Caribbean |
| EU Charter of Fundamental Rights | Charter of Fundamental Rights of the European Union |
| EU | European Union |
| European Commission | EU |
| Friendly-Relations Declaration | Declaration on Principles of International Law concerning Friendly Relations and Co-operation among States in accordance with the Charter of the UN |
| GHG | Greenhouse Gas |
| GPE | Global Pact for the Environment |
| Gt | Gigatons |
| HLPFSD | High-Level Political Forum on Sustainable Development |
| HRC | Human Rights Committee |
| IACHR | Inter-American Court of Human Rights |
| IAComHR | Inter-American Commission on Human Rights |
| ICCPR | International Covenant on Civil and Political Rights |
| ICESCR | International Covenant on Economic, Social and Cultural Rights |
| ICJ Statute | Statute of the International Court of Justice |
| ICJ | International Court of Justice |
| IDI | Institut de Droit International |
| ILA New Delhi Declaration | ILA New Delhi Declaration of Principles of International Law Relating to Sustainable Development |
| ILA Sofia Guiding Statements | ILA Sofia Guiding Statements on the Judicial Elaboration of the 2002 New Delhi Declaration |
| ILA | International Law Association |
| ILC | International Law Commission |
| IPBES | Intergovernmental Platform on Biodiversity and Ecosystem Services |
| IPCC | Intergovernmental Panel on Climate Change |

| | |
|---|---|
| IUCN | International Union for Conservation of Nature and Natural Resources |
| Kyoto Protocol | Kyoto Protocol to the United Nations Framework Convention on Climate Change |
| Moon Agreement | Agreement Governing the Activities of States on the Moon and Other Celestial Bodies |
| NGO (pl.: NGOs) | Non-governmental organisation(s) |
| OHCHR | Office of the High Commissioner for Human Rights |
| Protocol of San Salvador | Additional Protocol to the ACHR in the Area of Economic, Social and Cultural Rights |
| Protocol to the Espoo Convention | Protocol on Strategic Environmental Assessment to the Convention on Environmental Impact Assessment in a Transboundary Context |
| Revised Arab Charter | Revised Arab Charter on Human Rights |
| Rio Declaration | Rio Declaration on Environment and Development |
| Rome Statute | Rome Statute of the International Criminal Court |
| SDGs | Sustainable Development Goals |
| SIDS | Small Island Developing States |
| Stockholm Declaration | Declaration of the United Nations Conference on the Human Environment |
| Trusteeship Agreement | Trusteeship Agreement for the Territory of Nauru |
| TWAIL | Third World Approaches to International Law |
| UK | United Kingdom |
| UN Charter | Charter of the UN |
| UN Guiding Principles | Guiding Principles on Business and Human Rights |
| UN Watercourses Convention | UN Convention on the Law of Non-navigational Uses of International Watercourses |
| UN | United Nations |
| UNCCD | UN Convention to Combat Desertification in those Countries Experiencing Serious Drought and/or Desertification, Particularly in Africa |
| UNCED = Rio Conference = Earth Summit | UN Conference on Environment and Development |
| UNCLOS | United Nations Convention on the Law of the Sea |
| UNCSD = Rio+20 | UN Conference on Sustainable Development |
| UNEA | United Nations Environment Assembly |
| UNECE Water Convention | Convention on the Protection and use of transboundary waters and international Lakes |
| UNEP | United Nations Environment Programme |
| UNESCO Declaration | UNESCO Declaration on the Responsibilities of the Present Generations Towards Future Generations |

| | |
|---|---|
| UNESCO | UN Educational, Scientific and Cultural Organization |
| UNFCCC | UN Framework Convention on Climate Change |
| UNGA | UN General Assembly |
| UNSG | UN Secretary-General |
| US | United States |
| USA | United States of America |
| VCLT | Vienna Convention on the Law of Treaties |
| WCED | World Commission on Environment and Development |
| Whaling Convention | International Convention for the Regulation of Whaling |
| WHO | World Health Organization |
| WMO | World Meteorological Organization |
| World Heritage Convention | Convention Concerning the Protection of the World Cultural and Natural Heritage |
| WTO Agreement | Agreement Establishing the World Trade Organization |
| WTO | World Trade Organization |

# List of Figures

# Chapter 1
# Introduction

> *"If you travel back into your own past, that destination becomes your future, and your former present becomes the past, which can't now be changed by your new future."—Professor Hulk / Bruce Banner, 'The Avengers: Endgame', 2019.*
>
> *"If time travel is possible, where are the tourists from the future?"—Stephen Hawking, 'A Brief History of Time', 1988.*

Imagine it is the year 2100 on planet Earth…

*There is still human life on Earth but it has dramatically changed since the beginning of the twenty-first century.*[1] *Exponential advances in computing powers have allowed for an immense progress in many scientific areas, leading to positive technological innovation as well as more harmful developments. The implantation and integration of complex and sophisticated devices within the human body have resulted in a form of "transhumanism", for instance by successfully combatting disease, enhancing human senses and increasing the average life expectancy in many parts of the world. Artificial intelligence ('AI') has largely surpassed actual human intelligence, so that almost every high-level policy and business decision is directly or indirectly taken by sentient robots. These advances in AI have also allowed for a variety of scientific discoveries that go beyond the comprehension of human beings who increasingly depend on the super power of these AI entities. Overall, ultra-fast, ultra-intelligent machines and virtual entities have an extreme influence on world affairs in 2100.*

*Due to the increasing automation of most production processes, the world of labour has completely changed. In the year 2100, some sectors, such as manufacturing, are almost completely automatised and occupied by robots, so that many jobs have become redundant and unemployment has increased. At the same time, human employment in other, partly new, sectors has also increased. While the tremendous*

[1] The following paragraphs are a thought experiment and a fictional illustration of some aspects of how life on Earth might look like in the year 2100. The exemplary descriptions are based, *inter alia*, on Kaku (2011); Kaku (2015); Future Timeline Community (2024).



A. Bustami, *The Legal Relationship between Present and Future Generations*,
https://doi.org/10.1007/978-3-032-03345-1_1

*technological developments have contributed to higher human wealth for some parts of the world, these innovations and the extractivist ideology of the beginning twenty-first century have simultaneously aggravated inequalities and injustice within societies and globally. In reaction to this exacerbation of inequalities, the global economic system has adapted. In light of negative ecological impacts, resource scarcity and unequal distribution as well as global demographic trends, the system of turbo-capitalism that dominated large parts of the twentieth and of the early twenty-first century has proven unsuitable to address these challenges. Consequently, the predominant endless consumer culture and traditional free market capitalism have collapsed in the middle of the twenty-first century and were replaced by a new economic order that started to focus more on regionalism and a sustainable use of the remaining resources. Despite these promising developments, the twenty-first century has also seen wars as resource scarcity, environmental degradation and loss of living environment for millions of people have triggered regional as well as large-scale conflicts. Technological innovation has not only brought about positive progress but has also facilitated even more disastrous means of warfare: autonomous weapon systems, sophisticated cyberwarfare, the use of AI and biological and chemical warfare as well as nuclear proliferation.*

*Beyond these military threats to the international community, the most dramatic changes in the twenty-first century have occurred with regard to the global environment, particularly the exacerbation of climate change and the loss of biodiversity and ecosystems. Although the international community slowly steered onto a path of reducing greenhouse gas emissions from the 2020s onwards, past and additional emissions from the 2020s have still remained on an intermediate level causing additional global warming. This led to an increase of the global average temperature of around 2.0 °C by the mid-21st century and around 3.0 °C in the year 2100 compared to the period of 1850-1900.*[2] *Many land areas have become uninhabitable for human beings and other species due to temperature increases between 5 and 6.5 °C.*[3] *The frequency and intensity of hot extremes, marine heatwaves, heavy precipitation, regional agricultural and ecological droughts, intense tropical cyclones and the reduction of Arctic sea ice and permafrost have increased with*

[2]The following description of a fictional emission scenario is mainly based on the Working Group I contribution to the most recent Assessment Report of the Intergovernmental Panel on Climate Change ('IPCC'): IPCC (2021a). Therein, five illustrative scenarios attempt to cover the range of possible future developments of climate change, see IPCC (2021b), pp. 12–13. For the fictional description in this introduction, the author chooses the scenario with intermediate GHG emissions (SSP2-4.5), which largely exceeds the envisaged 1.5 °C and even the 2.0 °C path of the Paris Agreement, but does not reach the extreme scenarios of high emissions with between 2.8 to 5.7 °C increase of global surface temperature averaged compared to 1850–1900, cf. ibid., pp. 14–15. For a comparable categorisation in eight scenarios, see also IPCC (2022d), pp. 25–27. The following thought experiment of a time travel to the year 2100 thus assumes that the projected developments in the SSP2-4.5 scenario will come true. This does not deny the probabilities of even more extreme scenarios. Generally, on the methodology of global environmental scenarios, see Lucas et al. (2019), p. 488.

[3]Cf. IPCC (2019), p. 9.

*every 0.5 °C of global warming.*[4] *For instance, in 2100, hot temperature extremes occur around six times as often over land and they are around 3 °C hotter on average than in a climate without human influence.*[5]

*The rise of temperature to a global average of 3 °C in 2100 has triggered several disastrous effects on its way. The capacity of ocean and land carbon sinks has gradually decreased parallel to increasing $CO_2$ emissions in the twenty-first century.*[6] *Simultaneously, certain developments have had effects on the global climate system that are irreversible for centuries.*[7] *This includes changes in the global ocean temperature and deep ocean acidification as well as global mean sea level rise, which has reached around 0.7 metres in the year 2100.*[8] *Further, permafrost thaw in the Greenland Ice Sheet and the West Antarctic Ice Sheet in the course of the twenty-first century have caused irreversible loss of permafrost carbon.*[9] *The ongoing deforestation of the Amazon rainforest in the first half of the twenty-first century has exceeded a critical threshold, which has caused pronounced forest dieback, again destroying one of the most important carbon sinks.*[10]

*While the effects of climate change vary strongly from one region to the other, many regions of the Earth are affected to some degree.*[11] *Due to their lower coping capacities, developing countries are more vulnerable to these impacts of climate change.*[12] *Particularly, hurricanes and tropical cyclones have repeatedly struck States like the Philippines, Pakistan and Bangladesh; other States, such as Myanmar or Puerto Rico, were so strongly affected by exceptional and deadly catastrophes that they have been impaired on a long-term basis.*[13] *However, industrialised States have also increasingly been affected by extreme weather events, such as large forest fires that repeatedly caused extreme destruction of land, e.g., in Australia or the United States of America ('USA').*[14] *Extreme heatwaves of around 3 °C above average have also repeatedly struck European States, particularly in the South.*[15]

---

[4] IPCC (2021b), pp. 15–19.

[5] See also on other weather extremes, ibid., pp. 18–19.

[6] As to this effect, see ibid., pp. 19–21.

[7] For an overview, see Lee et al. (2021), pp. 633–635.

[8] IPCC (2021b), p. 21.

[9] Ibid.

[10] Hoegh-Guldberg et al. (2018), p. 263.

[11] See also IPCC (2019), p. 17.

[12] Eckstein et al. (2021), p. 5. On the inequalities of the effects of climate change, see also Human Rights Council (2019, paras. 11–15).

[13] Eckstein et al. (2019), pp. 9–10.

[14] On Australia in 2019–2020, see, e.g., Green (2020). On extreme heat waves and fires in North America in 2021, see, e.g., Warburton and Olmos (2021).

[15] On extreme heat waves in Europe in 2021 and 2022, see, e.g., The Guardian (2021); Demony and Pereira (2022).

*These extreme weathers have significantly increased in frequency and intensity during the first half of the twenty-first century.*[16]

*Indirect effects of global warming also impacted human civilisation: Exceeding 1.5 °C has led to much more human vector-borne diseases due to the spread of mosquitos in other parts of the world.*[17] *Hundreds of millions of people have additionally become at risk of hunger and more than two billion people are deprived of access to water as a result of climate change.*[18] *The continuing decrease of ecosystem quality is also unequally distributed among different regions of the world and among different segments of society.*[19] *All of these impacts of climate change have led to an exacerbation of poverty and inequality between different regions and people of the world. Several hundreds of millions of people have been pushed to poverty, particularly in the Global South.*[20] *Many of these pressures on the populations in affected States led to an extreme increase of environmentally induced migration and displacement in the middle of the twenty-first century.*[21] *Particularly, tropical populations have been forced to move great distances, which again intensified the socio-economic crisis due to higher population densities.*[22] *The establishment of space settlements by the mid-21st century has not been able to deal with this loss of inhabitable regions on Earth.*

*Additionally, biodiversity and ecosystem functions and services have deteriorated worldwide,*[23] *many of these contributions of nature being irreplaceable.*[24] *Human activities since the 1970s have contributed to further decline of biodiversity and have led to global extinction of more than one million species in the twenty-first century.*[25] *The main drivers of this mass extinction were immense changes in land and sea use, exploitation of organisms, climate change, pollution and invasion of alien species.*[26] *Climate change has not only contributed to biodiversity loss in general, but it has also exacerbated the impacts of the other drivers, leading to further chain reactions.*[27] *These developments have further deteriorated global food security and have undermined the resilience of agricultural systems worldwide.*[28] *Further*

[16] See IPCC (2019), pp. 14–16.

[17] World Health Organization (2014), p. 47; Hoegh-Guldberg et al. (2018), p. 241.

[18] See Human Rights Council (2019, para. 9 with further references).

[19] IPBES (2019), p. 10.

[20] See Human Rights Council (2019, para. 13).

[21] IPCC (2019), p. 18, 23. See also Hoegh-Guldberg et al. (2018), pp. 244–245. For a legal assessment of environmentally induced migration, see Palladino (2014).

[22] Hoegh-Guldberg et al. (2018), p. 245.

[23] Generally, see Stoett et al. (2019).

[24] IPBES (2019), p. 10.

[25] Ibid., pp. 11–12.

[26] Ibid., pp. 12–14.

[27] Ibid., 13, 16. See also IPCC (2022b), p. 11.

[28] IPBES (2019), p. 12.

*environmental degradation has had comparably dramatic effects on air quality, land resources, freshwater and ocean ecosystems.*[29]

*Some of these irreversible developments have exceeded climatic tipping points and other critical thresholds,*[30] *which have triggered partly abrupt changes in the global as well as regional ecosystems, further exacerbated global warming and threatened the livelihood of many millions more.*[31] *The human as well as the financial losses were already tremendous in the first two decades of the twenty-first century,*[32] *and they increased to more than two million people dead as well as financial losses of around 10 trillion US dollars until 2100 as a direct result of extreme weather events globally.*[33]

*Due to the enormous climatic changes and in light of the aforementioned changes in the global economic order, the international community of States has also profoundly changed in the second half of the twenty-first century.*[34] *Some States have literally vanished as a result of sea level rise, some States have become so uninhabitable that their populations were forced to leave their territories. In other States, food and water scarcity as well as the lack of other natural resources have caused armed conflicts and civil wars, which again led to the collapse of States worldwide. But the global climatic, technological and political developments have also initiated the restructuring of many States. Some States disintegrated into several smaller States, others united by creating new super-States. While former leading States have lost some of their influence and power, other world regions have gained new importance due to their population growth, technological innovations in their States, better adaptation capacities regarding environmental impacts as well as major geopolitical shifts in the distribution of global power.*

*Even the old post-war system of the United Nations ('UN') has not survived the massive restructuring of the international arena: As it has not sufficiently contributed to prevent or at least limit the climate crisis, the UN's power and influence has successively decreased during the first half of the twenty-first century. Particularly, the ongoing blockade of the UN Security Council's decisions due to the often-opposing interests of the five veto powers has further undermined its ability to successfully address the upcoming global challenges. The UN's loss of influence has increased with the Russian war of aggression against Ukraine in 2022, which illustrated the UN system's failure to achieve even its main goal "to save succeeding*

---

[29] In more detail, see United Nations Environment Programme (UNEP) (2019, Chapters 5–9).

[30] A tipping point is "a critical threshold beyond which a system reorganises, often abruptly and/or irreversibly", see Lee et al. (2021), p. 633. See also Hoegh-Guldberg et al. (2018), p. 262; UNEP (2012), p. 6.

[31] For an overview of potential tipping points, see Lenton et al. (2019); Potsdam Institute for Climate Impact Research (2024).

[32] Eckstein et al. (2021).

[33] These estimates are based on an analysis of the years 2000–2019 (ibid., p. 5), which have been roughly multiplied.

[34] The following fictional illustration of geopolitical developments are again mainly based on Future Timeline Community (2024, years 2060–2069).

*generations from the scourge of war" and "to maintain international peace and security".*[35] *This failure was further amplified in the context of Israel's war in the Gaza strip from October 2023 on, when the UN system failed to prevent the blatant and continuous violations of international humanitarian law with the plausible accusation of an ongoing genocide vis-à-vis the Palestinian people in Gaza.*[36] *In the years that followed, the UN has collapsed in the meantime and was replaced by new forms of international cooperation.*

*On 26 June 2056, 111 years after the adoption of the Charter of the United Nations ('UN Charter'), a new international organisation was established as its successor—named 'Union of Humankind'. While the former veto powers did not join the new organisation from the beginning, it has been broadly supported by many other States as the founders sought to shift the focus of international relations from a few super powers claiming certain privileges to equal distribution of power and influence between all States. In 2100, the Union's principal and decisive organ is the 'United Assembly of Humankind', which follows other rules than the former UN General Assembly ('UNGA'). The United Assembly shifted the internal power distribution of the institution towards a* per capita *representation of States and increased the participation of civil society. Thereby, it was able to realign the new international order towards a framework that understood the equality of human beings worldwide as its central concern. As a result, the organisation's new approaches to tackle global problems have strengthened its authority so that even the former veto powers eventually joined the Union of Humankind. The Union has made greater efforts to soften the catastrophic effects of climate change. But despite some smaller successes in adaptation in the twenty-first century,*[37] *the Union has not been able to reverse the grave and irreversible developments, which had been triggered by activities of past generations. Although policy-makers of the second half of the twenty-first century have begun to overcome the traditional growth economy and to establish new forms of global governance and economy, the seeds for many long-lasting harms had been planted before and irreversibly.*

*In the year 2100, the world faces many unalterable consequences of global warming and environmental degradation. On the basis of new scientific knowledge, the international community profoundly understands all of these planetary developments. Attribution science, which has emerged since the beginning of the twenty-first century,*[38] *has been further developed thanks to AI, so that it is possible to exactly attribute different climate change effects, such as droughts and hurricanes, to*

[35] *Charter of the United Nations* (UN Charter), adopted 26 June 1945, entered into force 24 October 1945, 1 UNTS XVI, Preamble.

[36] On the plausibility of the charge of genocide, see International Court of Justice, *Application of the Convention on the Prevention and Punishment of the Crime of Genocide in the Gaza Strip (South Africa v. Israel),* Order, 26 January 2024, retrieved 3 January 2025, from https://www.icj-cij.org/case/192/orders, paras. 35–59. On the consequences for international law, see, e.g., Bustami and Kahl (2024); Zarbiyev (2024).

[37] See IPCC (2022a).

[38] Chen et al. (2021), pp. 204–206.

*specific anthropogenic contributions to global warming. The scientific research clearly traces back the most detrimental effects on the global climate to the last decades of the twentieth century and the first decades of the twenty-first century. While the global cumulative $CO_2$ emissions in the 120 years between 1850 and 1970 added up to around 1000 gigatons ('Gt') of $CO_2$, an even greater amount of around 1390 Gt of $CO_2$ was emitted in the subsequent shorter period between 1970 and 2020.*[39] *Another 1000 Gt of $CO_2$ followed in the next 20 years until 2045.*[40]

*These insights cause the United Assembly of Humankind in 2100 to establish a subsidiary organ, the 'High Commissioner for Intergenerational Relations'. This organ is tasked with the examination of the intergenerational responsibility of these past generations between approximately 1970 and 2030 with regard to the consequences their actions had on the climate system and the global ecosystem in general. The Office of this High Commissioner immediately takes up its work and its findings are even more shocking than assumed before: Not only was a large part of the greenhouse gas ('GHG') emissions, which caused the aforementioned disastrous and partly irreversible impacts emitted from 1970 to 2030. The degree of human influence on global warming had also been known since the 1990s,*[41] *and unequivocally clear at least since the 2020s, as explicitly clarified by the sixth assessment report of the Intergovernmental Panel on Climate Change ('IPCC') in 2021.*[42] *According to that report, "observed increases in well-mixed greenhouse gas (GHG) concentrations since around 1750 are unequivocally caused by human activities".*[43] *First predictions of the increase in the global temperature had already been made in the 1970s,*[44] *which even culminated in a World Climate Conference Declaration in 1979.*[45] *Further research in the 1980s had led to a consensus on anthropogenic global warming,*[46] *leading to the establishment of the IPCC in 1988 by the World Meteorological Organization ('WMO') and the UN Environment Program ('UNEP'). The UNGA endorsed the IPCC and its task to coordinate the scientific assessments of the effects of climate change.*[47] *For the High Commissioner for Intergenerational Relations, the following six IPCC Assessment Reports from 1990 to 2022 illustrate very clearly the amount of knowledge this past generation had successively collected on the consequences of their activities.*[48] *Comparable*

---

[39] IPCC (2021b), p. 28.

[40] For scenario SSP2-4.5, cf. also ibid.

[41] See, e.g., IPCC (1992), pp. 66–67.

[42] IPCC (2021b), pp. 4–7.

[43] Ibid., p. 4.

[44] See, e.g., Sawyer (1972); Meadows et al. (1972).

[45] World Meteorological Organization (WMO) (1979).

[46] Hansen et al. (1981).

[47] United Nations General Assembly (1988, para. 5).

[48] IPCC (1992); IPCC (1995); IPCC (2001); IPCC (2007); IPCC (2014b); IPCC (2021a).

*knowledge had been gathered on the effects of continuing biodiversity loss triggered by human activities.*[49]

*In 2021, the global mean temperature was already measured at 1.11 °C above the 1850–1900 baseline.*[50] *Various mitigation pathways had been examined and suggested by scientists at that time in order to comply with the objective of the Paris Agreement*[51]*—"[to hold] the increase in the global average temperature to well below 2 °C above pre-industrial levels and [to pursue] efforts to limit the temperature increase to 1.5 °C above pre-industrial levels".*[52] *Nonetheless, this knowledge did not lead to consequent and sufficient global counter-measures in the following years; instead, the cumulative emissions still increased.*[53] *Based on these findings of the High Commissioner, the United Assembly of Humankind decides to widen the mandate of the High Commissioner to examine ways to hold the past generation of humankind accountable for its inaction in combating climate change, biodiversity loss and other intergenerational issues. In the view of the Assembly, the activities at the beginning of the twenty-first century were obviously in violation of the concept of intergenerational equity – a concept that governs fairness among all generations.*[54] *In order to better understand the political and legal motivations of the international community in this past generation, the Assembly decides to make use of a new technology, which has been developed with the help of transhuman AI at the end of the twenty-first century: time travel.*[55] *Although the decision-makers in the Assembly are aware of the complications related to time travel as well as the dangers of interference with the past,*[56] *they consider it absolutely necessary to travel back in time in order to confront the decision-makers in the beginning of the twenty-first century with the disastrous effects of their choices and activities on future generations.*[57] *Therefore, the High Commissioner is charged with the challenging task to represent the generation of the year 2100 on this time travel.*

---

[49] See, e.g., IPBES (2019).

[50] WMO (2022), p. 6.

[51] Most recently on these pathways, see IPCC (2022c). See also IPCC (2014a); Rogelj et al. (2018). See also.

[52] *Paris Agreement* (Paris Agreement), adopted 12 December 2015, entered into force 4 November 2016, UN Doc. FCCC/CP/2015/L.9/Rev.1.

[53] IPCC (2021b), p. 28.

[54] Brown Weiss (2021, para. 1).

[55] While most parts of the presented thought experiment are based on scientific predictions of future developments (e.g., in climate sciences), the present author does not claim that time travel will become possible in the future. Nonetheless, for the sake of illustration, the fictional thought experiment assumes that future AI and transhumanism might render time travel possible by the year 2100.

[56] On a philosophical manifestation of these concerns with regard to intergenerational justice, the non-identity problem, see *infra* in Sect. 3.2.1.

[57] *Alberto Szekely* fittingly stated: "Anyone belonging to the 'future generation' that we have so selfishly ignored, [...], will most likely judge us and condemn us as genocidal, for having departed from the path we had chosen in the post-war era [...]. How are they likely to see us then?", see Szekely (2008), p. 160.

*Due to the technological restraints of time travel, the earliest point in time to which time travel is possible is the year 2025. Therefore, the High Commissioner decides to confront the past generation with their omissions at the 2025 Conference of the Parties ('COP') to the United Nations Framework Convention on Climate Change ('UNFCCC')*[58] *in Brazil, the COP30. The IPCC had just published its sixth Assessment Report in 2022 so that the past generation's insights on the anthropogenic contributions to global warming and possible pathways of mitigation were already available to the respective decision-makers.*[59] *The COP26 in Glasgow had offered some careful promises with a view to raising the international community's awareness of the urgency of climate protection,*[60] *paralleled with some high-emitting States' pledges to put more effort in their reduction targets.*[61] *However, the subsequent actions and nationally determined contributions fell short of the sufficient efforts.*[62] *Even worse, the three subsequent COP, in Egypt (2022),*[63] *in the United Arab Emirates (2023)*[64] *and in Azerbaijan (2024)*[65] *had mostly resulted in less ambitious, merely formal, consensus declarations.*[66] *As the world was struggling with the effects of a global pandemic, Russia's war of aggression against Ukraine and escalating wars of Israel against neighbouring countries and people, the international community was in danger of undermining the necessary reduction targets and of falling back into old patterns.*[67] *Furthermore, the International Court of Justice ('ICJ') had just rendered an important advisory opinion on States' obligations in respect of climate change in 2025.*[68] *At this point in time, the High Commissioner for Intergenerational Relations deems the occasion appropriate for confronting the responsible States with their intergenerational duties and for encouraging them to build upon the envisaged plans of a green and sustainable*

---

[58] *United Nations Framework Convention on Climate Change* (UNFCCC), adopted 9 May 1992, entered into force 21 March 1994, 1771 UNTS 107.

[59] IPCC (2021a); IPCC (2022a); IPCC (2022c).

[60] UNFCCC Conference of the Parties 26 (2021a).

[61] For an overall analysis of updated emission reduction targets, see Climate Analytics and New Climate Institute (2024, see 2020/2021 updates (before COP26 Glasgow)). See, e.g., on the European Union Green Deal, European Commission (EC) (2019–2024).

[62] Climate Analytics and New Climate Institute (2022).

[63] See, e.g., Frenz (2023); Kronenberger (2022); Reeh (2022).

[64] See, e.g., van Asselt (2023); von Bernstorff (2023).

[65] See, e.g., Wewerinke-Singh and El Mahmoud (2024); Argueta and Batura (2024).

[66] Generally, on the history of climate change negotiations, see also Bodansky (2022); Maslin et al. (2023).

[67] For an analysis of potential policy rollbacks concerning the pandemic recovery, see Climate Analytics and New Climate Institute (2020).

[68] On the (currently still ongoing) proceedings, see Climate Change Litigation Databases (CCLD) (2023-today). In more detail, see *infra* in Sect. 5.3.3.2.1.

*recovery in the 2020s,*[69] *as it was still not too late to address the necessary system transformation in order to achieve the Paris objective.*[70]

*When the High Commissioner successfully completes her time travel and safely arrives in the year 2025, she immediately approaches the UN Secretary-General ('UNSG') with her unusual request. Soon thereafter, she is able to present this request before the 198 parties of the UNFCCC. After illustrating the upcoming developments in the twenty-first century including the disastrous and partly irreversible consequences for the global ecosystems and for humanity, the High Commissioner also clearly describes the present international community's contribution to these developments in the upcoming decades. She finishes her report with a provocative question to the representatives of the parties: "Why do you act in explicit violation of your responsibilities under the concept of intergenerational equity?"*

## 1.1 What Is Understood by Intergenerational Equity

Unfortunately, this intertemporal confrontation between the present and a future generation remains reserved for our imagination, as it will most likely not be possible to ever travel back in time. Nonetheless, the questions behind this fictional scenario are worth asking and merit answers from the present generation. While the question of "why" belongs to the realm of moral philosophy, a preliminary question should definitely be *whether* the present generation actually violates its obligations under intergenerational equity at all. This book attempts to give the answer to the latter question from an intertemporal perspective that always keeps in mind the idea behind the thought experiment: that the same question cannot only be asked from the perspective of the present generation but also from the perspective of future generations of humanity. Put differently, this work attempts to address *two* connected research questions. First, it analyses the legal contents and structures of the concept of intergenerational equity as of today. Second, it examines which legal understanding the present generation would and should base its answer on in the illustrated intertemporal confrontation between the present and the future.

Before turning to the intertemporal perspective, it is important to delimit what is exactly meant by the concept[71] of intergenerational equity. The most common formulation of the concept requires the present generation to abstain from

[69] See, e.g., UNFCCC COP 26 (2021b).

[70] See Rogelj et al. (2018); IPCC (2022d, pp. 21–43).

[71] In this book, the term "concept" is used in a non-technical way when referring to intergenerational equity or sustainable development. This does not anticipate their exact normative capacity but is understood as an umbrella term, since the issue of these concepts' normative capacity (as policy, principle or rule) is addressed at a later stage, see *infra* in Sect. 4.1.

"compromising the ability of future generations to meet their own needs".[72] Although the concept has often been linked to the conservation of the environment and the just distribution of natural resources,[73] intergenerational issues are neither limited to environmental law nor to the legal realm in general. Due to their close connection to considerations of justice, intergenerational relations have particularly occupied philosophers for centuries.[74] They have also been and still are an object of research in political[75] as well as economic sciences.[76] In regard to the *non-legal* perspectives on future generations, this book touches upon only the philosophical approaches to intergenerational justice,[77] and assumes that a concern for the long-term future should be "a key moral priority of our time".[78] There is obviously a strong link between international environmental law and its philosophical basis, which is mirrored in the discipline of environmental ethics.[79] In order to fully grasp the concept of intergenerational equity, a proper understanding of its ethical foundations is pivotal.[80]

Within the *legal* domain, intergenerational equity has also been discussed with regard to other fields than environmental law,[81] such as matters of budgetary law and public debt,[82] social security and pension systems.[83] This book does not address the non-environmental aspects of intergenerational relations but focuses solely on the questions of natural resources and environmental obligations. The foregoing fictional scenario in the year 2100 has illustrated that the impacts of anthropogenic global warming and climate change constitute the main and most serious case of

---

[72] World Commission on Environment and Development (WCED) (1987, Introduction, para. 27, Chapter 2, para. 1).

[73] Brown Weiss (2021, para. 1).

[74] See Meyer (2021, Introduction).

[75] See, e.g., Thompson (2010); Beckman (2015); Rose (2017).

[76] See, e.g., Fehr (2009); Wegner (2009); Stern (2011).

[77] For an overview, see Meyer (2021) For a variety of different philosophical approaches, see Tremmel (2006).

[78] Moorhouse (2021). In this sense, the present author and the thesis underlying this book can also be considered part of a longtermist approach to the law, even if the following chapters do not necessarily build upon the specific research of longtermism as such. On the foundations of longtermism, see generally Winter et al. (2021), pp. 13–17. On some contents of longtermist research, see, e.g., Greaves et al. (2020); Winter et al. (2021), pp. 35–121. The first contact the present author had with the research agenda of longtermism was during the 2022 Multidisciplinary Forum on Longtermism and the Law that took place in Hamburg from 9 to 11 June 2022. In this context, he was able to present and discuss the main findings of his thesis. This immensely helped to further shape some of the main findings in a (hopefully) more comprehensible and compelling way. As a result of the forum, a brief summary of the main ideas of the book has been published as part of a blog post debate on the *Verfassungsblog*, see Bustami (2022).

[79] Stone (2010); Brennan and Lo (2021).

[80] Lawrence (2012), pp. 23–24.

[81] For an overview, see, e.g., Heubach (2008), pp. 44–71; Shelton (2010), pp. 133–143.

[82] See, e.g., Süssmuth and von Weizsäcker (2006); Buchanan (2009); Catrina (2013).

[83] See, e.g., J. Thompson (2003); Doran (2008); Fuest (2009).

application for intergenerational problems. The UNGA already realised this connection in the 1980s,[84] and the connection is equally reflected in Art. 3(1) of the UNFCCC from 1992:

> The Parties should protect the climate system for the benefit of present and future generations of humankind, on the basis of equity and in accordance with their common but differentiated responsibilities and respective capabilities.

*Catherine Redgwell* noted that the UNFCCC "may be viewed as beginning the process of defining the obligations of the present generation to absorb the costs of reducing the risk of global warming for future generations."[85] The intention to protect the global climate for present as well as future generations of humankind was reaffirmed various times in the last decades.[86] The importance of global warming for the legal relationship between present and future generations has increased with the growing impact that human activities have on the future of the planet.[87] This results from the fact that most of these activities do not lead to an immediate environmental effect in the present, but rather constitute long-term degradations, which manifest only in the future and which are often irreversible.[88] As *Edith Brown Weiss* stated, "[n]o longer can we ignore the fact that climate change is an intergenerational problem and that the well-being of future generations depends upon actions that we take today."[89] In 2019, the UNGA President consequently underlined that "climate justice is intergenerational justice".[90]

Despite this most obvious connection between intergenerational equity and climate protection, climate change is not the only field of application for intergenerational equity. Instead, many environmental problems are at risk of threatening the needs of future generations.[91] These problems range from depletion of natural resources over the degradation in environmental quality to the discriminatory access and use of resources.[92] They touch upon areas as diverse as nuclear waste, conservation of renewable resources like forests and freshwater, and biodiversity loss.[93] *Brown Weiss* identified a broad variety of such issues:

> [W]astes that cannot with reasonable confidence be contained in impact either spatially or over time; damage to soils so extensive as to render them incapable of supporting plant or animal life; destruction of tropical forests that affect overall diversity of species in the region; pollution, land use transformation, use of fossil fuels and other practices sufficient to cause

[84] UNGA (1988, para. 1).

[85] Redgwell (1999), pp. 117–118.

[86] See, e.g., UNGA (2013, with further references).

[87] See also Fleurbaey et al. (2014), pp. 294–296.

[88] This was already clear in the 1980s, see Brown Weiss (1989), p. 23. Cf. also Gardiner (2006), pp. 150–152; Buchanan (2011), pp. 350–352.

[89] Brown Weiss (2008), p. 616.

[90] UNGA (2019).

[91] Cf. Beyerlin and Grote Stoutenburg (2013, para. 97).

[92] Brown Weiss (2010), pp. 100–102.

[93] In detail, see already Brown Weiss (1989), pp. 189–288.

> climate change; loss of knowledge essential for understanding natural and social systems; destruction of cultural monuments acknowledged by countries as part of the common heritage of humankind; and destruction of specific endowments established for the benefit of both present and future generations [...].[94]

In all of these areas, human activities have significantly contributed to a constant degradation of natural resources in the last decades, which will most probably compromise future generations in meeting their own needs. Moreover, the different environmental problems are not independent from each other, but there are many interrelations reciprocally amplifying each other. For instance, climate change is one of the main pressures on biodiversity that causes species movements due to global warming as well as extinction of many species.[95] At the same time, loss of biodiversity reduces the resilience of ecosystems, such as agricultural landscapes and forests,[96] and increases their vulnerability to further climate change.[97] The actual overlaps and feedback loops between the different pressures are even more complex and have partly unforeseeable long-term effects.[98]

This is why intergenerational equity is not only a climate change-related issue but an overarching concept that merits a holistic analysis. The present work thus examines a *universal* understanding of intergenerational equity, connected to all aspects of international environmental law. It exists beyond specific treaty regimes, such as the UNFCCC or the Convention on Biological Diversity ('CBD').[99] Of course, there are various links between the concept and its fields of application, so that the following chapters regularly refer to specific cases of intergenerational problems. For instance, the development of environmental treaties in specific fields is linked to the development and the legal nature of the concept of intergenerational equity.[100] Further, the book analyses, *inter alia*, some of the existing climate change litigation cases as far as they contribute to the implementation of intergenerational equity.[101] These references to specific fields of environmental law serve as illustration of the overarching concept of intergenerational equity. Due to this overarching character, intergenerational equity forms also part of the so-called principles of international environmental law.[102] In this regard, it is linked to other principles,

---

[94] Brown Weiss (2019), p. 57. See also Brown Weiss (2021, para. 10).

[95] Stoett et al. (2019), p. 152; IPBES (2019), p. 13.

[96] Stoett et al. (2019), pp. 161–162.

[97] Ibid., p. 142.

[98] Ibid., pp. 142, 148–149; IPBES (2019), p. 13.

[99] *Convention on Biological Diversity* (CBD), adopted 5 June 1992, entered into force 29 December 1993, 1760 UNTS 79, Preamble, Art. 1, 2.

[100] See *infra* in Sects. 2.1 and 4.2.

[101] See *infra* in Sect. 5.3.

[102] For an overview of the principles of international environmental law, see, e.g., Sands et al. (2018), pp. 197–250. At this point of the introduction, the term "principle" is used in a non-technical way and with regard to the totality of environmental "principles". Chapter 4 properly analyses the normative capacity of intergenerational equity and sustainable development with regard to their capacity as principles or rules, see *infra* in Sect. 4.1.

such as intra-generational equity, common but differentiated responsibilities and the notion of common concern of humankind. Most of all, it is strongly intertwined with the concept of sustainable development.[103] These interrelations must be examined in order to understand the exact scope and content of intergenerational equity that goes beyond the mere equation with sustainable development.

Starting with these first delimitations, the book attempts to address the *legal* questions underlying the provocative question of the fictional High Commissioner for Intergenerational Relations: Does the present generation act in violation of its responsibilities under the legal concept of intergenerational equity? The representatives of the UNFCCC parties at the COP30 would examine their intergenerational obligations in the year 2025 in order to know whether they act in violation of this concept. However, the question is not easily answered as it encompasses several follow-up questions: What exactly is the content of the concept of intergenerational equity? How is it related to other concepts of international environmental law? Does the concept have normative capacity and is it legally binding? In case there are any binding obligations, who would be the corresponding duty-bearers? Are future generations themselves right-holders in this relationship? How can intergenerational equity be implemented in an institutional framework by representation of future generations' interests? Would this institutional implementation be realised on the national or international level; and would it be limited to policy-making or include judicial enforcement of intergenerational equity?

## 1.2 State of the Art and Need for Further Research: What Has (Not) Been Written on Intergenerational Equity

Some of these questions on intergenerational equity have been discussed over the course of the last decades while the concept has emerged. In 1987, the well-known report of the World Commission on Environment and Development, the so-called 'Brundtland Report', was one of the first international documents that addressed the needs of future generations.[104] It underlined the necessity to abstain from "compromising the ability of future generations to meet their [own] needs".[105] Abundant sources have referred to the concept in the following decades until today. The most elaborate works have been written by *Edith Brown Weiss* who published her landmark book 'In Fairness to Future Generations' in 1989.[106] *Brown Weiss* established a doctrine of intergenerational equity that built upon various international documents and upon main philosophical approaches to

[103] See Brown Weiss (2021, para. 1).

[104] WCED (1987).

[105] Ibid., Introduction, para. 27, Chapter 2, para. 1.

[106] Brown Weiss (1989).

intergenerational justice.[107] She characterised intergenerational equity as an "obligation to future generations to pass on the natural and cultural resources of the planet in no worse condition than received and to provide reasonable access to the legacy for the present generation".[108] She identified three duties of conservation—conservation of options, of quality and of equitable access—which she specified in her work.[109] In her subsequent works, she further developed the doctrine and included references to more recent international documents;[110] one of the most recent being her contribution regarding the Global Pact for the Environment ('GPE').[111]

Virtually every subsequent work on intergenerational equity has addressed *Brown Weiss'* doctrine.[112] Some authors agreed with the conceptional basis put forward by *Brown Weiss* and assumed that it would be appropriate to address intergenerational issues.[113] Other authors further elaborated on the concept,[114] for instance, by emphasising its character as an intergenerational trust.[115] Not only legal scholarship has addressed intergenerational equity, but international courts and tribunals have also referred to the interests of future generations, although not necessarily to *Brown Weiss'* conception itself. The most noteworthy cases have been the 1996 *Nuclear Weapons* Advisory Opinion[116] and the 1997 *Gabčíkovo-Nagymaros Project* Judgment of the International Court of Justice ('ICJ').[117] Further, both *Judge Weeramantry* and *Judge Cançado Trindade* stressed the importance of the concept in some of their separate and dissenting opinions, in which they explicitly referred to

[107] Ibid., p. 24. Her works particularly referred to *John Rawls'* contractualist approaches, see Rawls (1971), p. 284.

[108] Brown Weiss (1989), pp. 37–38.

[109] Ibid., pp. 40–45, 49–86.

[110] See, e.g., Brown Weiss (1992); Brown Weiss (2010).

[111] Brown Weiss (2019). On the GPE, see International Group of Experts for the Pact (2017, Art. 4).

[112] In this context, the term "doctrine" is meant in the sense of a theory in scholarship and jurisprudence; the present work uses this denomination, as this constitutes an established term with regard to the conceptualisation of *Edith Brown Weiss*. The normative capacity of this doctrine is addressed in detail *infra* in Sect. 4.1.4.

[113] See, e.g., Collins (2007); Shelton (2010).

[114] See, e.g., Lawrence (2014). For a variety of different contributions on intergenerational equity, see, e.g., Cordonier Segger et al. (2021).

[115] Redgwell (1999). See also Slobodian (2020), pp. 580–582.

[116] ICJ, *Legality of the Threat or Use of Nuclear Weapons,* Advisory Opinion, 8 July 1996, ICJ Reports 1996, 226, paras. 29, 35–36. See also Brown Weiss (1999).

[117] ICJ, *Gabčíkovo-Nagymaros Project (Hungary v. Slovakia),* Judgment, 25 September 1997, ICJ Reports 1997, 7, para. 140.

*Brown Weiss.*[118] In 2013, the UNSG conducted an elaborate examination of intergenerational equity on the request of the UNGA.[119]

There has also been a lot of criticism of intergenerational equity on a conceptional as well as on a substantive basis.[120] This criticism ranges from doubts about the legal nature of intergenerational equity[121] and doubts about the possibility of rights of future generations[122] to criticism of the exact operationalisation of the concept.[123] *Zena Hadjiargyrou* summarised parts of the criticism as follows: "Intergenerational equity, […] though an admiral concept in thought, has proven to be chaotic in terms of understanding, implementation and elucidation both conceptually and in practice."[124] Many of the criticised aspects are not fully resolved today, much less have they been addressed consistently. There is still a lot of uncertainty on the concept's normative capacity and its legal status, and only few works properly distinguished between the two elements at all.[125] The analysis is often limited to the legal nature of sustainable development instead of intergenerational equity as such.[126] Due to these methodologically inaccurate examinations, the understanding of intergenerational equity remains partly incomplete or superficial. Therefore, *one* important contribution of this book is to offer a systematic analysis of the normative capacity and the legal status of intergenerational equity in order to properly understand the concept's role in international environmental law. At this point, the author identifies two different manifestations of intergenerational equity: a general conception that is rooted in sustainable development and a more specific doctrine of intergenerational equity that partly exceeds sustainable development in content as well as in its mechanisms of implementation.

Beyond the complexities of the concept's legal nature, the effective implementation of intergenerational equity contains many unresolved issues. These issues concern the identification of the responsible duty-bearers of intergenerational equity, the possibility of future generations to be right-holders and the existing or potential institutional frameworks of implementation and representation. There is a lot of

---

118 See, e.g., ICJ, *Legality of the Threat or Use of Nuclear Weapons,* Dissenting Opinion of Judge Weeramantry, 8 July 1996, ICJ Reports 1996, 429, p. 455; ICJ, *Gabčíkovo-Nagymaros Project (Hungary v. Slovakia),* Separate Opinion of Vice-President Weeramantry, 25 September 1997, ICJ Reports 1997, 88, pp. 109–110; ICJ, *Pulp Mills on the River Uruguay (Argentina v. Uruguay),* Separate Opinion of Judge Cançado Trindade, 20 April 2010, ICJ Reports 2010, 125, para. 114.

119 United Nations Secretary-General (2013). The task was described in the outcome document of the Rio+20 conference in 2012, see UNGA (2012, para. 86).

120 See, e.g., D'Amato (1990); Fitzmaurice (2008).

121 See, e.g., Lowe (1999).

122 See, e.g., Supanich (1992).

123 See, e.g., Beckman (2013), pp. 777–779.

124 Hadjiargyrou (2016), p. 277.

125 This book establishes an appropriate distinction *infra* in Sect. 4.1.1.

126 For one of the very few commentators explicitly distinguishing between the two concepts' legal nature, see Beyerlin (2010), p. 446.

literature on the conceptional capacity of future generations to be right-holders.[127] While *Edith Brown Weiss* and some other commentators argued in favour of granting rights to future generations,[128] most commentators remained critical.[129] Again, the comments against the existence of rights of future generations often remain methodologically inaccurate, as they confound pre-legal arguments of the conceptional possibility of rights of unborn generations with the legal assessment of the existence of such rights.[130] The present work attempts to offer a more accurate distinction between these two issues.

The assessment of the institutional framework for the representation of future generations is even more complex. It concerns the representation of future generations in policy-making as well as in judicial proceedings. Most contributions have so far either been interested in the existing frameworks of national ombudspersons,[131] or in the suggested establishment of an international representative for future generations.[132] Beyond policy-making, representation of future generations was also suggested in judicial proceedings on the inter-State level.[133] Eventually, an increasing amount of regional and national litigation, particularly in the context of climate change litigation,[134] has played an important role for the implementation of intergenerational equity.[135] The most popular example of individual complaints on behalf of future generations was the *Oposa v. Factoran* case before the Philippines Supreme Court.[136] Yet, many more decisions have referred to intergenerational equity although they did not always explicitly address the issue of representation

---

[127] Briefly, see UNSG (2013, paras. 19–22).

[128] See, e.g., Brown Weiss (1989), pp. 95–103; Shelton (1991), pp. 133–134; Schrijver (2009). See also ICJ, *Request for an Examination of the Situation in Accordance with Paragraph 63 of the Court's Judgment of 20 December 1974 in the Nuclear Tests (New Zealand v. France) Case*, Dissenting Opinion of Judge Weeramantry, 22 September 1995, ICJ Reports 1995, 317, p. 455.

[129] See, e.g., Norton (1982); Bobertz (1987); Malhotra (1998); Gosseries (2004); Merrills (2010), p. 672; Michallet (2018), p. 151.

[130] See, e.g., de George (1981), p. 159; Beckerman (2004), pp. 3–4. On the pre-legal assessment of this question, see *infra* in Sect. 3.2.2.

[131] For an overview, see, e.g., UNSG (2013, paras. 39–48); Anstee-Wedderburn (2014). See also various contributions in Cordonier Segger et al. (2021).

[132] For an overview, see, e.g., UNSG (2013, paras. 53–61); Pearce (2012). See also various contributions in Agius and Busuttil (1998, Chapters 10–14).

[133] See, e.g., Brown Weiss (1984), p. 273; Lawrence and Köhler (2017), p. 655. On the role of international courts themselves in the representation, see *Nuclear Weapons* (Dissenting Opinion of Judge Weeramantry), *supra* note 118, pp. 454–455.

[134] For an overview of recent climate change litigation, see UNEP (2020).

[135] See, e.g., Hadjiargyrou (2016), pp. 264–268; Burgers (2020), pp. 193–268; Niehaus and Davies (2021), pp. 241–245; Spentzou (2021).

[136] Republic of Philippines Supreme Court, *Oposa v. Factoran*, Decision, 30 July 1993, 33 International Legal Materials 173–206. For some comments on the decision, see, e.g., Manguiat and Yu (2003); Gatmaytan (2003).

and standing on behalf of future generations.[137] Overall, some of these aspects have been addressed separately in legal scholarship, but there is no comprehensive analysis of the different dimensions of representation so far. The present book thus offers an overarching assessment of the *status quo* of intergenerational equity with regard to its institutional implementation in policy-making and in judicial proceedings.

However, this *status quo* analysis is not the only focus of the book. Based on the introductory thought experiment of time travel, the second overarching research question takes an intertemporal perspective. The present author considers intergenerational equity to constitute an intertemporal relationship that links different generations across time. It is also intertemporal because the legal questions underlying the intertemporal confrontation are hypothetically asked by a representative of a future generation to members of the present generation. For this reason, the analysis of the legal contents of intergenerational equity as of today is only the necessary starting point for an intertemporal assessment. The author eventually attempts to answer which legal regime of intergenerational equity is temporally applicable to address the open issues of the intertemporal legal relationship between present and future generations. The following methodological considerations illustrate how this answer is to be found.

## 1.3 Methodology: How the Author Addresses Intergenerational Equity

As implied above, the first perspective on the research question must be based on the existing concept of intergenerational equity. Therefore, the author starts with an analysis of intergenerational equity *de lege lata*. It utilises a positivist approach to the assessment of international law, that means it starts with the "critical separation of law as it is from law as it ought to be – 'law as it is' being rules made up by the modern State".[138] From a positivist perspective, the existence and content of a legal norm depend on formalised criteria of validity and they are rooted in a voluntarist

[137] See, e.g., Hague District Court, *Urgenda Foundation v. The State of the Netherlands,* Judgment, 24 June 2015, European Case Law Identifier ECLI:NL:RBDHA:2015:7196; US District Court for the District of Oregon, 9th Circuit, *Juliana v. United States,* Opinion and Order, 10 November 2016, 217 F. Supp. 3d 1224; Supreme Court of Colombia, *Future Generations v. Ministry of the Environment and Others,* Decision, 5 April 2018, retrieved 3 January 2025, from https://climatecasechart.com/non-us-case/future-generation-v-ministry-environment-others/; Borgarting Court of Appeal, *Greenpeace Nordic Ass'n and Nature and Youth v. Ministry of Petroleum and Energy (People v. Arctic Oil),* Judgment, 23 January 2020, retrieved 3 January 2025, from https://climatecasechart.com/non-us-case/greenpeace-nordic-assn-and-nature-youth-v-norway-ministry-of-petroleum-and-energy/; Federal Constitutional Court of Germany, *Climate Change (Neubauer et al.),* Order, 24 March 2021, 74 (2021) NJW 1723–1751.

[138] Lachenmann (2012, para. 4). Generally on the characteristics of legal positivism, see ibid., paras. 2–5.

element of State will based on the sources of international law.[139] However, the book does not directly delve into the analysis of these legal sources, as this strict positivist focus would turn a blind eye to the historical and systemic context of intergenerational equity as well as to the non-positivist aspects, which have shaped the current meanings and contents of the concept. Therefore, this work begins the *lex lata* analysis with a more open-minded and mainly doctrinal analysis of the concept of intergenerational equity.[140] Doctrinal analysis "aims to give a systematic exposition of the principles, rules and concepts governing a particular legal field or institution and analyses the relationship between these principles, rules and concepts with a view to solving unclarities and gaps in the existing law".[141] A doctrinal analysis can assist in identifying the established public opinion on the existence of law among legal professionals.[142] This book thus relies on doctrinal analysis as an essential research method for the examination of the concept of intergenerational equity.[143]

The initial positivist and doctrinal assessment includes a historical outline of the relevance of "future generations" in international environmental law over the last decades. The historical outline is complemented by an overview of the assessment of intergenerational equity in legal scholarship, particularly shaped by the works of *Edith Brown Weiss*. Her doctrine of intergenerational equity as well as various judicial decisions serve as a solid source of knowledge for the purpose of understanding the concept of intergenerational equity as it stands today.[144] Due to the inherent connections between intergenerational equity and related environmental concepts, it is also necessary to include an evaluation of intergenerational equity vis-à-vis these other concepts. This systemic[145] analysis of the existing legal regime allows properly defining the actual research object of the present work in distinction to other notions of international environmental law. As long as it is not clear what exactly is meant by "intergenerational equity", a purely positivist approach based on the assessment of the legal sources would lack a precise research object. Furthermore, the doctrinal analysis of intergenerational equity and its links to sustainable development are also necessary for the distinction of the aforementioned two manifestations of intergenerational equity.

---

[139] Ibid., paras. 3, 28–40.

[140] On the connection between legal positivism and doctrinal analysis, see Cryer et al. (2011), p. 38.

[141] Smits (2017), p. 210. Cf. also Peczenik (2005), p. 1.

[142] See Koskenniemi (2007b, para. 12).

[143] Generally on the method of doctrinal analysis, see Smits (2017).

[144] This is also consistent with Article 38(1)(d) of the Statute of the International Court of Justice to take into consideration not only judicial decisions, but also "the teachings of the most highly qualified publicists of the various nations, as subsidiary means for the determination of rules of law", see *Statute of the International Court of Justice* (ICJ Statute), adopted 26 June 1945, entered into force 24 October 1945, 1 UNTS XVI, Art. 38(1)(d).

[145] In this book, "systemic" analysis means an analysis that looks at intergenerational equity within the contextual framework of international environmental law.

The foregoing *lex lata* perspective is then complemented by an interdisciplinary non-positivist perspective on intergenerational relations. Intergenerational equity is a concept of such an overarching and interdisciplinary nature that a mere legal analysis of positivist rules would disregard the concept's position between law and ethics, between present *status quo* and future ambition. Therefore, Chap. 3 of the book departs from the foregoing positivist approach. This chapter introduces elements of natural law approaches, which assume that certain norms are not relevant because they are laid down by the competent human authority, but because they are deducible from nature, reason or justice.[146] Natural law perspectives have shaped international law in different ways in its history, up until the twentieth century with representatives such as *Alfred Verdross* or *Hersch Lauterpacht*.[147] Although legal positivism constitutes the dominant approach in current international legal scholarship,[148] even in international environmental law,[149] natural law is still ubiquitous in the current international legal system.[150] Natural law elements have been particularly promoted in areas of international law that move away from mere bilateralism towards community interests.[151] In this sense, *Frauke Lachenmann* described that international law is "at least in parts, becoming an avowedly value-oriented system" that is increasingly committed "to extralegal considerations not based on the particular interests of individual States".[152]

Regardless of the accuracy of this assumption in general, notions of natural law certainly have a strong influence in the realm of international environmental law, as many environmental concepts, including sustainable development and intergenerational equity, combine legal elements with pre-legal ideas of ethics, justice and fairness.[153] This convergence of positivist and natural law methods[154] is inherent in international law, as *Martti Koskenniemi* fittingly stated:

> The labels 'natural law' and 'positivism' cover [...] a very wide spectrum of positions that are often hard to distinguish from one another. This is so because neither 'natural law' nor 'positivism' can be sustained without support from the other: a theory that begins by postulating a 'natural' law must prove itself by pointing to 'positive' evidence about its realization in history and practice; a theory that grounds itself in 'positive' facts of statehood – [e.g.] sovereign consent or interest – must derive its normative force from

[146] Orakhelashvili (2007, paras. 1–3). See also Koskenniemi (2007b, para. 5).

[147] For a historical overview, see Orakhelashvili (2007, paras. 7–28).

[148] Cryer et al. (2011), p. 39.

[149] For a critical comment on this omission in international environmental law scholarship, see Kotsakis (2017), pp. 341–345.

[150] Cryer et al. (2011), p. 35.

[151] Lachenmann (2012, para. 59).

[152] Ibid.

[153] See Stone (2010); Bosselmann (2009). Cf. also *Gabčíkovo-Nagymaros Project* (Separate Opinion of Vice-President Weeramantry), *supra* note 118, p. 90; Orakhelashvili (2007, para. 43).

[154] Generally on the convergence of different methods of international law, see Koskenniemi (2007b, paras. 23–25).

> outside such sovereignty, namely an 'external' criterion about when and to what extent sovereignty is to have such force.[155]

In order to find this normative force behind the relevant concept of intergenerational equity, Chap. 3 turns to its ethical foundations, which are influenced by divergent schools of thought as utilitarianism,[156] libertarianism,[157] contractualism[158] and communitarianism.[159] The author does not only describe these ethical foundations but also elaborates on the direct links between pre-legal approaches and their legal translation into international environmental law. Further, this is important, as many objections to the legal concept of intergenerational equity are actually based on an ethical assessment of intergenerational justice.

Building upon this historical, systemic and ethical overview, the fourth chapter of the book eventually turns to a purely positivist method that is based on the examination of the main sources of international law in order to determine their meaning and contents.[160] These sources of international law are declaratorily listed in Article 38(1) of the Statute of the International Court of Justice ('ICJ Statute').[161] This chapter only briefly looks at several international conventions (see Article 38(1)(a) of the ICJ Statute) that include references to future generations and intergenerational equity.[162] In this context, the methodological analysis makes use of the rules of treaty interpretation under the Vienna Convention on the Law of Treaties ('VCLT').[163] Yet, the work focuses on intergenerational equity as a concept of customary international law within the meaning of Article 38(1)(b) of the ICJ Statute,[164] as this reflects the holistic and universal character of intergenerational equity more adequately than focusing on particular treaty regimes.[165] For this

---

[155] Koskenniemi (2007a, para. 16). See also ibid., para. 33; Orakhelashvili (2007, para. 51).

[156] For an overview, see Nathanson (n.d.).

[157] For an overview, see van der Vossen (2023).

[158] For an overview, see Cudd and Eftekhari (2021).

[159] For an overview, see Bell (2024).

[160] See Cryer et al. (2011), p. 38. See also Koskenniemi (2007b, paras. 7–13).

[161] *Statute of the International Court of Justice* (ICJ Statute), adopted 26 June 1945, entered into force 24 October 1945, 1 UNTS XVI.

[162] See, e.g., Preamble of the CBD; Preamble and Art. 3(1) of the UNFCCC; *Convention on the Protection and Use of Transboundary Watercourses and International Lakes* (UNECE Water Convention), adopted 17 March 1992, entered into force 6 October 1996, 1936 UNTS 269, Art. 2(5)(c); *United Nations Convention to Combat Desertification in those Countries Experiencing Serious Drought and/or Desertification, Particularly in Africa* (UNCCD), adopted 17 June 1994, entered into force 26 December 1996, 1954 UNTS 3, Preamble; *Convention on Access to Information, Public Participation in Decision-making and Access to Justice in Environmental Matters* (Aarhus Convention), adopted 25 June 1998, entered into force 30 October 2001, 2161 UNTS 447, Preamble, Art. 1.

[163] *Vienna Convention on the Law of Treaties* (VCLT), adopted 23 May 1969, entered into force 27 January 1980, 1155 UNTS 331, Art. 31-33. For an overview, see Herdegen (2020, paras. 5–27).

[164] For an overview of the sources of international law, see Wolfrum (2011).

[165] See already *supra* notes 99–101.

purpose, an empirical assessment of the elements of customary international law would be relevant: State practice and *opinio iuris*.[166] However, the analysis of customary international law is limited to a number of exemplary statements, documents and other instances of practice and legal conviction, as it is beyond the scope of this work to offer a comprehensive sociological study of State practice and *opinio iuris* in the context of intergenerational equity.[167] The methodological references to specific instances of State practice and *opinio iuris* illustrate that international law must seek its persuasiveness not only from formalistic categories of legal sources, but also from the factual concretisation in international affairs.[168] In this regard, not only legally binding documents are relevant, but the analysis also turns to soft law documents and other instances of authority where this can be helpful for the assessment of the legal status of intergenerational equity.[169]

At this stage of the positivist analysis of intergenerational equity, the author makes an important conceptual distinction between the normative capacity of intergenerational equity and its legal status as a legally binding norm of international law.[170] While the second question (i.e., the legal status) depends on the illustrated assessment of the sources of international law, the first question (i.e., the normative capacity) requires characterising intergenerational equity as a mere policy, without normative capacity, or as a legal principle or rule according to the conception of *Ronald Dworkin*.[171] Only if the concept has normative capacity, it can be binding within the meaning of one of the sources of international law. Again, the assessment of normative capacity and legal status distinguishes between the general conception of intergenerational equity and the more specific doctrine.

While the foregoing methodological approaches aim at determining the legal contents of intergenerational equity *de lege lata*, the transition between *lex lata* and *lex ferenda* is often fluid and not as clear-cut as might be assumed.[172] Generally, *lex ferenda* refers to the law "as it ought to be" instead of the law "as it is".[173] However, in case of continuous developments of law over time, there is a certain "blurring of the lines" between these two statuses.[174] Intergenerational equity is a particularly

[166] For the elements of customary international law, see Treves (2006).

[167] See ICJ, *Barcelona Traction, Light and Power Company, Limited (Belgium v. Spain), Second Phase,* Separate Opinion of Judge Jessup, 5 February 1970, ICJ Reports 1970, 161, para. 60. For an overview of sociological theories of international law, see Carty (2008). As to a critical view on the academic tendency to excessively focus on epistemological scientific positivism, see Kotsakis (2017). On the assessment of customary international law, see Talmon (2015); Ryngaert and Hora Siccama (2018).

[168] See Koskenniemi (2007b, paras. 14–15).

[169] See, e.g., International Law Commission (2015, paras. 45–54); Boyle (1999), p. 906.

[170] On this distinction, see Beyerlin and Marauhn (2011), pp. 79–82; Proelß (2022), pp. 101, 147–148. See also Barral (2012), p. 383. See.

[171] Dworkin (1978), pp. 22–24. See also Beyerlin (2010), pp. 426–427.

[172] See Virally (1988), p. 73; von Arnauld (2021).

[173] Lachenmann (2012, para. 4).

[174] Von Arnauld (2021), p. 418. In more detail on these overlaps, see *infra* in Sect. 7.3.3.

fitting example for this blurring of lines due to its dynamic character. This becomes clear, on the one hand, with regard to the development between the aforementioned two manifestations of intergenerational equity. On the other hand, it is illustrated with regard to the unanswered structural issues of intergenerational equity in Chap. 5, meaning the concept's duty-bearers, the existence of corresponding right-holders and, most notably, the institutional frameworks of representation of future generations. To begin with, these three issues are assessed from a positivist and doctrinal perspective in order to demonstrate the *lex lata* status of implementation of intergenerational equity. This positivist assessment offers an important starting point for the presented legal analysis. At the same time, the fifth chapter serves the purpose of distinguishing between the legal structures of intergenerational equity *de lege lata* and *de lege ferenda*, as the issues of duty-bearers, right-holders and institutional implementation constantly evolve. Consequently, positivist legal research must be seen as "a prequel to, rather than a substitute for, the making of statements about what the law ought to be".[175] In this sense, Chap. 5 presents both the current *status quo* of these open issues as well as the potential *lex ferenda* that might emerge from existing developments.

Based on this interim result on the evolutive developments of intergenerational equity and on the interplay between *lex lata* and *lex ferenda* assessments, the book then turns to the methodological approach of its second main research question: the intertemporal perspective that has been metaphorically announced with the thought experiment of time travel. The so-called doctrine[176] of intertemporal law normally assists in determining the applicable *lex lata* as it addresses the delimitation of the temporal sphere of application of a norm.[177] The doctrine basically consists of two components—the principle of contemporaneity and evolutionary approaches.[178] By properly applying these two components, intertemporal law answers the question which legal regime is temporally applicable to a certain norm of international law if the legal regime that influenced this norm has changed over time. The doctrine of intertemporal law can thus assist in determining which legal regime the present generation must focus on when assessing its obligations under intergenerational equity in the illustrated intertemporal confrontation between the present and the future.

So far, the existing jurisprudence and scholarship on intergenerational equity lack a proper intertemporal assessment of the concept. Some aspects of intergenerational

---

[175] Cryer et al. (2011), p. 38. Cf. also Lachenmann (2012, para. 60); Koskenniemi (2007b, para. 5).

[176] Synonymously, the terms "theory", "principle" or "rule" of intertemporal law, or "of intertemporality" are used. The present book exclusively uses the most common denomination "doctrine of intertemporal law", in order to not further engage in the concept's normative capacity.

[177] Institut de Droit International (IDI) (1975, Preamble); Kotzur (2008, para. 1).

[178] The evolutionary approaches in the context of intertemporal law are strongly linked to some of the rules of treaty interpretation as codified in Art. 31, 32 of the VCLT. Therefore, these sections of the book again turn to a certain degree to a hermeneutic and doctrinal analysis of existing environmental treaties on the basis of these rules of interpretation. See, e.g., Fitzmaurice (2009); Arato (2018). Specifically on time elements in environmental treaties, see Tanaka (2013).

equity even hinder an unmodified application of the existing doctrine of intertemporal law to intergenerational disputes. For this reason, the book presents certain modifications of the doctrine in order to fit these particularities of intergenerational equity. These modifications require the departure from a strictly positivist *lex lata* approach to intergenerational equity. The modifications build upon the fluid boundaries between the law as it is and the law as it ought to be.[179] They also aim at better describing the intertemporal relationship between the present generation and unborn generations in the future. Would it be possible or even necessary to address the legal contents of intergenerational equity not only from the present but also from the perspective of future generations themselves? The suggested modified doctrine of intertemporal law answers this question from a future-oriented perspective. This new intertemporal perspective is based on the dichotomous manifestation of intergenerational equity in the form of the legally binding general conception (i.e., intergenerational equity *de lege lata*) and the still emerging specific doctrine of intergenerational equity (i.e., intergenerational equity *de lege ferenda*). In order to engage even more with the introduced thought experiment, this work also offers a more sophisticated methodological approach to anticipate general future developments of the concept of intergenerational equity—based on the methodological framework of legal change by *Paul F. Diehl* and *Charlotte Ku* in their work 'The Dynamics of International Law'.[180] In this sense, the present author agrees with *Martti Koskenniemi* with regard to the renewing endeavours of methodology in international law:

> Ideas about persuasive international law arguments have not remained static. Fashions change as professional focus shifts to new problems and issues, to be argued in novel ways. The ability to accommodate or discard novel vocabularies in reaction to the changing expectations remains an important asset in the search for persuasiveness.[181]

## 1.4 Structure: Which Steps Are Taken in the Analysis

In light of the foregoing methodological approaches and the two main research questions, the book is also divided into two substantive parts. While Part I offers an overarching analysis of the concept of intergenerational equity as it stands today (Chaps. 2 to 5), the intertemporal perspective on this concept is illustrated and methodologically developed in Part II (Chaps. 6 to 7).

Within Part I, the first four chapters primarily determine the legal contents of intergenerational equity *de lege lata* by analysing the historical and systemic developments and the legal status of the two manifestations of intergenerational equity from a positivist and sources-related perspective. Within this *lex lata* analysis, the

[179] See also Wheatley (2021).

[180] Diehl and Ku (2010).

[181] Koskenniemi (2007b, para. 25). On some examples of rethinking international law in such a forward-looking way, see Cassese (2012); Allott (2017); Theilen et al. (2017).

second chapter also links the positivist assessment of intergenerational equity with its natural law foundations of justice and fairness. More specifically, these methodological considerations lead to the following structure of the book. It begins with an analysis of the historical development of intergenerational equity as well as the assessment in legal scholarship and it relates the legal concern for future generations to other concepts of international environmental law, such as sustainable development (Chap. 2). The next chapter adds the ethical and philosophical foundations of intergenerational justice to the legal analysis, since these extra-legal influences shape the legal understanding of intergenerational equity (Chap. 3). Then, the work elaborates on the clear-cut distinction between the normative capacity and the legal status of intergenerational equity, before turning to a strictly positivist assessment of the sources of international law regarding intergenerational equity (Chap. 4). Finally, the examination of the *status quo* of intergenerational equity addresses the underlying structural issues of the concept—these include the issues of duty-bearers, right-holders and institutional frameworks of representation (Chap. 5). The latter chapter already illustrates the fluid transition between the *lex lata* contents and structures of intergenerational equity and its emerging developments *de lege ferenda*. It also points to the need for further research on intergenerational equity and its future development and operationalisation.

Based on these overlaps, the last two chapters in Part II then turn to an intertemporal perspective, which goes beyond the positivist assessment of the *status quo*. First, the well-established doctrine of intertemporal law is illustrated in order to understand its two-part approach between contemporaneity in the past and dynamic developments until the present (Chap. 6). Second, the last chapter demonstrates that an unmodified application of this doctrine to intergenerational problems lacks persuasiveness for several reasons, before the chapter elaborates in detail on the suggested modification of intertemporal law (Chap. 7). The book aims at establishing a methodological tool to determine which emerging and future developments of intergenerational equity *de lege ferenda* must or should already be relevant today in the legal assessment of the concept.

From this intertemporal perspective, the members of the present generation should hypothetically be able to answer the two main aspects underlying the provocative question of the time-traveling High Commissioner for Intergenerational Relations. Before reflecting upon the question *why* they violated their intergenerational responsibilities, they would be able to answer *whether* the present generation actually violates its obligations under intergenerational equity. And most importantly: Based on which legal considerations, this question is to be answered in the intertemporal confrontation between the present and the future?

## References


Agius, E., & Busuttil, S. (Eds.). (1998). *Future generations and international law: Proceedings of the international experts' meeting held by the future generations programme at the foundation for international studies, University of Malta*. Earthscan Publications Ltd.

Allott, P. (2017). *Eutopia: new philosophy and new law for a troubled world.* Edward Elgar Publishing.

Anstee-Wedderburn, J. (2014). Giving a voice to future generations: Intergenerational equity, representative of generations to come, and the challenge of planetary rights. *Australian Journal of Environmental Law, 1*(1), 37–70.

Arato, J. (2018). Accounting for difference in treaty interpretation over time. In A. Bianchi, D. Peat, & M. Windsor (Eds.), *Interpretation in international law* (Vol. 10, 1st ed., pp. 205–228). Oxford University Press.

Argueta, B. I., & Batura, J. (2024). Climate Justice or Market Expansion? Unpacking COP29's Financing Decisions: An Interview. *Völkerrechtsblog*. 28 November 2024. Retrieved 3 January 2025, from https://voelkerrechtsblog.org/de/climate-justice-or-market-expansion-unpacking-cop29s-financing-decisions/

Barral, V. (2012). Sustainable development in international law: Nature and operation of an evolutive legal norm. *European Journal of International Law, 23*(2), 377–400. https://doi.org/10.1093/ejil/chs016

Beckerman, W. (2004). Intergenerational justice. *Intergenerational Justice Review, 2*, 1–5.

Beckman, L. (2013). Democracy and future generations: Should the unborn have a voice? In J.-C. Merle (Ed.), *Spheres of global justice: Volume 2 fair distribution – global economic, social and intergenerational justice* (Vol. 62, pp. 775–788). Springer. https://doi.org/10.1007/978-94-007-5998-5_62

Beckman, L. (2015). Political representation of future generations and collective responsibility. *Jurisprudence, 6*(3), 516–534. https://doi.org/10.1080/20403313.2015.1065641

Bell, D. (2024). Communitarianism. In E. N. Zalta (Ed.). *The Stanford Encyclopedia of Philosophy.* ISSN 1095-5054. Retrieved 3 January 2025, from https://plato.stanford.edu/entries/communitarianism/. (Article last updated June 2024)

Beyerlin, U. (2010). Different types of norms in international environmental law policies, principles, and rules. In D. Bodansky, J. Brunnée, & E. Hey (Eds.), *The Oxford handbook of international environmental law* (Vol. 18, 1st ed., pp. 425–448). Oxford University Press.

Beyerlin, U., & Grote Stoutenburg, J. (2013). Environment, international protection. In A. Peters & R. Wolfrum (Eds.), *Max Planck Encyclopedia of public international law*. Oxford University Press. (Article last updated December 2013).

Beyerlin, U., & Marauhn, T. (2011). *International environmental law*. Hart Publishing.

Bobertz, B. C. (1987). Toward a better understanding of intergenerational justice. *Buffalo Law Review, 36*(1), 165–192.

Bodansky, D. (2022). The forever negotiations. *EJIL: Talk!* 19 December 2022. Retrieved 3 January 2025, from https://www.ejiltalk.org/the-forever-negotiations/

Bosselmann, K. (2009). Environmental ethics. In A. Peters & R. Wolfrum (Eds.), *Max Planck Encyclopedia of public international law*. Oxford University Press. (Article last updated January 2009).

Boyle, A. E. (1999). Some reflections on the relationship of treaties and soft law. *International and Comparative Law Quarterly, 48*, 901–913.

Brennan, A., & Lo, Y.-S. (2021). Environmental Ethics. In E. N. Zalta (Ed.). *The Stanford Encyclopedia of Philosophy.* ISSN 1095-5054. Retrieved 3 January 2025, from https://plato.stanford.edu/entries/ethics-environmental/. (Article last updated December 2021).

Brown Weiss, E. (1984). Conservation and equity between generations. In T. Buergenthal (Ed.), *Contemporary issues in international law: Essays in Honor of Louis B. Sohn* (pp. 245–289). Engel.

Brown Weiss, E. (1989). *In fairness to future generations: International law, common patrimony, and intergenerational equity*. Transnational Publishers, Inc.

Brown Weiss, E. (1992). Intergenerational equity and rights of future generations. In A. A. Cançado Trindade & E. Brown Weiss (Eds.), *Derechos Humanos, Desarrollo Sustentable y Medio Ambiente: Human rights, sustainable development and the environment* (pp. 71–81). Banco Interamericano de Desarrollo.

Brown Weiss, E. (1999). Opening the door to the environment and to future generations. In L. Boisson de Chazournes & P. Sands (Eds.), *International law, the international court of justice, and nuclear weapons* (Vol. 21, pp. 338–353). Cambridge University Press.

Brown Weiss, E. (2008). Climate change, intergenerational equity, and international law. *Vermont Journal of Environmental Law, 9*, 615–619.

Brown Weiss, E. (2010). Implementing intergenerational equity. In M. Fitzmaurice, D. Ong, & P. Merkouris (Eds.), *Research handbook on international environmental law* (Vol. 5, pp. 100–116). Edward Elgar Publishing.

Brown Weiss, E. (2019). Intergenerational equity. In Y. Aguila & J. E. Viñuales (Eds.). *A global pact for the environment: Legal foundations* (No. 5, pp. 51–58). Cambridge Centre for Environment, Energy and Natural Resource Governance (C-EENRG).

Brown Weiss, E. (2021). Intergenerational equity. In A. Peters & R. Wolfrum (Eds.), *Max Planck Encyclopedia of public international law*. Oxford University Press. (Article last updated April 2021).

Buchanan, N. H. (2009). What do we owe future generations? *George Washington Law Review, 77*(5-6), 1237–1297.

Buchanan, N. H. (2011). What kind of environment do we owe future generations? *Lewis & Clark Law Review, 15*(2), 339–367.

Burgers, L. (2020). *Justitia, the people's power and mother earth: Democratic legitimacy of judicial law-making in European private law cases on climate change*. Ipskamp Printing.

Bustami, A. (2022). An intertemporal perspective on intergenerational equity: How to assess the legal relationship between present and future generations. *Verfassungsblog*. 11 August 2022. Retrieved 3 January 2025, from https://verfassungsblog.de/an-intertemporal-perspective-on-intergenerational-equity/

Bustami, A., & Kahl, V. (2024). Intervention auf Irrwegen: Der Fall Südafrika gegen Israel und die problematische Rolle Deutschlands im Hauptverfahren. *Verfassungsblog*. 30 January 2024. Retrieved 3 January 2025, from https://verfassungsblog.de/intervention-auf-irrwegen/.

Carty, A. (2008). Sociological theories of international law. In A. Peters & R. Wolfrum (Eds.), *Max Planck Encyclopedia of public international law*. Oxford University Press. (Article last updated March 2008).

Cassese, A. (Ed.). (2012). *Realizing Utopia: The future of international law* (1st ed.). Oxford University Press. https://doi.org/10.1093/acprof:oso/9780199691661.001.0001

Catrina, I. L. (2013). Intergenerational equity of public debt. *European Journal of Science and Theology, 9*(2), 167–174.

Chen, D., Rojas, M., Samset, B. H., Cobb, K., Diongue-Niang, A., Edwards, P., Emori, S., Faria, S. H., Hawkins, E., Hope, P., Huybrechts, P., Meinshausen, M., Mustafa, S., Plattner, G.-K., & Treguier, A. M. (2021). Framing, context and methods. In V. Masson-Delmotte et al. (Eds.) IPCC, *climate change 2021 – The physical science basis: Working Group I Contribution to the IPCC Sixth Assessment Report* (pp. 147–286). Retrieved 3 January 2025, from https://www.ipcc.ch/report/ar6/wg1/downloads/report/IPCC_AR6_WGI_Chapter01.pdf

Climate Analytics, & New Climate Institute. (2020). Pandemic Recovery: Positive Intentions vs. Policy Rollbacks, With Just a Hint of Green: Warming Projections Global Update. *Climate Action Tracker*. September 2020. Retrieved 3 January 2025, from https://climateactiontracker.org/documents/790/CAT_2020-09-23_Briefing_GlobalUpdate_Sept2020.pdf

Climate Analytics, & New Climate Institute. (2022). Despite Glasgow Climate Pact 2030 Climate Target Updates Have Stalled: Mid-year Update. *Climate Action Tracker*. June 2022. Retrieved

3 January 2025, from https://climateactiontracker.org/documents/1051/CAT_2022-06-03_Briefing_MidYearUpdate_DespiteGlasgowTargetUpdatesStalled.pdf

Climate Analytics, & New Climate Institute. (2024). CAT Climate Target Update Tracker. *Climate Action Tracker*. December 2024. Retrieved 3 January 2025, from https://climateactiontracker.org/climate-target-update-tracker-2022/

Climate Change Litigation Databases. (2023-today). Request for an Advisory Opinion on the Obligations of States with Respect to Climate Change. *Sabin Center for Climate Change Law at Columbia Law School*. 2023-today. Retrieved 3 January 2025, from https://climatecasechart.com/non-us-case/request-for-an-advisory-opinion-on-the-obligations-of-states-with-respect-to-climate-change/

Collins, L. M. (2007). Revisiting the Doctrine of intergenerational equity in global environmental governance. *Dalhousie Law Journal, 30*(1), 73–134.

Cordonier Segger, M.-C., Szabó, M., & Harrington, A. R. (Eds.). (2021). *Intergenerational justice in sustainable development treaty implementation: Advancing future generations rights through national institutions*. Cambridge University Press.

Cryer, R., Hervey, T., Sokhi-Bulley, B., & Bohm, A. (2011). *Research methodologies in EU and international law*. Hart Publishing.

Cudd, A., & Eftekhari, S. (2021). Contractarianism. In E. N. Zalta (Ed.). *The Stanford Encyclopedia of Philosophy*. ISSN 1095-5054. Retrieved 3 January 2025, from https://plato.stanford.edu/entries/contractarianism/. (Article last updated September 2021)

D'Amato, A. (1990). Do we owe a duty to future generations to preserve the global environment? *American Journal of International Law, 84*, 190–198.

de George, R. (1981). The environment, rights, and future generations. In E. Partridge (Ed.), *Responsibilities to future generations: Environmental ethics* (pp. 157–166). Prometheus Books.

Demony, C., & Pereira, M. (2022). Scorching heat wave sparks wildfires in Europe. *REUTERS*. 14 July 2022. Retrieved 3 January 2025, from https://www.reuters.com/world/europe/wildfires-rage-heatwave-scorches-portugal-spain-2022-07-13/

Diehl, P. F., & Ku, C. (2010). *The dynamics of international law. Cambridge University Press.* https://doi.org/10.1017/CBO9780511817328

Doran, M. (2008). Intergenerational equity in fiscal policy reform. *Tax Law Review, 61*, 241–293.

Dworkin, R. (1978). *Taking rights seriously*. Harvard University Press.

Eckstein, D., Künzel, V., Schäfer, L., & Winges, M. (2019). *Global climate risk index 2020: Who suffers most from extreme weather events? Weather-related loss events in 2019 and 2000-2019.* Germanwatch e.V.

Eckstein, D., Künzel, V., & Schäfer, L. (2021). *Global climate risk index 2021: Who suffers most from extreme weather events? Weather-related loss events in 2019 and 2000-2019.* Germanwatch e.V.

European Commission. (2019–2024). A European Green Deal: Striving to be the First Climate-Neutral Continent. *European Union* (EU). 2019–2024. Retrieved 3 January 2025, from https://ec.europa.eu/info/strategy/priorities-2019-2024/european-green-deal_en

Fehr, H. (2009). Anmerkungen zum Generationenkonflikt aus Ökonomischer Perspektive. In N. Goldschmidt (Ed.), *Generationengerechtigkeit: Ordnungsökonomische Konzepte* (pp. 35–40). Mohr Siebeck.

Fitzmaurice, M. (2008). Intergenerational equity revisited. In I. Buffard, J. Crawford, A. Pellet, & S. Wittich (Eds.), *International law between universalism and fragmentation: Festschrift in Honour of Gerhard Hafner* (Vol. No. 11, pp. 195–229). Martinus Nijhoff Publishers.

Fitzmaurice, M. (2009). Dynamic (evolutive) interpretation of treaties: Part II. *Hague Yearbook of International Law, 22*, 3–31.

Fleurbaey, M., Kartha, S., Bolwig, S., Chee, Y. L., Chen, Y., Corbera, E., Lecocq, F., Lutz, W., Muylaert, M. S., Norgaard, R. B., Okereke, C., & Sagar, A. (2014). Sustainable development and equity. In O. Edenhofer et al. (Eds.) IPCC, *Climate Change 2014 – Mitigation of Climate Change: Working Group III Contribution to the Fifth Assessment Report of the*

*Intergovernmental Panel on Climate Change* (pp. 283–350). Retrieved 3 January 2025, from https://www.ipcc.ch/site/assets/uploads/2018/02/ipcc_wg3_ar5_chapter4.pdf

Frenz, W. (2023). COP 27 mit mageren Ergebnissen. *Natur Und Recht, 45*, 101–103. https://doi.org/10.1007/s10357-023-4138-5

Fuest, C. (2009). Sind Unsere Sozialen Sicherungssysteme Generationengerecht? In N. Goldschmidt (Ed.), *Generationengerechtigkeit: Ordnungsökonomische Konzepte* (pp. 153–178). Mohr Siebeck.

Future Timeline Community. (2024). *The Future Timeline*. 2024. Retrieved 3 January 2025, from https://www.futuretimeline.net/

Gardiner, S. M. (2006). Protecting future generations: Intergenerational buck-passing, theoretical ineptitude and a brief for a global core precautionary principle. In J. C. Tremmel (Ed.), *Handbook of intergenerational justice* (Vol. No. 8, pp. 148–169). Edward Elgar Publishing.

Gatmaytan, D. B. (2003). The illusion of intergenerational equity: Oposa v. Factoran as Pyrrhic Victory. *Georgetown International Environmental Law Review, 15*(3), 457–485.

Gosseries, A. (2004). constitutionalizing future rights? *Intergenerational Justice Review, 2*, 10–11.

Greaves, H., MacAskill, W., O'Keeffe-O'Donovan, R., Trammell, P., Tereick, B., Mogensen, A., Tarsney, C., Alexandrie, G., & Cugnon de Sévricourt, M. (2020). *A research Agenda for the global priorities institute*. Global Priorities Institute. October 2020. Retrieved 3 January 2025, from https://globalprioritiesinstitute.org/wp-content/uploads/GPI-research-agenda-version-2.1.pdf

Green, M. (2020). Australia's massive fires could become routine, Climate Scientists Warn. *REUTERS*. 14 January 2020. Retrieved 3 January 2025, from https://www.reuters.com/article/us-climate-change-australia-report/australias-massive-fires-could-become-routine-climate-scientists-warn-idUSKBN1ZD06W

Hadjiargyrou, Z. (2016). A conceptual and practical evaluation of intergenerational equity in international environmental law. *International Community Law Review, 18*, 248–277.

Hansen, J. E., Johnson, D., Lacis, A. A., Lebedeff, S. A., Lee, P., Rind, D. H., & Russell, G. L. (1981). Climate impact of increasing atmospheric carbon dioxide. *Science, 213*(4511), 957–966. https://doi.org/10.1126/science.213.4511.957

Herdegen, M. (2020). Interpretation in international law. In A. Peters & R. Wolfrum (Eds.), *Max Planck Encyclopedia of public international law*. Oxford University Press. (Article last updated November 2020).

Heubach, A. (2008). *Generationengerechtigkeit: Herausforderung für die Zeitgenössische Ethik*. V & R Unipress.

Hoegh-Guldberg, O., Jacob, D., Taylor, M., Bindi, M., Brown, S., Camilloni, I., Diedhiou, A., Djalante, R., Ebi, K. L., Engelbrecht, F., Guiot, J., Hijoka, Y., Mehrotra, S., Payne, A., Seneviratne, S. I., Thomas, A., Warren, R., & Zhou, G. (2018). Impacts of 1.5°C of Global Warming on Natural and Human Systems. In V. Masson-Delmotte et al. (Eds.), IPCC, *Global Warming of 1.5°C: An IPCC Special Report on the Impacts of Global Warming of 1.5°C Above Pre-Industrial Levels and Related Global Greenhouse Gas Emission Pathways, in the Context of Strengthening the Global Response to the Threat of Climate Change, Sustainable Development, and Efforts to Eradicate Poverty* (pp. 175–311). Retrieved 3 January 2025, from https://www.ipcc.ch/sr15/

Human Rights Council. (2019). *Climate Change and Poverty – Report of the Special Rapporteur on Extreme Poverty and Human Rights*, by P. Alston (17 July 2019). UN Doc. A/HRC/41/39.

Institut de Droit International. (1975). The Intertemporal Problem in Public International Law. 11 August 1975. Retrieved 3 January 2025, from https://www.idi-iil.org/app/uploads/2017/06/1975_wies_01_en.pdf

International Group of Experts for the Pact. (2017). Draft Global Pact for the Environment. *Global Pact for the Environment*. June 2017. Retrieved 3 January 2025, from https://globalpactenvironment.org/en/documents-en/the-pact-text/

International Law Commission. (2015). *Third Report by the Special Rapporteur on Identification of Customary International Law*, by M. Wood (27 March 2015). UN Doc. A/CN.4/682.

IPBES. (2019). Summary for policymakers. In intergovernmental platform on biodiversity and ecosystem services. In E. S. Brondízio, J. Settele, S. Diaz, & H. T. Ngo (Eds.), *Global assessment report on biodiversity and ecosystem services*. Retrieved 3 January 2025, from https://ipbes.net/global-assessment

IPCC. (June 1992). In B. Bolin et al. (Eds.) *Climate Change – The IPCC 1990 and 1992 Assessments: IPCC First Assessment Report Overview and Policymaker Summaries and 1992 IPCC Supplement*. Retrieved 3 January 2025, from https://www.ipcc.ch/report/climate-change-the-ipcc-1990-and-1992-assessments/

IPCC. (1995, October). In B. Bolin et al. (Eds.), *Climate Change 1995: Synthesis Report*. Retrieved 3 January 2025, from https://www.ipcc.ch/report/ar2/wg1/

IPCC. (2001, October). Climate Change 2001: Synthesis Report. In R. T. Watson et al. (Eds.), *Contributions of Working Groups I, II and III to the Third Assessment Report of the IPCC*. Retrieved 3 January 2025, from https://www.ipcc.ch/report/ar3/syr/

IPCC. (2007, September). Climate Change 2007: Synthesis Report. In Core Writing Team, R. K. Pachauri, & A. Reisinger (Eds.), *Contributions of Working Groups I, II and III to the Fourth Assessment Report of the IPCC*. Retrieved 3 January 2025, from https://www.ipcc.ch/report/ar4/syr/

IPCC. (2014a). In O. Edenhofer et al. (Eds.), *Climate Change 2014 – Mitigation of Climate Change: Working Group III Contribution to the Fifth Assessment Report of the Intergovernmental Panel on Climate Change*. Retrieved 3 January 2025, from https://www.ipcc.ch/report/ar5/wg3/.

IPCC. (October 2014b). Climate Change 2014: Synthesis Report. In Core Writing Team, R. K. Pachauri and L. Meyer (Eds.), *Contributions of Working Groups I, II and III to the Fifth Assessment Report of the Intergovernmental Panel on Climate Change*. Retrieved 3 January 2025, from https://www.ipcc.ch/report/ar5/syr/.

IPCC. (2019). Summary for Policymakers. In P. R. Shukla et al. (Eds.). IPCC, *Climate Change and Land: An IPCC Special Report on climate change, desertification, land degradation, sustainable land management, food security, and greenhouse gas fluxes in terrestrial ecosystems*. Retrieved 3 January 2025, from https://www.ipcc.ch/srccl/.

IPCC. (August 2021a). In V. Masson-Delmotte et al. (Eds.), *Climate Change 2021 – The Physical Science Basis: Working Group I Contribution to the IPCC Sixth Assessment Report*. Retrieved 3 January 2025, from https://www.ipcc.ch/report/sixth-assessment-report-working-group-i/

IPCC. (2021b). Summary for Policymakers. In V. Masson-Delmotte et al. (Eds.), IPCC, *Climate Change 2021 – The Physical Science Basis: Working Group I Contribution to the IPCC Sixth Assessment Report*. Retrieved 3 January 2025, from https://www.ipcc.ch/report/ar6/wg1/downloads/report/IPCC_AR6_WGI_SPM.pdf.

IPCC. (2022a, February ). In H.-O. Pörtner et al. (Eds.), *Climate Change 2022 – Impacts, Adaptation and Vulnerability: Working Group II Contribution to the IPCC Sixth Assessment Report*. Retrieved 3 January 2025, from https://www.ipcc.ch/report/sixth-assessment-report-working-group-ii/.

IPCC. (2022b). Summary for Policymakers. In H.-O. Pörtner et al. (Eds.), IPCC, *Climate Change 2022 – Impacts, Adaptation and Vulnerability: Working Group II Contribution to the IPCC Sixth Assessment Report* (pp. 1–35). Retrieved 3 January 2025, from https://www.ipcc.ch/report/ar6/wg2/downloads/report/IPCC_AR6_WGII_SummaryForPolicymakers.pdf.

IPCC. (April 2022c). In P. R. Shukla et al. (Eds.), *Climate Change 2022 – Mitigation of Climate Change: Working Group III Contribution to the IPCC Sixth Assessment Report*. Retrieved 3 January 2025, from https://www.ipcc.ch/report/sixth-assessment-report-working-group-3/

IPCC. (2022d). Summary for Policymakers. In P. R. Shukla et al. (Eds.), IPCC, *Climate Change 2022 – Mitigation of Climate Change: Working Group III Contribution to the IPCC Sixth Assessment Report* (pp. 1–52). Retrieved 3 January 2025, from https://www.ipcc.ch/report/ar6/wg2/downloads/report/IPCC_AR6_WGII_SummaryForPolicymakers.pdf

Kaku, M. (2011). *Physics of the future: How science will shape human destiny and our daily lives by the year 2100* (1st ed.). Doubleday.

Kaku, M. (2015). Life in the year 2100. *The Week*. 9 January 2015. Retrieved 3 January 2025, from https://theweek.com/articles/485908/life-year-2100.

Koskenniemi, M. (2007a). International legal theory and doctrine. In A. Peters & R. Wolfrum (Eds.), *Max Planck Encyclopedia of public international law*. Oxford University Press. (Article last updated November 2007).

Koskenniemi, M. (2007b). Methodology of international law. In A. Peters & R. Wolfrum (Eds.), *Max Planck Encyclopedia of public international law*. Oxford University Press. (Article last updated November 2007).

Kotsakis, A. (2017). On the relation between scholarship and action in environmental law: Method, theory, change. In A. Philippopoulos-Mihalopoulos & V. Brooks (Eds.), *Research methods in environmental law: A handbook* (Vol. 14, pp. 338–363). Edward Elgar Publishing.

Kotzur, M. (2008). Intertemporal law. In A. Peters & R. Wolfrum (Eds.), *Max Planck Encyclopedia of public international law*. Oxford University Press. (Article last updated April 2008).

Kronenberger, M. (2022). Dealing with loss and damage. *Völkerrechtsblog*. 18 November 2022. Retrieved 3 January 2025, from https://voelkerrechtsblog.org/dealing-with-loss-and-damage/

Lachenmann, F. (2012). Legal positivism. In R. Wolfrum (Ed.), *The Max Planck Encyclopedia of public international law*. Oxford University Press.

Lawrence, P. (2012). Justice for future generations: Environment discourses, international law and climate change. In B. Jessup & K. Rubenstein (Eds.), *Environmental Discourses in public and international law* (pp. 23–46). Cambridge University Press.

Lawrence, P. (2014). *Justice for future generations: Climate change and international law*. Edward Elgar Publishing.

Lawrence, P., & Köhler, L. (2017). Representation of future generations through international climate litigation: A normative framework. *German Yearbook of International Law, 60*, 640–667.

Lee, J.-Y., Marotzke, J., Bala, G., Cao, L., Corti, S., Dunne, J. P., Engelbrecht, F., Fischer, E., Fyfe, J. C., Jones, C., Maycock, A., Mutemi, J., Ndiaye, O., Panickal, S., & Zhou, T. (2021). Future Global Climate: Scenario-Based Projections and Near-Term Information. In V. Masson-Delmotte et al. (Eds.), *IPCC, Climate Change 2021 – The physical science basis: Working Group I Contribution to the IPCC Sixth Assessment Report* (pp. 553–672) Retrieved 3 January 2025, from https://www.ipcc.ch/report/sixth-assessment-report-working-group-i/

Lenton, T. M., Rockström, J., Gaffney, O., Rahmstorf, S., Richardson, K., Steffen, W., & Schellnhuber, H. J. (2019). Climate tipping points – too risky to bet against. *Nature, 575*(7784), 592–595. https://doi.org/10.1038/d41586-019-03595-0

Lowe, V. (1999). Sustainable development and unsustainable arguments. In A. E. Boyle & D. A. C. Freestone (Eds.), *International law and sustainable development: Past achievements and future challenges* (pp. 19–37). Oxford University Press.

Lucas, P., Hedden, S., van Vuuren, D., Calvin, K. V., Chung, S. H., Harfoot, M., Köberle, A. C., Moyer, J. D., & Wada, Y. (2019). Future developments without targeted policies. In United Nations Environment Programme (UNEP). In P. Ekins, J. Gupta, & P. Boileau (Eds.), *Global Environment Outlook 6 (GEO-6): Healthy Planet, Healthy People* (pp. 485–508) Retrieved 3 January 2025, from https://wedocs.unep.org/bitstream/handle/20.500.11822/27673/GEO6_CH21.pdf

Malhotra, A. (1998). A commentary on the status of future generations as a subject of international law. In E. Agius & S. Busuttil (Eds.), *Future generations and international law: Proceedings of the international experts' meeting held by the future generations programme at the foundation for international studies, University of Malta* (Vol. 5, pp. 39–50). Earthscan Publications Ltd..

Manguiat, M. S. Z., & Yu, V. P. B. (2003). Maximizing the value of Oposa v. Factoran. *Georgetown International Environmental Law Review, 15*(3), 487–496.

Maslin, M. A., Lang, J., & Harvey, F. (2023). A short history of the successes and failures of the international climate change negotiations. *UCL Open: Environment, 5*, e059. https://doi.org/10.14324/111.444/ucloe.000059

Meadows, D. H., Meadows, D. L., Randers, J., & Behrens, W. W., III. (1972). *The limits to growth: A report for the club of Rome's project on the predicament of mankind*. Universe Books.

Merrills, J. G. (2010). Environmental rights. In D. Bodansky, J. Brunnée, & E. Hey (Eds.), *The Oxford handbook of international environmental law* (Vol. 28, 1st ed., pp. 663–680). Oxford University Press. https://doi.org/10.1093/oxfordhb/9780199552153.013.0028

Meyer, L. H. (2021). Intergenerational Justice. In E. N. Zalta (Ed.). *The Stanford Encyclopedia of Philosophy*. ISSN 1095-5054. Retrieved 3 January 2025, from https://plato.stanford.edu/archives/sum2021/entries/justice-intergenerational/. (Article last updated May 2021)

Michallet, I. (2018). Equity and the interests of future generations. In L. Krämer & E. Orlando (Eds.), *Principles of environmental law* (pp. 150–160). Edward Elgar Publishing.

Moorhouse, F. (2021). What is Longtermism? 2021. Retrieved 3 January 2025, from https://longtermism.com/.

Nathanson, S. (n.d.). Utilitarianism: Act and Rule. In J. Fieser & B. Dowden (Eds.). *Internet Encyclopedia of Philosophy*. ISSN 2161-0002.

Niehaus, M., & Davies, K. J. (2021). Voices for the voiceless: Climate protection from the streets to the courts. *Journal of Human Rights and the Environment, 12*(2), 228–253. https://doi.org/10.4337/jhre.2021.02.04

Norton, B. G. (1982). Environmental ethics and the rights of future generations. *Environmental Ethics, 4*(4), 319–337. https://doi.org/10.5840/enviroethics1982444

Orakhelashvili, A. (2007). Natural law and justice. In A. Peters & R. Wolfrum (Eds.), *Max Planck Encyclopedia of public international law*. Oxford University Press. (Article last updated August 2007).

Palladino, R. (2014). Environmental changes and migration: Responses from Rio to Rio+20 and beyond. In M. Fitzmaurice, S. Maljean-Dubois, & S. Negri (Eds.), *Environmental protection and sustainable development from Rio to Rio+20: Protection de l'Environnement et Développement Durable de Rio à Rio+20* (pp. 239–263). Brill Nijhoff.

Pearce, C. (2012). Ombudspersons for future generations: A proposal for Rio+20: Bringing intergenerational justice into the heart of policy-making. *UN Environment Programme*. May 2012. Retrieved 3 January 2025, from https://wedocs.unep.org/20.500.11822/7444

Peczenik, A. (2005). Scientia juris: Legal doctrine as knowledge of law and as a source of law. In E. Pattaro (Ed.), *A treatise of legal philosophy and general jurisprudence* (Vol. 4). Springer.

Potsdam Institute for Climate Impact Research. (2024). *Tipping Elements: The Achilles Heels of the Earth System. 2024*. Retrieved 3 January 2025, from https://www.pik-potsdam.de/en/output/infodesk/tipping-elements

Proelß, A. (2022). Prinzipien des Internationalen Umweltrechts. In A. Proelß (Ed.), *Internationales Umweltrecht* (Vol. 3, 2nd ed., pp. 95–150). De Gruyter.

Rawls, J. (1971). *A theory of justice*. Harvard University Press.

Redgwell, C. (1999). *Intergenerational trusts and environmental protection*. Juris.

Reeh, G. (2022). Ernüchternde Klimakonferenz und ihre Lehren. *Verfassungsblog*. 28 November 2022. Retrieved 3 January 2025, from https://verfassungsblog.de/ernuchternde-klimakonferenz-und-ihre-lehren/

Rogelj, J., Shindell, D., Jiang, K., Fifita, S., Forster, P. M., Ginzburg, V., Handa, C., Kheshgi, H., Kobayashi, S., Kriegler, E., Mundaca, L., Séférian, R., & Vilariño, M. V. (2018). Mitigation pathways compatible with 1.5°C in the context of sustainable development. In V. Masson-Delmotte et al. (Eds) IPCC, *Global Warming of 1.5°C: An IPCC Special Report on the Impacts of Global Warming of 1.5°C Above Pre-Industrial Levels and Related Global Greenhouse Gas Emission Pathways, in the Context of Strengthening the Global Response to the Threat of Climate Change, Sustainable Development, and Efforts to Eradicate Poverty* (pp. 93–174). Retrieved 3 January 2025, from https://www.ipcc.ch/sr15/chapter/chapter-2/

Rose, M. (2017). *Zukünftige Generationen in der Heutigen Demokratie: Theorie und Praxis der Proxy-Repräsentation*. Springer.

Ryngaert, C. M. J., & Hora Siccama, D. W. (2018). Ascertaining customary international law: An Inquiry into the methods used by domestic courts. *Netherlands International Law Review, 65*(1), 1–25. https://doi.org/10.1007/s40802-018-0104-y

Sands, P., Peel, J., & Fabra, A. (2018). *Principles of international environmental law* (4th ed.). Cambridge University Press.

Sawyer, J. S. (1972). Man-made carbon dioxide and the "Greenhouse" effect. *Nature, 239*(5366), 23–26. https://doi.org/10.1038/239023a0

Schrijver, N. J. (2009). After us, the Deluge? The position of future generations of humankind in international environmental law. In M. A. R. M. Salih (Ed.), *Climate change and sustainable development: New challenges for poverty reduction* (Vol. No. 4, pp. 59–78). Edward Elgar Publishing.

Shelton, D. (1991). Human rights, environmental rights and the right to the environment. *Stanford Journal of International Law, 28*(1), 103–138.

Shelton, D. (2010). Intergenerational equity. In R. Wolfrum & C. Kojima (Eds.), *Solidarity: A structural principle of international law* (pp. 123–168). Springer.

Slobodian, L. (2020). Defending the future: Intergenerational equity in climate litigation. *Georgetown Environmental Law Review, 32*(3), 569–590.

Smits, J. M. (2017). What is legal doctrine? On the aims and methods of legal-dogmatic research. In R. van Gestel, H.-W. Micklitz, & E. L. Rubin (Eds.), *Rethinking scholarship: A transatlantic dialogue* (Vol. 5, pp. 207–228). Cambridge University Press.

Spentzou, D. (2021). Climate change litigation as a means to address intergenerational equity and climate change. *Queen Mary Law Journal, 2*, 153–183. https://doi.org/10.26494/QMLJ3944

Stern, N. H. (2011). *The economics of climate change: The stern review* (1st ed.). Cambridge University Press.

Stoett, P., Davies, J., Armenteras, D., Hills, J., McRae, L., & Zastavniouk, C. (2019). Biodiversity. In: P. Ekins, J. Gupta, & P. Boileau (Eds.) *Global Environment Outlook 6 (GEO-6): Healthy Planet, Healthy People* (pp. 141–173). United Nations Environment Programme (UNEP), Retrieved 3 January 2025, from https://wedocs.unep.org/bitstream/handle/20.500.11822/27659/GEO6_CH6.pdf

Stone, C. D. (2010). Ethics and international environmental law. In D. Bodansky, J. Brunnée, & E. Hey (Eds.), *The Oxford handbook of international environmental law* (Vol. No. 13, 1st ed., pp. 291–312). Oxford University Press.

Supanich, G. P. (1992). The legal basis of intergenerational responsibility: An alternative view – the sense of intergenerational identity. *Yearbook of International Environmental Law, 3*(1), 94–107. https://doi.org/10.1093/yiel/3.1.94

Süssmuth, B., & von Weizsäcker, R. K. (2006). Institutional determinants of public debt: A political economy perspective. In J. C. Tremmel (Ed.), *Handbook of intergenerational justice* (Vol. No. 9, pp. 170–184). Edward Elgar Publishing.

Szekely, A. (2008). The promise of the brundtland report: Honored or betrayed. *Pacific McGeorge Global Business and Development Law Journal, 21*, 159.

Talmon, S. (2015). Determining customary international law: the ICJ's methodology between induction, deduction and assertion. *European Journal of International Law, 26*(2), 417–443. https://doi.org/10.1093/ejil/chv020

Tanaka, Y. (2013). Reflections on time elements in the international law of the environment. *Zeitschrift Für Ausländisches Öffentliches Recht Und Völkerrecht, 73*, 139–175.

The Guardian. (2021). *Wildfires Burn Out of Control in Greece and Turkey as Thousands Flee*. 6 August 2021. Retrieved 3 January 2025, from https://www.theguardian.com/world/2021/aug/06/wildfires-out-of-control-greece-turkey-thousands-flee

Theilen, J. T., Hassfurther, I., & Staff, W. (2017). Guest Editors' introduction: Towards Utopia – rethinking international law. *German Yearbook of International Law, 60*, 315–334.

Thompson, D. F. (2010). Representing future generations: Political presentism and democratic trusteeship. *Critical Review of International Social and Political Philosophy, 13*(1), 17–37. https://doi.org/10.1080/13698230903326232

Thompson, J. (2003). Intergenerational equity: Issues of principle in the allocation of social resources between this generation and the next. *Information and Research Services Research Paper No. 7 2002-03.* 13 May 2003. Retrieved 3 January 2025, from https://apo.org.au/node/6952

Tremmel, J. C. (Ed.). (2006). *Handbook of intergenerational justice*. Edward Elgar Publishing.

Treves, T. (2006). Customary international law. In A. Peters & R. Wolfrum (Eds.), *Max Planck Encyclopedia of public international law*. Oxford University Press. (Article last updated November 2006).

UNFCCC Conference of the Parties 26. (2021a). *Glasgow Climate Pact* (13 November 2021). UN Doc. FCCC/PA/CMA/2021/10/Add.1.

UNFCCC Conference of the Parties 26. (2021b). *Supporting the conditions for a just transition internationally: Declaration*. 4 November 2021. Retrieved 3 January 2025, from https://ukcop26.org/supporting-the-conditions-for-a-just-transition-internationally/

United Nations Environment Programme. (2012). Summary for policymakers. In M. Billot et al. (Eds.). *Global Environment Outlook 5 (GEO-5): Environment for the Future We Want*. United Nations Environment Programme (UNEP), Retrieved 3 January 2025, from https://www.unep.org/resources/geo-5-summary-policy-makers.

United Nations Environment Programme. (2019). In P. Ekins, J. Gupta & P. Boileau (Eds.). *Global Environment Outlook 6 (GEO-6): Healthy Planet, Healthy People*. Retrieved 3 January 2025, from https://www.unep.org/resources/global-environment-outlook-6

United Nations Environment Programme. (2020). *Global Climate Litigation Report: 2020 Status Review*. UN Environment Programme.

United Nations General Assembly. (1988). *Protection of Global Climate for Present and Future Generations of Mankind* (6 December 1988). UN Doc. A/RES/43/53.

United Nations General Assembly. (2012). *The Future We Want* (27 July 2012). UN Doc. A/RES/66/288.

United Nations General Assembly. (2013). *Protection of Global Climate for Present and Future Generations of Humankind* (20 December 2013). UN Doc. A/RES/68/212.

United Nations General Assembly. (2019). Only 11 Years Left to Prevent Irreversible Damage from Climate Change, Speakers Warn during General Assembly High-Level Meeting: Seventy-Third Session, High-Level Meeting on Climate and Sustainable Development. *General Assembly Meetings Coverage*. 28 March 2019. Retrieved 3 January 2025, from https://www.un.org/press/en/2019/ga12131.doc.htm

United Nations Secretary-General. (2013). *Intergenerational Solidarity and the Needs of Future Generations, Report of the Secretary-General* (15 August 2013). UN Doc. A/68/322.

van Asselt, H. (2023). "Historic" or "Historic Failure"? Fossil Fuels at COP28. *EJIL: Talk!* 28 December 2023. Retrieved 3 January 2025, from https://www.ejiltalk.org/historic-or-historic-failure-fossil-fuels-at-cop28/

van der Vossen, B. (2023). Libertarianism. In E. N. Zalta (Ed.). *The Stanford Encyclopedia of Philosophy*. ISSN 1095-5054. Retrieved 3 January 2025, from https://plato.stanford.edu/entries/libertarianism/. (Article last updated August 2023)

Virally, M. (1988). To what extent are the traditional categories of Lex Lata and Lex Ferenda still viable? Ii. Discussion A. Lex Lata and Lex Ferenda. In A. Cassese & J. H. H. Weiler (Eds.), *Change and stability in international law making* (pp. 66–101). De Gruyter.

von Arnauld, A. (2021). How to illegalize past injustice: Reinterpreting the rules of intertemporality. *European Journal of International Law, 32*(2), 401–432.

von Bernstorff, J. (2023). A Fossil Fuel Ban Treaty: Corrective treaty-making beyond consensus. *EJIL: Talk!* 15 December 2023. Retrieved 3 January 2025, from https://www.ejiltalk.org/a-fossil-fuel-ban-treaty-corrective-treaty-making-beyond-consensus/

Warburton, M., & Olmos, S. (2021). Deaths surge in U.S. and Canada From worst heatwave on record. *REUTERS*. 1 July 2021. Retrieved 3 January 2025, from https://www.reuters.com/world/americas/dire-fire-warnings-issued-wake-record-heatwave-canada-us-2021-06-30/

Wegner, G. (2009). Der Gedanke der Nachhaltigkeit in der Ordnungsökonomik. In N. Goldschmidt (Ed.), *Generationengerechtigkeit: Ordnungsökonomische Konzepte* (pp. 277–280). Mohr Siebeck.

Wewerinke-Singh, M., & El Mahmoud, K. (2024). Missed opportunities in a microcosm of broader challenges. *Völkerrechtsblog*. 27 November 2024. Retrieved 3 January 2025, from https://voelkerrechtsblog.org/missed-opportunities-in-a-microcosm-of-broader-challenges/

Wheatley, S. (2021). Revisiting the doctrine of intertemporal law. *Oxford Journal of Legal Studies, 41*(2), 484–509. https://doi.org/10.1093/ojls/gqaa058

Winter, C., Schuett, J., Martínez, E., van Arsdale, S., Araújo, R., Hollman, N., Sebo, J., Stawasz, A., O'Keefe, C., & Rotola, G. (2021). Legal priorities research: A research Agenda. *Legal Priorities Project*. January 2021. Retrieved 3 January 2025, from https://papers.ssrn.com/sol3/papers.cfm?abstract_id=3931256

Wolfrum, R. (2011). Sources of international law. In A. Peters & R. Wolfrum (Eds.), *Max Planck Encyclopedia of public international law*. Oxford University Press. (Article last updated May 2011).

World Commission on Environment and Development (WCED). (1987). *Report of the World Commission on Environment and Development: Our Common Future (Brundtland Report)* (1987). UN Doc. A/42/427 Annex.

World Health Organization. (2014). *A Global Brief on Vector-Borne Diseases* (2014). WHO/DCO/WHD/2014.1.

World Meteorological Organization. (1979). World Climate Conference (A Conference of Experts on Climate and Mankind): Declaration and Supporting Documents. 12 February 1979. Retrieved 3 January 2025, from https://library.wmo.int/records/item/54699-world-climate-conference-declaration-and-supporting-documents

World Meteorological Organization. (2022). *State of the Global Climate 2021*. WMO.

Zarbiyev, F. (2024). Damaged Beyond Repair? International Law after Gaza. *EJIL: Talk!* 26 March 2024. Retrieved 3 January 2025, from https://www.ejiltalk.org/damaged-beyond-repair-international-law-after-gaza/

# Part I
# The Concept of Intergenerational Equity

The first part of this book offers an overarching analysis of the concept of intergenerational equity *de lege lata* in delimitation to potential developments *de lege ferenda*. "Intergenerational equity" has become a very prominent and multifaceted notion in the last century. The term referred to a confusingly broad variety of meanings in international law. These multifaceted understandings of intergenerational equity and the concern for future generations in international law complicate the proper delimitation of the present research object. An open-minded perspective on the contextual development of intergenerational equity is adequate and necessary in order to get a clear image of what could exactly be meant by "intergenerational equity". Therefore, this book starts with a doctrinal analysis of the historical and systemic contextualisation of intergenerational equity as well as the assessment of the concept in legal scholarship (Chap. 2). It then addresses the philosophical foundations of the concept that are necessary to properly understand the differences between the legal and the pre-legal realm of intergenerational relations (Chap. 3). Only based on these contextual assessments, the author subsequently turns to a strictly positivist analysis of the legal sources of international law, as enshrined in Article 38 of the ICJ Statute, while examining the legal nature of intergenerational equity (Chap. 4). The last chapter of this first part addresses the underlying structural open issues of intergenerational equity, meaning the identification of duty-bearers, the potential of future generations to become right-holders and the institutional implementation of the concept (Chap. 5).

# Chapter 2
# Intergenerational Equity in Its Historical, Scholarly and Systemic Contexts

This chapter serves as an introductory assessment of the historical roots of the concept[1] of intergenerational equity, its understanding in legal scholarship and of the system in which intergenerational equity operates. Its doctrinal analysis gives "a systematic exposition of the principles, rules and concepts governing a particular legal field or institution and [to analyse] the relationship between these principles, rules and concepts with a view to solving unclarities and gaps in the existing law".[2] The chapter begins with a historical account of intergenerational equity (Sect. 2.1). In order to fully understand the current state of the art of intergenerational equity, it is essential to look at the development of international environmental law that has framed the concern for future generations until today. This historical assessment primarily focuses on the mention of future generations and intergenerational equity in international documents (Sect. 2.1.1) and jurisprudence (Sect. 2.1.2).

The historical analysis is then complemented by a perspective on intergenerational equity in legal scholarship (Sect. 2.2). This section mainly examines the works of *Edith Brown Weiss* who has above all influenced the current understanding of intergenerational equity as "a concept of fairness among generations"[3] (Sect. 2.2.1). It then briefly turns to some reception and criticism in legal scholarship (Sect. 2.2.2).

[1] In this book, the term "concept" is used in a non-technical way when referring to intergenerational equity or sustainable development. The relevant concepts' normative capacity (as policy, principle or rule) is addressed *infra* in Sect. 4.1.

[2] Smits (2017), p. 210.

[3] Brown Weiss (2021a, para. 1).



A. Bustami, *The Legal Relationship between Present and Future Generations*,
https://doi.org/10.1007/978-3-032-03345-1_2

Eventually, the chapter turns to a contextualisation of intergenerational equity as the concept has many overlaps and interrelations with other concepts of international environmental law (Sect. 2.3). Based on the foregoing historical assessment and the analysis of legal scholarship on intergenerational equity, this section allows drawing some delimitations between related but different concepts of environmental law. Intergenerational equity has the most interrelations with the concept of sustainable development, which therefore constitutes the main focus of this third section (Sect. 2.3.1). However, it is similarly important to draw the lines between intergenerational equity and other notions, such as intra-generational equity (Sect. 2.3.2) or the common heritage and common concern of humankind (Sect. 2.3.3).

## 2.1 Historical Background: Future Generations Within the Development of International Environmental Law

The reference to the interests[4] of future generations has a long history in the evolution of humanity. Long before future generations entered the realm of international law, cultural and religious traditions already addressed the relationship towards the future. This has been the case for Judaism and Christianity as well as for Islam.[5] Similarly, forms of African customary law as well as Asian religious and philosophical traditions acknowledged a responsibility towards the future for a long time.[6] Indigenous communities in the Americas built their relations to the land on a spiritual element that obliges them to preserve their legacy for future generations.[7] Western liberal tradition as well as Marxism considered the present generation to

[4]International documents, jurisprudence and scholarship refer more or less interchangeable to "interests" or "needs" of future generations, so that these terms are also used as synonyms in this book. However, the idea of "rights of future generations" goes beyond these notions and explicitly refers to a rights-based approach, which is addressed in detail in a subsequent chapter, see *infra* in Sect. 5.2.

[5]For several perspectives, see Agius and Chircop (1998). For Judaism and Christianity, see Agius (1998). For an example in the Jewish Talmud, see De-Shalit (1995), p. 88. For Islam, see Ba Kader et al. (1983), p. 13; Khadduri (1984), pp. 137–138.

[6]See Brown Weiss (1989), p. 20. For Buddhism, see also Peek (1995), p. 529.

[7]See Inter-American Court of Human Rights, *Mayagna (Sumo) Awas Tingni Community v. Nicaragua (Merits, Reparations and Costs),* Judgment, 31 August 2001, OEA Series C No. 79, para. 149; IACHR, *Mayagna (Sumo) Awas Tingni Community v. Nicaragua (Merits, Reparations and Costs),* Joint Separate Opinion of Judges Cançado Trindade, Pacheco Gómez and Abreu Burelli, 31 August 2001, OEA Series C No. 79.

hold certain duties towards posterity.[8] While some of the more recent analyses of intergenerational equity in scholarship and jurisprudence also referred to these religious and cultural roots of the concept,[9] the history of international *legal* concern for future generations began in the last century, more specifically, in the last three decades of the twentieth century.[10]

These occurrences of "future generations" in international documents and jurisprudence were not always framed in the same wording and sometimes differed from document to document, from decision to decision. However, before analysing the legal significance of these different references in more detail in Chap. 4 below,[11] the following sections elaborate on the chronological development of concern for intergenerational issues in the course of the twentieth century until today. As these developments are intertwined with other developments of international environmental law, this historical account cannot address intergenerational equity separately, but must also consider developments of general environmental law where relevant.[12] However, the detailed positioning of intergenerational equity with relation to related concepts of international environmental law is presented at a later point.[13]

The first sub-section chronologically addresses the occurrence of future generations in international legal and policy documents (Sect. 2.1.1). Then, the analysis turns to the most relevant instances of international and national jurisprudence, in which future generations played a crucial role (Sect. 2.1.2).

### 2.1.1 International Legal and Policy Documents

A historical account of intergenerational equity in international law can hardly be exhaustive as the references to future generations are abundant. For instance, *Reinhard Bartholomäi* identified at least 35 international legal documents with references to the interests or concerns of future generations until 1995.[14] In the context of environmental law, the earliest mention of future generations can be found in the Preamble of the International Convention for the Regulation of Whaling ('Whaling Convention'), which recognised "the interest of the nations of the world in safeguarding for future generations the great natural resources represented by the

---

[8]For liberalism, see, e.g., Locke (1690, paras. 25, 31, 33). For Marxism, see Brown Weiss (1989), pp. 19–20.

[9]For such systematic overviews, see, e.g., International Court of Justice, *Gabčíkovo-Nagymaros Project (Hungary v. Slovakia),* Separate Opinion of Vice-President Weeramantry, 25 September 1997, ICJ Reports 1997, 88), pp. 97–109; Brown Weiss (1989), pp. 18–21; Collins (2007b), pp. 88–90.

[10]For an overview, see Brown Weiss (2010), pp. 103–108.

[11]See *infra* in Sect. 4.2.

[12]For a comparable overview, see also Cordonier Segger (2021), pp. 48–56.

[13]See *infra* in Sect. 2.3.

[14]Bartholomäi (1997), pp. 90–107.

whale stocks".[15] Some other early international treaties also referred to future generations in the context of conservation of natural resources,[16] natural and cultural heritage,[17] trade in endangered species[18] and activities on celestial bodies.[19]

The main part of relevant documents has started to evolve in the 1970s, which is why the following sub-sections turn to a chronological illustration of the occurrence of future generations from the beginning of modern international environmental law (Sect. 2.1.1.1), to the Rio conference (Sect. 2.1.1.2), the subsequent post-Rio process (Sect. 2.1.1.3), continuing with the beginning of the twenty-first century (Sect. 2.1.1.4) and ending with the most recent developments of the last years (Sect. 2.1.1.5).

#### 2.1.1.1 From the Beginning of Modern Environmental Law to the Brundtland Report

In the 1970s, the modern framework of international environmental law was born, starting with the UN Conference on the Human Environment in Stockholm in 1972.[20] The first two principles of the 'Stockholm Declaration' explicitly included the concern for future generations.[21] Principle 1 proclaims the "solemn responsibility to protect and improve the environment for present and future generations", while Principle 2 states that "the natural resources of the earth [...] must be safeguarded for the benefit of present and future generations through careful planning or

---

[15] *International Convention for the Regulation of Whaling* (Whaling Convention), adopted 2 December 1946, entered into force 10 November 1948, 161 UNTS 72, Preamble.

[16] *African Convention on the Conservation of Nature and Natural Resources* (African Nature Convention), adopted 15 September 1968, entered into force 16 June 1969, 1001 UNTS 3, Preamble. Moreover, see in its revised version: *Revised African Convention on the Conservation of Nature and Natural Resources* (Revised African Nature Convention), adopted 11 July 2003, entered into force 23 July 2016.

[17] *Convention Concerning the Protection of the World Cultural and Natural Heritage* (World Heritage Convention), adopted 16 November 1972, entered into force 17 December 1975, 1037 UNTS 151, Art. 4.

[18] *Convention on International Trade in Endangered Species of Wild Fauna and Flora* (CITES), adopted 3 March 1973, entered into force 1 July 1975, 993 UNTS 243, Preamble.

[19] *Agreement Governing the Activities of States on the Moon and Other Celestial Bodies* (Moon Agreement), adopted 5 December 1979, entered into force 11 July 1984, 1363 UNTS 3, Art. 4.

[20] Epiney (2022), p. 13.

[21] United Nations (1972, Principles 1, 2).

management, as appropriate". In the same year, the UNEP was founded as the United Nations' first institution for the global environment.[22] In its founding document, the UNGA similarly stressed the need to safeguard the environment for future generations.[23]

The Stockholm Conference was also one of the first occasions, in which the interrelation between environmental protection and economic and social development of States was seriously considered.[24] The conference thereby foreshadowed the core of sustainable development,[25] which has known a continuous evolution in environmental law ever since.[26] Some of the subsequent developments of intergenerational equity and sustainable development have gone hand in hand.[27]

This interrelation became particularly evident in the report 'Our Common Future' by the World Commission on Environment and Development ('WCED') in 1987, the so-called Brundtland Report.[28] The UNGA had welcomed the establishment of this special commission and suggested, *inter alia*, that it should propose strategies for achieving sustainable development.[29] In its report, the Commission redefined sustainable development as "development that meets the needs of the present without compromising the ability of future generations to meet their own needs".[30] It formulated two key concepts: the priority towards the essential needs of the world's poorer population, on the one hand, and the limitations on the environment's ability to meet the needs of present and future generations, on the other hand.[31] The WCED concluded:

> [S]ustainable development is a process of change in which the exploitation of resources, the direction of investments, the orientation of technological development; and institutional change are all in harmony and enhance both current and future potential to meet human needs and aspirations.[32]

---

[22] In detail, see, e.g., Ivanova (2020), pp. 342–344.

[23] United Nations General Assembly (1972, Preamble).

[24] UN (1972, Principles 9–11). See also "Founex Report on Development and Environment" (1972).

[25] Magraw and Hawke (2010), p. 615.

[26] Beyerlin and Marauhn (2011), p. 76; Epiney (2022), pp. 13–23; Proelß (2022), pp. 141–142.

[27] E.g., International Union for Conservation of Nature and Natural Resources (IUCN) et al. (1980, Chapter 1, para. 4); UNGA (1982).

[28] World Commission on Environment and Development (1987).

[29] UNGA (1983, paras. 2, 8). The report was later endorsed by the UN General Assembly: UNGA (1987).

[30] WCED (1987, Introduction, para. 27, Chapter 2, para. 1).

[31] Ibid., Chapter 2, para. 1.

[32] Ibid., Chapter 2, para. 15.

The report underlined the crucial interrelationship between the aspects of economic growth, social equality and environmental protection. More importantly, the WCED proposed a list of legal principles for environmental protection and sustainable development, which included intergenerational equity: "States shall conserve and use the environment and natural resources for the benefit of present and future generations."[33] For the Commission, this proposition was a logical consequence of the aspirations in the Stockholm Declaration and subsequent legal documents.[34] Overall, the Brundtland Report's references to the needs of future generations illustrate that intergenerational concerns are inherent to the concept of sustainable development.[35] This is why subsequent documents and works in scholarship on the status of future generations in international environmental law generally and necessarily referred to the Brundtland Report as an essential source.[36]

#### 2.1.1.2 The UN Conference on Environment and Development

A few years later, in 1992, the UN Conference on Environment and Development in Rio de Janeiro ('UNCED' or 'Rio Conference' or 'Earth Summit') continued the work of the Stockholm Conference and contributed significantly to the further evolution of international environmental law.[37] It was based on the preparatory work of the Brundtland Commission,[38] and it mainly focused on the links between environmental and development concerns. Thus, it further shaped the concept of sustainable development, which also influenced large parts of the conference's five outcome documents: three legally non-binding soft law documents and two major international environmental treaties.[39]

First, the Rio Declaration on Environment and Development outlined 27 key principles of international environmental and development law, including a variety of principles, which directly or indirectly shaped and still shape the concept of sustainable development.[40] While the more ambitious preparations of an Earth Charter prior to the Rio Conference were not successful,[41] the final declaration text constituted a compromise between competing views regarding the legal status

---

33 Ibid., Annex 1, Article 2.

34 Munro and Lammers (1987), pp. 43–44.

35 For a more detailed analysis of this relationship, see *infra* in Sect. 2.3.1.

36 Brown Weiss (1989), p. 39; Redgwell (1999), pp. 120–122.

37 Beyerlin (1994); Epiney (2022), pp. 17–18.

38 Kiss (1993), p. 64; Molinari (2015), p. 140.

39 Sand (1993); Epiney (2022), pp. 17–18.

40 UN Conference on Environment and Development (1992a, Principles 1, 3–5, 7–9, 12, 20–24, 27). See in detail Viñuales (2015).

41 Bosselmann (2009a, para. 2). See also *infra* notes 81–83.

of the document.[42] Principle 3 is the most pertinent part in the declaration text for the consideration of future generations.[43] It underlines the necessity to fulfil the right to development in a way which takes into account the "needs of present and future generations".[44] However, this importance for intergenerational equity was not clear from the beginning. During the preparations of the conference, developing and developed States disagreed on the inclusion of a right to development in the declaration.[45] In the end, Principle 3 accounted for the developing States' need for such a right, hence the choice of wording.[46] Yet, the developed States accepted this formulation only because "it was tempered by reference to the needs of future generations".[47] Despite this original focus on the right to development in the provision,[48] Principle 3 evolved into one of the textbook examples for the existence of intergenerational equity in international law.[49]

The Earth Summit's second outcome document, Agenda 21, was a detailed work programme on sustainable development for the twenty-first century. It addressed in 40 chapters all major areas affecting the environment and the economy.[50] It intended to mark "the beginning of a new global partnership for sustainable development" as a dynamic programme.[51] This is why some commentators considered it to be the most important outcome of the Earth Summit.[52] While none of its chapters explicitly dealt with intergenerational equity, there are several references to future generations.[53] Chapter 25 on children and youth in sustainable development shows the future-oriented approach taken by sustainable development.[54] Further, Chapter 38 set the basis for subsequent institutional arrangements; it recommended, *inter alia*, the establishment of a Commission on Sustainable Development ('CSD'). This Commission was supposed to ensure the effective follow-up of the Earth Summit and to enhance international cooperation in the field of sustainable development.[55]

---

[42]For more details on the competing interests at the Earth Summit, see Beyerlin and Marauhn (2011), p. 14; Shelton (2008, paras. 30–32).

[43]Boyle and Redgwell (2021), p. 121.

[44]UNCED (1992a, Principle 3). For another reference to "a better future for all", see ibid., Principle 21.

[45]Molinari (2015), pp. 141–142.

[46]Ibid. pp. 142–143.

[47]Ibid. p. 142.

[48]Wirth (1995), pp. 627–628.

[49]Molinari (2015), pp. 143–144.

[50]UNCED (1992b).

[51]Ibid., para. 1.6.

[52]Beyerlin (1994), p. 135; Freestone (1994), p. 201.

[53]UNCED (1992b, paras. 8.7, 8.31, 33.3, 33.4, 38.45).

[54]On the role of youth and children in the context of climate litigation, see *infra* in Sect. 5.3.3.3.2.

[55]Ibid., Chapter 38.11 The CSD was established by the UN Economic and Social Council, see United Nations Economic and Social Council (ECOSOC) (1993). For some of the CSD's work in connection with intergenerational equity, see *infra* note 76 and in Sect. 4.2.2.2.

The CSD accompanied the post-Rio implementation process for two decades,[56] before it was replaced by the new High-Level Political Forum on Sustainable Development ('HLPFSD') in 2013.[57] Other institutional initiatives, such as the proposal to establish a non-governmental Earth Council or a guardian for future generations, were not endorsed by the conference, but only taken note of.[58]

The third non-legally binding Rio document was the Statement of Forest Principles, which contained 15 globally applicable principles relating to forest management, conservation and sustainable development.[59] Principle 2 proclaimed that sustainable forest management aimed at "meet[ing] the social, economic, ecological, cultural and spiritual needs of present and future generations".[60]

Eventually, two binding international environmental treaties emerged from the Earth Summit,[61] which also have a strong link to the interests of future generations and sustainable development in general. The UNFCCC was adopted on 9 May 1992 in New York, followed by the CBD on 5 June 1992 in Nairobi. The sustainable use of the components of biological diversity is one of the CBD's main objectives, as stated in its Article 1; and the Preamble of the CBD declares the State parties' determination "to conserve and sustainably use biological diversity for the benefit of present and future generations". The UNFCCC also proclaims its State parties' determination to protect the climate system for future generations.[62] In contrast to the CBD, the UNFCCC goes beyond this mere preambular stipulation: Sustainable development is included in two substantive provisions, in the context of the convention's ultimate objective and as one of the leading principles.[63] Beyond this, Article 3(1) of the UNFCCC even explicitly refers to future generations by stating as a main principle that "[t]he Parties should protect the climate system for the benefit of present and future generations of humankind on the basis of equity and in accordance with their common but differentiated responsibilities and respective capabilities."[64] Due to the aforementioned strong links between intergenerational equity and the challenges posed by the negative effects of climate change,[65] the role of international climate protection law is crucial for the current and future

[56] Beyerlin and Marauhn (2011), p. 18. Cf. also Beyerlin (1994), pp. 143–144.

[57] See UN (n.d.). See also Epiney (2022), p. 43. For more details on the role of the HLPFSD, see *infra* notes 95–102.

[58] UNCED (1992b, para. 38.45).

[59] UNCED (1992d). Concerning the Statement in general, see Sand (1993), p. 383.

[60] UNCED (1992d, Principle 2(b)).

[61] Technically, both treaties had been elaborated and adopted prior to the conference. However, they had been signed by more than 150 States during the Earth Summit so that they are often seen as its outcome.

[62] *United Nations Framework Convention on Climate Change* (UNFCCC), adopted 9 May 1992, entered into force 21 March 1994, 1771 UNTS 107, Preamble.

[63] Art. 2, 3(4) of the UNFCCC.

[64] On the relevance of intergenerational equity for Art. 3(1) of the UNFCCC, see Redgwell (2016), pp. 193–195.

[65] See already *supra* in Sect. 1.1.

development of intergenerational equity. This is why the UNFCCC is discussed in more detail in Chap. 4 below.[66]

#### 2.1.1.3 The Post-Rio Process

Even though the Earth Summit fell short of some of the large expectations to which it had given rise,[67] it contributed to the further evolution of sustainable development and the concern for the interests of future generations.[68] In the aftermath of the Earth Summit, a variety of new global and regional agreements and protocols,[69] within and outside the environmental context, referred directly or indirectly to sustainable development, in their preambles or in their operative provisions.[70] Similarly, in the following years, several treaty provisions mentioned the needs of future generations.[71] Most of these references are again of a preambular nature; for example, provisions regularly stress the determination to achieve the treaties' respective goals "for the benefit of present and future generations".[72] However, both the Convention on the Protection and Use of Transboundary Watercourses and International Lakes ('UNECE Water Convention') as well as the Convention on Access to Information, Public Participation in Decision-making and Access to Justice in Environmental

---

[66] See *infra* in Sect. 4.2.1.

[67] For some of the shortcomings of the Rio Conference and the post-Rio process, see French (2010), p. 53. For a very critical appraisal of the post-Rio process, see Szekely (2008), pp. 161–163.

[68] Borg (1998), pp. 137–138.

[69] E.g., *Kyoto Protocol to the United Nations Framework Convention on Climate Change* (Kyoto Protocol), adopted 11 December 1997, entered into force 16 February 2005, 2303 UNTS 162, Art. 2(1); *Cartagena Protocol on Biosafety to the Convention on Biological Diversity* (Cartagena Protocol), adopted 29 January 2000, entered into force 11 September 2003, 2226 UNTS 208, Preamble.

[70] For an overview, see Magraw and Hawke (2010), pp. 622–623; Hunter et al. (2011), p. 170; Verschuuren (2016), pp. 283–287. In more detail, see also *infra* in Sect. 4.2.

[71] For an overview, see, e.g., Sands et al. (2018), pp. 221–222; Redgwell (1999), pp. 115–116.

[72] *United Nations Convention to Combat Desertification in those Countries Experiencing Serious Drought and/or Desertification, Particularly in Africa* (UNCCD), adopted 17 June 1994, entered into force 26 December 1996, 1954 UNTS 3, Preamble. See also *UN Convention on the Law of Non-Navigational Uses of International Watercourses* (UN Watercourses Convention), adopted 21 May 1997, entered into force 17 August 2014, 36 ILM 700, Preamble; *1996 Protocol to the Convention on the Prevention of Marine Pollution by Dumping of Wastes and Other Matter, 1972* (London Protocol), adopted 7 November 1996, entered into force 24 March 2006, 36 ILM 1, Preamble; *Convention on Access to Information, Public Participation in Decision-making and Access to Justice in Environmental Matters* (Aarhus Convention), adopted 25 June 1998, entered into force 30 October 2001, 2161 UNTS 447, Preamble; *Convention for the Protection of the Marine Environment of the North-East Atlantic* (OSPAR Convention), adopted 22 September 1992, entered into force 25 March 1998, 2354 UNTS 67, Preamble; *Protocol on Strategic Environmental Assessment to the Convention on Environmental Impact Assessment in a Transboundary Context* (Protocol to the Espoo Convention), adopted 21 May 2003, entered into force 11 July 2010, 2685 UNTS 140, Preamble.

Matters ('Aarhus Convention') contain explicit references even in their operative provisions to the protection of future generations' needs.[73]

These developments in international treaty law must be seen in light of the overall post-Rio process, in which sustainable development and the recognition of the needs of future generations also played a major role in several soft law developments. In 1995, the Copenhagen Declaration on Social Development reaffirmed, *inter alia*, the "responsibility for present and future generations by ensuring equity among generations and protecting the integrity and sustainable use of our environment".[74] Several declarations on the international and regional level similarly stressed the requirements to meet the needs of future generations[75]; among them two expert groups of the UN[76] as well as the UN Educational, Scientific and Cultural Organization ('UNESCO') Declaration on the Responsibilities of the Present Generations Towards Future Generations ('UNESCO Declaration'), which explicitly addresses the responsibilities of the present generations towards future generations.[77]

In 2000, the UN Millennium Declaration reaffirmed States' support for sustainable development,[78] despite the underrepresentation of environmental aspects in the Millennium Development Goals.[79] However, the declaration itself referred twice to the preservation of the Earth for "our descendants".[80] Furthermore, in 2000, the Earth Charter was adopted after a long drafting process of 7 years and although it had previously failed during the Rio Earth Summit.[81] It did not achieve legal or soft law status due to the lack of recognition by the international community as a whole, but it was endorsed by over 2000 organisations worldwide.[82] The Earth Charter demands to secure the Earth for present and future generations and stipulates further principles in order to meet this obligation towards future generations.[83]

---

[73] *Convention on the Protection and Use of Transboundary Watercourses and International Lakes* (UNECE Water Convention), adopted 17 March 1992, entered into force 6 October 1996, 1936 UNTS 269, Art. 2(5)(c); Art. 1 of the Aarhus Convention. See also *Regional Agreement on Access to Information, Public Participation and Justice in Environmental Matters in Latin America and the Caribbean* (Escazú Agreement), adopted 4 March 2018, entered into force 22 April 2021. Cf. also Redgwell (1999), p. 118. For a more detailed analysis of these provisions' relevance, see *infra* in Sect. 4.2.

[74] World Summit for Social Development (1995, paras. 6, 26). See also Magraw and Hawke (2010), pp. 616–617.

[75] See, e.g., World Conference on Human Rights (1993, para. 11); UN Conference on Human Settlements (1996, para. 10); UNESCO (1997); "Johannesburg Principles on the Role of Law and Sustainable Development" (2003), p. 108; Organization of American States (2007), pp. 3, 7; Association of Southeast Asian Nations (ASEAN) (2007, Preamble).

[76] UN Commission on Sustainable Development (CSD) (1996); UNEP (1996).

[77] UNESCO (1997). In more detail on these three documents, see *infra* in Sect. 4.2.2.2.

[78] UNGA (2000, paras. 21–23). See also United Nations Secretary-General (UNSG) (2001, Goal 7).

[79] Rehbinder (2012), p. 70.

[80] UNGA (2000, paras. 6, 21).

[81] Earth Charter Commission (2000). See also Bosselmann (2009a, para. 3) as well as *supra* note 41.

[82] Bosselmann (2009a, paras. 11–12.

[83] Earth Charter Commission (2000, Principles 4–8). See also Bosselmann (2009a, paras. 8–9).

#### 2.1.1.4 From the Johannesburg Summit to Rio+20

Ten years after the Earth Summit in Rio, the World Summit on Sustainable Development took place in 2002 in Johannesburg in order to evaluate the post-Rio process.[84] Although the summit's outcome documents[85] did not introduce any innovative improvements,[86] the Johannesburg Declaration at least contained two references to the long-term perspective of sustainable development and the responsibility towards the future.[87] Moreover, the International Law Association ('ILA') adopted the New Delhi Declaration of Principles of International Law Relating to Sustainable Development in 2002 ('ILA New Delhi Declaration').[88] Again, this declaration does not possess the status of a legally binding document,[89] but it is able to assist in shaping the contours of sustainable development. In its sections on the principle of equity, the declaration explicitly refers to inter- as well as intra-generational equity in the context of sustainable development.[90]

In 2012, the last big environmental conference in the post-Rio process took place, the UN Conference on Sustainable Development ('UNCSD' or 'Rio+20'). Due to controversies between the participating States, the conference did not create new approaches or obligations, but only reaffirmed the existing political commitment in international environmental law.[91] However, the outcome declaration with the hopeful title 'The Future We Want' starts with the "commitment to sustainable development and to ensuring the promotion of an economically, socially and environmentally sustainable future for our planet and for present and future generations".[92] The document further strengthens the governance role of the UNEP[93] and refers to the impacts on and the needs of future generations in nine more sections concerning different matters.[94]

---

[84] UNGA (2001); Beyerlin and Reichard (2003); Bosselmann (2002).

[85] World Summit on Sustainable Development (2002a); World Summit on Sustainable Development (2002b).

[86] See, e.g., Beyerlin and Marauhn (2011), p. 23. See also *Bosselmann* who sceptically observed: "While Rio aimed for sustainability to guide economic and social progress, Johannesburg aimed for economic and social progress to guide sustainability.", Bosselmann (2002), p. 314.

[87] World Summit on Sustainable Development (2002a, paras. 26, 37).

[88] ILA Committee on Legal Aspects of Sustainable Development (2002).

[89] Stein (2019, para. 9).

[90] ILA Committee on Legal Aspects of Sustainable Development (2002, 2.1–2.3). See also ILA Committee on International Law on Sustainable Development (2012b, Statement 4). In more detail, see *infra* in Sect. 4.2.2.2.

[91] Maier (2012); Rehbinder (2012); Negri and Maljean-Dubois (2014), p. 2; Verschuuren (2016), p. 279; Epiney (2022), pp. 20–21.

[92] UNGA (2012, para. 1).

[93] Ibid., para. 88 See also Qerimi (2014), p. 15. On a recent suggestion to further strengthen the UNEP's role as a global coordinator of environmental and climate protection, see Ivanova (2020).

[94] UNGA (2012, paras. 1, 13, 39, 50, 86, 108, 158, 191, 197, 230).

The aforementioned replacement of the CSD by the HLPFSD was one of the few visible innovations of the summit, if only as a minimal consensus.[95] After being established by the General Assembly,[96] the HLPFSD held its first meeting in September 2013.[97] The UNGA considered the HLPFSD to be a "guardian of the sustainable development agenda".[98] Although the High-Level Political Forum's mandate is not directly related to future generations,[99] its creation must be viewed in light of the various calls for the establishment of a representative of future generations prior to the UNCSD.[100] The original proposal in the Zero Draft of the outcome document had stipulated the agreement "to further consider the *establishment* of an Ombudsperson, or High Commissioner for Future Generations, to promote sustainable development" (emphasis added).[101] However, the final document only claimed to "consider the *need for promoting* intergenerational solidarity for the achievement of sustainable development, taking into account the needs of future generations, including by inviting the Secretary-General *to present a report* on this issue" (emphasis added).[102]

The UNSG subsequently presented a report on intergenerational solidarity and the needs of future generations in 2013.[103] The report had two purposes: to consider the need for intergenerational solidarity in international law and to evaluate ways how to address this need within the UN system.[104] It emphasised the interrelation between intergenerational equity and sustainable development.[105] The UNSG did not only consider sources of international law, but also addressed the conceptional, ethical and economic dimensions of intergenerational justice.[106] The report lists a broad variety of international agreements and declarations that refer to the needs of future generations, before turning to national legal provisions on their protection.[107] It further turns to possible institutional frameworks for the representation of future generations, starting with the existing institutions at the national level,[108] and then

---

[95] Ibid., paras. 84–86 See already *supra* notes 57–58 as well as Maier (2012), pp. 172–173; Beyerlin (2013, para. 8).

[96] UNGA (2013a).

[97] UNGA (2013b).

[98] Ibid., para. 8. See also UNGA (2015, paras. 82–90).

[99] However, with regard to its commitment to "heal and secure our planet for future generations", see: UNGA (2019b, para. 2). Cf. also ECOSOC (2016, para. 4).

[100] Anstee-Wedderburn (2014), pp. 56–59. For a detailed analysis, see *infra* in Sect. 5.3.2.2.

[101] Bureau of the Preparatory Process for the UNCSD (2012, para. 57).

[102] UNGA (2012, para. 86).

[103] UNSG (2013).

[104] Ibid., para. 2.

[105] Ibid., paras. 10, 15–16.

[106] Ibid., paras. 10–31 This conceptual analysis was particularly based on *Brown Weiss'* principles of conservation, see *infra* in Sect. 2.2.1.4.

[107] UNSG (2013, paras. 33–38).

[108] Ibid., paras. 39–48.

summarising proposals of representation on the international level.[109] The UNSG Report ends with the demonstration of multiple options for future developments within the UN system, including the establishment of a High Commissioner for Future Generations, an agenda item in the HLPFSD or a mere inter-agency coordination regarding the needs of future generations.[110] It constitutes an extensive and important assessment of the *status quo* of intergenerational equity at that time. Despite the comprehensive analysis and the forward-looking suggestions of the UNSG, the report has remained without much substantial impact so far. It was taken note of by the UNGA in 2013,[111] but none of the institutional options were implemented as of today. Some of the elements the UNSG analysed are addressed in more detail in subsequent chapters of this book.[112]

#### 2.1.1.5 Recent Developments Regarding Intergenerational Equity

The evolution of sustainable development continued with the 2030 Agenda for Sustainable Development, which was set in 2015 by the UNGA in its resolution 'Transforming Our World'.[113] The agenda contains 17 Sustainable Development Goals ('SDGs')[114] whose establishment intends to complement the achievements of Agenda 21 and the Millennium Development Goals of 2000.[115] While the latter had focused on the economic and social perspectives of sustainable development,[116] the new SDGs "should address and incorporate in a balanced way all three dimensions of sustainable development and their interlinkages".[117] Therefore, many of the SDGs cover different dimensions of sustainable development at the same time.[118] Nonetheless, three of the SDGs particularly address environmental objectives.[119] Future generations are not mentioned in the SDGs themselves,[120] but the underlying UNGA resolution explicitly states that the Agenda is to be implemented "for the full benefit of all, for today's generation and for future generations".[121]

---

[109] Ibid., paras. 53–61.

[110] Ibid., paras. 63–67.

[111] UNGA (2013c, para. 3).

[112] See, e.g., on the ethical foundations *infra* in Chap. 3, on the legal status of intergenerational equity *infra* in Chap. 4, and on the institutional frameworks *infra* in Sect. 5.3.2.2.

[113] UNGA (2015). See also UNGA (2014); UNSG (2014).

[114] UNGA (2015, paras. 54–59).

[115] UNGA (2012, paras. 245–246).

[116] Maier (2012), pp. 172–173.

[117] UNGA (2012, para. 246).

[118] Zsuzsanna (2016), pp. 189–190.

[119] UNGA (2015, Goals 13–15).

[120] For a proposition of an intergenerational perspective on the SDGs, see Vasconcellos Oliveira (2018).

[121] UNGA (2015, para. 18). See also ibid. p. 2 Cf. also Pogge and Sengupta (2015).

Additionally, other recent developments have contributed and are still contributing to the post-2015 agenda in the context of sustainable development and intergenerational equity. To begin with, climate change law again took the centre stage of international environmental law at the COP21 in the form of the 2015 Paris Agreement, which paved the way for further steps of climate protection.[122] After the long deadlock of the regime in the preceding years since the Kyoto Protocol,[123] the Paris Agreement came as a positive surprise despite its shortcomings.[124] Its objective is explicitly linked to sustainable development.[125] Like preceding instruments, which had highlighted the connection between climate protection and intergenerational equity,[126] the Paris Agreement was built on the general legal framework of the UNFCCC system.[127] Consequently, the Paris Agreement's objective also refers to the main objective of the UNFCCC,[128] which subjects the protection of the climate system in its substantive provision to the "benefit of present and future generations of humankind".[129] While there have been more ambitious proposals prior to the COP21,[130] the Paris Agreement only contains an explicit reference to future generations in its Preamble. It acknowledges "that climate change is a common concern of humankind" and states that "Parties should, when taking action to address climate change, respect, promote and consider their respective obligations on [...] intergenerational equity".[131] However, there are also more general references to the "principle of equity".[132] For instance, according to Article 2(2), the Paris Agreement "will be implemented to reflect equity". Overall, there is no doubt that the concern for future generations still plays an essential role in the

[122] For an overview, see, e.g., Bakker (2015); Böhringer (2016); Doelle (2016); Oberthür and Bodle (2016); Proelß (2016).

[123] Kyoto Protocol. For the development preceding the Paris Agreement, see: Böhringer (2016), pp. 757–760; Proelß (2016), pp. 61–62.

[124] Böhringer (2016), pp. 755–756; Doelle (2016), p. 17. For a more critical assessment, see Bakker (2015).

[125] *Paris Agreement* (Paris Agreement), adopted 12 December 2015, entered into force 4 November 2016, UN Doc. FCCC/CP/2015/L.9/Rev.1. On the links between the Paris Agreement and sustainable development, see Sindico (2016).

[126] See, e.g., UNGA (2013d, with further references). On this connection, see already *supra* in Sect. 1.1.

[127] See *supra* notes 62–64.

[128] Art. 2(1) of the Paris Agreement. with reference to Art. 2 of the UNFCCC.

[129] Art. 3(1) of the UNFCCC.

[130] Redgwell (2016), p. 200 with reference to UNFCCC Ad Hoc Working Group on the Durban Platform for Enhanced Action (2015). Cf. also Lepage and Drafting Committee (2015, Art. I, IV, VIII, XI).

[131] Recital 11 of the Preamble of the Paris Agreement. Apparently, some States rejected the inclusion of these concepts into the operative part of the agreement, see Morgenstern and Dehnen (2016), p. 133. Cf. also Redgwell (2016), p. 200.

[132] Recital 3 of the Preamble and Art. 2(2) of the Paris Agreement. See also Boer (2021), pp. 10–11, 21, 24.

current regime of climate protection law.[133] This was also confirmed by a recent work of the International Law Commission ('ILC'), which published its Draft Guidelines on the Protection of the Atmosphere in 2021.[134] Besides a preambular reference to the "interests of future generations of humankind", one guideline on the equitable and reasonable utilisation of the atmosphere required that "the atmosphere should be utilized in an equitable and reasonable manner, taking fully into account the interests of present and future generations."[135] The outcome document of the recent COP26 in Glasgow reaffirms the preambular recognition of intergenerational equity with similar wording as the Paris Agreement,[136] but it does not add anything new in this regard.

Beyond the developments in climate protection law, the recent proposals on the creation of a Global Pact for the Environment attempt to promote a systematic and coherent approach to international environmental law.[137] Among the suggested principles, Article 3 codifies sustainable development,[138] and Article 4 states:

> Intergenerational equity shall guide decisions that may have an impact on the environment. Present generations shall ensure that their decisions and actions do not compromise the ability of future generations to meet their own needs.[139]

While there were earlier proposals for comparable documents,[140] the initiative of the GPE itself originated from international civil society in 2015.[141] This triggered the establishment of an informal International Group of Experts for the Pact that published their Draft Zero for the GPE in June 2017.[142] The proposal entailed support as well as opposition within the international community.[143] Despite the criticism, the process was formalised in May 2018 by a UNGA Resolution 'Towards

---

[133] See also J. C. Wood (1996), pp. 304–305; Carazo Ortiz (2017), pp. 116–117. For more details on the relevance of climate protection law for intergenerational equity, see *infra* in Sect. 4.2.1.

[134] International Law Commission (2021). In December 2021, the UNGA took note of the draft guidelines, see UNGA (2021).

[135] ILC (2021, Guideline 6).

[136] UNFCCC COP 26 (2021a, Preamble). See *supra* note 131. Further, intergenerational equity is one of the guiding principles of the Glasgow Work Programme on Action for Climate Empowerment, see UNFCCC COP 26 (2021b, para. 3(d)).

[137] See also Parejo Navajas and Lobel (2018), pp. 44–46. For a detailed assessment of the process, see Tigre (2019).

[138] International Group of Experts for the Pact (2017, Art. 3). For a detailed analysis, see Barral and Dupuy (2019).

[139] International Group of Experts for the Pact (2017, Art. 4). For a detailed analysis, see Brown Weiss (2019). See also Kotzé and French (2018), pp. 826–827.

[140] E.g., UNEP (1993c, para. 9); IUCN and International Council of Environmental Law (1995/2015); Centre International de Droit Comparé de l'Environnement (CIDCE) (2015). See also Raith (2018), p. 5. On the Earth Charter, see *supra* notes 81–83.

[141] Tigre (2019), pp. 2–5.

[142] International Group of Experts for the Pact (2017).

[143] Tigre (2019), pp. 32–42.

a Global Pact for the Environment'.[144] This resolution requested the UNSG to submit a report that assessed possible gaps in international environmental law and environment-related instruments with a view to strengthening their implementation.[145] Although the UNSG Report did not explicitly recommend the adoption of a universal environmental agreement,[146] it revealed, *inter alia*, "significant gaps and deficiencies with respect to the applicable principles of environmental law" and concluded that "[a] comprehensive and unifying international instrument that gathers all the principles of environmental law could provide for better harmonization, predictability and certainty."[147] However, due to partly strong opposition to the negotiation of a legally binding agreement,[148] the General Assembly eventually endorsed the report of its open-ended working group,[149] which only recommended to the UN Environment Assembly ('UNEA') to prepare a political declaration for 2022.[150] This political declaration was adopted in March 2022.[151] It could have contributed to round off 50 years of progressive evolution of international environmental law since the Stockholm Conference in the form of a legally binding instrument.[152] However, the UNEA declaration fell short of the expectations that the draft GPE had raised.[153] The State representatives did not commit to new environmental principles and rules, but only reaffirmed pre-existing declarations.[154] Furthermore, there is only a brief preambular reference to future generations in the UNEA declaration.[155] Significantly, in June 2022, the so-called "Stockholm+50" Conference did not follow in the footsteps of its namesake either, as it did not even produce a common outcome document, but only ten "key recommendations" in the form of a summary provided by the conference's co-presidents.[156] Overall, although the GPE initiative did not result in an international agreement so far, the idea of addressing international environmental law in an overarching way is still on the

[144] UNGA (2018). For the process of formalisation of the GPE, see Juste Ruiz (2020), pp. 480–485.

[145] UNGA (2018, para. 1).

[146] However, this was the original intention of the draft, see Raith (2018), p. 4.

[147] UNSG (2018, paras. 100–102).

[148] Tigre (2019), pp. 137–154; Juste Ruiz (2020), pp. 488–489.

[149] See UNGA (2018, para. 2). In detail on the recommendations of this working group, see Tigre (2019), pp. 107–137. Interestingly, the first objective in these recommendations is the "protection of the environment for present and future generations", see UNGA (2019a, Annex para. 1).

[150] Ibid., Annex para. b.

[151] United Nations Environment Assembly (2022).

[152] *Maria Tigre* suggested to take the opportunity of the 50th anniversary of the Stockholm Conference and the 30th anniversary of the Rio Conference to organise a "mega-conference", see Tigre (2019), p. 190.

[153] Aguila and Chami (2022).

[154] Ibid.

[155] United Nations Environment Assembly (2022, Preamble).

[156] Ministry of the Environment of Sweden and Ministry of the Environment and Forestry of Kenya (2022). For the brief reference to "intergenerational responsibility", see ibid., para. 9.

agenda of civil society and might be successful at a later point.[157] This could potentially influence the legal nature of the concept of intergenerational equity, at least in the future.[158]

Eventually, the ongoing pursuit for the definition and delimitation of intergenerational equity can also be seen with view to the recent adoption of the Maastricht Principles on the Human Rights of Future Generations in February 2023.[159] The Maastricht Principles aim at a holistic codification of all aspects of intergenerational equity with a rights-based focus on future generations. According to their own purpose, they "seek to clarify the present state of international law as it applies to the human rights of future generations".[160] The Principles contain provisions on equal rights and non-discrimination of future generations,[161] intergenerational trusteeship,[162] different State obligations (to respect, protect and fulfil the rights of future generations),[163] the representation of future generations in decision-making processes[164] as well as duties of different non-State actors,[165] before even turning to possible remedies.[166] Many of the aspects formulated therein, coincide with the findings and some forward-looking suggestions on intergenerational equity in the following sections and chapters. Yet, the Maastricht Principles do not have any legally binding value as of today as they have emerged from the draft of a group of legal and human rights experts. Due to this lack of normative capacity, the current work does not refer in detail to the different aspects in the following chapters—although the Principles take indeed a convincing holistic approach to the codification of intergenerational equity.[167]

### 2.1.2 International and National Case Law: An Overview

The interests and needs of future generations have also been the object of several judicial proceedings in the last decades.[168] Generally, international courts and

[157] In favour of a legally binding agreement: Aguila (2020), pp. 9–11. In favour of an even more ambitious approach: Kotzé and French (2018), pp. 833–835. Critical of the benefits of a binding agreement: de Lassus St-Geniès (2020), pp. 4–8; Bodansky (2019), p. 20.

[158] See *infra* in Sect. 4.2.

[159] Liebenberg et al. (2023).

[160] Ibid., Introduction.

[161] Ibid., Principle 6.

[162] Ibid., Principle 8.

[163] Ibid., Principles 13, 16–21.

[164] Ibid., Principle 22.

[165] Ibid., Principles 25–27.

[166] Ibid., Principles 30–36.

[167] For some more references, see *infra* in Sect. 4.2.2.2 and Sect. 5.2.2.1.

[168] For an overview see Fitzmaurice (2008), pp. 223–228; Hadjiargyrou (2016), pp. 268–273.

tribunals that were concerned with environmental issues regularly faced an area with complex and intertwined principles, including sustainable development and intergenerational equity.[169] The exhaustive illustration of all environmental case law would by far exceed the scope of this work, so that the following analysis focuses exclusively on the existing jurisprudence with links to intergenerational equity and future generations.[170] The first explicit references in international case law to future generations and/or intergenerational equity have occurred in the 1990s, thus, in light of the parallel developments of international environmental law surrounding and following the Rio Conference. While the jurisprudence on intergenerational equity is examined in more detail in chapters below regarding the concept's legal nature,[171] the question of right-holders,[172] and particularly the institutional framework of implementation,[173] this section gives a brief introductory overview of the most important decisions that have similarly shaped and have been shaped by the works of scholarship on intergenerational equity.

In 1992, the International Court of Justice ('ICJ') made explicit reference to future generations for the first time in its *Phosphate Lands in Nauru* case.[174] In these proceedings, Nauru claimed that Australia had violated its obligations under the Trusteeship Agreement, which regulated Australia's obligations with regard to certain phosphate lands mined before the time of Nauru's independence.[175] According to Article 5(2)(a) of the Trusteeship Agreement, the Administering Authority was obliged to "take into consideration the customs and usages of the inhabitants of Nauru and respect the rights and safeguard the interests, both present *and future*, of the indigenous inhabitants of the Territory" (emphasis added). This obligation thus put both present and future generations of the Nauru people into the position of beneficiaries of the established trust.[176] The notion of a trust "for the benefit of [hu]mankind" had also been brought forward by the USA as early as 1893 in the *Pacific Fur Seal Arbitration* with the United Kingdom ('UK')[177]—although

[169] Bodansky (2020), p. 3. Generally on the relevance of international case law for sustainable development, see Ramlogan (2011); Verschuuren (2016), pp. 287–295; Cordonier Segger and Weeramantry (2017).

[170] For an overview of international case law in international environmental law, see, e.g., Mensah (2008); Stephens (2009), p. 346. As regards international dispute settlement and climate change, see Verheyen and Zengerling (2016).

[171] See *infra* in Chap. 4.

[172] See *infra* in Sect. 5.2.

[173] See *infra* in Sect. 5.3.

[174] ICJ, *Certain Phosphate Lands in Nauru (Nauru v. Australia),* Judgment (Preliminary Objections), 26 June 1992, ICJ Reports 1992, 240.

[175] *Trusteeship Agreement for the Territory of Nauru* (Trusteeship Agreement), adopted 21 October 1947, entered into force 1 Novemver 1947, 10 UNTS 3.

[176] Hadjiargyrou (2016), pp. 272–273; Fitzmaurice (2008), pp. 226–228.

[177] Arbitral Tribunal, *Fur Seal Arbitration: Proceedings of the Tribunal of Arbitration,* Memorial of the United States of America, 1895, pp. 300–301. *Zena Hadjiargyrou* addressed this argument's links to intergenerational equity: Hadjiargyrou (2016), p. 264. See also Fitzmaurice (2008), p. 212.

the arbitral tribunal itself did not refer to intergenerational issues when dealing with the sustainable use of natural resources.[178] The idea of an intergenerational trust also became an important element of *Brown Weiss'* doctrine of intergenerational equity that is addressed in more detail below.[179]

In 1996, the ICJ was again concerned with intergenerational equity, when it issued its *Nuclear Weapons Advisory Opinion*.[180] The ICJ had to answer the question whether the possession, use or threat of use of nuclear weapons were prohibited under international law. In this context, it pinpointed the manifold dangers of nuclear weapons for the environment. According to the ICJ, the environment consists of "the living space, the quality of life and the very health of human beings, including generations unborn".[181] Further, the Court underlined the specific dangers nuclear weapons pose for future generations since their "destructive power [...] cannot be contained in either space or time".[182] Consequently, the ICJ acknowledged:

> [I]n order correctly to apply to the present case the Charter law [...], it is imperative for the Court to take account of the unique characteristics of nuclear weapons, and in particular their destructive capacity, their capacity to cause untold human suffering, and their ability to cause damage to generations to come.[183]

Although the ICJ did not explicitly recognise "intergenerational equity" as a concept, *Brown Weiss* suggested that its findings could represent at least "an implicit recognition of the interests of future generations and of our obligation to consider these interests [...]".[184]

One year later, in its *Gabčíkovo-Nagymaros Project* case, the ICJ again had the opportunity to adjudicate on a case in the realm of international environmental law.[185] The dispute submitted to the ICJ concerned a treaty between Czechoslovakia[186] and Hungary from 1977 on the construction and operation of a dam system along the Danube river.[187] Subsequent political and economic changes in both States

---

[178] Arbitral Tribunal, *Pacific Fur Seal Arbitration (United States of America v. Great Britain)*, Arbitral Award, 15 August 1893, RIAA XXVIII (1893), 263.

[179] See *infra* in Sect. 2.2.1.3.

[180] ICJ, *Legality of the Threat or Use of Nuclear Weapons*, Advisory Opinion, 8 July 1996, ICJ Reports 1996, 226, paras. 29, 35–36. See also Brown Weiss (1999).

[181] *Nuclear Weapons* (Advisory Opinion), *supra* note 180, para. 29.

[182] Ibid., para. 35.

[183] Ibid., para. 36.

[184] Brown Weiss (1999), pp. 349–350.

[185] ICJ, *Gabčíkovo-Nagymaros Project (Hungary v. Slovakia)*, Judgment, 25 September 1997, ICJ Reports 1997, 7.

[186] In 1993, Czechoslovakia broke up into the Czech Republic and Slovakia, with Slovakia becoming the successor into said treaty, ibid., para. 123.

[187] *Treaty between the Hungarian People's Republic and the Czechoslovak Socialist Republic concerning the Construction and Operation of the Gabčíkovo-Nagymaros System of Locks* (1977 Treaty concerning the Gabčíkovo-Nagymaros System), entered into force 16 September 1977, 32 ILM 1247.

and new scientific knowledge with regard to the environmental impacts of the project led to unilateral activities and suspension of activities on the project by Hungary.[188] In those parts of the judgment, in which the ICJ addressed environmental issues,[189] it pointed to the often irreversible damage to the environment resulting from human activity and to the "growing awareness of the risks for [hu] mankind – for present and future generations".[190] Without explicitly referring to intergenerational equity as such,[191] the ICJ stressed the new norms and standards that had developed in environmental law due to that awareness and new scientific knowledge.[192]

All in all, these references to the interests of future generations by the ICJ remained limited and superficial so far.[193] *Malgosia Fitzmaurice* stated in this regard: "The Court's invocation of the concept of intergenerational equity appears to be confined only in considering it as one of the factors to be taken into account in relation to environmental issues."[194] This reluctance was also underlined in the Court's more recent decision in the *Pulp Mills* case.[195] Although it would have been a fitting opportunity, the Court made not a single reference to future generations in its whole decision.[196]

Notwithstanding this, clarification can be sought from several separate and dissenting opinions issued in the aforementioned and other proceedings. Among these individual opinions, *Judge Weeramantry* was probably the strongest proponent of an acceptance of intergenerational equity in the realm of international law. Starting in a separate opinion in a maritime delimitation case in 1993, he listed "respect for the rights of future generations" among those "principles whose fuller implications have yet to be woven into the fabric of international law",[197] before

---

188 For a case summary, see Boisson de Chazournes and Mbengue (2017), pp. 436–437.

189 Some of the other issues in the case that concerned treaty law and treaty interpretation are addressed *infra* in Sect. 6.2.4.

190 *Gabčíkovo-Nagymaros Project* (Judgment), *supra* note 185, para. 140.

191 For a critical assessment of the court's only vague references, see, e.g., Mbengue (2020), p. 184.

192 *Gabčíkovo-Nagymaros Project* (Judgment), *supra* note 185, para. 140. The Court only explicitly mentioned the concept of sustainable development. On the relationship between intergenerational equity and sustainable development, see *infra* in Sect. 2.3.1.

193 ILA Committee on International Law on Sustainable Development (2012a), p. 15; French (2017), p. 179.

194 Fitzmaurice (2008), p. 225. See also Ramlogan (2011), p. 215.

195 ICJ, *Pulp Mills on the River Uruguay (Argentina v. Uruguay),* Judgment, 20 April 2010, ICJ Reports 2010, 14.

196 See ICJ, *Pulp Mills on the River Uruguay (Argentina v. Uruguay),* Separate Opinion of Judge Cançado Trindade, 20 April 2010, ICJ Reports 2010, 125, para. 119. Critical on this reluctance, see ILA Committee on International Law on Sustainable Development (2012a), p. 16. For an analysis of the principle of sustainable development in this case, see Tladi (2017).

197 ICJ, *Maritime Delimitation in the Area between Greenland and Jan Mayen (Denmark v. Norway),* Separate Opinion of Judge Weeramantry, 14 June 1993, ICJ Reports 1993, 211, para. 240.

elaborating on the deep historical roots of intergenerational equity.[198] Comparably, three other of his individual opinions included references either to intergenerational equity, the rights of future generations or an intergenerational trust.[199] For instance, in his dissenting opinion to the *Nuclear Weapons Advisory Opinion*, he clarified that "rights of future generations have passed the stage when they were merely an embryonic right struggling for recognition. They have woven themselves into international law [...]".[200] In his separate opinion to the *Gabčíkovo-Nagymaros Project* case, *Weeramantry* referred both to the "principle of intergenerational rights" and the "principle of trusteeship of earth resources".[201] Since these cases were all decided in the 1990s, the influence of the Rio Conference was clearly visible in *Weeramantry's* reasoning.[202]

In the same tradition, in 2010, *Judge Cançado Trindade* dedicated a whole section of his separate opinion in the *Pulp Mills* case to the analysis of intergenerational equity and stipulated that "it can hardly be doubted that the acknowledgement of inter-generational equity forms part of conventional wisdom in International Environmental Law [sic.]".[203] In 2014, in a separate opinion to the *Whaling in the Antarctic* case, he reaffirmed his prior position and again referred to many of the aforementioned international documents that would illustrate the legal relevance of intergenerational equity.[204] Particularly these separate and dissenting opinions of *Weeramantry* and *Cançado Trindade* shaped the discussion on the contents and the means of implementation of intergenerational equity; thus, they are examined in more detail in following chapters of the book.[205]

Last but not least, the ICJ will certainly have the opportunity to pronounce in more detail on intergenerational equity in the context of the currently pending advisory proceeding initiated by the UNGA in March 2023 on the obligations of

---

[198] Ibid., paras. 241–243.

[199] ICJ, *Request for an Examination of the Situation in Accordance with Paragraph 63 of the Court's Judgment of 20 December 1974 in the Nuclear Tests (New Zealand v. France) Case,* Dissenting Opinion of Judge Weeramantry, 22 September 1995, ICJ Reports 1995, 317, pp. 341–342; ICJ, *Legality of the Threat or Use of Nuclear Weapons,* Dissenting Opinion of Judge Weeramantry, 8 July 1996, ICJ Reports 1996, 429, pp. 454–455; *Gabčíkovo-Nagymaros Project* (Separate Opinion of Vice-President Weeramantry), *supra* note 9, pp. 109–110.

[200] *Nuclear Weapons* (Dissenting Opinion of Judge Weeramantry), *supra* note 199, p. 455. On the intergenerational aspect of nuclear weapons and disarmament, see also ICJ, *Obligations concerning Negotiations Relating to Cessation of the Nuclear Arms Race and to Nuclear Disarmament (Marshall Islands v. United Kingdom),* Dissenting Opinion of Judge Cançado Trindade, 5 October 2016, ICJ Reports 2016, 907, paras. 180–187.

[201] *Gabčíkovo-Nagymaros Project* (Separate Opinion of Vice-President Weeramantry), *supra* note 9, p. 110. On *Brown Weiss'* concept of a planetary trust, see *infra* in Sect. 2.2.1.3.

[202] See, e.g., *Gabčíkovo-Nagymaros Project* (Separate Opinion of Vice-President Weeramantry), *supra* note 9, pp. 93–94.

[203] *Pulp Mills* (Separate Opinion of Judge Cançado Trindade), *supra* note 196, paras. 114–124.

[204] ICJ, *Whaling in the Antarctic (Australia v. Japan: New Zealand intervening),* Separate Opinion of Judge Cançado Trindade, 31 March 2014, ICJ Reports 2014, 348, paras. 41–47.

[205] See *infra* in Chap. 4 and Sects. 5.2 and 5.3.

States in respect of climate change.[206] This advisory proceeding is also addressed in more detail below – although the recent findings of the court rendered in 2025 will have to be analysed on another occasion.[207]

There are some other international and regional courts and tribunals that have referred to intergenerational equity and future generations in their decisions. For instance, future generations played a role in the *Iron Rhine Arbitration* between Belgium and the Netherlands,[208] in an opinion of the Advocate General of the Court of Justice of the European Union ('CJEU'),[209] as well as in decisions issued by the Inter-American Court of Human Rights ('IACHR').[210]

Eventually, there is abundant jurisprudence with references to future generations on the domestic level.[211] Many of the recent cases with intergenerational aspects concern climate change litigation, which is assessed in more detail below in regard to the judicial representation of future generations.[212] Nonetheless, at least one important decision is briefly presented at this point due to its almost emblematic significance for intergenerational equity: the decision of the Philippines Supreme Court in *Oposa v. Factoran* from 1993.[213] A group of Philippine children had been acting as representatives in a class action for themselves and future generations. They sought to stop the cutting of remaining national forests by government licensees. The Supreme Court stated:

> Petitioners minors assert that they represent their generation as well as generations yet unborn. We find no difficulty in ruling that they can, for themselves, for others of their generation and for the succeeding generations, file a class suit. Their personality to sue in behalf of the succeeding generations can only be based on the concept of intergenerational responsibility insofar as the right to a balanced and healthful ecology is concerned. Such a

[206] ICJ, *Obligations of States in Respect of Climate Change*, UNGA Request for Advisory Opinion, 29 March 2023, UN Doc. A/RES/77/276. On the status of the proceeding, see Climate Change Litigation Databases (CCLD) (2023-today).

[207] See *infra* in Sect. 5.3.3.2.1.

[208] Permanent Court of Arbitration, *Award in the Arbitration regarding the Iron Rhine ("Ijzeren Rijn") Railway between the Kingdom of Belgium and the Kingdom of the Netherlands,* Arbitral Award, 24 May 2005, RIAA XXVII (2005), 35, paras. 58–59. In more detail, see Verschuuren (2016), pp. 288–289.

[209] Court of Justice of the European Union, *First Corporate Shipping,* Opinion of Advocate General Léger, 7 March 2000, European Case Law Identifier ECLI:EU:C:2000:108, paras. 54–58.

[210] *Mayagna Awas Tingni Community v. Nicaragua* (Judgment), *supra* note 7, para. 149; *Mayagna Awas Tingni Community v. Nicaragua* (Joint Separate Opinion of Judges Cançado Trindade, Pacheco Gómez and Abreu Burelli), *supra* note 7, paras. 9–10; IACHR, *The Environment and Human Rights (Requested by the Republic of Colombia),* Advisory Opinion, 15 November 2017, retrieved 3 January 2025, from https://www.corteidh.or.cr/docs/opiniones/seriea_23_ing.pdf, para. 59. See also Kahl (2019), p. 116.

[211] For an overview, see Ramlogan (2011), pp. 222–230; Molinari (2015, 145–146, 152–154); Brown Weiss (2021a, paras. 36–48).

[212] See *infra* in Sect. 5.3.3.3.3. The prominent *Urgenda* case in the Netherlands has been one of the more recent examples, see CCLD (2015–2020).

[213] Republic of Philippines Supreme Court, *Oposa v. Factoran,* Decision, 30 July 1993, 33 International Legal Materials 173–206.

> right [...] indispensably include[s], inter alia, the judicious disposition, utilization, management, renewal and conservation of the country's forest, mineral, land, waters, fisheries, wildlife, off-shore areas and other natural resources to the end that their exploration, development and utilization be equitably accessible to the present as well as future generations. Needless to say, every generation has a responsibility to the next to preserve that rhythm and harmony for the full enjoyment of a balanced and healthful ecology. Put a little differently, the minors' assertion of their right to a sound environment constitutes, at the same time, the performance of their obligation to ensure the protection of that right for the generations to come.[214]

The decision was one of the first domestic cases that addressed intergenerational equity in such an explicit and direct way. It reflected important components of the concept, which have also been formulated by *Edith Brown Weiss* in her works,[215] but it also constituted an important example of procedural representation for future generations. While some commentators expressed critical concerns as to the practical and conceptional relevance of this decision,[216] other commentators as well as subsequent judicial references demonstrated the decision's impact on the concept of intergenerational equity.[217] The relevance of the decision is assessed in more detail in Chap. 5 below.[218]

### 2.1.3 Summary

The foregoing sections have illustrated the many occurrences of future generations within international legal and policy documents, within treaty law and jurisprudence. They have illustrated how intergenerational equity rapidly gained significance and how it developed within the broader framework of international environmental law. It started in the form of first incidental references in some treaty documents; it evolved to the core element of the sustainable development definition in the Brundtland Report; and it directly or indirectly shaped many subsequent documents of environmental law in the last decades, including the Rio Declaration and the climate protection regime of the UNFCCC. The brief overview of the existing international case law has shown that future generations also found their way into the legal reasoning of the ICJ as well as other courts and tribunals. While the references in most decisions remained vague and unspecific, separate and dissenting opinions contributed to a more distinctive elaboration of intergenerational equity.

---

[214] Ibid., p. 185.

[215] See *infra* in Sect. 2.2.1.

[216] Lowe (1999), p. 27; Gatmaytan (2003).

[217] Manguiat and Yu (2003), pp. 492–494; Brown Weiss (2010), pp. 111–112; Gaillard (2011, para. 655). See also Molinari (2015), pp. 152–153. with further references.

[218] See *infra* in Sect. 5.3.3.3.3.1.1. On some relevant subsequent case law referring to *Oposa*, see *supra* in Sect. 5.3.3.3.3.2.

Several historical developments in the last years could be meaningless or become more promising, depending on the future direction of international environmental law. With regard to climate protection law, the Paris Agreement reaffirms the responsibility of protecting the climate for the benefit of future generations. The proposal of a GPE illustrates the attempts of promoting intergenerational equity even more directly. The proposed pact would have included, *inter alia*, an explicit provision on the concept of intergenerational equity; notwithstanding the low likelihood of its future adoption as a binding document.

Despite the important historical assessment of intergenerational equity, the foregoing sections have also illustrated the immense differences with regard to the notion's specificity and contents. The historical perspective has only provided an overview but does not explain the concept's exact legal contents or its legal nature. Therefore, based on this important foundation, the following section now turns to the assessment of intergenerational equity in legal scholarship.

## 2.2 The Doctrine of Intergenerational Equity: The Analysis of Intergenerational Equity in Legal Scholarship

In order to understand today's notion of "intergenerational equity", an analysis of legal scholarship in the sense of an overall doctrinal research is indispensable. This analysis is essential in the context of intergenerational equity, as the early works of *Edith Brown Weiss* have not only built on the developing legal and non-legal documents of that time;[219] they have also undoubtedly shaped the evolving understanding of the concept since its origins—most of all her 1989 monograph 'In Fairness to Future Generations'.[220]

For a start, *Brown Weiss'* idea of equity could be summarised as "fairness among all generations".[221] This is in line with a common understanding of the more general term of equity "as a synonym for fairness or justice".[222] The ICJ considered equity to be a "direct emanation of the idea of justice".[223] In some domestic legal systems, equity is contrasted with positive law, that means as a basis for judicial decisions in the absence of law (equity *praeter legem*) or against positive law (equity *contra legem*).[224] Yet, this meaning is foreign to international law.[225] Equity in

[219] See, e.g., Brown Weiss (1984a); Brown Weiss (1987).

[220] Brown Weiss (1989).

[221] Ibid., p. 21.

[222] Shelton (2010a), p. 640. See also Franck (1997), pp. 7–9; Francioni (2020, para. 1).

[223] ICJ, *Case concerning the Continental Shelf (Tunisia v. Libyan Arab Jamahiriya),* Judgment (Merits), 24 February 1982, ICJ Reports 1982, 18, para. 71.

[224] Ibid; Shelton (2010a), pp. 641–642; Francioni (2020, paras. 17–21).

[225] *Continental Shelf, Tunisia v. Libya* (Judgment (Merits)), *supra* note 223, para. 71. For an exception that has not been applied so far, see *Statute of the International Court of Justice* (ICJ

international law is strongly linked to international environmental law in general and to the idea of environmental justice in particular.[226] Environmental justice aims at justly sharing the natural resources of the planet and at guaranteeing a just allocation of benefits and harm in the sense of distributive justice.[227] Despite the sometimes synonymous use of the terms "equity" and "justice", "intergenerational equity" is normally used in a legal context, while "intergenerational justice" has a more general meaning and has particularly been shaped in the context of philosophical approaches.[228]

In the context of international environmental law, equity includes two dimensions: intergenerational and intra-generational equity.[229] While intra-generational equity aims at justice among living human beings of the present generation,[230] intergenerational equity regulates the relationship of human beings of different generations "as regards the right, correct or just handling [...] of planetary resources".[231] Based on these introductory remarks, the following section is mainly dedicated to the more specific illustration of *Brown Weiss'* doctrine of intergenerational equity (Sect. 2.2.1), before then turning to a brief overview of scholarly reactions to her doctrine (Sect. 2.2.2).

### *2.2.1 Contents of* **Brown Weiss'** *Doctrine*

The doctrine[232] of intergenerational equity builds upon the idea that every generation holds the Earth in common with members of the present generation and with other generations, past and future.[233] *Brown Weiss* first introduced her doctrine with the following words:

> [E]ach generation receives a natural [...] legacy in trust from previous generations and holds it in trust for future generations. This relationship imposes upon each generation certain planetary obligations to conserve the natural [...] resource base for future generations and also gives each generation certain planetary rights as beneficiaries of the trust to benefit from

Statute), adopted 26 June 1945, entered into force 24 October 1945, 1 UNTS XVI, Art. 38(2). Cf. also Shelton (2010a), p. 646.

[226] CSD (1996, paras. 38–41). See generally Gonzales (2013).

[227] See Shelton (2010a), pp. 640–641. See generally on distributive justice in international law: ibid., pp. 647–652. However, intergenerational equity can also contain corrective justice elements, see *infra* in Sect. 3.1.

[228] These philosophical approaches to intergenerational justice are addressed *infra* in Sect. 3.3.

[229] Ibid., p. 642.

[230] Ibid., pp. 642–643; Brown Weiss (1989), p. 21. For an assessment of the relationship between both concepts, see *infra* in Sect. 2.3.2.

[231] Hadjiargyrou (2016), p. 249. See also UNSG (2013, para. 10).

[232] This book uses the term "doctrine" in this context in the sense of a theory in scholarship and jurisprudence, as this denomination constitutes an established term with regard to *Brown Weiss'* conceptualisation. See also *infra* in Sect. 2.3.1.2.

[233] Brown Weiss (2021a, para. 1). See also Shelton (2010a), p. 643.

> the legacy of their ancestors. These planetary obligations and planetary rights form the corpus of a proposed doctrine of intergenerational equity, or justice between generations.[234]

Put differently, *Brown Weiss* understood intergenerational equity as "obligation to future generations to pass on the natural and cultural resources of the planet in no worse condition than received".[235] Several elements of her doctrine can be deduced from these formulations. First, it is important to analyse the environmental element of her doctrine by taking a look at her understanding of "natural resources of the planet" (Sect. 2.2.1.1). Second, the notion of "future generations" is assessed in order to define its meaning within the doctrine of intergenerational equity (Sect. 2.2.1.2). Third, *Brown Weiss'* built her doctrine on the idea of a planetary trust (Sect. 2.2.1.3). Eventually, according to *Brown Weiss*, intergenerational equity consists of three intergenerational principles or obligations, which build the core of the doctrine, thus, also the focus of the following analysis (Sect. 2.2.1.4). At this point, it is important to note that this chapter is not yet concerned with the exact questions of implementation of the presented doctrine of intergenerational equity, but puts an emphasis on its normative contents. Whether and to what extent these normative elements result in specific implementation mechanisms is the object of Chap. 5 below.[236]

#### 2.2.1.1 Natural Resources and Environmental Degradation

For *Brown Weiss*, intergenerational equity refers to the protection of "the natural and cultural resources of the planet".[237] This focus on natural resources is justified by her assessment that the main intergenerational equity issues today are inherently linked to environmental degradation in general and natural resources in particular: depletion of resources, degradation in environmental quality and a discriminatory access and use of the natural resources.[238] These environmental issues are strongly linked to the regime of natural resources conservation and biological diversity,[239] but they must be understood in a broad and all-encompassing sense since "natural resources are integral parts of ecosystems".[240] Natural resources include "the atmosphere, the oceans, plant and animal life, water, soils, and other natural resources, both

---

[234] Brown Weiss (1989), p. 2.

[235] Ibid., pp. 37–38. See also Brown Weiss (2008), p. 616.

[236] See also Brown Weiss (1989), pp. 119–168.

[237] Ibid., pp. 37–38 See also Brown Weiss (2021a, para. 1).

[238] Brown Weiss (2010), pp. 100–102.

[239] Beyerlin and Holzer (2013); Matz-Lück (2008, paras. 3–4).

[240] Beyerlin and Holzer (2013, para. 3).

renewable and exhaustible".[241] They encompass not only living organisms[242] but also non-living elements of the environment, such as water, soil and land.[243]

In this sense, the degradation of the existing resources also correlates with other intergenerational issues, such as climate change. For instance, depletion of natural resources influences the ability of ecosystems to adapt to climate change and the increase of greenhouse gases in the atmosphere equally affects ecosystems and has negative impacts on natural resources and environmental quality in general.[244] Interrelations like these are mirrored in the long-established connection between the protection of natural resources and the concerns for future generations and sustainable development in the realm of international environmental law.[245] According to *Dinah Shelton*, intergenerational protection of natural resources is therefore based on three assumptions:

> that human life emerged from, and is dependent upon, the Earth's natural resource base, including its ecological processes, and is thus inseparable from environmental conditions; that human beings have a unique capacity to alter the environment upon which life depends; and that no generation has a superior claim to the Earth's resources because humans did not create them, but inherited them.[246]

All in all, *Brown Weiss'* doctrine of intergenerational equity with regard to natural resources must thus be understood as the just allocation of environmental benefits (resources) as well as burdens between generations.[247]

Apart from natural resources, the doctrine originally also included the conservation of cultural resources,[248] which includes "the intellectual, artistic, social, and historical record of [hu]mankind".[249] In her 1989 treatise, *Brown Weiss* still dedicated a whole chapter to the specific application of intergenerational equity to cultural resources.[250] But mostly, her works addressed cultural resources only incidentally within the umbrella term of "natural and cultural resources" without addressing particular obligations concerning cultural conservation in detail.[251] In *Brown Weiss'* more recent works on intergenerational equity, the concept is further

241 Brown Weiss (1984b), p. 495.

242 These are sometimes referred to as "biological resources", see Beyerlin and Holzer (2013, para. 1).

243 Ibid. Cf. also WCED (1987, Chapter 6, para. 1).

244 Brown Weiss (2010), pp. 101–102.

245 See Schrijver (2008, para. 16); Beyerlin and Holzer (2013, para. 10). More generally, see also Borg (1998).

246 Shelton (2010b), p. 143.

247 Collins (2007b), pp. 95–96. See also Brown Weiss (2021a, para. 3).

248 See Brown Weiss (1984b); Brown Weiss (1989), pp. 21, 257–289.

249 Brown Weiss (1984b), p. 495.

250 Brown Weiss (1989), pp. 257–289. Cf. also Taylor (2013). For an overall approach on natural and cultural resources, see, e.g., World Heritage Convention.

251 See, e.g., Brown Weiss (1990); Brown Weiss (2010).

limited to the environmental aspects of natural resource conservation.[252] Likewise, the present book focuses on the environmental aspects of intergenerational equity and leaves out any other intergenerational concerns.[253]

#### 2.2.1.2 Future Generations

As far as the doctrine of intergenerational equity describes the just and fair relationship between all generations,[254] this raises two questions with regard to the meaning of "generations". First, the anthropocentric focus of intergenerational equity is addressed (Sect. 2.2.1.2.1). Second, the author offers a temporal delimitation between the "present generation" and "future generations" (Sect. 2.2.1.2.2).

##### 2.2.1.2.1 Anthropocentrism: Future Generations of Human Beings

*Brown Weiss's* understanding of intergenerational equity primarily refers to the relationship between generations of *human* beings: "We, as a species, hold the natural [...] environment of our planet in common [...]".[255] She further clarified:

> We also hold it in common with other living species. Human beings are part of the biosphere. As the only intelligent spokesman for all living things, we have a special responsibility toward them. The intergenerational implications of this, however, are reserved for subsequent analysis. The theory developed here focuses on intergenerational relationships of the human species in keeping with the focus of international law on states and people.[256]

Therefore, *Brown Weiss'* theory is purely anthropocentric,[257] although she did not deny a special responsibility of humankind to care for the planet.[258] Already in the 1980s, she admitted that there were other, non-anthropocentric approaches of environmental protection, which focused on the obligations owed towards all living species or the ecosystems as such.[259] In this context, different non-anthropocentric approaches can be distinguished, such as pathocentrism (i.e., ethical value of all sentient beings), biocentrism (i.e., ethical value of all living beings) and pure ecocentrism (i.e., ethical value of ecological wholes like species and ecosystems,

---

[252] Brown Weiss (2019), p. 49; Brown Weiss (2021a, para. 1). Cf. also Collins (2007b), p. 96.

[253] For an initial delimitation to other areas of intergenerational concern, see already *supra* in Sect. 1.1 Further, the limitation of intergenerational equity to environmental concerns is taken up with respect to the intertemporal character of environmental treaties, *infra* in Sect. 6.2.4.

[254] Brown Weiss (1989), p. 21.

[255] Ibid., p. 17. See also Brown Weiss (1984b), p. 498.

[256] Brown Weiss (1989), p. 17 (at footnote 2).

[257] Brown Weiss (1984b), p. 498 (at footnote 13).

[258] See, e.g., Brown Weiss (1992), p. 72.

[259] Brown Weiss (1984b), pp. 498–499 (at footnote 14). with reference to Stone (1972).

regardless of their character as living or non-living forms of nature).[260] Nonetheless, *Brown Weiss'* doctrine of intergenerational equity focused on the common understanding of intergenerational equity as the relationship between present and future generations of *humankind*.[261]

This approach is not obligatory for the concept of intergenerational equity or a planetary trust that is illustrated in detail below.[262] For instance, *Ulrich Beyerlin* as well as *Klaus Bosselmann* argued in favour of conceiving intergenerational equity in an ecocentric, or at least biocentric, manner.[263] In this sense, the planetary trust would constitute a trust for all living species or the whole Earth;[264] a possibility that was also seen by *Brown Weiss* in the form of a separate trust or the extension of her concept.[265] Even more than in the 1980s, environmental ethics have developed since then and ecocentric approaches of environmental law have emerged.[266] They criticise the biased focus of anthropocentrism on the interests of humankind that ignores the important "ecological correlations and networks, of which humankind is only one aspect".[267]

With regard to pathocentrism and biocentrism, the research field of animal law has further evolved in the last years and addressed the inclusion of nonhuman animals into existing or new ethical, political and legal frameworks.[268] For instance, *Elien Verniers* suggested to "bring[…] animal welfare under the umbrella of sustainable development".[269] Beyond this, some rights-based approaches have argued for the acceptance of animal rights in order to overcome anthropocentrism.[270] In 1974, *Joel Feinberg* was one of the first who addressed the idea of rights of future generations and rights of animals together.[271] While these discussions have often been separated from each other in the last decades, *Andrew Stawasz* and *Jeff Sebo* recently argued in favour of bringing together the legal consideration of future

[260] Bosselmann (2009b, paras. 23–42) with further distinctions. This book does not elaborate in detail on this distinction.

[261] Brown Weiss (1989), p. 17 (at footnote 2). Cf. also Shelton (2010b), p. 128.

[262] See *infra* in Sect. 2.2.1.3.

[263] Beyerlin (2006), p. 275; Bosselmann (2017), pp. 120–123. For the philosophical discussion, see, e.g., Birnbacher (2006), p. 30.

[264] Cf. Bosselmann (2020). who addressed "environmental trusteeship" in a broader sense with fiduciary duties not only to (future) humanity but to the Earth as a whole.

[265] Brown Weiss (1984b, 498–499 (at footnote 14) with further references). See also Shelton (2010b), p. 128.

[266] For an overview, see Bosselmann (2009b).

[267] Ibid., para. 15. For a recent proponent of more ecocentric environmental law, see, e.g., Kotzé (2020).

[268] For philosophical approaches, see, e.g., Andrews et al. (2019). For a political doctrine, see, e.g., Donaldson and Kymlicka (2014). For recent legal approaches, see, e.g., Pietrzykowski (2020); Bradshaw (2020).

[269] Verniers (2021).

[270] See, e.g., Stucki (2020), Pietrzykowski (2020), Bielefeldt (2021).

[271] Feinberg (1974).

generations of human beings with animal law.[272] They suggested to extend the view of legal longtermism[273] from only future human beings "to *all* distant-future sentient beings" (emphasis in the original).[274]

The present author considers that the aforementioned pathocentric, biocentric and ecocentric approaches to environmental law and the extension of intergenerational considerations to nonhuman animals are convincing in many regards. These approaches deserve support and they have already been advocated for elsewhere.[275] It is true that the predominant anthropocentric accounts of international law in general and international environmental law in particular "have led to major environmental destruction in practice".[276] In the view of the present author, not only ethical reasons speak in favour of a legally stronger protection of nonhuman animals today and in the future,[277] but also the commonly shared interests between future human beings and nonhuman animals.[278] In this sense, intergenerational equity could also be viewed to describe the relationship between present and future generations of all species. Despite these convincing arguments, the existing doctrine of intergenerational equity remains a mainly anthropocentric concept so far—from *Brown Weiss'* perspective but even more so in its international legal and non-legal foundations. Therefore, the present book equally focuses on this anthropocentric understanding as a relationship between present and future generations of humankind. This understanding does not deny the potential to develop intergenerational equity further towards a pathocentric, biocentric or ecocentric responsibility towards future generations of all human and non-human (sentient) species.[279] In subsequent chapters, this tendency is addressed where relevant, but it is not the focus of the present work.[280]

#### 2.2.1.2.2 Temporal Delimitation: Present and Future Generations

The environmental obligation to pass on the natural resources to future generations also depends on the exact understanding of the term "future generations", which constitutes the central reference point of intergenerational equity. More generally,

[272] Stawasz and Sebo (2022). In more detail, see also Winter et al. (2021), pp. 113–120 with further references.

[273] *Stawasz* and *Sebo* discussed their approach in the context of legal longtermism, see already briefly *supra* in Sect. 1.1 [note 78].

[274] Stawasz and Sebo (2022).

[275] See Bustami and Hecken (2021), pp. 165–168.

[276] Bosselmann (2009b, paras. 18–22) See also Feinberg (1974), pp. 66–67; Kotzé (2020), p. 101.

[277] See Andrews et al. (2019); Pietrzykowski (2020), pp. 243–246.

[278] See Sebo (2022).

[279] See Brown Weiss (1984b), p. 498 (at footnote 14).

[280] With regard to the rights-based approach of intergenerational equity, see *infra* in Sect. 5.2. With regard to some more ecocentric jurisprudential approaches, see *infra* in Sect. 5.3.3.3.3 [notes 950–960].

the term of "generations" is ambiguous and can be understood in different ways.[281] *Ajai Malhotra* suggested as a starting point "a body of individuals born at about the same time".[282] However, it has been emphasised that "popular ideas about generations are somewhat muddled".[283]

This is why *Lawrence Solum* distinguished between three different meanings: demographic cohort generations, lineal descent generations and unborn future generations.[284] Demographic cohort generations are separated from each other on the basis of demographic and societal, or cultural factors, such as the "Baby Boomer generation" or "Generation X".[285] Lineal descent generations take the perspective of familial relations and can be divided into the generation of grandparents, parents, children and so on.[286] These two categorisations are inherently vague with regard to the demarcation of different generations.[287] *Malhotra* observed that "the present generation, its successor, as well as, in turn, every following generation constitute a continuum in generations, and it is well nigh impossible to separate specific collective persons from such a continuum".[288] Another problem is that, in the first two of *Solum's* categorisations, the group of "future generations" includes currently living children. While some of the existing international documents and scholarship include youth and children within the scope of intergenerational issues,[289] this understanding of "future generations" is prone to mixing up issues of intergenerational equity with concerns between contemporaries whose lives' partly overlap.[290] When addressing moral obligations towards partly overlapping generations of children and grand-children, some philosophical objections arise to a different degree than towards more remote future generations.[291]

---

[281] Stone (1998), p. 68; Malhotra (1998), pp. 40–41; Tremmel (2003), pp. 30–32; Hadjiargyrou (2016), pp. 249–250.

[282] Malhotra (1998), p. 41.

[283] Solum (2001), p. 169. Cf. also Malhotra (1998), p. 40.

[284] Solum (2001), pp. 169–171. For a similar distinction, see also Tremmel (2009), pp. 19–24.

[285] Solum (2001), p. 169.

[286] Ibid., p. 170. In this categorisation, future generations would rather be framed as "succeeding generations", see Tremmel (2006), pp. 205–206.

[287] In more detail: Solum (2001), pp. 169–170.

[288] Malhotra (1998), p. 41 with reference to Attard (1991), p. 29. Cf. also Kiss (1996), p. 21; Gewirth (2001/2014), p. 118.

[289] For this understanding of "future generations" in the context of intergenerational justice, see UNSG (2013, paras. 12–14); Tremmel (2006), pp. 205–206; Tremmel (2009), p. 22.

[290] As to the different intergenerational problems arising towards adjacent or distant future generations, see, e.g., Brown Weiss (1984b), p. 506 (at footnote 51); Stone (1998), p. 68.

[291] In more detail, these philosophical considerations are examined *infra* in Sect. 3.2. Furthermore, the overlap between succeeding but contemporary generations complicates the distinction between intergenerational and intra-generational equity, which is addressed *infra* in Sect. 2.3.2. Nonetheless, there are certain overlaps between the interests of children already born and future unborn generations, and currently living younger generations of children play an important role in the context of representation, which is addressed in more detail *infra* in Sect. 5.3.3.3.

Therefore, *Lukas Meyer* drew a clear distinction between intergenerational issues between contemporaries and between non-contemporaries.[292] Similarly, most theories of intergenerational justice and intergenerational equity refer to *Solum's* third aforementioned meaning of future generations as "unborn future generations". This means all persons "who will exist in the future but who are not yet born".[293] Beyond this, it is possible to even narrow this definition down: "future generations" could then encompass only persons "who will not be born during the lifetime of the speaker and her audience, or even during the lifetime of any person now alive".[294] While the present author considers the latter narrow understanding to be too restrictive, it certainly fits the concept of intergenerational equity better to include only unborn future generations within its scope of protection. *Brown Weiss* comparably understood future generations as "all those generations that do not exist yet" and she explicitly considered that multiple (demographic cohort or lineal descent) generations belonged to her concept of the present generation.[295]

This conceptional separation between living younger generations and unborn future generations is reasonable because it better distinguishes between environmental degradations that already have consequences in the present and those impacts in the long-term future. Further, it corresponds better with the aforementioned philosophical discussions that distinguish between moral obligations towards the children and grand-children of currently living human beings and more remote future individuals.[296] The suggested understanding of future generations does not entirely resolve the difficulty that different intergenerational problems could arise with respect to different remote future generations.[297] However, it better emphasises the particularities of a longtermist approach to intergenerational equity, which constitutes the basis of this book.[298] Therefore, similar to *Brown Weiss'* doctrine, any theory of intergenerational equity should build upon this general understanding of future generations as encompassing *all*, but only, unborn generations. The present work also follows this understanding.[299] Although the term "unborn future generations" would thus describe the research object more specifically, the more common term of "future generations" is used in the subsequent chapters with a similar meaning.

---

[292] *Meyer* distinguished between intergenerational equity and "*Altersgruppengerechtigkeit*" (translation: "equity between age groups"), see Meyer (2009), p. 282. See also Tremmel (2003), p. 32.

[293] Solum (2001), pp. 170–171. See also Malhotra (1998), p. 41; Scheyli (2008), pp. 349–350; Meyer (2009), pp. 282–283; Tremmel (2009), p. 24. More recently, cf. also Nolan (2022).

[294] Solum (2001), pp. 170–171; Hadjiargyrou (2016), p. 250.

[295] Brown Weiss (2021a, para. 4).

[296] In more detail, see *infra* in Sect. 3.2.

[297] Stone (1998), p. 68. See also Brown Weiss (1984b), p. 505 (at footnote 47).

[298] Winter et al. (2021), pp. 15–16. See already *supra* in Sect. 1.1 [note 78].

[299] When it comes to the representation of future generations, some overlaps can be observed with regard to currently living children and youth, particularly in the context of climate litigation. These overlaps are addressed in more detail *infra* in Sect. 5.3.3.3.

Based on the foregoing definition of future generations, the present book chooses the year 2100 at several occasions as a reference point in the future for the purpose of illustration,[300] although most of the following chapters generally concern *all* future generations. The future generation in the year 2100 combines two important criteria: it covers an *unborn* future generation, on the one hand, and it meets a minimum of predictability, on the other hand. With regard to the criteria of an *unborn* generation, addressing an overlapping generation in around 20 to 30 years as illustrative example would include the currently living younger generation. In contrast, a time span of 200, 300 or even 1000 years from today would be too far in the future and result in complete unpredictability.[301] The chosen time frame of approximately 80 years, from 2025 to 2100 ('generation X+80'),[302] lies in between these extremes. With regard to a global average life expectancy between 70 and 75 years,[303] and not beyond 89 years average in any State,[304] only very few and very young members of the present generation will still be alive in the year 2100.[305] Consequently, generation X + 80 is dissimilar to most members of the current generation. At the same time, the limitations of present-day scientific knowledge justify not to pick generations further in the future. Current scientific knowledge and predictions on factual developments in the future are more or less specific and reliable with regard to the next 70 to 80 years.[306] This is particularly evident with regard to climate science, as most scientific predictions on climate change assess the potential developments and irreversible threats of the ecosystems until the end of the twenty-first century.[307] The year 2100 thus coincides with many current insights on this important area of intergenerational equity. For these reasons, the year 2100 constitutes a particularly fitting reference point for the purpose of illustration.

#### 2.2.1.3 Planetary Trust

For her concept of intergenerational equity, *Brown Weiss'* assumed that every generation of the human species holds the Earth in common as a trust for all generations of humankind.[308] This is also reflected in the main obligation to pass

300 See already in the thought experiment *supra* in Chap. 1 and *infra* in Chap. 7.

301 Generally, on the objection of uncertainty, see *infra* in Sect. 3.2.4.

302 Chapter 7 refers to 'generation X+80' in its illustrations; this constitutes an approximate denomination that points to the future generation of the year 2100.

303 World Health Organization (WHO) (2019).

304 Central Intelligence Agency (2022).

305 This perspective assumes that technological and medical progress will not decisively prolong human life for a majority of the *present* generation.

306 For some examples of (partly) scientific predictions of the future, see Kaku (2011); Future Timeline Community (2024).

307 See, e.g., Lee et al. (2021), pp. 570–612.

308 Brown Weiss (1984b), p. 498. Sometimes, synonyms such as custodianship or stewardship are used, see Fitzmaurice (2008), p. 217.

on this trust to future generations "in no worse condition than received".[309] This understanding of intergenerational equity as a fiduciary relationship between generations is at the core of her whole concept.[310] Accordingly, every present generation is at the same time beneficiary of the planetary resources and trustee of these resources with an obligation to guard them for future generations who are also the trust's beneficiaries.[311]

*Brown Weiss* derived the fiduciary nature of intergenerational equity from a "nearly universal recognition and acceptance among peoples of an obligation to protect the natural and cultural heritage for future generations".[312] She used socio-biological and psychological theory as well as considerations of community life and social value as an aid for the foundation of her theory.[313] The historical, cultural and religious traditions would further reflect an "implied declaration by each generation that it holds the [planetary resources] in trust for future generations", thereby creating the planetary trust.[314] *Brown Weiss* conceptualised the "planetary trust" of intergenerational equity by borrowing from domestic doctrines of trust law.[315] Under Anglo-American trust law, a private trust is "an equitable obligation, binding a person [trustee] to deal with property over which he [or she] has control [trust property] either for the benefit of persons [beneficiaries] [...], or for a charitable purpose [...]".[316] Intergenerational equity originally borrows from the trust concept of a charitable trust,[317] or the United States public trust doctrine respectively.[318] While some works on intergenerational equity rather refer to the concept of public trusts,[319] the following assessment uses *Brown Weiss'* terminology of a charitable trust.[320]

---

309 Brown Weiss (1989), pp. 37–38.

310 For a detailed analysis, see Redgwell (1999). See also Wood (2009a, 2009b).

311 Brown Weiss (1989), p. 17. In detail, see Brown Weiss (1984b), pp. 504–508.

312 Ibid., p. 500.

313 Ibid., pp. 499–502. See also Shelton (2010b), pp. 123–124.

314 Brown Weiss (1984b), p. 504. See also Redgwell (1999), p. 73. *Brown Weiss* was mostly influenced by *John Rawls'* theory of justice as well as by communitarian approaches of intergenerational justice, which is assessed in more detail below, see *infra* in Sects. 3.3.3 and 3.3.4.

315 Brown Weiss (1984b), p. 503. In her first works, *Brown Weiss* referred to Restatement (Second) of Trusts (1959) in order to give references for Anglo-American trust law. This book subsequently refers to the respective counterparts in the more recent Restatement (Third) of Trusts (2003).

316 Pettit (2005), p. 23; Redgwell (1999), p. 8. See also Restatement (Third) of Trusts § 2 (2003).

317 Fitzmaurice (2008), p. 213. In detail on charitable trusts, see Restatement (Third) of Trusts § 28 (2003); Redgwell (1999), pp. 13–17.

318 Brown Weiss (1984b), p. 523 (at footnote 148). See also Redgwell (2016), p. 191.

319 See, e.g., Sand (2004); Bosselmann (2020), p. 55.

320 On the parallels between charitable and public trusts, see Hadjiargyrou (2016), p. 252. Arguing that the public trust doctrine would not adequately fit the idea of intergenerational equity, see Redgwell (1999), pp. 68–70; Redgwell (2016), pp. 191–192.

Charitable trusts differ from traditional private trusts in various ways, which render them particularly fitting for the adoption to intergenerational equity.[321] While private trusts normally require definite beneficiaries,[322] charitable trusts do not need ascertainable beneficiaries.[323] While private trusts are subject to a temporal limitation, called the "rule against perpetuities", charitable trusts can be of unlimited duration.[324] Furthermore, charitable trusts must aim at a charitable purpose,[325] meaning an objective that is of social interest and beneficial to the community.[326] Since there often are no identifiable beneficiaries, the enforcement of a charitable trust is normally realised at the instance of the Attorney General.[327]

According to *Brown Weiss*, all the criteria of a charitable trust can be used as a basis for the development of a doctrine of planetary trust. The present generation would be in the position of a trustee for the planetary trust. It would owe the fiduciary duties to the trust's beneficiaries, namely future generations.[328] Since a charitable trust does not require identifiable beneficiaries, this concept would allow that future (unborn) generations can become beneficiaries of the planetary trust.[329] Particularly, as in a charitable trust, the planetary trust obligations would not distinguish between different generations of trust beneficiaries, but would be owed towards all future generations alike.[330] At the same time, the present generation would also be a *beneficiary* of the planetary trust, thus, it would be entitled to an equitable access to the planetary resources.[331] Despite this double function as beneficiary and trustee, the present generation in its function as trustee is bound to manage the trust property, namely the planetary resources, in a way as to fulfil the trust's purpose.[332] In order to fulfil this purpose, a certain standard of behaviour is required by a trustee.[333] Further, *Brown Weiss* established that the planetary trust of intergenerational equity aims at "[...] purposes beneficial to the community",[334] namely "to sustain the welfare of

[321] Brown Weiss (1984b), pp. 503–504; Redgwell (1999), pp. 72–73, 176.

[322] Restatement (Third) of Trusts § 44 (2003).

[323] Restatement (Third) of Trusts § 28 (2003), p. 13.

[324] Ibid.

[325] Ibid., pp. 21–24.

[326] Ibid., p. 10.

[327] Ibid., p. 13; Brown Weiss (1984b), p. 503 (at footnote 36). In detail, see Redgwell (1999), pp. 84–93.

[328] Brown Weiss (1984b), pp. 504–505.

[329] Ibid., pp. 505–506.

[330] Ibid., 505 (at footnote 48).

[331] Ibid., 499, 507. See also Brown Weiss (1989), pp. 37–38.

[332] Brown Weiss (1984b), pp. 507–508.

[333] When developing her concept of a planetary trust, *Brown Weiss* referred to the trust law standard of the "Prudent Man Rule" ("of prudent persons dealing with their own property"), see ibid., 507 (at footnote 59) with reference to Restatement (Second) of Trusts (1959), § 227(a). For the more developed standard under the Restatement Third, see Restatement (Third) of Trusts § 90 (2003), Chapter 17: Investment of Trust Funds (The "Prudent Investor Rule").

[334] Restatement (Third) of Trusts § 28 (2003), 10, 21–22.

future generations".[335] This purpose would further promote the social interest of the community in its broadest sense by including all future parts of the human community.[336]

The concept of intergenerational equity as a planetary trust has been examined, *inter alia*, by *Catherine Redgwell* who concluded that trust doctrine offered:

> 1) an intertemporal approach with intergenerational and intragenerational dimensions; 2) acknowledgement of the need for the standing and/or representation of the interests of future generations in the present; 3) a legal mechanism for operationalising intergenerational concerns through trust institutions and trust funds. It is a doctrine particularly well suited to the contemporary challenge of global environmental problems requiring a community response.[337]

*Redgwell* further found that the notion of trust is not foreign to international environmental law.[338] Although there is no coherent institutional framework of the trust concept in international law,[339] several decisions of international courts and tribunals referred to different conceptions of trusts,[340] some of which are addressed in more detail in Chap. 5.[341] Furthermore, her analysis illustrates that the concept of an intergenerational trust is not only used as a metaphor,[342] but that it can also entail elements of operationalisation and enforcement, such as judicial representation or a trust fund.[343] Some of these potential elements are examined in more detail at a later point.[344] Then, it will become clear that certain differences remain between the charitable or public trust concept on a national level and the idea of a global and intergenerational trust *Brown Weiss* offered.[345]

Most importantly, however, *Brown Weiss* further built on the idea of a planetary trust when she assessed alternative approaches for the management of trust resources for future generations,[346] before she developed specific proposals for obligations of the trustees.[347] Due to the "dual role of each generation as trustee of the planet for

---

[335] Brown Weiss (1984b), pp. 508–509.

[336] Ibid., p. 509 As to the anthropocentric focus of *Brown Weiss'* trust conception, see *supra* notes 255–279.

[337] Redgwell (1999), p. 184.

[338] See ibid., Chapter 6.

[339] Ibid., 183–184.

[340] *Pacific Fur Seal Arbitration* (Arbitral Award), *supra* note 178; ICJ, *South West Africa, Second Phase (Ethiopia v. South Africa; Liberia v. South Africa),* Judgment, 18 July 1966, ICJ Reports 1966, 6; *Phosphate Lands in Nauru* (Judgment (Preliminary Objections)), *supra* note 174.

[341] See *infra* in Sect. 5.3.3.2. See also already *supra* notes 174–178.

[342] For critical remarks as to the frequent metaphorical use of the trust concept: Sand (2004), pp. 54–55; Lowe (1999), p. 27.

[343] For the parallels to a charitable trust, see also Redgwell (1999), pp. 72–73; Fitzmaurice (2008), pp. 213–214.

[344] See in detail *infra* in Sect. 5.3.3.3.3.2.1.

[345] Cf. ibid., p. 218.

[346] Brown Weiss (1984b), pp. 510–523.

[347] Ibid., pp. 523–540; Brown Weiss (1989), pp. 40–45.

present and future generations and as beneficiary of the planetary legacy", each generation is bound by these obligations as well as asserted certain rights.[348] Consequently, *Brown Weiss* named them "planetary" or "intergenerational" rights and obligations.[349] The planetary obligations of the present generation constitute the core of *Brown Weiss'* doctrine of intergenerational equity, thus, they are presented in the following section, whereas the aspect of planetary rights is addressed in more detail below in Chap. 5.[350]

#### 2.2.1.4 Principles of Intergenerational Equity and Planetary Obligations

According to *Brown Weiss*, the main purpose of the planetary trust[351] contains three aspects: "to sustain the life-support systems of the planet; to sustain the ecological processes, environmental conditions and cultural resources necessary for the survival of the human species; and to sustain a healthy and decent human environment".[352] From this purpose, she deduced the fiduciary duty of each generation "to pass on the natural and cultural resources of the planet in no worse condition than received".[353] *Brown Weiss* suggested three basic "principles"[354] of intergenerational equity to achieve this fiduciary duty: conservation of options, conservation of quality of the environment, and conservation of an equitable access of all generations to the planetary resources.[355]

First, conservation of options requires present generations to conserve the diversity of the natural and cultural resources base to offer future generations the same possibilities that arise from the condition of the environment as have been available to the present generation.[356] In this context, diversity is meant to strengthen the robustness of the environment and thereby to increase the opportunities of future generations to live a decent life.[357] However, *Brown Weiss* emphasised that conservation of options does not mean conservation of the *status quo*, but that change is an

---

348 Ibid., p. 45. See also Fitzmaurice (2008), p. 218.

349 Brown Weiss (1989), p. 45.

350 See *infra* in Sect. 5.2.

351 See *supra* note 335: "to sustain the welfare of future generations".

352 Ibid., p. 37.

353 Ibid., pp. 37–38.

354 At this point, the term "principle" is not used in a technical way, but in the sense that *Brown Weiss* utilised in the elaboration of her doctrine. Chapter 4 properly analyses the normative capacity of norms and the distinction between policies, principles and rules, see *infra* in Sect. 4.1.

355 Two of these principles were already developed in 1984: Brown Weiss (1984b), pp. 523–540., but further elaborated and complemented by the third principle in her main work: Brown Weiss (1989), pp. 40–45.

356 Ibid., 38, 40–42.

357 Ibid., p. 40. Referring to "preservation of opportunities", see also Page (1983).

essential part of this obligation.[358] The conservation of the diversity of the resource base has to be achieved by combining the conservation of existing resources with more efficient exploitation of existing resources and new technological developments.[359] In this regard, she stressed from the beginning that future generations are only entitled "to diversity *comparable* to that of previous generations" (emphasis added);[360] an aspect she put forward more distinctly in later works by explicitly referring to "comparable options" instead.[361]

Second, conservation of quality demands of the present generation to maintain a quality of the Earth, which is in no worse condition than the present generation benefitted from it.[362] Degradation of natural resources is thus the opposite of this duty. Again, this obligation does not require an unchanged environment for the future, which is why *Brown Weiss* later mainly referred to "comparable quality".[363] A balancing is necessary between, on the one hand, a reasonable degradation caused by the present generation and, on the other hand, benefits passed on to future generations, such as higher capital and knowledge that allows for a development of substitutes for the degraded resources.[364] In the context of these benefits, *Brown Weiss* focused on the necessity of prediction of future technological change and of future breaking points (i.e., critical ecosystem thresholds or tipping points) in natural and social systems.[365]

Third, conservation of equitable access obliges present generations to grant a non-discriminatory minimum level of access to the common natural resources to all members of the present generation. At the same time, present generations have to guarantee that such minimum access remains possible for future generations as well.[366] This duty of conservation of equitable access consists of intergenerational as well as *intra*-generational components, an indispensable interrelationship that

[358] She thereby explicitly rejects the preservationist model, see Brown Weiss (1989), pp. 22–23 with further references.

[359] Ibid., pp. 41–42.

[360] Ibid., p. 38.

[361] E.g., Brown Weiss (2010), pp. 102–103; Brown Weiss (2021a, paras. 8–9). See also Redgwell (2016), p. 190.

[362] Brown Weiss (1989), pp. 38, 42–43.

[363] E.g., Brown Weiss (2010), pp. 102–103; Brown Weiss (2021a, paras. 8–9).

[364] Brown Weiss (1989), pp. 42–43. For a critical perspective on comparable arguments of "weak sustainability", see Dernbach and Cheever (2015), pp. 274–276.

[365] Brown Weiss (1989), p. 43. with references to catastrophe theory and complex systems theory. With regard to these aspects, however, it must be noticed that technological progress has not only contributed to positive effects on environmental protection, but instead, it has often been part of very adverse effects on the environment, for a comprehensive analysis, see Dwivedi et al. (2022). Therefore, an exaggerated confidence in future technological progress could potentially lead to the transgression of irreversible planetary thresholds, which would reduce any further attempts of intergenerational responsibility to absurdity. Technological restraint might also be necessary to some degree and in certain areas, see, e.g., Maas (2022).

[366] Brown Weiss (1989), pp. 38, 43–45.

*Brown Weiss* stressed throughout her works.[367] She pointed out the obligation of wealthier communities of the present generation to give assistance to the poorest communities and to ensure that all members of the present generation have at least a minimum level of access to the planet's natural resources.[368] In consequence, the compliance with this intra-generational duty allows wealthier and poorer members of the present generation to meet their own conservation obligations towards future generations.[369] Since the present generation is not only trustee but at the same time beneficiary of the planetary trust,[370] *Brown Weiss'* third principle perfectly fits into the concept of trust law by obliging the members of the present generation to assure equality and impartiality among the beneficiaries.[371]

The aforementioned three principles of conservation are the basis of *Brown Weiss'* doctrine. They directly translate into so-called "planetary obligations", as they also constitute duties of conservation—of comparable options, of comparable quality and of equitable access.[372] These duties are primarily owed by the State,[373] although the duty-bearers might include all members of the present generation.[374] Subsequently, *Brown Weiss* further specified these planetary obligations by elaborating more specific sub-duties that arise from the three main obligations.[375] These sub-duties are designed to achieve the purpose of the planetary trust and they define the exact contents of the duties of the present generation towards future generations.[376] *Brown Weiss* identified five of these sub-duties: the duty to conserve both renewable and non-renewable resources,[377] the duty to ensure equitable access to and use of the planetary resources within and between generations,[378] the duty to avoid adverse impacts from the present generation's actions on the environment,[379] the duty to prevent disasters, minimise damage and provide emergency assistance,[380] and the duty to compensate for environmental harm.[381] The detailed elaboration of these sub-duties illustrates the specific character of *Brown Weiss'* doctrine as well as the interrelatedness with other areas of international

[367] Ibid., p. 21; Brown Weiss (2021a, para. 12) In more detail, see *infra* in Sect. 2.3.2.

[368] Brown Weiss (1989), pp. 44–45.

[369] Ibid.

[370] Brown Weiss (2021a, para. 8).

[371] Redgwell (1999), p. 78.

[372] See Collins (2007b), p. 98.

[373] Brown Weiss (1989), p. 48.

[374] Collins (2007b), p. 99. For a detailed analysis of the potential duty-bearers, see *infra* in Sect. 5.1.

[375] Brown Weiss (1989), pp. 45–46; Collins (2007b), pp. 98–99.

[376] Brown Weiss (1989), p. 46.

[377] Ibid., pp. 50–55.

[378] Ibid., pp. 55–59.

[379] Ibid., pp. 59–69.

[380] Ibid., pp. 70–79. See also UNSG (2013, para. 25).

[381] Brown Weiss (1989), pp. 79–86.

environmental law—such as procedural environmental rights,[382] the precautionary approach,[383] the principle of prevention,[384] or environmental liability regimes.[385] However, for the purpose of the present analysis, a more detailed assessment of the sub-duties is not necessary as the main contents of *Brown Weiss'* doctrine still build upon the three main principles of conservation.[386]

The doctrine of intergenerational equity does not only consist of planetary obligations of the present generation. It is based on a dichotomy between these obligations and corresponding planetary rights, which are owed by the planetary trustees, the present generation, to the trust's beneficiaries, future generations.[387] These planetary rights are integrally linked to the planetary obligations and mirror them to a great extent.[388] Therefore, *Brown Weiss* described them as "the basic right to live on a planet with as good environmental quality and natural [...] resource diversity as previous generations had and the right to have equitable access to the benefits and use of these resources".[389] She subsequently conceptualised the nature of these planetary rights as collective rights, their exact contents and potential mechanisms of enforcement.[390] While the idea of "rights of future generations" is one of the aspects of her doctrine that has been criticised most, it is examined in more detail in Chap. 5 below due to the numerous philosophical and conceptional implications that are equally assessed below.[391] So far, the overview of *Brown Weiss'* principles of intergenerational equity and the resulting duties of conservation is sufficient to understand the normative framework of her doctrine.

### 2.2.2 *Criticism and Summary of* Brown Weiss' *Doctrine*

*Brown Weiss'* doctrine constitutes without doubt one of the most influential works on intergenerational equity. There is no academic contribution to the discourse that does not address her doctrine at one point or the other. Not only legal scholarship

[382] Ibid., pp. 60–62. See also Collins (2007b), p. 98.

[383] Brown Weiss (1989), pp. 67–69. See also *infra* notes 411–415.

[384] Ibid., pp. 70–73. See also Collins (2007b), p. 99.

[385] Brown Weiss (1989), pp. 79–84.

[386] In later works, *Brown Weiss* rarely referred to the specific sub-duties, see, e.g., Brown Weiss (2010), p. 103.

[387] Brown Weiss (1989), pp. 45–46; Brown Weiss (2021b), p. 22. On this understanding of rights and obligations, see Redgwell (1999), p. 84.

[388] Brown Weiss (1989), p. 45, 104; Collins (2007b), p. 99.

[389] Brown Weiss (1989), p. 104.

[390] Ibid., pp. 95–114.

[391] See *infra* in Sect. 3.2.2 and Sect. 5.2.

largely builds on her theory,[392] but past jurisprudence has also referred to her doctrine, particularly the aforementioned individual opinions of judges *Weeramantry* and *Cançado Trindade*.[393] Further, some official reports of international institutions have based their analysis of intergenerational equity on *Brown Weiss'* doctrine, *inter alia*, the aforementioned Expert Group Report of the CSD[394] as well as the 2013 Report of the UNSG on intergenerational solidarity and the needs of future generations.[395]

Beside much support for her work and continuing doctrinal research on intergenerational equity, many commentators have also criticised her doctrine, either on a conceptional or on a substantive basis.[396] *Zena Hadjiargyrou* summarised parts of the criticism as follows: "Intergenerational equity, […] though an admiral [sic.] concept in thought, has proven to be chaotic in terms of understanding, implementation and elucidation both conceptually and in practice."[397] Most of the critical commentators had doubts concerning the conceptional ideas *behind* her theory of intergenerational equity and justice.[398] For instance, they criticised the idea of "rights of future generations",[399] or they suggested to solve the intergenerational challenges from a perspective of *intra*-generational rights and duties instead.[400] Others focused on the vagueness and the missing clarity of the doctrine's legal content,[401] or the lack of effective and adequate implementation and representation.[402]

It is true that many issues of intergenerational equity still remain unresolved as of today.[403] However, the often-cited criticism mostly refers to specific elements of the doctrine, which have not been illustrated yet, so that it would be inconclusive and confusing to address them in more detail at this point of the work. Instead, this book addresses all of the critical observations at the relevant positions in the subsequent

---

[392] See, e.g., Redgwell (1999); Fitzmaurice (2008); Shelton (2010b); Hadjiargyrou (2016); Michallet (2018).

[393] *Maritime Delimitation in the Area* (Separate Opinion of Judge Weeramantry), *supra* note 197, para. 242; *Nuclear Tests 1995* (Dissenting Opinion of Judge Weeramantry), *supra* note 199, p. 341; *Pulp Mills* (Separate Opinion of Judge Cançado Trindade), *supra* note 196, para. 114. See *supra* notes 197–204.

[394] CSD (1996, paras. 41–47).

[395] UNSG (2013, para. 24). See already *supra* note 106.

[396] For an overview of some of the most common critiques, see, e.g., Collins (2007b), pp. 102–110.

[397] Hadjiargyrou (2016), p. 277.

[398] E.g., D'Amato (1990). For some counter-arguments in direct reaction to *D'Amato's* contribution, see also Brown Weiss (1990).

[399] E.g., Supanich (1992); Beckerman (2006); Merrills (2010), pp. 669–672.

[400] E.g., Barresi (1997); Barresi (1998). For some counter-arguments in direct reaction to *Barresi's* first contribution, see also Brown Weiss (1997). In detail, see *infra* in Sect. 2.3.2.

[401] E.g., Lowe (1999); Hadjiargyrou (2016).

[402] E.g., Supanich (1992), pp. 97–98; Beckerman (2006), p. 60; Beckman (2013), pp. 777–779. For criticism on judicial representation due to separation of powers, see, e.g., Wegener (2019).

[403] Fitzmaurice (2008), p. 210.

chapters, for instance regarding the ethical foundations of intergenerational justice,[404] the legal nature of intergenerational equity,[405] the discussion of intergenerational rights,[406] and the possible institutional frameworks of implementation.[407]

While the unresolved issues of intergenerational equity—particularly the issues of implementation and operationalisation—thus become part of this research in subsequent chapters, the foregoing sections have focused on the substantive content of *Brown Weiss'* doctrine and have presented a basic understanding of intergenerational equity. From this point on, the term of intergenerational equity only refers to the protection and conservation of natural resources and the environmental quality of the Earth for present and future generations. The concept in this research is limited to an anthropocentric perspective on future generations of human beings and it leaves the perspective of other living species or the ecosystems in general to other research, which is though explicitly welcomed. According to the doctrine of intergenerational equity, the term "future generations" refers to future *unborn* generations. At the core of the doctrine, the relationship between present and future generations is considered a planetary trust, which is held by all generations in common. In this trust concept, every present generation becomes simultaneously a beneficiary and a trustee of the trust, and is obliged in its position as trustee to pass on the planetary resources to future generations in no worse condition than received. From this fiduciary duty, *Brown Weiss* has derived three main principles of intergenerational equity, which can also be translated into planetary or intergenerational obligations: conservation of comparable resource diversity, conservation of comparable quality of the environment, and conservation of an equitable access of all generations to the planetary resources.

## 2.3 Systemic Framework: Interrelation Between Intergenerational Equity and Related Concepts of International Environmental Law

Having illustrated the basic pillars of *Brown Weiss'* doctrine of intergenerational equity, it has to be contextualised within the framework of international environmental law. As had been implied above, intergenerational equity does not operate in a vacuum, but is embedded within a variety of related environmental concepts.[408]

[404] See *infra* in Sect. 3.2.

[405] See *infra* in Chap. 4.

[406] See *infra* in Sect. 5.2.

[407] See *infra* in Sect. 5.3.

[408] These concepts are mostly labelled "principles of environmental law" in a non-technical manner. The normative capacity of intergenerational equity and sustainable development as principles or rules is addressed *infra* in Sect. 4.1.

The historical analysis of the concept's development has already revealed the inherent links between the interests of future generations and sustainable development. Beyond this, there are other concepts of environmental law that either have important overlaps with intergenerational equity or complement it. Therefore, the following systemic evaluation of intergenerational equity within the framework of general international environmental law serves both the contextual understanding of its contents and the exact definition of this book's scope of analysis in delimitation to other concepts of international environmental law.

The next section thus starts with the most complex relationship between intergenerational equity and sustainable development (Sect. 2.3.1). Then, the notions of intra-generational equity and common but differentiated responsibilities are illustrated, as they are often treated like opposites to intergenerational equity (Sect. 2.3.2). Last, the notions of common heritage and common concern of humankind are addressed since they contain important overlaps and parallels with the concept of intergenerational equity (Sect. 2.3.3).

Certainly, intergenerational equity has links with other concepts of international environmental law.[409] For instance, the right to a healthy environment could also be mentioned here, but it is instead addressed below in connection to the issue of right-holders of intergenerational equity.[410] Furthermore, the precautionary approach also has an important impact on the interests of future generations.[411] It requires that, "[w]here there is a risk of serious or irreversible damage, lack of scientific certainty shall not be used as a reason for postponing the adoption of effective and proportionate measures to prevent environmental degradation."[412] The link to future generations becomes obvious considering the approach's objective to avoid irreversible harm in the future.[413] The UNSG Report on intergenerational solidarity fittingly observed: "where risks to the interests of future generations are reasonably clear and consequential, present generations should exercise forbearance, foregoing some benefits. This finds its expression in the precautionary principle [...]."[414] However, as precaution takes another approach to intergenerational problems than the concept of intergenerational equity, the present book does not contain a detailed illustration of the former, but addresses the precautionary approach below with

---

409 For an overview of principles of international environmental law, see, e.g., Sands et al. (2018), pp. 197–250.

410 In more detail, see *infra* in Sect. 5.2.2.2. On the connection between such a right and intergenerational equity, see Brown Weiss (2021a, para. 15).

411 On the connection between the precautionary approach and future generations, see Kiss (1996), p. 27; Cameron et al. (1998), pp. 110–113; Redgwell (1999), pp. 138–140. Cf. also Tanaka (2013), p. 167.

412 See, e.g., UNCED (1992a, Principle 15); International Group of Experts for the Pact (2017, Art. 6). In detail, see also Mbengue (2019), p. 74.

413 On the connection between irreversible and long-term damage to intergenerational equity, see already *supra* in Sect. 1.1.

414 UNSG (2013, para. 26). See also Prakash (1995), p. 428.

respect to irreversibility and only inasmuch as it becomes relevant for the present work.[415]

## 2.3.1 *Sustainable Development*

The relationship between sustainable development and intergenerational equity is most intertwined in international environmental law. In order to better understand this relationship, the following sub-section gives a brief overview of the content of sustainable development as such (Sect. 2.3.1.1), before turning to the specific intergenerational component of sustainable development and the consequences for the concept of intergenerational equity as a whole (Sect. 2.3.1.2).

### 2.3.1.1 The Components of Sustainable Development

The 1987 Brundtland Report was one of the first documents that defined sustainable development: "Sustainable development is development that meets the needs of the present without compromising the ability of future generations to meet their own needs".[416] The concept was subsequently elaborated in the report,[417] and it shaped the international discourse on the reconciliation between economic development and environmental protection in the following years.[418] Subsequent international documents as well as jurisprudence have further stressed the balancing character of sustainable development regarding economic and environmental concerns.[419] In 1995, the World Summit for Social Development explicitly added and underlined the dimension of *social* development to the understanding of sustainable development.[420] According to *Dire Tladi*, sustainable development shifted the paradigm of international law from a situation, in which development trumped environmental and social protection, to an understanding, which focused on social and environmental concerns instead.[421]

However, beyond the consensus on the three dimensions of sustainable development, there is no common understanding of its specific contents. Sustainable

---

[415] In more detail, see *infra* in Sect. 7.2.3.

[416] WCED (1987, Chapter 2, para. 1). On the Brundtland Commission, see already *supra* notes 28–36.

[417] Ibid., Chapter 2.

[418] Magraw and Hawke (2010), p. 615.

[419] See, e.g., UNCED (1992a, Principle 4); *Pulp Mills* (Judgment), *supra* note 195, para. 177; *Iron Rhine Railway* (Arbitral Award), *supra* note 208, para. 59. For an overview of relevant case law, see Voigt (2009), pp. 171–177; Verschuuren (2016), pp. 287–295.

[420] World Summit for Social Development (1995, para. 6). On the necessary inclusion of social concerns, see Tladi (2017), p. 253.

[421] Tladi (2007), pp. 34–37.

development is subject to controversies and uncertainties, to a high level of abstraction and generality.[422] Furthermore, due to its abstract character, it is open to easy abuse.[423] Consequently, it has often been criticised for its vagueness[424] as well as for its allegedly strong focus on economic growth.[425] In the latter sense, *Louis Kotzé* criticised that sustainable development actually had perpetuated the current socio-ecological destruction of the planet.[426] He observed with regard to several environmental concepts, including sustainable development, that they were "based on a green-washed neoliberal anthropocentric ethic, devoid of a deeper sense of ecological obligation."[427]

Despite this criticism and despite the relative vagueness of sustainable development, certain core elements have been deduced in the last decades. While differing in detail,[428] commentators have identified the following fundamental and undisputed components of sustainable development: (i) the need to take into account the interests of future generations (intergenerational equity); (ii) the duty of every State to exploit and use its natural resources in a "sustainable" way (sustainable use);[429] (iii) the duty of each State to take into account the interests of other States, particularly the world's poor, in the utilisation of the natural resources (intragenerational equity);[430] and (iv) the duty of States to incorporate environmental considerations into their economic and development policies (integration).[431]

Other sources included additional components to sustainable development, for instance a right to development itself,[432] or procedural elements, such as obligations of cooperation, environmental impact assessment ('EIA'),[433] public participation and access to information.[434] The ILA New Delhi Declaration is exemplary for a very comprehensive account of sustainable development. Its Preamble expressed:

---

[422] Barral (2018), pp. 106–107.

[423] Dupuy and Viñuales (2018), p. 91.

[424] See, e.g., Lowe (1999), p. 34 and in more detail *infra* in Sect. 4.1.2.

[425] See, e.g., Szekely (2008), pp. 161–163.

[426] Kotzé (2019a), p. 17. On an alternative approach of "Earth System Law", see also briefly *infra* in Sect. 7.3.2 [notes 213–215].

[427] Ibid. See also Kotzé (2019b), p. 222.

[428] See Barral (2018), p. 107.

[429] This aspect of sustainability already existed in international law much earlier than the development of modern international environmental law, see *Pacific Fur Seal Arbitration* (Arbitral Award), *supra* note 178.

[430] This is sometimes also referred to as the notion of "equitable use", see Sands (1995), pp. 60–61; Sands et al. (2018), p. 219.

[431] Dupuy and Viñuales (2018), p. 92. See also Sands (1995), pp. 58–62; Magraw and Hawke (2010), p. 619; Barral (2018), p. 108; Sands et al. (2018), p. 219; Boyle and Redgwell (2021), pp. 117–125; Proelß (2022), p. 143.

[432] Boyle and Redgwell (2021), pp. 119–120; Proelß (2022), p. 143.

[433] On the connection between sustainable development and EIA, see Tladi (2017), pp. 248–250.

[434] Boyle and Redgwell (2021), p. 125.

> The objective of sustainable development involves a comprehensive and integrated approach to economic, social and political processes, which aims at the sustainable use of natural resources of the Earth and the protection of the environment on which nature and human life as well as social and economic development depend and which seeks to realize the right of all human beings to an adequate living standard on the basis of their active, free and meaningful participation in development and in the fair distribution of benefits resulting therefrom, with due regard to the needs and interests of future generations.[435]

This paragraph of the ILA New Delhi Declaration contained the aforementioned four undisputed components of sustainable development; but it went beyond them and also included the principle of common but differentiated responsibilities,[436] the precautionary approach,[437] and the principle of good governance.[438] The inherent variability of the components of sustainable development led *Virginie Barral* to observe that "it is by nature an evolutive concept and its components must thus evolve accordingly if sustainable development is to be achieved".[439]

Regardless of the variable components, the element of integration was often presumed to be at the heart of sustainable development.[440] According to Principle 4 of the Rio Declaration, integration requires that "environmental protection shall constitute an integral part of the development process and cannot be considered in isolation from it".[441] This focus of sustainable development on integration is reflected in Article 3 of the GPE[442] as well as in the case law on sustainable development.[443] In the *Gabčíkovo-Nagymaros Project* case, the ICJ stated that the "need to reconcile economic development with protection of the environment is aptly expressed in the concept of sustainable development."[444] According to the decision in the *Pulp Mills* case, the "interconnectedness between equitable and reasonable utilization of a shared resource and the balance between economic development and environmental protection [...] is the essence of sustainable development."[445] Consequently, integration can be considered the "key technique for the

[435] ILA Committee on Legal Aspects of Sustainable Development (2002, Preamble). For a comparably comprehensive understanding of sustainable development, see also *Fourth ACP-EEC Convention* (1989 Lomé Convention), adopted 15 December 1989, entered into force 1 September 1991, 1924 UNTS 4, Art. 33.

[436] See *infra* in Sect. 2.3.2.

[437] See *supra* notes 411–415.

[438] ILA Committee on Legal Aspects of Sustainable Development (2002, Principles 3, 4, 6).

[439] Barral (2018), p. 107. See also Barral (2012), pp. 382–383.

[440] Barral (2018), pp. 108–109; Dupuy and Viñuales (2018), p. 91; Proelß (2022), p. 144.

[441] UNCED (1992a, Principle 4). See also Barral and Dupuy (2015).

[442] International Group of Experts for the Pact (2017, Art. 3). For a detailed analysis, see Barral and Dupuy (2019).

[443] See *supra* note 169.

[444] *Gabčíkovo-Nagymaros Project* (Judgment), *supra* note 185, 140. See also *Iron Rhine Railway* (Arbitral Award), *supra* note 208, para. 59.

[445] *Pulp Mills* (Judgment), *supra* note 195, para. 177. As to the shortcomings of the Court with regard to sustainable development, see *Pulp Mills* (Separate Opinion of Judge Cançado Trindade), *supra* note 196), pp. 184–190.

realisation of the objective of sustainable development".[446] Nonetheless, sustainable development goes far beyond the mere balancing of economic, social and environmental considerations.[447] Of the other three main components of sustainable development, the intergenerational element is most relevant for the present work. This is why the next section turns to this element and addresses the specific relationship between sustainable development and intergenerational equity.

#### 2.3.1.2 The Intergenerational Component of Sustainable Development and Beyond: Two Manifestations of Intergenerational Equity

Beside the important component of integration, intergenerational equity constitutes another essential component of sustainable development.[448] Some commentators considered it to be the core element of sustainable development, since it introduced the concerns of future generations into the realm of international environmental law.[449] The birth document of both intergenerational equity and sustainable development, namely the Brundtland Report, is evidence of this strong connection. As far as sustainable development was first defined as "development that meets the needs of the present without compromising the ability of future generations to meet their own needs",[450] its content seemed to coincide with that of intergenerational equity.[451] This overlap of sustainable development and intergenerational equity is also reflected in many of the international documents analysed above, which refer to future generations in the same context as they refer to other aspects of sustainable development.[452] This led *Pierre-Marie Dupuy* and *Jorge Viñuales* to observe that the principle of intergenerational equity "can be considered as a manifestation of the old idea of nature conservation and the more recent concept of sustainable development".[453]

This finding could lead to the assumption that the various documents referring to sustainable development in general or future generations in particular reflect the aforementioned contents of intergenerational equity, including *Brown Weiss'* ideas

---

[446] Barral (2012), pp. 380–381.

[447] Ibid.

[448] See, e.g., Atapattu (2006), pp. 114–115; Molinari (2015), p. 151 with further references.

[449] Howarth and Norgaard (1992), p. 473; Brown Weiss (1995), pp. 21–22; Bartholomäi (1997), pp. 83–84; Dupuy (1997), p. 887; Epiney and Scheyli (1998), p. 45; Beder (2000), p. 227; Scheyli (2008), pp. 341–348; Handl (2011), p. 158. Cf. also Borg (1998), pp. 139–140.

[450] WCED (1987, Chapter 2 para. 1).

[451] Bartholomäi (1997), pp. 83–84; Redgwell (1999), pp. 127–128.

[452] E.g., UNCED (1992d, Principle 2(b)); World Summit for Social Development (1995, paras. 6, 26); UNEP (2006, paras. 20–23); UNGA (2012, para. 1).

[453] Dupuy and Viñuales (2018), p. 88. See also *Catherine Redgwell*: "Intergenerational equity is the international legal articulation of sustainable development", Redgwell (1991), p. 42; and *Rajendra Ramlogan*: "intergenerational equity is irretrievably woven into the fabric of sustainable development", Ramlogan (2011), p. 213.

of a planetary trust and duties of conservation. However, a detailed look at these documents suggests a more cautious approach than simply equating every reference to future generations in international documents with the doctrine elaborated by *Brown Weiss*. *Zena Hadjiargyrou* fittingly described the confusion on this equation as follows:

> The general trend of content however wherever the concept is invoked, be it in hard law or soft law documents, is almost half-hearted. The sentiment of intergenerational equity is raised, but only elements of it are traceable rather than its holistic embodiment. [...], the term 'intergenerational equity' is seldom used, the obligations are not termed as imperatives but as guidance, the concept is entwined into others such as sustainable development, the global public trust mechanism is not referred to and the specific rights and duties of generations are hardly expressed.[454]

Indeed, on closer examination, it turns out that there are several manifestations of intergenerational equity, generally speaking, which differ in international treaties, documents, jurisprudence and scholarship.[455] Two legal manifestations of intergenerational equity can be distinguished from the foregoing analysis.[456] On one side of the spectrum, there are numerous vague references to the needs, concerns or interests of future generations that ought to be respected.[457] These references represent a general conception of intergenerational equity,[458] which is also encompassed in the overarching concept of sustainable development. It can be summarised as the "need to take into account the interests of future generations"[459] or the "notion of environmental responsibility towards the future".[460] On the other side of the spectrum, *Brown Weiss'* doctrine is framed in a context of planetary trust with the obligation "to pass on the natural and cultural resources of the planet in no worse condition than received".[461]

The general conception of intergenerational equity remains superficial and differs much between the various documents. It does not pronounce obligations towards future generations, and even less mentions the notion of rights of future generations.[462] In contrast, the doctrine of *Brown Weiss* is elaborated in much detail with regard to planetary rights and specific duties of conservation. While the general

454 Hadjiargyrou (2016), p. 264.

455 Fitzmaurice (2008), p. 211. See also Hadjiargyrou (2016), p. 264; Dupuy and Viñuales (2018), p. 89; Collins (2007b), pp. 126–127.

456 *Malgosia Fitzmaurice* identified "at least three ways", whereas she also referred to intergenerational equity as a philosophical concept; see Fitzmaurice (2008), p. 211. This philosophical concept is addressed *infra* in Chap. 3; as to the differentiation, see already *supra* in context with note 228. *Daniel Bertram* identified "four historical incarnations of intergenerational equity", see Bertram (2023).

457 Exemplarily, see UNCED (1992a, Principle 3).

458 Collins (2007b), p. 127. See also Hadjiargyrou (2016), p. 264.

459 Dupuy and Viñuales (2018), p. 92.

460 Collins (2007b), p. 118.

461 Brown Weiss (1989), pp. 37–38.

462 Collins (2007b), p. 127; Hadjiargyrou (2016), p. 264.

conception was included in a variety of documents,[463] only a small number of documents since the Stockholm Declaration mirrored the more specific doctrine of intergenerational equity so far.[464]

This does not mean that intergenerational equity, as understood by *Brown Weiss*, is completely independent from the intergenerational component of sustainable development. In contrast, *Brown Weiss* based her doctrine on a variety of international legal and non-legal sources, which illustrates the deep historical roots of the concern for future humanity.[465] Both manifestations of intergenerational equity operate in a broader legal framework, which encompasses sustainable development but also other concepts of international environmental law. While the general conception of intergenerational equity remains a sub-principle and one of the main components of sustainable development,[466] *Brown Weiss* clarified that her doctrine of planetary rights goes "beyond what has customarily been considered as part of sustainable development."[467] Both manifestations, the specific doctrine and the intergenerational component of sustainable development, can be understood as nuances of the general idea of fairness among present and future generations, but they have developed to a different extent in specificity and contents.

In the following chapters, the terms "intergenerational equity" and "concept of intergenerational equity" are used as an overall notion, which includes both manifestations,[468] while "general conception of intergenerational equity" refers to the component of sustainable development and "specific doctrine of intergenerational equity" refers to *Brown Weiss'* doctrine. After the overall assessment of the philosophical and ethical foundations of intergenerational equity in Chap. 3, Chap. 4 addresses in more detail the legal nature of both manifestations separately. Chapter 7 further builds on the distinction, as it examines whether and how far it is possible that the general conception evolves into the specific doctrine on the international level. Before these perspectives in the different chapters, the following sections turn to the interrelations between intergenerational equity and two other concepts of international environmental law.

---

[463] Generally, see *supra* in Sect. 2.1.1. In more detail, see *infra* in Sect. 4.2.2.1.

[464] Boyle and Redgwell (2021), pp. 121–122. These documents are characterised in more detail *infra* in Sect. 4.2.2.2. In contrast, see Bartholomäi (1997), pp. 134–139.

[465] Brown Weiss (2019), pp. 51–53. See also Bartholomäi (1997), pp. 135–139.

[466] Sands et al. (2018), p. 219.

[467] Brown Weiss (2010), p. 109 See also Collins (2007b), pp. 125–126.

[468] On the use of the term "concept" in this book, see already *supra* note 1.

### 2.3.2 *Intra-Generational Equity and Common But Differentiated Responsibilities*

Intergenerational equity and intra-generational equity together constitute the two dimensions of equity or environmental justice.[469] While intergenerational equity envisages fairness among generations, intra-generational equity aims to assure a just distribution among human beings that are alive today.[470] Both notions of equity constitute components of sustainable development.[471] This connection of both dimensions of equity also becomes obvious in various international documents, which refer to the needs of present *and* future generations in one breath.[472] For instance, the Brundtland Report understood sustainable development as "meet[ing] the needs of the present without compromising the ability of future generations to meet their own needs".[473] Due to this historical and conceptual connection, intergenerational equity must also be assessed in relation to its intra-generational counterpart,[474] although it exceeds the present book's scope of analysis to address the contents of intra-generational equity in detail.[475]

Intra-generational equity is understood as "fairness in utilization and enjoyment of resources as well as in enduring the costs for degradation, disposal, and rehabilitation of resources, among all persons and groups both domestically and internationally."[476] It requires an equitable share and use of natural resources in the relationship to other States.[477] With regard to *Brown Weiss'* doctrine of intergenerational equity, several commentators have criticised its alleged incompatibility with a fair distribution of resources within the present generation.[478] According to these commentators, it is unbearable to oblige the present generation to address the needs of future generations as long as there is not even a fair distribution of resources within the same generation.[479] Further, a focus on obligations towards the future would lead to an instrumentalisation of the present

---

[469] Shelton (2010a), p. 642; Nanda and Pring (2013), p. 33.

[470] Shelton (2010a), p. 642.

[471] Beyerlin (2006), p. 275; Nanda and Pring (2013), pp. 32–33. See also *supra* note 431.

[472] E.g., Preamble and Art. 3(2) of the UNFCCC; UNCED (1992a, Principle 3); UNESCO (1997, Article 1). See also Maggio (1997).

[473] WCED (1987, Introduction para. 27).

[474] See Malhotra (1998), p. 47; Collins (2007b), pp. 107–110; Brown Weiss (2021a, para. 12).

[475] For a detailed analysis of environmental inter-State justice, including intra-generational equity, see Bartenstein (2022). See also Lammers (2008).

[476] Maggio (1997), p. 193. Cf. also Shelton (2010a), p. 642; Barral (2012), p. 380.

[477] Sands et al. (2018), pp. 219, 225–227.

[478] E.g., Gündling (1990), p. 211; Barresi (1997); Mayeda (2004); Anstee-Wedderburn (2014), p. 66; Boyle and Redgwell (2021), p. 124. For another challenge, often discussed within environmental ethics, see Gosseries (2001), p. 332. on the relation between intergenerational justice and population ethics.

[479] Gündling (1990), p. 211.

generation as a mere means to the end of future generations' happiness; such an approach would "undermin[e] the importance of human dignity and equal worth of all".[480]

This criticism has a certain validity, as the equitable distribution of natural resources within one generation and the equitable distribution among generations can conflict if intergenerational equity is applied in an unjust manner.[481] Members of the present generation who are living in extreme poverty would be obliged in their position as trustees to safeguard the scarce existing resources in order to conserve them for members of future generations who could possibly be much better off than them.[482] This is why particularly developing States have been reluctant to a level of environmental protection for the future that would be too ambitious and could endanger their economic development.[483] Notwithstanding this, people in poor societies are most vulnerable and least resilient to environmental degradation not only today,[484] but even more so in the future.[485] With regard to the impacts of climate change, the UN Special Rapporteur on Extreme Poverty and Human Rights stated in a 2019 report:

> Climate change threatens to undo the last 50 years of progress in development, global health and poverty reduction. [...] The World Bank estimates that without immediate action, climate change could push 120 million more people into poverty by 2030, likely an underestimate, and rising in subsequent years. In South Asia alone, 800 million people live in climate hotspots and will see their living conditions decline sharply by 2050.[486]

Many environmental problems have intergenerational *and* intra-generational impacts on the same parts of the world population, present and future alike.[487] Therefore, it is neither mandatory nor persuasive to play off both dimensions of equity against each other.

*Brown Weiss'* doctrine itself offered counter-arguments against this criticism. As one of the preliminary criteria for her doctrine, she clarified that the elements of intergenerational equity "neither authorize unreasonable exploitation by the present generation nor impose unreasonable burdens on it".[488] This is consistent with her

480 Mayeda (2004), p. 45. A somehow similar objection was often raised against the philosophical approach of utilitarianism in the context of intergenerational justice, cf. in detail Birnbacher (2006), pp. 32–33 as well as *infra* in Sect. 3.3.1.

481 Collins (2007b), pp. 97–98, 109–110; Redgwell (1999), p. 110; Nanda and Pring (2013), p. 35.

482 Collins (2007b), p. 109.

483 See, e.g., Lammers (2008), pp. 32–39. See also *supra* notes 45–49.

484 See, e.g., UN Department of Economic and Social Affairs (2016), pp. 21–46; Abeygunawardena et al. (2009). In the 1980s and 1990s, poverty was also still considered a major factor for environmental degradation, see WCED (1987, Introduction, para. 8, Chapter 1, para. 17). However, this direction of the interrelationship has been refuted, see, e.g., Satterthwaite (2002), pp. 28–31.

485 Human Rights Council (2019, paras. 8–15); Scheyli (2008), p. 342; Brown Weiss (1995), p. 21.

486 Human Rights Council (2019, para. 13).

487 Brown Weiss (1992), p. 74; Malhotra (1998), pp. 47–48; Redgwell (1999), p. 110; Shelton (2010b), p. 133.

488 Brown Weiss (2021a, para. 8).

notion of a planetary trust, which envisages present generations both as beneficiaries and as trustees.[489] Explicitly, she underlined that intergenerational equity "encompasses a parallel set of planetary obligations and planetary rights that are intragenerational."[490] The fact that the present generation has an obligation towards succeeding generations does not indicate anything about the distribution of the intergenerational burdens within the present generation.[491] *Brown Weiss* understood the danger of an inequitable distribution of burdens in the present, which is why she specified:

> The quest for intergenerational equity requires that intragenerational equity issues be addressed. In practice, the two kinds of equity are joined, because poor communities cannot be expected to fulfil intergenerational obligations if they are not able to meet basic needs today.[492]

Consequently, the balanced approach between present and future generations became clear in all three of *Brown Weiss'* basic principles.[493] Conservation of options does not require a standstill at the *status quo* to the detriment of poorer people of the present generation[494]; and conservation of quality allows for inevitable trade-offs in order to achieve benefits for both the present and the future.[495] Particularly, the third intergenerational principle, conservation of equitable access, includes a strong intra-generational perspective. It requires that the members of the present generation first have a reasonable, non-discriminatory right of access to the natural resources of the planet.[496] Only secondly, it addresses the same right of equitable access of future generations.[497] *Brown Weiss* further underlined that developed States have a special responsibility to help poorer parts of the present generation to gain equitable access to the natural resources of the planet.[498]

Although the concept of intergenerational equity remains primarily future-oriented and addresses intra-generational aspects rather incidentally,[499] it does not solve equity concerns to the detriment of disadvantaged parts of the present generation. Generally, intergenerational equity is open to interaction with present-orientated concerns of intra-generational distribution of resources.[500] Particularly,

---

[489] Brown Weiss (1989), p. 17. Cf. also Brown Weiss (1992), pp. 74–75.

[490] Brown Weiss (1989), p. 21.

[491] Ibid.

[492] Brown Weiss (2021a, para. 12). Cf. also Brown Weiss (2019), p. 55.

[493] In detail, see already *supra* in Sects. 2.2.1.3 and 2.2.1.4.

[494] Brown Weiss (1989), pp. 41–42.

[495] Ibid., pp. 42–43.

[496] Ibid., 43–44, 55. On distributive principles in allocating natural resources, see Shelton (2010a), pp. 647–649.

[497] Brown Weiss (1989), p. 44.

[498] Brown Weiss (1992), p. 75; Brown Weiss (1989), p. 45.

[499] Redgwell (1999), p. 109 (at footnote 208).

[500] *Maritime Delimitation in the Area* (Separate Opinion of Judge Weeramantry), *supra* note 197, para. 242; Collins (2007b), pp. 110, 128; Collins (2007a), p. 323.

it is embedded in the larger framework of sustainable development, which is able to balance competing interests with each other.[501] Since sustainable development encompasses intergenerational as well as intra-generational components, it can equally contribute to achieve the necessary balance between both dimensions of equity.[502]

With regard to the intertwined relationship between sustainable development, intergenerational and intra-generational equity, the concept of Common But Differentiated Responsibilities ('CBDR') comes into play.[503] It was explicitly stated in Principles 6 and 7 of the Rio Declaration.[504] Principle 7 provides:

> States shall co-operate in a spirit of global partnership to conserve, protect and restore the health and integrity of the Earth's ecosystem. In view of the different contributions to global environmental degradation, States have common but differentiated responsibilities. The developed countries acknowledge the responsibility that they bear in the international pursuit of sustainable development in view of the pressures their societies place on the global environment and of the technologies and financial resources they command.[505]

The general idea behind this concept was the fair distribution of responsibilities and burdens for environmental protection amongst States with due regard to existing differences between developing and developed States.[506] Although the notion of CBDR and its legal status were and still are disputed between developing and developed States,[507] CBDR has found its way into international environmental law and governance.[508] As it is itself a principle of equity and balance,[509] it is

[501] Dupuy and Viñuales (2018), p. 62. See also Malhotra (1998), p. 48.

[502] Shelton (2010a), pp. 642–643. See also Brown Weiss (2019), pp. 57–58.

[503] Hey and Paulini (2021, para. 5). In general on the concept, see also Cullet (2010); Sands et al. (2018), pp. 244–248; Bartenstein (2022), pp. 64–89.

[504] See also Hey and Paulini (2021, para. 4).

[505] UNCED (1992a, Principle 7). See also ibid., Principle 6; UN (1972, Principle 23); UNGA (1974, Art. 30); *Montreal Protocol on Substances that Deplete the Ozone Layer* (Montreal Protocol), adopted 16 September 1987, entered into force 1 January 1989, 1522 UNTS 3, Art. 5.

[506] Shelton (2010a), p. 657; Hey and Paulini (2021, para. 5); Bartenstein (2022), pp. 68–69.

[507] Shelton (2010a), pp. 656–658; Maggio (1997), p. 207; Bartenstein (2022), p. 73. The USA was specifically concerned with Principle 7 of the Rio Declaration and issued an interpretative statement denying any legal obligation or any diminution in the responsibility of developing countries arising from this Principle: UNCED (1992c), pp. 17–18; French (2000), p. 37. Particularly, the issue of historical responsibility of developed States for past environmental degradation is controversial: in favour of a moral relevance of the past, see Mayeda (2004), pp. 54–56.; in favour of a differentiated treatment due to different historical contributions, see Najam (1994), p. 24.

[508] In detail, see Hey and Paulini (2021, para. 19).

[509] Dupuy and Viñuales (2018), pp. 81, 83–84; Shelton (2010a), p. 656.

strongly connected to intra-generational equity,[510] and sometimes even considered to be a synonym.[511] *Ellen Hey* and *Sophia Paulini* noted in this context:

> The interrelationship [...] can be characterized as follows: the concept of common but differentiated responsibilities constitutes a means of translating the concept of inter- and intra-generational equity to the inter-State level [...] with a view to attaining sustainable development [...].[512]

While the international community has a common responsibility for certain environmental goods and natural resources,[513] the intra-generational component of common but differentiated responsibilities stipulates differences between the States with regard to their legal obligations that result from this common responsibility.[514] The exact operationalisation of common but differentiated responsibilities largely depends on the relevant treaty regime, in which it is incorporated.[515] Differentiated environmental standards can apply to different States dependent on various factors, such as specific needs, circumstances and capacities.[516] *Brown Weiss* went beyond this and clarified that intergenerational equity also required wealthier States "to contribute to the costs incurred by poor countries and communities in protecting [the natural] resources".[517]

Overall, CBDR constitutes a framework, which allows for an equitable share of the burdens of environmental degradation among the present generation. While it does not explicitly regulate past, historical responsibilities,[518] it regulates the extent of State obligations with regard to environmental protection for the future.[519] This is consistent with *Brown Weiss'* third intergenerational principle, the equitable access to the planetary resources for all members of the present generation.[520] Therefore, CBDR can be a helpful instrument to resolve the potential conflict between the interests and capacities of the present generation and the needs of future generations.[521] As demonstrated, intergenerational equity is not necessarily in

---

[510] Malhotra (1998), p. 47; Redgwell (1999), p. 140; Nanda and Pring (2013), pp. 42–43; Hey and Paulini (2021, para. 5). See also Collins (2007b), p. 110.

[511] Nanda and Pring (2013), pp. 42–43; Dupuy and Viñuales (2015), p. 71. However, this synonymous understanding was apparently dropped in the subsequent edition: Dupuy and Viñuales (2018), p. 81.

[512] Hey and Paulini (2021, para. 5).

[513] Sands et al. (2018), p. 245. On the familiar concepts of "common heritage of humankind" and "common concern of humankind", see *infra* in Sect. 2.3.3.

[514] Ibid., pp. 246–247.

[515] Hey and Paulini (2021, para. 7) For an overview of treaties that explicitly or implicitly incorporated the concept, see Sands et al. (2018), p. 246. The Paris Agreement is a recent example that incorporated CBDR, see Preamble and Art. 2(2) of the Paris Agreement.

[516] Redgwell (1999), pp. 141–142; Sands et al. (2018), p. 246.

[517] Brown Weiss (1989), pp. 27–28.

[518] See *supra* note 507.

[519] Shelton (2010a), p. 657; Bartenstein (2022), pp. 73–74.

[520] Cf. Brown Weiss (2021a, para. 20).

[521] Collins (2007b), pp. 127–128; Maggio (1997), pp. 206–207.

contradiction to equity within the present generation, since it operates within a broader framework with other concepts of international environmental law, such as intra-generational equity and common but differentiated responsibilities.[522] Consequently, any further elaboration on the concept of intergenerational equity must always be considered to also include an equitable sharing of resources and burdens within the present generation. Yet, this intra-generational perspective is not in the focus of this book.

### *2.3.3 Common Heritage and Common Concern of Humankind*

The idea of common but differentiated responsibilities is based on the understanding that certain areas and/or environmental goods and resources are governed by a *common* responsibility shared by all States.[523] This idea of a shared responsibility is connected to familiar notions of international environmental law, such as the common heritage of humankind and the common concern of humankind.[524] It is also rooted in communitarian concepts of the relationship between human beings.[525]

The status of a common heritage of humankind is normally attributed to areas and/or resources beyond national jurisdiction of any State and which exist for the benefit of all.[526] Core features of the concept are: the area's or the resources' freedom from State sovereignty, a system of global governance and management, the sharing of any economic benefits derived from its utilisation and its use for solely peaceful purposes.[527] So far, the domains of international law of outer space[528] and the law of the sea[529] have shaped the common heritage of humankind.

However, the concept was rejected with regard to general international environmental law.[530] This is due to the concept's connection to geographical areas outside

[522] See also Collins (2007b), pp. 97–98, 110, 128.

[523] Sands et al. (2018), p. 245. See also Soltau (2016), p. 210.

[524] Brunnée (2010), p. 566; Sands et al. (2018), p. 245. For the related notion of "common interest", see Feichtner (2007, para. 25) In this book, the more contemporary term of "humankind" is used in relation to both concepts, although some (particularly older) sources still referred to the common heritage of "mankind".

[525] In more detail, see *infra* in Sect. 3.3.4.2.

[526] Nanda and Pring (2013), p. 37.

[527] Ibid., p. 38; Proelß and Haake (2017), pp. 183–184.

[528] Art. 11(1) of the Moon Agreement. See also Matte (1987); Cançado Trindade (2020), pp. 329–331.

[529] *United Nations Convention on the Law of the Sea* (UNCLOS), adopted 10 December 1982, entered into force 16 November 1994, 1833 UNTS 3, Art. 136–149. See also Cançado Trindade (2020), pp. 331–336.

[530] Wolfrum (2009, para. 9). See, however, with regard to related concepts: Cançado Trindade (2020), pp. 339–344.

national jurisdiction.[531] Therefore, its extension to areas of biological diversity or climate protection met with strong sovereignty-based opposition.[532] Consequently, the global dimension of many environmental problems led to the introduction of other references to humankind in a variety of international documents on the environment.[533] In 1988, the UNGA recognised that climate change was a "common concern of [hu]mankind",[534] before the UNFCCC acknowledged this status in its Preamble.[535] The same reference to the common concern of humankind exists in the CBD with regard to the conservation of biological diversity.[536] The central idea of the common concern of humankind is the cooperation of States by concerted actions, so that the burdens of environmental protection are equitably shared among States.[537] Contrary to the notion of common heritage, the understanding of the climate system as common concern of humankind did not interfere with national sovereignty and shifted the emphasis away from mere exploitation of natural resources.[538] Overall, the common concern concept is more adequate to deal with issues of climate change or biological diversity.[539]

Despite certain parallels, there are decisive distinctions between these two notions so that they do not overlap but coexist.[540] While common heritage refers to geographical areas outside of particular national jurisdiction, common concern typically regulates environmental problems of natural resources in areas *within* State jurisdiction, but which have global impacts and are considered to be the concern of the international community as a whole.[541] While the former has a specific link to the distribution of resources and its benefits,[542] the latter primarily aims at the fair distribution of responsibility and burdens for environmental protection between States.[543] Therefore, there are strong connections between the common concern of humankind and the aforementioned idea of common but differentiated responsibilities.[544]

---

531 Redgwell (1999), p. 130; Proelß and Haake (2017), pp. 173, 178.

532 Nanda and Pring (2013), p. 39; Proelß and Haake (2017), pp. 188–189. However, see Malta's request in 1988: UNGA (1988a). Also arguing in favour of the global climate as common heritage, see Sobrino Heredia (2014), p. 78.

533 Cançado Trindade (2020), p. 339. See also Wood (1996), p. 325.

534 UNGA (1988b, para. 1).

535 See also Preamble of the Paris Agreement.

536 *Convention on Biological Diversity* (CBD), adopted 5 June 1992, entered into force 29 December 1993, 1760 UNTS 79, Preamble.

537 Cançado Trindade (2020), p. 344.

538 Ibid., 340, 344.

539 Borg (1998), p. 137. Cf. also Wood (1996), pp. 321–325.

540 Proelß and Haake (2017), pp. 191–192; Cançado Trindade (2020), p. 348.

541 Proelß and Haake (2017), p. 189; Brunnée (2010), pp. 564–565; Nanda and Pring (2013), p. 39; Dupuy and Viñuales (2018), p. 98.

542 Ibid., p. 96.

543 Borg (1998), p. 137; Proelß and Haake (2017), p. 191; Cançado Trindade (2020), p. 340.

544 Brunnée (2010), p. 566; Proelß and Haake (2017), pp. 191–192.

More importantly, both notions have significant intergenerational components.[545] The notion of "heritage" has a strong temporal connotation, as it generally describes the relationship of inheritance between a testator and an heir. In the context of international law, the (common) heritage could include present as well as future generations as beneficiaries.[546] This intergenerational component is even stronger with regard to the notion of humankind, which encompasses both present and future generations.[547] In the 1990s, a group of legal experts of the UNEP addressed in the 1990s the implications of common concern of humankind on environmental issues and particularly underlined the concept's temporal elements, which arose from long-term consequences of many environmental challenges.[548]

Comparable to *Edith Brown Weiss'* notion of an intergenerational trust, the common heritage of humankind can be based on explanatory concepts of a public trust and of universal solidarity among successive generations.[549] Originally, *Brown Weiss'* was of the opinion that "the common heritage of [hu]mankind anticipates the need for planetary obligations"[550] and suggested:

> [It] could be viewed as encompassing the concerns for future generations [...]. If we were to rely on the doctrine, countries should reaffirm explicitly that the common heritage is directed to the welfare of future as well as present generations. It should extend to all natural and cultural resources, wherever located, that are internationally important for the well-being of future generations. [...] In the intergenerational context, our planet is a global commons shared by each generation.[551]

However, this extension of the common heritage concept to all environmental issues has not been accepted by the international community.[552] *Catherine Redgwell* even doubted whether the notion of common heritage constituted an intergenerational trust or just a trust of *intra*-generational equity instead.[553] Later, *Brown Weiss* admitted that common heritage, while related to intergenerational equity, has remained limited to the specific areas mentioned above.[554] Consequently, the stronger connection exists between intergenerational equity and the concept of common concern of humankind, which developed later and which also put the interests of present and future generations of humankind in the centre of attention of the

---

545 Borg (1998), pp. 135–137; Fitzmaurice (2012); Proelß and Haake (2017), p. 191.

546 Kiss (1982), pp. 240, 243; Wolfrum (2009, para. 22); Cançado Trindade (2020), p. 328. See also Redgwell (1999), p. 130. Cf. also Sobrino Heredia (2014).

547 Nagy (1988), p. 321 (at footnote 29); Nagy (1998), p. 60; Proelß and Haake (2017), p. 179; Cançado Trindade (2020), p. 347.

548 UNEP (1993a, paras. 3–5); UNEP (1993b, para. 5) Related to this, some commentators even assumed a general temporal character of all international treaties on environmental matters, see Tanaka (2013), pp. 156–158. and in more detail *infra* in Sect. 6.2.4.

549 Kiss (1982), pp. 113, 229–231; Cançado Trindade (2020), pp. 327–328.

550 Brown Weiss (1989), p. 48.

551 Ibid., p. 49.

552 See *supra* notes 530–532.

553 Redgwell (1999), pp. 131–132.

554 Brown Weiss (2021a, para. 18).

international community.[555] The broad reference to—present and future generations of—humankind also brings together issues of intergenerational equity and intra-generational equity. Finally, the aspect of common goods and interests of humanity is also related to a notion of obligations *erga omnes*,[556] meaning obligations that are owed to the international community as a whole.[557] The relevance of this kind of obligations for intergenerational equity is addressed in more detail in Chap. 5.[558]

### 2.3.4 Summary

The foregoing sections have illustrated that intergenerational equity operates within a multifaceted legal framework of international environmental law. It is related to other concepts, most importantly to sustainable development, intra-generational equity, common but differentiated responsibilities and common heritage as well as common concern of humankind.

The overarching framework of sustainable development[559] has the most complex interrelation with intergenerational equity. Sustainable development consists of several elements, such as integration and intergenerational as well as intra-generational equity. The strong interrelation with intergenerational equity is already reflected in the common birth document of both concepts, the Brundtland Report. This is why intergenerational equity has often been considered to be the main content of sustainable development. However, an accurate analysis has demonstrated that there are at least *two* manifestations of intergenerational equity in international documents, jurisprudence and scholarship, which differ in the degree of specificity with regard to their exact contents. On the one hand, a general conception of intergenerational equity constitutes one of the components of sustainable development: the requirement to take into account the needs of future generations. On the other hand, the doctrine of intergenerational equity, as elaborated by *Edith Brown Weiss*, encompasses a planetary trust and intergenerational rights and obligations, and therefore exceeds the intergenerational component of sustainable development. This means that intergenerational equity exists both as a sub-principle of sustainable development and as an independent notion of international environmental law. Therefore, intergenerational equity definitely merits a distinct legal analysis, which surpasses the analysis of sustainable development in international

---

[555] Cançado Trindade (2020), pp. 344, 347. As to the parallels, see also Brown Weiss (2021a, para. 19).

[556] Fitzmaurice (2010), p. 1020; Cançado Trindade (2020), p. 347.

[557] ICJ, *Barcelona Traction, Light and Power Company, Limited (Belgium v. Spain), Second Phase*, Judgment, 5 February 1970, ICJ Reports 1970, 3, para. 33. See also Kammerhofer (2024).

[558] See *infra* in Sect. 5.3.3.2.2.

[559] On the normative capacity of this framework, see *infra* in Sect. 4.1.2.

law. The exact differences between these two manifestations with regard to their legal nature are addressed in Chap. 4 below.

Besides this interrelation between intergenerational equity and sustainable development, intergenerational equity touches upon other concepts of international environmental law. The relationship between intra-generational and intergenerational equity seems to be problematic at first glance. Some commentators have criticised that a strong focus on intergenerational concerns, particularly *Brown Weiss'* doctrine, would ignore the need to provide for fairness among the members of the present generation. However, the foregoing analysis has demonstrated that these objections are neither mandatory nor persuasive. First, *Brown Weiss'* doctrine also addresses intra-generational aspects in order to allow wealthier and poorer members of the present generation to meet their conservation obligations towards future generations. Second, the idea of common but differentiated responsibilities of different States of the present generation is also applicable to the present generation's planetary obligations towards the future. Third, the framework of sustainable development allows for a balancing process to consolidate inter- and intra-generational concerns, as both forms of equity are included in the components of sustainable development.

Lastly, the foregoing section has illustrated the strong intergenerational elements of the environmental concepts of common heritage and common concern of humankind. While they address different substantial areas and consist of different mechanisms, both concepts rely on a universal understanding of "humankind" as beneficiary of these regimes. This means that the common heritage and the common concern pertain to present and future generations of humankind alike. Intergenerational equity is partly based on the same underlying rationale, including ideas of a public planetary trust, international and intergenerational solidarity, and a general concern for the needs of future generations.

The foregoing sections have not only illustrated the interrelation and overlaps of intergenerational equity with several other concepts of international environmental law. They have also served as a proper delimitation of the present work's research object. This research object does neither focus on the overall framework of sustainable development and its other components nor does it assess problems of intra-generational equity in detail. Further, it is not focusing on the idea of common heritage or common concern of humankind as alternative mechanisms of guaranteeing the interests of future generations. The focus remains on the concept of intergenerational equity, including both manifestations elaborated in the foregoing analysis. Nonetheless, this does not exclude these related notions as far as they play a role in the course of the book.

## 2.4 Conclusion of This Chapter

This chapter has introduced the analysis of the concept of intergenerational equity in international environmental law. The historical analysis has examined the references to the interests, needs or rights of future generations in the development of international environmental law. While the responsibility towards future generations had always played a role in cultural and religious traditions, the interests of future generations have started to increasingly influence the realm of international law since the 1980s. The notions of intergenerational equity and sustainable development have shaped international binding and non-binding documents a lot in the 1990s, beginning with the Rio Conference. But this influence has continued in the twenty-first century and until today, the interests of future generations are included in most documents of environmental concern. Further, a brief overview of international jurisprudence has illustrated that future generations have also played a role in some environmental cases and advisory opinions; although more explicitly in several individual opinions. Most recently, two examples have demonstrated the relevance of intergenerational equity in international environmental law: the current climate change law, building on the 1992 UNFCCC and revived by the 2015 Paris Agreement, touches upon matters of direct intergenerational concern; further, the draft proposal of a Global Pact for the Environment includes intergenerational equity as a decisive principle.

Most of these historical and jurisprudential references to future generations remained vague and superficial, while they did not stipulate specific obligations or rights or mechanisms of implementation. In contrast, at the centre of the works on intergenerational equity, *Edith Brown Weiss* has elaborated a sophisticated doctrine of intergenerational equity, which builds on the "obligation to future generations to pass on the natural and cultural resources of the planet in no worse condition than received".[560] According to this doctrine, intergenerational equity regulates the fair distribution of natural resources and environmental quality between present and future generations of humanity. It is conceived as a planetary trust between all generations, whereas the present generation is beneficiary and trustee of the trust at the same time and holds the planetary resources in trust for the benefit of future generations. *Brown Weiss* derived three main principles and duties of conservation from this planetary trust: conservation of comparable options of the resource base, conservation of environmental quality and conservation of equitable access to the natural resources by present and future generations. Conversely, intergenerational rights of future generations complement these obligations. There has been a lot of support but also much criticism of *Brown Weiss'* doctrine, which is addressed at later points of the book, where adequate.

---

[560] Brown Weiss (1989), pp. 37–38.

So far, the historical illustration, and the doctrinal analysis in general, have focused on the substantive components of a potential norm of intergenerational equity. Operating mechanisms of implementation, such as the question of right-holders and duty-bearers as well as the institutional frameworks of representation and implementation, have not been examined in this first chapter, but they are addressed in detail in Chap. 5.[561]

In order to fully grasp the legal contents of intergenerational equity, its position within international environmental law is important. The concern for future generations in international law exists in a multifaceted framework of international environmental law with parallels and overlaps to many related concepts. The contextualisation of intergenerational equity within this framework also serves as a delimitation of this book's scope of analysis. The strongest interrelations exist between intergenerational equity and sustainable development, as was already obvious from the historical perspective. It has become clear that these two notions are not completely identical but that sustainable development contains a general conception of intergenerational equity as one of its main components. This general conception must be distinguished from another, more specific manifestation of intergenerational equity, as mirrored in the doctrine of *Edith Brown Weiss*. Both manifestations can be understood as nuances of the general idea of fairness among present and future generations, but they have developed to a different extent in specificity and contents. The legal nature of these two manifestations and the possible evolution of international law from one manifestation to the other constitute the research object of following chapters.[562] Beyond sustainable development, the most relevant conflicts and parallels exist between intergenerational equity and intragenerational equity as well as the concepts of common heritage and common concern of humankind.

The foregoing chapter has already contributed to a legal contextualisation of intergenerational equity as well as to its delimitation from other concepts of international environmental law. However, there is one *non*-legal perspective that is equally important to the understanding of intergenerational equity: the philosophical approaches to intergenerational justice. In order to better grasp the legal concept of intergenerational equity and to distinguish it from pre-legal considerations, its ethical foundations must be analysed appropriately. Therefore, Chap. 3 illustrates the philosophical perspectives on intergenerational justice, before Chap. 4 turns to the actual positivist analysis of intergenerational equity.

[561] As to the interrelation between the presented normative elements of intergenerational equity and its operating framework, see briefly *infra* in Sect. 7.3.4.

[562] As to the legal nature, see *infra* in Chap. 4; as to the future evolutions of these manifestations, see *infra* in Chap. 7.

## References

Abeygunawardena, P., Vyas, Y., Knill, P., Foy, T., Harrold, M., Steele, P., Tanner, T., Hirsch, D., Oosterman, M., Rooimans, J., Debois, M., Lamin, M., Liptow, H., Mausolf, E., Verheyen, R., Agrawala, S., Caspary, G., Paris, R., Kashyap, A. et al. (2009). *Poverty and climate change: Reducing the vulnerability of the poor through adaptation*. OECD. 2009. Retrieved 3 January 2025, from https://documents.worldbank.org/en/publication/documents-reports/documentdetail/534871468155709473/poverty-and-climate-change-reducing-the-vulnerability-of-the-poor-through-adaptation

Agius, E. (1998). The earth belongs to all generations: Moral challenges of sustainable development. In E. Agius & L. Chircop (Eds.), *Caring for future generations: Jewish, Christian and Islamic perspectives* (p. 103). Praeger Publishers.

Agius, E., & Chircop, L. (Eds.). (1998). *Caring for future generations: Jewish, Christian and Islamic perspectives*. Praeger Publishers.

Aguila, Y. (2020). A global pact for the environment: The logical outcome of 50 years of international environmental law. *Sustainability, 12*(14), 5636. https://doi.org/10.3390/su12145636

Aguila, Y., & Chami, L. (2022). The global pact for the environment: Where to? *Jus Mundi Blog*. 17 March 2022. Retrieved 3 January 2025, from https://blog.jusmundi.com/global-pact-for-the-environment-where-to/

Andrews, K., Comstock, G., Crozier, G., Donaldson, S., & Fenton, A. (2019). *Chimpanzee rights: The philosophers' brief*. Routledge Taylor & Francis Group.

Anstee-Wedderburn, J. (2014). Giving a voice to future generations: Intergenerational equity, representative of generations to come, and the challenge of planetary rights. *Australian Journal of Environmental Law, 1*(1), 37–70.

Association of Southeast Asian Nations. (2007). *ASEAN Declaration on Environmental Sustainability*. 20 November 2007. Retrieved 3 January 2025, from https://asean.org/asean-declaration-on-environmental-sustainability/

Atapattu, S. A. (2006). *Emerging principles of international environmental law*. Transnational Publishers, Inc. https://doi.org/10.1163/ej.9781571051820.i-536

Attard, D. J. (Ed.). (1991). *The meeting of the group of legal experts to examine the concept of the common concern of mankind in relation to global environmental issues: University of Malta, Malta, 13-15 December, 1990*. UN Environment Programme.

Ba Kader, A. B. A., Al Sabbagh, A. L. T. E. S., Al Glenid, M. A. S., & Izzidien, M. Y. S. (1983). *Basic paper on the islamic principles for the conservation of the natural environment*. International Union for Conservation of Nature. https://doi.org/10.2305/IUCN.CH.2015.EPLP.31/rev4.en.

Bakker, C. (2015). The Paris Agreement on climate change: Balancing legal force and geographical scope. *Italian Yearbook of International Law, 25*, 299–310.

Barral, V. (2012). Sustainable development in international law: Nature and operation of an evolutive legal norm. *European Journal of International Law, 23*(2), 377–400. https://doi.org/10.1093/ejil/chs016

Barral, V. (2018). The principle of sustainable development. In L. Krämer & E. Orlando (Eds.), *Principles of environmental law* (pp. 103–114). Edward Elgar Publishing.

Barral, V., & Dupuy, P.-M. (2015). Principle 4. In J. E. Viñuales (Ed.), *The rio declaration on environment and development: A commentary* (1st ed., pp. 157–179). Oxford University Press.

Barral, V., & Dupuy, P.-M. (2019). Sustainable development and integration. In Y. Aguila & J. E. Viñuales (Eds.). *A global pact for the environment: Legal foundations* (Vol. 4, pp. 44–50). Cambridge Centre for Environment, Energy and Natural Resource Governance (C-EENRG).

Barresi, P. A. (1997). Beyond fairness to future generations: An intragenerational alternative to intergenerational equity in the international environmental arena. *Tulane Environmental Law Journal, 11*(1), 59–88.

Barresi, P. A. (1998). Advocacy, frame, and the intergenerational imperative: A reply to Professor Weiss on "Beyond Fairness to Future Generations". *Tulane Environmental Law Journal, 11*, 425–439.

Bartenstein, K. (2022). Zwischenstaatliche Umweltgerechtigkeit. In A. Proelß (Ed.), *Internationales Umweltrecht* (Vol. 2, 2nd ed., pp. 53–94). De Gruyter.

Bartholomäi, R. (1997). *Sustainable Development und Völkerrecht: Nachhaltige Entwicklung und Intergenerative Gerechtigkeit in der Staatenpraxis* (1st ed.). Nomos.

Beckerman, W. (2006). The impossibility of a theory of intergenerational justice. In J. C. Tremmel (Ed.), *Handbook of intergenerational justice* (Vol. 3, pp. 53–71). Edward Elgar Publishing.

Beckman, L. (2013). Democracy and future generations: Should the unborn have a voice? In J.-C. Merle (Ed.), *Spheres of global justice: Volume 2 fair distribution – global economic, social and intergenerational justice* (Vol. 62, pp. 775–788). Springer. https://doi.org/10.1007/978-94-007-5998-5_62

Beder, S. (2000). Costing the earth: Equity, sustainable development and environmental economics. *New Zealand Journal of Environmental Law, 4*, 227–244.

Bertram, D. (2023). "For You Will (Still) Be Here Tomorrow": The many lives of intergenerational equity. *Transnational Environmental Law, 12*(1), 121–149.

Beyerlin, U. (1994). Rio-Konferenz 1992: Beginn einer Neuen Globalen Umweltrechtsordnung? *Zeitschrift Für Ausländisches Öffentliches Recht Und Völkerrecht, 54*, 124–149.

Beyerlin, U. (2006). Bridging the North-South divide in international environmental law. *Zeitschrift Für Ausländisches Öffentliches Recht Und Völkerrecht, 66*, 259–296.

Beyerlin, U. (2013). Sustainable development. In A. Peters & R. Wolfrum (Eds.), *Max Planck Encyclopedia of public international law*. Oxford University Press. (Article last updated October 2013).

Beyerlin, U., & Holzer, V. (2013). Conservation of natural resources. In A. Peters & R. Wolfrum (Eds.), *Max Planck Encyclopedia of public international law*. Oxford University Press. (Article last updated October 2013).

Beyerlin, U., & Marauhn, T. (2011). *International environmental law*. Hart Publishing.

Beyerlin, U., & Reichard, M. (2003). The Johannesburg Summit: Outcome and overall assessment. *Zeitschrift Für Ausländisches Öffentliches Recht Und Völkerrecht, 63*, 213–237.

Bielefeldt, H. (2021). Moving beyond anthropocentrism? Human rights and the charge of speciesism. *Human Rights Quarterly, 43*(3), 515–537. https://doi.org/10.1353/hrq.2021.0038

Birnbacher, D. (2006). Responsibility for future generations – scope and limits. In J. C. Tremmel (Ed.), *Handbook of intergenerational justice* (Vol. 1, pp. 23–38). Edward Elgar Publishing.

Bodansky, D. (2019). Top 10 developments in international environmental law. *Yearbook of International Environmental Law, 30*(1), 3–21. https://doi.org/10.2139/ssrn.3644557

Bodansky, D. (2020). The role and limits of the international court of justice in international environmental law. In E. Carlos & K. Partlett (Eds.), *The Cambridge companion to the international court of justice*. Cambridge University Press.

Boer, B. (2021). The preamble. In G. van Calster & L. Reins (Eds.), *Paris agreement on climate change: A commentary* (pp. 5–32). Edward Elgar Publishing.

Böhringer, A.-M. (2016). Das Neue Pariser Klimaübereinkommen: Eine Kompromisslösung mit Symbolkraft und Verhaltenssteuerungspotential. *Zeitschrift Für Ausländisches Öffentliches Recht Und Völkerrecht, 76*, 753–795.

Boisson de Chazournes, L., & Mbengue, M. M. (2017). Gabčíkovo-Nagymaros Project (Hungary/Slovakia) (1997). In C. Miles & E. Bjorge (Eds.), *Landmark cases in public international law* (Vol. 18, pp. 435–453). Bloomsbury Publishing PLC.

Borg, S. (1998). Guarding intergenerational rights over natural resources. In E. Agius & S. Busuttil (Eds.), *Future generations and international law: Proceedings of the International Experts' Meeting Held by the Future Generations Programme at the Foundation for International Studies, University of Malta* (Vol. 11, pp. 127–141). Earthscan Publications Ltd.

Bosselmann, K. (2002). Rio+10: Any closer to sustainable development? *New Zealand Journal of Environmental Law, 6*, 297–317.

Bosselmann, K. (2009a). Earth charter (2000). In A. Peters & R. Wolfrum (Eds.). *Max Planck Encyclopedia of public international law*. Oxford University Press. (Article last updated March 2009)
Bosselmann, K. (2009b). Environmental ethics. In A. Peters & R. Wolfrum (Eds.), *Max Planck Encyclopedia of public international law*. Oxford University Press. (Article last updated January 2009).
Bosselmann, K. (2017). *The principle of sustainability: Transforming law and governance* (2nd ed.). Routledge Taylor & Francis Group.
Bosselmann, K. (2020). Environmental trusteeship and state sovereignty: Can they be reconciled? *Transnational Legal Theory, 11*(1–2), 47–61. https://doi.org/10.1080/20414005.2020.1757862
Boyle, A. E., & Redgwell, C. (2021). *Birnie, Boyle, and Redgwell's international law and the environment* (4th ed.). Oxford University Press.
Bradshaw, K. (2020). *Wildlife as property owners: A new conception of animal rights*. University of Chicago Press. https://doi.org/10.7208/9780226571539.
Brown Weiss, E. (1984a). Conservation and equity between generations. In T. Buergenthal (Ed.), *Contemporary issues in international law: Essays in Honor of Louis B. Sohn* (pp. 245–289). Engel.
Brown Weiss, E. (1984b). The planetary trust: Conservation and intergenerational equity. *Ecology Law Quarterly, 11*, 495–582.
Brown Weiss, E. (1987). Intergenerational equity in international law. *American Society of International Law Proceedings, 81*, 126–132.
Brown Weiss, E. (1989). *In fairness to future generations: International law, common patrimony, and intergenerational equity*. Transnational Publishers, Inc.
Brown Weiss, E. (1990). Our rights and obligations to future generations for the environment. *American Journal of International Law, 84*(1), 198–207. https://doi.org/10.2307/2203020
Brown Weiss, E. (1992). Intergenerational equity and rights of future generations. In A. A. Cançado Trindade & E. Brown Weiss (Eds.), *Derechos Humanos, Desarrollo Sustentable y Medio Ambiente: Human rights, sustainable development and the environment* (pp. 71–81). Banco Interamericano de Desarrollo.
Brown Weiss, E. (1995). Environmental equity: The imperative for the twenty-first century. In W. Lang (Ed.), *Sustainable development and international law* (Vol. 2, pp. 17–28). Graham & Trotman.
Brown Weiss, E. (1997). A Reply to Barresi's "Beyond Fairness to Future Generations". *Tulane Environmental Law Journal, 11*(1), 89–97.
Brown Weiss, E. (1999). Opening the door to the environment and to future generations. In L. Boisson de Chazournes & P. Sands (Eds.), *International law, the international court of justice, and nuclear weapons* (Vol. No. 21, pp. 338–353). Cambridge University Press.
Brown Weiss, E. (2008). Climate change, intergenerational equity, and international law. *Vermont Journal of Environmental Law, 9*, 615–619.
Brown Weiss, E. (2010). Implementing intergenerational equity. In M. Fitzmaurice, D. Ong, & P. Merkouris (Eds.), *Research handbook on international environmental law* (Vol. 5, pp. 100–116). Edward Elgar Publishing.
Brown Weiss, E. (2019). Intergenerational equity. In Y. Aguila & J. E. Viñuales (Eds.). *A global pact for the environment: Legal foundations* (Vol. 5, pp. 51–58). Cambridge Centre for Environment, Energy and Natural Resource Governance (C-EENRG).
Brown Weiss, E. (2021a). Intergenerational equity. In A. Peters & R. Wolfrum (Eds.), *Max Planck Encyclopedia of public international law*. Oxford University Press. (Article last updated April 2021).
Brown Weiss, E. (2021b). The theoretical framework for international legal principles of intergenerational equity and implementation through national institutions. In M.-C. Cordonier Segger, M. Szabó, & A. R. Harrington (Eds.), *Intergenerational justice in sustainable development treaty implementation: Advancing future generations rights through national institutions* (Vol. 2, pp. 16–43). Cambridge University Press.

Brunnée, J. (2010). Common areas, common heritage, and common concern. In D. Bodansky, J. Brunnée, & E. Hey (Eds.), *The Oxford handbook of international environmental law* (Vol. 23, 1st ed., pp. 550–572). Oxford University Press.

Bureau of the Preparatory Process for the UNCSD. (2012). The Future We Want – Zero Draft of the Outcome Document. *UN Conference on Sustainable Development*. 10 January 2012. Retrieved 3 January 2025, from https://www.researchgate.net/publication/330443876_The_Future_We_Want_-_Zero_Draft_of_the_Outcome_Document

Bustami, A., & Hecken, M.-C. (2021). Perspectives for a new international crime against the environment: International criminal responsibility for environmental degradation under the Rome statute. *Goettingen Journal of International Law, 11*(1), 145–189.

Cameron, J., Wade-Gery, W., & Abouchar, J. (1998). Precautionary principle and future generations. In E. Agius & S. Busuttil (Eds.), *Future generations and international law: Proceedings of the international experts' meeting held by the future generations programme at the foundation for international studies, University of Malta* (Vol. 9, pp. 93–113). Earthscan Publications Ltd..

Cançado Trindade, A. A. (2020). *International law for humankind: Towards a New Jus Gentium* (3rd ed.). Brill Nijhoff.

Carazo Ortiz, M. P. (2017). Contextual provisions (preamble and Article 1). In D. R. Klein, M. P. Carazo Ortiz, M. Doelle, J. Bulmer, & A. Higham (Eds.), *The Paris Agreement on climate change: Analysis and commentary* (Vol. 6, pp. 107–122). Oxford University Press.

Central Intelligence Agency. (2022). *The World Factbook: Life Expectancy at Birth*. 2022. Retrieved 3 January 2025, from https://www.cia.gov/the-world-factbook/field/life-expectancy-at-birth

Centre International de Droit Comparé de l'Environnement. (2015). *Draft of the International Covenant on the Human Right to the Environment*. 2015. Retrieved 3 January 2025, from https://cidce.org/wp-content/uploads/2016/08/Draft-of-the-International-Covenant-on-the-Human-Right-to-the-Environment_15.II_.2017_EN.pdf

Climate Change Litigation Databases. (2015–2020). Urgenda Foundation v. State of the Netherlands. *Sabin Center for Climate Change Law at Columbia Law School*. 2015-2020. Retrieved 3 January 2025, from http://climatecasechart.com/non-us-case/urgenda-foundation-v-kingdom-of-the-netherlands/

Climate Change Litigation Databases. (2023-today). Request for an Advisory Opinion on the Obligations of States with Respect to Climate Change. *Sabin Center for Climate Change Law at Columbia Law School*. 2023-today. Retrieved 3 January 2025, from https://climatecasechart.com/non-us-case/request-for-an-advisory-opinion-on-the-obligations-of-states-with-respect-to-climate-change/

Collins, L. M. (2007a). Environmental rights for the future? Intergenerational equity in the EU. *Review of European, Comparative and International Environmental Law, 16*(3), 321–331. https://doi.org/10.1111/j.1467-9388.2007.00568.x

Collins, L. M. (2007b). Revisiting the doctrine of intergenerational equity in global environmental governance. *Dalhousie Law Journal, 30*(1), 73–134.

Cordonier Segger, M.-C. (2021). International treaty law and policy for future generations. In M.-C. Cordonier Segger, M. Szabó, & A. R. Harrington (Eds.), *Intergenerational justice in sustainable development treaty implementation: Advancing future generations rights through national institutions* (Vol. 3, pp. 47–67). Cambridge University Press.

Cordonier Segger, M.-C., & Weeramantry, C. G. (Eds.). (2017). *Sustainable development principles in the decisions of international courts and tribunals: 1992-2012*. Routledge Taylor & Francis Group.

Cullet, P. (2010). Common but differentiated responsibilities. In M. Fitzmaurice, D. Ong, & P. Merkouris (Eds.), *Research handbook on international environmental law* (Vol. 8, pp. 161–181). Edward Elgar Publishing.

D'Amato, A. (1990). Do we owe a duty to future generations to preserve the global environment? *American Journal of International Law, 84*, 190–198.

de Lassus St-Geniès, G. (2020). The outcome of the negotiations on the global pact for the environment: A commentary. *Sustainability, 12*(3), 877. https://doi.org/10.3390/su12030877

Dernbach, J. C., & Cheever, F. (2015). Sustainable development and its discontents. *Transnational Environmental Law, 4*(2), 247–287. https://doi.org/10.1017/S2047102515000163

De-Shalit, A. (1995). *Why posterity matters: Environmental policies and future generations*. Routledge Taylor & Francis Group.

Doelle, M. (2016). The Paris Agreement: Historic breakthrough or high stakes experiment? *Climate Law, 6*(1-2), 1–20. https://doi.org/10.1163/18786561-00601001

Donaldson, S., & Kymlicka, W. (2014). *Zoopolis: A political theory of animal rights*. (Reprinted). Oxford University Press.

Dupuy, P.-M. (1997). Où en est Le Droit International de L'Environnement à la Fin du Siècle? *Revue Générale De Droit International Public, 101*, 873.

Dupuy, P.-M., & Viñuales, J. E. (2015). *International environmental law*. Cambridge University Press.

Dupuy, P.-M., & Viñuales, J. E. (2018). *International environmental law* (2nd ed.). Cambridge University Press.

Dwivedi, Y. K., Hughes, L., Kar, A. K., Baabdullah, A. M., Grover, P., Abbas, R., Andreini, D., Abumoghli, I., Barlette, Y., Bunker, D., Chandra Kruse, L., Constantiou, I., Davison, R. M., De', R., Dubey, R., Fenby-Taylor, H., Gupta, B., He, W., Kodama, M., et al. (2022). Climate change and COP26: Are digital technologies and information management part of the problem or the solution? An editorial reflection and call to action. *International Journal of Information Management, 63*, 102456. https://doi.org/10.1016/j.ijinfomgt.2021.102456

Earth Charter Commission. (2000). Earth Charter. March 2000. Retrieved 3 January 2025, from https://earthcharter.org/read-the-earth-charter/download-the-charter/.

Epiney, A. (2022). Gegenstand, Entwicklung, Quellen und Akteure des Internationalen Umweltrechts. In A. Proelß (Ed.), *Internationales Umweltrecht* (Vol. 1, 2nd ed., pp. 1–51). De Gruyter.

Epiney, A., & Scheyli, M. (1998). *Strukturprinzipien des Umweltvölkerrechts* (1st ed.). Nomos.

Feichtner, I. (2007). Community interest. In A. Peters & R. Wolfrum (Eds.), *Max Planck Encyclopedia of public international law*. Oxford University Press. (Article last updated February 2007).

Feinberg, J. (1974). The rights of animals and unborn generations. In W. Blackstone (Ed.), *Philosophy and environmental crisis* (pp. 43–68). University of Georgia Press.

Fitzmaurice, M. (2008). Intergenerational equity revisited. In I. Buffard, J. Crawford, A. Pellet, & S. Wittich (Eds.), *International law between universalism and fragmentation: Festschrift in Honour of Gerhard Hafner* (Vol. 11, pp. 195–229). Martinus Nijhoff Publishers.

Fitzmaurice, M. (2010). International responsibility and liability. In D. Bodansky, J. Brunnée, & E. Hey (Eds.), *The Oxford handbook of international environmental law* (Vol. 44, 1st ed., pp. 1011–1034). Oxford University Press.

Fitzmaurice, M. (2012). Some reflections on legal and philosophical foundations of international environmental law. *Polish Yearbook of International Law, 32*, 89–110.

Founex Report on Development and Environment: Submitted by a Panel of Experts Convened by the Secretary-General of the United Nations Conference on the Human Environment 4-12 June 1971, Founex, Switzerland (1972). *International Conciliation, 39*, 7–36.

Francioni, F. (2020). Equity in international law. In A. Peters & R. Wolfrum (Eds.), *Max Planck Encyclopedia of public international law*. Oxford University Press. (Article last updated November 2020).

Franck, T. M. (1997). *Fairness in international law and institutions*. (First issued new as paperback). Clarendon Press.

Freestone, D. A. C. (1994). The Road from Rio: International environmental law after the earth summit. *Journal of Environmental Law, 6*, 193–218.

French, D. (2000). Developing states and international environmental law: The importance of differentiated responsibilities. *International and Comparative Law Quarterly, 49*(1), 35–60.

French, D. (2010). Sustainable development. In M. Fitzmaurice, D. Ong, & P. Merkouris (Eds.), *Research handbook on international environmental law* (Vol. 3, pp. 51–68). Edward Elgar Publishing.
French, D. (2017). The Sofia guiding statements on sustainable development principles in the decisions of international tribunals. In M.-C. Cordonier Segger & C. G. Weeramantry (Eds.), *Sustainable development principles in the decisions of international courts and tribunals: 1992-2012* (Vol. 7, pp. 177–241). Routledge Taylor & Francis Group.
Future Timeline Community. (2024). *The future timeline*. 2024. Retrieved 3 January 2025, from https://www.futuretimeline.net/
Gaillard, É. (2011). *Générations Futures et Droit Privé: Vers un Droit des Générations Futures*. LGDJ Lextenso Éditions.
Gatmaytan, D. B. (2003). The illusion of intergenerational equity: Oposa v. Factoran as Pyrrhic Victory. *Georgetown International Environmental Law Review, 15*(3), 457–485.
Gewirth, A. (2014). Human rights and future generations: (2001). In M. Boylan (Ed.), *Environmental ethics* (2nd ed., pp. 118–121). Wiley Blackwell.
Gonzales, C. G. (2013). Environmental justice and international environmental law. In S. Alam (Ed.), *Routledge handbook of international environmental law* (Vol. 5, pp. 77–98). Routledge Taylor & Francis Group.
Gosseries, A. (2001). What do we owe the next generation(s). *Loyola of Los Angeles Law Review, 35*, 293–354.
Gündling, L. (1990). Our responsibility to future generations. *American Journal of International Law, 84*(1), 207–212.
Hadjiargyrou, Z. (2016). A conceptual and practical evaluation of intergenerational equity in international environmental law. *International Community Law Review, 18*, 248–277.
Handl, G. (2011). Environmental security and global change: The challenge to international law. In J. H. H. Weiler & A. T. Nissel (Eds.), *International law: Critical concepts in law* (Vol. 48, pp. 143–175). Routledge Taylor & Francis Group.
Hey, E., & Paulini, S. (2021). Common but differentiated responsibilities. In A. Peters & R. Wolfrum (Eds.), *Max Planck Encyclopedia of public international law*. Oxford University Press. (Article last updated October 2021).
Howarth, R. B., & Norgaard, R. B. (1992). Environmental valuation under sustainable development. *The American Economic Review, 82*(2), 473–477.
Human Rights Council. (2019). *Climate Change and Poverty – Report of the Special Rapporteur on Extreme Poverty and Human Rights*, by P. Alston (17 July 2019). UN Doc. A/HRC/41/39.
Hunter, D. B., Salzman, J., & Zaelke, D. (2011). *international environmental law and policy* (4th ed.). Foundation Press.
ILA Committee on International Law on Sustainable Development. (2012a). Sofia Conference (2012) – International Law on Sustainable Development: Final Report. *International Law Association*. 2012a. Retrieved 3 January 2025, from https://www.ila-hq.org/en/committees/international-law-on-sustainable-development
ILA Committee on International Law on Sustainable Development. (2012b). *2012 Sofia Guiding Statements on the Judicial Elaboration of the 2002 New Delhi Declaration of Principles of International Law Relating to Sustainable Development: Resolution 7/2012*. International Law Association. 30 August 2012b. Retrieved 3 January 2025, from https://www.ila-hq.org/en/committees/international-law-on-sustainable-development
ILA Committee on Legal Aspects of Sustainable Development. (2002). *New Delhi Declaration of Principles of International Law Relating to Sustainable Development: Resolution 3/2002*. International Law Association. 6 April 2002. Retrieved 3 January 2025, from https://www.ila-hq.org/en_GB/documents/conference-resolution-english-new-delhi-2002-3
International Group of Experts for the Pact. (2017). Draft Global Pact for the Environment. *Global Pact for the Environment*. June 2017. Retrieved 3 January 2025, from https://globalpactenvironment.org/en/documents-en/the-pact-text/

International Law Commission (2021). *Draft Guidelines on the Protection of the Atmosphere, with Commentaries thereto* (2021). UN Doc. A/76/10.
International Union for Conservation of Nature and Natural Resources, & International Council of Environmental Law. (2015). *Draft International Covenant on Environment and Development: Implementing Sustainability*. (5th ed.). International Union for Conservation of Nature. https://doi.org/10.2305/IUCN.CH.2015.EPLP.31/rev4.en. (Original work published 13 March 1995).
International Union for Conservation of Nature and Natural Resources, United Nations Environment Programme, & World Wildlife Fund. (1980). *World Conservation Strategy: Living Resources Conservation for Sustainable Development*. International Union for Conservation of Nature.
Ivanova, M. (2020). Fighting fire with a thermometer? Environmental efforts of the United Nations. *Ethics and International Affairs, 34*(3), 339–349. https://doi.org/10.1017/S0892679420000404
Johannesburg Principles on the Role of Law and Sustainable Development: Adopted at the Global Judges Symposium, 18-20 August 2002 (2003). *Journal of Environmental Law, 15*(1), 107–110.
Juste Ruiz, J. (2020). The process towards a global pact for the environment at the United Nations: From legal ambition to political dilution. *Review of European, Comparative and International Environmental Law, 29*(3), 479–490. https://doi.org/10.1111/reel.12331
Kahl, V. (2019). Ökologische Revolution am Interamerikanischen Gerichtshof für Menschenrechte: Besprechung des Rechtsgutachtens Nr. 23 "Umwelt und Menschenrechte" (OC-23/17). *Zeitschrift Für Europäisches Umwelt- Und Planungsrecht, 17*(2), 110–131.
Kaku, M. (2011). *Physics of the future: How science will shape human destiny and our daily lives by the year 2100* (1st ed.). Doubleday.
Kammerhofer, J. (2024). Obligations erga omnes. In A. Peters & R. Wolfrum (Eds.), *Max Planck Encyclopedia of public international law*. Oxford University Press. (Article last updated February 2024).
Khadduri, M. (1984). *The Islamic conception of justice*. Johns Hopkins University Press.
Kiss, A. (1982). La Notion de Patrimoine Commun de L'Humanité. *Recueil Des Cours, 175*(II), 99–256.
Kiss, A. (1993). Le Droit International à Rio de Janeiro et à Côté de Rio de Janeiro. *Revue Juridique De L'environnement, 18*(1), 45–74. https://doi.org/10.3406/rjenv.1993.2925
Kiss, A. (1996). The rights and interests of future generations and the precautionary principle. In D. A. C. Freestone (Ed.), *The precautionary principle and international law: The challenge of implementation* (Vol. 2, pp. 19–28). Kluwer Law International.
Kotzé, L. J. (2019a). A global environmental constitution for the anthropocene? *Transnational Environmental Law, 8*(1), 11–33. https://doi.org/10.1017/S2047102518000274
Kotzé, L. J. (2019b). International environmental law's lack of normative ambition: An opportunity for the global pact for the environment? *Journal for European Environmental and Planning Law, 16*(3), 213–236. https://doi.org/10.1163/18760104-01603002
Kotzé, L. J. (2020). Earth system law for the anthropocene: Rethinking environmental law alongside the earth system metaphor. *Transnational Legal Theory, 11*(1–2), 75–104. https://doi.org/10.1080/20414005.2020.1776556
Kotzé, L. J., & French, D. (2018). A critique of the global pact for the environment: A stillborn initiative or the foundation for lex anthropocenae? *International Environmental Agreements, 18*, 811–838. https://doi.org/10.1007/s10784-018-9417-x
Lammers, J. G. (2008). Equity in international environmental law and the special position of developing countries. *Hague Yearbook of International Law, 21*, 9–40.
Lee, J.-Y., Marotzke, J., Bala, G., Cao, L., Corti, S., Dunne, J. P., Engelbrecht, F., Fischer, E., Fyfe, J. C., Jones, C., Maycock, A., Mutemi, J., Ndiaye, O., Panickal, S., & Zhou, T. (2021). Future Global Climate: Scenario-Based Projections and Near-Term Information. In V. Masson-Delmotte et al. (Eds.). IPCC, *Climate Change 2021 – The Physical Science Basis: Working Group I Contribution to the IPCC Sixth Assessment Report* (pp. 553–672). Retrieved 3 January 2025, from https://www.ipcc.ch/report/sixth-assessment-report-working-group-i/

Lepage, C., & Drafting Committee. (2015). Universal Declaration of Humankind Rights: Draft Presented Under the Aegis of Corinne Lepage, Commissioned by the President of the French Republic. *Alliance DDHU 2022*. 25 September 2015. Retrieved 3 January 2025, from https://ddhu.org/la-declaration/

Liebenberg, S., Khalfan, A., Kothari, M., Muffett, C., Sepúlveda Carmona, M., Venne-Manyfingers, S., & Wewerinke-Singh, M. (2023). *Maastricht principles on the human rights of future generations*. Maastricht University. 3 February 2023. Retrieved 3 January 2025, from https://www.rightsoffuturegenerations.org/the-principles

Locke, J. (1690). *Two treatises of government: An essay concerning the true original, extent and end of civil government (second treatise)*. Awnsham Churchill.

Lowe, V. (1999). Sustainable development and unsustainable arguments. In A. E. Boyle & D. A. C. Freestone (Eds.), *International law and sustainable development: Past achievements and future challenges* (pp. 19–37). Oxford University Press.

Maas, M. (2022). Paths Untaken: The History, Epistemology and Strategy of Technological Restraint, and Lessons for AI. *Verfassungsblog*. 9 August 2022. Retrieved 3 January 2025, from https://verfassungsblog.de/paths-untaken/

Maggio, G. F. (1997). Inter/intra-generational equity: Current applications under international law for promoting the sustainable development of natural resources. *Buffalo Environmental Law Journal, 4*, 161–223. https://doi.org/10.1515/9783110571028-toc

Magraw, D. B., & Hawke, L. D. (2010). Sustainable development. In D. Bodansky, J. Brunnée, & E. Hey (Eds.), *The Oxford handbook of international environmental law* (Vol. 26, 1st ed., pp. 613–638). Oxford University Press.

Maier, J. (2012). UN-Konferenz über Nachhaltige Entwicklung (Rio+20): 20–22. Juni 2012. *Vereinte Nationen, 4*, 171–173.

Malhotra, A. (1998). A commentary on the status of future generations as a subject of international law. In E. Agius & S. Busuttil (Eds.), *Future generations and international law: Proceedings of the international experts' meeting held by the future generations programme at the foundation for international studies, University of Malta* (Vol. 5, pp. 39–50). Earthscan Publications Ltd..

Manguiat, M. S. Z., & Yu, V. P. B. (2003). Maximizing the value of Oposa v. Factoran. *Georgetown International Environmental Law Review, 15*(3), 487–496.

Matte, N. M. (1987). *The common heritage of mankind and outer space: Toward a new international order for survival* (pp. 313–337). *Annals of Air and Space Law*.

Matz-Lück, N. (2008). Biological diversity, international protection. In A. Peters & R. Wolfrum (Eds.), *Max Planck Encyclopedia of public international law*. Oxford University Press. (Article last updated December 2008).

Mayeda, G. (2004). Where should johannesburg take us? Ethical and legal approaches to sustainable development in the context of international environmental law. *Colorado Journal of International Environmental Law and Policy, 15*(1), 29–70.

Mbengue, M. M. (2019). Precaution. In Y. Aguila, & J. E. Viñuales (Eds.). *A global pact for the environment: Legal foundations* (Vol. 8, pp. 73–78). Cambridge Centre for Environment, Energy and Natural Resource Governance (C-EENRG).

Mbengue, M. M. (2020). On sustainable development: A conversation with Judge Weeramantry. In S. Forlati, M. M. Mbengue, & B. K. McGarry (Eds.), *The Gabčíkovo-Nagymaros judgment and its contribution to the development of international law* (Vol. 12, pp. 166–192). Brill Nijhoff.

Mensah, T. A. (2008). Using judicial bodies for the implementation and enforcement of international environmental law. In I. Buffard, J. Crawford, A. Pellet, & S. Wittich (Eds.), *International law between universalism and fragmentation: Festschrift in Honour of Gerhard Hafner* (Vol. 40, pp. 797–815). Martinus Nijhoff Publishers.

Merrills, J. G. (2010). Environmental rights. In D. Bodansky, J. Brunnée, & E. Hey (Eds.), *The Oxford handbook of international environmental law* (Vol. 28, 1st ed., pp. 663–680). Oxford University Press. https://doi.org/10.1093/oxfordhb/9780199552153.013.0028

Meyer, L. H. (2009). Intergenerationelle Suffizienzgerechtigkeit. In N. Goldschmidt (Ed.), *Generationengerechtigkeit: Ordnungsökonomische Konzepte* (pp. 281–322). Mohr Siebeck.

Michallet, I. (2018). Equity and the interests of future generations. In L. Krämer & E. Orlando (Eds.), *Principles of environmental law* (pp. 150–160). Edward Elgar Publishing.

Ministry of the Environment of Sweden, & Ministry of the Environment and Forestry of Kenya. (2022). Stockholm Agenda: Key Recommendations for Accelerating Action Towards a Healthy Planet for the Prosperity of All. *Stockholm+50*. 8 June 2022. Retrieved 3 January 2025, from https://www.stockholm50.global/presidents-final-remarks-plenary-key-recommendations-accelerating-action-towards-healthy-planet

Molinari, C. (2015). Principle 3. In J. E. Viñuales (Ed.), *The Rio Declaration on environment and development: A commentary* (1st ed., pp. 139–156). Oxford University Press.

Morgenstern, L., & Dehnen, M. (2016). Eine Neue Ära für den internationalen Klimaschutz: Das Übereinkommen von Paris. *Zeitschrift Für Umweltrecht*, 131–138.

Munro, R. D., & Lammers, J. G. (1987). *Environmental protection and sustainable development: Legal principles and recommendations*. Graham & Trotman.

Nagy, B. (1988). Common heritage of mankind: The status of future generations. *Proceedings on the Law of Outer Space, 31*, 319–325.

Nagy, B. (1998). Speaking without a voice. In E. Agius & S. Busuttil (Eds.), *Future generations and international law: Proceedings of the international experts' meeting held by the future generations programme at the foundation for international studies, University of Malta* (Vol. 6, pp. 51–64). Earthscan Publications Ltd..

Najam, A. (1994). *International environmental negotiation: The case for a South Secretariat: Research Report*. Sustainable Development Policy Institute.

Nanda, V. P., & Pring, G. (Eds.). (2013). *International environmental law for the 21st century* (2nd ed.). Martinus Nijhoff Publishers.

Negri, S., & Maljean-Dubois, S. (2014). Introduction. In M. Fitzmaurice, S. Maljean-Dubois, & S. Negri (Eds.), *Environmental protection and sustainable development from Rio to Rio+20: Protection de l'Environnement et Développement Durable de Rio à Rio+20* (pp. 1–5). Brill Nijhoff.

Nolan, A. (2022). The children are the future – Or not? Exploring the complexities of the relationship between the rights of children and future generations. *EJIL: Talk!* 26 May 2022. Retrieved 3 January 2025, from https://www.ejiltalk.org/the-children-are-the-future-or-not-exploring-the-complexities-of-the-relationship-between-the-rights-of-children-and-future-generations/

Oberthür, S., & Bodle, R. (2016). Legal form and nature of the paris outcome. *Climate Law, 6*(1–2), 40–57. https://doi.org/10.1163/18786561-00601003

Organization of American States. (2007). *Inter-American Program for Sustainable Development (2006-2009)* (11 May 2007). OEA/XLIII.1.

Page, T. (1983). Intergenerational justice as opportunity. In D. MacLean & P. G. Brown (Eds.), *Energy and the future* (pp. 38–58). Rowman & Littlefield.

Parejo Navajas, T., & Lobel, N. (2018). Framing the global pact for the environment: Why it's needed, what it does, and how it does it. *Fordham Environmental Law Review, 30*(1), 32–62.

Peek, J. M. (1995). Buddhism, human rights and the Japanese State. *Human Rights Quarterly, 17*(3), 527–540.

Pettit, P. H. (2005). *Equity and the law of trusts* (10th ed.). Oxford University Press.

Pietrzykowski, T. (2020). Animal rights. In A. von Arnauld, K. von der Decken, & M. Susi (Eds.), *The Cambridge handbook of new human rights: Recognition, novelty, rhetoric* (Vol. 18, pp. 243–252). Cambridge University Press. https://doi.org/10.1017/9781108676106.019

Pogge, T. W., & Sengupta, M. (2015). The sustainable development goals (SDGS) As drafted: Nice idea, poor execution. *Washington International Law Journal, 24*, 571–589.

Prakash, S. (1995). The right to the environment. Emerging implications in theory and Praxis. *Netherlands Quarterly of Human Rights, 13*(4), 403–433. https://doi.org/10.1177/016934419501300403

Proelß, A. (2016). Klimaschutz im Völkerrecht nach dem Paris Agreement: Durchbruch oder Stillstand? *Zeitschrift Für Umweltpolitik & Umweltrecht, Sonderheft*, 58–71.

Proelß, A. (2022). Prinzipien des Internationalen Umweltrechts. In A. Proelß (Ed.), *Internationales Umweltrecht* (Vol. 3, 2nd ed., pp. 95–150). De Gruyter.

Proelß, A., & Haake, C. (2017). Gemeinschaftsräume in der Entwicklung: Von der Res Communis Omnium zum Common Heritage of Mankind. In A. von Arnauld (Ed.), *Völkerrechtsgeschichte (n): Historische Narrative und Konzepte im Wandel* (pp. 171–192). Duncker & Humblot.

Qerimi, Q. (2014). Sustainable development in international law: From origin to operation. *City University of Hong Kong Law Review, 5*(1), 1–29.

Raith, J. (2018). The "Global Pact for the Environment": A new instrument to protect the planet? *Journal for European Environmental and Planning Law, 15*(1), 3–23. https://doi.org/10.1163/18760104-01501002.

Ramlogan, R. (2011). *Sustainable development: Towards a judicial interpretation.* Martinus Nijhoff Publishers.

Redgwell, C. (1991). Intergenerational equity and global warming. In R. R. Churchill & D. A. C. Freestone (Eds.), *International law and global climate change* (p. 42). Graham & Trotman.

Redgwell, C. (1999). *Intergenerational trusts and environmental protection.* Juris.

Redgwell, C. (2016). Principles and emerging norms in international law: Intra- and inter-generational equity. In C. P. Carlarne, K. R. Gray, & R. Tarasofsky (Eds.), *The Oxford handbook of international climate change law* (Vol. 9, 1st ed., pp. 185–201). Oxford University Press.

Rehbinder, E. (2012). The Outcome of the UN Conference on sustainable development "Rio+20": Some critical comments. *Environmental Law Network International Review,* 2, 68–73.

Restatement (Second) of Trusts (1959).

Restatement (Third) of Trusts (2003).

Restatement (Third) of Trusts § 2 (2003).

Restatement (Third) of Trusts § 28 (2003).

Restatement (Third) of Trusts § 44 (2003).

Restatement (Third) of Trusts § 90 (2003).

Sand, P. H. (1993). International environmental law after Rio. *European Journal of International Law, 4*(3), 377–389. https://doi.org/10.1093/oxfordjournals.ejil.a035836

Sand, P. H. (2004). Sovereignty bounded: Public trusteeship for common pool resources? *Global Environmental Politics, 4*(1), 47–71. https://doi.org/10.1162/152638004773730211

Sands, P. (1995). International law in the field of sustainable development: Emerging legal principles. In W. Lang (Ed.), *Sustainable development and international law* (Vol. 5, pp. 53–66). Graham & Trotman.

Sands, P., Peel, J., & Fabra, A. (2018). *Principles of international environmental law* (4th ed.). Cambridge University Press.

Satterthwaite, D. (2002). The Ten and a Half Myths That May Distort the Urban Policies of Governments and International Agencies. *International Institute for Environment and Development.* January 2002. Retrieved 3 January 2025, from https://pubs.iied.org/g03188.

Scheyli, M. (2008). *Konstitutionelle Gemeinwohlorientierung im Völkerrecht: Grundlagen Völkerrechtlicher Konstitutionalisierung am Beispiel des Schutzes der Globalen Umwelt* (1st ed.). Duncker & Humblot. https://doi.org/10.3790/978-3-428-52826-4

Schrijver, N. J. (2008). Permanent sovereignty over natural resources. In A. Peters & R. Wolfrum (Eds.), *Max Planck Encyclopedia of public international law.* Oxford University Press. (Article last updated June 2008).

Sebo, J. (2022). *Saving animals, saving ourselves: Why animals matter for pandemics, climate change, and other catastrophes.* Oxford University Press. https://doi.org/10.1093/oso/9780190861018.001.0001

Shelton, D. (2008). Stockholm Declaration (1972) and Rio Declaration (1992). In A. Peters & R. Wolfrum (Eds.). *Max Planck Encyclopedia of public international law.* Oxford University Press. (Article last updated July 2008).

Shelton, D. (2010a). Equity. In D. Bodansky, J. Brunnée, & E. Hey (Eds.), *The Oxford handbook of international environmental law* (Vol. 27, 1st ed., pp. 639–662). Oxford University Press. https://doi.org/10.1093/oxfordhb/9780199552153.013.0027

Shelton, D. (2010b). Intergenerational equity. In R. Wolfrum & C. Kojima (Eds.), *Solidarity: A structural principle of international law* (pp. 123–168). Springer.

Sindico, F. (2016). Paris, climate change, and sustainable development. *Climate Law, 6*(1–2), 130–141. https://doi.org/10.1163/18786561-00601009

Smits, J. M. (2017). What is legal doctrine? On the aims and methods of legal-dogmatic research. In R. van Gestel, H.-W. Micklitz, & E. L. Rubin (Eds.), *Rethinking scholarship: A transatlantic dialogue* (Vol. 5, pp. 207–228). Cambridge University Press.

Sobrino Heredia, J. M. (2014). The heritage dimension of the climate system and its protection for the benefit of Mankind. In M. Fitzmaurice, S. Maljean-Dubois, & S. Negri (Eds.), *Environmental protection and sustainable development from Rio to Rio+20: Protection de l'Environnement et Développement Durable de Rio à Rio+20* (pp. 65–79). Brill Nijhoff.

Soltau, F. (2016). Common concern of humankind. In C. P. Carlarne, K. R. Gray, & R. Tarasofsky (Eds.), *The Oxford handbook of international climate change law* (Vol. 10, 1st ed., pp. 202–212). Oxford University Press.

Solum, L. B. (2001). To our children's children's children: The problems of intergenerational ethics. *Loyola of Los Angeles Law Review, 35*, 163–233.

Stawasz, A., & Sebo, J. (2022). Bridging legal longtermism and animal law. *Verfassungsblog*. 19 August 2022. Retrieved 3 January 2025, from https://verfassungsblog.de/bridging-legal-longtermism-and-animal-law/

Stein, T. (2019). International law association (ILA). In A. Peters & R. Wolfrum (Eds.), *Max Planck Encyclopedia of public international law*. Oxford University Press. (Article last updated May 2019).

Stephens, T. (2009). *International courts and environmental protection*. Cambridge University Press. https://doi.org/10.1017/CBO9780511576034.

Stone, C. D. (1972). Should trees have standing? Toward legal rights for natural objects. *Southern California Law Review, 45*, 450–501.

Stone, C. D. (1998). Safeguarding future generations. In E. Agius & S. Busuttil (Eds.), *Future generations and international law: Proceedings of the international experts' meeting held by the future generations programme at the foundation for international studies, University of Malta* (Vol. 7, pp. 65–79). Earthscan Publications Ltd..

Stucki, S. (2020). Towards a theory of legal animal rights: Simple and fundamental rights. *Oxford Journal of Legal Studies, 40*(3), 533–560.

Supanich, G. P. (1992). The legal basis of intergenerational responsibility: An alternative view – the sense of intergenerational identity. *Yearbook of International Environmental Law, 3*(1), 94–107. https://doi.org/10.1093/yiel/3.1.94

Szekely, A. (2008). The promise of the brundtland report: Honored or betrayed. *Pacific McGeorge Global Business and Development Law Journal, 21*, 159.

Tanaka, Y. (2013). Reflections on time elements in the international law of the environment. *Zeitschrift Für Ausländisches Öffentliches Recht Und Völkerrecht, 73*, 139–175.

Taylor, J. (2013). Intergenerational justice: A useful perspective for heritage conservation. *Conservation, Exposition, Restauration d'Objets d'Art* (CeROArt). 30 October 2013. Retrieved 3 January 2025, from http://journals.openedition.org/ceroart/3510.

Tigre, M. A. (2019). *Gaps in international environmental law: Toward a global pact for the environment*. Environmental Law Institute.

Tladi, D. (2007). *Sustainable development in international law: An analysis of key enviro-economic instruments*. Pretoria University Law Press.

Tladi, D. (2017). The principles of sustainable development in the case concerning Pulp Mills on the River Uruguay. In M.-C. Cordonier Segger & C. G. Weeramantry (Eds.), *Sustainable development principles in the decisions of international courts and tribunals: 1992-2012* (Vol. 8, pp. 242–254). Routledge, Taylor & Francis Group.

Tremmel, J. C. (2003). Generationengerechtigkeit: Versuch einer Definition. In J. C. Tremmel (Ed.), *Handbuch Generationengerechtigkeit* (2nd ed., pp. 27–79). ökom Verlag.

Tremmel, J. C. (2006). Establishing intergenerational justice in national constitutions. In J. C. Tremmel (Ed.), *Handbook of intergenerational justice*. Edward Elgar Publishing.

Tremmel, J. C. (2009). *A theory of intergenerational justice*. Earthscan Publications Ltd. https://doi.org/10.4324/9781849774369.

UN Commission on Sustainable Development (CSD). (1996). Report of the Expert Group Meeting on Identification of Principles of International Law for Sustainable Development, Geneva, Switzerland, 26-28 September 1995: Background Paper, Prepared by the Division for Sustainable Development for the Commission on Sustainable Development, Fourth Session. 3 May 1996. Retrieved 3 January 2025, from https://digitallibrary.un.org/record/212979/

UN Conference on Environment and Development (UNCED). (1992a). *Rio Declaration on Environment and Development* (1992). UN Doc. A/CONF.151/26 (Vol. I).

UN Conference on Environment and Development (UNCED). (1992b). *Agenda 21* (June 1992). UN Doc. A/CONF.151/26 (Vol. II).

UN Conference on Environment and Development (UNCED). (1992c). *Report of the UN Conference on Environment and Development* (3 June 1992). A/CONF.151/26 (Vol. II).

UN Conference on Environment and Development (UNCED). (1992d). *Non-Legally Binding Authoritative Statement of Principles for a Global Consensus on the Management, Conservation and Sustainable Development of All Types of Forests* (14 August 1992). UN Doc. A/CONF.151/26 (Vol. III).

UN Conference on Human Settlements. (1996). *Istanbul Declaration on Human Settlements and the Habitat Agenda* (3 June 1996). A/CONF.165/14 (1996).

UN Department of Economic and Social Affairs. (2016). *World Economic and Social Survey 2016: Climate Change Resilience – An Opportunity for Reducing Inequalities*. United Nations Publication.

UNFCCC Ad Hoc Working Group on the Durban Platform for Enhanced Action. (2015). *Scenario Note on the Tenth Part of the Second Session of the Ad Hoc Working Group on the Durban Platform for Enhanced Action: Note by the Co-Chairs* (24 July 2015). ADP.2015.4.InformalNote.

UNFCCC Conference of the Parties 26. (2021a). *Glasgow Climate Pact* (13 November 2021). UN Doc. FCCC/PA/CMA/2021/10/Add.1.

UNFCCC Conference of the Parties 26. (2021b). *Glasgow Work Programme on Action for Climate Empowerment*. 13 November 2021. Retrieved 3 January 2025, from https://unfccc.int/documents/310896.

United Nations. (1972). *Declaration of the United Nations Conference on the Human Environment* (16 June 1972). UN Doc. A/Conf.48/14/Rev. 1 (1973).

United Nations. (n.d.). *High-Level Political Forum on Sustainable Development: Official Website*. n. d. Retrieved 3 January 2025, from https://hlpf.un.org/

United Nations Economic and Social Council (ECOSOC). (1993). *Establishment of the Commission on Sustainable Development* (12 February 1993). UN Doc. E/1993/207.

United Nations Economic and Social Council (ECOSOC). (2016). *Ministerial Declaration of the High-Level Segment of the 2016 Session of the Economic and Social Council on the Annual Theme "Implementing the Post-2015 Development Agenda: Moving from Commitments to Results"* (29 July 2016). UN Doc. E/HLS/2016/1.

United Nations Educational, Scientific and Cultural Organization. (1997). *Declaration on the Responsibilities of the Present Generations Towards Future Generations* (12 November 1997). UNESCO Doc. 29/C Resolution 44.

United Nations Environment Assembly. (2022). *Political Declaration of the Special Session of the United Nations Environment Assembly to Commemorate the Fiftieth Anniversary of the Establishment of the United Nations Environment Programme* (3 March 2022). UN Doc. UNEP/EA.SS.1/4.

United Nations Environment Programme. (1993a). Note of the Executive Director of UNEP on the Implications of the "Common Concern of Mankind" Concept on Global Environmental Issues: (To the UNEP Group of Legal Experts Meeting of Malta, of 13–15 December 1990). In A. A. Cançado Trindade (Ed.). *Direitos Humanos e Meio Ambiente: Paralelo dos Sistemas de Proteção Internacional* (Anexo V, pp. 273–275). S.A. Fabris Editor.

United Nations Environment Programme. (1993b). Report of the I Meeting of the UNEP Group of Legal Experts to Examine the Implications of the "Common Concern of Mankind" Concept on Global Environmental Issues: (Malta, 13-15 December 1990). In A. A. Cançado Trindade (Ed.). *Direitos Humanos e Meio Ambiente: Paralelo dos Sistemas de Proteção Internacional* (Anexo VI, 276–281). S.A. Fabris Editor.

United Nations Environment Programme. (1993c). Report of the II Meeting of the UNEP Group of Legal Experts to Examine the Implications of the "Common Concern of Mankind" Concept on Global Environmental Issues: (Geneva, 20-22 March 1991). In A. A. Cançado Trindade (Ed.). *Direitos Humanos e Meio Ambiente: Paralelo dos Sistemas de Proteção Internacional* (Anexo VII, pp. 282–287). S.A. Fabris Editor.

United Nations Environment Programme. (1996). *Final Report of the Expert Group Workshop on International Environmental Law Aiming at Sustainable Development* (4 October 1996). UN Doc. UNEP/IEL/WS/3/2.

United Nations Environment Programme. (2006). Training Manual on International Environmental Law. 2006. Retrieved 3 January 2025, from https://wedocs.unep.org/20.500.11822/20599

United Nations General Assembly. (1972). *Institutional and Financial Arrangements for International Environmental Cooperation* (15 December 1972). UN Doc. A/RES/2997(XXVII).

United Nations General Assembly. (1974). *Charter of Economic Rights and Duties of States* (12 December 1974). UN Doc. A/RES/3281 (XXIX).

United Nations General Assembly. (1982). *World Charter for Nature* (28 October 1982). UN Doc. A/RES/37/7.

United Nations General Assembly. (1983). *Process of Preparation of the Environmental Perspective to the Year 2000 and Beyond* (19 December 1983). UN Doc. A/RES/38/161.

United Nations General Assembly. (1987). *Report of the World Commission on Environment and Development* (11 December 1987). UN Doc A/RES/42/187.

United Nations General Assembly (1988a). *Declaration Proclaiming Climate as Part of the Common Heritage of Mankind (Letter dated 9 September 1988 from the Permanent Representative of Malta to the UN addressed to the Secretary-General)* (12 September 1988). UN Doc. A/43/241.

United Nations General Assembly. (1988b). *Protection of Global Climate for Present and Future Generations of Mankind* (6 December 1988). UN Doc. A/RES/43/53.

United Nations General Assembly. (2000). *United Nations Millennium Declaration* (18 September 2000). UN Doc. A/RES/55/2.

United Nations General Assembly. (2001). *Ten-Year Review of Progress Achieved in the Implementation of the Outcome of the United Nations Conference on Environment and Development* (5 February 2001). UN Doc. A/RES/55/199.

United Nations General Assembly. (2012). *The Future We Want* (27 July 2012). UN Doc. A/RES/66/288.

United Nations General Assembly. (2013a). *Format and Organizational Aspects of the High-Level Political Forum on Sustainable Development. Resolution Adopted by the General Assembly on 9 July 2013* (23 August 2013). UN Doc. A/RES/67/290.

United Nations General Assembly. (2013b). *Summary of the First Meeting of the High-Level Political Forum on Sustainable Development* (13 November 2013). UN Doc. A/68/588.

United Nations General Assembly. (2013c). *Implementation of Agenda 21, the Programme for the Further Implementation of Agenda 21 and the outcomes of the World Summit on Sustainable Development and of the United Nations Conference on Sustainable Development* (20 December 2013). UN Doc. A/RES/68/210.

United Nations General Assembly. (2013d). *Protection of Global Climate for Present and Future Generations of Humankind* (20 December 2013). UN Doc. A/RES/68/212.

United Nations General Assembly. (2014). *Report of the Open Working Group of the General Assembly on Sustainable Development Goals* (12 August 2014). UN Doc. A/68/970.

United Nations General Assembly. (2015). *Transforming Our World: The 2030 Agenda for Sustainable Development* (21 October 2015). UN Doc. A/RES/70/1.

United Nations General Assembly. (2018). *Towards a Global Pact for the Environment* (14 May 2018). UN Doc. A/RES/72/277.

United Nations General Assembly. (2019a). *Follow-up to the Report of the Ad hoc Open-Ended Working Group Established Pursuant to General Assembly Resolution 72/277* (5 September 2019). UN Doc. A/RES/73/333.

United Nations General Assembly. (2019b). *Political Declaration of the High-Level Political Forum on Sustainable Development Convened under the Auspices of the General Assembly* (21 October 2019). UN Doc. A/RES/74/4.

United Nations General Assembly. (2021). *Protection of the Atmosphere* (9 December 2021). UN Doc. A/RES/76/112.

United Nations Secretary-General. (2001). Millennium Development Goals. 2001. Retrieved 3 January 2025, from http://www.un.org/millenniumgoals/

United Nations Secretary-General. (2013). *Intergenerational Solidarity and the Needs of Future Generations, Report of the Secretary-General* (15 August 2013). UN Doc. A/68/322.

United Nations Secretary-General. (2014). *The Road to Dignity by 2030: Ending Poverty, Transforming All Lives and Protecting the Planet. Synthesis Report of the Secretary-General on the Post-2015 Sustainable Development Agenda* (4 December 2014). UN Doc. A/69/700.

United Nations Secretary-General. (2018). *Gaps in International Environmental Law and Environment-related Instruments: Towards a Global Pact for the Environment* (30 November 2018). UN Doc. A/73/419.

Vasconcellos Oliveira, R. (2018). Back to the future: The potential of intergenerational justice for the achievement of the sustainable development goals. *Sustainability, 10*(2), 427–442. https://doi.org/10.3390/su10020427

Verheyen, R., & Zengerling, C. (2016). International dispute settlement. In C. P. Carlarne, K. R. Gray, & R. Tarasofsky (Eds.), *The Oxford handbook of international climate change law* (Vol. 19, 1st ed., pp. 417–440). Oxford University Press.

Verniers, E. (2021). Bringing animal welfare under the Umbrella of sustainable development: A legal analysis. *Review of European, Comparative and International Environmental Law, 30*(3), 349–362. https://doi.org/10.1111/reel.12414

Verschuuren, J. (2016). The growing significance of sustainable development as a legal norm. In D. E. Fisher (Ed.), *Research handbook on fundamental concepts of environmental law* (pp. 276–305). Edward Elgar Publishing.

Viñuales, J. E. (Ed.). (2015). *The Rio Declaration on environment and development: A commentary. Oxford commentaries on international law*. Oxford University Press.

Voigt, C. (2009). *Sustainable development as a principle of international law: Resolving conflicts between climate measures and WTO law*. Martinus Nijhoff Publishers. https://doi.org/10.1163/ej.9789004166974.i-428

Wegener, B. W. (2019). Urgenda – world rescue by court order? The "Climate Justice"-movement tests the limits of legal protection. *Journal for European Environmental and Planning Law, 16*(2), 125–147.

Winter, C., Schuett, J., Martínez, E., van Arsdale, S., Araújo, R., Hollman, N., Sebo, J., Stawasz, A., O'Keefe, C., & Rotola, G. (2021). Legal Priorities Research: A Research Agenda. *Legal Priorities Project*. January 2021. Retrieved 3 January 2025, from https://papers.ssrn.com/sol3/papers.cfm?abstract_id=3931256

Wirth, D. A. (1995). The Rio declaration on environment and development: Two steps forward and one back, or vice versa? *Georgia Law Review, 29*(3), 599–654.

Wolfrum, R. (2009). Common heritage of mankind. In A. Peters & R. Wolfrum (Eds.), *Max Planck Encyclopedia of public international law*. Oxford University Press. (Article last updated November 2009).
Wood, J. C. (1996). Intergenerational equity and climate change. *Georgetown International Environmental Law Review, 8*, 293–332.
Wood, M. C. (2009a). Advancing the sovereign trust of government to safeguard the environment for present and future generations: Part I: ecological realism and the need for a paradigm shift. *Environmental Law, 39*(1), 43–90.
Wood, M. C. (2009b). Advancing the sovereign trust of government to safeguard the environment for present and future generations: Part II: Instilling a fiduciary obligation in governance. *Environmental Law, 39*(1), 91–140.
World Commission on Environment and Development. (1987). *Report of the World Commission on Environment and Development: Our Common Future (Brundtland Report)* (1987). UN Doc. A/42/427 Annex.
World Conference on Human Rights. (1993). *Vienna Declaration and Programme of Action* (25 June 1993). UN Doc. A/CONF.157/23.
World Health Organization. (2019). *The Global Health Observatory: Global Health Estimates – Life Expectancy and Leading Causes of Death and Disability. 2019*. Retrieved 3 January 2025, from https://www.who.int/data/gho/data/themes/mortality-and-global-health-estimates.
World Summit for Social Development. (1995). *Copenhagen Declaration on Social Development* (14 March 1995). UN Doc. A/CONF.166/9.
World Summit on Sustainable Development. (2002a). *Johannesburg Declaration on Sustainable Development* (4 September 2002). UN Doc. A/CONF.199/20.
World Summit on Sustainable Development. (2002b). *Plan of Implementation of the World Summit on Sustainable Development* (4 September 2002). UN Doc. A/CONF.199/20.
Zsuzsanna, H. (2016). Transforming our world: New Agenda and goals for sustainable development. *Hungarian Yearbook of International Law and European Law*, 167–194.

# Chapter 3
# A Philosophical Perspective on Intergenerational Justice

From a purely positivist perspective, the analysis of intergenerational equity would only require an assessment of the existing sources of international law.[1] Such a positivist analysis is undertaken in Chap. 4, but this book is not limited to legal positivism. Instead, certain norms are not only relevant because they are laid down by the competent human authority, but because they are deducible from nature, reason or justice.[2] Without doubt, international environmental law is a domain strongly connected to questions of ethics, fairness and justice.[3] This natural law character is particularly evident in environmental concepts such as sustainable development and intergenerational equity.[4] Intergenerational equity itself aims at the just distribution of natural resources among generations,[5] which necessarily requires considerations of environmental justice and ethics.[6] It constitutes an explicit manifestation of distributive justice.[7] Due to this connection and its interdisciplinary character, the concept cannot be assessed separately from its ethical and philosophical foundations.[8] *Peter Lawrence* even considered that "[to] solve global environment challenges it is essential that international environmental treaties be strengthened on the basis of the ethics and justice discourse."[9]

---

1 See Cryer et al. (2011), p. 38.

2 Orakhelashvili (2007, paras. 1–3). For a comparable non-positivist perspective, cf. also Kleiber (2014), pp. 43–44.

3 See Stone (2010); Bosselmann (2009); Gillespie (2021).

4 Stephens (2010); Orakhelashvili (2007, para. 43).

5 Hadjiargyrou (2016), p. 249.

6 See, e.g., Stone (2010), pp. 292, 304–311.

7 Shelton (2010a), pp. 640–641 On the general connection between equity and justice, see International Court of Justice, *Case concerning the Continental Shelf (Tunisia v. Libyan Arab Jamahiriya),* Judgment (Merits), 24 February 1982, ICJ Reports 1982, 18, para. 71.

8 See, e.g., Collins (2007), pp. 94–95; Shelton (2010b), pp. 131–133.

9 Lawrence (2012), p. 46.



A. Bustami, *The Legal Relationship between Present and Future Generations*,
https://doi.org/10.1007/978-3-032-03345-1_3

This kind of non-positivist analysis has also been mirrored in former studies on intergenerational equity. *Edith Brown Weiss* explicitly addressed the long history of cultural and religious traditions referring to the relationship between present and future generations,[10] and her doctrine was influenced by several philosophical approaches to intergenerational justice.[11] In the UNSG Report on intergenerational solidarity from 2013, the Secretary-General stated that "a dedication to future generations is visible worldwide and across cultures. It is a value universally shared by humanity."[12] The report then examined the ethical dimensions of intergenerational equity.[13]

The following chapter takes a comparable approach and turns to the philosophical concepts of "intergenerational justice"[14] as a foundation of the legal concern for future generations.[15] This approach has two reasons. It shows which discussions on the plausibility of a theory of intergenerational equity belong to the realm of philosophy and ethics, and which other aspects are actually part of the legal discourse. Many of the common objections to intergenerational equity in legal doctrine do not properly distinguish between these two dimensions, although they primarily address the philosophical, pre-legal foundations of intergenerational relations.[16] The second reason for this natural law analysis of intergenerational equity lies in the inherent influences the philosophical foundations already had on the development of the concept. By understanding these foundations, many of the aforementioned legal developments become much clearer. These parallels between the philosophical and the legal realm and their impact on each other thus form the core of this chapter.[17]

Philosophy would first have to address *why* the present generation should care for the future from a moral point of view.[18] This preliminary question is also reflected in the provocative question of the High Commissioner for Intergenerational Relations in the introductory thought experiment of time travel. Nonetheless, this issue is not addressed in much detail in the next sections, as it would exceed the scope of a primarily legal analysis. A brief preliminary answer very much relates to the metaphysical consideration that human survival is a good thing,[19] or even that

[10] See, e.g., Brown Weiss (1989), pp. 18–21 as well as *supra* in Sect. 2.1 [notes 5–9].

[11] See Brown Weiss (1989), pp. 23–24.

[12] United Nations Secretary-General (2013, para. 3).

[13] Ibid., paras. 8–28.

[14] Despite the sometimes synonymous use of the terms "equity" and "justice", "intergenerational justice" has a more general meaning and has particularly been shaped in the context of philosophical approaches, while "intergenerational equity" is normally used in a legal context.

[15] With a similar reasoning, see Stone (2010), pp. 304–311; Tremmel (2009), p. 63; Kleiber (2014), pp. 43–59.

[16] See *infra* in Sect. 3.2.

[17] See *infra* in Sects. 3.3.1.2, 3.3.2.2, 3.3.3.2 and 3.3.4.2.

[18] See, e.g., Partridge (1981).

[19] Kavka (1981), pp. 116–118; Collins (2007), p. 94; Shelton (2010b), p. 131.

humanity has an obligation to endure.[20] For instance, *Hans Jonas* justified his ethics of responsibility with the metaphysical condition that there is a responsibility to ensure the existence of humanity.[21] Another important argument is the temporal equality of human beings, put differently: there is no ethical foundation for a moral distinction between human beings depending on their date of birth.[22] This argument is linked to the foundational conception of human rights, which is already stipulated in the Universal Declaration of Human Rights: “All human beings are born free and equal in dignity and rights. They are endowed with reason and conscience and should act towards one another in a spirit of brotherhood.”[23] This life in dignity also includes the dignity of future human beings[24] and it demands the present generation to care for future generations based on the respect owed to human dignity.[25] The universal dedication to future generations, mentioned by the UNSG,[26] is also articulated within the philosophical framework of “longtermism”,[27] which considers the concern for the long-term future “a key moral priority of our time”.[28] Whether based on religious or cultural beliefs, on human dignity as a foundational concept or on the idea of longtermism, most philosophical approaches to intergenerational justice start with this preliminary understanding of responsibility towards future generations.[29]

Although the following sections do not explicitly address this preliminary question in more detail, they might give implicit answers as far as these are necessary to understand the respective philosophical approach. The following chapter starts with an introduction of some basic terminology (Sect. 3.1), before turning to several objections that are generally raised against the existence of any moral obligations towards future generations. It is thus examined why there should *not* be any moral obligation to the future (Sect. 3.2). As far as these objections can be overcome, four main philosophical schools of thought on intergenerational justice are presented in overview in order to illustrate the different perspectives on *how* the moral duties towards future generations must be conceptualised (Sect. 3.3). Of course, the present chapter cannot offer an exhaustive analysis of the philosophical approaches to

---

[20] Carson (1962), pp. 5–13.; quoting Jean Rostand. For a critical counterargument concluding that there is no obligation to the future at all, see Thompson (1981).

[21] Jonas (1979), pp. 34–36. See also Heubach (2008), pp. 165–167.

[22] UNSG (2013, para. 13); Brown Weiss (1992), pp. 72–73; Ekeli (2006), pp. 402–403; Shelton (2010b), p. 131. See also Lepage and Drafting Committee (2015, Art. IV). On intergenerational discounting, see Birnbacher (1989), p. 103.

[23] United Nations General Assembly (1948, Art. 1).

[24] Shelton (2010b), p. 131; Woods (2016).

[25] In more detail, see, e.g., Düwell (2014); Düwell (2016).

[26] UNSG (2013, para. 3).

[27] See already *supra* in Sect. 1.1 [note 78]. Generally, on the paradigm of longtermism, see, e.g., Winter et al. (2021), pp. 13–22.

[28] Moorhouse (2021). Recent studies have confirmed the underlying conviction among both legal professionals and laypersons, see Martínez and Winter (2022).

[29] For a similar introductory assessment, see Nagy (1998), pp. 53–55.

intergenerational justice, much less establish a proper philosophical theory of it. Instead, it gives an overview of the most important philosophical approaches that have influenced the legal domain. It is not necessary either for the subsequent legal development to take position between the different philosophical approaches. The chapter illustrates that the existing legal concepts of intergenerational equity are based on several of these philosophical approaches and that there are certain parallels between the philosophical and the legal concepts of intergenerational justice and equity.

## 3.1 Basic Terminology and Distinctions

The overall idea of "justice" is at the core of intergenerational justice. From a legal standpoint, justice constitutes the ultimate object and purpose of legal norms,[30] so that the interpretation of positive law must always aim "to be closest to the requirements of justice".[31] Beyond this, definitions of justice have varied since the times of Aristotle.[32] In ancient Roman law, justice was defined as "the constant and perpetual wish to render every one his due."[33] Put in other words, *Thomas Scanlon* understood justice as "what we owe to each other".[34]

In the context of justice in international environmental law, corrective justice (or commutative justice) and distributive justice must be distinguished.[35] Corrective justice is based on reciprocity as an element of justice,[36] and it aims at rectifying fair transactions between individuals and at righting particular wrongs.[37] Meanwhile, distributive justice concerns the just distribution of benefits and burdens between human beings.[38] As environmental law and ethics address the just handling of natural resources, distributive justice often is at the core of environmental norms.[39] Similarly, intergenerational equity aims at the just allocation of natural resources

---

[30] Orakhelashvili (2007, para. 48). For a detailed assessment of the interrelationship between international law and international justice, see Mégret (2019).

[31] *Continental Shelf, Tunisia v. Libya* (Judgment (Merits)), *supra* note 7, para. 71.

[32] For an overview, see Miller (2021).

[33] See ibid., Section 1 with reference to Justinian (1893). See also Aristotle (1980, Book V, Chapters 1–2).

[34] Scanlon (1998).

[35] This distinction between "iustitia commutativa" and "iustitia distributiva" was first drawn by Aristotle (1980, Book V, Chapter 2)., and it is still relevant today, see Solum (2001), p. 174; Hadjiargyrou (2016), p. 257.

[36] On the relevance of "reciprocity" for a theory of justice, see *infra* in Sect. 3.2.3.

[37] Aristotle (1980, Book V, Chapter 2). See also Solum (2001), p. 174.

[38] Aristotle (1980, Book V, Chapter 2).

[39] Shelton (2010a), p. 642; Scholtz (2021), pp. 336–337; Bartenstein (2022), pp. 68–69 For a comprehensive analysis of distributive justice principles and their significance for sustainable development, see Vasconcellos Oliveira (2018), pp. 431–433.

between present and future generations and, thus, mainly contains elements of distributive justice.[40] *Brown Weiss'* doctrine of intergenerational equity also contains elements of corrective justice.[41] Most notably, the idea of an intergenerational trust is corrective, as it includes a trust fund to compensate future generations for injuries caused by the present generation.[42] *Zena Hadjiargyrou* also considered that "if a wrong does occur, an ombudsman will step into the shoes of a future generation to correct it so that corrective justice here achieves distributive justice", which is why "[t]he trust poses an intricate intermingling of both concepts of justice."[43]

Still, the core idea of intergenerational equity remains distributive. Therefore, the focus of this chapter is on the philosophical origins of these distributive justice elements. The philosophical basis of distributive justice does not rely on one single school of thought, but on different philosophical approaches to intergenerational distribution of resources,[44] such as utilitarianism, libertarianism, social contract theories and communitarianism. Nonetheless, a preliminary distinction of distributive justice arguments into egalitarian and sufficientarian approaches is helpful,[45] since the specific schools of thought can normally be affiliated to egalitarian and/or sufficientarian principles of justice.[46]

Egalitarianism in general and strict egalitarianism in particular consider that equality is of an intrinsic value as such.[47] Therefore, justice is furthered by means, which render human beings more equal and less different.[48] In a distributive context, this means that diminishing inequalities between humans would always lead to a better, a more just, society. Egalitarianism has often faced much criticism based on the so-called levelling-down-objection: Since strict egalitarian reasoning *always* prefers equality over inequality, this would even prefer to worsen those who are better off until they are on an equal footing with the worst-off in society—even when this might not make anyone better off in an absolute understanding.[49] This is why *Derek Parfit* attempted to reformulate strict egalitarianism by advocating a weaker

---

[40] Collins (2007), p. 95; Shelton (2010a), pp. 640–641. Generally on distributive justice in international environmental law, see Czarnecki (2008); Shelton (2010a), pp. 647–652.

[41] Solum (2001), pp. 174–175; Fitzmaurice (2008), pp. 198–199, 212, 226; Shelton (2010b), p. 132; Hadjiargyrou (2016), pp. 257–258.

[42] Fitzmaurice (2008), p. 212. See also Solum (2001), p. 175. On the planetary trust, see *supra* in Sect. 2.2.1.3.

[43] Hadjiargyrou (2016), p. 258.

[44] Ibid.

[45] In detail, see Meyer and Roser (2009), p. 220. See also Vasconcellos Oliveira (2018), pp. 431–432.

[46] For the specific categorisation, see *infra* in Sect. 3.3.

[47] Vasconcellos Oliveira (2018), pp. 432–433. Cf. Arneson (2013, Section 1).

[48] Therefore, egalitarianism is also qualified as a comparative theory of justice, see Miller (2021, Section 2.4).

[49] Meyer and Roser (2009), pp. 220–221

form, called the priority view.[50] Prioritarians do not consider equality itself an absolute value.[51] They are not exposed to the criticism of the levelling-down objection, although they have a natural tendency towards equality.[52] According to the priority view, "to benefit persons matters more the worse off the person is to whom the benefits accrue, the more people are being benefited and the greater the benefits in question."[53] Put differently, they favour welfare for the worst-off people more than for other persons.[54]

Contrary to these egalitarian concepts, sufficientarian principles of justice do not value equality in general.[55] Instead, concerns of inequality only matter when they fall below a specific threshold.[56] Therefore, sufficientarianism assumes that benefitting people who are worse off contributes to a greater degree to justice, but only with regard to persons below this threshold.[57] The key characteristic of sufficientarian views of justice is thus the minimum threshold, which should be reached by as many as possible to achieve a sufficient level of justice.[58] The exact determination of the threshold is subject to debate and could depend on different factors.[59] Below this threshold, the priority view remains valid, that means priority should be given to benefiting those who are worse off. Above the threshold, however, there are no priorities; this distinguishes sufficientarianism from the priority view.[60]

Sufficientarian approaches are nuanced between weak and strong sufficientarianism.[61] Weak sufficientarianism still ascribes some relevance to the quantity of persons who are benefitted as well as to the amount of benefit reached by an action.[62] Thereby, it does not consider that it has absolute priority to benefit those below the threshold.[63] In contrast, the main characteristic of strong sufficientarianism is the absolute prohibition of trade-offs between persons above

---

50 Parfit (1997), p. 213 with further references. See also Raz (1988, Chapter 9). For an overview, see Meyer and Roser (2009), pp. 222, 226.

51 Cf. Meyer (2021, Section 4.2).

52 Meyer and Roser (2009), pp. 221–222; Mulgan (2014), p. 336.

53 Meyer and Roser (2009), p. 221. See also Meyer (2021, Section 4.2); Parfit (1997), pp. 213–214.

54 Vasconcellos Oliveira (2018), p. 433.

55 Frankfurt (1987), pp. 32–33.

56 Meyer and Roser (2009), p. 226; Philips (2016), pp. 90–91.

57 In detail on intergenerational sufficientiarianism, see Meyer (2009).

58 Cf. Vasconcellos Oliveira (2018), p. 433. Sufficientarian concepts of justice are often non-comparative: Miller (2021, Section 2.4).

59 See, e.g., Meyer (2009), pp. 300–304; Spengler (2016), pp. 924–925. See also *infra* note 128.

60 Meyer and Roser (2009), p. 222. Cf. also Casal (2007), pp. 297–298.

61 Meyer and Roser (2009), pp. 222–224.

62 Ibid., p. 222.

63 Ibid., pp. 223–224. See, e.g., Beckerman and Pasek (2001, Chapter 4).

and persons below the threshold: persons below the threshold enjoy lexical priority to all those above the threshold.[64]

This preliminary distinction between egalitarian and sufficientarian concepts of distributive justice can both help in the understanding of the following objections to intergenerational justice (II.), and it can support the characterisation of the subsequently illustrated philosophical approaches as either egalitarian or sufficientarian principles (III.).

## 3.2 Objections to a Theory of Intergenerational Justice

Even if a moral responsibility towards future generations is generally assumed, this does not necessarily establish the moral status of future generations. This moral status is questioned from several conceptional points of view due to the particularities of intergenerational justice in comparison to matters of justice between living persons.[65] For some commentators, these particularities render an appropriate theory of justice with obligations of the present towards future generations impossible. Often, these objections are also raised legally although they concern the pre-legal realm. This is why their illustration in the following sections serves as an important factor in understanding the conceptional basis for intergenerational equity. As far as they can be refuted in this chapter, they do not impede the existence of a legal concept of intergenerational equity. Four main objections are discussed in the following: the non-identity problem (Sect. 3.2.1), the problem of non-existence (Sect. 3.2.2), the lack of reciprocity (Sect. 3.2.3) and the element of uncertainty (Sect. 3.2.4).[66] This strict distinction is not mandatory as the different objections are interrelated and sometimes addressed jointly.

### *3.2.1 Non-Identity Problem*

The "non-identity problem" is the most prominent argument against a theory of intergenerational justice.[67] It was first expressed by *Derek Parfit* in the 1970s.[68] Since then, several philosophers have addressed this problem, using different

[64] Meyer and Roser (2009), p. 224. On the different manifestations of sufficientarianism, see also Spengler (2016), pp. 924–925.

[65] For an overview, see Shrader-Frechette (2004), pp. 603–604; Meyer (2005), pp. 18–19; Partridge (2007), pp. 378–379; Cochrane (n.d., Section 1.a).

[66] However, these objections are interrelated and are sometimes addressed in a conjunctive way. The relationship between intergenerational justice and population ethics is another issue often addressed as an objection to responsibility for the future.

[67] Roberts (2024)—on which the following explanations are based.

[68] Parfit (1976); Parfit (1982).

terminology such as non-identity argument, future individuals paradox, possible people-dilemma, or contingency problem.[69] The non-identity problem is based on two important premises. First, according to traditional ideas of moral behaviour, a moral obligation to refrain from an act only exists if that act is morally wrong, thus, if it harms some existing or future individual.[70] To harm individuals means that the act makes them worse off than they would otherwise have been without that act.[71] Consequently, "wrongs require victims",[72] which constitutes a person-affecting view of morality.[73]

Second, the non-identity problem is based on the fact that even slight changes in two persons' manner of procreation would lead to a different partner for reproduction, a different time or manner of conception (*in vitro*, *coitus*), which in consequence would result in a distinct individual being born from different genetic material.[74] This contingency between current decisions on procreation and future individuals is at the core of the non-identity problem. If certain acts and policy decisions of the present generation can have an impact on the conception of a specific future individual,[75] this leads to the following observation: On the one hand, future individuals might suffer from negative impacts of the present generation's actions or inactions, which would lead to flawed existences. On the other hand, if these flaws were to be avoided by taking alternative actions, this would unavoidably lead to bringing different individuals into existence than would have existed in the first place.[76] In the words of *Derek Parfit:* "It may help to think about this question: how many of us could truly claim, 'Even if railways and motor cars had never been invented, I would still have been born'?"[77] However, if the originally flawed existence was nonetheless worth living, the flawed existence would still be preferable to not existing at all; at least, the flawed existence could not constitute a "harm" to that *specific* future individual.[78]

At this point, *Derek Parfit* introduced a distinction between "same people choices" and "different people choices".[79] While "different people choices" have an impact on the identities and possibly also the number of future people, a "same people choice" does not have any influence on the composition, number and identity of future humans. Therefore, the non-identity argument is irrelevant in the case of

---

[69] See, e.g., Schwartz (1978), pp. 10–11; Kavka (1982); Woodward (1986); Elliot (1989).

[70] See Roberts (2024, Section 1).

[71] Parfit (1982), p. 117; Kavka (1982), p. 93; Kleiber (2014), pp. 49–50; Parfit (2017), pp. 118–119.

[72] Parfit (1982), p. 117.

[73] Roberts (2009), pp. 201–202; Roberts (2024, Section 1). In more detail on this premise, see *infra* notes 101–128.

[74] Kavka (1982), p. 94; Roberts (2024, Section 2).

[75] Kavka (1982), p. 94.

[76] Parfit (1982), p. 115; Roberts (2024, Section 1).

[77] Parfit (1982), p. 115.

[78] Roberts (2024, Section 1). See also, e.g., Kavka (1981), p. 115.

[79] Parfit (1984), pp. 355–356.

"same people choices"[80]: If the act that caused a flawed existence of future individuals could be avoided without any impact on number and identities of these future individuals, then the act is morally wrong.[81] For illustration of "same people choices", commentators have often referred to the examples of a nuclear technician,[82] to the time bomb example,[83] or to a comparison between two different cases of birth diseases.[84]

The non-identity problem only is relevant in case of "different people choices", on which the exact number and identities of future individuals depend.[85] In the literature on the non-identity problem, several illustrations exist, for instance examples of depletion,[86] the slave child example,[87] and the wrongful life example.[88] For environmental decision-making on basis of a moral responsibility to the future, the consideration of two alternative environmental policies can be helpful[89]: Policy 1 is favourable to the current generation. But due to degradation of the natural resources, it will lead to suffering for future individuals A, B and C, who will be born in 80 years from today. Policy 2 is much more sustainable and will lead to a higher standard of living for any individuals living in 80 years from now. However, it has monetary impacts on present individuals, which thus influences their decisions in a way that causes them either to decide against having children or to procreate at a later point in time. Due to these impacts, individuals A, B and C will never come into existence in the scenario of Policy 2. Instead, individuals D, E and F would be born from distinct genetic material. Therefore, comparing the two policies, the sustainable Policy 2 will cause less suffering for D, E and F than A, B and C would have suffered under Policy 1. However, it cannot easily be claimed that Policy 1 thereby would harm individuals A, B and C, if an alternative Policy 2 caused them to never have existed at all. On basis of these reflections, proponents of the non-identity argument concluded that even a policy, which causes suffering of future humans, cannot be considered morally wrong.[90] A case of intergenerational justice would be illogical

---

[80] Kleiber (2014), pp. 51–52.

[81] Parfit (1982, p. 114).

[82] Ibid., pp. 113–114.

[83] Feinberg (1986), p. 154; Meyer (2005), p. 27.

[84] Boonin (2008), pp. 127–129; Rivera-López (2009), p. 338.

[85] For more details on the distinction between "same number different people choices" and "different number different people choices", see Parfit (1984), p. 356.

[86] Ibid., p. 362; Roberts (2024, Section 2.1).

[87] Kavka (1982), pp. 100–101; Roberts (2024, Section 2.2).

[88] Parfit (1984), pp. 367–368; Gosseries (2004), p. 10; Boonin (2008), pp. 127–132; Roberts (2024, Section 2.4).

[89] This example is based on *Derek Parfit's* risky policy example (Parfit 1984, pp. 371–372), which was applied to the context of climate change by Broome (1992), p. 34.

[90] See Heyd (1992), pp. 30–33; Boonin (2008); Heyd (2009b), pp. 170–176; Heyd (2009a); Roberts (2024, Section 3.1).

and paradox in itself; thus, moral obligations to future generations could not be based on a theory of justice.[91]

However, these findings are not compulsory, some are not even persuasive, which is why most literature on intergenerational ethics rejected the conclusions from the non-identity problem.[92] One of the assumptions for the illustration of the non-identity problem was that the flawed existences caused by a certain action or inaction today would still be worth living.[93] Only then, no "harm" could be found in choosing this action/inaction for the future human being's flawed existence. Yet, if the flawed existence was less than worth living, this existence would constitute a "harm" and it would be morally wrong to bring this individual into existence.[94] This assumption of the existence worth having could turn out to be wrong in the case of environmental policies, if the actions or inactions of the present generation had such a dire impact on the planet that any human life became steadily less worthy of living due to catastrophic scenarios of resource scarcity, natural disasters, sea-level rise, increasingly extreme weather events and other consequences of climate change. Since these scenarios are becoming more likely in context of insufficient climate change policies,[95] one of the main premises of the non-identity problem might prove to be irrelevant for philosophical considerations of intergenerational justice.[96]

Further, even if the assumption remained correct, this does not necessarily lead to the impossibility of a moral theory of intergenerational justice. Quite the opposite, the conclusions derived from the non-identity problem seem to be counterintuitive and implausible,[97] since they give a free moral pass to almost every act that has an impact on timing and manner of conception.[98] *Edith Brown Weiss* correctly pointed out that "[v]irtually every policy decision of government and business affects the composition of future generations, whether or not they are taken to ensure their rights."[99] *Parfit* himself rejected the conclusions of the non-identity problem and put forward the "No-Difference View": Despite the non-identity of future individuals in cases of "different people choices", there is no difference in the present generation's moral responsibility towards the future.[100] Therefore, he suggested the quest for a new moral principle, "Theory X", to define these intergenerational obligations in a

[91] See, e.g., Schwartz (1978), pp. 11–13; D'Amato (1990), pp. 192–194; Beckerman and Pasek (2001, Chapter 2); Beckerman (2004).

[92] See, e.g., Kavka (1982); Parfit (1984); Carter (2001); Ekeli (2005), p. 444; Partridge (2007); Tremmel (2009), p. 46.

[93] Kavka (1982), p. 94; Roberts (2024, Section 1 (intuition 2)).

[94] In more detail, see Steinbock (2009); Roberts (2011b); Roberts (2011a).

[95] In detail, see *supra* in Chap. 1.

[96] For a comparable conclusion, cf. Steinbock (2009), pp. 163–166.

[97] See Kavka (1982), p. 95; Parfit (1984), pp. 363, 366–367; Gündling (1990), p. 210; Carter (2001), p. 433; Ekeli (2005), p. 444.

[98] Roberts (2024, Section 3.1). Referring to historical injustices as an illustrating example: Visser 't Hooft (1999), p. 51.

[99] Brown Weiss (1990), p. 206. See also Gündling (1990), p. 210.

[100] Parfit (1984), pp. 366–371.

way, which does not rely on the narrow person-affecting view initially presented.[101] According to this view, morally relevant harm requires that an act makes individuals worse off than they would otherwise have been without that act.[102]

Various solutions have been presented in order to address "different people choices".[103] Impersonal concepts of justice constitute one possible alternative to the comparative narrow person-affecting understanding of harm.[104] These views do not derive morality from effects on individuals but on impersonal effects on a general level of well-being in the world.[105] Utilitarian concepts of justice are typical examples of impersonal views of morality, as they assess the morality of an act by its contribution to the overall well-being of human beings.[106] Although they overcome the non-identity problem, they have other disadvantages in the context of intergenerational justice,[107] as shown in more detail below.[108] *Parfit* accepted such an impersonal concept only with regard to "different people *but* same number choices"[109]: "If in either of two outcomes the same number of people would ever live, it would be bad if those who live are worse off, or have a lower quality of life, than those who would have lived."[110] By comparing different states of the future with each other, this conception goes beyond the mere comparison of the personal impact on specific individuals.[111]

However, applied to "different people *and* different number choices", impersonal utilitarian concepts of morality would lead to the so-called "repugnant conclusion"[112]: "Compared with the existence of many people whose quality of life would be very high, there is some much larger number of people whose existence would be better, even though these people's lives would be barely worth living."[113] This is why *Parfit* continued to search for a better approach to different number choices, which would not lead to the repugnant conclusion.[114] As a result, he

[101] Ibid., 361, 370. For a very early discussion of alternative concepts, see Narveson (1978), pp. 41–56.

[102] Parfit (1982), p. 117. See *supra* notes 71–73.

[103] For an overview, see: Roberts (2024, Sections 3.2–3.6).

[104] Ibid., Section 3.2.

[105] Kleiber (2014), p. 50.

[106] Birnbacher (1988), pp. 58–59; Howarth (2011), pp. 342–343; Mulgan (2014), pp. 326–330; Roberts (2024, Section 3.2.1). For an overview, see Miller (2021, Section 4).

[107] See Birnbacher (2006), pp. 31–33; Roberts (2024, Section 3.2.1).

[108] See *infra* in Sect. 3.3.1.

[109] For this distinction, see Parfit (1984), p. 356.

[110] Ibid., pp. 369–370.

[111] Kleiber (2014), pp. 51–52.

[112] *Derek Parfit* particularly referred to the "Impersonal Total Principle": Parfit (1984), p. 387., which is similar to the total utility utilitarianism, see also Roberts (2024, Section 3.2.1). See also *infra* notes 251–255. As to his objections to the "Impersonal Average Principle", see, e.g., Parfit (1982), p. 159.

[113] Parfit (2017), p. 153; Parfit (1984), p. 388. In more detail, see Arrhenius et al. (2017).

[114] Parfit (1984), pp. 389–390; Parfit (2017), pp. 149–157.

suggested a combination of wide person-affecting views, the Wide Dual Person-Affecting Principle: "One of two outcomes would be in one way better if this outcome would together benefit people more, and in another way better if this outcome would benefit each person more."[115] There are other non-utilitarian impersonal approaches, which attempt to solve the non-identity problem, such as *Janna Thompson's* approach based on humanitarian duties.[116] According to *Jeffrey Reiman*, *John Rawls'* theory of justice,[117] emanating from the original position, could also be seen as such an (impersonal) conception of intergenerational relations, which does not depend on specific individuals.[118]

Finally, there are also person-affecting views of morality, which depend on the effects on individuals, but which do not require a person to be "worse off" in a comparative sense. Some of these views consider that wrongful acts can occur without the necessity of a "harm".[119] For instance, *Marc Davidson* suggested an "*in dubio pro futura*"-approach as a solution for the non-identity-problem in the context of climate change: "It justifies a 'precautionary' approach, in which climate damage is treated *as if* it were a wrongful harm to future generations until such time as coherence between theory and intuition is regained" (emphasis in the original).[120] Other proponents of person-based views referred to rights-based accounts of wrongdoing.[121] Some of them argued that a future person is wronged if the act that resulted in their existence at the same time caused the flaws of this existence.[122] Others construed a prohibition of discrimination or exploitation between generations: if future people are treated in a discriminatory way as compared to existing people, these future people are wronged.[123]

Alternatively, some person-affecting approaches considered "harm" to be a necessary requirement for the identification of a morally wrongful act, but offered non-comparative conceptions of "harm".[124] For instance, *Lukas Meyer* advocated

---

[115] Ibid., pp. 154–157.

[116] J. Thompson (2009b), p. 149. Cf. also De-Shalit (1995), pp. 62–65. For other impersonal approaches, see: Roberts (2024, Section 3.2.2).

[117] In more detail on *John Rawls'* approach to intergenerational justice, see *infra* in Sect. 3.3.3.

[118] Reiman (2007), p. 89.

[119] Kleiber (2014), p. 54; Roberts (2024, Section 3.3.1). For other concepts based on the present generation's reasons and intentions rather than the harmful outcomes themselves, see: ibid., Section 3.6.

[120] Davidson (2008), p. 482.

[121] See Roberts (2024, Section 3.3.1). Cf. also Meyer (2019), pp. 134–135.

[122] Smolkin (1999), p. 206; Beyleveld et al. (2015), pp. 553–556. See also Woodward (1986), pp. 817–818.

[123] Kavka (1982), pp. 106–109; Tremmel (2004, p. 7); Heubach (2008), pp. 124–125.

[124] Roberts (2024, Section 3.3.2). See, e.g., Harman (2009), p. 139. In general on these conceptions, see Gardner (2015).

for a threshold approach of harm,[125] which is based on a sufficientarian concept of justice.[126] According to this threshold notion, a person is harmed by an act only if that act makes that person's well-being level fall below "some normal threshold of quality of life".[127] Of course, any such threshold approach would have to elaborate on how exactly the threshold level of well-being is defined.[128] *Rita Vasconcellos Oliveira* offered an example of such a definition by elaborating a theory of "intergenerational sufficientarianism".[129]

Overall, the non-identity problem is a sophisticated challenge in the conception of a theory of intergenerational justice. At first sight, it seems to be an obstacle that hinders the existence of moral obligations towards the future, but the foregoing solutions have illustrated that this obstacle is not insurmountable. Quite the opposite, most philosophers so far have explicitly countered the objections of the non-identity problem and have offered more or less convincing alternatives on how to justify a moral obligation to not ignore the interests of future people. While this book does not assume to choose one of these solutions over the others or to offer its own concept, the foregoing observations have shown that the non-identity problem does in fact not hinder a philosophical theory of intergenerational justice.[130]

### *3.2.2 Non-Existence Argument*

Non-existence (or non-actuality) is the second common objection raised against those theories of intergenerational justice that are based on rights of future generations.[131] According to this objection, only individuals who currently exist can be bearers of rights, as could allegedly be deduced from the present tense form of the wording "to have rights".[132] Although the acceptance of rights of future generations

---

[125] Meyer (2004); Meyer (2005), pp. 36–38; Meyer and Roser (2009), pp. 227–232; Meyer (2009), pp. 295–296. See also Rivera-López (2009), p. 342; Steinbock (2009), pp. 163–165; Derek Bell (2011), pp. 109–110.

[126] See already *supra* notes 55–64.

[127] Rivera-López (2009), p. 337. Discussing particularly the advantages of such a threshold notion to overcome the difficulties posed by the non-identity problem: Meyer and Roser (2009), pp. 226–232; Meyer (2009), pp. 294–299.

[128] For some attempts to elaborate such thresholds, see Roberts (2024, Section 3.3.2). See also Steinbock (2009), pp. 163–165 as well as *supra* note 59.

[129] Vasconcellos Oliveira (2018), pp. 433–437.

[130] See also Ekeli (2005), p. 444; Heubach (2008), p. 125; Tremmel (2009), p. 48; Kleiber (2014), p. 55.

[131] See, e.g., de George (1981); Kleiber (2014), pp. 55–57.

[132] De George (1981), p. 159; Beckerman (2004), pp. 3–4; Beckerman (2006), pp. 54–56; Herstein (2009), pp. 1181–1182. See also Gosseries (2008a), pp. 453–457; Anstee-Wedderburn (2014), pp. 61–62.

is not a necessary condition for a theory of intergenerational justice,[133] it is often included in the existing theories, particularly in *Brown Weiss'* specific doctrine of intergenerational equity.[134] There are important differences between, on the one hand, concepts which only entail moral or legal obligations without the corresponding rights, and, on the other hand, concepts which confer corresponding moral or legal rights on individuals or groups. While Chap. 5 addresses these differences in more detail with regard to intergenerational equity,[135] the argument of non-existence is connected to the rights-based concepts, thus, to the conceptional (im-)possibility of future generations to be right-holders. Since these questions are of a preliminary, conceptional character and concern both the moral and the legal sphere,[136] they are addressed in the following.

Rights are considered as entitlements vis-à-vis others to perform or not to perform certain actions.[137] They are an important element of structuring modern societies between freedom and authority, between permissible and prohibited behaviour.[138] This general idea of rights is also relevant in human rights law[139] as well as increasingly in environmental law.[140] According to *Joseph Raz'* conception of rights, "an individual or a group has a right is to say that an aspect of their well-being is a ground for holding another to be under a duty".[141] While obligations do not necessarily entail corresponding rights, a right is always associated with a duty.[142]

This is why legal positivists, such as *John Austin* and *Hans Kelsen*, often rejected legal rights connected to legal obligations.[143] They built their theories on absolute obligations "without a corresponding reflex right",[144] especially regarding duties towards animals, plants and inanimate objects.[145] Similarly, there are some commentators who explicitly rejected a rights-based conception of intergenerational

---

[133] Tremmel (2004), p. 7; Heubach (2008), pp. 112–113.

[134] Brown Weiss (1989), pp. 99–100.

[135] See *infra* in Sect. 5.2.

[136] On the overlaps and distinctions between moral rights and legal rights, see, e.g., Tremmel (2009), pp. 47–48.

[137] Wenar (2020, Introduction). Cf. also Dworkin (1978), p. 85. For the comparable Hohfeldian notion of "claim-rights", cf. also Hohfeld (1913). and in more detail, see Wenar (2005), pp. 229–230.

[138] Wenar (2020, Introduction).

[139] See, e.g., Nickel (2024, Section 1).

[140] See, e.g., Merrills (2010), p. 665.

[141] Raz (1984a), p. 1.

[142] Dworkin (1978), p. 85; Brandt (1983), p. 29; Raz (1984a), p. 1. See also Brown Weiss (2021, para. 13). For different correlations, see Tremmel (2009), pp. 54–55.

[143] Brown Weiss (1989), p. 99.

[144] Austin (1873), pp. 413–415; Kelsen (1969), p. 62.

[145] Ibid.

justice due to the non-existence of future generations.[146] For instance, *Bryan Norton* referred to the "modern liberal tradition in ethics" and its individualistic conception of rights, which would be incompatible with the idea of future generations as right-holders.[147]

It is true that a strict focus on the present existence of specific right-holders is supported by traditional libertarian concepts of rights.[148] However, *Joel Feinberg* has for instance illustrated in his time bomb example why the non-existence of future generations could be irrelevant for the consideration of moral rights:

> A wicked misanthrope desires to blow up a school house in order to kill or mutilate the pupils. He conceals a bomb in a closet in the kindergarten room and sets a timing device to go off in six years. It goes off on schedule, killing or multilating [sic.] dozens of five year old children. It was the evil action of the wicked criminal six years earlier, before they were even conceived, that harmed them. It set in train a causal sequence that led directly to the harm.[149]

Based on this illustration, other commentators have derived that the children were wrongfully harmed by the misanthrope's action regardless of their non-existence at the time of the action, thus, there would also be no logical impediment to the moral consideration of future generations already today.[150]

At this point, two opposing theories of rights come into play, which decisively influence the question of whether non-existent future persons or generations can conceptionally be right-holders[151]: the will theory and the interest theory of rights.[152] "Which theory offers the better account of the functions of rights has been the subject of spirited dispute"[153]—thus, it cannot be said that the existence of the right-holder would be a necessary condition in any case. The difference between both theories can be summarised as follows:

> For the Interest Theorists, the essence of a legal right consists in its tendency to safeguard some aspect of the well-being of its holder; for the Will Theorists, contrariwise, the essence of a legal right consists in its provision of opportunities for its holder to make significant choices.[154]

---

[146] De George (1981), p. 159; Norton (1982), pp. 335–336; Bobertz (1987), pp. 191–192; D'Amato (1990), p. 198; Beckerman (2004). Referring to positivism, see also Burchardt (2012), p. 194.

[147] Norton (1982), p. 336. On this individualist understanding of rights, cf. also Donnelly (2003), p. 25.

[148] Steiner and Vallentyne (2009), p. 55.

[149] Feinberg (1986), p. 154.

[150] See, e.g., Davidson (2008), pp. 474–475; Kleiber (2014), pp. 56–57; Heubach (2008), p. 115.

[151] Steiner and Vallentyne (2009), p. 55.

[152] Meyer (2021, Section 1). For a general overview, see Campbell (2017, Section 2); Wenar (2020, Section 2.2.2) "Will theory" and "choice theory" are normally used synonymously; hereafter, the term "will theory" is used.

[153] Ibid. On the current validity of both theories, see Kramer and Steiner (2005).

[154] Kramer (2013), p. 248.

Will theorists, such as *Herbert L.A. Hart*,[155] *Carl Wellman*,[156] and *Hillel Steiner*,[157] assumed that the function of a right is to give its holder control over another person's duty.[158] Right-holders would have to be able to enforce or waive such a right on their own.[159] Any being that is not capable of making such choices or expressing its will could thus not be a right-holder according to will theory.[160] Future individuals do not exist today, thus, they do not possess said capacity to exercise any control over their potential rights today, which is why they would be excluded as holders of rights.[161] While this conclusion is clear with regard to individual rights of future generations, rights-based concepts of intergenerational justice and equity are often based on the idea of future generations as holders of collective or group rights.[162] Group rights are rights "possessed by a group *qua* group rather than by its members severally."[163]

For most will theorists, influenced by libertarian individualist conceptions of rights,[164] group rights for future generations are problematic since a group must fulfil certain criteria in order to hold rights.[165] First, a group right can exist independently from the aggregation of its members' individual rights, if the respective collective entity remains identifiable as the same entity regardless of changes in its members.[166] As future generations constitute the aggregation of all unborn future individuals regardless of their exact identity and composition,[167] they fulfil this first criteria to qualify as right-holders of group rights. Second, a will theory of rights requires that the group has a capacity for agency,[168] (i.e., a sufficient organisational structure and collective decision-making procedures[169]) in order to "be represented

155 Hart (1982), p. 183.

156 Wellman (1985).

157 Steiner (1994), pp. 68–73.

158 Wenar (2020, Section 2.2.2).

159 Kramer (2013), p. 248. This correlates with the Hohfeldian analytics of rights (Hohfeld (1913)), i.e. will theory requires a power over a claim-right, see Herstein (2009), pp. 1196–1197; Lewis (2018), p. 106,108. On the contrary, for interest theories, see *infra* note 185.

160 Steiner and Vallentyne (2009), p. 55.

161 Most prominently, see Beckerman (2006), pp. 59–60. See also Herstein (2009), p. 1202). Cf. Gosseries (2008a), pp. 453–454.

162 Explicitly, see Brown Weiss (1989), p. 98; Brown Weiss (2021, para. 13). See also UNSG (2013, para. 22). In more detail on rights of future generations as group rights, see *infra* in Sect. 5.2. 1.1.

163 Jones (2022, Section 1). See also Wenzel (2011, para. 2).

164 Cf. van Dyke (1982); Freeman (1995).

165 For an overview, see Jones (2022, Section 3).

166 Graham (2002), pp. 68–69; Newman (2011), p. 4. For general criteria for the existence of group rights, see

167 For the term of "future generations", see Brown Weiss (2021, para. 4) and already *supra* in Sect. 2.2.1.2.2.

168 P. A. French (1984), p. 32, 38.

169 Merrills (2010), pp. 670–671; Preda (2012), pp. 247–253. Cf. also Galenkamp (1993), pp. 62, 71–73, 101–110.

by legitimatized members".[170] Future generations, as a collective, lack these additional factors due to their non-existence; they do not have collective decision-making procedures, which would amount to the necessary agency competent to represent their interests.[171] This is why *John Merrills* concluded that "there can be no useful debate about rights in [the] context [of future generations]".[172]

Interest theorists, such as *Jeremy Bentham*[173] or *Neil MacCormick*,[174] objected to this focus on a potential right-holder's will and its exercise and underlined the weaknesses of will theories of rights.[175] Particularly, will theorists must accept that children and persons suffering from mental diseases would not qualify as right-holders according to their conception,[176] which was rejected by several commentators.[177] Further, a will theory of rights would mix up the actual existence of a specific right with issues of legal standing.[178] *Brown Weiss* formulated in this regard:

> The fact that the holder of the right lacks the standing to bring grievances forward and hence must depend upon the decision of the representative to do so does not affect the existence of the right or the obligation associated with it.[179]

Consequently, interest theorists maintain that the ability to exercise or waive one's right is not a precondition for its existence.[180] Instead, the function of a right is to further the right-holder's benefits or interests.[181] This means that only beings that have interests can have rights.[182] As *Joseph Raz* put it: "To assert that an individual has a right is to indicate [...] that an aspect of his well-being is a ground for a duty on another person. The specific role of rights [...] is, therefore, the grounding of duties in the interests of other beings."[183] While this approach also can have conceptional

---

[170] Wenzel (2011, para. 3).

[171] Merrills (2010), p. 671. For a similar argumentation, see also Supanich (1992), pp. 98–99; Ekardt (2021), p. 297.

[172] Merrills (2010), p. 672.

[173] Hart (1982), pp. 168–169, 174–182 with references, *inter alia*, to Bentham and Hart (1970), p. 84, 220.

[174] MacCormick (1977).

[175] See, e.g., MacCormick (1976); Freeman and Lloyd of Hampstead (1994), p. 388; Davidson (2008), pp. 473–475; Kramer (2013), pp. 247–258, 262–263.

[176] Wellman (1995), pp. 113–125; Beckerman (2006), p. 59.

[177] See, e.g., Tremmel (2009), pp. 51–52; Lewis (2018), p. 109. *Joel Feinberg* also acknowledged an interest theory approach concerning the issue of *holding* rights, although he was a will theorist with regard to the *nature* of rights, see Feinberg (1974), pp. 45–51.

[178] Freeman and Lloyd of Hampstead (1994), p. 388. See also Campbell (2017, Section 3).

[179] Brown Weiss (1989), p. 97. See also explicitly Nagy (1998), p. 57.

[180] See, e.g., Tremmel (2009), p. 52; Meyer (2021, Section 1).

[181] Wenar (2020, Section 2.2.2).

[182] Steiner and Vallentyne (2009), p. 55.

[183] Raz (1984b), pp. 207–208. See also Raz (1984a), p. 1. For an alternative wording, see Kramer (2013), p. 246.

difficulties,[184] the dichotomy between will theory and interest theory still remains relevant today.[185]

According to the interest theory, future generations would be potential right-holders if they had identifiable interests.[186] At this point, it becomes relevant again that rights of future generations are generally conceived as collective rights.[187] For interest theorists, a collective entity neither needs capacity for agency nor collective decision-making procedures in order to hold rights. Beyond unity and identity of the group,[188] it is sufficient that the group has a moral status and interests as a group, which go beyond the aggregated interests of its individual members.[189] Although the exact identity of future individuals as well as their exact interests is still unclear today,[190] *Joel Feinberg* stated in this regard: "whoever these human beings may turn out to be, and whatever they might reasonably be expected to be like, they will have interests that we can affect, for better or worse, right now."[191] Proponents of intergenerational rights supported this by stressing that future generations will in any case have certain interests in the diversity and quality of the planet, including basic physiological needs, such as clean air.[192] These interests could be "judged by objective, independent criteria", and they do not depend on the number or kinds of future individuals.[193]

Overall, it is true in light of any will theory of rights that the current non-existence of future generations remains an obstacle for their consideration as right-holders today. Nonetheless, most commentators have objected to the inevitable validity of such strict will theories and instead offered a variety of possible solutions regarding the moral consideration of future generations.[194] Most of these views are based on an interest theory of rights and illustrate the fact that future generations certainly share

---

[184] This led to some hybrid approaches, see, e.g., Sreenivasan (2005); Wenar (2005); Steiner and Vallentyne (2009), p. 56.

[185] Kramer and Steiner (2005). Contrary to the will theory of rights (see *supra* notes 137, 159), an interest theory "right" interchangeably correlates only with a "claim" in the sense of a Hohfeldian framework (Hohfeld (1913).), see Kramer (2013), p. 248.

[186] Brown Weiss (1989), p. 96; Lawrence (2012), pp. 38–39.

[187] See already *supra* note 162.

[188] See *supra* note 166.

[189] McDonald (1998), pp. 315–316; Graham (2002), pp. 89–93; Newman (2011, Part I). See also Jones (2022, Section 3).

[190] As to their identity, see *supra* in Sect. 3.2.1. on the non-identity problem. As to the uncertainty concerning the future, see also *infra* in Sect. 3.2.4.

[191] Feinberg (1974), p. 65. See also Davidson (2008), p. 473; Kleiber (2014), pp. 56–57; Lewis (2018), p. 110. For the opposing view, see, e.g., Herstein (2009), p. 1205.

[192] Brown Weiss (1989), pp. 98–99. See also UNSG (2013, para. 22); Barry (1989), pp. 274–275; Ekeli (2007), pp. 388–389; Birnbacher (2008), pp. 26–27; Lawrence (2012), p. 40.

[193] Brown Weiss (1989), p. 96, 99. See also Gewirth (2001/2014), p. 120. In opposition to an understanding of future generations as a universal group, see Herstein (2009), pp. 1175–1187. who categorised future generations into "types of future people", see ibid.), p. 1182.

[194] For another, constitutional, approach to this matter, see Riley (2016).

certain common interests, which are increasingly affected by the behaviour of present generations.[195] While the "non-actuality" of these interests led some authors to doubt any intergenerational moral obligations based on a duties-rights-relationship, interest theories offer at least two solutions to this challenge: Either it is assumed that there can be *present* rights of future generations despite their non-existence today,[196] or it is accepted that there are only *future* rights of future generations, but that these future rights can trigger obligations of the present generation already today.[197] In this sense, *Joerg Tremmel* stated:

> [Non-existence of future generations] does not necessarily imply that [...] the present generation, cannot violate future individuals' rights today [...]. That would only be the case if we conceded that present rights alone can constrain present actions [...]. But future rights can also constitute present obligations.[198]

This brief overview of the non-existence problem and its counterarguments introduced another challenge of a philosophical theory of intergenerational justice, which also has a strong impact on the legal concept. While, at first glance, the non-existence of future generations today could prevent such a theory of justice, at least based on intergenerational duties and rights, several possible solutions speak in favour of the moral consideration of future generations despite all challenges. Based on the interest theory of rights, this book assumes in the following that the non-existence argument is no sufficient objection against any concept of intergenerational justice, regardless of whether such a concept requires rights of future generations or not. In detail, Chap. 5 turns to the question of whether such intergenerational rights are actually legally anchored in public international law.[199]

### 3.2.3 Lack of Reciprocity

There is a third common objection to moral obligations vis-à-vis future generations that is linked to the non-existence argument[200]: the lack of reciprocity in intergenerational relations.[201] According to this line of reasoning, rights and

---

[195] Lawrence (2012), pp. 38–39. On the consequences of this affectedness of future persons by today's actions in the context of representation of future generations' interests, see *infra* in Sect. 5.3.1.

[196] On this "non-concessional view", see Elliot (1989), pp. 161–162.

[197] Ibid. p. 162; Gosseries (2008a), pp. 455–457; Derek Bell (2011), p. 105. In this sense, speaking of pre-effects ("Vorwirkung") of future rights of future generations, cf. also Ekardt (2021), pp. 297–300.

[198] Tremmel (2009), p. 53.

[199] See *infra* in Sect. 5.2.2.

[200] Kleiber (2014), pp. 55–56.

[201] See, e.g., Gosseries (2009); Gaillard (2011), pp. 337–340; Lawrence (2014), pp. 48–50. Connected to this, on the problem of asymmetry, see Birnbacher (2008), p. 30.

obligations must be in a reciprocal relationship to each other; a person could not have a right without having a correlating obligation because relations of justice would be built on reciprocity.[202] Since future generations cannot offer anything to the present generation in return for the latter's obligations, there could not be any obligation towards the future based on a theory of justice.[203] An alternative argument would be that the present generation cannot be obliged to bear the whole costs of mitigation of environmental problems today since future generations would then only unilaterally profit from the benefits.[204] *Gareth Davies* formulated this objection in a very pointed way by asking: "What can the future do for us?"[205] These objections are particularly relevant in case of social contract theories of justice, which are based on concepts of mutual advantage.[206]

However, this approach was often criticised for being unpersuasive: First, it is already inconclusive that a theory of intergenerational justice must be based on reciprocity.[207] As illustrated above, environmental ethics and intergenerational justice are primarily based on elements of distributive justice as opposed to the reciprocal concept of corrective justice.[208]

Second, even if one considered reciprocity a necessary condition for any theory of justice, several models of adapted reciprocity have been proposed for the intergenerational context. For overlapping generations, the classic direct model of reciprocity still holds true since children will feel obliged towards their parents in their old days because the latter cared for them when they were young.[209] In the case of non-overlapping generations, only broader concepts can resolve the issue of non-reciprocity, such as indirect descending reciprocity, indirect ascending reciprocity and direct double reciprocity.[210] Indirect descending reciprocity is the most suitable type of reciprocity for intergenerational justice: a specific present generation owes something (and as much) to future generations because past generations had transferred something to the present generation.[211] The reciprocal relationship is indirect because the final beneficiary is not identical to the initial benefactor; it is descending because it refers to transfers from one generation to the next one.[212]

[202] Barry (1989), p. 189. See also Narveson (1978), p. 38; Golding (1981), p. 65; Beckerman (2006), p. 56.

[203] Mulgan (2014), p. 331. See also Lawrence (2014), pp. 48–49; Gosseries (2008b), pp. 63–65.

[204] See Davies (2020).

[205] Davies (2022).

[206] Barry (1989), pp. 234–254; Mulgan (2014), p. 331; Hadjiargyrou (2016), pp. 260–261. In more detail, see *infra* in Sect. 3.3.3.

[207] Gosseries (2008b), p. 64. *Michael Kleiber* instead compared intergenerational justice to (non-reciprocal) moral obligations towards non-human animals, see Kleiber (2014), p. 58.

[208] See *supra* notes 35–43.

[209] Tremmel (2004), p. 6. However, this consideration does not provide an answer for the understanding of "future generations" in this book, see *supra* in Section 2.2.1.2.2.

[210] For an overview, see Gosseries (2009), pp. 123–126; Lawrence (2014), pp. 48–50.

[211] Gosseries (2008b), p. 63; Gosseries (2009), p. 123. Cf. also Nagy (1998), p. 59.

[212] Gosseries (2009), p. 123.

*Peter Lawrence* illustrated this kind of indirect reciprocity with reference to the carob tree narrative in the Talmud: "An old man is asked why he is planting a carob tree, as after all, he will not live to see this tree bloom. He answers: 'When I was born the world was full of blooming carob trees'".[213]

Transferred to the relation between present and future generations, *Boldizsár Nagy* observed: "[…] if future generations perform an obligation vis a vis [sic.] their successors as a counter-performance for the service which they have received from the present generation then the reciprocal element is established."[214] By connecting each of these indirect reciprocation steps, it becomes possible to bind successive generations to each other by some kind of chain of reciprocity.[215] It is not a coincidence that *Brown Weiss'* understanding of intergenerational equity as a planetary trust between generations builds on a similar idea of intergenerational relationship.[216]

All in all, it depends on the respective philosophical approach to intergenerational justice whether reciprocity is even a necessary requirement at all, or whether it can be adapted to the context of future generations.[217] Generally, lack of direct reciprocity between present and future generations is not an absolute hindrance to moral obligations vis-à-vis the future. Instead, indirect models of reciprocity have been and can be developed in order to explain intergenerational relationships of justice.[218] Consequently, this objection cannot persuasively negate the existence of any theory of intergenerational justice.

### 3.2.4 Lack of Knowledge and Uncertainties

Lastly, a theory of intergenerational justice can be challenged with reference to prognostic uncertainties regarding the future: it is not possible to predict with certainty how long future generations of humankind will exist, or which interests and needs they will have.[219] The members of the present generation do not know which knowledge future individuals will still acquire or whether they will be better

[213] Lawrence (2014), p. 49.

[214] Nagy (1998), p. 59.

[215] Gosseries (2009), p. 123; Gaillard (2011), p. 339.

[216] Brown Weiss (1984), p. 498; Brown Weiss (1989), p. 17. *Brown Weiss* was also inspired by Judeo-Christian precedents on intergenerational relations, see ibid. p. 19. This kind of transgenerational connection is also reflected in communitarian approaches to intergenerational justice, see *infra* note 493.

[217] Where necessary, this aspect is addressed in more detail in this chapter in the context of the respective philosophical approaches, see *infra* in Sects. 3.3.3 and 3.3.4.

[218] Kleiber (2014), p. 58.

[219] Anstee-Wedderburn (2014), pp. 63–65. For an overview, see also Kleiber (2014), p. 59.

or worse off than the present generation.[220] Some commentators go beyond this criticism and declare that a theory of intergenerational justice could even be "used as a way to import present values and impose these on the future".[221] According to this objection, the lack of knowledge and the significant uncertainties would render any theory of intergenerational justice meaningless.[222] The argument is linked to the non-identity problem, which refers to the uncertainty of future individuals as well as their contingency on present behaviour.[223]

Definitely, such uncertainty of the future is an inherent characteristic of any moral or legal theory of intergenerational justice. Uncertainty is also not unfamiliar to international environmental law in general, as the precautionary approach is "evidence of the incorporation of such indeterminacy into environmental decision-making."[224] Consequently, uncertainties about the future must not necessarily hinder a theory of intergenerational justice.[225] The objection underrates the actual knowledge today and further misconceives aspirations of a justice theory. It is not necessary to know and to envisage exact needs and interests of future generations in order to establish moral obligations towards the future; to the contrary, this would unjustly impose present values on the future.[226] Further, as *Lynda Collins* correctly stated with regard to the uncertainty of future generations' preferences:

> It is simply impossible to stay out of the affairs of future generations. The only question is whether the present generation will consciously consider future interests, or simply allow the future to unfold randomly, with potentially devastating impacts on unborn generations.[227]

As long as it is possible to determine certain minimum anthropological characteristics, which will shape the existence of future generations, it is possible to discuss and specify intergenerational obligations towards these generations.[228] This knowledge already exists today, so that the basic interests of future generations as well as the impacts of present behaviour on these interests can be foreseen.[229] These interests will certainly include basic physiological needs for fresh air, water and food as well as elementary psychological needs, such as security, appreciation and affection.[230] It

---

[220] Birnbacher (1988), pp. 140, 152–155; Supanich (1992), pp. 97–98; Birnbacher (2003b), p. 99 (on optimistic and pessimistic perspectives: pp. 86–89)).

[221] Mayeda (2004), p. 61. Cf. also Brown Weiss (2021, para. 11). *Lynda Collins* countered this argument, which she referred to as "intertemporal imperialism", see Collins (2007), p. 106.

[222] See Gillespie (2014), p. 120; Anstee-Wedderburn (2014), pp. 63–64.

[223] In detail, see *supra* in Sect. 3.2.1.

[224] Redgwell (1999), p. 97. On overlaps with and a delimitation to intergenerational equity, see briefly *infra* in Sect. 7.2.3.

[225] Kavka (1981), p. 111.

[226] Kleiber (2014), p. 59. Cf. Brown Weiss (2021, para. 11).

[227] Collins (2007), p. 106.

[228] Redgwell (1999), p. 97; Birnbacher (2008), p. 26; Brown Weiss (2021, para. 11).

[229] Collins (2007), pp. 105–106; Ekeli (2007), pp. 388–389.

[230] Kavka (1981), p. 111; Ekeli (2007), pp. 388–389; Birnbacher (2008), pp. 26–27; Kleiber (2014), pp. 59–60. See already *supra* notes 191–193.

is difficult or impossible to determine specific interests of future individuals beyond these basic interests,[231] which remains a challenge for any theory of intergenerational justice. However, the remaining uncertainties and lack of knowledge about the future do not preclude moral obligations towards these uncertain future generations. If uncertainty were to lead to the impossibility of intergenerational justice, this would result in a moral lacuna or ignorance towards the future, which is neither persuasive nor morally tolerable.[232] Consequently, most commentators reject the argument of uncertainty in the context of intergenerational justice.[233]

### *3.2.5 Interim Conclusion*

The particularities of intergenerational relations have led to several objections that question whether a theory of intergenerational justice could be conceptually possible at all. Four main objections have been illustrated in the foregoing sections. The non-identity problem, the argument of non-existence, the lack of reciprocity between non-overlapping generations as well as current uncertainties about the future have posed severe challenges to the establishment of a theory of justice. These objections have also been raised against any *legal* argument of intergenerational equity.

Although the conceptional challenges remain to a certain degree, the foregoing sections have illustrated that none of these objections necessarily render the moral basis of intergenerational justice impossible. In contrast, many of the objections are counterintuitive to the moral premises most human beings might feel towards future generations. Even the seemingly logical non-identity problem can be countered with some effort, as *Derek Parfit* himself established with his no-difference view on intergenerational justice.[234] Similar solutions have been offered vis-à-vis the other three objections.

Since the present work does not attempt to comprehensively address all the issues in this regard, the foregoing section was meant to give an overview of the arguments and counterarguments. It is sufficient to demonstrate that thus far, there is no persuasive reason to reject the further discussion of a theory of intergenerational justice—neither within the ethical realm nor with regard to the legal concepts of intergenerational equity. Both a moral and a legal theory of intergenerational justice and equity are conceptually possible. The following section thus turns to the different philosophical approaches to the formulation of such a theory while

[231] Heubach (2008), pp. 126–127.

[232] Ibid.), p. 128.

[233] See, e.g., Kavka (1981), p. 113; Birnbacher (1988), p. 143; Redgwell (1999), p. 97; Collins (2007), pp. 105–106; Ekeli (2007), p. 389; Heubach (2008), pp. 126–128; Kleiber (2014), p. 60; Ekardt (2021), pp. 304–305.

[234] Parfit (1984), pp. 366–371.

simultaneously demonstrating the parallels to and consequences for the legal concepts of intergenerational equity.

## 3.3 Philosophical Approaches to Intergenerational Justice and Their Relevance for the Legal Analysis

This chapter's introductory remarks have already pointed to the inherent influences between the development of the legal concept of intergenerational equity and several ethical and philosophical approaches to intergenerational justice. Many of the modern philosophical works on intergenerational justice have also been published in the 1970s and 1980s, parallel to the development of intergenerational equity. Based on these historical parallels, this chapter turns to some of the main philosophical schools of thought on intergenerational justice in order to analyse their explicit or implicit impacts on legal reasoning in the context of intergenerational equity. This book does not assume to present an exhaustive analysis of the philosophical debates, let alone a proper philosophical argument and opinion. Instead, the main philosophical approaches to intergenerational justice are presented in overview: Starting with utilitarianism (Sect. 3.3.1), libertarian approaches (Sect. 3.3.2) and social contract theory (Sect. 3.3.3) are illustrated, before ending with communitarian approaches (Sect. 3.3.4).[235]

While this overview briefly illustrates the different approaches to intergenerational justice as well as their potential challenges and critics, it does not take position for one or the other.[236] More interestingly, every section subsequently addresses the parallels between the respective philosophical approach and the legal concept of intergenerational equity and examines whether intergenerational equity is based on one or more of the illustrated approaches. Some of these parallels and the consequences drawn might serve as potential starting points for further legal analysis in subsequent chapters.[237]

### *3.3.1 Utilitarianism*

Utilitarianism is a form of consequentialist moral theory, which means that the righteousness of an action is exclusively derived from this action's consequences.[238]

[235] For an overview of different approaches, see, e.g., Gosseries (2008b).

[236] For a similar introductory assessment, see Nagy (1998), pp. 53–55.

[237] With regard to social contract theories and communitarian approaches in the context of intertemporal law, see *infra* in Sects. 7.2.2.2 and 7.3.3.3.

[238] Sinnott-Armstrong (2023, Section 1).

In contrast to deontological theories,[239] the moral reasons for a certain behaviour are not taken into consideration for their own sake, but only in context with the behaviour's effects.[240] The aim of utilitarianism is the maximisation of utility in these effects, meaning the largest amount of good for human beings.[241] Therefore, it becomes crucial for utilitarianism to define "the good" for human beings.[242] Classic utilitarianism understands this from a hedonistic perspective as "pleasure", "happiness" or "well-being" of persons.[243] For instance, *Jeremy Bentham* has addressed this "greatest happiness principle" as one of the first: "the greatest happiness of all those whose interest is in question, [is] the right and proper, and only right and proper and universally desirable, end of human action [...] in every situation".[244] More comprehensively, utilitarianism aims at producing well-being or diminishing ill-being.[245]

#### 3.3.1.1 Utilitarianism as an Aggregative Account of Intergenerational Justice

From a utilitarian perspective, justice is achieved as long as every action increases an overall well-being of human beings.[246] The utilitarian understanding of justice is aggregative: it is based on the assumption that the total amount of well-being is the only relevant element of justice and that it is not necessary to take into account the distribution of well-being between persons.[247] In the intragenerational context, this aggregative view has already been criticised because it is susceptible to a sacrificial exploitation of a minority to the benefit of the well-being of the majority.[248] The same concern was raised in respect of intergenerational justice: Applied to an intergenerational context, utilitarianism requires achieving the most possible happiness for the totality of human beings—in their temporal as well as spatial totality.[249] Since the number of future generations is either infinite or at least indefinite, the

---

[239] On deontological ethics, see Alexander and Moore (2024, Sections 1, 2).

[240] Sinnott-Armstrong (2023).

[241] Nathanson (n.d.). First proponents of utilitarianism have been: Bentham (1789); Mill (1863); Sidgwick (1874).

[242] Nathanson (n.d., Section 1.a.).

[243] Sinnott-Armstrong (2023, Section 3) In the following, these terms are used synonymously in the context of utilitarianism.

[244] Bentham (1789, Chapter 1, Note added 1822).

[245] Nathanson (n. d., Section 1.a). Cf. also Sinnott-Armstrong (2023, Section 1).

[246] Miller (2021, Section 4).

[247] Gosseries (2008b), p. 65; Ashford and Mulgan (2018, Section 3); Miller (2021, Sections 1.1, 4.2).

[248] See Williams (1973); Gosseries (2008b), p. 65; Lamont and Favor (2017, Section 5); Miller (2021, Section 4.2).

[249] On the differences between "total utility" and "average utility", see *infra* note 251.

aggregative utilitarian idea of well-being is susceptible to prioritising the interests of the majority of future generations to those of the minoritarian present generation.[250]

In this regard, average utility utilitarianism and total utility utilitarianism can be distinguished. Average utility utilitarianism aims at maximising only the average happiness of human beings, as opposed to total utility utilitarianism, which aims at maximising the total happiness of humans.[251] For average utility utilitarianism, the present's responsibility towards the future is limited to those future people who will live anyway.[252] As long as their average well-being is maximised, it is irrelevant how many human beings will live in the future or whether humanity will survive at all.[253] For total utility utilitarianism, every present generation has an obligation to guarantee the survival of humankind in order to accumulate total utility over the future.[254] The more human beings, the higher their well-being will be in absolute terms.[255]

The tendency towards maximisation results in an unequal and unreasonable distribution of welfare to the pure benefit of the future by disadvantaging present persons, which is a consequence of utilitarianism's aggregative character and its ignorance of interpersonal aspects of justice.[256] As *Parfit* has also criticised with regard to the non-identity problem,[257] impersonal utilitarian concepts of justice cannot solve this "repugnant conclusion".[258] *Axel Gosseries* formulated that this application of utilitarianism might "[force] us into everlasting sacrifices, since there is no way of knowing where [coming generations] should stop".[259] This is particularly true for the present generation's poorest members who would be equally restrained to the benefit of—possibly better off—generations to come.[260]

Proponents of utilitarianism have offered several suggestions how to solve this failure of utilitarianism. First, the idea of "diminishing marginal utility" stipulates that the utility attributed to a certain increase of well-being of a person depends on that person's original level of well-being: "the more a person has of a given good, the less the additional good will bring her additional utility".[261] The attributed utility

250 Partridge (2007), p. 380; Gosseries (2008b), p. 65.

251 Smart (1973), pp. 27–28.

252 Birnbacher (2006), p. 31; Mulgan (2014), pp. 333–335.

253 Birnbacher (2006), p. 31.

254 Ibid.), p. 32.

255 Partridge (2007), p. 380.

256 Birnbacher (2006), p. 32; Howarth (2011), p. 343. For the intra-generational context, see already *supra* note 248.

257 See *supra* notes 105–110.

258 Parfit (1984), p. 388; Parfit (2017), p. 153.

259 Gosseries (2008b), p. 65.

260 Birnbacher (2006), pp. 32–33; Howarth (2011), pp. 343–344.

261 Gosseries (2008b), p. 65.

diminishes linearly to the achieved well-being of a person.[262] This approach resembles the reasoning of prioritarian views of justice.[263] Consequently, the incidental utilitarian preference towards the quantitatively bigger group of future people can be attenuated for a fairer coexistence between generations, since more focus is put on aspects of minimum needs.

Second, a social discount rate has been proposed in order to respond to the repugnant conclusion. Such a discount rate would define to what extent utility in the future is considered to have a lesser value than the same utility unit in the present.[264] The further into the future a certain impact on utility comes up, the less value it has today, whereas the same utility impact in the present might still have a high value. At first sight, such a discount rate might seem attractive and a possible solution to the utilitarian time preference for the future. However, it causes certain problems itself, as it establishes a new time preference to the benefit of the present generation and thereby disregards the moral basis of intergenerational justice—the idea of same human value of present and future human beings.[265]

#### 3.3.1.2 Parallels to and Consequences for Intergenerational Equity

As utilitarianism in its different manifestations has influenced philosophical thinking for a long time,[266] it must be assessed how far current legal concepts of intergenerational equity have also been influenced by utilitarianism. On the one hand, utilitarianism promotes a strong case for the well-being of future human beings since their simple number quantitatively outweighs the well-being of the smaller present generation. On the other hand, this strong case for a maximisation of total utility over generations is the main reason for criticism due to its potential ignorance of the well-being of the present generation. The proposed solutions—diminishing marginal utility and the social discount rate—could be considered successful possibilities to attenuate utilitarianism's negative aspects; but they could also constitute inefficient attempts to change an incorrect system, which is not conceived for intergenerational concerns.[267]

In any case, utilitarian concepts of justice differ from other approaches to intergenerational justice as subsequently described. They also mainly differ from most legal accounts of intergenerational equity. Due to their impersonal approach to

[262] See also Gauthier (1986), pp. 304–305; Singer (2002), p. 42; Mulgan (2014), pp. 335–336; Miller (2021, Section 4.2).

[263] Parfit (1997), p. 213. See *supra* in Sect. 3.1.

[264] Cowen and Parfit (1992); Birnbacher (2003a); Wallack (2006), pp. 87–88; Mulgan (2014), p. 337.

[265] Parfit (1984), p. 357; Rawls (1971/1999), p. 262; Gosseries (2008b), p. 66. See also *supra* notes 22–25. On the other hand, if assumed that future people will be better off due to technological developments, this can be a sound utilitarian reason to discount, cf. Mulgan (2014), p. 337.

[266] Sinnott-Armstrong (2023, Section 1).

[267] Arguing for the latter, see Rawls (1971/1999), p. 262; Gosseries (2008b), p. 66.

justice, any rights-based account of intergenerational relations is already incompatible with utilitarian views.[268] Particularly, utilitarianism is an aggregative theory of justice rather than a distributive one.[269] This is an important distinction vis-à-vis intergenerational equity, which is primarily a distributive concept that aims at justly sharing the natural resources of the planet between generations.[270] Since utilitarian concepts of intergenerational justice do not contain distributive elements and do not address questions of interpersonal distribution, they can neither be characterised as egalitarian nor as sufficientarian approaches.[271] Their aggregative character largely disqualifies them as a fitting basis for legal concepts of intergeneration relations, so that they have had no great impact on the development of intergenerational equity.

### *3.3.2 Libertarianism*

The rejection of utilitarian concepts of intergenerational justice constitutes a point of departure for the analysis of further philosophical schools of thought since some of these have been established explicitly or implicitly in opposition to utilitarianism.[272] This is true for libertarianism, a view of political philosophy that understands individual freedom as the most important value. Libertarianism is closely related to classic liberal theory, as it prioritises individual liberties and private property over State coercion.[273] Self-ownership is the starting point of all libertarian theories, as they consider "that people have a very stringent [...] set of rights over their persons, giving them the kind of control over themselves that one might have over possessions they own."[274] The following observations focus on the (neo-)Lockean form of libertarianism, building on the works of *John Locke*.[275]

[268] Cf. Howarth (2011), p. 344. On the rights-based character of intergenerational equity, see already briefly *supra* in Sect. 3.2.2 and *infra* in Sect. 5.2.

[269] See Ashford and Mulgan (2018, Section 3).

[270] Shelton (2010a), pp. 640–641.

[271] On distributive justice as well as this distinction, see *supra* in Sect. 3.1.

[272] E.g., Alexander and Moore (2024, Section 1); Ashford and Mulgan (2018, Section 3).

[273] Van der Vossen (2023, Introduction).

[274] Ibid., Section 1 with references to Nozick (1974).

[275] See, e.g., Locke (1690).

#### 3.3.2.1 Libertarian Approaches to Intergenerational Justice

Beyond the self-ownership over internal resources,[276] libertarian perspectives of justice turn to the applicable allocation of external resources.[277] In general, libertarians consider that external resources are originally unallocated, thus, that they do not belong to anyone.[278] Therefore, acquisition of property by individuals would be possible without the consent of any prior owner or any collective of owners.[279] For libertarians, the distribution of external resources by any sort of institutionalised entity constitutes an unwanted constraint to individual liberties and private property, which they tend to reject.[280]

However, in most libertarian theories of justice, this rejection is not absolute. Rather, corrective reflections of distribution remain possible.[281] The most common restriction to free appropriation is the so-called "Lockean proviso". It is based on the understanding that "God [has] given the world to men [sic.] in common".[282] According to the Lockean proviso, initial appropriation is permissible "at least where there is enough, and as good left in common for others".[283] This limitation is based on the idea that others equally have basic rights and liberties, as libertarianism is a primarily rights-based theory of justice.[284]

It is subject to debate how to interpret the original Lockean proviso, that means how much is "enough" for others in the allocation of external resources.[285] On the one hand, weaker versions of this proviso, so-called right-libertarianism,[286] only require the observance of a sufficientarian minimum baseline. In appropriating unowned goods, it is necessary to ensure that others still have access to a "decent share", which enables them to no less than decent initial lifetime opportunities to use their internal resources,[287] or to a "minimally adequate" or "sufficient" quality of life

[276] In detail, see van der Vossen (2023, Section 1). Intergenerational issues with regard to the violation of self-ownership of future generations are left aside in the following, see also Steiner and Vallentyne (2009), p. 57.

[277] Gosseries (2008b), p. 66; Steiner and Vallentyne (2009), p. 57.

[278] Gosseries (2008b), p. 66.

[279] Van der Vossen (2023, Section 2).

[280] Ibid.

[281] For the right-wing, extreme position that denies any constraints on use or appropriation, see Narveson (1992, Chapter 7); van der Vossen (2023, Section 4 with further references).

[282] Locke (1690, paras. 24–25, 33). In 1789, *Thomas Jefferson* formulated similarly that "the earth belongs in usufruct to the living", see Howarth (2011), p. 345).

[283] Locke (1690, para. 26). See also Nozick (1974), pp. 174–182; Gosseries (2008b), pp. 66–67; Steiner and Vallentyne (2009), p. 53; van der Vossen (2023, Section 4).

[284] Howarth (2011), pp. 344–347.

[285] See Gosseries (2008b), p. 66.

[286] Van der Vossen (2023, Section 4).

[287] Underlining the ability to exercise one's rights of self-ownership: Mack (1995).

respectively.[288] On the other hand, the stronger concepts of left-libertarianism propose an egalitarian share proviso[289]: for them, the Lockean proviso requires enabling equally valuable shares for everyone.[290]

The application of a Lockean proviso to the intergenerational domain turns to the constraints, which restrict resource appropriation in order to leave "enough and as good" for future generations.[291] According to the weak version of the Lockean proviso, the present generation must be able to use and appropriate the natural resources as long as future generations are not left with less than a decent share of initial opportunities to use natural resources themselves.[292] According to an egalitarian understanding of the Lockean proviso, this is not enough. Instead, the present generation can use the existing resources only to such a degree that it leaves an equally valuable share of resources for future generations.[293] The exact content of the egalitarian version depends on whether the equally valuable shares refer to equivalence of resources between generations in total or between all individuals of all generations.[294] Further, it is unclear whether innovations can partially compensate for an excess of resources, as far as they improve the totality of resources.[295]

For instance, *Axel Gosseries* examined in detail different possible interpretations of the Lockean proviso in the context of relations between generations.[296] He concluded that the present generation should neither be held accountable for natural causes of improvement or degradation,[297] nor should the present generation be obliged to compensate for degradations caused by their predecessor generations since they could not have influenced these degradations.[298] However, the present generation would also not be allowed to reverse any improvements created by preceding generations.[299] *Gosseries* thus suggested to apply the following version of the Lockean proviso to intergenerational relations:

[288] Steiner and Vallentyne (2009), pp. 59–60; Wendt (2017). For a comparable phrasing of an "intergenerational principle of liberty", see also Ekeli (2006), pp. 405–406.

[289] This left-libertarianism could also be conceived as a form of liberal egalitarianism, see Steiner and Vallentyne (2009), p. 61 (at footnote 21)); Arneson (2013, Section 3.1).

[290] Ackerman (1980), p. 208; Otsuka (1998), p. 89; Steiner and Vallentyne (2009), p. 60; van der Vossen (2023, Section 4); Otsuka (2018).

[291] In general, see Elliot (1986); Steiner and Vallentyne (2009), pp. 58–63.

[292] See, e.g., Beckerman and Pasek (2001), p. 68. For a more detailed explanation, see Steiner and Vallentyne (2009), pp. 59–60.

[293] See ibid. p. 60.

[294] For the former, see, e.g., Gosseries (2001), pp. 310–311. For the latter, see, e.g., Arneson (1991), p. 53; Steiner and Vallentyne (2009), pp. 63–64.

[295] See Partridge (2007), p. 385; Steiner and Vallentyne (2009), p. 61.

[296] Gosseries (2001), pp. 303–311.

[297] Ibid. 306–307.

[298] Ibid. p. 309.

[299] Ibid. pp. 308–309. While *Axel Gosseries* assumed that the present generation could use its own improvements as it wishes (ibid. pp. 307–308), this does not mean that these improvements could

> [E]ach generation must leave to the next at least as much as what the next generation could have appropriated if the current generation had not contributed by its action to a net improvement or deterioration of what the following generation would otherwise have inherited.[300]

Several objections have been raised against libertarian theories of justice, but their detailed analysis goes far beyond the scope of this book.[301] One problem could be that libertarian ethics are primarily Eurocentric and that it is at least questionable whether its ideas are applicable to all political communities.[302] The main criticism addresses the individualistic perspective of libertarianism, which is said to restrict human nature to pure individual interests while ignoring the social and collective nature of human beings and societies.[303] Based on this objection, communitarian schools of philosophical thought have emerged in opposition to classical libertarian theories.[304] The meaning of these communitarian approaches for intergenerational justice is addressed in more detail below in a separate section.[305]

#### 3.3.2.2 Parallels to and Consequences for Intergenerational Equity

Despite the conclusive objections to the Eurocentric as well as individualistic focus of libertarian theories of justice, the current international legal system in general and the (human) rights-based frameworks in particular were certainly influenced by classic liberal theory.[306] Since the French Revolution, the idea that liberty consists of doing anything which does not harm others shaped liberal democracies. This means that the only boundaries for the exercise of individual rights were the boundaries that assure other members of society the fruition of these same rights.[307] Based on this rights-based understanding of justice, libertarian justice theories start with a non-distributive perspective, in which all initial external resources can be allocated to individuals by their actions. However, additional distributive elements restrict the individual liberal appropriation and use of these resources.

---

not be used to compensate for proper degradations of the present generation, see Steiner and Vallentyne (2009), p. 61

[300] Gosseries (2008b), pp. 66–67. See also Gosseries (2001), pp. 308–309; Steiner and Vallentyne (2009), p. 63.

[301] See, e.g., Gaus et al. (2022, Section 3.4).

[302] See ibid., Section 4.1 with further references. For instance, *John Rawls* denied such a universalistic understanding of liberal theories, see Rawls (1999), p. 66. In contrast, *Martha Nussbaum* advocated for a version of moral universalism in regard to liberalism and human rights, see Nussbaum (2002). More specifically, see *infra* in Sect. 3.3.4.1 and in Sect. 5.2.1.

[303] Ritchie (1891), p. 13.

[304] Gutmann (1985); Gaus et al. (2022, Section 3.4).

[305] See *infra* in Section 3.3.4.

[306] See Theilen (2021), p. 833.

[307] *Déclaration des Droits de l'Homme et du Citoyen* (DDHC), entered into force 26 August 1789.

Thereby, libertarianism in its distributive sense fits much better into environmental justice theories than aggregative utilitarianism.[308] This distributive version of libertarian theories is also mirrored in the legal concept of intergenerational equity, as can be illustrated with regard to the phrasing in the Brundtland Report.[309] While the first part of the wording—"[to meet] the needs of the present"—amounts to the libertarian focus on individual self-ownership and basic liberties, the second part—"-without compromising the ability of future generations to meet their own needs"—can be seen as a perfect Lockean limitation of these liberties.[310]

The degree of the distributive restrictions further depends on whether weak or strong Lockean provisos are applied. While weak provisos only require a minimum guarantee for a sufficient quality of life, stronger provisos aim at an equal distribution of resources.[311] The approach reflected in the Brundtland report is sufficientarian rather than egalitarian.[312] It does not envisage to establish equality between all human beings but focuses on the guarantee of a minimum safeguard to future generations for the enjoyment of their basic needs.[313] As *Herman Daly* put it in relation to the achievement of basic needs: "the basic needs of the present should always take precedence over the basic needs of the future but the basic needs of the future should take precedence over the extravagant luxury of the present".[314] This purely sufficientarian approach to intergenerational justice has been criticised from egalitarian perspectives for being unjust since it neglects any improvements of life conditions beyond said minimum basic needs.[315]

Turning to *Edith Brown Weiss'* doctrine of intergenerational equity, it is not primarily influenced by libertarian theories. Instead, the following two sections illustrate her inspiration from social contract theories as well as communitarianism.[316] Nonetheless, there are certain parallels between her doctrine and libertarian concepts of justice. First, *Brown Weiss'* notion of a planetary trust[317] resembles *John Locke's* as well as *Thomas Jefferson's* understanding that the planetary resources do not simply belong to the present generation alone but that they constitute a form of

---

308 Howarth (2011), p. 348.

309 World Commission on Environment and Development (1987).

310 Birnbacher (2006), p. 33.

311 See van der Vossen (2023, Section 4) as well as *supra* notes 285–290.

312 Birnbacher (2006), p. 33; Gosseries (2008b), pp. 68–69. Regarding the UNFCCC, cf. also Howarth (2011), p. 346. With regard to the SDGs, *Rita Vasconcellos Oliveira* assessed that they are mainly based on egalitarian and prioritarian principles of distributive justice, see Vasconcellos Oliveira (2018), p. 433.

313 Gosseries (2008b), p. 69.

314 Daly (1996), p. 36.

315 Gosseries (2005).

316 See *infra* in Sects. 3.3.3.2 and 3.3.4.2.

317 Brown Weiss (1989), p. 17., according to which the human species holds "the natural and cultural environment of our planet in common, both with other members of the present generation and with other generations, past and future".

usufruct rights.[318] This parallel illustrates that there can be certain overlaps between a trust-based concept and a rights-based approach of intergenerational equity.[319] Second, *Brown Weiss'* intergenerational duty "to pass on the natural and cultural resources of the planet in no worse condition than received"[320] can also be found in *Axel Gosseries'* proposition of an intergenerational Lockean proviso.[321] However, *Brown Weiss* considered that "all generations are entitled to at least the minimum level that the first generation in time had",[322] while *Gosseries* explicitly rejected such a reading of the Lockean proviso.[323]

It is even more difficult to attribute *Brown Weiss'* doctrine to either sufficientarian or egalitarian Lockean provisos. Her theory contains some egalitarian aspects, such as the duty to grant equitable access to all generations.[324] This "minimum equality among generations"[325] refers, however, only to a just distribution between generations rather than individuals.[326] Further, most passages of her doctrine point to a sufficientarian understanding of intergenerational distribution. For instance, the conservation of equitable access only requires "at least a minimum level of access to the common patrimony" to all members of present and future generations.[327] This reflects a sufficientarian understanding of distributive justice between generations.[328]

These tentative comparisons between intergenerational equity and libertarian theories illustrate that the general conception of intergenerational equity, as enshrined in the Brundtland Report, has certainly been influenced by classic liberal theory in the form of a sufficientarian understanding of the Lockean proviso. At the same time, the more specific doctrine of intergenerational equity cannot be easily identified within a libertarian framework of justice. It was at least not directly inspired by libertarian philosophy but rather by a mixture of social contract theories and communitarianism, as demonstrated in the following two sections.

---

[318] See Howarth (2011), p. 345. In more detail on the concept of usufructuary rights, see Wolf (1995), pp. 814–818.

[319] Howarth (2011), pp. 345–346. However, for the communitarian elements of this understanding, see *infra* in Sect. 3.3.4.2.

[320] Brown Weiss (1989), pp. 37–38.

[321] Gosseries (2001), pp. 308–309. See also *supra* note 300.

[322] Brown Weiss (1989), p. 25.

[323] Gosseries (2008b), pp. 66–67. Insofar, *Brown Weiss'* conception rather resembles *Gosseries'* first or second (rejected) interpretations of the intergenerational Lockean proviso, see Gosseries (2001), pp. 305, 307.

[324] Brown Weiss (1989), pp. 43–45.

[325] Ibid. p. 25.

[326] In contrast to this, see Steiner and Vallentyne (2009), pp. 63–64.

[327] Brown Weiss (1989), pp. 38, 43–45.

[328] *Richard Howarth* is referring to a "safe minimum standard": Howarth (2011), p. 346.

### 3.3.3 Social Contract Theories

Social contract theories are related to liberal political theories, as they assume that liberal individuals are best capable of deciding in a free state of mind about the best rules of life.[329] Beyond this, contract theories take a different approach to intergenerational justice than the aforementioned libertarian theories. All contract theories have in common that they derive the normative force of moral norms from the idea of a contract or mutual agreement.[330] Different models of a just society can arise from this mutual agreement.[331]

Among social contract theories, "contractarianism" and "contractualism" differ in what they consider to be the driving factor behind mutual agreement of individuals.[332] While contractarianism considers that self-interest and its maximisation are the primary driving factors for human behaviour,[333] contractualism is based on rationality instead of mere self-interest, which would require our respect towards other beings with an equal moral status.[334] Due to this variety of social contract theories, the present work focuses solely on *John Rawls'* contractualist approach to justice and intergenerational justice, since he is without doubt the most influential social contract theorist,[335] who systematically analysed intergenerational obligations in the context of a justice theory.[336] He first developed his justice theory in his work 'A Theory of Justice' from 1971,[337] which was later revised.[338]

---

[329] Gaus et al. (2022, Section 1.1).

[330] Cudd and Eftekhari (2021, Introduction); Friend (n.d.).

[331] The exact theory of justice resulting from this mutual agreement depends on the respective approach taken. As not all approaches result in libertarian concepts of justice, this is one decisive difference between classic liberal theory in general and certain social contract theories, see Solum (2001), p. 202; Cudd and Eftekhari (2021, Section 1). For a libertarian critique of Rawls, see, e.g., Nozick (1974).

[332] Ashford and Mulgan (2018, Section 2); Cudd and Eftekhari (2021, Introduction).

[333] The political theory of *Thomas Hobbes* is the origin of contractarianism: Hobbes (1651/1651). See also Hampton (1986). For more recent representatives of contractarianism, see Gauthier (1986); Narveson (1992).

[334] Contractualism is based on the ethics of *Immanuel Kant*, as it contains elements of his discussions on the Categorical Imperative, see Kant (1785). See also Ashford and Mulgan (2018, Section 2). For more recent representatives of contractualism: Rousseau (1762/1968); Rawls (1980); Scanlon (1998).

[335] Ashford and Mulgan (2018, Section 2). For another recent approach to intergenerational justice, see Gauthier (1986), pp. 298–305.

[336] Meyer (2021, Introduction, Section 4.5).

[337] Rawls (1971).

[338] Rawls (1971/1999). The following references primarily refer to this revised edition.

#### 3.3.3.1 *John Rawls'* Theory of Intergenerational Justice

For *Rawls*, principles of justice can only result from consensual decisions of free and equal human beings. Since individuals are mainly driven by their rationality, they know that respect of every free and equal being is a crucial condition for their proper self-interest, which requires them to justify the standards of their morality.[339] In order to arrive at such a mutual consent on the rules of justice, *Rawls* established the idea of a hypothetical contract situation of all deciding parties, which he called the original position.[340] While other social contract theorists sometimes built their theories on comparable initial situations under different nominations,[341] *Rawls'* original position remained hypothetical and a nonhistorical thought experiment, which constituted the basis of his theory of justice.[342] In this original position, there are no unfair bargaining advantages or any threats of force, coercion, deception or fraud.[343] Therefore, an agreement on the principles of justice can be reached under fair conditions for everyone, which is why *Rawls'* understanding of justice is one of "justice as fairness".[344] He envisaged that only free and equal negotiations under fair circumstances could lead to the establishment of rational rules of justice.[345]

However, to achieve equal and fair conditions, it is necessary to place all hypothetically negotiating parties behind a "veil of ignorance".[346] Behind this veil of ignorance, the negotiating parties lack knowledge of certain information on their particular situation, such as information on gender, race, talents or disabilities, age, social status or the specific political system and structure of the society they are living in.[347] Instead, the parties are only aware of general facts and of common sense about human social life as well as general conclusions of science that are uncontroversial; they know that all citizens have an interest in more primary goods and that the society is under conditions of moderate scarcity.[348]

For *Rawls*, two main principles would emerge as result from this hypothetical original position, the two principles of justice.[349] First, "each person is to have an

[339] Cudd and Eftekhari (2021, Introduction).

[340] Rawls (1971/1999), pp. 15–19.

[341] Cudd and Eftekhari (2021, Section 1); Wenar (2021, Section 4.6). See, e.g., Gauthier (1986), pp. 14–16, 131–134.

[342] Rawls and Kelly (2001), pp. 16–17. See also Partridge (2007), pp. 381–382; Solum (2001), p. 206.

[343] Rawls and Kelly (2001), p. 15.

[344] Wenar (2021, Section 4.6). In this sense, *Rawls'* theory follows a typical Kantian ethics approach, see Ashford and Mulgan (2018, Section 2).

[345] Wenar (2021, Section 4.6).

[346] Rawls (1971/1999), pp. 118–123.

[347] Ibid. pp. 118–119; Wenar (2021, Section 4.6).

[348] Rawls and Kelly (2001), pp. 86–88. Moderate scarcity is understood in the sense that "there is enough to go around, but not enough for everyone to get what they want", see Wenar (2021, Section 4.6).

[349] Rawls (1971/1999), p. 52.

equal right to the most extensive scheme of equal basic liberties compatible with a similar scheme of liberties for others."[350] Second:

> Social and economic inequalities are to satisfy two conditions: [...] they are to be attached to offices and positions open to all under conditions of fair equality of opportunity; and [...] they are to be to the greatest benefit of the least advantaged members of society (the difference principle).[351]

The first principle addresses a constitutional basis of basic rights and liberties and has priority over the second.[352] It illustrates that *Rawls* was also a liberal philosopher.[353] The second principle is one of distributive justice, which addresses the fair distribution of resources and opportunities among human beings.[354] In order to achieve fair distribution, the first part of the second principle only allows for social inequalities if they are attached to positions open to all under fair equality of opportunity.[355] This equality of opportunity is not limited to formal equality, but requires that all persons "should have a fair chance" to actually attain these positions.[356] If the first principle and this principle of fair equality of opportunity are satisfied,[357] the second part of the second principle, the so-called difference principle, becomes relevant.[358] It addresses the distributive equality of income and wealth in a just society, as it requires that any social inequality must always be "to the greatest benefit of the least-advantaged members of society".[359]

Originally, *Rawls'* principles of justice were primarily construed to cover justice in an *intra*-generational context.[360] However, the difference principle does not only require considering the social minimum of the worst off in the *present* generation but also to consider the "long-term prospects of the least favoured extending over generations".[361] This leads to *Rawls'* "just savings principle", which requires each generation to "put aside in each period of time a suitable amount of real capital accumulation".[362] The savings rate also aims at acquiring a fair distribution over generations.[363] In contrast to utilitarian concepts of justice,[364] the determination of

[350] Ibid. p. 53.

[351] Rawls and Kelly (2001), pp. 42–43. Cf. also Rawls (1971/1999), p. 53.

[352] Rawls and Kelly (2001), pp. 44–47.

[353] On the relationship between libertarian and social contract theories, see *supra* note 329.

[354] Wenar (2021, Section 4.3).

[355] Rawls and Kelly (2001), pp. 42–43.

[356] Ibid. pp. 43–44.

[357] Ibid. pp. 61–63.

[358] See for an example Wenar (2021, Section 4.3).

[359] Rawls and Kelly (2001), pp. 42–43.

[360] Gardiner (2009), pp. 114–116; Heyd (2009b), pp. 169–170.

[361] Rawls (1971/1999), p. 252.

[362] Ibid. On *Brown Weiss'* extension of this principle to natural resources, see *infra* note 417.

[363] Ibid. pp. 252–253; Rawls and Kelly (2001), pp. 159–160.

[364] These are based on the maximisation of wealth of all human beings across time, see Rawls (1971/1999), pp. 19, 228, 257; Heyd (2009b), p. 171. See also *supra* in Sect. 3.3.1.

the specific rate of just savings must again be the outcome of hypothetical negotiations of all parts of society in fair and equal conditions.[365]

At this point, *Rawls'* theory of justice must be slightly adapted to the intergenerational context.[366] Despite the inherent difficulties of some social contract theories in dealing with intergenerational problems,[367] *Rawls* chose to do so by adjusting his circumstances of justice.[368] To understand Rawls' contract theory in regard to intergenerational justice, it is important that his hypothetical original position was "not to be thought of as a general assembly which includes at one moment everyone who will live at some time; or, much less, as an assembly of everyone who could live at some time. It is not a gathering of all actual or possible persons."[369] Instead, the original position is based on the present time of entry interpretation, which means that it can hypothetically be entered at any time but only includes persons who are contemporaries in a specific generation.[370] Therefore, every representative in the original position lacks knowledge of her own generation and has to choose for all generations yet to come.[371] However, one could object that the representatives in this original position may not have any rational reason to care for savings for the future at all. Since they are part of the same temporal generation, they know that "earlier generations will have either saved or not [and that] there is nothing the parties can do to affect that."[372]

For this reason, the original position does not offer a suitable starting point for the consideration of intergenerational problems. Instead, *Rawls* decided to add two other constraints to the original position[373]: First, he introduced a Kantian approach to universal justice[374] by stipulating that the representatives in the original position must decide on the just savings rate "on the assumption that all other generations have saved, or will save, in accordance with the same criterion".[375] Thereby, they can reach hypothetical agreement on a principle, which "the members of any generation [...] would adopt as the principle they would want preceding generations

---

[365] Rawls and Kelly (2001), pp. 80–134.

[366] Rawls (1971/1999), pp. 251–262.

[367] Heyd (2009b), pp. 169–170. In general on these difficulties, see Gardiner (2009), pp. 97–114; Ashford and Mulgan (2018, Section 13). *Lawrence Solum* argued that *Rawls'* theory avoids these difficulties, see Solum (2001), pp. 207–208.

[368] On other possibilities of adjustment, see Heyd (2009b), pp. 169–170.

[369] Rawls (1971/1999), p. 120; Rawls and Kelly (2001), p. 86.

[370] Rawls (1971/1999), p. 121; Rawls and Kelly (2001), p. 86. In more detail, cf. Heyd (2009b), pp. 172–174.

[371] Rawls (1971/1999), p. 121. See also Rawls and Kelly (2001), p. 160.

[372] Rawls (1971/1999), pp. 254–255. See also Redgwell (1999), pp. 104–105; Heyd (2009b), p. 174.

[373] *Rawls* added these additional assumptions in his later works. This distinguishes them from his original account on intergenerational justice in Rawls (1971).

[374] See Wallack (2006), pp. 90–91.

[375] Rawls (1971/1999), p. 255.

to have followed".[376] Second, *Rawls* added a motivational assumption to the individuals in the original position, namely, that they are not only interested in their proper self-interest, but that they are naturally motivated by the well-being of their direct progeny.[377] Thereby, Rawls understood that the contractors in the original position are also in the role of "head[s] of a family" who are driven by their concern for immediate future generations.[378]

Limited by these two additional assumptions, the representatives in the hypothetical original position would decide that the principles of justice must contribute to a just distribution of resources between all ever existing generations; any generation would have to decide the fairest solution for all.[379] Since it would not satisfy the fair conditions of negotiation to discount people's value on merely temporal grounds,[380] the just savings principle would be the result of fair negotiations in the original position.[381] It complements the difference principle and consists of two phases.[382] The first phase is a phase of accumulation, in which a just savings rate is established until a position with just institutions is achieved. As soon as this is reached, the steady state phase begins, in which savings are no longer required to guarantee a fair distribution as long as the minimum standard of justice is safeguarded.[383]

It is not easy to attribute *Rawls'* theory of justice to a purely egalitarian or purely sufficientarian understanding. Some commentators considered *Rawls* to be a typical egalitarian, as many of his philosophical reflections relied on a focus of equality between human beings.[384] This can already be seen in the introduction to his two principles of justice:

> All social values – liberty and opportunity, income and wealth, and the bases of self-respect – are to be distributed equally unless an unequal distribution of any, or all, of these values is to everyone's advantage. Injustice, then, is simply inequalities that are not to the benefit of all.[385]

---

[376] Rawls and Kelly (2001), p. 160; Rawls (1993/2005), p. 274. With this adaptation, *Rawls* agreed to earlier arguments of *Derek Parfit* and *Thomas Nagel*, see Rawls and Kelly (2001), p. 160 (at footnote 39). Cf. also English (1977), p. 98. In more detail, see *infra* notes 402–411.

[377] Rawls (1971/1999), pp. 121, 255. For a critical rejection of this assumption, see Tremmel (2013), pp. 485–486.

[378] Heyd (2009b), pp. 174–175 However, this motivational assumption has been partly revoked by *Rawls* in a later work, and he rather focused on the first assumption that the contracting parties "would want preceding generations to have followed (and later generations to follow) [the reached principles], [...]", see Rawls (1993/2005), p. 274.

[379] Rawls (1971/1999), p. 255.

[380] Tremmel (2013), pp. 484–485.

[381] Rawls (1971/1999), pp. 259–262.

[382] *Joerg Tremmel* understood the just savings principle rather as a limitation of the difference principle: Tremmel (2013), p. 484.

[383] Rawls (1971/1999), p. 255. See also Gosseries (2001), p. 317; Wenar (2021, Section 4.9); Meyer (2021, Section 4.5).

[384] Gosseries (2001), p. 311); Gosseries (2008b), pp. 67–68; Arneson (2013, Sections 3.5, 5); Hadjiargyrou (2016), pp. 258–260.

[385] Rawls (1971/1999), p. 54.

The first principle of justice requires equal basic liberties for everyone, the second demands fair equality of opportunity.[386] In this sense, *Rawls'* theory of justice could be seen as egalitarian.[387] However, his perspective on human equality did not necessarily aim at an equal distribution of resources as is typical for egalitarian views. Instead, according to *Rawls*, social inequalities can be justified if they are to the benefit of everyone, particularly the least well off.[388] His understanding of distribution did not entail a reduction of the wealth of the best off towards the worst off in a way that would lead to an equal level of wealth or income.[389] Therefore, his theory cannot be considered purely egalitarian in terms of distributive justice. It rather aims at procedural equality. In many regards, *Rawls'* approach leans on sufficientarian ideas of distribution, e.g., regarding the minimum requirement of just institutions.[390] Further, the just savings principle aims at finding a just social minimum of savings for future generations, realised by the two phases of accumulation and steady state.[391] Consequently, in distributive terms, *Rawls'* social contract theory remains largely sufficientarian when it comes to intergenerational justice.[392]

Although *John Rawls* is one of the most influential social contract theorists,[393] many commentators have criticised various aspects of his theory.[394] To begin with, some commentators have generally criticised the inadequacy of social contract theories in an intergenerational context due to the lack of reciprocity between present and future generations.[395] For instance, *Peter Lawrence* stated:

> Theories of justice resting on a contractual or reciprocal basis [...] cannot establish a basis of an obligation towards future generations based on justice [because] these theories involve direct reciprocity in the sense that justice requires the possibility of a mutual exchange of advantages.[396]

*Brian Barry* similarly concluded that intergenerational justice "is not a matter of justice between generations. (Other generations are not, after all, parties to the agreement.) It is, rather, a matter of justice *with respect to* future generations" (emphasis in the original).[397]

---

386 Rawls and Kelly (2001), pp. 42–43.

387 *Thomas Scanlon* is considered to be an egalitarian social contractualist, see Scanlon (2005).

388 Rawls (1971/1999), pp. 70–72.

389 Ibid. p. 252. See also Gosseries (2001), pp. 314–315.

390 Rawls (1971/1999), pp. 244–251.

391 Ibid. pp. 251–252.

392 See also Wallack (2006), p. 94; Meyer (2009), p. 281; Birnbacher (2006), p. 34.

393 Ashford and Mulgan (2018, Section 2).

394 See, e.g., Barry (1989), pp. 179–202; Dierksmeier (2006); Wallack (2006); Attas (2009); Gardiner (2009); Heyd (2009b), pp. 170–177; Gardiner (2011); Tremmel (2013), pp. 485–487.

395 Narveson (1978), p. 38; Solum (2001), pp. 203–205; Lawrence (2014), p. 48; Hadjiargyrou (2016), pp. 260–262. See already *supra* note 206. Cf. also Cudd and Eftekhari (2021, Section 6).

396 Lawrence (2014), pp. 48–49.

397 Barry (1989), p. 192.

However, the issue of reciprocity is no absolute obstacle for theories of intergenerational justice, as has been demonstrated above in regard to alternative models of indirect reciprocity.[398] Furthermore, *Rawls'* contractualist approach avoids typical difficulties of other social contract theories, as his theory of justice emanates from the hypothetical conditions of the original position, which is not based on a strict understanding of actual reciprocity.[399] This is particularly the case with regard to the added motivational assumption "that all other generations have saved, or will save, in accordance with the same criterion".[400] Consequently, the lack of reciprocity is no sufficient reason to discard *Rawls'* contractualist theory of justice vis-à-vis future generations.[401]

Notwithstanding this, some commentators have criticised *Rawls* exactly for this additional motivational assumption, which deviated from his original circumstances of justice.[402] Changing from the idea of self-interested and rational human beings in the original position to adding his motivational assumption, *Rawls* would get back to ideal theory,[403] in contradiction to his primarily non-metaphysical philosophy.[404] As *Michael Wallack* put it: "[…] if people could be assumed to be Kantian as well as rational and reasonable there would be no need for 'A Theory of Justice' as a guide to deliberation."[405]

The introduction of a motivational assumption by *Rawls* became only necessary due to the present time of entry interpretation of the original position.[406] In the alternative interpretation, an assembly of all generations, there would be no need for an additional assumption, because the representatives behind the veil or ignorance could actually belong to successive generations.[407] *Rawls* only rejected the idea of a "general assembly" between members of all generations, past, present and future, because this would "stretch fantasy too far; the conception would cease to be a natural guide to intuition".[408] This argument seems at least debatable with some commentators arguing in favour of the general assembly interpretation, which

[398] See already *supra* in Sect. 3.2.3. Cf. also Tritschoks (2018), pp. 454–458.

[399] Solum (2001), pp. 205–208. See also Redgwell (1999), pp. 106–107.

[400] Rawls (1971/1999), p. 255.

[401] As already demonstrated *supra* in Sect. 3.2.1, particularly note 118, the non-identity problem can equally be solved within *Rawls'* social contract theory; see Reiman (2007), p. 89. Cf. also Ashford and Mulgan (2018, Section 13).

[402] Tremmel (2013), pp. 485–486; Heyd (2009b), pp. 170–176.

[403] Gosseries (2001), p. 312. Cf. also Ekardt (2021), pp. 287–288.

[404] Dierksmeier (2006), pp. 78–80; Wallack (2006), pp. 90–93; Tremmel (2013), p. 487.

[405] Wallack (2006), p. 93.

[406] Rawls (1971/1999), p. 121. See also *supra* notes 369–372.

[407] Cf. Solum (2001), p. 204.

[408] Rawls (1971), p. 139.

hypothetically brings together representatives of *all* generations.[409] According to *Joerg Tremmel*:

> Whether a thought experiment is 'far-fetched' or 'very far-fetched' is irrelevant, as long as it is a guideline for deriving principles of justice. This guideline is that rational and self-interested actors have to be in a situation that does not allow an individual to translate his bargaining power into personal advantage.[410]

Consequently, *Joerg Tremmel* based his theory of intergenerational justice on an original position in the form of a hypothetical gathering of "representatives of all past, present, and future generations [who] do not know which generation they belong to and will later live as".[411]

Despite the criticism and remaining challenges of *Rawls'* motivational assumptions, his version of a social contract theory can still be considered an adequate basis of intergenerational justice. All in all, his philosophical approach to justice, including intergenerational justice, remains one of the most referenced works in intergenerational ethics. This is also mirrored in the impact it had on the legal concept of intergenerational equity, as illustrated in the following section.

#### 3.3.3.2 Parallels to and Consequences for Intergenerational Equity

There is no doubt that *Edith Brown Weiss'* doctrine was mainly influenced by *John Rawls'* philosophical works on intergenerational justice.[412] Her works referred to *Rawls'* idea of the original position and the veil of ignorance at several instances.[413] Building on this original position, she elaborated:

> [It] is appropriate to assume the perspective of a generation that is placed somewhere along the spectrum of time, but does not know in advance where it will be located. Such a generation would want to inherit the common patrimony of the planet in as good condition as it has been for any previous generation and to have as good access to it as previous generations.[414]

---

[409] Tremmel (2013), p. 487; Gardiner (2009), pp. 114–116. *Axel Gosseries* was also critical and questioned whether "it [would] really stretch fantasy much further [...] than considering people as members of the same—but possibly remotely future-generation"; he concluded that "[w]e should probably not attach too much importance then to this 'present time of entry' assumption", see Gosseries (2001), p. 312.

[410] Tremmel (2013), p. 487.

[411] Ibid., 485, 487–497.

[412] For some analysis, see Redgwell (1999), pp. 100–105; Collins (2007), pp. 94–95; Fitzmaurice (2012), pp. 107–109; Hadjiargyrou (2016), p. 261.

[413] See, e.g., Brown Weiss (1984), p. 532; Brown Weiss (1989), p. 24; Brown Weiss (1992), pp. 73–74.

[414] Brown Weiss (1989), p. 24.

Consequently, she assumed that her principles of intergenerational equity would equally result from considerations in a just and fair setting of the original position.[415] While *Rawls* focused on a national context and did not explicitly refer to natural resources as part of the material capital,[416] *Brown Weiss* extended his just savings principle to the environmental context of natural resources and applied it to the global level.[417] Her conclusion is that each generation should leave to the succeeding generation a planet in at least as good a condition as that generation received it.[418] Further, *Brown Weiss* deduced from the thought experiment the three intergenerational duties of conservation: to conserve the diversity of the natural and cultural resources base (conservation of options), to maintain a certain quality of the Earth (conservation of quality), and to grant a minimum and non-discriminatory access to the common patrimony to all members of present and future generations (conservation of equitable access).[419]

*Brown Weiss'* doctrine thereby primarily resembles the second phase in *Rawls'* just savings principle, the steady state phase,[420] in which each generation must leave to the next at least the equivalent of what it has received.[421] As illustrated, both of *Rawls'* just savings phases aim at a just social minimum of savings for future generations,[422] meaning they are mainly sufficientarian.[423] In this regard, *Brown Weiss'* doctrine, which includes egalitarian and sufficientarian aspects,[424] also fits the general idea behind *Rawls'* principles of justice.

Beyond these obvious influences, there is another less apparent parallel between *Rawls'* just savings principle and certain legal concepts of intergenerational equity. In the accumulation phase, the present generation is required to save enough capital to maintain effective and just institutions.[425] These just institutions are a prerequisite to guaranteeing the minimum safeguards of equal basic liberties. Institutions also play a decisive role in the legal perspective on intergenerational equity. The general conception of intergenerational equity has not envisaged a specific institutional framework for the implementation of intergenerational equity so far,[426] whereas *Brown Weiss'* doctrine is in favour of an institutionalised representation of future

---

[415] UNSG (2013, para. 24); Redgwell (1999), p. 108.

[416] Brown Weiss (1984), p. 532 (at footnote 178); Partridge (2007), p. 382.

[417] UNSG (2013, para. 24); Partridge (2007), p. 382. *Zena Hadjiagyrou* criticised this extension to the intergenerational context: Hadjiargyrou (2016), pp. 261–262.

[418] Brown Weiss (1989), pp. 37–38. See also UNSG (2013, para. 24).

[419] Brown Weiss (1989), pp. 38, 40–45. In more detail, see *supra* in Sect. 2.2.1.4.

[420] Cf. UNSG (2013, para. 24).

[421] Gosseries (2001), p. 317. See *supra* note 383.

[422] Rawls (1971/1999), pp. 251–252.

[423] See *supra* notes 390–392 as well as on the partly egalitarian aspects, see *supra* notes 384–386.

[424] See *supra* notes 324–328.

[425] Rawls (1971/1999), pp. 256–258. See also UNSG (2013, para. 24).

[426] On the distinction between the two manifestations of intergenerational equity, see *supra* in Sect. 2.3.1.2.

generations' interests.[427] Although *Rawls* did not discuss this question in his works at all, one could argue that his just savings principle and the requirement to establish and maintain just institutions would also be in favour of some form of institutionalised representation of future generations. This aspect of intergenerational equity is discussed in more detail below in the context of the open issues of intergenerational equity.[428]

Eventually, *Rawls'* understanding of the original position allows for another consequence in the subsequent legal analysis. While his contractualist approach is based on the idea of a contract between all representatives in the original position, it must be recalled that this is *not* considered an actual contract between generations in a legal sense.[429] *Lawrence Solum* fittingly explained:

> Unborn future generations cannot agree to a social contract with current and past generations, either explicitly or tacitly. Time travel is science fiction, and the impossibility of contracting with distant generations is a fact of nature.[430]

Therefore, *Rawls'* social generational contract emanates from a hypothetical thought experiment, which aims at establishing fair conditions for the hypothetical negotiation of principles of justice, including intergenerational justice.[431] This aspect of "justice as fairness"[432] can serve as a helpful mechanism in order to evaluate the methodological assessment of the legal concept of intergenerational equity. The present book focuses on the question of the intertemporally applicable law for the legal assessment of intergenerational equity in Part 2 below. In this context, the intertemporal relationship between present and future generations is an important aspect for the establishment of the inherently intertemporal nature of intergenerational equity.[433] The perspective from *Rawls'* original position behind a veil of ignorance can then serve as a decisive argument for the proposed intertemporal assessment of the concept. For this reason, the distinction between *Rawls'* present time of entry interpretation of the original position[434] and the alternative idea of a "general assembly" between all generations[435] becomes relevant

---

427 Brown Weiss (1989), pp. 120–126. See also Brown Weiss (2021, paras. 49–51).

428 See *infra* in Sect. 5.3.

429 It might be an interesting approach to further develop this idea of a (quasi-legal) "contract between generations" to some kind of new source of international law, beyond the regime of international treaties under Article 38(1)(a) of the ICJ Statute. However, the present book resists this innovative idea and focuses on a traditional positivist analysis of intergenerational equity based on the existing sources of international law, see *infra* in Sect. 4.2.

430 Solum (2001), p. 203. *Lawrence Solum* further elaborated in more detail on the difficulties of social contract theories due to this factual impossibility of intergenerational negotiations, see ibid. pp. 203–205.

431 Rawls and Kelly (2001), pp. 16–17.

432 See Wenar (2021, Section 4.6).

433 See *infra* in Sects. 7.2.2.2 and 7.3.3.3.

434 Rawls (1971/1999), pp. 120–121; Rawls and Kelly (2001), p. 86. In more detail, see *supra* notes 369–370.

435 Tremmel (2013), pp. 485, 487–497. In more detail, see *supra* notes 406–411.

again in Chap. 7. Despite its hypothetical character, the idea of a social contract between all generations certainly merits a second look and constitutes at least an initial starting point.

Overall, it is clear that *Rawls'* theory of justice has influenced the legal concept of intergenerational equity, particularly in the form of *Brown Weiss'* doctrine. But the latter did not exclusively rely on social contract theory. As *Catherine Redgwell* correctly pointed out: "unlike *Rawls*, *[Brown Weiss]* views the human community as a partnership among generations, with the purpose of human society 'to realize and protect the welfare and well-being of every generation'".[436] While *Rawls'* original position has served as a starting point for her principles of justice, her doctrine further contained elements of a planetary trust. As demonstrated in the following section, this idea was also inspired by communitarian concepts of justice.

## 3.3.4 Communitarianism

Communitarian concepts of justice developed as a direct response to and criticism of liberal theories of justice.[437] Instead of focusing on the individual as the only entity of considerations of justice,[438] they considered individuals to be embedded in a community with its own moral feelings about the individuals' position in this community.[439] Consequently, not the mere self-interest of every individual becomes the driving factor of justice, but the inherent social obligations derived from one's affiliation to a certain community.[440] Such communities are tied to each other by interaction as well as sentiments and emotions, often by historical relations, but also by cultural interaction and moral similarities.[441] They can constitute a family, a village, an academic community, a religion as well as a nation.[442]

### 3.3.4.1 Communitarian Approaches to Intergenerational Relations

Communitarian concepts of justice can be distinguished in categories of strong or weak communitarianism.[443] Strong communitarianism is based on the primacy of the community and denies the value of individualism; thus, it stands in strong

[436] Redgwell (1999), p. 75.

[437] J. Thompson (2009a), pp. 27–28; Daniel Bell (2024).

[438] J. Thompson (2009a), p. 26.

[439] Ibid. p. 28.

[440] De-Shalit (1995), pp. 14–15.

[441] Ibid., 16–17, 21–31.

[442] See, e.g., ibid., 65 (at footnote 5).

[443] J. Thompson (2009a), pp. 29–33.

opposition to liberal theories of justice.[444] In contrast, weak communitarianism is not necessarily irreconcilable with liberal ideas of justice. Rather, it combines community values with liberal ideas about individual rights.[445] There could even be overlaps between weak communitarian approaches and certain contractualist approaches to justice, insofar as the latter stress the rational respect of every individual towards other beings with an equal moral status.[446] While stronger versions of communitarianism have provoked considerable criticism,[447] forms of weak communitarianism were invoked to attenuate the libertarian exclusive focus on individual liberty by establishing a theory of intergenerational justice that is based on community interests.

From a communitarian perspective, individuals always derive their proper self also from a community identity.[448] Intergenerational communitarians, such as *Avner De-Shalit*, tried to extend the communitarian approach to the idea of a "transgenerational community".[449] First notions of such an intergenerational community can already be found in *Edmund Burke's* understanding of intergenerational relations as "a partnership not only between those who are living but between those who are living, those who are dead, and those who are to be born".[450] Further, some of the religious and cultural origins of intergenerational justice relied on the communitarian idea that humanity holds the world in common to pass it on to each generation.[451]

Although the relationship between the present generation and future generations lacks some of the typical elements of a "community",[452] *Avner De-Shalit* has tried to overcome this lack of interaction by referring to existing cultural interaction, moral similarity and the role of reflection between generations.[453] For *Janna Thompson*, the core driving factor for individuals in a transgenerational community was the existence of "lifetime-transcending interests".[454] This means that most individuals have a certain concern for events or objects that existed before their lifetime or that will exist in the future after their lifetime.[455] These lifetime-transcending interests

[444] Ibid. p. 29.

[445] Ibid.

[446] On this characteristic of contractualist theories, see Ashford and Mulgan (2018, Section 2). See also *supra* note 334.

[447] See, e.g., Buchanan (1989).

[448] J. Thompson (2009a), p. 30.

[449] De-Shalit (1995), pp. 13–50.

[450] Burke (1790/1986), p. 110.

[451] For further references to Christian, Islamic and African customary traditions, see, e.g., UNSG (2013, para. 12); Brown Weiss (1989), pp. 18–21 with reference to Obeng (1980).

[452] This is why some authors denied the existence of transgenerational obligations: De-Shalit (1995), pp. 17–21 (with further references); Golding (1981).

[453] De-Shalit (1995), pp. 21–50.

[454] J. Thompson (2009a), pp. 33–38; Thompson (2009b), pp. 39–54.

[455] J. Thompson (2009a), p. 34.

result in the existence of a transgenerational community between past, present and future generations over time.[456] *Gary Supanich* had a similar idea, which he framed as an "extended human community across time".[457] Similarly, *Emmanuel Agius* construed a relational theory of intergenerational justice, which started with a critique of individualist (liberal) theories of justice and focused on the relational character of human beings.[458] These human relations "extend not only over space but also across time" and, thus, result in an intergenerational community.[459]

Communitarian theories address issues of distributive justice between generations; yet, they cannot easily be attributed to either egalitarian or sufficientarian approaches, since their proponents rarely elaborated on the exact manner of distribution. *De-Shalit's* and *Thompson's* understanding of obligations in a transgenerational community manifested certain sufficientarian ideas. *Thompson* concluded that there is a duty to ensure that future generations "have sufficient means; at least they cannot be miserable, poor or preoccupied by problems of survival".[460] While *De-Shalit's* wording was not as clear, his theory differentiated between the rather egalitarian distribution of goods between adjacent generations and the merely sufficientarian obligation towards the remote future to prevent certain catastrophic scenarios.[461]

Parallel and related to communitarianism, feminist ethics have also developed as a counter-reaction to utilitarian and libertarian concepts of justice and morality.[462] From a broader perspective, both schools of thought take a critical view of traditional doctrinal approaches, also in international law, as far as the latter often remained Eurocentric and did not sufficiently consider non-Western traditions.[463] Care ethics have been part of these feminist approaches to environmental ethics.[464] Their proponents criticised the focus of traditional ethics on individualism and reason, and they attempted to shift this focus to human interdependence and relationships between one another.[465] For instance, *Marion Blondel* suggested to use the notion of vulnerability as a legal concept in order to reshape the protection of individuals in

[456] Ibid. pp. 43–45. Cf. also Gewirth (2001/2014), p. 119.

[457] Supanich (1992), pp. 101–103 with reference to Stone (1987), pp. 89–91. See also Redgwell (1999), pp. 93–94.

[458] Agius (2006), pp. 325–328.

[459] Ibid. p. 328.

[460] Thompson (2009a), p. 44.

[461] De-Shalit (1995), pp. 64–65. On *De-Shalit's* differentiation between these duties, see *infra* notes 490–492.

[462] Norlock (2019, Section 2.4). See also Groves (2014), pp. 26–49.

[463] Cf. Koskenniemi (2007, para. 14); Daniel Bell (2024, Section 1) On this criticism of Eurocentric individualistic approaches, see also *infra* in Sect. 5.2.1.2.

[464] Norlock (2019, Section 2.2); Warren (2015, Section 3.8). For the first representative of care ethics, see Gilligan (1982).

[465] Norlock (2019, Section 2.2).

international law through a care ethic approach instead of a pure focus on individualism and autonomy.[466]

While care ethics have generally remained silent on intergenerational relations,[467] a few commentators addressed this issue.[468] For instance, *Christopher Grove* criticised certain traditional theories of intergenerational justice for their failures and then offered a theory of future care ethics himself.[469] Similarly, *Ruth Makoff* and *Rupert Read* pointed out several difficulties and flaws of libertarian distributive and procedural justice theories.[470] Instead, they elaborated that care ethics were more appropriate to address issues of intergenerational relations, as "future generations should not be thought of as a distinct society or group living at a different temporal 'location', but as what/*who we will become*, emerging from our generation, and the future identity of our society(ies)" (emphasis in the original).[471] *Thomas Randall* examined the insufficiency of most care ethics in the context of intergenerational relations,[472] and rejected *Groves'* approach in detail.[473] He then suggested alternative future care ethics, which mainly focused on two premises: There is an intergenerational relational interdependency that is based on an "imaginal content with future generations" and that is "real enough to be normatively relevant in the care framework".[474] From this normative relevance of future generations, he deduced a sufficientarian theory of intergenerational obligations: "the present generation ought to ensure the conditions that enable good caring relations to flourish for posterity".[475] More interestingly, *Randall* explicitly based his first conclusion regarding the normative relevance of future generations on *De-Shalit's* communitarian reasoning of a transgenerational community.[476] This illustrates the parallels between a care theory of intergenerational ethics and communitarian approaches.[477] Although these parallels were not universally accepted,[478] the following paragraphs address care ethics as part of the broader idea of communitarian approaches.

---

[466] Blondel (2018), pp. 202–204 with further references.

[467] Randall (2019), p. 528.

[468] Groves (2014); Makoff and Read (2017); Randall (2019).

[469] Groves (2014), pp. 26–49. See also.

[470] Makoff and Read (2017), pp. 229–249.

[471] Ibid. p. 254.

[472] Randall (2019), pp. 528–532.

[473] Ibid. pp. 533–536 with reference to Groves (2014), pp. 131–180.

[474] Randall (2019), pp.536, 538–541.

[475] Ibid., 537, 541.

[476] De-Shalit (1995), pp. 15–17. While *Ruth Makoff* and *Rupert Read* positively referred to *De-Shalit*, they also criticised him for remaining trapped by traditional (communitarian) concepts of distributive justice, see Makoff and Read (2017), p. 251. Instead, *Makoff* and *Read* advocated for a care-related intergenerational ethics without the limitations of intergenerational justice regimes. This critique of *De-Shalit's* theory seems misplaced with regard to his approach to remote future generations, see *infra* notes 490–492.

[477] Cf. Randall (2019), p. 540; Norlock (2019, Section 1.3).

[478] See Makoff and Read (2017), p. 251.

Communitarian approaches also faced certain criticism with regard to intergenerational issues. For instance, *Norman Care* argued that there could not be any bonds of love or concern for indefinite future persons, since there is no kind of community bond or no sense of identification with a joint intertemporal enterprise.[479] However, this lack of confidence in human care for transgenerational humanity seems to be based on the strictly individualistic understanding of ethics.[480] It was this focus on self-interested and rational individuals that both communitarian approaches and care ethics criticised with respect to liberal and social contract theories of justice.[481] Communitarians mainly objected to the idea of an intergenerational contract based on rationality, since such notions lacked mutual advantage and a necessary motivational bond.[482] Present individuals simply would not have any reason to care for the well-being of future generations in a contractual conception of justice.[483] This critique is based on the inexistence of direct reciprocal relations between the present and the future and on the rejection of artificial indirect reciprocity.[484] Instead of relying on allegedly inappropriate solutions to the motivational lacunae, communitarian concepts of morality derived the need to care for the future directly from every individual's affiliation to a transgenerational community.[485] In opposition to *Norman Care's* and *Garrit Hardin's* pessimistic accounts of human (self-)interests,[486] *Ernest Partridge* established a concept of self-transcendence:

> [A]s a result of the psychodevelopmental sources of the self and the fundamental dynamics of social experience, well-functioning human beings identify with, and seek to further, the well-being, preservation, and endurance of communities, locations, causes, artifacts, institutions, ideals, and so on, that are outside themselves and that they hope will flourish beyond their own lifetimes.[487]

Communitarian concepts of intergenerational justice have also been criticised for not sufficiently taking into account intergenerational duties towards more remote generations as well as for environmental concerns in general.[488] Therefore, most communitarians acknowledged the decreasing nature of obligations towards future

---

[479] Care (1982), pp. 207–213. See also Hardin (1977), pp. 78–79.

[480] See already *supra* notes 437–440.

[481] See De-Shalit (1995), pp. 110–111); Thompson (2009a), pp. 27–28); Daniel Bell (2024).

[482] See, e.g., Makoff and Read (2017), pp. 242–249. For comparable criticism, cf. *supra* notes 395–397.

[483] See De-Shalit (1995), pp. 87–111; Partridge (2007), pp. 382–383.

[484] Makoff and Read (2017), pp. 242–244. On the lack of reciprocity issue, see *supra* in Sect. 3.2.3.

[485] De-Shalit (1995), p. 124.

[486] See Partridge (2007), pp. 382–383.

[487] Partridge (1981), pp. 204–206. On an intergenerational continuum of transcendence, cf. also Nagy (1998), p. 59).

[488] UNSG (2013, para. 23); De-Shalit (1995), p. 14; Thompson (2009a), p. 46.

persons the more remote these future generations were from the present.[489] For instance, *De-Shalit* distinguished between, on the one hand, basic obligations of justice in regard to immediate future generations belonging to the transgenerational community, and, on the other hand, mere obligations "out of humanity", instead of justice, towards remote future generations.[490] The obligations to the near future would be negative and positive alike, thus, include the pursuance of active policies.[491] However, the obligations to the distant future would primarily consist of the negative duty to refrain from causing severe predictable harm.[492] *Thompson* took a different approach and regarded even remote generations "as successors, as participants in a never-ending chain of relationships in which each generation fulfils moral requirements in respect to its predecessors and successors".[493] While *De-Shalit's* differentiation could possibly avoid the reciprocity problem of intergenerational relations, *Thompson's* chain of intergenerational relationships has certain similarities with concepts of indirect reciprocity.[494]

Overall, communitarian theories as well as care ethics encompass a broad reasoning for intergenerational ethics. This can constitute an advantage in comparison to liberal and social contract theories, as these often fail to present convincing arguments without contradicting themselves.[495] Weak forms of communitarianism, as proposed by *De-Shalit* or *Thompson*, contain sufficientarian aspects as far as they primarily demand ensuring a sufficient level of prerequisites for immediate and remote future generations in order to fulfil the present generation's duty in a transgenerational community.

#### 3.3.4.2 Parallels to and Consequences for Intergenerational Equity

As pointed out above, *Brown Weiss'* doctrine of intergenerational equity was built on a *Rawlsian* original position only as a starting point in order to establish the principles of justice between generations.[496] From this, *Brown Weiss* deduced that every generation of the human species holds the Earth in common as a trust for all generations of humankind.[497] This fiduciary planetary trust is at the core of her concept.[498] She viewed "the human community as a partnership among all

[489] De-Shalit (1995), pp. 13–14. Cf. also *Makoff* and *Read* who mainly addressed relations between present and directly subsequent generations: Makoff and Read (2017), pp. 250–254.

[490] De-Shalit (1995), pp. 62–65.

[491] Ibid., p. 64.

[492] Ibid., 13, 63.

[493] J. Thompson (2009a), p. 47.

[494] See *supra* in Sect. 3.2.3.

[495] De-Shalit (1995), pp. 124–128.

[496] Redgwell (1999), pp. 77, 108–109.

[497] See, e.g., Brown Weiss (1984), p. 498.

[498] For a detailed explanation of the planetary trust, see *supra* in Sect. 2.2.1.3.

generations"[499] and called for the recognition of a "planetary citizenship for all members of the human species".[500] The communitarian notion of the planetary trust was also expressed by *Brown Weiss'* explicit references to several religious and cultural roots,[501] but also to *Burke*[502] who observed that the partnership of the human community "becomes a partnership [...] between those who are living, those who are dead, and those who are to be born".[503] The planetary trust concept was also based on the "psychological need to transcend the self by relating to the future",[504] which is comparable to *Partridge's* idea of human self-transcendence or *Thompson's* "lifetime-transcending interests".[505] The doctrine of intergenerational equity is thus strongly inspired by a communitarian understanding of justice.[506]

Beyond this, other international documents on intergenerational equity have manifested communitarian notions of intergenerational equity as well. For instance, the UNSG Report from 2013 explicitly considered communitarianism an influential view on the legal notion of intergenerational equity[507]: "In this view, humanity as a whole forms an intergenerational community in which all members respect and care for one another, achieving the common goal of survival of humankind."[508] These connections further illustrate the inherent links between intergenerational equity and the concepts of common heritage and common concern of humankind.[509] *Agius* elaborated on the central notion of "common good" in his relational theory of intergenerational justice.[510] He observed:

> The common good is the good of [hu]mankind as a whole. Relational metaphysics gives a philosophical reason for the broadening in scope of the notion of common good from a national to the supranational, from the supranational to the common good of [hu] mankind.[511]

From this, *Agius* deduced that the natural resources constitute shared goods of all generations and concluded an "intergenerational solidarity with the whole family of

499 Brown Weiss (1992), p. 73.

500 Brown Weiss (1989), p. 165.

501 Ibid. pp. 18–21. See also UNSG (2013, para. 12).

502 See, e.g., Brown Weiss (1989), p. 23; Brown Weiss (1992), p. 73. See also Redgwell (1999), p. 75.

503 Burke (1790/1986), p. 110.

504 Brown Weiss (1984), p. 500.

505 Partridge (1981), pp. 204–206; Thompson (2009a), pp. 33–38; J. Thompson (2009b), pp. 39–54.

506 Collins (2007), p. 94. Cf. also.

507 UNSG (2013, paras. 8, 23) with reference to World Summit for Social Development (1995, para. 26(b)).

508 UNSG (2013, para. 8).

509 In detail, see *supra* in Sect. 2.3.3.

510 Agius (2006), pp. 328–330.

511 Ibid., p. 328.

humankind", which is again very much linked to *Brown Weiss'* concept of intergenerational equity.[512]

Consequently, the parallels between intergenerational equity and communitarianism are even more obvious than the former's connections to *Rawls'* social contract theory. However, it is not contradictory for *Brown Weiss'* concept to rely on both contractualist and communitarian ideas alike, since at least weak communitarianism is not in complete opposition to liberal concepts of justice.[513] Further, it can be distinguished between the hypothetical original position *Brown Weiss* relied on as a starting point for the establishment of principles of justice and the fiduciary trust she established as a communitarian result.[514]

Eventually, the communitarian core of intergenerational equity as a partnership among all generations can also serve as the basis of the intertemporal perspective taken on intergenerational equity in Chapters 6 and 7 in this book. Comparable to *Rawls'* hypothetical thought experiment of a contract between generations, the image of an intergenerational partnership of the whole human community could also help to establish the inherently intertemporal nature of intergenerational equity.[515]

## 3.4 Conclusion of This Chapter

This chapter has shifted the perspective from the introductory legal overview of intergenerational equity to its pre-legal foundations in environmental ethics and philosophy. This is important due to the inherent links of intergenerational equity to distributive justice. A purely positivist perspective, as undertaken in Chap. 4, would fall short of the multidisciplinary and philosophical character of any concept of intergenerational distribution of natural resources, very much linked to considerations of natural law.

Within the philosophical discussions of intergenerational justice, four main objections have led some commentators to the conclusion that a theory of justice with obligations of the present towards future generations is inappropriate. As these objections are often also raised in legal discussions of intergenerational equity, it is crucial to understand and possibly solve them in order to be able to address the legal concept of intergenerational equity. Most prominently, the non-identity problem has concerned philosophers and environmentalists for a long time: the fact that the composition, number and identity of future generations are contingent upon the activities of the present generation would lead to the impossibility of "harming" future generations by these activities. Although the non-identity argument seemingly

---

[512] Ibid., p. 330.

[513] J. Thompson (2009a), p. 29.

[514] Redgwell (1999), p. 109. Cf. also Ackerman (1980), p. 225.

[515] See *infra* in Sects. 7.2.2.2 and 7.3.3.3.

complicates some approaches to intergenerational justice, it does not constitute an insurmountable obstacle to any such theory. Instead, many commentators have demonstrated how it is possible to conceptionally overcome the challenges of the non-identity problem. The same is true for the non-existence argument, the lack of reciprocity in intergenerational relations and the lack of certain knowledge about the future. Consequently, the following chapters consider these objections not to be critical for the assessment of the present's moral and legal obligations towards future generations. The remaining parts of the book thus assume the conceptional possibility of a moral status of future generations regardless of the non-identity problem, the non-existence of future generations, the lack of reciprocity or the present-day uncertainties on the exact future developments.

Having overcome these main objections, it is important to understand the inherent links and parallels between philosophical and legal considerations on intergenerational issues in the last decades. Four philosophical schools of thought have offered different approaches to intergenerational justice. While utilitarian concepts of aggregative justice seem unfit to solve problems of intergenerational relations, libertarian approaches and social contract theories have evolved principles of distributive justice to balance the interests and needs of present and future generations. Eventually, communitarian approaches have developed as counter-reaction to utilitarian and deontological ethics while focusing on the human affiliation to a transgenerational community. All of these philosophical approaches offer convincing arguments, but they also face certain criticism and challenges.

The present chapter has neither offered an exhaustive analysis of all philosophical approaches nor has it taken position for one of them, since this is not necessary for the subsequent legal development. It has only given an overview of the most important ideas that have influenced the legal domain. Consequently, the sub-sections on the respective parallels to and consequences for the legal concept of intergenerational equity constitute the most relevant parts for the remaining analysis.[516] Most importantly, intergenerational equity is not based on *one* of the philosophical approaches exclusively. It is rather inspired by several of the approaches to different degrees. While the general conception of the Brundtland Report is mainly libertarian, in form of a sufficientarian version of the Lockean proviso, *Brown Weiss'* doctrine of intergenerational equity combines various approaches to intergenerational justice. It is egalitarian in some respects, but sufficientarian in others. It can also be understood as a form of Lockean proviso. However, the specific doctrine is mainly based on *Rawls'* social contract approach as well as on communitarian notions of a transgenerational community. On the one hand, *Brown Weiss* established a sufficientarian version of the just savings principle in form of her duties of conservation. On the other hand, her concept of a planetary trust resembles the communitarian idea of a partnership between all generations.

All in all, this third chapter has distinguished between the non-positivist, philosophical analysis of intergenerational justice and the legal questions of

[516] See *supra* Sects. 3.3.1.2, 3.3.2.2, 3.3.3.2, and 3.3.4.2 respectively.

intergenerational equity, which are often not clearly distinguished in scholarship. Despite the imminent distinctions, this preliminary natural law perspective was necessary for a comprehensive understanding of the partly overlapping arguments and challenges intergenerational relations face in philosophy and law. Based on this, the following chapter turns back to the legal concept of intergenerational equity as introduced in Chap. 2. The findings of this third chapter become particularly important again with regard to the rights-based operationalisation of intergenerational equity[517] as well as its inherently intertemporal nature.[518]

## References


Ackerman, B. A. (1980). *Social justice in the Liberal state*. Yale University Press.

Agius, E. (2006). Intergenerational justice. In J. C. Tremmel (Ed.), *Handbook of intergenerational justice* (Vol. 16, pp. 317–332). Edward Elgar Publishing.

Alexander, L., & Moore, M. (2024). Deontological ethics. In E. N. Zalta (Ed.). *The Stanford encyclopedia of philosophy*. ISSN 1095-5054. Retrieved 3 January 2025, from https://plato.stanford.edu/entries/ethics-deontological/. (Article last updated December 2024).

Anstee-Wedderburn, J. (2014). Giving a voice to future generations: Intergenerational equity, representative of generations to come, and the challenge of planetary rights. *Australian Journal of Environmental Law, 1*(1), 37–70.

Aristotle (1980). *The Nicomachean ethics: Translated with an introduction into English by David Ross.* (Reprint). Oxford University Press.

Arneson, R. J. (1991). Lockean self-ownership: Towards a demolition. *Political Studies, 39*(1), 36–54. https://doi.org/10.1111/j.1467-9248.1991.tb00580.x

Arneson, R. J. (2013). Egalitarianism. In E. N. Zalta (Ed.). *The Stanford encyclopedia of philosophy.* ISSN 1095-5054. Retrieved 3 January 2025, from https://plato.stanford.edu/entries/egalitarianism/. (Article last updated April 2013).

Arrhenius, G., Ryberg, J., & Tännsjö, T. (2017). The repugnant conclusion. In E. N. Zalta (Ed.). *The Stanford encyclopedia of philosophy.* ISSN 1095-5054. Retrieved 3 January 2025, from https://plato.stanford.edu/entries/repugnant-conclusion/. (Article last updated January 2017).

Ashford, E., & Mulgan, T. (2018). Contractualism. In E. N. Zalta (Ed.). *The Stanford encyclopedia of philosophy.* ISSN 1095-5054. Retrieved 3 January 2025, from https://plato.stanford.edu/entries/contractualism/. (Article last updated April 2018).

Attas, D. (2009). A transgenerational difference principle. In A. Gosseries & L. H. Meyer (Eds.), *Intergenerational justice* (Vol. 7, pp. 189–218). Oxford University Press.

Austin, J. (1873). *Lectures on jurisprudence*. Henry Holt and Company.

Barry, B. M. (1989). *Theories of justice*. University of California Press.

Bartenstein, K. (2022). Zwischenstaatliche Umweltgerechtigkeit. In A. Proelß (Ed.), *Internationales Umweltrecht* (Vol. 2, 2nd ed., pp. 53–94). De Gruyter.

Beckerman, W. (2004). Intergenerational Justice. *Intergenerational Justice Review, 2*, 1–5.

Beckerman, W. (2006). The impossibility of a theory of intergenerational justice. In J. C. Tremmel (Ed.), *Handbook of intergenerational justice* (Vol. 3, pp. 53–71). Edward Elgar Publishing.

Beckerman, W., & Pasek, J. (2001). Justice, posterity, and the environment. *Oxford University Press.* https://doi.org/10.1093/0199245088.001.0001


517 See *infra* in Sect. 5.2.

518 See *infra* in Sects. 7.2.2.2 and 7.3.3.3.

Bell, D. [Derek] (2011). Does anthropogenic climate change violate human rights? Critical Review of International Social and Political Philosophy, 14(2), 99–124. https://doi.org/10.1080/13698230.2011.529703.

Bell, D. [Daniel]. (2024). Communitarianism. In E. N. Zalta (Ed.). *The Stanford Encyclopedia of Philosophy.* ISSN 1095–5054. Retrieved 3 January 2025, from https://plato.stanford.edu/entries/communitarianism/. (Article last updated June 2024).

Bentham, J. (1789). *An introduction to the principles of morals and legislation.* T. Payne and Son.

Bentham, J., & Hart, H. L. A. (1970). *Of laws in general.* Athlone Press.

Beyleveld, D., Düwell, M., & Spahn, A. (2015). Why and how should we represent future generations in policymaking? *Jurisprudence, 6*(3), 549–566. https://doi.org/10.1080/20403313.2015.1065642

Birnbacher, D. (1988). *Verantwortung für Zukünftige Generationen.* Reclam.

Birnbacher, D. (1989). Intergenerationelle Verantwortung oder: Dürfen Wir die Zukunft der Menschheit Diskontieren? In R. Kümmel (Ed.), *Umweltschutz und Marktwirtschaft: Aus der Sicht unterschiedlicher Disziplinen* (Vol. 7, pp. 101–116). Königshausen & Neumann.

Birnbacher, D. (2003a). Can discounting be justified? *International Journal of Sustainable Development, 6*(1), 42. https://doi.org/10.1504/IJSD.2003.004222

Birnbacher, D. (2003b). Verantwortung für Zukünftige Generationen: Reichweite und Grenzen. In J. C. Tremmel (Ed.), *Handbuch Generationengerechtigkeit* (2nd ed., pp. 81–104). ökom Verlag.

Birnbacher, D. (2006). Responsibility for future generations—Scope and limits. In J. C. Tremmel (Ed.), *Handbook of intergenerational justice* (Vol. 1, pp. 23–38). Edward Elgar Publishing.

Birnbacher, D. (2008). Langzeitverantwortung – das Problem der Motivation. In C. F. Gethmann & J. Mittelstraß (Eds.), *Langzeitverantwortung: Ethik, Technik, Ökologie* (pp. 23–39). Wissenschaftliche Buchgesellschaft.

Blondel, M. (2018). Vulnerability as a virtue: An attempt to transpose the Care ethic in international law. *Baltic Yearbook of International Law Online, 17*(1), 197–221. https://doi.org/10.1163/22115897_01701_010

Bobertz, B. C. (1987). Toward a better understanding of intergenerational justice. *Buffalo Law Review, 36*(1), 165–192.

Boonin, D. (2008). How to solve the non-identity problem. *Public Affairs Quarterly, 22*(2), 127–157.

Bosselmann, K. (2009). Environmental ethics. In A. Peters & R. Wolfrum (Eds.), *Max Planck encyclopedia of public international law*. Oxford University Press. (Article last updated January 2009).

Brandt, R. B. (1983). The concept of a moral right and its function. *The Journal of Philosophy, 80*(1), 29–45. https://doi.org/10.2307/2026285

Broome, J. (1992). *Counting the cost of global warming: A report to the economic and social research council.* White Horse Press.

Brown Weiss, E. (1984). The planetary trust: Conservation and intergenerational equity. *Ecology Law Quarterly, 11*, 495–582.

Brown Weiss, E. (1989). *In fairness to future generations: International law, common patrimony, and intergenerational equity.* Transnational Publishers, Inc.

Brown Weiss, E. (1990). Our rights and obligations to future generations for the environment. *American Journal of International Law, 84*(1), 198–207. https://doi.org/10.2307/2203020

Brown Weiss, E. (1992). Intergenerational equity and rights of future generations. In A. A. Cançado Trindade & E. Brown Weiss (Eds.), *Derechos Humanos, Desarrollo Sustentable y Medio Ambiente: Human rights, sustainable development and the environment* (pp. 71–81). Banco Interamericano de Desarrollo.

Brown Weiss, E. (2021). Intergenerational equity. In A. Peters & R. Wolfrum (Eds.), *Max Planck encyclopedia of public international law*. Oxford University Press. (Article last updated April 2021).

Buchanan, N. H. (1989). Assessing the communitarian critique of liberalism. *Ethics, 99*(4), 852–882.

Burchardt, D. (2012). Zukünftige Generationen—Träger Kollektiver Rechte? In Junge Wissenschaft im Öffentlichen Recht e.V. (Ed.). *Kollektivität—Öffentliches Recht zwischen Gruppeninteressen und Gemeinwohl: 52. Assistententagung Öffentliches Recht* (pp. 187–209). Nomos.

Burke, E. (1986). Reflections on the revolution in France. In *And on the proceedings in certain societies in London relative to that event* (1st ed.). Penguin Books. (Original work published 1790).

Campbell, K. (2017). Legal rights. In E. N. Zalta (Ed.). *The Stanford encyclopedia of philosophy.* ISSN 1095-5054. Retrieved 3 January 2025, from https://plato.stanford.edu/archives/win2022/entries/legal-rights/. (Article last updated November 2017).

Care, N. S. (1982). Future generations, public policy, and the motivation problem. *Environmental Ethics, 4*(3), 195–213. https://doi.org/10.5840/enviroethics19824327

Carson, R. (1962). *Silent spring*. Houghton Mifflin Company.

Carter, A. (2001). Can we harm future people? *Environmental Values, 10*(4), 429–454.

Casal, P. (2007). Why sufficiency is not enough. *Ethics, 117*(2), 296–326. https://doi.org/10.1086/510692

Cochrane, A. (n.d.). Environmental ethics. In J. Fieser & B. Dowden (Eds.). *Internet Encyclopedia of Philosophy*. ISSN 2161-0002.

Collins, L. M. (2007). Revisiting the doctrine of intergenerational equity in global environmental governance. *Dalhousie Law Journal, 30*(1), 73–134.

Cowen, T., & Parfit, D. (1992). Against the social discount rate. In P. Laslett & J. S. Fishkin (Eds.), *Philosophy, politics, and society, sixth series: Justice between age groups and generations* (Vol. 7, pp. 144–161). Yale University Press. https://doi.org/10.2307/j.ctt211qw3x.11

Cryer, R., Hervey, T., Sokhi-Bulley, B., & Bohm, A. (2011). *Research methodologies in EU and international law*. Hart Publishing.

Cudd, A., & Eftekhari, S. (2021). Contractarianism. In E. N. Zalta (Ed.). *The Stanford encyclopedia of philosophy.* ISSN 1095-5054. Retrieved 3 January 2025, from https://plato.stanford.edu/entries/contractarianism/. (Article last updated September 2021).

Czarnecki, R. (2008). *Verteilungsgerechtigkeit im Umweltvölkerrecht: Dogmatik und Umsetzung*. Duncker & Humblot.

D'Amato, A. (1990). Do we owe a duty to future generations to preserve the global environment? *American Journal of International Law, 84*, 190–198.

Daly, H. E. (1996). *Beyond growth: The economics of sustainable development*. Beacon Press.

Davidson, M. D. (2008). Wrongful harm to future generations: The case of climate change. *Environmental Values, 17*(4), 471–488. https://doi.org/10.3197/096327108X368494

Davies, G. (2020). Climate change and reversed intergenerational equity: The problem of costs now, for benefits later. *Climate Law, 10*(3–4), 266–281. https://doi.org/10.1163/18786561-10030002

Davies, G. (2022). Solidarity across time: What can the future do for us? *Verfassungsblog*. 10 August 2022. Retrieved 3 January 2025, from https://verfassungsblog.de/solidarity-across-time/

de George, R. (1981). The environment, rights, and future generations. In E. Partridge (Ed.), *Responsibilities to future generations: Environmental ethics* (pp. 157–166). Prometheus Books.

De-Shalit, A. (1995). *Why posterity matters: Environmental policies and future generations*. Routledge Taylor & Francis Group.

Dierksmeier, C. (2006). John Rawls on the rights of future generations. In J. C. Tremmel (Ed.), *Handbook of intergenerational justice* (Vol. 4, pp. 72–85). Edward Elgar Publishing.

Donnelly, J. (2003). *Universal human rights in theory and practice* (2nd ed.). Cornell University Press.

Düwell, M. (2014). Human dignity and future generations. In M. Düwell et al. (Eds.), *The Cambridge handbook of human dignity: Interdisciplinary perspectives* (Vol. 62, pp. 551–558). Cambridge University Press.

Düwell, M. (2016). Human dignity and intergenerational human rights. In G. Bos & M. Düwell (Eds.), *Human rights and sustainability: Moral responsibilities for the future* (Vol. 6, pp. 69–81). Routledge Taylor & Francis Group.

Dworkin, R. (1978). *Taking rights seriously*. Harvard University Press.

Ekardt, F. (2021). *Theorie der Nachhaltigkeit: Ethische, Rechtliche, Politische und transformative Zugänge – Am Beispiel von Klimawandel, Ressourcenknappheit und Welthandel* (2nd ed.). Nomos. https://doi.org/10.5771/9783845254593

Ekeli, K. S. (2005). Giving a voice to posterity: Deliberative democracy and representation of future people. *Journal of Agricultural and Environmental Ethics, 18*(5), 429–450. https://doi.org/10.1007/s10806-005-7048-z

Ekeli, K. S. (2006). The principle of liberty and legal representation of posterity. *Res Publica, 12*(4), 385–409. https://doi.org/10.1007/s11158-006-9021-8

Ekeli, K. S. (2007). Green constitutionalism: The constitutional protection of future generations. *Ratio Juris, 20*(3), 378–401. https://doi.org/10.1111/j.1467-9337.2007.00366.x

Elliot, R. (1986). Future generations, Locke's proviso and libertarian justice. *Journal of Applied Philosophy, 3*(2), 217–227. https://doi.org/10.1111/j.1468-5930.1986.tb00421.x

Elliot, R. (1989). The rights of future people. *Journal of Applied Philosophy, 6*(2), 159–169. https://doi.org/10.1111/j.1468-5930.1986.tb00421.x

English, J. (1977). Justice between generations. *Philosophical Studies, 31*(2), 91–104. https://doi.org/10.1007/BF01857179

Feinberg, J. (1974). The rights of animals and unborn generations. In W. Blackstone (Ed.), *Philosophy and environmental crisis* (pp. 43–68). University of Georgia Press.

Feinberg, J. (1986). Wrongful life and the counterfactual element in harming. *Social Philosophy and Policy, 4*(1), 145–178. https://doi.org/10.1017/S0265052500000467

Fitzmaurice, M. (2008). Intergenerational equity revisited. In I. Buffard, J. Crawford, A. Pellet, & S. Wittich (Eds.), *International law between universalism and fragmentation: Festschrift in honour of Gerhard Hafner* (Vol. 11, pp. 195–229). Martinus Nijhoff Publishers.

Fitzmaurice, M. (2012). Some reflections on legal and philosophical foundations of international environmental law. *Polish Yearbook of International Law, 32*, 89–110.

Frankfurt, H. (1987). Equality as a moral ideal. *Ethics, 98*, 21–43.

Freeman, M. D. A. (1995). Are there collective human rights? *Political Studies, 43*(1), 25–40. https://doi.org/10.1111/j.1467-9248.1995.tb01734.x

Freeman, M. D. A., & Lloyd of Hampstead, D. L. (1994). *Lloyd's introduction to jurisprudence* (6th ed.). Sweet & Maxwell.

French, P. A. (1984). *Collective and corporate responsibility*. Columbia University Press.

Friend, C. (n.d.). Social contract theory. In J. Fieser & B. Dowden (Eds.). *Internet Encyclopedia of Philosophy*. ISSN 2161-0002.

Gaillard, É. (2011). *Générations Futures et Droit Privé: Vers un Droit des Générations Futures*. LGDJ Lextenso Éditions.

Galenkamp, M. (1993). *Individualism versus collectivism: The concept of collective rights*. Erasmus Universiteit, Faculteit der Wijsbegeerte.

Gardiner, S. M. (2009). A contract on future generations? In A. Gosseries & L. H. Meyer (Eds.), *Intergenerational justice* (Vol. 3, pp. 77–118). Oxford University Press.

Gardiner, S. M. (2011). Rawls and climate change: Does Rawlsian political philosophy pass the global test? *Critical Review of International Social and Political Philosophy, 14*(2), 125–151. https://doi.org/10.1080/13698230.2011.529705

Gardner, M. (2015). A harm-based solution to the non-identity problem. *Ergo – an Open Access. Journal of Philosophy, 2*(17). https://doi.org/10.3998/ergo.12405314.0002.017

Gaus, G., Courtland, S. D., & Schmidtz, D. (2022). Liberalism. In E. N. Zalta (Ed.). *The Stanford encyclopedia of philosophy*. ISSN 1095-5054. Retrieved 3 January 2025, from https://plato.stanford.edu/entries/liberalism/. (Article last updated February 2022).

Gauthier, D. P. (1986). *Morals by agreement*. Clarendon Press.

Gewirth, A. (2014). Human rights and future generations: (2001). In M. Boylan (Ed.), *Environmental ethics* (2nd ed., pp. 118–121). Wiley Blackwell.
Gillespie, A. (2014). *International environmental law, policy, and ethics* (2nd ed.). Oxford University Press.
Gillespie, A. (2021). Ethical considerations. In L. Rajamani & J. Peel (Eds.), *The Oxford handbook of international environmental law* (Vol. 13, 2nd ed., pp. 217–232). Oxford University Press.
Gilligan, C. (1982). *In a different voice: Psychological theory and women's development* (38th ed.). Harvard University Press.
Golding, M. P. (1981). Obligations to future generations. In E. Partridge (Ed.), *Responsibilities to future generations: Environmental ethics* (pp. 61–72). Prometheus Books.
Gosseries, A. (2001). What do we owe the next generation(s). *Loyola of Los Angeles Law Review, 35*, 293–354.
Gosseries, A. (2004). Constitutionalizing future rights? *Intergenerational Justice Review, 2*, 10–11.
Gosseries, A. (2005). The egalitarian case against Brundtland's sustainability. *Gaia, 14*(1), 40–46.
Gosseries, A. (2008a). On future generations' future rights. *Journal of Political Philosophy, 16*(4), 446–474. https://doi.org/10.1111/j.1467-9760.2008.00323.x
Gosseries, A. (2008b). Theories of intergenerational justice: A synopsis. *Surveys and Perspectives Integrating Environment and Society, 1*(1), 61–71.
Gosseries, A. (2009). Three models of intergenerational reciprocity. In A. Gosseries & L. H. Meyer (Eds.), *Intergenerational justice* (Vol. 4, pp. 119–146). Oxford University Press.
Graham, K. (2002). Practical reasoning in a social world: How we act together. *Cambridge University Press.* https://doi.org/10.1017/CBO9780511487408
Groves, C. (2014). *Care, Uncertainty and intergenerational ethics*. Palgrave Macmillan.
Gündling, L. (1990). Our responsibility to future generations. *American Journal of International Law, 84*(1), 207–212.
Gutmann, A. (1985). Communitarian critics of liberalism. *Philosophy and Public Affairs, 14*(3), 308–322.
Hadjiargyrou, Z. (2016). A conceptual and practical evaluation of intergenerational equity in international environmental law. *International Community Law Review, 18*, 248–277.
Hampton, J. (1986). *Hobbes and the social contract tradition*. Cambridge University Press. https://doi.org/10.1017/CBO9780511625060.
Hardin, G. J. (1977). *The limits of altruism: An ecologist's view of survival.* Indiana University Press.
Harman, E. (2009). Harming as causing harm. In M. A. Roberts & D. T. Wasserman (Eds.), *Harming future persons: Ethics, genetics and the nonidentity problem* (Vol. 7, pp. 137–154). Springer.
Hart, H. L. A. (1982). *Essays on Bentham: Studies in jurisprudence and political theory*. Clarendon Press.
Herstein, O. J. (2009). The identity and (legal) rights of future generations. *George Washington Law Review, 77*(5–6), 1173–1215.
Heubach, A. (2008). *Generationengerechtigkeit: Herausforderung für die Zeitgenössische Ethik*. V & R Unipress.
Heyd, D. (1992). *Genethics: Moral issues in the creation of people*. University of California Press.
Heyd, D. (2009a). The intractability of the nonidentity problem. In M. A. Roberts & D. T. Wasserman (Eds.), *Harming future persons: Ethics, genetics and the nonidentity problem* (Vol. 1, pp. 3–25). Springer.
Heyd, D. (2009b). A value or an obligation? Rawls on justice to future generations. In A. Gosseries & L. H. Meyer (Eds.), *Intergenerational justice* (Vol. 6, pp. 167–188). Oxford University Press.
Hobbes, T. (1651). *Leviathan: Or the matter, forme, & power of a commonwealth ecclasiasticall and civil*. Printed for Andrew Crooke. (Original work published 1651).
Hohfeld, W. N. (1913). Some fundamental legal conceptions as applied in judicial reasoning. *Yale Law Journal, 23*(1), 16–59. https://doi.org/10.2307/786270

Howarth, R. B. (2011). Intergenerational justice. In J. S. Dryzek, R. B. Norgaard, & D. Schlosberg (Eds.), *The Oxford handbook of climate change and society* (Vol. 23, pp. 338–353). Oxford University Press. https://doi.org/10.1093/oxfordhb/9780199566600.003.0023

Jonas, H. (1979). *Das Prinzip Verantwortung: Versuch einer Ethik für die technologische Zivilisation* (1st ed.). Insel-Verlag.

Jones, P. (2022). Group rights. In E. N. Zalta (Ed.). *The Stanford encyclopedia of philosophy*. ISSN 1095-5054. Retrieved 3 January 2025, from https://plato.stanford.edu/entries/rights-group/. (Article last updated August 2022).

Justinian, F. (1893). The Institutes of Justinian (Sixth Century Codification Justinian of Roman Law): Translated into English by John B. Moyle. *Project Gutenberg*. 1893. Retrieved 3 January 2025, from https://www.gutenberg.org/files/5983/5983-h/5983-h.htm

Kant, I. (1785). *Grundlegung zur Metaphysik der Sitten*. J. F. Hartknoch.

Kavka, G. S. (1981). The futurity problem. In E. Partridge (Ed.), *Responsibilities to future generations: Environmental ethics* (pp. 109–122). Prometheus Books.

Kavka, G. S. (1982). The paradox of future individuals. *Philosophy and Public Affairs, 11*(2), 93–112.

Kelsen, H. (1969). *Pure theory of law*. University of California Press.

Kleiber, M. (2014). *Der Grundrechtliche Schutz Künftiger Generationen*. Mohr Siebeck.

Koskenniemi, M. (2007). International legal theory and doctrine. In A. Peters & R. Wolfrum (Eds.), *Max Planck encyclopedia of public international law*. Oxford University Press. (Article last updated November 2007).

Kramer, M. H. (2013). Some doubts about alternatives to the interest theory of rights. *Ethics, 123*(2), 245–263. https://doi.org/10.1086/668705

Kramer, M. H., & Steiner, H. (2005). Theories of rights: Is there a third way? *Oxford Journal of Legal Studies, 27*(2), 281–310. https://doi.org/10.1093/ojls/gqi039

Lamont, J., & Favor, C. (2017). Distributive justice. In E. N. Zalta (Ed.), *The Stanford encyclopedia of philosophy*. ISSN 1095-5054. Retrieved 3 January 2025, from https://plato.stanford.edu/entries/justice-distributive/. (Article last updated September 2017).

Lawrence, P. (2012). Justice for future generations: Environment discourses, international law and climate change. In B. Jessup & K. Rubenstein (Eds.), *Environmental discourses in public and international law* (pp. 23–46). Cambridge University Press.

Lawrence, P. (2014). *Justice for future generations: Climate change and international law*. Edward Elgar Publishing.

Lepage, C., & Drafting Committee. (2015). Universal Declaration of Humankind Rights: Draft Presented Under the Aegis of Corinne Lepage, Commissioned by the President of the French Republic. *Alliance DDHU* 2022. 25 September 2015. Retrieved 3 January 2025, from https://ddhu.org/la-declaration/

Lewis, B. (2018). *Environmental human rights and climate change: Current status and future prospects*. Springer. https://doi.org/10.1007/978-981-13-1960-0

Locke, J. (1690). *Two treatises of government: An essay concerning the true original, extent and end of civil government (second treatise)*. Awnsham Churchill.

MacCormick, D. N. (1976). Children's rights: A test-case for theories of right. *Archiv Für Rechts-Und Sozialphilosophie, 62*(3), 305–317.

MacCormick, D. N. (1977). Rights in legislation. In P. M. S. Hacker & J. Raz (Eds.). *Law, morality, and society: Essays in Honour of H. L. A. Hart* (Vol. 11, pp. 189–209). Clarendon Press.

Mack, E. (1995). The self-ownership proviso: A new and improved Lockean proviso: A new and improved Lockean proviso. *Social Philosophy and Policy, 12*(1), 186–218. https://doi.org/10.1017/S0265052500004611

Makoff, R., & Read, R. (2017). Beyond just justice: Creating space for a future-Care ethic. *Philosophical Investigations, 40*(3), 223–256. https://doi.org/10.1111/phin.12138

Martínez, E., & Winter, C. (2022). Is legal Longtermism common sense? *Verfassungsblog*. 9 August 2022. Retrieved 3 January 2025, from https://verfassungsblog.de/is-legal-longtermism-common-sense/

Mayeda, G. (2004). Where should Johannesburg take us? Ethical and legal approaches to sustainable development in the context of international environmental law. *Colorado Journal of International Environmental Law and Policy, 15*(1), 29–70.

McDonald, L. (1998). Can collective and individual rights coexist? *Melbourne University Law Review, 22*(2), 310–336. https://doi.org/10.1163/174552412X625736

Mégret, F. (2019). Justice. In J. d'Aspremont & S. Singh (Eds.), *Concepts for international law: Contributions to disciplinary thought* (Vol. 38, pp. 585–606). Edward Elgar Publishing.

Merrills, J. G. (2010). Environmental rights. In D. Bodansky, J. Brunnée, & E. Hey (Eds.), *The Oxford handbook of international environmental law* (Vol. 28, 1st ed., pp. 663–680). Oxford University Press. https://doi.org/10.1093/oxfordhb/9780199552153.013.0028

Meyer, K. (2019). Précis zu Was Schulden Wir Künftigen Generationen? Herausforderung Zukunftsethik. *Zeitschrift Für Philosophische Forschung, 73*(1), 133–137. https://doi.org/10.3196/004433019825852330

Meyer, L. H. (2004). Compensating wrongless historical emissions of greenhouse gases. *Ethical Perspectives, 11*(1), 20–35. https://doi.org/10.2143/EP.11.1.504778

Meyer, L. H. (2005). *Historische Gerechtigkeit.* De Gruyter. https://doi.org/10.1515/9783110927498.

Meyer, L. H. (2009). Intergenerationelle Suffizienzgerechtigkeit. In N. Goldschmidt (Ed.), *Generationengerechtigkeit: Ordnungsökonomische Konzepte* (pp. 281–322). Mohr Siebeck.

Meyer, L. H. (2021). Intergenerational Justice. In E. N. Zalta (Ed.). *The Stanford encyclopedia of philosophy.* ISSN 1095-5054. Retrieved 3 January 2025, from https://plato.stanford.edu/archives/sum2021/entries/justice-intergenerational/. (Article last updated May 2021)

Meyer, L. H., & Roser, D. (2009). Enough for the future. In A. Gosseries & L. H. Meyer (Eds.), *Intergenerational justice* (Vol. 8, pp. 219–248). Oxford University Press.

Mill, J. S. (1863). *Utilitarianism.* West Strand.

Miller, D. (2021). Justice. In E. N. Zalta (Ed.). *The Stanford encyclopedia of philosophy.* ISSN 1095-5054. Retrieved 3 January 2025, from https://plato.stanford.edu/entries/justice/. (Article last updated August 2021)

Moorhouse, F. (2021). *What is longtermism? 2021.* Retrieved 3 January 2025, from https://longtermism.com/

Mulgan, T. (2014). Utilitarianism and our obligations to future people. In B. Eggleston (Ed.), *The Cambridge companion to utilitarianism* (pp. 325–347). Cambridge University Press. https://doi.org/10.1017/CCO9781139096737.017

Nagy, B. (1998). Speaking without a voice. In E. Agius & S. Busuttil (Eds.). *Future generations and international law: Proceedings of the international experts' meeting held by the future generations Programme at the Foundation for International Studies, University of Malta* (Vol. 6, pp. 51–64). Earthscan Publications Ltd.

Narveson, J. (1978). Future people and us. In R. I. Sikora & B. M. Barry (Eds.), *Obligations to future generations* (pp. 38–60). Temple University Press.

Narveson, J. (1992). The libertarian idea. *The Philosophical Review, 101*(2), 470. https://doi.org/10.2307/2185579

Nathanson, S. (n.d.). Utilitarianism: Act and rule. In J. Fieser & B. Dowden (Eds.). *Internet encyclopedia of philosophy.* ISSN 2161-0002.

Newman, D. (2011). *Community and collective rights: A theoretical framework for rights held by groups.* Hart Publishing.

Nickel, J. W. (2024). Human rights. In E. N. Zalta (Ed.). *The Stanford encyclopedia of philosophy.* ISSN 1095-5054. Retrieved 3 January 2025, from https://plato.stanford.edu/entries/rights-human/. (Article last updated May 2024).

Norlock, K. (2019). Feminist ethics. In E. N. Zalta (Ed.). *The Stanford encyclopedia of philosophy.* ISSN 1095-5054. Retrieved 3 January 2025, from https://plato.stanford.edu/entries/feminism-ethics/. (Article last updated 27 May 2019).

Norton, B. G. (1982). Environmental ethics and the rights of future generations. *Environmental Ethics, 4*(4), 319–337. https://doi.org/10.5840/enviroethics1982444

Nozick, R. (1974). *Anarchy, state, and utopia*. Blackwell Publishers.
Nussbaum, M. (2002). Women and the law of peoples. *Politics, Philosophy and Economics, 3*, 283–306.
Obeng, L. (1980). Benevolent yokes in different worlds. In C. N. McRostie, B. Commoner, & G. A. College (Eds.), *Global resources: Perspectives and alternatives* (pp. 21–32). University Park Press.
Orakhelashvili, A. (2007). Natural law and justice. In A. Peters & R. Wolfrum (Eds.), *Max Planck encyclopedia of public international law*. Oxford University Press. (Article last updated August 2007).
Otsuka, M. (1998). Self-ownership and equality: A Lockean reconciliation. *Philosophy and Public Affairs, 27*(1), 65–92. https://doi.org/10.1111/j.1088-4963.1998.tb00061.x
Otsuka, M. (2018). Appropriating Lockean appropriation on behalf of equality. In J. E. Penner & M. Otsuka (Eds.), *Property theory: Legal and political perspectives* (pp. 121–137). Cambridge University Press. https://doi.org/10.1017/9781108500043.007
Parfit, D. (1976). On doing the best for our children. In M. D. Bayles (Ed.), *Ethics and population* (pp. 100–115). Schenkman.
Parfit, D. (1982). Future generations, further problems. *Philosophy and Public Affairs, 11*(2), 113–172.
Parfit, D. (1984). *Reasons and persons*. Clarendon Press.
Parfit, D. (1997). Equality and priority. *Ratio, 10*(3), 202–221. https://doi.org/10.1111/1467-9329.00041
Parfit, D. (2017). Future people, the non-identity problem, and person-affecting principles. *Philosophy and Public Affairs, 45*(2), 118–157. https://doi.org/10.1111/papa.12088
Partridge, E. (1981). Why Care about the future? In E. Partridge (Ed.), *Responsibilities to future generations: Environmental ethics* (pp. 203–220). Prometheus Books.
Partridge, E. (2007). Future generations. In D. Jamieson (Ed.), *A companion to environmental philosophy* (2nd ed., pp. 377–389). Blackwell Publishers. https://doi.org/10.1002/9780470751664.ch26
Philips, J. (2016). Human rights and threats concerning future people: A Sufficientarian proposal. In G. Bos & M. Düwell (Eds.), *Human rights and sustainability: Moral responsibilities for the future* (Vol. 7, pp. 82–94). Routledge Taylor & Francis Group.
Preda, A. (2012). Group rights and group agency. *Journal of Moral Philosophy, 9*(2), 229–254. https://doi.org/10.1163/174552412X625736
Randall, T. (2019). Care ethics and obligations to future generations. *Hypatia, 34*(3), 527–545. https://doi.org/10.1111/hypa.12477
Rawls, J. (1971). *A theory of justice* (Revised edn). Harvard University Press (Original work published 1971).
Rawls, J. (1980). Kantian constructivism in moral theory: Rational and full autonomy. *The Journal of Philosophy, 77*(9), 515. https://doi.org/10.2307/2025790
Rawls, J. (1999). *The law of peoples: With "The Idea of Public Reason Revisited"*. Harvard University Press.
Rawls, J. (2005). *Political liberalism*. Columbia University Press (Original work published 1993).
Rawls, J., & Kelly, E. (2001). *Justice as fairness: A restatement* (2nd ed.). Harvard University Press.
Raz, J. (1984a). Legal rights. *Oxford Journal of Legal Studies, 4*(1), 1–21. https://doi.org/10.1093/ojls/4.1.1
Raz, J. (1984b). On the nature of rights. *Oxford Journal of Legal Studies, 93*(370), 194–214. https://doi.org/10.1093/ojls/4.1.1
Raz, J. (1988). *The morality of freedom*. Clarendon Press.
Redgwell, C. (1999). *Intergenerational trusts and environmental protection*. Juris.
Reiman, J. (2007). Being fair to future people: The non-identity problem in the original position. *Philosophy and Public Affairs, 35*(1), 69–92. https://doi.org/10.1111/j.1088-4963.2007.00099.x

Riley, S. (2016). International human rights and duties to future generations: The role of an international constitution. In G. Bos & M. Düwell (Eds.), *Human rights and sustainability: Moral responsibilities for the future* (Vol. 5, pp. 53–66). Routledge Taylor & Francis Group.

Ritchie, D. G. (1891). *The principles of state interference: Four essays on the political philosophy of Mr. Herbert Spencer, J. S. Mill, and T. H. Green*. Swan Sonnenschein & Co.

Rivera-López, E. (2009). Individual procreative responsibility and the non-identity problem. *Pacific Philosophical Quarterly, 90*(3), 336–363. https://doi.org/10.1111/j.1468-0114.2009.01344.x

Roberts, M. A. (2009). The nonidentity problem and the two envelope problem: When is one act better for a person than another? In M. A. Roberts & D. T. Wasserman (Eds.), *Harming future persons: Ethics, genetics and the nonidentity problem* (Vol. 10, pp. 201–229). Springer.

Roberts, M. A. (2011a). The asymmetry: A solution. *Theoria, 77*(4), 333–367. https://doi.org/10.1111/j.1755-2567.2011.01117.x

Roberts, M. A. (2011b). An asymmetry in the ethics of procreation. *Philosophy Compass, 6*(11), 765–776. https://doi.org/10.1111/j.1747-9991.2011.00435.x

Roberts, M. A. (2024). The Nonidentity Problem. In E. N. Zalta (Ed.). *The Stanford Encyclopedia of Philosophy*. ISSN 1095-5054. Retrieved 3 January 2025, from https://plato.stanford.edu/entries/nonidentity-problem/. (Article last updated July 2024).

Rousseau, J.-J. (1968). *The social contract* (1st ed.). Penguin Books. (Original work published 1762).

Scanlon, T. M. (1998). *What we owe to each other*. Belknap Press of Harvard University Press.

Scanlon, T. M. (2005). When Does Equality Matter? 2005. Retrieved 3 January 2025, from https://law.yale.edu/sites/default/files/documents/pdf/Intellectual_Life/ltw-Scanlon.pdf

Scholtz, W. (2021). Equity. In L. Rajamani & J. Peel (Eds.), *The Oxford handbook of international environmental law* (Vol. 20, 2nd ed., pp. 335–349). Oxford University Press.

Schwartz, T. (1978). Obligations to posterity. In R. I. Sikora & B. M. Barry (Eds.), *Obligations to future generations* (pp. 3–13). Temple University Press.

Shelton, D. (2010a). Equity. In D. Bodansky, J. Brunnée, & E. Hey (Eds.), *The Oxford handbook of international environmental law* (Vol. 27, 1st ed., pp. 639–662). Oxford University Press. https://doi.org/10.1093/oxfordhb/9780199552153.013.0027

Shelton, D. (2010b). Intergenerational equity. In R. Wolfrum & C. Kojima (Eds.), *Solidarity: A structural principle of international law* (pp. 123–168). Springer.

Shrader-Frechette, K. (2004). Ethical theory versus unethical practice: Radiation protection and future generations. In R. J. Goldstein (Ed.), *Environmental ethics and law* (Vol. 16, pp. 593–614). Ashgate.

Sidgwick, H. (1874). *The methods of ethics* (7th ed.). MacMillan and.

Singer, P. (2002). *One world: The ethics of globalization*. Yale University Press.

Sinnott-Armstrong, W. (2023). Consequentalism. In E. N. Zalta (Ed.). *The Stanford encyclopedia of philosophy*. ISSN 1095-5054. Retrieved 3 January 2025, from https://plato.stanford.edu/entries/consequentialism/. (Article last updated October 2023).

Smart, J. J. C. (1973). An outline of a system of utilitarian ethics. In J. J. C. Smart & B. Williams (Eds.), *Utilitarianism: For and against* (pp. 1–74). Cambridge University Press.

Smolkin, D. (1999). Toward a rights-based solution to the non-identity problem. *Journal of Social Philosophy, 30*(1), 194–208.

Solum, L. B. (2001). To our children's children's children: The problems of intergenerational ethics. *Loyola of Los Angeles Law Review, 35*, 163–233.

Spengler, L. (2016). Two types of 'Enough' sufficiency as minimum and maximum. *Environmental Politics, 25*(5), 921–940. https://doi.org/10.1080/09644016.2016.1164355

Sreenivasan, G. (2005). A hybrid theory of claim-rights. *Oxford Journal of Legal Studies, 25*(2), 257–274. https://doi.org/10.1093/ojls/gqi013

Steinbock, B. (2009). Wrongful life and procreative decisions. In M. A. Roberts & D. T. Wasserman (Eds.), *Harming future persons: Ethics, genetics and the nonidentity problem* (Vol. 8, pp. 155–178). Springer.

Steiner, H. (1994). *An essay on rights*. Blackwell Publishers.

Steiner, H., & Vallentyne, P. (2009). Libertarian theories of intergenerational justice. In A. Gosseries & L. H. Meyer (Eds.), *Intergenerational justice* (Vol. 2, pp. 50–76). Oxford University Press.

Stephens, T. (2010). Sustainability discourses in international courts: What place for global justice? In D. French (Ed.), *Global justice and sustainable development* (Vol. 2, pp. 39–56). Martinus Nijhoff Publishers.

Stone, C. D. (1987). *Earth and other ethics: The case for moral pluralism* (1st ed.). Harper & Row.

Stone, C. D. (2010). Ethics and international environmental law. In D. Bodansky, J. Brunnée, & E. Hey (Eds.), *The Oxford handbook of international environmental law* (Vol. 13, 1st ed., pp. 291–312). Oxford University Press.

Supanich, G. P. (1992). The legal basis of intergenerational responsibility: An alternative view—The sense of intergenerational identity. *Yearbook of International Environmental Law, 3*(1), 94–107. https://doi.org/10.1093/yiel/3.1.94

Theilen, J. T. (2021). The inflation of human rights: A deconstruction. *Leiden Journal of International Law, 34*(4), 831–854. https://doi.org/10.1017/S0922156521000297

Thompson, J. (2009a). Identity and obligation in a transgenerational polity. In A. Gosseries & L. H. Meyer (Eds.), *Intergenerational justice* (Vol. 1, pp. 25–49). Oxford University Press. https://doi.org/10.1093/acprof:oso/9780199282951.003.0002

Thompson, J. (2009b). *Intergenerational justice: Rights and responsibilities in an intergenerational polity*. Routledge Taylor & Francis Group.

Thompson, T. H. (1981). Are we obligated to future others? In E. Partridge (Ed.), *Responsibilities to future generations: Environmental ethics* (pp. 195–202). Prometheus Books.

Tremmel, J. C. (2004). Is a theory of intergenerational justice possible? A response to Beckerman. *Intergenerational Justice Review, 2*, 6–9.

Tremmel, J. C. (2009). A theory of intergenerational justice. *Earthscan Publications Ltd.* https://doi.org/10.4324/9781849774369

Tremmel, J. C. (2013). The convention of representatives of all generations under the "Veil of Ignorance". *Constellations, 20*(3), 483–502. https://doi.org/10.1111/1467-8675.12049

Tritschoks, A. (2018). Rethinking justice in international environmental negotiations: Toward a more comprehensive framework. *International Negotiation, 23*(3), 446–477. https://doi.org/10.1163/15718069-23031159

United Nations General Assembly. (1948). *Universal Declaration of Human Rights* (10 December 1948). UN Doc. A/RES/217(III).

United Nations Secretary-General. (2013). *Intergenerational Solidarity and the Needs of Future Generations, Report of the Secretary-General* (15 August 2013). UN Doc. A/68/322.

van der Vossen, B. (2023). Libertarianism. In E. N. Zalta (Ed.). *The Stanford encyclopedia of philosophy.* ISSN 1095-5054. Retrieved 3 January 2025, from https://plato.stanford.edu/entries/libertarianism/. (Article last updated August 2023).

van Dyke, V. (1982). Collective entities and moral rights: Problems in Liberal-democratic thought. *The Journal of Politics, 44*(1), 21–40. https://doi.org/10.2307/2130282

Vasconcellos Oliveira, R. (2018). Back to the future: The potential of intergenerational justice for the achievement of the sustainable development goals. *Sustainability, 10*(2), 427–442. https://doi.org/10.3390/su10020427

Visser 't Hooft, H. P. (1999). *Justice to future generations and the environment.* Spring https://doi.org/10.1007/978-94-015-9103-4.

Wallack, M. (2006). Justice between generations: The limits of procedural justice. In J. C. Tremmel (Ed.), *Handbook of intergenerational justice* (Vol. 5, pp. 86–105). Edward Elgar Publishing.

Warren, K. J. (2015). Feminist environmental philosophy. In E. N. Zalta (Ed.). *The Stanford encyclopedia of philosophy.* ISSN 1095-5054. Retrieved 3 January 2025, from https://plato.stanford.edu/entries/feminism-environmental/. (Article last updated April 2015).

Wellman, C. (1985). *A theory of rights: Persons under Laws, institutions, and morals*. Rowman & Littlefield.

Wellman, C. (1995). *Real rights.* Oxford University Press.

Wenar, L. (2005). The nature of rights. *Philosophy and Public Affairs, 33*(3), 223–252. https://doi.org/10.1111/j.1088-4963.2005.00032.x

Wenar, L. (2020). Rights. In E. N. Zalta (Ed.). *The Stanford encyclopedia of philosophy.* ISSN 1095-5054. Retrieved 3 January 2025, from https://plato.stanford.edu/entries/rights/. (Article last updated February 2020).

Wenar, L. (2021). John Rawls. In E. N. Zalta (Ed.). *The Stanford encyclopedia of philosophy.* ISSN 1095-5054. Retrieved 3 January 2025, from https://plato.stanford.edu/entries/rawls/. (Article last updated April 2021).

Wendt, F. (2017). The sufficiency proviso. In J. Brennan, B. van der Vossen, & D. Schmidtz (Eds.), *The Routledge handbook of libertarianism* (Vol. 12, 1st ed., pp. 169–183). Routledge Taylor & Francis Group.

Wenzel, N. (2011). Group rights. In A. Peters & R. Wolfrum (Eds.), *Max Planck encyclopedia of public international law*. Oxford University Press. (Article last updated January 2011).

Williams, B. (1973). A critique of utilitarianism. In J. J. C. Smart & B. Williams (Eds.), *Utilitarianism: For and against* (pp. 75–150). Cambridge University Press.

Winter, C., Schuett, J., Martínez, E., van Arsdale, S., Araújo, R., Hollman, N., Sebo, J., Stawasz, A., O'Keefe, C., & Rotola, G. (2021). Legal Priorities Research: A Research Agenda. *Legal Priorities Project*. January 2021. Retrieved 3 January 2025, from https://papers.ssrn.com/sol3/papers.cfm?abstract_id=3931256.

Wolf, C. (1995). Contemporary property rights, Lockean provisos, and the interests of future generations. *Ethics, 105*(4), 791–818.

Woods, K. (2016). The rights of (future) humans qua humans. *Journal of Human Rights, 15*(2), 291–306. https://doi.org/10.1080/14754835.2015.1106310

Woodward, J. (1986). The non-identity problem. *Ethics, 96*(4), 804–831.

World Commission on Environment and Development. (1987). *Report of the World Commission on Environment and Development: Our Common Future (Brundtland Report)* (1987). UN Doc. A/42/427 Annex.

World Summit for Social Development. (1995). *Copenhagen Declaration on Social Development* (14 March 1995). UN Doc. A/CONF.166/9.

# Chapter 4
# Legal Nature of Intergenerational Equity: Normative Capacity and Legal Status

Chapter 2 has offered a doctrinal analysis of the historical development and systemic framework of intergenerational equity. Chapter 3 has demonstrated the overlaps between the moral sphere and its legal counterpart as well as the important influence different philosophical schools of thought have had on the legal discussion of intergenerational relations. The overlaps between legal normativity and its pre-legal foundations are also relevant in this chapter, which turns back to the legal assessment of intergenerational equity. The present chapter focuses on a mainly positivist analysis of intergenerational equity, which is based on the overview of the historical, scholarly and systemic contexts in Chap. 2. In order to fully understand how exactly intergenerational equity takes effect in the international legal system, its legal nature must be analysed. This is important with regard to the open issues addressed in Chap. 5, but also as far as the potential consequences of its legal nature for the development of intertemporal law in Chaps. 6 and 7 are concerned.

Legal nature, as understood in this book, encompasses two different notions.[1] First, it is important whether the concept of intergenerational equity is structured in a way that has normative capacity, or normativity, at all.[2] Normative capacity implies that the concept has the "capacity to directly or indirectly steer the behaviour of its addressees",[3] and it can exist in the form of principles or rules. Normative capacity is not limited to the examination of legally binding documents, but focuses on the exact contents of the respective concept. Therefore, various non-binding documents, the case law of international bodies and legal scholarship equally play a role in the analysis of normative capacity. In this regard, the method of doctrinal analysis

[1] Barral (2012), p. 383.

[2] Often, the term "normative quality" is used in academic literature, see, e.g., Beyerlin and Marauhn (2011), p. 79. However, in this book, the terms "normative capacity" and "normativity" are used interchangeably since they better describe the meaning intended for the present analysis.

[3] Beyerlin (2010), p. 428; Beyerlin and Marauhn (2011), p. 79.



A. Bustami, *The Legal Relationship between Present and Future Generations*,
https://doi.org/10.1007/978-3-032-03345-1_4

provides a suitable tool to analyse the contents and interrelations between potential principles, rules and non-legal policies without normative capacity.[4]

The second aspect of legal nature answers whether intergenerational equity is legally binding or not. It can only be answered if the concept of intergenerational equity has normative capacity in a first step.[5] This second issue, often referred to as the "legal status" of a norm, only exists if the norm falls under one of the sources of international law. Consequently, the second section of the chapter turns to a traditional positivist method of analysis by examining the main sources of international law, listed in Article 38(1) of the ICJ Statute.[6] More importantly, a positivist assessment of the potential customary nature of intergenerational equity requires an examination of the empirical existence of State practice and *opinio iuris*.[7] Yet, as the present work cannot offer a comprehensive sociological study of State practice in the context of intergenerational equity,[8] the empirical evidence used in the following analysis must be limited to a number of exemplary statements, documents and other instances of practice and legal conviction.[9]

Unfortunately, legal scholarship does not always properly make the mentioned distinction between the normative capacity and the legal status of a norm.[10] Moreover, terminological differences exist with regard to both issues, so that a doctrinal analysis of intergenerational equity's legal nature is difficult.[11] Additionally, the two manifestations of intergenerational equity, which have been illustrated in Chap. 2,[12] must be distinguished in the context of the question of its legal nature. The general conception of intergenerational equity might have another normative capacity than the specific doctrine established by *Brown Weiss*. One of them might be legally binding as a treaty or a customary norm while the other is not.

Consequently, the following sections use the terminology introduced in this chapter and are structured alongside these two distinctions. First, this chapter assesses the normative capacity of intergenerational equity (Sect. 4.1). Second, the analysis turns to the issue of intergenerational equity's legal status in light of the

---

[4]Cf. Smits (2017), p. 210.

[5]Epiney and Scheyli (2000), pp. 40, 76; Beyerlin and Marauhn (2011), pp. 79–82; Proelß (2022), pp. 101, 146.

[6]See Cryer et al. (2011), p. 38.

[7]For the elements of customary international law, see, e.g., Treves (2006). In more detail, see *infra* in Sect. 4.2.2.

[8]For an overview of sociological theories of international law, see Carty (2008). For criticism of the common methods of empirical assessment in international law, see Talmon (2015).

[9]Cf. International Court of Justice, *Barcelona Traction, Light and Power Company, Limited (Belgium v. Spain), Second Phase,* Separate Opinion of Judge Jessup, 5 February 1970, ICJ Reports 1970, 161, para. 60.

[10]Generally on the terminological inconsistencies, see Beyerlin (2010), pp. 429–432, 438–439.

[11]For instance, *Virginie Barral* used the term "legal scope" instead of "normative capacity", see Barral (2012), p. 383.

[12]See *supra* in Sect. 2.3.1.2.

sources of international law (Sect. 4.2). In both sections, the distinction between the two manifestations of intergenerational equity is of particular relevance.[13]

## 4.1 Normative Capacity

So far, this book has used the term "concept" in a non-technical way with regard to sustainable development or intergenerational equity.[14] Both concepts are often considered to be part of what is called "principles of environmental law".[15] However, the term "principle" is at least ambiguous and may refer to different notions.[16] "General principles of law recognized by civilized nations"[17] is not the only relevant meaning in this context.[18] In the context of environmental law, the term "principle" is predominantly used in a less technical way and does not necessarily entail a characterisation of a concept's normative capacity.[19] In contrast, the following analysis of intergenerational equity's normative capacity is based on *Ronald Dworkin's* typology, which distinguished three different types of concepts: policies, principles and rules (Sect. 4.1.1).[20] Due to the strong connections and overlaps between the general conception of intergenerational equity and the overarching framework of sustainable development,[21] the subsequent analysis starts with an examination of the normative capacity of sustainable development (Sect. 4.1.2), before it turns to the related general conception of intergenerational equity (Sect. 4.1.3). Finally, the specific doctrine of intergenerational equity is assessed separately with regard to its normativity (Sect. 4.1.4).

---

[13]For such a differentiation, see also Redgwell (1999), pp. 128, 143; Beyerlin (2010), pp. 446, 447; Dupuy and Viñuales (2018), p. 62.

[14]See *supra* in Chap. 2 [note 1].

[15]See, e.g., Proelß (2022), p. 103.

[16]Crawford and Brownlie (2019), p. 34.

[17]*Statute of the International Court of Justice* (ICJ Statute), adopted 26 June 1945, entered into force 24 October 1945, 1 UNTS XVI, Art. 38(1)(d).

[18]Crawford and Brownlie (2019), p. 34; Brunnée (2017), pp. 973–974.

[19]See also Beyerlin (2010), pp. 429–432, 438–439.

[20]Dworkin (1978), p. 22.

[21]See *supra* in Sect. 2.3.1.

### 4.1.1 A Typology of Normative Capacity: Policies, Principles and Rules

*Ronald Dworkin* distinguished between policies, legal principles and legal rules.[22] While some commentators refer to "concepts" instead of "policies" with respect to a similar notion,[23] the present author uses "concept" in a non-technical manner. Instead, the threefold division of *Dworkin's* terminology is consistently used in the following sections. According to *Dworkin*, the normative capacity of a concept depends on whether it constitutes a legal principle or a legal rule or whether it is a mere policy. While rules and principles have the "capacity to directly or indirectly steer the behaviour of their addressees",[24] a policy constitutes a "standard that sets out a goal to be reached, generally an improvement in some economic, political or social feature of the community".[25] In contrast to principles and rules, policies lack normative capacity in a legal sense.[26]

Although principles and rules both have normative capacity, the question remains in which way the respective norm influences the behaviour of its addressee. This depends on whether the norm concerned establishes a principle or a rule.[27] This norm structure helps in determining the exact consequences of the norm's application.[28] *Dworkin* defined a principle as a norm "that is to be observed, [...] because it is a requirement of justice or fairness or some other dimension of morality".[29] The inherent relationship between legal principles and their moral foundations is particularly obvious in the realm of international environmental law.[30]

---

[22] Ibid.

[23] Dupuy and Viñuales (2018), pp. 59–62; Kiss and Beurier (2010), p. 129.

[24] Beyerlin (2010), p. 428; Beyerlin and Marauhn (2011), p. 79.

[25] Dworkin (1978), p. 22.

[26] Instead of distinguishing between "policies" and "principles", some authors preferred a distinction between legal principles and mere moral principles, see Alexy (1995), p. 177; Rauber (2018), pp. 155–157, 227–229. Some commentators have labelled policies that influence the behaviour of States in a political-moral but extra-legal sense as "soft law", see Beyerlin (2010), p. 427. However, the characterisation as soft law does not concern the normative capacity of a concept but the question of a document's legally non-binding character, see also Thürer (2009), paras. 1–3; for different meanings of soft law, see in detail Boyle (1999), pp. 901–913. This means that soft law documents can incorporate policies without normative capacity as well as principles and rules that have normative capacity. The character as soft law refers only to the legal status of the document itself, which cannot establish legal bindingness. Therefore, the notion of soft law is addressed below with regard to the legal status of intergenerational equity, see *infra* in Sect. 4.2.2.

[27] See, e.g., Eggett (2019), pp. 202–205.

[28] Schröter (2015), p. 122.

[29] Dworkin (1978), p. 22. See also Permanent Court of Arbitration, *Gentini Case (of a general nature) (Italy v. Venezuela)*, Arbitral Award, 13 February 1903, RIAA X (1903), 551, p. 556.

[30] See Stone (2010), p. 292 as well as *supra* in Chap. 3 [notes 3–9].

In contrast to principles, rules are norms that entail directly binding effects that direct States to a specific act or behaviour.[31] Rules and principles particularly differ in their structure[32]: Rules apply in an "all-or-nothing fashion", meaning that a rule supplies a clear answer as to its consequences if the facts of the rule are given.[33] They have a narrower scope and a more clearly defined normative message.[34] In contrast, principles do "not set out legal consequences that follow automatically when the conditions provided are met".[35] As stated by *Dworkin*:

> [A principle] states a reason that argues in one direction, but does not necessitate a particular decision. [...] There may be other principles or policies arguing in the other direction [...]. If so, our principle may not prevail, but that does not mean that it is not a principle of our legal system, because in the next case, when these contravening considerations are absent or less weighty, the principle may be decisive. [...] the principle is one which officials must take into account, if it is relevant, as a consideration inclining in one way or another.[36]

The respective principle is ascribed a certain weight and importance,[37] and it sets a certain goal that should be achieved to the greatest extent legally and factually possible.[38] Put briefly, it could be said that principles are norms of a more general character that provide guidance on State behaviour, while rules are the "practical formulation of the principles".[39]

Legal scholarship has often referred to *Dworkin's* typology of policies, principles and rules.[40] Some scholars have suggested other categorisations,[41] which sometimes only adapted *Dworkin's* distinction,[42] but sometimes also objected to it due to its alleged inflexibility.[43] Even though some of these objections may be legitimate, they do not necessarily offer a better distinction but give rise to other difficulties.[44] This is why there is no need to address them in more detail in the present book. Rather, the author takes *Dworkin's* distinction between non-normative policies and principles

---

[31] Beyerlin (2010), p. 428.

[32] For other distinctions, see Alexy (2000), pp. 295–298; Eggett (2019), pp. 202–204.

[33] Dworkin (1978), p. 24.

[34] See de Castro (1997), p. 28.

[35] Dworkin (1978), p. 25.

[36] Ibid., p. 26.

[37] Ibid., pp. 25–26.

[38] Ibid; Beyerlin (2010), p. 433; Eggett (2019), p. 203. Cf. Schröter (2015), pp. 122–124.

[39] Cheng (1994), p. 376; Lang (1999), p. 159.

[40] See, e.g., Bodansky (1993), p. 501; Sands (1995), pp. 54–55; Verschuuren (2003), pp. 19, 38, 41; Scheyli (2008), pp. 293–302; Beyerlin (2010), pp. 435–438; Eggett (2019), pp. 202–205.

[41] For an overview with more references, see Beyerlin (2010), pp. 434–435.

[42] See, e.g., Alexy (1995), p. 177; Alexy (2006), pp. 88–90; Rauber (2018), pp. 160–179. For *Alexy's* distinction between definitive commands and optimisation commands, see Alexy (2000), p. 295. For an overview and comparison of *Ronald Dworkin's* and *Robert Alexy's* theories, see Schröter (2015), pp. 124–138.

[43] See, e.g., Aarnio (1990); de Sadeleer (2005), p. 308. Cf. also Lowe (1999), p. 31.

[44] In more detail, see Beyerlin (2010), pp. 435–438.

and rules *with* normative capacity as a basis for the further analysis of the concepts of intergenerational equity and sustainable development.

### 4.1.2 Sustainable Development

As has been illustrated in Chap. 2, the need to take into account the interests of future generations is part of the overarching framework of sustainable development.[45] This general conception of intergenerational equity is sometimes even considered to constitute the core of sustainable development.[46] The strong interrelation between the two notions could also influence the normative capacity of the general conception of intergenerational equity. The normative capacity of sustainable development could have an indicative effect on the normative capacity of intergenerational equity. Even if both concepts were independent in this regard, the analysis of normativity of sustainable development would remain essential for any further understanding of the general conception of intergenerational equity. Therefore, the following analysis first assesses the normativity of sustainable development as a starting point.

The initial question is whether sustainable development has the capacity to influence the behaviour of its addressees in a legal sense. If it did not have such normative capacity, it would constitute a mere policy. Provided that it has the necessary normative capacity, it could either qualify as a principle or as a rule.

International treaties in the context of sustainable development usually do not give much indication on the concept's normativity.[47] Most references exist in the respective treaties' preambles and with rather unclear wording.[48] Some of these references stipulate the promotion of sustainable development as their "objective".[49]

---

[45] See *supra* in Sect. 2.3.1.

[46] Sands et al. (2018), p. 219.

[47] Beyerlin and Marauhn (2011), p. 79.

[48] E.g., *Agreement Establishing the World Trade Organization* (WTO Agreement), adopted 15 April 1994, entered into force 1 January 1995, 33 ILM 1125, Preamble; *Convention on the Protection and Use of Transboundary Watercourses and International Lakes* (UNECE Water Convention), adopted 17 March 1992, entered into force 6 October 1996, 1936 UNTS 269, Preamble; *Convention on Access to Information, Public Participation in Decision-making and Access to Justice in Environmental Matters* (Aarhus Convention), adopted 25 June 1998, entered into force 30 October 2001, 2161 UNTS 447, Preamble; *Rotterdam Convention on the Prior Informed Consent Procedure for Certain Hazardous Chemicals and Pesticides in International Trade* (Rotterdam Convention), adopted 10 September 1998, entered into force 24 February 2004, 2244 UNTS 337, Preamble; *Protocol on Strategic Environmental Assessment to the Convention on Environmental Impact Assessment in a Transboundary Context* (Protocol to the Espoo Convention), adopted 21 May 2003, entered into force 11 July 2010, 2685 UNTS 140, Preamble.

[49] *United Nations Framework Convention on Climate Change* (UNFCCC), adopted 9 May 1992, entered into force 21 March 1994, 1771 UNTS 107, Art. 2; *United Nations Convention to Combat Desertification in those Countries Experiencing Serious Drought and/or Desertification, Particularly in Africa* (UNCCD), adopted 17 June 1994, entered into force 26 December 1996, 1954 UNTS

Only Article 3 of the UNFCCC goes beyond such preambular stipulation or reference to a mere objective and proclaims as one of its "principles":

> The Parties have a right to, and should, promote sustainable development. Policies and measures to protect the climate system against human-induced change should be appropriate for the specific conditions of each Party and should be integrated with national development programmes, taking into account that economic development is essential for adopting measures to address climate change.[50]

Regardless of the denomination as an "objective" or as a "principle", this denomination cannot necessarily be understood in the sense of a normative typology. Instead, the concept's normative capacity must be assessed based on its content rather than on what it is called.[51]

International jurisprudence is hardly more instructive in this respect. The International Court of Justice in its *Gabčíkovo-Nagymaros Project* decision referred very clearly to sustainable development as a "need to reconcile economic development with protection of the environment".[52] Although the Court framed sustainable development as a "concept",[53] this formulation was not meant as a declaration on the normative character; the Court rather was "careful not to become entangled in questions of qualification and doctrinal refinement".[54] *Judge Weeramantry's* separate opinion shed more light on the issue, as it categorised sustainable development as "a principle with normative value"[55] rather than a mere concept. Further, *Judge Weeramantry* classified sustainable development as "an integral part of modern international law".[56] However, based on the wording of the Court's judgment, it is not clear whether this categorisation was shared by the majority in the case, a question which has given rise to much academic debate.[57]

The more recent *Pulp Mills* decision of the ICJ also addressed a variety of concepts related to and complementing sustainable development, such as the

---

3, Art. 2; Preamble of the WTO Agreement; Art. 1 of the Protocol to the Espoo Convention. With regard to "sustainable use", see *Convention on Biological Diversity* (CBD), adopted 5 June 1992, entered into force 29 December 1993, 1760 UNTS 79, Art. 1.

[50] Art. 3(4) of the UNFCCC.

[51] Magraw and Hawke (2010), p. 623.

[52] ICJ, *Gabčíkovo-Nagymaros Project (Hungary v. Slovakia),* Judgment, 25 September 1997, ICJ Reports 1997, 7, para. 140.

[53] Ibid.

[54] De Castro (1997), p. 28. See also Beyerlin and Marauhn (2011), p. 79.

[55] ICJ, *Gabčíkovo-Nagymaros Project (Hungary v. Slovakia),* Separate Opinion of Vice-President Weeramantry, 25 September 1997, ICJ Reports 1997, 88, p. 88. Cf. also Weeramantry (2004), pp. 432–434.

[56] *Gabčíkovo-Nagymaros Project* (Separate Opinion of Vice-President Weeramantry), *supra* note 55, 89, 95.

[57] Considering the majority judgment in the same sense, see de Castro (1997), pp. 28–29; Sands et al. (2018), p. 220. Denying this meaning of the judgment, see Beyerlin and Marauhn (2011), pp. 79–80; Mbengue (2020), pp. 184–185. Generally on the normative vagueness in the decision, see McGarry (2020).

principle of prevention, the precautionary approach or the requirement to conduct an EIA.[58] However, indications on the normative capacity of sustainable development as such remained scarce. The Court referred, *inter alia*, to the "objective of sustainable development",[59] and again refrained from offering the expected clarification.[60] Instead, *Judge Cançado Trindade*, again in a separate opinion, examined the aforementioned concepts in detail, including sustainable development and even intergenerational equity.[61] He underlined that the disputing parties' acknowledged the normative significance of sustainable development.[62] Moreover, he concluded that "there are strong reasons for recognizing sustainable development as a guiding general principle for the consideration of environmental and developmental issues".[63] It is not clear whether the Court itself was of that same opinion, or whether its reference to an "objective" must rather be understood as a denial of any normativity of sustainable development.[64]

At first glance, the arbitral award in the *Iron Rhine* case shed some light on the issue of normative capacity when it stated:

> Environmental law and the law on development stand not as alternatives but as mutually reinforcing, integral concepts, which require that where development may cause significant harm to the environment there is a duty to prevent, or at least mitigate, such harm [...]. This duty, in the opinion of the Tribunal, has now become a principle of general international law.[65]

This has been interpreted as a confirmation of *Judge Weeramantry's* assessment of sustainable development as a principle with normative capacity.[66] However, *Ulrich Beyerlin* and *Thilo Marauhn* pointed out that this qualification by the arbitral tribunal only referred to the "no harm" principle and left the normativity of sustainable development undecided.[67] This interpretation is backed by the tribunal's preceding

---

[58] ICJ, *Pulp Mills on the River Uruguay (Argentina v. Uruguay),* Judgment, 20 April 2010, ICJ Reports 2010, 14, paras. 101, 160–164, 203–219. The denomination as "principle" of prevention is not meant technically in the sense of *Dworkin's* typology.

[59] Ibid., para. 177.

[60] Tladi (2017), p. 250.

[61] ICJ, *Pulp Mills on the River Uruguay (Argentina v. Uruguay),* Separate Opinion of Judge Cançado Trindade, 20 April 2010, ICJ Reports 2010, 125, paras. 114–147.

[62] Ibid., paras. 141–147.

[63] Ibid., para. 139. However, *Judge Cançado Trindade* discussed this question with regard to an attribution to the sources of international law within the meaning of Article 38(1)(c) of the ICJ Statute, which seems to confound the issues of normative capacity and legal status, cf. ibid., paras. 39–44, 48, 51–53. See also *infra* in Sect. 4.2.3.

[64] Tladi (2017), pp. 252–254; Boyle and Redgwell (2021), p. 127. See also ILA Committee on International Law on Sustainable Development (2012a), pp. 15–16.

[65] PCA, *Award in the Arbitration regarding the Iron Rhine ("Ijzeren Rijn") Railway between the Kingdom of Belgium and the Kingdom of the Netherlands,* Arbitral Award, 24 May 2005, RIAA XXVII (2005), 35, para. 59.

[66] Dupuy and Viñuales (2018), pp. 92–93. See also Barral (2012), p. 387.

[67] Beyerlin and Marauhn (2011), p. 80.

observation, according to which "[t]he emerging principles, *whatever their current status*, make reference to [...], notions of prevention and sustainable development, and protection for future generations" (emphasis added).[68]

Overall, international jurisprudence on this matter has remained unclear, open to interpretation and inconsistent.[69] Concerning legal scholarship, *Beyerlin* and *Marauhn* observed that the "spectrum of doctrinal views on the normative content and status of sustainable development [...] is broad and multifaceted".[70] When dealing with the legal nature of sustainable development, many scholars either based their analysis on a different typology of norms,[71] or they did not distinguish between the normative capacity and the legal status of a norm at all.[72]

Some commentators rejected that sustainable development has any normative capacity and qualified it as a "political ideal"[73] or "programme"[74] due to the concept's inherent vagueness.[75] According to *Dworkin's* typology, they attributed sustainable development to the category of mere policies.[76] Other observers did not deny normativity of sustainable development *per se* but remained vague as to a specific classification[77]; or they categorised it as "neither a concept nor a principle but [falling] somewhere between the two".[78] A third group of scholars referred to

[68] *Iron Rhine Railway* (Arbitral Award), *supra* note 65, para. 58.

[69] Cf. Dupuy and Viñuales (2018), pp. 93–94. See also the following case law: World Trade Organization Appellate Body, *United States – Import Prohibition of Certain Shrimp and Shrimp Products,* Report of the Appellate Body, 12 October 1998, WTO Doc. WT/DS58/AB/R, para. 129; PCA, *In the Matter of the Indus Waters Kishenganga Arbitration before the Court of Arbitration constituted in accordance with the Indus Waters Treaty 1960 between the Government of India and the Government of Pakistan signed on 19 September 1960 (Islamic Republic of Pakistan v. Republic of India),* Partial Award, 18 February 2013, Retrieved January 3, 2025, from https://pcacases.com/web/sendAttach/1681, paras. 448–453.

[70] Beyerlin and Marauhn (2011), p. 80. For another comprehensive overview of literature, see also Atapattu (2006), pp. 182–194.

[71] See, e.g., Proelß (2022), p. 100 who referred to Alexy (1995), pp. 177–212. See also *supra* notes 26, 41–44.

[72] See, e.g., Beaucamp (2002), pp. 80–87; Cordonier Segger and Khalfan (2004), pp. 45–50; Dupuy (2010), pp. 461–462. As to this distinction, see Proelß (2022), pp. 101–102. Cf. also Dupuy et al. (2021), pp. 391–392.

[73] Verschuuren (2003), pp. 20–25; Mensah (2008), p. 52; Beyerlin (2010), pp. 444–445; Beyerlin and Marauhn (2011), p. 81; Beyerlin and Grote Stoutenburg (2013), para. 28.

[74] Dupuy and Viñuales (2018), p. 90. Cf. also Beaucamp (2002), pp. 84–86.

[75] In more detail, see Dernbach and Cheever (2015), pp. 272–279.

[76] *Jonathan Verschuuren* defined "ideals" as "values that are implicit or latent in the law, or the public and moral culture of a society or group that usually cannot be fully realized, and that partly transcend contingent, historical formulations, and implementations in terms of rules and principles and policies", Verschuuren (2003), p. 20. Although there are parallels to *Dworkin's* "policies", *Verschuuren* himself distinguished between these two terms, see ibid., pp. 41–42.

[77] Cordonier Segger and Khalfan (2004), p. 46; Louka (2006), p. 53; Magraw and Hawke (2010), p. 624; Nanda and Pring (2013), p. 22. *Nora Ait-Aissi Paillon* doubted the concept's "*maturité juridique*", see Ait-Aissi Paillon (2018), pp. 97–98.

[78] Atapattu (2006), pp. 186–187, 191.

sustainable development as a "constitutional leading concept"[79] or a "meta principle",[80] which would set the terms of the debate for the creation of true primary norms.[81] As such, sustainable development would at least have limited "normative force" in a moral-political sense as it would influence State and judicial decision-making.[82] However, the latter assumption is rather inconsistent in light of the foregoing typology.

On the other end of the spectrum of legal scholarship, scholars emphasised the normative capacity of sustainable development but disagreed on the degree of specificity—as principle or rule.[83] Among them, some commentators referred to sustainable development as a legal principle that sets standards without requiring specific automatic consequences of its application.[84] In this sense, *Vaughan Lowe* stated:

> [Sustainable development] acquires a kind of normativity within the process of judicial decision-making […] It will colour the understanding of the norms that it modifies. It is in these senses that the concept of sustainable development has real normative force.[85]

Other commentators affirmed sustainable development's normative capacity and considered it to be a legal rule of international law,[86] even if it only constituted an obligation of achieving "ideal standards".[87]

This analysis of the discussion on the normative capacity of sustainable development illustrates the complexity of the question. With regard to the numerous legal documents, which have been influenced by the concept of sustainable development and which have contributed to influencing the behaviour of States, the better reasons speak in favour of accepting at least a certain degree of normativity. At the same

---

[79] Scheyli (2008), pp. 296–298, 337–357. Cf. also Epiney and Scheyli (1998), p. 171.

[80] Lowe (1999), p. 31. In this sense, cf. also Bodansky (2010), p. 203; Dupuy (2010), p. 462; Boyle and Redgwell (2021), p. 129.

[81] Cf. Sands (1995), pp. 57–58, 62; Verschuuren (2003), pp. 27–31; Collins (2007b), pp. 126–127. In this sense, see potentially also Viñuales (2021), pp. 292–293; but *Viñuales* then softened the normative impact he ascribed to sustainable development, see ibid., pp. 296–299.

[82] Epiney and Scheyli (1998), pp. 83–84, 171; Lowe (1999), p. 34; Verschuuren (2016), pp. 296–297. In this direction, see also Cordonier Segger and Khalfan (2004), p. 46; Cordonier Segger (2008), p. 118.

[83] See, e.g., Barral (2012), p. 383.

[84] *Gabčíkovo-Nagymaros Project* (Separate Opinion of Vice-President Weeramantry), *supra* note 55, p. 88; de Castro (1997), pp. 28–29; Tladi (2007), pp. 101–104; Gärditz (2008), p. 167; Voigt (2009), pp. 165–166; Bosselmann (2017), p. 66; Mbengue (2020), pp. 191–192. See also Epiney and Scheyli (2000), p. 76.

[85] Lowe (1999), p. 34. Although *Lowe* only accepted a very limited normativity of sustainable development (see *supra* note 82), this classification as a "meta-principle" could equally be attributed to the norm of a legal principle in the sense of *Dworkin's* typology.

[86] Schröter (2015), pp. 319–320; Rauber (2018), pp. 484–485 as well as Proelß (2022), pp. 145–146 with references to *Gabčíkovo-Nagymaros Project* (Judgment), *supra* note 52, para. 140; Court of Justice of the European Union, *First Corporate Shipping,* Opinion of Advocate General Léger, 7 March 2000, European Case Law Identifier ECLI:EU:C:2000:108, para. 54.

[87] Proelß (2022), p. 145.

time, due to its indeterminacy, its flexibility, and its character as a framework for balancing opposing interests, sustainable development has normative capacity in the form of a legal principle rather than a rule.[88] It thus constitutes a "requirement of justice or fairness or some other dimension of morality".[89] As far as some commentators insisted on the qualification of sustainable development as a legal rule, they admitted that its normative content is not very hard, which is why their qualification might result from a gradually different distinction between principles and rules.[90]

### 4.1.3 The General Conception of Intergenerational Equity

This section turns to the normative capacity of the general conception of intergenerational equity, which constitutes a sub-concept of sustainable development.[91] It is possible to draw two different conclusions from the foregoing analysis of sustainable development. On the one hand, if one affirmed the normativity of sustainable development in the sense of a principle or a rule, this could have an indicative effect on the normative capacity of its sub-concepts. For instance, *Pierre-Marie Dupuy* and *Jorge Viñuales* concluded that "when applied as a principle, sustainable development means the application of other principles of international environmental law with solid customary grounding".[92] The present book also understands sustainable development in this sense as a legal principle that goes beyond a mere political ideal. Nonetheless, the abstract framework of sustainable development would necessarily require more specific normative principles (or rules) in order to be properly applied.[93]

On the other hand, even if one denied the normative capacity of sustainable development, this would not necessarily mean that intergenerational equity could not constitute or develop into a norm with normative capacity itself.[94] This is indirectly supported by those commentators who ascribed a certain meta-normativity to sustainable development without explicitly acknowledging its normative capacity[95]: For instance, *Beyerlin* described sustainable development's function as "catalyst in

[88] Voigt (2009), p. 165.

[89] Dworkin (1978), p. 22.

[90] See, e.g., Proelß (2022), p. 145 who referred rather to *Robert Alexy's* typology, see Alexy (1995).

[91] See *supra* in Sect. 2.3.1.

[92] Dupuy and Viñuales (2018), p. 93.

[93] Cf. Atapattu (2006), p. 182. For instance, *Alexander Proelß* derived the normative capacity of sustainable development (as a rule) from the clear-cut rule character of the integration principle: Proelß (2022), pp. 145–146. This could also be understood as supporting the necessity of more specific sub-principles with proper normative capacity.

[94] See Collins (2007b), pp. 125–127; Beyerlin and Marauhn (2011), pp. 81–82.

[95] See *supra* notes 79–82.

the process of further developing international law"[96] and as "an apt source from which subsequent legal norms may flow".[97] This means that the framework character of sustainable development—as a principle or even as a policy—allows for the identification of sub-concepts with independent normativity, irrespective of the framework's normative capacity as a whole.[98] While it has been essential to analyse and understand the normativity and structure of sustainable development in order to be able to examine its sub-concepts, including intergenerational equity, the following analysis focuses on the normative capacity of the general conception of intergenerational equity as such.

As in the case of sustainable development, the relevant legal documents remain silent on the normative capacity of intergenerational equity. Denominations as "principles"[99] cannot necessarily be understood as technical terms in the sense of *Dworkin*.[100] Within legal scholarship, only a small number of commentators explicitly addressed the issue of the normativity of intergenerational equity.[101] Most commentators either directly commented on its legally binding character as a norm of customary international law (i.e., the second level of analysis), or they confused the issue of legal status with the preliminary question of normative capacity.[102] Among those who commented on the normativity of intergenerational equity, *Lowe* stated that "the principle of inter-generational equity is, in normative terms, a chimera."[103] For him, it was not clear which obligations exactly resulted from this concept, as too many questions would remain unanswered.[104] *Lowe* concluded that "inter-generational equity can scarcely be more than a weak injunction to take into account the interest of future generations when engaging in, or permitting others to engage in, present activities. It lacks normative status."[105] Similarly, *Zena Hadjiargyrou* agreed and stated:

> Intergenerational equity, [...], though an admiral [sic.] concept in thought, has proven to be chaotic in terms of understanding, implementation and elucidation both conceptually and in

---

[96] Beyerlin (2010), p. 445.

[97] Ibid., p. 447. See also Boyle and Redgwell (2021), p. 129.

[98] Beyerlin and Marauhn (2011), p. 82.

[99] See, e.g., UN Conference on Environment and Development (1992), Principle 3; Art. 3(1) of the UNFCCC; *Regional Agreement on Access to Information, Public Participation and Justice in Environmental Matters in Latin America and the Caribbean* (Escazú Agreement), adopted 4 March 2018, entered into force 22 April 2021.

[100] See already *supra* note 51.

[101] For one of the very few instances, which explicitly addressed the concept's normative capacity separately from its status under customary international law, see Beyerlin (2010), p. 446.

[102] See, e.g., Redgwell (1999), pp. 115–122; Collins (2007b), pp. 115–121; Anstee-Wedderburn (2014), pp. 48–51.

[103] Lowe (1999), p. 27.

[104] Ibid., p. 28. Cf. also Kiss and Beurier (2010), p. 129.

[105] Lowe (1999), pp. 28–29. See also Boyle (1999), pp. 908–909; Anstee-Wedderburn (2014), pp. 50–51. Cf. Lawrence (2012), pp. 32–33.

> practice. [...] Only through such clarity and consistency can intergenerational equity be recognised as a true and obligatory guiding principle.[106]

*Claire Molinari* stated:

> [I]ntergenerational equity [cannot] be described categorically as a legal 'principle' in the narrow, strong sense described by *Ronald Dworkin*, [...]. Instead, it is more likely to be construed as a concept or principle in a broader sense: one that guides interpretation and provides context for decisions in international environmental law [...].[107]

In contrast, other observers affirmed such normativity with respect to intergenerational equity and considered it "a 'guiding principle' in the application of substantive norms [...] under international law."[108] For *Winfried Lang*, intergenerational equity was "already well beyond the realm of a political postulate. It reflects much more than aspirations."[109] While he still doubted its "full legal value and binding force" in 1999,[110] *Lang* preferred to use the terminology of "principles and/or concepts" in order to avoid "drawing a line between them as regards their normative value [...]".[111] Nonetheless, he classified intergenerational equity as an "emerging principle of International Environmental Law [sic.]".[112]

Further, as *Beyerlin* put it:

> [I]ntergenerational equity is designed to guide the discretion of states in international environmental and developmental decision-making processes, it appears to surmount the threshold of normativity and can therefore be considered a principle. If incorporated into an international environmental agreement, this principle gives meaningful legal guidance for the parties to that agreement and, in this sense, is a legal principle. It may lead parties to interpret and apply open or unclear treaty rules in such a way that the interests and needs of future generations will be met as best as possible.[113]

While *Beyerlin's* remark on the incorporation into treaty law pointed to the legally binding effect as a second step,[114] his observations concerning the concept's normative capacity as a legal principle are convincing. The general conception of intergenerational equity has moved beyond a mere political ideal and it fits much better into *Dworkin's* typology of a legal principle, meaning "a requirement of

[106] Hadjiargyrou (2016), p. 277. Cf. also Scholtz (2021), p. 341.

[107] Molinari (2015), p. 144.

[108] Redgwell (1999), p. 123, 143; Redgwell (2016), p. 199. See also ICJ, *Request for an Examination of the Situation in Accordance with Paragraph 63 of the Court's Judgment of 20 December 1974 in the Nuclear Tests (New Zealand v. France) Case,* Dissenting Opinion of Judge Weeramantry, 22 September 1995, ICJ Reports 1995, 317, p. 341; Beyerlin (2010), p. 446.

[109] Lang (1999), p. 166.

[110] Ibid.

[111] Ibid., p. 164.

[112] Ibid., p. 171. Cf. also Lawrence (2012), pp. 32–33. These classifications again mix up the issues of normative capacity and legally binding character; for the latter, see *infra* in Sect. 4.2.

[113] Beyerlin (2010), p. 446.

[114] See *infra* in Sect. 4.2.1.

justice or fairness [...]".[115] This is particularly obvious with respect to intergenerational equity's strong connection to distributive environmental justice,[116] but also in the context of the philosophical analysis in Chap. 3. The need to take into account the interests of future generations is exactly such a requirement of intergenerational justice in the sense of *Dworkin*. It does not require an automatic legal consequence or applies in an "all or nothing fashion", as a legal rule would.[117] However, it stipulates a normative goal, namely the consideration of future generations' interests, which should be achieved to the greatest extent legally and factually possible. This responsibility for future generations constitutes one consideration in the balancing process of decision-makers without defining a particular outcome.[118] Consequently, the general conception of intergenerational equity constitutes a principle with normative capacity.

### 4.1.4 The Doctrine of Intergenerational Equity

As has been illustrated in Chap. 2, both manifestations of intergenerational equity represent nuances of the general idea of fairness among present and future generations, which have developed to a different extent in specificity and contents. While the general conception of intergenerational equity constitutes a sub-concept of sustainable development, the specific doctrine of intergenerational equity, as elaborated by *Edith Brown Weiss*, has exceeded this intergenerational component of sustainable development.[119] Consequently, its normative capacity should be examined independently from the normative capacity of the general conception.[120]

However, the existing references to intergenerational equity do not offer much assistance in this regard. First, most international documents only refer to the general conception of intergenerational equity,[121] and second, their terminology is inconsistent and not based on *Dworkin's* typology of policies, principles and rules.[122] The aforementioned normative classifications of intergenerational equity in legal scholarship also mostly referred to the general conception.[123] Even *Brown Weiss'*

---

[115] Dworkin (1978), p. 22.

[116] See, e.g., Stone (2010), p. 292; Shelton (2010), pp. 640–641.

[117] See Beyerlin (2010), p. 433; Eggett (2019), p. 203.

[118] Beyerlin (2010), p. 446. Cf. also Fitzmaurice (2008), p. 225.

[119] Collins (2007b), pp. 125–126; Brown Weiss (2010), p. 109. In more detail, see also *supra* in Sect. 2.3.1.2.

[120] Cf. Collins (2007b), pp. 125–127; Beyerlin (2010), pp. 446, 447; Beyerlin and Marauhn (2011), pp. 81–82.

[121] In detail see *infra* in Sect. 4.2.2.

[122] See already *supra* note 51.

[123] See *supra* notes 101–113.

denomination of intergenerational equity as a "principle"[124] should not necessarily be understood in a technical manner. In lack of more consistency in the doctrinal literature, it is necessary to directly examine the doctrine of intergenerational equity in light of *Dworkin's* threefold typology. Only if it has the capacity to influence the behaviour of the present generation, it goes beyond a mere policy, meaning that it has normativity either in the form of a legal principle or a legal rule.

The doctrine of intergenerational equity stipulates an obligation of present generations "to pass on the natural and cultural resources of the planet [to future generations] in no worse condition than received".[125] It further includes specific conservation duties: conservation of options, conservation of quality and conservation of equitable access.[126] These planetary obligations are embedded in a concept of planetary trust, which also includes opposing planetary rights of future generations.[127] Thereby, the structure of the doctrine of intergenerational equity is much more sophisticated than that of sustainable development or the general conception of intergenerational equity. Indeed, the elaborate doctrine of intergenerational equity does not display the same level of abstraction as sustainable development, which had led to the latter's categorisation as mere political ideal by some commentators.[128] The indeterminacy and lack of clarity of intergenerational equity, which some commentators criticised,[129] primarily referred to the vague formulations in international documents,[130] thus to the *general* conception only. The determinate and clear language and contents of *Brown Weiss'* doctrine shapes planetary rights and obligations, so that this doctrine goes beyond a vague political ideal or mere policy.[131]

The next step would be to assess whether the doctrine constitutes a legal principle (i.e., a goal to be achieved to the greatest extent possible[132]) or a legal rule (i.e., a more practical formulation that directs its addressees to a specific act or behaviour[133]). While the present work has classified the general conception of intergenerational equity as a legal principle above, the three intergenerational duties of conservation go beyond mere normative goals; they oblige their addressees to act in specific ways.[134] For instance, conservation of options requires maintaining on balance the diversity of the resource base for the benefit of future generations.[135] In contrast to a mere principle, it is not at the discretion of the addressee whether and

[124] E.g., Brown Weiss (2019), p. 51.

[125] Brown Weiss (1989), pp. 37–38.

[126] Ibid., pp. 38–45.

[127] Ibid., pp. 95–109.

[128] See *supra* notes 73–80.

[129] See *supra* notes 103–106.

[130] See, e.g., Anstee-Wedderburn (2014), pp. 41–51.

[131] Cf. Borg (1998), p. 132.

[132] See Dworkin (1978), pp. 25–26; Beyerlin (2010), p. 433.

[133] See Cheng (1994), p. 376; Beyerlin (2010), p. 428.

[134] Collins (2007a), p. 331. In detail on the three duties of conservation, see *supra* in Sect. 2.2.1.4.

[135] Brown Weiss (1989), pp. 41–42.

how far the diversity of options is maintained. The planetary obligation is quite clear and thus applies in an "all-or-nothing-fashion".[136] Of course, conservation of options does not predetermine which specific action the addressees must take. It establishes a duty of conduct instead of a duty of result, but this does not prevent the existence of a legal rule.[137] In case that a behaviour in the present has potential long-term consequences, this triggers the application of the intergenerational duty for the present generation. It automatically follows that this behaviour must conform to the conservation of diversity of the resource base for future generations. This is an example for the rule character of the duties of conservation. The doctrine of intergenerational equity could thus be considered a "coherent and practicable set of legal rules".[138]

Of course, certain issues of intergenerational equity remain still unanswered, also with regard to *Brown Weiss'* specific doctrine—as illustrated in Chap. 5 below. Yet, these open issues primarily concern structural questions, such as the potential of future generations to be right-holders or the exact institutional framework and representation of future generations. In contrast, the normative contents of intergenerational equity are clearly defined within *Brown Weiss'* doctrine.[139] Further, normativity does not require clarity of a rule in absolute terms, so that the remaining open issues would not hinder the normative capacity of the doctrine of intergenerational equity. The doctrine constitutes a legal rule according to *Dworkin's* typology.

### *4.1.5 Summary*

The foregoing sections have illustrated the complexity in assessing the normative capacity of the concepts of sustainable development and intergenerational equity. Based on *Ronald Dworkin's* typology, this book has distinguished between mere political policies without normative capacity and legal norms in the form of principles and rules. Although the existing international documents and case law do not offer a consistent answer and despite the disagreement and inconsistency in legal scholarship, several observations can be made on sustainable development as well as on the two manifestations of intergenerational equity.

The present work has characterised sustainable development as a principle that goes beyond a mere political ideal. Regardless of whether it is conceived as a legal principle or as a non-normative "meta principle",[140] its framework character

[136] Dworkin (1978), p. 24.

[137] With regard to sustainable development, see Proelß (2022), pp. 145–146.

[138] Collins (2007b), p. 133. See also Redgwell (1999), p. 126.

[139] On the distinction between normative and operating system elements in intergenerational equity, see *infra* in Sect. 7.3.4.1.

[140] See Lowe (1999), p. 31.

definitely allows for the identification of sub-concepts with independent normativity.[141] This is why the two manifestations of intergenerational equity have been examined next. Both manifestations of intergenerational equity possess the normative capacity to influence their respective addressees' behaviour, but they differ in their degree of specificity and constitute different kinds of legal norms. The general conception of intergenerational equity (i.e., one of the sub-concepts of sustainable development that requires taking into account the needs of future generations) constitutes a legal principle in the sense of *Dworkin*, as it provides general legal guidance to its addressees without setting specific legal consequences.[142] On the other side of the spectrum, the more specific manifestation of intergenerational equity encompasses a planetary trust and intergenerational rights and obligations; it exceeds the intergenerational component of sustainable development. This doctrine of intergenerational equity consists of a set of legal rules that oblige their addressees to specific legal consequences in an "all-or-nothing-fashion".[143]

## 4.2 Legal Status

These two manifestations cannot be regarded as completely independent from one another. They constitute nuances of the overall notion of intergenerational equity, two nuances on the same scale of a general idea of fairness among present and future generations. Both manifestations are inspired by the various legal, philosophical, cultural and religious instances of intergenerational responsibility. However, they might be rooted to a different extent in these instances, particularly in the existing documents of international law and governance. As both manifestations of intergenerational equity have normative capacity, this only means that they are capable of influencing their addressees' behaviour in an *abstract* sense. This does not yet answer the question whether they are actually part of international law in a legally *binding* sense. Whether intergenerational equity plays a legally binding role as a legal principle or whether the doctrine of intergenerational equity guides the present generation's behaviour as a legal rule—this depends on the legal status that both manifestations of intergenerational equity have or have not achieved.[144]

---

[141] Beyerlin and Marauhn (2011), p. 82.

[142] Beyerlin (2010), p. 446.

[143] Dworkin (1978), p. 24.

[144] Epiney and Scheyli (2000), pp. 40, 76; Proelß (2022), pp. 101, 147. Due to the inconsistency in legal scholarship, different terms for this same issue exist, e.g., "legal status", "legal effects" or "legally binding character", which are further often mixed up with the aspect of normative capacity, see *supra* notes 10–11. The present work uses the term "legal status" for assessing the existence of intergenerational equity in the sources of international law.

The legal status is to be assessed on the basis of the existing sources of public international law.[145] This analysis is positivist, as it focuses on the examination of the sources of international law as listed in Article 38(1) of the ICJ Statute.[146] The first sub-section addresses the references to future generations in treaty law within the meaning of Article 38(1)(a) of the ICJ Statute (Sect. 4.2.1). The second sub-section constitutes the focus of the analysis: whether and to what degree intergenerational equity has become part of customary international law within the meaning of Article 38(1)(b) of the ICJ Statute (Sect. 4.2.2). Both sub-sections distinguish between the general conception and the specific doctrine of intergenerational equity in order to answer which of these two manifestations may already have become a legally binding norm of international law. The last sub-section briefly analyses whether intergenerational equity could also be a general principle of law within the meaning of Article 38(1)(c) of the ICJ Statute (Sect. 4.2.3).

### *4.2.1 Intergenerational Equity in Treaty Law*

Intergenerational equity could have become a binding part of certain treaty regimes. The following paragraphs analyse various international agreements, which refer to the concern for future generations and which have already been mentioned above in this book.[147] They encompass various areas of international environmental law and range from the International Whaling Convention[148] to the UNFCCC.[149] The analysis presented here gives an overview of the similarities between the references as well as the particularities in certain treaty regimes. It assesses whether the respective references incorporate a legally binding treaty norm of intergenerational equity and whether these incorporations point to the general conception (i.e., a normative principle) or to the specific doctrine of intergenerational equity (i.e., a normative rule). Overall, the book does *not* focus on the analysis of the treaty-based legal status of intergenerational equity, but focuses—in a subsequent step in the next section—on the customary legal status of the concept. Therefore, the following observations on different treaty regimes remain in parts superficial. They are nevertheless an important starting point for both the analysis of the customary norm of

[145] Beyerlin and Marauhn (2011), pp. 79–82; Proelß (2022), p. 101.

[146] See Cryer et al. (2011), p. 38.

[147] See *supra* in Sect. 2.1.1.

[148] *International Convention for the Regulation of Whaling* (Whaling Convention), adopted 2 December 1946, entered into force 10 November 1948, 161 UNTS 72, Preamble.

[149] Art. 3(1) of the UNFCCC.

intergenerational equity and for the intertemporal law perspective in Chaps. 6 and 7.[150]

Most of the agreements mention future generations only in their preambular provisions,[151] which decreases the reference's normative weight.[152] Others include future generations in their operative parts. The first global agreement in this regard was the Convention Concerning the Protection of the World Cultural and Natural Heritage ('World Heritage Convention'), which prescribes in its Article 4:

> Each State Party to this Convention recognizes that the duty of ensuring the identification, protection, conservation, presentation and transmission to future generations of the cultural and natural heritage [...] situated on its territory, belongs primarily to that State.

Article 4 of the Agreement Governing the Activities of States on the Moon and Other Celestial Bodies ('Moon Agreement') states that "[d]ue regard shall be paid to the interests of present and future generations [...]"[153] and Article 2(5)(c) of the UNECE Water Convention mirrors in parts the wording of the Brundtland Report, stipulating that "[w]ater resources shall be managed so that the needs of the present generation are met without compromising the ability of future generations to meet their own needs."[154] Some documents of the European Union ('EU') also refer to future generations[155]: For instance, the Charter of Fundamental Rights of the European Union ('EU Charter of Fundamental Rights'), though in its Preamble, underlines the responsibilities towards future generations.[156]

As demonstrated, the UN climate protection regime is the most relevant framework for intergenerational issues.[157] The UNFCCC contains not one but two references to future generations. Its Preamble emphasises the parties' determination "to protect the climate system for present *and future* generations" (emphasis added).

---

150 On the difficulties of applying intertemporal law to intergenerational equity, see *infra* in Sect. 7.2.1.

151 See, e.g., Preamble of the UNCCD; *UN Convention on the Law of Non-Navigational Uses of International Watercourses* (UN Watercourses Convention), adopted 21 May 1997, entered into force 17 August 2014, 36 ILM 700, Preamble as well as *supra* in Sect. 2.1.1.3.

152 Magraw and Hawke (2010), p. 622.

153 *Agreement Governing the Activities of States on the Moon and Other Celestial Bodies* (Moon Agreement), adopted 5 December 1979, entered into force 11 July 1984, 1363 UNTS 3, Art. 4.

154 Art. 2(5)(c) of the UNECE Water Convention. See also Redgwell (1999), p. 118; Fitzmaurice (2012), p. 109.

155 For a detailed assessment of the relevance of intergenerational equity in the EU, see Collins (2007a).

156 *Charter of Fundamental Rights of the European Union* (EU Charter of Fundamental Rights), adopted 7 December 2000, entered into force 1 December 2009, EU OJ C 326, 395. See also *Declaration of the Council of the European Communities and of the Representatives of the Governments of the Member States Meeting in the Council of 22 November 1973 on the Programme of Action of the European Communities on the Environment* adopted 22 November 1973, EU OJ C 112/1.

157 See already *supra* in Sect. 1.1.

More importantly, Article 3(1) of the UNFCCC lists the following provision among its principles:

> The Parties should protect the climate system for the benefit of present and future generations of humankind, on the basis of equity and in accordance with their common but differentiated responsibilities and respective capabilities.

*Catherine Redgwell* concluded that this central position of future generations in the UNFCCC constituted the "beginning [of] the process of defining the obligations of the present generation to absorb the costs of reducing the risk of global warming for future generations".[158] This process was continued with the Paris Agreement from 2015,[159] which stipulates in its Preamble:

> Acknowledging that climate change is a common concern of humankind, Parties should, when taking action to address climate change, respect, promote and consider their respective obligations on human rights, [...], as well as gender equality, empowerment of women and intergenerational equity.

As intergenerational equity is thereby largely limited to the Preamble instead of operative provisions,[160] its binding character in the Paris Agreement has been questioned.[161] *Bridget Lewis* demonstrated how the references to future generations were watered down during the drafting process due to opposition of some States.[162] Yet, she further elaborated on how the Paris Agreement's final text nonetheless incorporates the concern for future generations.[163] For instance, the formulation in the Preamble is unusual for a preambular provision.[164] According to *María Pía Carazo*, it "embodies the will of the negotiating parties that it be used as a guide for the implementation of the Agreement and, as such, breaks new ground".[165] Moreover, it builds on the respect for future generations in the UNFCCC, so that the relevance of intergenerational equity in the climate protection regime is generally confirmed by the Paris Agreement.[166]

A closer look at the formulations in the Paris Agreement as well as in most other treaty examples again results in a differentiated analysis. In some treaties, intergenerational equity has been incorporated as a legally binding treaty norm. For instance, the World Heritage Convention and the UNFCCC refer to future generations in their objectives and principles and claim that that the respective

---

[158] Redgwell (1999), pp. 117–118. Cf. also Collins (2007b), p. 118; Redgwell (2016), pp. 190–195.

[159] In more detail, see Cordonier Segger (2021b).

[160] For two other references to "equity" as such, see *Paris Agreement* (Paris Agreement), adopted 12 December 2015, entered into force 4 November 2016, UN Doc. FCCC/CP/2015/L.9/Rev.1. See also Rajamani and Guérin (2017), pp. 87–88.

[161] Doelle (2016), p. 16. Cf. also Boer (2021), p. 22.

[162] Lewis (2018), pp. 72–75.

[163] Ibid., pp. 75–78.

[164] Carazo Ortiz (2017), pp. 114–115. Cf. Lewis (2018), p. 76.

[165] Carazo Ortiz (2017), pp. 114–115. See also Boer (2021), p. 21.

[166] Cf. Cordonier Segger (2021b), pp. 740–741; Boer (2021), p. 24.

regimes should serve the interests of future generations. In this sense, natural and cultural heritage is to be transmitted to future generations[167]; the climate system must be protected for their benefit.[168] Thanks to this incorporation in operative treaty provisions, the needs and interests of future generations have become a main part of the considerations of the respective treaty regimes.[169] As *Alan Boyle* stated with regard to the UNFCCC:

> At the very least Article 3 is relevant to interpretation and implementation of the Convention as well as creating expectations concerning matters which must be taken into account in good faith in the negotiation of further instruments.[170]

Notwithstanding these incorporations, these references are usually accompanied by wording such as "due regard shall be paid" or "without compromising the ability".[171] These are typical for the general conception of intergenerational equity. All of these legally binding treaty norms are an expression of the legal principle to "take into account the interests of future generations",[172] and they enshrine the "notion of environmental responsibility towards the future".[173] Accordingly, they must be understood in the sense of the general conception of intergenerational equity.[174] In contrast, they do *not* incorporate specific obligations that would result from the legal rule of *Brown Weiss'* doctrine of intergenerational equity.[175] With regard to the Paris Agreement, the aforementioned preambular recital does explicitly not refer to rights of future generations due to the many contested issues in the context of the doctrine of intergenerational equity.[176] Rather, it only incorporates the more abstract legal principle of intergenerational equity.[177]

Yet, there are two regional treaties, which might go beyond the general conception of intergenerational equity. The Aarhus Convention, in its Preamble, refers to the "duty, [. . .] to protect and improve the environment for the benefit of present and future generations", which is in line with the aforementioned references to the general conception of intergenerational equity. Beyond this preambular reference, the Aarhus Convention's objective is described as follows: "In order to contribute to the protection of the right of every person of present *and future* generations to live in an environment adequate to his or her health and well-being [. . .]" (emphasis

---

[167] *Convention Concerning the Protection of the World Cultural and Natural Heritage* (World Heritage Convention), adopted 16 November 1972, entered into force 17 December 1975, 1037 UNTS 151, Art. 4.

[168] Art. 3(1) of the UNFCCC. See also Stoll and Krüger (2022), pp. 434–435.

[169] Boyle (1999), pp. 907–908.

[170] Ibid., p. 908.

[171] See, e.g., Art. 4 of the Moon Agreement; Art. 2(5)(c) of the UNECE Water Convention.

[172] Dupuy and Viñuales (2018), p. 92.

[173] Collins (2007b), p. 118.

[174] Ibid. For the UNFCCC, see Boyle (1999), pp. 908–909.

[175] Cf. Redgwell (2016), pp. 193–195.

[176] See Lewis (2018), pp. 77–78.

[177] Carazo Ortiz (2017), p. 117.

added).[178] Further, the Regional Agreement on Access to Information, Public Participation and Justice in Environmental Matters in Latin America and the Caribbean ('Escazú Agreement') states, in similar terms, that its objective aims at "contributing to the protection of the right of every person of present *and future* generations to live in a healthy environment and to sustainable development" (emphasis added).[179] Both references could be understood as incorporating a specific legal right to a healthy environment for future generations,[180] which would resemble *Brown Weiss'* doctrine of intergenerational equity more so than the general conception enshrined in most other treaties. This would mean that the Aarhus Convention, and later the Escazú Agreement, was the "first hard-law text to recognize the rights of future generations".[181] While references to the general conception of intergenerational equity can be found in a variety of international treaties, the Aarhus Convention could be the "first international legal instrument to extend this concept to a set of legal obligations".[182]

However, these observations are not obligatory. First, the Convention text presupposes the existence of a right to live in an environment adequate to one's health and well-being,[183] although such a right is strongly contested in international law.[184] Second, certain doubts have been articulated that the formulations in Article 1 of the Aarhus Convention were not intended to refer to an existing right, but rather aimed at strengthening the meaning and importance of the procedural rights in the treaties.[185] Based on these doubts, Article 1 would only constitute an abstract objective without legally binding character in the sense of an enforceable rule.[186] Overall, the provisions in both the Aarhus Convention and the Escazú Agreement are definitely framed in a more specific way than the aforementioned treaty regimes and they possibly refer to the more specific legal rule of intergenerational equity. However, their legally binding character can be doubted, as they primarily establish procedural

[178] Art. 1 of the Aarhus Convention.

[179] Art. 1 of the Escazú Agreement. Generally on the relation between the Aarhus Convention and the Escazú Agreement, see Barritt (2020).

[180] Cf. Knox (2019), p. 42.

[181] Ebbesson et al. (2014), p. 30.

[182] Ibid., p. 42.

[183] See ibid.; Stec and Jendrośka (2019), p. 538.

[184] Epiney et al. (2018), p. 92. In more detail on the relevance of such a right in the context of intergenerational equity, see *infra* in Sect. 5.2.

[185] Ibid., p. 93. In this sense, cf. also CJEU, *The Queen, on the application of David Edwards and Lilian Pallikaropoulos v Environment Agency and Others,* Opinion of Advocate General Kokott, 18 October 2012, European Case Law Identifier ECLI:EU:C:2012:645, para. 41; CJEU, *Gemeinde Altrip, Gebrüder Hört GbR, Willi Schneider v Land Rheinland-Pfalz,* Opinion of Advocate General Cruz Villalón, 20 June 2013, European Case Law Identifier ECLI:EU:C:2013:422, para. 96; CJEU, *Council of the European Union, European Parliament, European Commission v Vereniging Milieudefensie and Stichting Stop Luchtverontreiniging Utrecht,* Opinion of Advocate General Jääskinen, 8 May 2014, European Case Law Identifier ECLI:EU:C:2014:310, paras. 87–89.

[186] Epiney et al. (2018), pp. 92–93. Cf. also Collins (2007a), p. 325.

environmental rights.[187] The strengthening of these procedural rights could inspire potential institutional frameworks of representation of future generations in the future,[188] but they do not establish such frameworks based on their current legal status. Further, as both treaties constitute regional agreements, they are only binding on the 47 States or entities, or 12 respectively, which have become parties to these treaties as of this date.

This observation leads to the most recent attempt of *universal* codification of general concepts of international environmental law, the Global Pact for the Environment.[189] The draft GPE aims at the codification of legal principles and rules of international environmental law through a holistic and cross-sectoral approach.[190] Its Article 4 explicitly includes intergenerational equity:

> Intergenerational equity shall guide decisions that may have an impact on the environment. Present generations shall ensure that their decisions and actions do not compromise the ability of future generations to meet their own needs.[191]

An assessment of Article 4 of the draft largely depends on the question whether the GPE will be adopted as a legally binding instrument of treaty law or, at least, be proclaimed in the form of a non-binding but holistic political declaration in the future. This book does not address the potential additional value and the disadvantages or problems of the GPE's approach to international environmental law or of its envisaged legal status.[192] Instead, it focuses on the question whether the currently existing formulation in Article 4 of the draft GPE, if adopted as a treaty, would incorporate the general conception or even the specific doctrine of intergenerational equity. On the one hand, the proposal in the draft GPE was certainly inspired by *Brown Weiss'* doctrine and would thus include specific planetary rights and obligations.[193] It is also framed in a legally binding way, as intergenerational equity "shall guide decisions […]" and present generations "shall ensure […]" that the ability of future generations to meet their own needs is not compromised.[194] However, even *Brown Weiss* admitted with respect to the GPE that "[w]hether [intergenerational equity] conveys rights as well as responsibilities is not well established."[195]

[187] Cf. also Ebbesson et al. (2014), p. 42; Stec and Jendrośka (2019), p. 538.

[188] See Fülöp (2016), pp. 248–250. On the institutional frameworks of representation on the national level, see *infra* in Sect. 5.3.2.1.

[189] International Group of Experts for the Pact (2017). For details on its genesis, see already *supra* in Sect. 2.1.1.5.

[190] In more detail, see Aguila (2020).

[191] International Group of Experts for the Pact (2017), Art. 4.

[192] Rather in favour of the GPE's approach, see, e.g., Parejo Navajas and Lobel (2018); Aguila (2020). Rather critical of the GPE's approach, see, e.g., Biniaz (2017); Kotzé and French (2018), pp. 827–829; Raith (2018), pp. 21–22.

[193] See in detail Brown Weiss (2019), pp. 55–57 with reference to United Nations Secretary-General (2013), para. 24.

[194] International Group of Experts for the Pact (2017), Art. 4.

[195] Brown Weiss (2019), p. 56.

Moreover, the formulations of the GPE are rather abstract, so that some commentators have interpreted most of its stipulations as normative, but only as general environmental principles without specific obligations.[196] For instance, *Jasmin Raith* stated with regard to the environmental principles in the GPE:

> [T]heir main function will likely be to guide policy development. In that sense, their codification adds little value to the existing state of play. Already now, although only enshrined in soft law instruments like the Rio Declaration, these principles have an important policy-guiding function.[197]

*Louis Kotzé* and *Duncan French* even considered that the Pact constituted "a clear regression from the well-established [international environmental law] principles of inter- and intra-generational equity".[198] From this perspective, the GPE would—even in case of its timely adoption as a legally binding treaty—only incorporate the general conception of intergenerational equity; although this would be at a universal and cross-sectoral level in contrast to the aforementioned treaty examples. As of March 2022, the UNEA failed the expectations for a legally binding codification as it only adopted a political declaration that did not even take up all of the suggested principles of the draft GPE.[199] The adoption of the GPE as a treaty in the near future is thus unlikely,[200] so that this book does not address this issue further.

Overall, most of the aforementioned treaties refer to intergenerational equity in a legally binding way—at least if the references are not of mere preambular character. This means that intergenerational equity constitutes a binding part of these treaty regimes in the form of a treaty norm. However, in most, if not all, of these treaties, only the general manifestation in the form of a legal principle of intergenerational equity has achieved the legal status of a treaty norm. Beyond this, the *doctrine* of intergenerational equity has not yet become part of treaty law. The only potential exceptions could be the treaty regimes of the Aarhus Convention and the Escazú Agreement, but the aforementioned counter-arguments militate against the incorporation of the specific doctrine of intergenerational equity through these conventions. Finally, the effect of a future adoption of a GPE would depend on the exact formulation and subsequent interpretation of such a future treaty norm.

It is beyond the scope of the present work to assess the exact application of intergenerational equity in these respective treaty regimes in more detail. Since the climate regime is most important with respect to intergenerational effects, the subsequent chapters nonetheless regularly refer to developments in international climate protection law.[201] As the book aims at examining intergenerational equity

---

[196] See Raith (2018), pp. 14–15, 19; Kotzé and French (2018), p. 827; Aguila (2020), p. 8.

[197] Raith (2018), p. 14. In more detail on this existing "state of play" in customary international law, see *infra* in Sect. 4.2.2.

[198] Kotzé and French (2018), p. 827.

[199] United Nations Environment Assembly (2022). On the criticism, see, e.g., Aguila and Chami (2022) and *supra* in Sect. 2.1.1.5.

[200] See already Tigre (2019).

[201] On the relevance of climate litigation, see *infra* in Sect. 5.3.3.

in its holistic and general character, covering many aspects of international environmental law, the next section focuses on the potential customary nature of intergenerational equity—either in its general manifestation as a principle or in the form of the more specific doctrine of intergenerational equity.

### 4.2.2 Intergenerational Equity as Customary International Law

Beyond certain treaty provisions, intergenerational equity could also have achieved legally binding force in the form of a norm of customary international law within the meaning of Article 38(1)(b) of the ICJ Statute. In order to assess the existence of a customary norm, positivist analysis turns to the empirical existence of two elements: *opinio iuris* and general State practice.[202] Although this dichotomy is generally accepted in international law,[203] it is not always strictly applied by the judiciary.[204] Often, international courts and tribunals tend to focus on aspects of *opinio iuris* more than on State practice.[205] For instance, *Judge Jessup* has stated in a separate opinion:

> No survey of State practice can, strictly speaking, be comprehensive and the practice of a single State may vary from time to time – perhaps depending on whether it is in the position of plaintiff or defendant. However, I am not seeking to marshal all the evidence necessary to establish a rule of customary international law. Having indicated the underlying principles and the bases of the international law regarding [...], I need only cite some examples to show that these conclusions are not unsupported by State practice and doctrine.[206]

While some commentators criticised this oversimplification in judicial reasoning with regard to the establishment of customary international law,[207] others have concluded that modern forms of customary international law would depend primarily on State conviction and less on actual practice.[208] Regardless of the position vis-à-vis the relevance of both components of customary international law, it is clear that the assessment of exhaustive sociological evidence of *opinio iuris* and State

---

[202] ICJ, *North Sea Continental Shelf Cases (Germany v. Denmark; Germany v. Netherlands),* Judgment (Merits), 20 February 1969, ICJ Reports 1969, 3, paras. 74, 77; ICJ, *Case concerning Military and Paramilitary Activities in and against Nicaragua (Nicaragua v. United States of America),* Judgment (Merits), 27 June 1986, ICJ Reports 1986, 14, paras. 184–186. See also Treves (2006).

[203] See Pellet (2012), p. 814.

[204] Talmon (2015); Ryngaert and Hora Siccama (2018).

[205] Condorelli (2012), p. 150.

[206] *Barcelona Traction* (Separate Opinion of Judge Jessup), *supra* note 9, para. 60.

[207] See Dupuy et al. (2021), pp. 389–391.

[208] Roberts (2001); Diehl and Ku (2010), p. 40.

practice is not easy in international law.[209] These difficulties exist also, and perhaps particularly, in the context of international environmental law.[210]

For *opinio iuris* to exist, States must act in a specific way because they believe in the existence of a rule of international law that requires them to do so.[211] Several factors can serve as indicators of the existence of *opinio iuris*, for instance resolutions of international organisations,[212] documents of the ILC,[213] or certain treaties if they codify pre-existing *opinio iuris*.[214] Further, soft law documents may also give important indications as to the legal convictions of States.[215] The present author understands "soft law" only in its meaning as non-binding documents, thus, in contrast to treaties or other written sources of international law.[216] Soft law documents include, for instance, inter-governmental conference declarations, UNGA resolutions or guidelines and recommendations of international organisations.[217] Despite the non-binding character of these documents themselves, they can contribute to the evidence of *opinio iuris*.[218] On the one hand, this recourse to soft law instruments illustrates the fluid boundaries between legal norms of international law and the non-legal realm of political and social systems alongside the international legal system.[219] The importance of soft law for international law in general and for the development of customary international law in particular has increased over the past decades.[220] In international environmental law, soft law documents play a particularly important role for the development of customary norms.[221] On the other hand, a certain measure of self-restraint should be shown with respect to carelessly equating soft law instruments with legally binding expression of *opinio*

[209] Cf. Talmon (2015), pp. 421–423. For an overview of sociological theories of international law, see Carty (2008).

[210] Dupuy (2010), pp. 450–454; Dupuy et al. (2021), pp. 389–392.

[211] *North Sea Continental Shelf* (Judgment (Merits)), *supra* note 202, para. 77. Generally on *opinio iuris*, see Pellet (2012), pp. 818–826.

[212] See, e.g., ICJ, *Legality of the Threat or Use of Nuclear Weapons,* Advisory Opinion, 8 July 1996, ICJ Reports 1996, 226, para. 70.

[213] See, e.g., *Gabčíkovo-Nagymaros Project* (Judgment), *supra* note 52, paras. 47, 50–54, 58.

[214] For several examples, see Pellet (2012), pp. 821–823. See also *infra* note 229.

[215] ILC (2015), paras. 45–54; Boyle (1999), p. 906; Barral (2012), pp. 387–388; Epiney (2022), pp. 36–37. More critically, see Dupuy et al. (2021), p. 391.

[216] See Boyle (1999), pp. 902–906. See also *supra* note 26.

[217] Ibid., p. 902.

[218] Ibid., p. 906.

[219] Diehl and Ku (2010), pp. 51–53. On the permeable boundaries between both systems, see also *infra* in Sect. 7.3.4.

[220] See Chinkin (2000), pp. 27–28; Ku (2005), pp. 639–641.

[221] Redgwell (2017), pp. 951, 955.

*iuris*.[222] Most importantly, the attitude of States regarding these instruments is of particular relevance as it directly reflects their legal opinions.[223]

With respect to State practice, a proper analysis of existing evidence is even more difficult. Generally, national administrative acts, legislation or case law can serve as sources of State practice, as well as the occurrence of the relevant norms in international treaties.[224] However, State practice can often be incoherent and contradictory.[225] Therefore, the ICJ pointed out in the *Military and Paramilitary Activities in Nicaragua* case:

> It is not to be expected that in the practice of States the application of the rules in question should have been perfect, in the sense that States should have refrained, with complete consistency, from [acting against that rule]. The Court does not consider that, for a rule to be established as customary, the corresponding practice must be in absolutely rigorous conformity with the rule. In order to deduce the existence of customary rules, the Court deems it sufficient that the conduct of States should, in general, be consistent with such rules, [...].[226]

Due to this inconsistency, international courts and tribunals have often based their main arguments rooted in customary international law on the existence of sufficient *opinio iuris* or have directly turned to other instances of alleged evidence of State practice, such as treaties, doctrine or other judicial decisions.[227] While treaties can contain norms that are at the same time part of customary international law,[228] not every treaty reflects the pre-existence of the respective norm under customary international law. Rather, this depends on whether the treaty codifies an already existing customary law norm, or whether it aims at establishing a new legally binding norm of treaty law.[229]

All in all, the analysis of customary international law is thus much more complicated than the assessment of a legally binding treaty norm. As it is beyond the scope of the present work to provide an exhaustive sociological study of international relations in the context of intergenerational equity, it is limited to a number of exemplary statements, documents and other instances of practice and legal conviction. The author is aware of the aforementioned methodological difficulties, which is why the following sub-sections nonetheless attempt to give an appropriate overview

---

[222] See ILC (2015), para. 47; Dupuy (2010), pp. 458–460; Ryngaert and Hora Siccama (2018), pp. 10–14; Dupuy et al. (2021), pp. 390–391.

[223] *Military and Paramilitary Activities in Nicaragua* (Judgment (Merits)), *supra* note 202, para. 188; ILC (2015), para. 47. Stressing this requirement, see Pellet (2012), pp. 824–825.

[224] Shaw (2008), p. 82; Pellet (2012), pp. 815–816.

[225] Dupuy (2010), pp. 459–460; Talmon (2015), pp. 422–423.

[226] *Military and Paramilitary Activities in Nicaragua* (Judgment (Merits)), *supra* note 202, para. 186. Cf. also Brierly and Clapham (2012), pp. 59–60.

[227] Condorelli (2012), pp. 150–151; Ryngaert and Hora Siccama (2018).

[228] *North Sea Continental Shelf* (Judgment (Merits)), *supra* note 202, para. 71; *Military and Paramilitary Activities in Nicaragua* (Judgment (Merits)), *supra* note 202, para. 175.

[229] ICJ, *Case concerning Ahmadou Sadio Diallo (Republic of Guinea v. Democratic Republic of the Congo)*, Preliminary Objections, Judgment, 24 May 2007, ICJ Reports 2007, 582, para. 90; Pellet (2012), p. 816; Dupuy et al. (2021), pp. 389–390.

of the most representative instances of *opinio iuris* and current practice. Most importantly, the following two sub-sections explicitly distinguish between the two manifestations of intergenerational equity, although the inconsistency in doctrinal analysis so far renders such an examination a challenging endeavour. First, the following sub-section analyses the customary nature of the general conception of intergenerational equity (Sect. 4.2.2.1), before the analysis turns to a brief assessment of the more elaborate doctrine of intergenerational equity in a second step (Sect. 4.2.2.2).

#### 4.2.2.1 The General Conception of Intergenerational Equity

The second chapter of this book has illustrated the long history of concern for future generations in detail. The following section examines whether these instances constitute evidence of sufficient *opinio iuris* and State practice regarding the general conception of intergenerational equity.

Generally speaking, there is certainly no lack of references to the "need to take into account the interests of future generations" in various international and national texts.[230] In the words of the UNSG: "A dedication to future generations is visible worldwide and across cultures. It is a value universally shared by humanity."[231] Following the Stockholm Declaration (e.g., "solemn responsibility to protect and improve the environment for present and future generations"),[232] the Brundtland Report shaped in 1987 the main expression of intergenerational equity as a main component of sustainable development: "development that meets the needs of the present without compromising the ability of future generations to meet their own needs".[233] Many other soft law documents have used comparable formulations, which reflect the increasing legal conviction of States that the interests and needs of future generations should be taken into account in environmental governance.[234] The documents themselves, although formally non-binding, have contributed in their totality to the evolution of the relevant *opinio iuris*.[235]

Several UNGA resolutions explicitly considered that the benefit for future generations was a driving factor of international actions. This includes the World Charter for Nature,[236] the resolution accompanying the SDGs,[237] and two more

---

230 Dupuy and Viñuales (2018), p. 92.

231 UNSG (2013), para. 3.

232 United Nations (1972), Principle 1.

233 World Commission on Environment and Development (WCED) (1987), Introduction, para. 27, Chap. 2, para. 1.

234 See, e.g., UNCED (1992), Principles 3, 21; United Nations General Assembly (UNGA) (2012); World Summit for Social Development (1995), paras. 6, 26.

235 Tladi (2007), p. 98. Cf. also Atapattu (2006), pp. 114–115.

236 UNGA (1982), Preamble.

237 UNGA (2015), Preamble, Declaration para. 18.

recent resolutions on the protection of the global climate for present and future generations of humankind[238] and on the protection of the atmosphere.[239] Already in 1980, the UNGA had proclaimed "the historical responsibility of States for the preservation of nature for present and future generations".[240] If the GPE were adopted in the form of a non-binding document in the future, its Article 4 would constitute another example of an existing conviction that present decisions and actions shall "not compromise the ability of future generations to meet their own needs".[241] Further, the parties in two relevant environmental disputes before the ICJ implicitly or explicitly acknowledged the applicability of intergenerational equity, or sustainable development respectively.[242]

As demonstrated, the establishment of coherent State practice to confirm this legal conviction is more difficult.[243] Treaty provisions could constitute evidence of State practice, but only if their provisions actually mirror an existing customary norm and do not merely aim at establishing a new treaty norm of intergenerational equity that surpasses the existing custom.[244] The references to future generations in treaties of the last decades are as frequent as the aforementioned soft law references.[245] These treaties do not intend to proclaim a new or more specific norm of intergenerational equity, which would go beyond the existing legal regime of international environmental law. In contrast, the foregoing analysis of the treaty provisions has demonstrated that most of them made recourse to the general idea of responsibility towards future generations, thereby incorporating the "need to take into account the interests of future generations"[246] into the respective treaty regimes. Despite the methodological difficulties of referring to treaty law in this context,[247] the widespread occurrence of relevant treaties with nearly identical wording is a strong indication of State practice.[248] The GPE, if adopted as a treaty with (quasi-) universal application, could reaffirm this practice. However, these instances are only sufficient to establish customary international law if they are supported by enough

---

[238] UNGA (2013).

[239] UNGA (2021), Annex Preamble, Guideline 6. On the explicit references of the ILC guidelines to the general conception of intergenerational equity, see ILC (2021), Preamble para. 9, Guideline 6 para. 3.

[240] UNGA (1980), paras. 1–3.

[241] International Group of Experts for the Pact (2017), Art. 4. In more detail, see *supra* notes 189–200.

[242] See *Gabčíkovo-Nagymaros Project* (Separate Opinion of Vice-President Weeramantry), *supra* note 55, pp. 89–90; *Pulp Mills* (Separate Opinion of Judge Cançado Trindade), *supra* note 61, paras. 123, 146–147.

[243] See *supra* notes 225–229.

[244] *Diallo* (Preliminary Objections, Judgment), *supra* note 229, para. 90.

[245] See, e.g., Art. 2(5)(c) of the UNECE Water Convention; Art. 3(1) of the UNFCCC. See already *supra* notes 148–159.

[246] Dupuy and Viñuales (2018), p. 92.

[247] See Dupuy et al. (2021), p. 390.

[248] Cf. Collins (2007b), p. 118.

*opinio iuris* independent from the treaty provisions. Otherwise, the compliance with these provisions would in itself not suffice to establish *opinio iuris*—the States would probably rather feel obliged by the binding treaty regime.[249] Additional indications are necessary to illustrate sufficient State practice.

National legislation and domestic case law confirm a widespread acceptance of the general conception of intergenerational equity in many States. The respect for the interests of future generations is enshrined in many national constitutional or legislative texts.[250] In 2007, *Lynda Collins* listed already more than twenty States with constitutional provisions for the benefit of future generations.[251] While some of these provisions even stipulate specific rights of future generations or established institutional frameworks for the representation of future generations,[252] most of them remain abstract and thus point to the general conception of intergenerational equity. From this, *Collins* concluded that "the prevalence of intergenerational concern in recently enacted constitutions arguably supports the emergence of a broad principle of environmental responsibility towards future generations as a principle of customary international law."[253] Further, manifold and increasing national case law supports the existence of some kind of responsibility towards future generations in the practice of States.[254] This case law is examined in more detail in Chap. 5 below.[255]

Consequently, there is sufficient evidence of both *opinio iuris* and State practice, which confirms the existence of a general conception of intergenerational equity. These findings are also supported by international jurisprudence and legal scholarship. While the ICJ's jurisprudence is not always clear on the concept of intergenerational equity,[256] some examples point to the existence of a customary principle[257] of international law. Several references in the *Nuclear Weapons Advisory Opinion*[258] indicate "an implicit recognition of the interests of future generations and of our obligation to consider these interests [...]".[259] In the *Gabčíkovo-Nagymaros Project* case, the ICJ mentioned the "growing awareness of the risks for [hu]mankind – for present and future generations".[260] Other bodies have

[249] On the evidence of *opinio iuris*, see *supra* notes 230–242.

[250] For an overview, see, e.g., UNSG (2013), paras. 37–48; Tremmel (2006), pp. 203–205; Fitzmaurice (2009), pp. 148–168.

[251] Collins (2007b), pp. 130–131.

[252] UNSG (2013), paras. 39–48; Collins (2007b), pp. 131–132. For a detailed assessment of these institutional frameworks, see *infra* in Sect. 5.3.2.

[253] Collins (2007b), p. 131. Cf. also Lee (2000), p. 339.

[254] For an overview, see, e.g., Collins (2007b), pp. 129–130; Hadjiargyrou (2016), pp. 264–267.

[255] For a detailed assessment of this case law, see *infra* in Sect. 5.3.3.3.3.

[256] For an overview, see already *supra* in Sect. 2.1.2.

[257] On the normative capacity indicated in the relevant case law, see already *supra* in Sect. 4.1.3.

[258] *Nuclear Weapons* (Advisory Opinion), *supra* note 212, paras. 29–36.

[259] Brown Weiss (1999), pp. 349–350.

[260] *Gabčíkovo-Nagymaros Project* (Judgment), *supra* note 52, para. 140.

also referred to the protection of future generations.[261] *Judge Weeramantry* further elaborated on the concept of intergenerational equity in several of his individual opinions,[262] although some of them went beyond the general conception and included more specific elements, such as rights of future generations or an intergenerational trust. For instance, he elaborated on the "juristic opinion" with regard to intergenerational equity in his dissenting opinion to the *Nuclear Weapons Advisory Opinion*:

> Juristic opinion is now abundant, with several major treatises appearing upon the subject and with such concepts as intergenerational equity and the common heritage of [hu]mankind being academically well established. Moreover, there is a growing awareness of the ways in which a multiplicity of traditional legal systems across the globe protect the environment for future generations. To these must be added a series of major international declarations commencing with the 1972 Stockholm Declaration on the Human Environment.[263]

At the doctrinal level, the assessment of intergenerational equity as a norm of customary international law remains ambiguous and unclear. As far as commentators distinguished between the concept's normative capacity and its legal status at all,[264] they often did not clarify whether their assessment referred to the general conception of intergenerational equity or to the more specific doctrine as introduced by *Brown Weiss*. Some observers rejected the customary nature of any form of intergenerational equity.[265] Other classifications were less obvious.[266] *Redgwell* stated that "in no case has the principle of inter-generational equity formed the legal basis for resolution of the dispute before [the ICJ] nor has any case before an international tribunal expressly recognized the rights of future generations."[267] Although the first part of her statement seems to refer to intergenerational equity in general, the second part explicitly referred to the rights-based approach, which is typical for the specific doctrine of intergenerational equity.[268] Similarly, *Malgosia Fitzmaurice* found that "[t]he Court's invocation of the concept of intergenerational

---

[261] See, e.g., *Iron Rhine Railway* (Arbitral Award), *supra* note 65, para. 58.

[262] ICJ, *Maritime Delimitation in the Area between Greenland and Jan Mayen (Denmark v. Norway),* Separate Opinion of Judge Weeramantry, 14 June 1993, ICJ Reports 1993, 211, para. 240; *Nuclear Tests 1995* (Dissenting Opinion of Judge Weeramantry), *supra* note 108, pp. 341–342; ICJ, *Legality of the Threat or Use of Nuclear Weapons,* Dissenting Opinion of Judge Weeramantry, 8 July 1996, ICJ Reports 1996, 429, pp. 454–455; *Gabčíkovo-Nagymaros Project* (Separate Opinion of Vice-President Weeramantry), *supra* note 55, pp. 109–110. For the classification of *Judge Cançado Trindade's* in the *Pulp Mills* case, see *infra* in Sect. 4.2.3.

[263] *Nuclear Weapons* (Dissenting Opinion of Judge Weeramantry), *supra* note 262, pp. 455–456.

[264] As to this problem, see *supra* note 72. Not distinguishing, see, e.g., Redgwell (1999), pp. 115–122.

[265] See, e.g., Beaucamp (2002), pp. 88–91; Anstee-Wedderburn (2014), pp. 48–51. Cf. also Szekely (2008), p. 159.

[266] For instance, in 1999, *Winfried Lang* characterised intergenerational equity as an "emerging" principle of international environmental law without clarifying whether this analysis referred to the general conception or the specific doctrine, see Lang (1999), p. 171.

[267] Redgwell (2016), p. 198.

[268] See also ibid., p. 196.

equity appears to be confined only in considering it as one of the factors to be taken into account in relation to environmental issues."[269] Although she concluded that international law would "not have such a suitable mechanism to accommodate such claims [of the representation of future generations]",[270] this observation was again connected to the specific means of implementation before judicial bodies.[271] Yet, her initial observation could even be understood positively with regard to the more general conception of intergenerational equity, which only requires taking into account the needs of future generations.

Furthermore, since the general conception of intergenerational equity is tantamount to the intergenerational component of sustainable development,[272] proponents of a customary nature of sustainable development[273] must be mentioned in favour of a customary nature of intergenerational equity.[274] However, most of them relied primarily on the component of integration in their analysis instead of intergenerational equity.[275]

There are also some commentators who addressed the legal status of the general conception of intergenerational equity more directly. For instance, *Collins* explicitly distinguished between the two manifestations of intergenerational equity and affirmed the legal status of the general conception (the "environmental responsibility towards the future"[276]) as a norm of customary international law.[277] *Boyle* and *Redgwell* also clarified in their standard work that "the essential point of the theory, that [hu]mankind has a responsibility for the future, and that this is an inherent component of sustainable development, is incontrovertible, however expressed."[278]

Overall, the abundant references to the needs of future generations in international soft law documents, UNGA resolutions, treaty law, and domestic legislation as well as national and international jurisprudence militate in favour of the existence of a customary norm of international law with regard to future generations. This responsibility towards the future began to develop in the 1990s with an increasing number of international documents and events referring to future generations, as illustrated in the second chapter. Since then, this responsibility to the future has

---

[269] Fitzmaurice (2008), p. 225. See also Ramlogan (2011), p. 215.

[270] Fitzmaurice (2008), p. 228.

[271] In detail on these institutional issues, see *infra* in Sect. 5.3.3.

[272] See, e.g., Howarth and Norgaard (1992), p. 473; Dupuy (1997), p. 887; Epiney and Scheyli (1998), p. 45.

[273] In favour of such a customary nature, see, e.g., Tladi (2007), pp. 99–104; Barral (2012), p. 388. Against such a customary nature, see, e.g., Beyerlin and Marauhn (2011), pp. 79–81. For an overview on the customary nature of sustainable development with further references, see Collins (2007b), p. 125 (at footnote 282)); Magraw and Hawke (2010), pp. 623–625.

[274] In this sense, see, e.g., Cordonier Segger (2021a), p. 65.

[275] See, e.g., Sands et al. (2018), p. 219; Proelß (2022), pp. 146–147.

[276] Collins (2007b), p. 114.

[277] Ibid., 114, 118, 130–132. Cf. also Borg (1998), p. 135; Hadjiargyrou (2016), pp. 263–264.

[278] Boyle and Redgwell (2021), p. 122. Cf. also Atapattu (2006), p. 118.

successively evolved into a customary norm in the last three decades.[279] However, these references only point to the existence of a general conception of intergenerational equity as it is also enshrined in the concept of sustainable development. Taken together with the observations on the normative capacity of this general conception, a legally binding principle has emerged in customary international law, which incorporates the responsibility to future generations into the international legal system, or the need to take into account the interests of future generations respectively.

#### 4.2.2.2 The Doctrine of Intergenerational Equity

The general conception of intergenerational equity thus already forms part of customary international law, but the same cannot necessarily be said of the legal status of the specific doctrine. It is possible that this customary norm has evolved from including the general conception only to a more specific manifestation of intergenerational equity in the form of the specific doctrine. While the mentioned instances of *opinio iuris* and State practice only constitute evidence of the customary nature of the *general* conception, other instances could point to *opinio iuris* and State practice incorporating the specific doctrine of intergenerational equity. This would require explicit references to intergenerational rights and obligations or to an intergenerational trust, as elaborated by *Brown Weiss* since the 1980s.[280]

With regard to the existing treaties, it has already been demonstrated that the doctrine of intergenerational equity is not yet included in them in a binding form. To the extent that the Aarhus Convention or the Escazú Agreement possibly include more specific elements of intergenerational equity,[281] these regionally and substantively limited treaties would not constitute sufficient evidence of existing State practice with regard to the doctrine of intergenerational equity. Yet, they could be an indicator for an increasing custom, if there are further instances of *opinio iuris* and State practice.

The first examples of potential *opinio iuris* can be addressed in context with the Rio Conference and its preparations. With respect to Principle 3 of the Rio Declaration,[282] some States, such as Japan, had suggested more specific wordings preceding the summit:

> Today and in the future, the individual has both a fundamental right to benefit from the common resources of humankind, which constitute the global environment, and at the same

[279] This time period is of relevance below, when it comes to the intertemporal assessment of intergenerational equity, as it describes the time contemporary with the norm's creation, see *infra* in Sects. 7.1.2 and 7.3.1.1.

[280] See, e.g., Brown Weiss (1989), pp. 47–86, 95–108.

[281] In detail, see *supra* in Sect. 4.2.1.

[282] "The right to development must be fulfilled so as to equitably meet developmental and environmental needs of present and future generations", see UNCED (1992), Principle 3.

> time a responsibility to protect, restore and improve them for present and future generations.[283]

These statements did not succeed in convincing the majority of States and a compromise was agreed on in the final Rio Declaration, which rather pointed to the general conception of intergenerational equity.[284] Nonetheless, many commentators subsequently interpreted Principle 3 as evidence of intergenerational equity rather than a right to development.[285] This is an interesting indicator with regard to the Principle's relevance for customary international law. In the years following the Rio Conference, two expert groups of the UN addressed the issues of sustainable development and intergenerational equity.[286] While the expert group report of the UNEP mentioned the protection of future generations only as a component of the principle of equity in international environmental law,[287] the expert group of the CSD went further and endorsed the notion of intergenerational equity as "a partnership that extends across time in relation to [all generations'] human environment".[288] The CSD report referred to various legal and soft law documents and even endorsed the doctrine of *Brown Weiss* while explicitly referring to the three components of comparable quality, option and access of all generations.[289] However, as *Winfried Lang* observed, there are certain differences between, on the one hand, these non-political documents drafted by lawyers and environmentalists and, on the other hand, political documents such as conference declarations.[290] While conference declarations carry more political weight, as they reflect the conviction of States more directly, *Lang* continued:

> [Political documents] do not necessarily reflect the state of international law, or the direction into which international law is moving. The [...] texts emanating from expert bodies [...] are largely based on the political consensus achieved in the previously mentioned texts, but they try to refine thinking; they try to link lofty ideals and ideas to reality, especially when one considers their focus on implementation, compliance-control etc.[291]

The ILA adopted in 2002 the New Delhi Declaration, another example for such a non-political document, which also attempted to link ideas to reality.[292] The ILA New Delhi Declaration addresses principles relating to sustainable development.[293]

---

[283] Preparatory Committee for the United Nations Conference on Environment and Development (1992), para. 17. See Molinari (2015), p. 142.

[284] See *supra* note 234.

[285] Cf. Molinari (2015), pp. 143–144.

[286] See Brown Weiss (1999), p. 352; Lang (1999), pp. 165–166.

[287] United Nations Environment Programme (1996), Principle 6. See also UNEP (2006), paras. 20–23.

[288] UN Commission on Sustainable Development (CSD) (1996), para. 42.

[289] Ibid., paras. 41–47. See also Brown Weiss (1999), p. 352.

[290] Lang (1999), p. 165.

[291] Ibid.

[292] See already *supra* in Sect. 2.1.1.4.

[293] ILA Committee on Legal Aspects of Sustainable Development (2002).

Beside some general references to future generations,[294] the declaration also explicitly refers to the "right of future generations to enjoy a fair level of the common patrimony" and the obligation of the present generation "to take into account the long-term impact of its activities and to sustain the resource base and the global environment for the benefit of future generations of humankind."[295] Although these formulations go beyond the general conception of intergenerational equity, the 2012 Sofia Guiding Statements on the Judicial Elaboration of the 2002 New Delhi Declaration ('ILA Sofia Guiding Statements') were framed more reluctantly; Statement 4 reads:

> The principle of equity (incorporating notions of intergenerational equity, intragenerational equity and substantive equality) [...] should, *where appropriate*, contextualise and inform judicial and quasi-judicial decision-making when matters of sustainable development are raised. Although judicial bodies and quasi-judicial bodies *cannot* alone address the social, economic, governance and political issues that invariably form key aspects of such disputes, it is *nevertheless* incumbent upon judicial and quasi-judicial bodies to further such principles of equity and fairness in exercising their judicial function (emphasis added).[296]

The ILA Sofia Guiding Statement's aim is to study the legal status and implementation of sustainable development and to observe the legal developments with regard to the concepts enshrined in the ILA New Delhi Declaration.[297] In the accompanying Sofia Conference Report, the ILA explicitly observed that the "principle" of equity "remains a multi-layered principle for which jurisprudence remains sporadic, inchoate and ultimately not fully reflective of the broad-ambition of the New Delhi principle itself."[298] Nonetheless, the foregoing Statement 4 contains in its second sentence a certain forward-looking optimism regarding the consequences of intergenerational equity for the judiciary.[299]

Beyond these expert group declarations and reports, the UNESCO Declaration is arguably the most relevant document in this context.[300] With respect to the 193 Member States of the UNESCO,[301] the Declaration can serve as a helpful indicator of an emerging *opinio iuris* concerning the responsibility towards future generations.[302] Although the Declaration remains silent on the issue of *rights* of future generations, it incorporates many of the planetary duties as enshrined in

[294] Ibid., para. 1.2.

[295] Ibid., paras. 2.1–2.3 See also Cordonier Segger (2021a), pp. 63–65.

[296] ILA Committee on International Law on Sustainable Development (2012b), Statement 4.

[297] ILA Committee on International Law on Sustainable Development (2012a), pp. 1–2; French (2017), p. 178.

[298] ILA Committee on International Law on Sustainable Development (2012a), p. 15. See also French (2017), p. 179.

[299] Cf. French (2017), p. 179.

[300] UNESCO (1997), p. 69.

[301] UNESCO (n.d.).

[302] Collins (2007b), p. 121.

*Brown Weiss'* doctrine.[303] Its Article 1 stipulates the present generation's "responsibility of ensuring that the needs and interests of present and future generations are fully safeguarded".[304] Furthermore, the Declaration elaborates on specific obligations, which resulted from this responsibility. In this respect, the present generation must "make every effort to ensure" the freedom of choice of future generations.[305] This is equivalent to *Brown Weiss'* conservation of comparable options principle, which also aims at offering future generations the same opportunities to live a decent life.[306]

Article 4 of the UNESCO Declaration prohibits to damage the Earth irreversibly and obliges the present generation to "take care to use natural resources reasonably and ensure that life is not prejudiced by harmful modifications of the ecosystems [...]".[307] Further, Article 5 explicitly requires the preservation of the quality and integrity of the environment and the natural resources necessary for sustaining human life.[308] Thereby, both provisions reflect the duty of conservation of quality, which also prohibits the degradation of natural resources.[309]

Lastly, *Brown Weiss'* third intergenerational duty can also be found in the UNESCO Declaration, which emphasised the need to safeguard access of the present generation to the common heritage of humankind.[310] The declaration text further ensures the "conditions of equitable, sustainable and universal socio-economic development of future generations [...] in particular through a fair and prudent use of available resources for the purpose of combating poverty" within the present generation.[311] Additionally, Article 11 stipulates the requirement of non-discrimination within generations.[312] These provisions mirror the duty of conservation of equitable access, both in the form of its inter- as well as its intragenerational components.[313] From these parallels, *Collins* concluded that the declaration "provides some evidence of emerging *opinio juris* concerning present environmental duties towards future generations".[314] Again, the GPE could be referred to in this context: If it were adopted as a non-binding document in the future, it would become relevant as potential evidence of universal *opinio iuris*. If it were adopted as a binding treaty, it could be considered widespread State practice. However, it is not yet clear whether and to what extent it would also be evidence of the existence of a

[303] Ibid., pp. 119–121.

[304] UNESCO (1997), Art. 1.

[305] Ibid., Art. 2.

[306] Brown Weiss (1989), pp. 38, 40–42.

[307] UNESCO (1997), Art. 4.

[308] Ibid., Art. 5(1), 5(3).

[309] Brown Weiss (1989), pp. 38, 42–43.

[310] UNESCO (1997), Art. 8.

[311] Ibid., Art. 10(1).

[312] Ibid., Art. 11.

[313] Brown Weiss (1989), p. 21; Brown Weiss (2021), para. 12.

[314] Collins (2007b), p. 121.

specific doctrine of intergenerational equity in customary international law, as the exact contents of its Article 4 are still controversial and depend on the subsequent interpretation and application of the GPE.[315]

Beyond these political and expert group documents, there have been several other initiatives for a more specific codification of intergenerational equity in the last decades, which were more or less inspired by *Brown Weiss'* doctrine. In 1988, an Advisory Group of the UN University Project, headed by *Brown Weiss*, issued the 'Goa Guidelines on Intergenerational Equity'.[316] Although these guidelines contain the contents of the doctrine of intergenerational equity, the authors explicitly considered them an "innovative response [...] which attempts to introduce *for the first time* in a systematic and comprehensive manner, a long-term temporal dimension into international law [...]" (emphasis added).[317]

In 1991, the Cousteau Society initiated a petition for a draft UNGA Resolution in the form of an international 'Bill of Rights for Future Generations', which proclaimed the right of future generations "to an uncontaminated and undamaged Earth and to its enjoyment [...]".[318] The draft resolution also considered the relationship between generations to be a planetary trust.[319] Although the petition was signed by nine million people in a short time and was formally accepted by the UNSG in 2001, it never was adopted by the UNGA.[320]

In 2016, the environmental lawyer and former French Minister of the Environment *Corinne Lepage* presented a draft for a 'Universal Declaration of Humankind Rights', which she had elaborated at the request of the former French President.[321] The declaration prominently referred to future generations and intergenerational equity several times.[322] For instance, it proclaimed a "principle of non-discrimination between generations"[323] and stated that humankind had a "right to the preservation of common goods, [...] and the right to universal and effective access to vital resources"; further, that future generations were "entitled to their transmission".[324] The declaration was originally conceived as a potential outcome document for the COP21 in Paris in 2015,[325] but it was ultimately not considered for this purpose. Until today, it did not achieve political approval by any

---

[315] In more detail, see *supra* in Sect. 4.2.1. On the unlikelihood of the adoption of the GPE as a treaty, see already *supra* in Sect. 2.1.1.5.

[316] Brown Weiss et al. (1988).

[317] Ibid.

[318] Cousteau (1991, Art. 1).

[319] See ibid., Art. 2.

[320] See Collins (2007b), pp. 118–119; Brown Weiss (2010), p. 109.

[321] Lepage and Drafting Committee (2015). See also Lepage (2015).

[322] Lepage and Drafting Committee (2015), Art. I, IV, VIII, XI.

[323] Ibid., Art. IV.

[324] Ibid., Art. VIII.

[325] See Guenfoud (2015).

State or international organisation, but remained a civil society petition with signatories from municipalities, corporations and public figures.

Comparably, the Maastricht Principles on the Human Rights of Future Generations from February 2023 address several issues that can easily be matched with the notions of *Brown Weiss'* specific doctrine of intergenerational equity.[326] For instance, the Principles contain a provision on "equality and non-discrimination" between generations, resembling *Brown Weiss'* equality of options.[327] The "obligation to respect the human rights of future generations" includes, *inter alia*, the duty not to unstainably use or deplete natural resources, to degrade ecosystems, to contribute to a decline in biodiversity or to engage in conduct that results in discriminatory access to natural resources.[328] These aspects of the stipulated State obligations mirror in large parts the three conservation duties in *Brown Weiss'* doctrine. The Maastricht Principles further refer to an intergenerational trusteeship, as "[d]uring their time on Earth, each generation must act as trustees of the Earth for future generations [...] in harmony with all living beings and Nature".[329] Although the Principles "seek to clarify the present state of international law as it applies to the human rights of future generations", they remain the "result of a process [...] of research, dialogue and collective brainstorming" of academic experts and civil society actors without any binding character.[330]

Generally, while all of these civil society initiatives demonstrate an increasing public consciousness for the responsibilities towards the future, they can at best indirectly influence the development of the customary nature of a norm since they did not emanate from State conduct at all.[331]

Finally, the customary nature of the specific doctrine of intergenerational equity could be supported by jurisprudence and legal doctrine. With regard to jurisprudence, the explicit references to future generations only reflect a general conception of intergenerational equity, as has been illustrated above. One exception at the international level can be found in an advisory opinion of the IACHR from 2017.[332] Therein, the IACHR recognised a human right to a healthy environment in the system of the American Convention on Human Rights ('ACHR')[333] and explicitly stated that "[i]n its collective dimension, the right to a healthy environment constitutes a universal value that is owed to both present *and future* generations"

[326] Liebenberg et al. (2023). See already *supra* in Sect. 2.1.1.5.

[327] Ibid., Principle 6.

[328] Ibid., Principles 16–17.

[329] Ibid., Principle 8.

[330] Ibid., Introduction.

[331] Cf. Pellet (2012), pp. 823–824.

[332] Inter-American Court of Human Rights, *The Environment and Human Rights (Requested by the Republic of Colombia),* Advisory Opinion, 15 November 2017, Retrieved January 3, 2025, from https://www.corteidh.or.cr/docs/opiniones/seriea_23_ing.pdf, para. 59.

[333] Ibid., paras. 57–63. See also V. Kahl (2019), pp. 115–117.

(emphasis added).[334] Furthermore, two individual opinions in cases before the ICJ are worth analysing in the present context. First, *Judge Weeramantry* explained in his dissenting opinion to the *Nuclear Weapons Advisory Opinion*:

> It is to be noted in this context that the *rights* of future generations have passed the stage when they were merely an embryonic right struggling for recognition. They have woven themselves into international law through major treaties, through juristic opinion [...] (emphasis added).[335]

Second, *Judge Cançado Trindade* added 14 years later that "it can hardly be doubted that the acknowledgement of inter-generational equity forms part of conventional wisdom in International Environmental Law [sic.]",[336] although he apparently considered intergenerational equity a general principle of law.[337]

As *Judge Weeramantry* explicitly referred to the "rights" of future generations, it can be assumed that his dissenting opinion argued in favour of a more sophisticated understanding of intergenerational equity as part of the "juristic opinion", thus, customary international law. *Judge Cançado Trindade* also attempted to draw a more detailed picture of the existence of intergenerational notions in the development of international environmental law.[338] Both judges explicitly referred to the works of *Brown Weiss'* works.[339] At the same time, both statements could also be understood in terms of the general conception of intergenerational equity, as enshrined in many international environmental law documents.

Due to the inconsistencies in doctrinal accounts of intergenerational equity, most assessments did not properly distinguish between the manifestations of the concept. On the one hand, those commentators that already rejected the existence of the general conception in customary international law would all the more reject its specific manifestation.[340] The implicit rejections by *Fitzmaurice* and *Redgwell* with respect to the specific doctrine have also already been illustrated above.[341] On the other hand, there have also been some observers who explicitly analysed the customary nature of the specific doctrine of intergenerational equity with its planetary rights and obligations. For instance, *Reinhard Bartholomäi* assessed a broad number of treaties and soft law documents, which he explicitly attributed to one of the three planetary duties of *Brown Weiss'* doctrine.[342] He concluded that this

[334] *The Environment and Human Rights* (Advisory Opinion), *supra* note 332, para. 59. On the relationship between this human right and intergenerational equity, see *infra* in Sect. 5.2.2.

[335] *Nuclear Weapons* (Dissenting Opinion of Judge Weeramantry), *supra* note 262, pp. 455–456.

[336] *Pulp Mills* (Separate Opinion of Judge Cançado Trindade), *supra* note 61, para. 122.

[337] For a critical assessment of this assumption, see *supra* note 63 and *infra* in Sect. 4.2.3.

[338] He referred to a "long-term temporal dimension", see *Pulp Mills* (Separate Opinion of Judge Cançado Trindade), *supra* note 61, paras. 114–131.

[339] See, e.g., *Nuclear Weapons* (Dissenting Opinion of Judge Weeramantry), *supra* note 262, p. 455; *Pulp Mills* (Separate Opinion of Judge Cançado Trindade), *supra* note 61, para. 114.

[340] On these commentators, see already *supra* notes 265–266.

[341] Fitzmaurice (2008), pp. 225, 228; Redgwell (2016), pp. 196–198. See also *supra* notes 267–271.

[342] Bartholomäi (1997), pp. 134–139.

doctrine was mirrored in *opinio iuris* and State practice.[343] However, the enumerated documents, while illustrating some examples of environmental conservation duties, did neither encompass any planetary rights nor frameworks of intergenerational representation. Therefore, they did "not demonstrate that future generations have been endowed with justiciable rights in international law".[344] They have been attributed rather to the general conception of intergenerational equity in this book, although they could eventually contribute to the further development of intergenerational equity. So far, it seems more convincing to conclude that the specific manifestation of intergenerational equity is not yet part of but constitutes an emerging norm of customary international law.[345] *Redgwell* stated in 1999:

> Whilst intergenerational equity has not yet achieved the status of a binding rule (or, perhaps more accurately, set of rules) under international law, a process of 'creeping intergenerationalisation' may be observed […].[346]

In 2019, *Kotzé* considered intergenerational justice in a more elaborate sense to form part of the currently "unmentionable norms", meaning norms that have not yet been agreed to by the international community.[347] Even *Brown Weiss* herself considered in 1989 that intergenerational rights and obligations did not yet constitute legal rights and obligations, but remained of moral value and were still in the process of developing into binding law.[348]

More than 30 years later, the general conception of intergenerational equity has definitely become part of customary international law.[349] In contrast, there is still not enough evidence to confirm the existence of sufficient *opinio iuris* and State practice with respect to the more specific doctrine as formulated by *Brown Weiss*. First indications for emerging *opinio iuris* and State practice exist in this regard, particularly the illustrations in the UN expert group reports, the ILA New Delhi Declaration and the UNESCO Declaration. The potential further development of the GPE could be another example for the emergence of a customary norm of intergenerational equity in its more specific manifestation.

Overall, the legal status of *Brown Weiss'* doctrine as customary international law cannot be confirmed with certainty at present. However, it is possible that the future development of international environmental law will cause intergenerational equity to evolve from its general to a more specific manifestation, which contains corresponding rights and obligations as well as frameworks of representation. Chapter 7 below turns to the question of whether this will be the case and which

---

[343] Ibid., pp. 139–140.

[344] Boyle and Redgwell (2021), p. 122.

[345] See Lang (1999), p. 171; Molinari (2015), p. 155. However, *Winfried Lang* did not clarify to which conception of intergenerational equity he was referring, see *supra* note 266.

[346] Redgwell (1999), p. 126.

[347] Kotzé (2019), pp. 216, 220, 223.

[348] Brown Weiss (1989), pp. 102–103. See also Brown Weiss (1984), pp. 504, 564.

[349] Brown Weiss (2010), p. 114.

consequences such an emergence might already have today.[350] Beforehand, the next section addresses the potential legal status of intergenerational equity as a general principle of law.

### *4.2.3 Intergenerational Equity as a General Principle of International Law*

Eventually, intergenerational equity could also constitute a "general principle[…] of law recognized by civilized nations" within the meaning of Article 38(1)(c) of the ICJ Statute. This source of international law has its origins in municipal legal systems; if a legal principle is recognised in all or most domestic legal systems and if it can be analogously applied to the international legal system, then it is considered a general principle in the sense of Article 38 of the ICJ Statute.[351] The reference to municipal law for the establishment of such general principles by the ICJ has remained quite limited so far.[352] Instead, the ICJ often recurred to such general principles of international law without thorough analysis of parallels in municipal law.[353] Particularly with respect to international environmental law, *Tullio Treves* analysed that international courts and tribunals often avoided to explicitly refer to general principles under Article 38 of the ICJ Statute in their assessment of environmental concepts:[354]

> [I]n alluding to general international law […] and not engaging directly in speaking of customary international law, the ICJ takes into consideration the difficulties alluded to by scholarly opinion. It avoids engaging in the discussion as to whether these principles are customary international law or general principles of law referred to in [A]rticle 38 of its Statute. It seems to prefer the former classification but does not exclude the second altogether as 'general international law' might encompass it. In so doing it remains close to the notion used by specialists of international environmental law of 'principles' or 'general principles' of international environmental law […]. It may also be surmised that the Court adopts this terminology in order to leave open the discussion about the difference between general principles to be imported into international law from domestic legal systems and more general legal propositions, difficult to distinguish from customary rules, but for which the ascertainment of the requirements of general practice and *opinio juris* may be less rigorously pursued. […][355]

---

350 When it comes to the intertemporal assessment of intergenerational equity, the future development of the specific doctrine plays a decisive role, see *infra* in Sect. 7.3.3.2.

351 The exact functioning and origins of these principles are controversial until today. In more detail with further examples, see, e.g., Shaw (2008), pp. 98–105; Pellet (2012), pp. 832–841; Gaja (2020), paras. 4–16.

352 Gaja (2020), paras. 7–16.

353 See ibid., paras. 17–20.

354 Treves (2019), pp. 385–388.

355 Ibid., p. 387.

Consequently, it is difficult to establish the legal status of a certain concept of international environmental law from the jurisprudence of the ICJ,[356] which is also the reason for the inconsistencies in the aforementioned case law.[357] Nonetheless, some commentators have suggested a classification as a general principle of law for either sustainable development or intergenerational equity.[358] Most prominently, *Judge Cançado Trindade* argued in favour of such a legal status for both sustainable development and intergenerational equity in his separate opinion in the *Pulp Mills* case.[359] He stated, *inter alia*:

> Principles of international law are guiding principles of general content, and, in that, they differ from the norms or rules of positive international law, and transcend them. As basic pillars of the international legal system (as of any legal system), those principles give expression to the *idée de droit*, and furthermore to the *idée de justice*, reflecting the conscience of the international community.[360]

However, this categorisation is erroneous as it misunderstands the character of general principles under Article 38 of the ICJ Statute as a completely distinct source of international law.[361] While these principles are not created by State practice on the international field but result from domestic law,[362] sustainable development and intergenerational equity are concepts, which have primarily arisen from *international* developments.[363] Even though aspects of both concepts can indeed be found in domestic legal systems all over the world,[364] this does not alter the legal status of sustainable development or the general conception of intergenerational equity. They remain norms of customary nature.[365] For instance, although *Judge Weeramantry* extensively illustrated the occurrence of future generations in various traditional

---

[356] See also Fitzmaurice (2019), p. 446.

[357] See *supra* notes 256–263.

[358] With regard to sustainable development, see Voigt (2009), pp. 145–186. See also Tladi (2007), pp. 102–103 with reference to Lowe (2009), p. 216. With regard to the principle of environmental protection ("Umweltprinzip"), cf. also Rauber (2018), pp. 454–476.

[359] *Pulp Mills* (Separate Opinion of Judge Cançado Trindade), *supra* note 61, paras. 39–44, 48, 51–53.

[360] Ibid., para. 39.

[361] See Tladi (2007), pp. 102–103; Proelß (2022), pp. 102–103. In the sense of this distinction, cf. Redgwell (2017), pp. 952–953.

[362] See explicitly Brierly and Clapham (2012), p. 64 (at footnote 23). Opposing this "minimalistic view" of Art. 38(1)(c) of the ICJ Statute, see *Pulp Mills* (Separate Opinion of Judge Cançado Trindade), *supra* note 61, para. 39; Voigt (2009), pp. 154–157.

[363] See *supra* in Sect. 2.1 and in Sect. 4.2.2.

[364] See *Gabčíkovo-Nagymaros Project* (Separate Opinion of Vice-President Weeramantry), *supra* note 55, pp. 97–110.

[365] Concerning the generally minor role of general principles in international environmental law, see Epiney (2022), p. 35. As to the (mainly academic) dispute concerning the distinction between general principles and customary norms Mbengue and McGarry (2019), pp. 414–423.

systems, he did *not* consider sustainable development to be a general principle of law,[366] but as a principle of customary international law.[367]

By referring to intergenerational equity as a general principle in the sense of Article 38(1)(c) of the ICJ Statute, *Judge Cançado Trindade* confused the issue of normative capacity with the characterisation of legal sources. Although he explicitly based his analysis on Article 38(1)(c),[368] his reference to the "*idée de justice*" and the "conscience of the international community" with regard to general principles[369] illustrates that he actually used the distinction between rules and principles according to *Ronald Dworkin's* terminology. His classification of intergenerational equity as a "principle" of international law must thus be understood in the context of this principle/rule dichotomy, not in the sense of the sources of law under Article 38 of the ICJ Statute.[370] Furthermore, at least with respect to intergenerational equity, *Judge Cançado Trindade* was not entirely consistent in his classification. While he started by listing sustainable development and intergenerational equity together with prevention and precaution among the general principles of law,[371] he later only addressed prevention and precaution under this heading,[372] before returning again to intergenerational equity without explicit reference to the latter as a "general principle".[373] Instead, intergenerational equity would constitute "part of conventional wisdom in International Environmental Law [sic.]",[374] which could equally be understood in a customary sense.[375] All in all, intergenerational equity is no general principle of law within the meaning of Article 38(1)(c) of the ICJ Statute—neither in its general nor in its specific manifestation—as it primarily belongs to the source of customary international law.

[366] *Gabčíkovo-Nagymaros Project* (Separate Opinion of Vice-President Weeramantry), *supra* note 55, 109–110.

[367] Ibid., p. 95.

[368] See, e.g., *Pulp Mills* (Separate Opinion of Judge Cançado Trindade), *supra* note 61, para. 40.

[369] Ibid., para. 39. See also *supra* note 360.

[370] Convincingly, see Tladi (2007), p. 103; Proelß (2022), pp. 102–103. For an overview of the inconsistencies with regard to general principles in international environmental law, see Brunnée (2017), pp. 973–975.

[371] *Pulp Mills* (Separate Opinion of Judge Cançado Trindade), *supra* note 61, paras. 51–53.

[372] Ibid., paras. 54–96.

[373] Ibid., paras. 114–140.

[374] Ibid., para. 122.

[375] See already *supra* notes 336–337.

## 4.3 Conclusion of Chap. 4

Chapter 4 has extensively analysed the legal nature of the concept of intergenerational equity, distinguishing between the concept's normative capacity and its legal status within the sources of international law. The existence of two manifestations of intergenerational equity with different levels of specificity complicated this analysis. The general conception of intergenerational equity (i.e., the need to take into account the interests of future generations) mirrors the intergenerational component of sustainable development. While this chapter has concluded—in the highly disputed question—that sustainable development constitutes a legal principle with normative capacity and not a mere political policy, this finding was not a necessary precondition for the following assessment of intergenerational equity. Sustainable development's sub-concepts could evolve into independent legal principles and rules that are not limited by the normative capacity of sustainable development. Notwithstanding this, the general conception of intergenerational equity also constitutes a legal principle, meaning a requirement of justice that stipulates a normative goal to be achieved to the greatest extent legally and factually possible.

On the second step, the general conception achieved legal status in the sense of Article 38 of the ICJ Statute. While the classification of intergenerational equity as a general principle of law (Article 38(1)(c) of the ICJ Statute) was briefly rejected due to conceptional confusions, intergenerational equity is a legally binding norm of both treaty law (Article 38(1)(a) of the ICJ Statute) and customary international law (Article 38(1)(b) of the ICJ Statute). The focus of this book lies on this customary norm rather than the various pertinent treaty regimes.

The specific doctrine of intergenerational equity, as elaborated by *Edith Brown Weiss*, has exceeded the general conception of intergenerational equity in several regards. It contains more specific intergenerational obligations—the duties of conservation of options, environmental quality and equitable access—as well as intergenerational rights, and it is embedded in a planetary trust, which also requires an institutional framework of representation of future generations. Due to these much more elaborated planetary duties, this doctrine has undoubtedly normative capacity. The doctrine constitutes a set of legal rules in the sense of *Ronald Dworkin's* typology, that means a set of practical formulations that direct its addressees to a specific act or behaviour.

The legal status of the specific doctrine of intergenerational equity is less clear than with regard to the general manifestation. In contrast to the general responsibility towards the future, the specific planetary duties and rights as well as the institutional framework are only to be found in very few international documents. Particularly, there is not sufficient evidence to support a legal rule of customary international law with regard to the doctrine of intergenerational equity. The illustrated developments point to an emerging norm of customary law, which could achieve the sufficient legal status in the future; but *Brown Weiss'* doctrine of intergenerational equity does not constitute a legally binding norm yet.

The illustrated distinctions between the two manifestations of intergenerational equity constitute essential foundations for the further assessment in the next chapters. The two manifestations are not two opposite or completely independent notions but rather constitute two nuances on the same scale of the overall idea of intergenerational equity. While the general conception has become a legally binding norm of international law, the more specific manifestation has not yet emerged as such a customary norm. However, as illustrated above, it is certainly possible that the general conception will evolve into the more specific set of legal rules in the next years and decades. The legally binding manifestation of intergenerational equity would then contain duties of conservation, attribute legal rights to future generations and operationalise an institutional form of representation of these rights. The evolutionary character of these two manifestations is of importance in the context of the intertemporal perspective taken in Chaps. 6 and 7. As far as the potential evolutionary development of intergenerational equity is analysed, the two manifestations constitute the essential reference points for a modified doctrine of intertemporal law.[376]

Furthermore, the foregoing chapter has contributed to the distinction between the concept of intergenerational equity *de lege lata* and the potential prospects of intergenerational equity *de lege ferenda*. While the general conception of intergenerational equity is part of the current law, the specific doctrine of *Brown Weiss* is only an emerging norm and could shape the law in the future. In order to fully understand how exactly this legal regime of intergenerational equity could develop in the future, it is important to assess the aspects of the doctrine more thoroughly that do not constitute part of the existing law yet. So far, these more specific components of the doctrine have only been illustrated in an overview, e.g., with regard to the planetary duties.[377] These duties of conservation of comparable options, environmental quality and equitable access constitute substantive standards for accepted behaviour with regard to the specific doctrine; they are part of a normative sub-system of intergenerational equity.[378] It is a question of this normative sub-system whether intergenerational equity takes effect as a legal principle, as is currently the case, or whether it develops into a legal rule in the future. The relationship of the two manifestations of intergenerational equity as well as the emerging character of the doctrine are visualised in Fig. 4.1.[379]

Beyond these substantive aspects, the doctrine also raises certain operational issues. In Chap. 7, these issues are framed as parts of the "operating system" of intergenerational equity, meaning the structural dimensions that govern the functioning of the substantive norms of intergenerational equity.[380] In this context, three

[376] See *infra* in Sect. 7.3.3.2.

[377] See *supra* in Sect. 2.2.1.4.

[378] Diehl and Ku (2010), pp. 29–35. In detail on this classification, see *infra* in Sect. 7.3.4.1.

[379] Chapters 5 and 7 take this illustration up again for further development, see *infra* in Sect. 5.4, Fig. 5.1, and in Sect. 7.3.4.3, Fig. 7.9.

[380] See *supra* note 378.

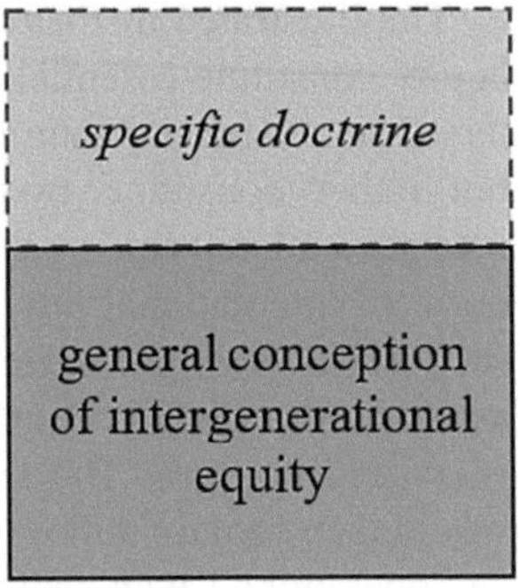


**Fig. 4.1** The Two Manifestations of Intergenerational Equity

main questions are still unanswered. First, the doctrine of intergenerational equity incorporates planetary obligations of "the present generation", so that it must be addressed which persons or entities could be fitting duty-bearers of the concept. Second, the doctrine construes a planetary trust with future generations as holders of intergenerational rights—another controversial issue. Third, the implementation of these more specific rights and obligations is based on an institutionalised framework of representation, as future generations cannot act for themselves. The next chapter turns to the detailed assessment of these open issues of intergenerational equity.

## References

Aarnio, A. (1990). Taking rules seriously. In W. Maihofer & G. Sprenger (Eds.), *Law and the states in modern times: Proceedings of the 14th IVR World Congress in Edinburgh, August 1989* (pp. 180–192). Steiner.

Aguila, Y. (2020). A global pact for the environment: The logical outcome of 50 years of international environmental law. *Sustainability, 12*(14), 5636. https://doi.org/10.3390/su12145636

Aguila, Y., & Chami, L. (2022, March 17). The global pact for the environment: Where to? *Jus Mundi Blog*. Retrieved January 3, 2025, from https://blog.jusmundi.com/global-pact-for-the-environment-where-to/.

Ait-Aissi Paillon, N. (2018). Le Pacte Mondial pour L'Environnement: Un Appui à La Gouvernance Mondiale de L'Environnement? *Revue Québécoise De Droit International, 31*(2), 71–102.

Alexy, R. (1995). *Recht, Vernunft, Diskurs: Studien zur Rechtsphilosophie* (1st ed.). Suhrkamp.

Alexy, R. (2000). On the structure of legal principles. *Ratio Juris, 13*(3), 294–304.

Alexy, R. (2006). *Theorie der Grundrechte* (1st ed.). Suhrkamp.

Anstee-Wedderburn, J. (2014). Giving a voice to future generations: Intergenerational equity, representative of generations to come, and the challenge of planetary rights. *Australian Journal of Environmental Law, 1*(1), 37–70.

Atapattu, S. A. (2006). *Emerging principles of international environmental law*. Transnational Publishers. https://doi.org/10.1163/ej.9781571051820.i-536

Barral, V. (2012). Sustainable development in international law: Nature and operation of an evolutive legal norm. *European Journal of International Law, 23*(2), 377–400. https://doi.org/10.1093/ejil/chs016

Barritt, E. (2020). Global values, transnational expression: From Aarhus to Escazú. In V. Heyvaert & L.-A. Duvic-Paoli (Eds.), *Research handbook on transnational environmental law* (Vol. 12, pp. 198–214). Edward Elgar Publishing.

Bartholomäi, R. (1997). *Sustainable development und Völkerrecht: Nachhaltige Entwicklung und Intergenerative Gerechtigkeit in der Staatenpraxis* (1st ed.). Nomos.

Beaucamp, G. (2002). *Das Konzept der Zukunftsfähigen Entwicklung im Recht: Untersuchungen zur Völkerrechtlichen, Europarechtlichen, Verfassungsrechtlichen und Verwaltungsrechtlichen Relevanz eines Neuen Politischen Leitbildes*. Mohr Siebeck.

Beyerlin, U. (2010). Different types of norms in international environmental law policies, principles, and rules. In D. Bodansky, J. Brunnée, & E. Hey (Eds.), *The Oxford handbook of international environmental law* (Vol. 18, 1st ed., pp. 425–448). Oxford University Press.

Beyerlin, U., & Grote Stoutenburg, J. (2013). Environment, international protection. In A. Peters & R. Wolfrum (Eds.), *Max Planck encyclopedia of public international law*. Oxford University Press. (Article last updated December 2013).

Beyerlin, U., & Marauhn, T. (2011). *International environmental law*. Hart Publishing.

Biniaz, S. (2017, August). *10 questions to ask about the proposed "global pact for the environment*. Sabin Center for Climate Change Law at Columbia Law School. Retreived January 3, 2025, from http://columbiaclimatelaw.com/files/2017/08/Biniaz-2017-08-Global-Pact-for-the-Environment.pdf

Bodansky, D. (1993). The United Nations framework convention on climate change: A commentary. *Yale Journal of International Law, 18*(2), 451–558.

Bodansky, D. (2010). *The art and craft of international environmental law*. Harvard University Press.

Boer, B. (2021). The preamble. In G. van Calster & L. Reins (Eds.), *Paris agreement on climate change: A commentary* (pp. 5–32). Edward Elgar Publishing.

Borg, S. (1998). Guarding intergenerational rights over natural resources. In E. Agius & S. Busuttil (Eds.), *Future generations and international law: Proceedings of the international experts' meeting held by the future generations programme at the foundation for international studies, University of Malta* (Vol. 11, pp. 127–141). Earthscan Publications Ltd..

Bosselmann, K. (2017). *The principle of sustainability: Transforming law and governance* (2nd ed.). Routledge Taylor & Francis Group.

Boyle, A. E. (1999). Some reflections on the relationship of treaties and soft law. *International and Comparative Law Quarterly, 48*, 901–913.

Boyle, A. E., & Redgwell, C. (2021). *Birnie, Boyle, and Redgwell's international law and the environment* (4th ed.). Oxford University Press.

Brierly, J. L., & Clapham, A. (2012). *Brierly's law of nations: An introduction to the role of international law in international relations* (7th ed.). Oxford University Press.

Brown Weiss, E. (1984). The planetary trust: Conservation and intergenerational equity. *Ecology Law Quarterly, 11*, 495–582.

Brown Weiss, E. (1989). *In fairness to future generations: International law, common patrimony, and intergenerational equity*. Transnational Publishers.

Brown Weiss, E. (1999). Opening the door to the environment and to future generations. In L. Boisson de Chazournes & P. Sands (Eds.), *International law, the international court of justice, and nuclear weapons* (Vol. 21, pp. 338–353). Cambridge University Press.

Brown Weiss, E. (2010). Implementing intergenerational equity. In M. Fitzmaurice, D. Ong, & P. Merkouris (Eds.), *Research handbook on international environmental law* (Vol. 5, pp. 100–116). Edward Elgar Publishing.

Brown Weiss, E. (2019). Intergenerational equity. In Y. Aguila & J. E. Viñuales (Eds.), *A global pact for the environment: Legal foundations* (Vol. 5, pp. 51–58). Cambridge Centre for Environment, Energy and Natural Resource Governance (C-EENRG).

Brown Weiss, E. (2021). Intergenerational equity. In A. Peters & R. Wolfrum (Eds.), *Max Planck encyclopedia of public international law*. Oxford University Press. (Article last updated April 2021).

Brown Weiss, E., Cançado Trindade, A. A., Kiss, A., Peng Cheng, L., Ploman, E. W., & Pathak, R. S. (1988, February 15). *Goa guidelines on intergenerational equity: Statement of the United Nations University Project on "International Law, Common Patrimony and Intergenerational Equity"*. United Nations University Project. Retrieved January 3, 2025, from http://goenchimati.org/the-goa-guidelines-on-intergenerational-equity/.

Brunnée, J. (2017). Sources of international environmental law: Interactional law. In J. d'Aspremont & S. Besson (Eds.), *The Oxford handbook on the sources of international law* (Vol. 44, pp. 960–983). Oxford University Press.

Carazo Ortiz, M. P. (2017). Contextual provisions (preamble and article 1). In D. R. Klein, M. P. Carazo Ortiz, M. Doelle, J. Bulmer, & A. Higham (Eds.), *The Paris agreement on climate change: Analysis and commentary* (Vol. 6, pp. 107–122). Oxford University Press.

Carty, A. (2008). Sociological theories of international law. In A. Peters & R. Wolfrum (Eds.), *Max Planck encyclopedia of public international law*. Oxford University Press. (Article last updated March 2008).

Cheng, B. (1994). *General principles of law as applied by international courts and tribunals*. (Reprint). Cambridge University Press.

Chinkin, C. (2000). Normative development in the international legal system. In D. Shelton (Ed.), *Commitment and compliance: The role of non-binding norms in the international legal system* (Vol. 1, pp. 21–42). Oxford University Press.

Collins, L. M. (2007a). Environmental rights for the future? Intergenerational equity in the EU. *Review of European, Comparative and International Environmental Law, 16*(3), 321–331. https://doi.org/10.1111/j.1467-9388.2007.00568.x

Collins, L. M. (2007b). Revisiting the doctrine of intergenerational equity in global environmental governance. *Dalhousie Law Journal, 30*(1), 73–134.

Condorelli, L. (2012). Customary international law: The yesterday, today, and tomorrow of general international law. In A. Cassese (Ed.), *Realizing Utopia: The future of international law* (Vol. 12, 1st ed., pp. 147–157). Oxford University Press.

Cordonier Segger, M.-C. (2008). Sustainable development in international law. In H. C. Bugge & C. Voigt (Eds.), *Sustainable development in international and national law: What did the Brundtland report do to legal thinking and legal development, and where can we go from here?* (pp. 85–199). Europa Law Publishing.

Cordonier Segger, M.-C. (2021a). International treaty law and policy for future generations. In M.-C. Cordonier Segger, M. Szabó, & A. R. Harrington (Eds.), *Intergenerational justice in sustainable development treaty implementation: Advancing future generations rights through national institutions* (Vol. 3, pp. 47–67). Cambridge University Press.

Cordonier Segger, M.-C. (2021b). lntergenerational justice in the Paris agreement on climate change. In M.-C. Cordonier Segger, M. Szabó, & A. R. Harrington (Eds.), *Intergenerational justice in sustainable development treaty implementation: Advancing future generations rights through national institutions* (Vol. 37, pp. 731–753). Cambridge University Press.

Cordonier Segger, M.-C., & Khalfan, A. (2004). *Sustainable development law: Principles, practices and prospects*. Oxford University Press.

Cousteau, J.-Y. (1991). *A bill of rights for future generations: Draft general assembly resolution*. Cousteau Society. Retrieved January 3, 2025, from https://archivos.juridicas.unam.mx/www/bjv/libros/8/3635/12.pdf

Crawford, J., & Brownlie, I. (2019). *Brownlie's principles of public international law* (9th ed.). Oxford University Press.

Cryer, R., Hervey, T., Sokhi-Bulley, B., & Bohm, A. (2011). *Research methodologies in EU and international law*. Hart Publishing.

de Castro, P. C. (1997). The judgment in the case concerning the Gabčíkovo-Nagymaros project: Positive signs for the evolution of international water law. *Yearbook of International Environmental Law, 8*(1), 21–31. https://doi.org/10.1093/yiel/8.1.21

de Sadeleer, N. (2005). *Environmental principles: From political slogans to legal rules*. Oxford University Press.

Dernbach, J. C., & Cheever, F. (2015). Sustainable development and its discontents. *Transnational Environmental Law, 4*(2), 247–287. https://doi.org/10.1017/S2047102515000163

Diehl, P. F., & Ku, C. (2010). *The dynamics of international law*. Cambridge University Press. https://doi.org/10.1017/CBO9780511817328

Doelle, M. (2016). The Paris agreement: Historic breakthrough or high stakes experiment? *Climate Law, 6*(1–2), 1–20. https://doi.org/10.1163/18786561-00601001

Dupuy, P.-M. (1997). Où en est Le Droit International de L'Environnement à la Fin du Siècle? *Revue Générale De Droit International Public, 101*, 873.

Dupuy, P.-M. (2010). Formation of customary international law and general principles. In D. Bodansky, J. Brunnée, & E. Hey (Eds.), *The Oxford handbook of international environmental law* (Vol. 19, 1st ed., pp. 449–466). Oxford University Press.

Dupuy, P.-M., Le Moli, G., & Viñuales, J. E. (2021). Customary international law and the environment. In L. Rajamani & J. Peel (Eds.), *The Oxford handbook of international environmental law* (Vol. 23, 2nd ed., pp. 385–401). Oxford University Press.

Dupuy, P.-M., & Viñuales, J. E. (2018). *International environmental law* (2nd ed.). Cambridge University Press.

Dworkin, R. (1978). *Taking rights seriously*. Harvard University Press.

Ebbesson, J., Gaugitsch, H., Jendrośka, J., Marshall, F., & Stec, S. (2014). *The Aarhus Convention: An implementation guide* (2nd ed.). United Nations Publication.

Eggett, C. (2019). The role of principles and general principles in the "constitutional processes" of international law. *Netherlands International Law Review, 66*(2), 197–217. https://doi.org/10.1007/s40802-019-00139-1

Epiney, A. (2022). Gegenstand, Entwicklung, Quellen und Akteure des Internationalen Umweltrechts. In A. Proelß (Ed.), *Internationales Umweltrecht* (Vol. 1, 2nd ed., pp. 1–51). De Gruyter.

Epiney, A., Diezig, S., Pirker, B., & Reitemeyer, S. (2018). *Aarhus-Konvention: Handkommentar*. Nomos; Manz; Helbing & Lichtenhahn.

Epiney, A., & Scheyli, M. (1998). *Strukturprinzipien des Umweltvölkerrechts* (1st ed.). Nomos.

Epiney, A., & Scheyli, M. (2000). *Umweltvölkerrecht: Völkerrechtliche Bezugspunkte des Schweizerischen Umweltrechts*. Stämpfli Verlag.

Fitzmaurice, M. (2008). Intergenerational equity revisited. In I. Buffard, J. Crawford, A. Pellet, & S. Wittich (Eds.), *International law between Universalism and Fragmentation: Festschrift in Honour of Gerhard Hafner* (Vol. 11, pp. 195–229). Martinus Nijhoff Publishers.

Fitzmaurice, M. (2009). *Contemporary issues in international environmental law*. Edward Elgar Publishing.

Fitzmaurice, M. (2012). Some reflections on legal and philosophical foundations of international environmental law. *Polish Yearbook of International Law, 32*, 89–110.

Fitzmaurice, M. (2019). Conclusions: General principles and developing areas of international law. In M. T. Andenæs, M. Fitzmaurice, A. Tanzi, & J. Wouters (Eds.), *General principles and the coherence of international law* (Vol. 24, pp. 442–447). Brill Nijhoff. https://doi.org/10.1163/9789004390935_026

French, D. (2017). The sofia guiding statements on sustainable development principles in the decisions of international tribunals. In M.-C. Cordonier Segger & C. G. Weeramantry (Eds.), *Sustainable development principles in the decisions of international courts and tribunals: 1992–2012* (Vol. 7, pp. 177–241). Routledge Taylor & Francis Group.

Fülöp, S. (2016). In fairness to future generations: Building effective public participation. *Hungarian Yearbook of International Law and European Law*, 231–250.

Gaja, G. (2020). General principles of law. In A. Peters & R. Wolfrum (Eds.), *Max Planck encyclopedia of public international law*. Oxford University Press. (Article last updated April 2020).

Gärditz, K. F. (2008). Nachhaltigkeit und Völkerrecht. In W. Kahl (Ed.), *Nachhaltigkeit als Verbundbegriff* (pp. 137–179). Mohr Siebeck.

Guenfoud, I. (2015, November 6). The universal declaration of the rights of humankind: Big words, small effect. *Verfassungsblog*. Retrieved January 3, 2025, from https://verfassungsblog.de/the-universal-declaration-of-the-rights-of-humankind-big-words-small-effect/

Hadjiargyrou, Z. (2016). A conceptual and practical evaluation of intergenerational equity in international environmental law. *International Community Law Review, 18*, 248–277.

Howarth, R. B., & Norgaard, R. B. (1992). Environmental valuation under sustainable development. *The American Economic Review, 82*(2), 473–477.

ILA Committee on International Law on Sustainable Development. (2012a). *Sofia Conference (2012) – International law on sustainable development: Final report*. International Law Association. Retrieved January 3, 2025, from https://www.ila-hq.org/en/committees/international-law-on-sustainable-development

ILA Committee on International Law on Sustainable Development. (2012b, August 30). *2012 Sofia guiding statements on the judicial elaboration of the 2002 New Delhi Declaration of Principles of International Law relating to sustainable development: Resolution 7/2012*. International Law Association. Retrieved January 3, 2025, from https://www.ila-hq.org/en/committees/international-law-on-sustainable-development

ILA Committee on Legal Aspects of Sustainable Development. (2002, April 6). New Delhi Declaration of principles of international law relating to sustainable development: Resolution 3/2002. *International Law Association*. Retrieved January 3, 2025, from https://www.ila-hq.org/en_GB/documents/conference-resolution-english-new-delhi-2002-3.

International Group of Experts for the Pact. (2017, June). Draft global pact for the environment. *Global Pact for the Environment*. Retrieved January 3, 2025, from https://globalpactenvironment.org/en/documents-en/the-pact-text/

International Law Commission. (2015, March 27). *Third Report by the Special Rapporteur on Identification of Customary International Law*, by M. Wood. UN Doc. A/CN.4/682.

International Law Commission. (2021). *Draft Guidelines on the Protection of the Atmosphere, with Commentaries thereto*. UN Doc. A/76/10.

Kahl, V. (2019). Ökologische Revolution am Interamerikanischen Gerichtshof für Menschenrechte: Besprechung des Rechtsgutachtens Nr. 23 "Umwelt und Menschenrechte" (OC-23/17). *Zeitschrift Für Europäisches Umwelt- Und Planungsrecht, 17*(2), 110–131.

Kiss, A., & Beurier, J.-P. (2010). *Droit International de L'Environnement* (4th ed.). Editions A. Pedone.

Knox, J. H. (2019). The global pact for the environment: At the crossroads of human rights and the environment. *Review of European, Comparative and International Environmental Law, 28*(1), 40–47. https://doi.org/10.2139/ssrn.3357868

Kotzé, L. J. (2019). International environmental law's lack of normative ambition: An opportunity for the global pact for the environment? *Journal for European Environmental and Planning Law, 16*(3), 213–236. https://doi.org/10.1163/18760104-01603002

Kotzé, L. J., & French, D. (2018). A critique of the global pact for the environment: A stillborn initiative or the foundation for lex anthropocenae? *International Environmental Agreements, 18*, 811–838. https://doi.org/10.1007/s10784-018-9417-x

Ku, C. (2005). Forging a multilayered system of global governance. In R. S. J. Macdonald & D. M. Johnston (Eds.), *Towards world constitutionalism: Issues in the legal ordering of the world community* (Vol. 23, pp. 631–651). Martinus Nijhoff Publishers.

Lang, W. (1999). UN-principles and international environmental law. *Max Planck United Nations Year Book, 3*, 157–172.

Lawrence, P. (2012). Justice for future generations: Environment discourses, international law and climate change. In B. Jessup & K. Rubenstein (Eds.), *Environmental discourses in public and international law* (pp. 23–46). Cambridge University Press.

Lee, J. (2000). The underlying legal theory to support a well-defined human right to a healthy environment as a principle of customary international law. *Columbia Journal of Environmental Law, 25*(2), 283–346.

Lepage, C. (2015, September 25). Déclaration Universelle des Droits de l'Humanité: Rapport à L'Attention de Monsieur le Président de la République. *République Française – Vie Publique*. Retrieved January 3, 2025, from https://www.vie-publique.fr/rapport/35202-declaration-universelle-des-droits-de-lhumanite

Lepage, C., & Drafting Committee (2015, September 25). Universal Declaration of Humankind Rights: Draft Presented Under the Aegis of Corinne Lepage, Commissioned by the President of the French Republic. *Alliance DDHU 2022*. Retrieved January 3, 2025, from https://ddhu.org/la-declaration/

Lewis, B. (2018). The rights of future generations within the post-Paris Climate Regime. *Transnational Environmental Law, 7*(1), 69–87. https://doi.org/10.1017/S2047102517000243

Liebenberg, S., Khalfan, A., Kothari, M., Muffett, C., Sepúlveda Carmona, M., Venne-Manyfingers, S., & Wewerinke-Singh, M. (2023, February 3). *Maastricht Principles on the Human Rights of Future Generations*. Maastricht University. Retrieved January 3, 2025, from https://www.rightsoffuturegenerations.org/the-principles.

Louka, E. (2006). *International environmental law: Fairness, effectiveness, and world order*. Cambridge University Press. https://doi.org/10.1017/CBO9780511618109

Lowe, V. (1999). Sustainable development and unsustainable arguments. In A. E. Boyle & D. A. C. Freestone (Eds.), *International law and sustainable development: Past achievements and future challenges* (pp. 19–37). Oxford University Press.

Lowe, V. (2009). The politics of law-making: Are the method and character of norm creation changing? In M. Byers (Ed.), *The role of law in international politics: Essays in international relations and international law*. (Reprint) (pp. 207–226). Oxford University Press.

Magraw, D. B., & Hawke, L. D. (2010). Sustainable development. In D. Bodansky, J. Brunnée, & E. Hey (Eds.), *The Oxford handbook of international environmental law* (Vol. 26, 1st ed., pp. 613–638). Oxford University Press.

Mbengue, M. M. (2020). On sustainable development: A conversation with Judge Weeramantry. In S. Forlati, M. M. Mbengue, & B. K. McGarry (Eds.), *The Gabčíkovo-Nagymaros judgment and its contribution to the development of international law* (Vol. 12, pp. 166–192). Brill Nijhoff.

Mbengue, M. M., & McGarry, B. K. (2019). General principles of international environmental law in the case law of international courts and tribunals. In M. T. Andenæs, M. Fitzmaurice, A. Tanzi, & J. Wouters (Eds.), *General principles and the coherence of international law* (Vol. 23, pp. 408–441). Brill Nijhoff. https://doi.org/10.1163/9789004390935_025

McGarry, B. K. (2020). Norms, standards, and the elusive nomenclature of the Gabčíkovo-Nagymaros judgment. In S. Forlati, M. M. Mbengue, & B. K. McGarry (Eds.), *The Gabčíkovo-Nagymaros judgment and its contribution to the development of international law* (Vol. 14, pp. 207–228). Brill Nijhoff.

Mensah, T. A. (2008). Soft law: A fresh look at an old mechanism. *Environmental Policy and Law, 38*(1–2), 50–56.

Molinari, C. (2015). Principle 3. In J. E. Viñuales (Ed.), *The Rio declaration on environment and development: A commentary* (1st ed., pp. 139–156). Oxford University Press.

Nanda, V. P., & Pring, G. (Eds.). (2013). *International environmental law for the 21st century* (2nd ed.). Martinus Nijhoff Publishers.

Parejo Navajas, T., & Lobel, N. (2018). Framing the global pact for the environment: Why it's needed, what it does, and how it does it. *Fordham Environmental Law Review, 30*(1), 32–62.

Pellet, A. (2012). Art. 38. In A. Zimmermann et al. (Eds.), *The statute of the international court of justice: A commentary* (2nd ed., pp. 731–870). Oxford University Press.

Preparatory Committee for the United Nations Conference on Environment and Development. (1992, April 1). *Draft Report of Working Group III*. UN Doc A/CONF.151/PC/WG.III/L.34.

Proelß, A. (2022). Prinzipien des Internationalen Umweltrechts. In A. Proelß (Ed.), *Internationales Umweltrecht* (Vol. 3, 2nd ed., pp. 95–150). De Gruyter.

Raith, J. (2018). The "global pact for the environment": A new instrument to protect the planet? *Journal for European Environmental and Planning Law, 15*(1), 3–23. https://doi.org/10.1163/18760104-01501002

Rajamani, L., & Guérin, E. (2017). Central concepts in the Paris agreement and how they evolved. In D. R. Klein, M. P. Carazo Ortiz, M. Doelle, J. Bulmer, & A. Higham (Eds.), *The Paris agreement on climate change: Analysis and commentary* (Vol. 4, pp. 74–90). Oxford University Press.

Ramlogan, R. (2011). *Sustainable development: Towards a judicial interpretation*. Martinus Nijhoff Publishers.

Rauber, J. (2018). *Strukturwandel als Prinzipienwandel: Theoretische, Dogmatische und Methodische Bausteine eines Prinzipienmodells des Völkerrechts und seiner Dynamik*. Springer. https://doi.org/10.1007/978-3-662-55471-5

Redgwell, C. (1999). *Intergenerational trusts and environmental protection*. Juris.

Redgwell, C. (2016). Principles and emerging norms in international law: Intra- and intergenerational equity. In C. P. Carlarne, K. R. Gray, & R. Tarasofsky (Eds.), *The Oxford handbook of international climate change law* (Vol. 9, 1st ed., pp. 185–201). Oxford University Press.

Redgwell, C. (2017). Sources of international environmental law: Formality and informality in the dynamic evolution of international environmental law norms. In J. d'Aspremont & S. Besson (Eds.), *The Oxford handbook on the sources of international law* (Vol. 43, pp. 939–959). Oxford University Press.

Roberts, A. E. (2001). Traditional and modern approaches to customary international law: A reconciliation. *American Journal of International Law, 95*(4), 757–791.

Ryngaert, C. M. J., & Hora Siccama, D. W. (2018). Ascertaining customary international law: An inquiry into the methods used by domestic courts. *Netherlands International Law Review, 65*(1), 1–25. https://doi.org/10.1007/s40802-018-0104-y

Sands, P. (1995). International law in the field of sustainable development: Emerging legal principles. In W. Lang (Ed.), *Sustainable development and international law* (Vol. 5, pp. 53–66). Graham & Trotman.

Sands, P., Peel, J., & Fabra, A. (2018). *Principles of international environmental law* (4th ed.). Cambridge University Press.

Scheyli, M. (2008). *Konstitutionelle Gemeinwohlorientierung im Völkerrecht: Grundlagen Völkerrechtlicher Konstitutionalisierung am Beispiel des Schutzes der Globalen Umwelt* (1st ed.). Duncker & Humblot. https://doi.org/10.3790/978-3-428-52826-4

Scholtz, W. (2021). Equity. In L. Rajamani & J. Peel (Eds.), *The Oxford handbook of international environmental law* (Vol. 20, 2nd ed., pp. 335–349). Oxford University Press.

Schröter, J. (2015). *Strukturprinzipien des Umweltvölkerrechts und ihr Beitrag zur Eindämmung des Klimawandels*. Erich Schmidt Verlag.

Shaw, M. N. (2008). *International law* (6th ed.). Cambridge University Press.

Shelton, D. (2010). Equity. In D. Bodansky, J. Brunnée, & E. Hey (Eds.), *The Oxford handbook of international environmental law* (Vol. 27, 1st ed., pp. 639–662). Oxford University Press. https://doi.org/10.1093/oxfordhb/9780199552153.013.0027

Smits, J. M. (2017). What is legal doctrine? On the aims and methods of legal-dogmatic research. In R. van Gestel, H.-W. Micklitz, & E. L. Rubin (Eds.), *Rethinking scholarship: A transatlantic dialogue* (Vol. 5, pp. 207–228). Cambridge University Press.

Stec, S., & Jendrośka, J. (2019). The Escazú Agreement and the regional approach to Rio Principle 10: Process, innovation, and shortcomings. *Journal of Environmental Law, 31*(3), 533–545. https://doi.org/10.1093/jel/eqz027

Stoll, P.-T., & Krüger, H. (2022). Klimawandel. In A. Proelß (Ed.), *Internationales Umweltrecht* (Vol. 9, 2nd ed., pp. 423–473). De Gruyter.

Stone, C. D. (2010). Ethics and international environmental law. In D. Bodansky, J. Brunnée, & E. Hey (Eds.), *The Oxford handbook of international environmental law* (Vol. 13, 1st ed., pp. 291–312). Oxford University Press.

Szekely, A. (2008). The promise of the Brundtland report: Honored or betrayed. *Pacific McGeorge Global Business and Development Law Journal, 21*, 159.

Talmon, S. (2015). Determining customary international law: The ICJ's methodology between induction, deduction and assertion. *European Journal of International Law, 26*(2), 417–443. https://doi.org/10.1093/ejil/chv020

Thürer, D. (2009). Soft law. In A. Peters & R. Wolfrum (Eds.), *Max Planck encyclopedia of public international law*. Oxford University Press. (Article last updated March 2009).

Tigre, M. A. (2019). *Gaps in international environmental law: Toward a global pact for the environment*. Environmental Law Institute.

Tladi, D. (2007). *Sustainable development in international law: An analysis of key enviro-economic instruments*. Pretoria University Law Press.

Tladi, D. (2017). The principles of sustainable development in the case concerning pulp mills on the River Uruguay. In M.-C. Cordonier Segger & C. G. Weeramantry (Eds.), *Sustainable development principles in the decisions of international courts and tribunals: 1992–2012* (Vol. 8, pp. 242–254). Routledge Taylor & Francis Group.

Tremmel, J. C. (2006). Establishing intergenerational justice in national constitutions. In J. C. Tremmel (Ed.), *Handbook of intergenerational justice*. Edward Elgar Publishing.

Treves, T. (2006). Customary international law. In A. Peters & R. Wolfrum (Eds.), *Max Planck encyclopedia of public international law*. Oxford University Press. (Article last updated November 2006).

Treves, T. (2019). Environmental impact assessment and the precautionary approach: Why are international courts and tribunals reluctant to consider them as general principles of law? In M. T. Andenæs, M. Fitzmaurice, A. Tanzi, & J. Wouters (Eds.), *General principles and the coherence of international law* (Vol. 21, pp. 379–388). Brill Nijhoff. https://doi.org/10.1163/9789004390935_023

UN Commission on Sustainable Development. (1996, May 3). Report of the Expert Group Meeting on Identification of Principles of International Law for Sustainable Development, Geneva, Switzerland, 26–28 September 1995: Background Paper, Prepared by the Division for Sustainable Development for the Commission on Sustainable Development, Fourth Session. Retrieved January 3, 2025, from https://digitallibrary.un.org/record/212979/

UN Conference on Environment and Development. (1992). *Rio Declaration on Environment and Development*. UN Doc. A/CONF.151/26 (Vol. I).

United Nations. (1972, June 16). *Declaration of the United Nations conference on the human environment*. UN Doc. A/Conf.48/14/Rev. 1 (1973).

United Nations Educational, Scientific and Cultural Organization. (1997, November 12). *Declaration on the responsibilities of the present generations towards future generations*. UNESCO Doc. 29/C Resolution 44.

United Nations Educational, Scientific and Cultural Organization. (n.d.). *Member states List*. Retrieved January 3, 2025, from https://en.unesco.org/countries.

United Nations Environment Assembly. (2022, March 3). *Political Declaration of the Special Session of the United Nations Environment Assembly to Commemorate the Fiftieth Anniversary of the Establishment of the United Nations Environment Programme*. UN Doc. UNEP/EA.SS.1/4.

United Nations Environment Programme. (1996, October 4). *Final report of the expert group workshop on international environmental law aiming at sustainable development*. UN Doc. UNEP/IEL/WS/3/2.

United Nations Environment Programme. (2006). Training Manual on International Environmental Law. Retrieved January 3, 2025, from https://wedocs.unep.org/20.500.11822/20599.

United Nations General Assembly. (1980, October 30). *Historical Responsibility of States for the Preservation of Nature for Present and Future Generations*. UN Doc. A/RES/35/8.

United Nations General Assembly. (1982, October 28). *World charter for nature*. UN Doc. A/RES/37/7.

United Nations General Assembly. (2012, July 27). *The future we want*. UN Doc. A/RES/66/288.

United Nations General Assembly. (2013, December 20). *Protection of Global Climate for Present and Future Generations of Humankind*. UN Doc. A/RES/68/212.

United Nations General Assembly. (2015, October 21). *Transforming our world: The 2030 agenda for sustainable development*. UN Doc. A/RES/70/1.

United Nations General Assembly. (2021, December 9). *Protection of the atmosphere*. UN Doc. A/RES/76/112.

United Nations Secretary-General. (2013, August 15). *Intergenerational solidarity and the needs of future generations, report of the Secretary-General*. UN Doc. A/68/322.

Verschuuren, J. (2003). *Principles of environmental law: The ideal of sustainable development and the role of principles of International, European, and National Environmental Law* (1st ed.). Nomos.

Verschuuren, J. (2016). The growing significance of sustainable development as a legal norm. In D. E. Fisher (Ed.), *Research handbook on fundamental concepts of environmental law* (pp. 276–305). Edward Elgar Publishing.

Viñuales, J. E. (2021). Sustainable development. In L. Rajamani & J. Peel (Eds.), *The Oxford handbook of international environmental law* (Vol. 17, 2nd ed., pp. 285–301). Oxford University Press.

Voigt, C. (2009). *Sustainable development as a principle of international law: Resolving conflicts between climate measures and WTO law*. Martinus Nijhoff Publishers. https://doi.org/10.1163/ej.9789004166974.i-428

Weeramantry, C. G. (2004). *Universalising International Law*. Martinus Nijhoff Publishers.

World Commission on Environment and Development. (1987). *Report of the World Commission on Environment and Development: Our Common Future (Brundtland Report)*. UN Doc. A/42/427 Annex.

World Summit for Social Development. (1995, March 14). *Copenhagen Declaration on Social Development*. UN Doc. A/CONF.166/9.

# Chapter 5
# Open Issues of the Operational Framework of Intergenerational Equity

After the normative assessment of the legal nature of both manifestations of intergenerational equity in Chap. 4, this fifth chapter addresses the parallel structural issues of the concept—this means the identification of duty-bearers, the potential of future generations as right-holders and the institutional framework of their representation. These structural issues particularly concern the effective implementation of the specific doctrine of intergenerational equity. The latter's emerging character implies that the structural issues are not yet part of the legal concept of intergenerational equity *de lege lata*; at least not in their entirety. Yet, there are certain developments in these contexts on the international and national level. At the same time, they are still extremely controversial and source of further academic and practical debate. Therefore, this fifth chapter turns to an analysis of exactly these operational issues by examining whether, and if so, how far they are already becoming part of international law. For this purpose, existing international documents and proposals, international and national case law and scholarly approaches are examined in detail. As far as the respective issues cannot be consistently answered in the affirmative, the following sections illustrate potential future developments of intergenerational equity *de lege ferenda*.

First, the planetary obligations, enshrined in *Edith Brown Weiss'* doctrine, can be addressed at several potential duty-bearers (Sect. 5.1). Second, the legal personality of future generations (i.e., their capacity to hold rights) is extremely controversial (Sect. 5.2).[1] Third, the implementation of intergenerational equity raises several issues, which are directly linked to the frameworks of representation for the interests of future generations (Sect. 5.3); this topic is addressed both with regard to implementation in policy-making and in judicial proceedings.

[1] For this reason, the thesis underlying this book was originally started as a project on the *human rights* of future generations, before the focus shifted from this original approach to a broader and intertemporal perspective.



A. Bustami, *The Legal Relationship between Present and Future Generations*,
https://doi.org/10.1007/978-3-032-03345-1_5

## 5.1 The Present Generation as Duty-Bearer of Intergenerational Equity

So far, only the contents of the general conception of intergenerational equity as well as *Edith Brown Weiss'* planetary duties have been illustrated. Under the general conception, there is an obligation to take into account the interests of future generations and present actions must not compromise the ability of future generations to meet their own needs.[2] But it has not been answered so far who exactly is obliged by these intergenerational obligations: Is it "the present generation" as a whole and what would that mean? Are States the obliged entities of intergenerational equity? Or is every entity and every individual of the present generation a duty-bearer of intergenerational obligations?[3] The question of the duty-bearers of intergenerational equity can be answered regardless of whether the concept is considered to be a rights-based approach, since obligations can exist independent of corresponding rights.[4] These obligations would either be owed to future generations, if the latter are potential right-holders,[5] or to the international community in general without a specific right-holder.

*Brown Weiss* did not address the question of duty-bearers of intergenerational equity in much detail in her works; also, most commentators remained silent on the issue. Instead of speaking of specific duty-bearers for the intergenerational obligation, *Brown Weiss* considered the role of the present generation as "trustee"[6] of the planet or referred to the State as "primary guarantor of the planetary rights".[7] Despite this lack of systematic analysis, the present book sheds some light on the potential duty-bearers of intergenerational equity in order to answer who exactly is obliged by these intergenerational obligations.

One possibility would be to take the formulations in several documents seriously that refer to the responsibility of "present generations" to not compromise the ability of future generations; thus, to the present generation as a whole.[8] However, there is little evidence that the concept of intergenerational equity was meant in this abstract way. Such an understanding could also weaken the effectiveness of implementation

[2] See, e.g., World Commission on Environment and Development (1987), Introduction, para. 27, Chap. 2, para. 1; Dupuy and Viñuales (2018), p. 92.

[3] In this chapter, the terms "duty-bearer", "obliged entity" or "obliged person" are used interchangeably as synonyms for the persons and entities that can be bound by the existing (and future) obligations of intergenerational equity. Particularly, "duty-bearer" is not used in a strict sense of a mandatory counter-part to "right-holders".

[4] Austin (1873), pp. 413–415; Kelsen (1969), p. 62. See also Brown Weiss (2021a), para. 13.

[5] See *infra* in Sect. 5.2.

[6] Brown Weiss (1989), p. 45.

[7] Ibid., p. 95.

[8] See, e.g., United Nations (1972), Principle 1: "Man [sic.] [...] bears a solemn responsibility [...]"; United Nations Secretary-General (2013), para. 24: "each generation should bequeath to its successors [...]"; International Group of Experts for the Pact (2017), Art. 4: "Present generations shall ensure that [...]".

of intergenerational obligations if the international community was the obliged entity in a collective way, as no specific duty-bearer would then be identifiable. Instead, it seems more adequate to consider specific actors within the present generation to be duty-bearers of intergenerational equity. This is also supported by an almost incidental reference of *Brown Weiss*, which mentioned that "all actors in the international community – States, transnational corporations, other nongovernmental [sic.] organizations and individuals – must respect planetary obligations".[9] The following sections take up this perspective. First, the analysis turns to the principal subjects of public international law and assesses the role of States as duty-bearers (Sect. 5.1.1). Second, it is assessed whether private actors could be considered duty-bearers of intergenerational equity today (Sect. 5.1.2).

### *5.1.1 States as Duty-Bearers of Intergenerational Obligations*

An entity that has capacity to possess international rights and obligations and to be responsible for the breaches of such obligations constitutes a subject of international law.[10] States are the principal subjects of public international law in this sense.[11] They are also the primary addressees of environmental obligations in general.[12] In the context of intergenerational equity, *Brown Weiss* stated that "[t]he State theoretically serves as the primary guarantor of the planetary rights of both present and future generations".[13] In this function, States would be bound by the general conception of intergenerational equity under customary international law. The same is true for all relevant treaty references to the general conception of intergenerational equity, which explicitly oblige the respective State parties.[14] States must take into account the interests of future generations in their activities and they must consider these interests to the greatest extent legally and factually possible.[15] In their pursuit of economic and social development, they must not compromise the

[9]Brown Weiss (1989), p. 48.

[10]Crawford and Brownlie (2019), p. 105. See also Kau (2024), p. 211.

[11]Crawford and Brownlie (2019), pp. 105–106. The present book does not address the role of international (governmental) organisations as actors and subjects of public international law, see, e.g., ibid., Chap. 7.

[12]Boyle and Redgwell (2021), pp. 107–219.

[13]Brown Weiss (1989), pp. 48, 95. See also Collins (2007), p. 99.

[14]See, e.g., *Convention Concerning the Protection of the World Cultural and Natural Heritage* (World Heritage Convention), adopted 16 November 1972, entered into force 17 December 1975, 1037 UNTS 151, Art. 4; *United Nations Framework Convention on Climate Change* (UNFCCC), adopted 9 May 1992, entered into force 21 March 1994, 1771 UNTS 107, Art. 3(1); *Convention on the Protection and Use of Transboundary Watercourses and International Lakes* (UNECE Water Convention), adopted 17 March 1992, entered into force 6 October 1996, 1936 UNTS 269, Art. 2(5) (c).

[15]Dupuy and Viñuales (2018), p. 92. See already *supra* in Sect. 4.1.3.

ability of future generations to meet their own needs.[16] The intergenerational obligations of States guide their discretion in all relevant decision-making processes.[17] Further, if the specific doctrine of intergenerational equity achieves legal status in the future,[18] these general obligations will turn into more specific planetary duties of States.[19]

Consequently, States are the primary duty-bearers of intergenerational equity, so that they are also responsible for breaches of this obligation. Forms of enforcement can and should be addressed at States, as is illustrated below in the context of institutional representation.[20] The following paragraphs analyse in which constellations States are actually responsible for a breach of their intergenerational obligations. This depends on the regime of State responsibility in international law, mainly reflected in the ILC's Draft Articles on the Responsibility of States for Internationally Wrongful Acts ('ARSIWA', 'Articles on State Responsibility'),[21] which have been taken note of in a UNGA Resolution,[22] and which constitute customary international law in large parts.[23]

According to these rules, a State is responsible for any violation of its international obligations. Two constellations can be distinguished. First, a State is responsible if certain violating acts are attributable to this State under the law of State responsibility.[24] In most instances, the State itself does not *directly* contribute to the deterioration of the natural environment to the detriment of future generations, but rather private entities that operate on its territory.[25] The acts of these private entities are normally not directly attributable to the State, except for the narrow conditions set out in Articles 4–8 of the ARSIWA.[26] For State-owned enterprises, such attribution is possible if they exercise elements of governmental authority within the meaning of Article 5 of the ARSIWA or if the specific conduct is directed or controlled by a State (Article 8 of the ARSIWA).[27] Further, State-owned enterprises could exceptionally qualify as *de facto* organs if they "act in 'complete dependence'

---

[16] WCED (1987), Chap. 2, para. 1.

[17] Beyerlin (2010), p. 446.

[18] See *supra* in Sect. 4.2.2.2.

[19] See Brown Weiss (1989), pp. 49–86 as well as *supra* in Sect. 2.2.1.4.

[20] See *infra* in Sects. 5.3.3.2 and 5.3.3.3.

[21] International Law Commission (2001b), p. 26.

[22] United Nations General Assembly (2002).

[23] Crawford (2006), para. 3; Crawford and Brownlie (2019), p. 524.

[24] Crawford (2006), para. 18; Schmalenbach (2022b), pp. 336–338.

[25] Brown Weiss (1989), p. 88; Schmalenbach (2022b), p. 338.

[26] Schmalenbach (2022b), p. 338.

[27] ILC (2001b), 48, Art. 8 para. 6.

on the State, of which they are ultimately merely the instrument".[28] In these cases, the private act would become an act attributable to the respective State, so that the State violated its obligations under intergenerational equity. Beyond this, acts of private corporations and individuals cannot be directly attributed to the State of territory or jurisdiction under the law of State responsibility.[29]

Notwithstanding this, there is a second constellation, in which a State's responsibility can extend to activities in connection with private entities' behaviour. As the ICJ stipulated in its *Nuclear Weapons Advisory Opinion*, there is a "general obligation of States to ensure that activities within their jurisdiction and control respect the environment of other States or of areas beyond the national control".[30] Such obligations of due diligence constitute a commonly accepted concept of preventive duties in international environmental law.[31] Due diligence is strongly intertwined with the environmental law principle of no harm or prevention,[32] which essentially is an obligation of due diligence by nature.[33] It requires States to prevent harm that results from private entities on their territory.[34] However, this due diligence obligation does explicitly *not* lead to an attribution of these private acts to the State.[35] Instead, the State is only accountable for its proper misconduct if it did not exercise the due diligence required by its own international obligations.[36]

Due diligence obligations in general do not constitute separate principles with a proper content, but describe the nature, or direction respectively, of many substantive treaty and customary norms of international environmental law.[37] They constitute obligations of conduct rather than of result.[38] This means that a State is not

---

[28] International Court of Justice, *Application of the Convention on the Prevention and Punishment of the Crime of Genocide (Bosnia and Herzegovina v. Serbia and Montenegro),* Judgment, 26 February 2007, ICJ Reports 2007, 43, para. 392. See also Schmalenbach (2022b), pp. 337–338.

[29] Cf. Kees (2011), para. 1.

[30] See already ICJ, *Legality of the Threat or Use of Nuclear Weapons,* Advisory Opinion, 8 July 1996, ICJ Reports 1996, 226, para. 29.

[31] ILC (2001a), Art. 3 para. 8; Koivurova and Singh (2022), paras. 28–32. For due diligence obligations in human rights law, see Riddell (2016), p. 65.

[32] ILC (2001a), Art. 3; Beyerlin and Marauhn (2011), p. 39; Koivurova and Singh (2022), paras. 28–29; Proelß (2022), pp. 104–120.

[33] ICJ, *Pulp Mills on the River Uruguay (Argentina v. Uruguay),* Judgment, 20 April 2010, ICJ Reports 2010, 14, para. 101; ILC (2001a), Art. 3 para. 7; Beyerlin and Marauhn (2011), p. 42; Lawrence and Köhler (2017), p. 658; Koivurova and Singh (2022), paras. 28–29; Sands et al. (2018), p. 211.

[34] Arbitral Tribunal, *Trail Smelter Arbitration,* Arbitral Award, 16 April 1938, RIAA III (1938), 1905; ICJ, *Corfu Channel Case (Merits),* Judgment, 9 April 1949, ICJ Reports 1949, 4, p. 22; *Pulp Mills* (Judgment), *supra* note 33, para. 101. See also UN (1972), Principle 21.

[35] Koivurova and Singh (2022), para. 2.

[36] ILC (1975), Art. 11 para. 4; Koivurova and Singh (2022), para. 2. Cf. also de La Fayette (2010), p. 329.

[37] Koivurova and Singh (2022), para. 4.

[38] Schmalenbach (2017b), p. 219; Koivurova and Singh (2022), paras. 1–2; Proelß (2022), pp. 106–110.

required to achieve a specific result with regard to a primary norm nor that the State is automatically liable in case of any environmental harm, which occurs by actions on its territory.[39] Instead, States are only required to exert their best possible efforts while attempting to prevent harm.[40] International courts and tribunals have confirmed this understanding concerning the prevention principle on various occasions.[41] States have to comply with an objective standard by taking all reasonable measures to control and restrain likely harmful activities on their territory.[42] This standard can vary in different contexts or in relation to the risks involved, and it may change over time, e.g., due to new scientific or technological knowledge.[43]

Under due diligence obligations, States are obliged not only to adopt appropriate rules and measures, but also to observe a certain level of vigilance in their enforcement and the exercise of administrative control applicable to public and private operators.[44] Consequently, State responsibility for an internationally wrongful act may occur if the State did not enact necessary legislation, did not enforce its laws against persons acting on its territory, or did not punish the person or corporation responsible for an illegal activity.[45]

As States are the principal subjects of international law and the primary duty-bearers of international environmental obligations, including intergenerational equity, their intergenerational obligations must necessarily encompass a due diligence obligation vis-à-vis private activities on their territory and under their jurisdiction. States must take the interests of future generations into account in all their activities and must attempt to achieve intergenerational equity to the greatest extent legally and factually possible.[46] This includes their national policies and regulation of private activities. Beyond this general conception of intergenerational equity, some specific planetary duties explicitly constitute due diligence obligations, such as

---

[39] Sands et al. (2018), pp. 747–748.

[40] ILC (2001a), Art. 3 para. 7; Proelß (2022), pp. 105–106.

[41] *Pulp Mills* (Judgment), *supra* note 33, para. 101; International Tribunal for the Law of the Sea, *Responsibilities and obligations of States sponsoring persons and entities with respect to activities in the Area (Request for Advisory Opinion submitted to the Seabed Disputes Chamber),* Advisory Opinion, 1 February 2011, ITLOS Reports 2011, 10, para. 110. For an exception, see Lawrence and Köhler (2017), pp. 658–659 with reference to ICJ, *Certain Activities Carried Out by Nicaragua in the Border Area (Costa Rica v. Nicaragua) and Construction of a Road in Costa Rica along the San Juan River (Nicaragua v. Costa Rica),* Judgment, 16 December 2015, ICJ Reports 2015, 665, paras. 196, 207, 213, 216–217.

[42] Pisillo Mazzeschi (1991), pp. 16–17; Beyerlin and Marauhn (2011), p. 42; Schmalenbach (2022b), p. 339.

[43] *Activities in the Area* (Advisory Opinion), *supra* note 41, para. 117; ILC (2001b), p. 34, Art. 2 para. 3.

[44] *Pulp Mills* (Judgment), *supra* note 33, para. 197; Sands et al. (2018), p. 748; Douhan (2019), para. 24.

[45] Restatement (Third) of Foreign Relations Law § 601 (1987), Comment d. On the consequences of these domestic legislations, see *infra* in Sect. 5.1.2.2, notes 117–120.

[46] Cf. Dupuy and Viñuales (2018), p. 92.

the duty to avoid adverse impacts on the environment[47] or the duty to prevent disasters.[48]

This is also reflected in *Brown Weiss'* observation that "States must be responsible for their own actions and for taking the measures necessary and practicable to ensure compliance of private actors with relevant international duties".[49] After referring, *inter alia*, to Principle 21 of the Stockholm Declaration,[50] she further concluded that a State "is responsible for its own activities and for those of persons, whether they be individuals or private or public corporations, so long as the activities are under the state's jurisdiction or control".[51] As illustrated, this responsibility of States with regard to private activities on their territory does *not* amount to a strict form of responsibility in regard to all private actions.[52] It must rather be understood in the sense of a due diligence dimension of intergenerational equity. As private actions increasingly gain in importance with regard to the deterioration of planetary resources, these due diligence obligations of States also become particularly relevant in international environmental law in order to hold States accountable for violations of international law by private persons under their exclusive jurisdiction and control.[53]

### 5.1.2 *Private Actors as Duty-Bearers of Intergenerational Obligations*

Beyond States as primary subjects of international law, the next section turns to the question whether private actors can also be considered duty-bearers of intergenerational equity. Building upon the idea of "the present generation" as trustee of planetary resources,[54] this could generally include all members of the present generation, meaning States, international organisations,[55] non-governmental organisations ('NGO', 'NGOs'), corporations and individuals.

With regard to the general conception, most documents explicitly only referred to States as the addressees of intergenerational equity. The relevant treaties, as treaty

[47] Brown Weiss (1989), pp. 59–69.

[48] Ibid., pp. 70–73.

[49] Ibid., p. 86. See also Restatement (Third) of Foreign Relations Law § 601 (1987), Subsection (1).

[50] Brown Weiss (1989), pp. 86–89 with reference to UN (1972), Principle 21. See also UN Conference on Environment and Development (1992a), Principle 2; Proelß (2022), pp. 105–106.

[51] Brown Weiss (1989), p. 89.

[52] De La Fayette (2010), p. 329.

[53] Koivurova and Singh (2022), para. 44.

[54] See, e.g., Brown Weiss (1984b), p. 507.

[55] See *supra* note 11.

law and evidence of State practice,[56] obliged their respective State parties, not private persons.[57] Similarly, many declarations, reports and other soft law documents pointed to States as duty-bearers.[58] For instance, a UNGA Resolution from 1980 proclaimed "the historical responsibility of States for the preservation of nature for present and future generations".[59] However, a few documents widened this focus on State responsibility to *all* members of the international community. The Brundtland Report's formulation is ambiguous, as the report stated that "*humanity* has the ability to make development sustainable to ensure that it meets the needs of the present without compromising the ability of future generations to meet their own needs" (emphasis added)[60]—without limitation to States alone. The World Charter for Nature, another UNGA Resolution, was clearer as it concluded that "[e]ach person has a duty to act in accordance with the provisions of the present Charter; acting individually, [...], each person shall strive to ensure that the objectives and requirements of the present Charter are met."[61]

Similarly, *Brown Weiss* explicitly included all actors of the international community as duty-bearers in her doctrine—"States, transnational corporations, other nongovernmental organizations and individuals".[62] While some documents that generally support the specific doctrine only pointed to States as duty-bearers,[63] Article 12(1) of the UNESCO Declaration reads:

> States, the United Nations system, other intergovernmental and non-governmental organizations, individuals, public and private bodies should assume their full responsibilities in promoting, in particular through education, training and information, respect for the ideals laid down in this Declaration, and encourage by all appropriate means their full recognition and effective application.[64]

Despite these rare references to individuals and private corporations as obliged entities of intergenerational equity, it is far from clear whether private persons could be considered to be potential duty-bearers in the context of international environmental law at all. This is a structural question of international law and depends on the general possibility of private persons to become subjects of international law.[65] So far, the legal personality of individuals—natural persons and corporations alike—has remained limited in international law. On the one hand, individuals as well as corporations can be holders of human rights under international law.[66] On the other

[56] See *supra* in Sect. 4.2.2.

[57] See, e.g., Art. 4 of the World Heritage Convention; Art. 3(1) of the UNFCCC; Art. 2(5)(c) of the UNECE Water Convention.

[58] See, e.g., UNCED (1992a), Principle 3; World Summit on Sustainable Development (2002), para. 37; UNGA (2015), para. 18.

[59] UNGA (1980), paras. 1–3.

[60] WCED (1987), Introduction, para. 27.

[61] UNGA (1982), para. 24.

[62] See Brown Weiss (1989), p. 48.

[63] See ILA Committee on Legal Aspects of Sustainable Development (2002), para. 1.2.

[64] UNESCO (1997), Art. 12(1).

[65] Generally, see McCorquodale (2018).

[66] Ibid., pp. 264–265.

hand, their individual responsibility resulting from international law obligations exists only in very few areas.[67] This is addressed, first, with respect to individuals (Sect. 5.1.2.1) and second, to private corporations (Sect. 5.1.2.2).

#### 5.1.2.1 Individuals

Beginning with individuals, their role as subjects of international law mainly results from the development of their individual liability due to the violation of international criminal law.[68] Under the Rome Statute of the International Criminal Court ('Rome Statute'), individuals can be responsible for the violation of the crime of genocide, crimes against humanity, war crimes and the crime of aggression.[69] They are duty-bearers of international legal obligations without the intermediate stage of domestic law. International criminal law could thus *prima facie* be considered to be a potential precedent for the individual responsibility of private persons—also in the context of intergenerational equity. However, this would only be the case if intergenerational equity established duties of individuals within international criminal law.

*De lege lata*, the Rome Statute does not include a specific and overall environmental crime, even less an intergenerational crime.[70] The only explicit environmental-related crime, in Article 8(2)(b)(iv) of the Rome Statute, concerns wartime scenarios and remains rather narrow;[71] particularly, it has no link to the interests of future generations. In 1989, *Brown Weiss* still considered that crimes against humanity could lead to a recognition of an individual obligation towards humanity as a whole, including present as well as future generations.[72] This assumption was based on the original proposals of the ILC since the 1970s to include the wilful causation of "widespread, long-term and severe damage to the natural environment" as an international crime.[73] However, despite long and intensive discussions to include such a crime into international criminal law,[74] it was not incorporated in the final draft of the Rome Statute in 1998.[75] Until today, suggestions for a new crime against the environment have not been successful on the international level.[76]

---

[67] For individuals see Gorski (2013), paras. 44–51. For corporations see Muchlinski (2014), paras. 30–51.

[68] McCorquodale (2018), pp. 265–266. For criminal liability of corporations in international law, see Muchlinski (2014), paras. 47–48.

[69] *Rome Statute of the International Criminal Court Rome, 17 July 1998* (Rome Statute), adopted 17 July 1998, entered into force 1 July 2002, 2187 UNTS 3, Art. 5.

[70] For an overview of the contemporary protection of the environment in international criminal law, see Bustami and Hecken (2021), pp. 153–162.

[71] Ibid., pp. 156–158.

[72] Brown Weiss (1989), pp. 91–92.

[73] ILC (1995), draft Article 26, paras. 119–125.

[74] See ILC (1996b), paras. 24–30.

[75] ILC (1996a), pp. 17–56.

[76] See Bustami and Hecken (2021), pp. 170–171. For one of the first and most relevant proposals, see Higgins (2016), p. 61.

There have been suggestions for the extension of the crimes against humanity to proper "crimes against future generations",[77] which would have stated:

> Crimes against future generations means any of the following acts within any sphere of human activity, [...], when committed with knowledge of the substantial likelihood of their severe consequences on the long-term health, safety, or means of survival of any identifiable group or collectivity: [...][78]

Although this proposal drew on the concept of intergenerational equity,[79] it only incidentally relied on actual long-term harm on future generations and instead considered that the notion of "future generations" was "of conceptual, rather than legal, importance".[80] There was only one single criminal act in the suggested list that did not require immediate victims alive at the time of the commission of the crime, but referred to severe environmental harm in general.[81] Consequently, it could already be doubted whether this suggestion would actually be capable of implementing the concept of intergenerational equity into international criminal law.[82] In any way, these suggestions of "crimes against future generations" have not led to any considerable success until today.[83]

Instead, and more promisingly, proposals for the introduction of a crime of "ecocide" have recently been raised by several actors.[84] In 2021, an independent expert panel published a proposition for a legal definition of ecocide and suggested the inclusion of a new Article 8ter into the Rome Statute:

> For the purpose of this Statute, 'ecocide' means unlawful or wanton acts committed with knowledge that there is a substantial likelihood of severe and either widespread or long-term damage to the environment being caused by those acts.[85]

Other comparable suggestions have accompanied these developments, both on the international and on the national level.[86] The difference between this crime of ecocide and an intergenerational crime is the lack of explicit reference to future

[77] Jodoin (2010); Jodoin and Saito (2011); Gaillard (2012).

[78] Jodoin and Saito (2011), p. 127.

[79] Jodoin (2010), pp. 20–22.

[80] Jodoin and Saito (2011), p. 129. Critical and advocating for another approach, see Mégret (2015), pp. 160–162.

[81] Jodoin and Saito (2011), pp. 128–129.

[82] Mégret (2015), pp. 160–162. Cf. also Bustami and Hecken (2021), pp. 167–168.

[83] Atapattu (2019), pp. 178–179; Schmalenbach (2022b), p. 363.

[84] See, e.g., Rauxloh (2011); Mwanza (2018); Bustami and Hecken (2021), p. 171 with further references.

[85] Independent Expert Panel for the Legal Definition of Ecocide (2021), p. 5. For a partly different suggestion, see, e.g., Bustami and Hecken (2021), pp. 172–185.

[86] See O'Brien (2021). For current developments, see also Stop Ecocide Foundation (n.d.).

generations or human harm in general. Ecocide is an ecocentric crime,[87] which would not depend on the harm to specific (present or future) human individuals, but which "primarily focuses on the protection of the environment" itself.[88] Nonetheless, it aims, *inter alia*, at preventing long-term damage to the environment, that means damage that is "irreversible or which cannot be redressed through natural recovery within a reasonable period of time".[89] Therefore, ecocide has a certain temporal element,[90] and it could thus become a tool for the protection of the interests of future generations. As the process of actually introducing ecocide into binding international criminal law is at least full of obstacles, if not unlikely to succeed,[91] the crime does not constitute a basis for individual responsibility for intergenerational equity at the moment. It could establish such individual obligations *de lege ferenda* in the future.

#### 5.1.2.2 Private Corporations

Apart from obligations of all individual members of the present generation, at least corporations could be considered duty-bearers of intergenerational obligations.[92] From a pragmatic point of view, this would be a logical consideration, since private corporations are the main contributors to the deterioration of future natural resources, e.g., regarding their greenhouse gas emissions.[93]

Originally, private corporations have not been considered subjects of public international law, so that they could not have been duty-bearers of international obligations.[94] But the issue of international legal personality of private corporations was increasingly discussed in the last years and decades, particularly with regard to State-investor-treaties.[95] On the one hand, certain objections have been raised against the recognition of international legal personality of private corporations under international investment law.[96] On the other hand, investor-State-agreements constitute contracts between States and private corporations, which are subject to

[87] In favour of an ecocentric crime of ecocide, see Bustami and Hecken (2021), pp. 165–167.

[88] Pezzot and Graf (2022).

[89] Independent Expert Panel for the Legal Definition of Ecocide (2021), Art. 8ter(2)(d).

[90] Ibid., p. 9.

[91] Sceptical in this regard, see Heller (2021); Ambos (2021). On the advantages, see, e.g., Rauxloh (2011), pp. 445–446.

[92] See Brown Weiss (1989), pp. 48–49.

[93] Ibid., p. 88; Schmalenbach (2022b), p. 338.

[94] Crawford and Brownlie (2019), pp. 111–112.

[95] McCorquodale (2018), pp. 272–273; Muchlinski (2014), paras. 26–29.

[96] Crawford and Brownlie (2019), pp. 111–112. See also Portmann (2010), pp. 124–125 with references to international commercial jurisprudence, see, e.g., International Centre for Settlement of Investment Disputes (ICSID), *Compañia de Aguas del Aconquijia S.A. and Vivendi Universal (formerly Compagnie Générale des Eaux v. Argentine Republic,* Decision on Annulment, Award, 3 July 2002, ICSID Case No. ARB/97/3, paras. 96–98.

international law and confer substantive enforceable rights to the corporations; thus, it is convincing to acknowledge their international legal capacity in this context.[97] This being said, this does not mean that private corporations have international legal personality in regard to *all* subject matters.[98] Rather, the scope of their legal personality in international law must be assessed on a case-by-case basis with regard to every single domain of international law.[99]

With regard to intergenerational obligations of corporations, it must be assessed whether private corporations can directly be bound by international environmental law obligations. This issue has often been addressed with respect to transnational corporations, or multinational enterprises respectively.[100] While there are some reflections regarding international environmental law,[101] most discussion and progress has been made in the context of human rights obligations of transnational corporations.[102] First, transnational corporations have been the addressees of an increasing number of international soft law instruments, which have stipulated their responsibility for the respect of human rights or the environment.[103] Most importantly, the Human Rights Council endorsed the UN Guiding Principles on Business and Human Rights ('UN Guiding Principles') in 2011, which stipulated that "business enterprises should respect human rights".[104] In 2000, the UN created a corporate sustainability initiative, the UN Global Compact, in order to encourage and support corporations in adopting sustainable policies.[105] Besides human rights norms, the ten principles of the Global Compact include three environmental

---

[97] See, e.g., Arbitral Tribunal, *Dispute between Texaco Overseas Petroleum Company / California Asiatic Oil Company and the Government of the Libyan Arab Republic (Compensation for Nationalized Property),* Arbitral Award on the Merits, 19 January 1977, (1978) 17 International Legal Materials 1, para. 47; Arbitral Tribunal, *Revere Copper and Brass Inc. v. Overseas Private Investment Corporation,* Arbitral Award, 24 August 1978, (1978) 56 International Law Reports 258, paras. 46–49; ICSID, *Corn Products International Inc. v. United Mexican States,* Decision on Responsibility, Award, 15 January 2008, ICSID Case No. ARB (AF)/04/01, paras. 173–174; Ijalaye (1978), pp. 221–232; Seidl-Hohenvelden (1987), pp. 12–14.

[98] *Texaco Overseas Petroleum Company* (Arbitral Award on the Merits), *supra* note 97, paras. 47–48; Muchlinski (2014), para. 7.

[99] Clapham (2010), p. 26; Muchlinski (2014), para. 25. This also holds true if one considers the simple subject/object-dichotomy to be inappropriate for the characterisation of actors on the international plane. For instance, *Rosalyn Higgins* advocated to distinguish with regard to the character as "participants" in the decision-making process of international law, see Higgins (1995), pp. 50–51. In more detail, see also Portmann (2010), pp. 208–242; López Latorre (2020), pp. 60–65.

[100] See Muchlinski (2014), para. 5; Schmalenbach (2022b), p. 363.

[101] For an overview, see Muchlinski (2014), paras. 42–46.

[102] See, e.g., International Council on Human Rights (2002); Tomuschat (2010), p. 322; Riddell (2016), pp. 54–55; Lambooy and Palm (2016); Chiussi Curzi and Malafosse (2022).

[103] See, e.g., UN Sub-Commission on the Promotion and Protection of Human Rights (2003), paras. 2, 4; Organisation for Economic Co-operation and Development (OECD) (2023), Chaps. IV, VI.

[104] Human Rights Council (2011). See also Riddell (2016), pp. 61–62.

[105] UN Global Compact (2000). See, e.g., Evaristus (2007).

principles to guide corporate policies.[106] In 2015, the Office of the High Commissioner for Human Rights ('OHCHR') stated that "businesses are also duty bearers".[107] However, these instruments are not legally binding, but voluntary and without mandatory duties for the corporations.[108]

This is why, second, the Human Rights Council initiated an open-ended intergovernmental working group in 2014, which was mandated to elaborate a legally binding instrument to regulate the activities of transnational corporations and other business enterprises in international human rights law.[109] From 2018 to 2021, the working group presented several revised drafts for such a legally binding instrument.[110] Although the proposed instrument focuses on human rights obligations, there is at least one reference to environmental rights.[111] While a more detailed analysis of these (still) non-binding instruments in international human rights law exceeds the scope of the present analysis, the instrument's impact on the current status of legal personality of corporations as duty-bearers in international law remains limited for two reasons. First, the draft document has not been adopted yet and it is not clear whether it will be in the near future,[112] so that there is currently no internationally binding legal instrument, which would impose legal obligations on multinational enterprises with regard to the protection of the environment.[113] Notwithstanding this, in its advisory opinion from 2017, the IACHR took at least note of the UN Guiding Principles and observed an international tendency of regulation of corporate activity with regard to human rights.[114]

Second, even the draft legal instrument does not impose *direct* obligations on corporations, but rather obliges States to take certain measures in order to guarantee the respect of human rights by business corporations and to establish a domestic system of legal liability.[115] This approach of the draft instrument with regard to human rights law is consistent with a general tendency of corporate liability in the realm of international environmental law. The fact that corporations are not directly

[106] UN Global Compact (2000), Principles 7–9.

[107] Office of the High Commissioner for Human Rights (OHCHR) (2015), p. 4. See also Toft (2020).

[108] Tomuschat (2010), pp. 327–328; Perry-Kessaris (2010), pp. 367–373. See also Pribytkova (2020), pp. 421–423.

[109] Human Rights Council (2014).

[110] For the third revised draft, see Human Rights Council (2021c). Generally on the draft's chances of success, see Bialek (2019). Critical, see Kampourakis (2019), pp. 556–559.

[111] Human Rights Council (2021c), Art. 1.2. See also Krajewski (2021), pp. 21–22.

[112] In detail, see Karska (2021); Chiussi Curzi and Malafosse (2022).

[113] Nollkaemper (2006); Tomuschat (2010), p. 328; Muchlinski (2014), para. 42; Boyle and Redgwell (2021), p. 346; Schmalenbach (2022b), pp. 362–364.

[114] Inter-American Court of Human Rights, *The Environment and Human Rights (Requested by the Republic of Colombia),* Advisory Opinion, 15 November 2017, Retrieved January 3, 2025, from https://www.corteidh.or.cr/docs/opiniones/seriea_23_ing.pdf, paras. 151, 155.

[115] See, e.g., Human Rights Council (2021c), Art. 6, 8. See also Bialek (2019), pp. 518–524; Schmalenbach (2022b), pp. 363–364.

obliged by international environmental or human rights law does not exempt them from any legal obligations in these fields. Instead, international law indirectly triggers legal consequences for private corporations in case of environmental damage caused by them.[116] These consequences arise from the domestic law of the corporation's home State. States themselves often are subject to due diligence obligations to adequately regulate private persons' activities on their territory.[117] These duties of due diligence require States to adopt and enforce appropriate legislation in order to fulfil the protective purpose of environmental law.[118] They also include the duty to hold private actors accountable for violations of international environmental law;[119] which is related but not equivalent to the environmental polluter pays principle.[120]

So far, there is no consistent and universal customary law norm on mandatory civil liability,[121] as stipulated e.g., in Principle 13 of the Rio Declaration. Several multilateral environmental treaties aimed at the harmonisation of national civil liability regimes, so that corporations under the State parties' jurisdiction can be held liable for damage caused by their activities.[122] The existing liability regimes may be applicable to environmental damage caused both by lawful or wrongful acts.[123] However, these treaty regimes only established civil liability with a view to addressing damage that was caused by specific types of activities,[124] such as oil pollution,[125] disposal of hazardous wastes and substances,[126] or nuclear pollution.[127]

[116]Ibid., pp. 364–365.

[117]See already *supra* in Sect. 5.1.1, notes 31–45.

[118]Cf. UN (1972), Principle 21.

[119]With examples of involvement of private actors in the implementation of international environmental obligations, see Muchlinski (2014), para. 44.

[120]De La Fayette (2010), p. 328; Boyle and Redgwell (2021), pp. 335, 341–345; Proelß (2022), pp. 136–141. On the distinctions between corporate liability and polluter pays principle, see Proelß (2022), p. 140.

[121]Douhan (2019), para. 31.

[122]In detail, see Beyerlin and Marauhn (2011), pp. 368–373; Muchlinski (2014), para. 45; Boyle and Redgwell (2021), pp. 335–341; Schmalenbach (2022b), pp. 367–372.

[123]Douhan (2019), paras. 11–13.

[124]De La Fayette (2010), pp. 330–346; Douhan (2019), paras. 6, 31; Schmalenbach (2022b), pp. 369–372. For an analysis of liability for damage caused by stratospheric aerosol injection as well as an overview of further examples, see Saxler et al. (2015), pp. 136–145.

[125]*International Convention on Civil Liability for Oil Pollution Damage* (CLC), adopted 29 November 1969, entered into force 19 June 1975, 973 UNTS 3; *Protocol of 1992 to Amend the International Convention on Civil Liability for Oil Pollution Damage, 1969* (1992 Protocol), adopted 27 November 1992, entered into force 30 May 1996, 1956 UNTS 255.

[126]Not yet in force: *International Convention on Liability and Compensation for Damage in Connection with the Carriage of Hazardous and Noxious Substances by Sea, 2010* (2010 HNS Convention), adopted 30 April 2010, entered into force not yet in force.

[127]*Vienna Convention on Civil Liability for Nuclear Damage* (Vienna Convention on Nuclear Damage), adopted 21 May 1963, entered into force 12 November 1977, 1063 UNTS 265; *Protocol to Amend the Vienna Convention on Civil Liability for Nuclear Damage* (1997 Vienna Protocol), adopted 29 September 1997, entered into force 4 October 2003, 2241 UNTS 270.

There is no universal liability regime yet with regard to environmental damage.[128] In 1993, the Convention on Civil Liability for Damage Resulting from Activities Dangerous to the Environment was adopted as an attempt to codify a universal regime on the Council of Europe level,[129] but it did not enter into force until today.[130] Currently, the European Commission is working on a new regulatory framework for sustainable corporate governance, which would establish corporate obligations with regard to social and human rights, climate change and the environment.[131] Beyond this, codification attempts resulted in the ILC's 'Draft Principles on the Allocation of Loss in the Case of Transboundary Harm arising out of Hazardous Activities',[132] which the General Assembly took note of.[133] These draft principles have never been transformed into a treaty document.[134]

Consequently, regardless of the partial legal personality of private corporations in some specific areas of international law, no direct legal obligations of national or transnational corporations have yet been accepted in the field of international environmental law. The fragmented civil liability frameworks in specific treaty regimes must not be confused with direct international responsibility of private corporations, as they only oblige the respective State parties to harmonise their national liability regimes.[135] These national liability regimes differ in detail,[136] although there are some common requirements for civil liability of corporations under national law.[137]

Generally, the focus on national civil liability is confirmed by the increasing amount of domestic judicial proceedings against private corporations based on their liability for environmental damage,[138] since this case law is eventually based on the legal personality of corporations under national law.[139] Two recent Dutch decisions in the case *Milieudefensie v. Royal Dutch Shell* constitute a rare exception to this

---

[128] Douhan (2019), paras. 30–31.

[129] *Convention on Civil Liability for Damage Resulting from Activities Dangerous to the Environment* (Lugano Convention), adopted 21 June 1993, 32 ILM 1228.

[130] See Schmalenbach (2022b), p. 368. However, it led to the adoption of the EU Environmental Liability Directive, see *Directive 2004/35/CE of the European Parliament and of the Council on environmental liability with regard to the prevention and remedying of environmental damage* (EU Environmental Liability Directive), adopted 21 April 2004, EU OJ L 143, 56–75.

[131] For the current status, see European Commission (EC) (2020-2022). See also Rosini (2022).

[132] ILC (2006).

[133] UNGA (2006).

[134] Douhan (2019), para. 10; Schmalenbach (2022b), pp. 364–365.

[135] See Turner and Bright (2022), p. 161. For three recent national codifications on corporate liability in supply chains, see ibid., pp. 154–155.

[136] De La Fayette (2010), p. 324.

[137] See, e.g., ibid., pp. 324–330; Douhan (2019), paras. 14–29.

[138] For a pending German case, see Climate Change Litigation Databases (CCLD) (2015b-today).

[139] In more detail on some relevant proceedings against private corporations in the context of intergenerational equity, see *infra* in Sect. 5.3.3.4.

observation.[140] The Dutch courts had to decide whether Royal Dutch Shell, a private corporation,[141] had violated a duty of care and human rights obligations by failing to take adequate action to address climate change. The district court confirmed this claim in 2021 by ruling that Royal Dutch Shell had violated its obligations and it obliged the company to reduce its greenhouse gas emissions by 45% by 2030.[142] Although the corporation's duty of care primarily emanated from the Dutch Civil Code,[143] the court had to interpret the unwritten standard of care. In its interpretation, the court drew, *inter alia*, on the corporation's international human rights obligations[144] as well as the content of the UN Guiding Principles.[145] It admitted that the UN Guiding Principles constituted a soft law instrument and that it did "not create any new right nor establish legally binding obligations".[146] Nonetheless, it observed with regard to the responsibility of private corporations:

> The responsibility of business enterprises to respect human rights, as formulated in the [UN Guiding Principles], is a global standard of expected conduct for all business enterprises wherever they operate. It exists independently of States' abilities and/or willingness to fulfil their own human rights obligations, and does not diminish those obligations. And it exists over and above compliance with national laws and regulations protecting human rights. Therefore, it is not enough for companies to monitor developments and follow the measures states take; they have an *individual responsibility*. (emphasis added)[147]

In November 2024, the Hague Court of Appeal overturned this decision as it refused to impose a specific emission reduction target of 45% by 2030 on Shell as requested by the plaintiffs.[148] However, it upheld the district court's findings on the individual responsibility of Shell generally, which it also deduced from the UN Guiding Principles as well as the OECD Guidelines for Multinational Enterprises.[149] It specifically concluded on Shell's obligations:

---

[140] For an overview on this proceeding in *Milieudefensie v. Royal Dutch Shell*, see CCLD (2019a-today).

[141] In detail, see Hague District Court, *Vereniging Milieudefensie* et al. *v. Royal Dutch Shell plc.*, Judgment, 26 May 2021, European Case Law Identifier ECLI:NL:RBDHA:2021:5339, paras. 2.2.1–2.2.3.

[142] Ibid., para. 5.3.

[143] See ibid., para. 4.4.1.

[144] Ibid., paras. 4.4.9–4.4.10.

[145] Ibid., paras. 4.4.11–4.4.21 with reference to Human Rights Council (2011). See also Hösli (2021), pp. 199–200; Nollkaemper (2021).

[146] *Hague District Court, Milieudefensie v. Shell* (Judgment), *supra* note 141, para. 4.4.11 (court translation).

[147] Ibid., para. 4.4.13 (court translation).

[148] Hague Court of Appeal, *Vereniging Milieudefensie* et al. *v. Royal Dutch Shell plc.*, Judgment, 12 November 2024, European Case Law Identifier ECLI:NL:GHDHA:2024:2100, paras. 7.68–7.111. For an overview of the reasons for this overturning, see CCLD (2019a-today).

[149] *Hague Court of Appeal, Milieudefensie v. Shell* (Judgment), *supra* note 148, paras. 7.18–7.27., yet, still with reference to the foregoing OECD (2011).

> [...] Especially companies whose products have contributed to the creation of the climate problem and have it in their power to contribute to combating it are obliged to do so vis-à-vis other inhabitants of the earth, even when (public law) rules do not necessarily compel them to do so. This follows from the instruments discussed above, including the OECD guidelines and the UNGP, to which Shell has subscribed. Those instruments place responsibility for protection against dangerous climate change also on (large) companies and call on them to take appropriate measures themselves to counter dangerous climate change.[150]

This reasoning illustrates the strong interpretative force soft law instruments can have on the national level.[151] At the same time, the Dutch courts' far-reaching conclusions have also been criticised for their untechnical reliance on soft law documents without elaboration on their status as actual reflection of the existing standard of care.[152] Still, these conclusions remain valid for a Dutch legal perspective on international law despite Shell's success before the Hague Court of Appeal. While it is beyond the scope of this work to further assess the significance of the appeal decision on climate litigation against private corporations in general,[153] it is to be observed whether the strong reliance on the UN Guiding Principles will be followed by other courts in the future.

There is another forward-looking attempt in the Philippines to hold private actors accountable for violations of human rights and environmental standards. In 2015, the NGO Greenpeace Southeast Asia and other plaintiffs filed a petition to the Philippines' Commission on Human Rights.[154] The plaintiffs asked the Commission to assess the responsibility of the 50 Carbon Majors for human rights violations resulting from the impacts of climate change.[155] They argued that the Carbon Majors should be held accountable for these violations and they based their argumentation, *inter alia*, on intergenerational equity.[156] The Commission published its detailed final report in May 2022 after it had already announced its main findings in 2019.[157] Besides extensive observations on the human rights issues linked to climate change,

---

[150] *Hague Court of Appeal, Milieudefensie v. Shell* (Judgment), *supra* note 148, para. 7.26.

[151] Macchi and Zeben (2021), pp. 412–413. In favour of an even stronger approach to "climate due diligence" of corporations, see Macchi (2021).

[152] Weller and Tran (2021), p. 354. Cf. also Ekardt (2021b).

[153] For some initial analysis, see, e.g., Legal Tribune Online (2024); Nollkaemper (2024); Hilson (2024); Paiement (2024); Giabardo (2024). Further, it is not yet clear whether Milieudefensie will appeal against the last decision, see CCLD (2019a-today).

[154] Commission on Human Rights of the Republic of the Philippines, *Requesting for Investigation of the Responsibility of the Carbon Majors for Human Rights Violations or Threats of Violations Resulting from the Impacts of Climate Change,* Petition, 12 May 2015, Retrieved January 3, 2025, from https://climatecasechart.com/non-us-case/in-re-greenpeace-southeast-asia-et-al/

[155] For an overview, see CCLD (2015-2022). See also Toft (2020), pp. 8–9.

[156] *Carbon Majors for Human Rights Violations* (Petition), *supra* note 154, 6, 21, 30.

[157] Commission on Human Rights of the Republic of the Philippines, *Requesting for Investigation of the Responsibility of the Carbon Majors for Human Rights Violations or Threats of Violations Resulting from the Impacts of Climate Change,* Memorandum, 19 September 2019, Retrieved January 3, 2025, from https://climatecasechart.com/non-us-case/in-re-greenpeace-southeast-asia-et-al/. See CCLD (2015-2022).

including the rights of future generations and intergenerational equity,[158] the Commission also elaborated in its final report on the role of business enterprises in general and the Carbon Majors in particular.[159] Interestingly, the final report analysed the existing international standards and guidelines that govern the responsibility of private corporations under international law,[160] such as the UN Guiding Principles and the UN Global Compact. Despite the non-binding nature of these documents,[161] the Commission incorporated certain human rights due diligence obligations of private corporations into Philippine law,[162] comparable to the Dutch district court. The Commission's detailed assessment of climate change-related obligations both of the Philippine government and private corporations contributes to the further legal understanding of these obligations, although the findings are not binding in the Philippines.

Apart from these two instances, the case law for direct environmental law obligations of private corporations under international law remains weak so far. Overall, as far as *Brown Weiss* considered that "transnational corporations […] must respect planetary obligations",[163] this does not find a consistent basis in international environmental law. Instead, corporations cannot be considered duty-bearers of intergenerational equity, as the current operating system (i.e., the structural framework) of international law does not provide for the sufficient structural basis. The environmental (and human rights) obligations of private corporations are still based on the domestic implementation of international law into domestic civil liability regimes.

### *5.1.3 Summary*

The idea that all actors of the present generation are duty-bearers of intergenerational obligations has proven to be too abstract in light of the existing legal regime. A proper analysis has illustrated that States remain today the primary actors and subjects of public international law. They are the unequivocal duty-bearers of intergenerational equity and can be responsible for violations of these duties. This includes both their attributable activities that directly disrespect the needs of future

[158] Commission on Human Rights of the Republic of the Philippines, *Requesting for Investigation of the Responsibility of the Carbon Majors for Human Rights Violations or Threats of Violations Resulting from the Impacts of Climate Change,* Final Report, 6 May 2022, Retrieved January 3, 2025, from https://climatecasechart.com/non-us-case/in-re-greenpeace-southeast-asia-et-al/, pp. 67–69; *Carbon Majors for Human Rights Violations* (Memorandum), *supra* note 157, paras. 8.51, 8.63, 8.65.

[159] *Carbon Majors for Human Rights Violations* (Final Report), *supra* note 158, pp. 88–115.

[160] Ibid., pp. 90–94.

[161] Pribytkova (2020), pp. 421–423.

[162] *Carbon Majors for Human Rights Violations* (Final Report), *supra* note 158, pp. 110–114.

[163] Brown Weiss (1989), pp. 48–49.

generations and potential violations of their due diligence obligations, which oblige them to prevent harmful activities of private actors under their jurisdiction. This primarily State-centred understanding of intergenerational equity is not necessarily in opposition to *Brown Weiss'* observations, as she also considered States the most relevant actors.[164] She further stated "[s]ince States are continuing entities, they represent past, present and future generations",[165] which is also an illustrative remark with respect to the intertemporal perspective of this book.[166]

Beyond States as duty-bearers, several proposals exist to establish a direct international responsibility both of individuals under international criminal law and of private corporations under certain soft law and governance regimes. Despite these cautious developments, these efforts have not been successful so far, so that neither individuals nor corporations can be considered appropriate duty-bearers in the context of intergenerational equity today.

## 5.2 Future Generations as Right-Holders of Intergenerational Equity

First of all, any legal concept of intergenerational equity creates responsibility and duties of the present generation towards the future—which has been examined in the foregoing section. Such duties can exist independently of corresponding rights,[167] as theorists like *Hans Kelsen* or *John Austin* have generally clarified.[168] Intergenerational duties without corresponding right-holders would then be owed to the international community in general. For instance, *Gary Supanich* suggested:

> Instead of appealing to the legal rights of future generations as the basis of intergenerational responsibility, this view identifies the legal source of that responsibility in the moral-psychological harm to our self-image as members of a species whose situation on this planet is unique.[169]

However, at least the specific doctrine of intergenerational equity, as elaborated by *Brown Weiss*, was built on planetary rights that mirrored the planetary duties.[170] Therefore, the following section turns to the analysis of this rights-based approach in order to assess the current status of international law in regard to the existence of rights of future generations *de lege lata*, and to illustrate the possibilities of rights of

---

[164] Ibid., 48, 95.

[165] Ibid., 48. On the continuity of States, see also Crawford and Brownlie (2019), pp. 132, 412.

[166] See *infra* in Sect. 7.2.2.1.

[167] UNSG (2013), para. 21; Brown Weiss (2021a), para. 13. Originally, *Brown Weiss* assumed a reciprocal interdependence of rights and duties, see Brown Weiss (1989), p. 99.

[168] Austin (1873), pp. 413–415; Kelsen (1969), p. 62.

[169] Supanich (1992), p. 101. For an analysis of *Supanich*, see also Redgwell (1999), pp. 93–97. Cf. also D'Amato (1990), pp. 197–198.

[170] See Brown Weiss (1989), pp. 95–109.

future generations *de lege ferenda*. It starts with a conceptional perspective on potential obstacles for a rights-based approach to intergenerational equity (Sect. 5.2.1), before examining the legal basis in existing documents, jurisprudence and doctrine regarding the rights of future generations (Sect. 5.2.2).

### 5.2.1 Conceptional Obstacles for a Rights-Based Approach to Intergenerational Equity

If intergenerational equity is conceived as a rights-based concept of international law, this means that future generations are right-holders of specific intergenerational rights. In this sense, a right is "an interest that is sufficient ground for holding another subject to a duty".[171] Consequently, such a right of future generations cannot exist without a correlative duty.[172] This notion of right is equivalent to *Wesley Hohfeld's* concept of "claim-rights" (i.e., entitlements vis-à-vis others to perform or not to perform certain actions).[173] The most important form of such claim-rights probably are human rights.[174] The human rights discourse plays a decisive role in the context of environmental law,[175] as is discussed further below.[176]

However, rights in the environmental context could also be conferred to other right-holders, such as animals[177] or even nature itself.[178] Some commentators have insisted on the necessarily anthropocentric character of human rights law.[179] Other commentators have argued that the purely anthropocentric focus of human rights law would ignore the decisive nonhuman aspects of the environment and would thus be inappropriate for the latter's protection.[180] As illustrated in Chap. 2 above,[181] the concept of intergenerational equity itself remains mainly anthropocentric with future human beings as potential right-holders.[182] While the present author considers

171 Ibid., p. 99 with reference to Raz (1984), p. 1.

172 Dworkin (1978), p. 85; Brandt (1983), p. 29; Raz (1984), p. 1. See also Brown Weiss (1989), p. 99; Redgwell (1999), p. 84.

173 Hohfeld (1913). See also Wenar (2020), Sect. 2.1.2.

174 On their conceptional basis, see, e.g., Nickel (2024), Sect. 1.

175 Generally, see Merrills (2010); Nickel (2024), Sect. 3.4.

176 See *infra* in Sect. 5.2.2.

177 See, e.g., Feinberg (1974) and more recently Pietrzykowski (2020); Stucki (2020).

178 See, e.g., Stone (1972). and more recently Burdon and Williams (2016); Tabios Hillebrecht and Berros (2017); Schimmöller (2020); Tănăsescu (2020).

179 See, e.g., Bielefeldt (2021).

180 See, e.g., Norton (1982), p. 337; D'Amato (1990), p. 196; Boyle (1998), pp. 51–53; Redgwell (1998); Wolfe (2003), p. 58; Bosselmann (2009), para. 15. Cf. also Brown Weiss (1989), p. 100 (at footnote 12).

181 See *supra* in Sect. 2.2.1.2.1.

182 See ibid., p. 17.

ecocentric and animal rights approaches to international environmental law to be reasonable and adequate, the following sub-sections focus on the anthropocentric character of *human* rights. This does not exclude a future development of intergenerational equity towards a more biocentric, pathocentric or ecocentric concept that allows for rights of human and nonhuman beings alike.[183] *Andrew Stawasz* and *Jeff Sebo* suggested in this regard "to develop frameworks that extend appropriate consideration to *all* distant-future sentient beings" (emphasis in the original).[184] The potentials of such a future development of intergenerational equity for the present research question are briefly mentioned in Chap. 8 below.

Despite the conceptional proximity of future generations' rights to human rights law, the rights-based character of *Brown Weiss'* doctrine has been the cause of much dispute since its origins.[185] While the intergenerational duties of the present generation have generally been accepted—at least in the context of the general conception of intergenerational equity—there have been many objections to future generations as potential right-holders in this context. Probably, this issue is the most controversial part of the specific doctrine.

Most objections against this understanding of intergenerational equity have been raised on a conceptional basis,[186] denying that future generations could have the ability to hold rights at all.[187] These doubts have often been articulated in connection with the so-called non-existence argument: only individuals who currently exist could be bearers of rights, as was deduced from the present tense form of the formulation "to have rights".[188] While the arguments against this objection have been presented in the chapter on philosophical perspectives of intergenerational justice,[189] the main analysis is recalled here. If one subscribed to a will theory of rights, right-holders would have to be able to enforce or waive their rights on their own;[190] so that future generations could not be right-holders under intergenerational equity, neither as individuals nor as a group.[191] According to an interest theory of rights, the ability to enforce or waive a right is irrelevant for the question of right-holders; but any beings that have interests can have rights.[192] Consequently, future generations can be right-holders of intergenerational rights as they have identifiable

[183] Pietrzykowski (2020); Bernet Kempers (2022).

[184] Stawasz and Sebo (2022). who argued in favour of a combination of animal law and "legal longtermism" (i.e., a legal consideration of the long-term future). See also Winter et al. (2021), pp. 113–122. Cf. also Bertram (2023), pp. 145–146.

[185] For one of the first critics, see D'Amato (1990).

[186] See also UNSG (2013), paras. 19–22.

[187] These objections often constitute pre-legal arguments, which have already been addressed in the context of moral objections to intergenerational equity, see *supra* in Sect. 3.2.

[188] See, e.g., de George (1981), p. 159; Beckerman (2004), pp. 3–4.

[189] See *supra* in Sect. 3.2.2.

[190] Kramer (2013), p. 248.

[191] Merrills (2010), pp. 671–672.

[192] Steiner and Vallentyne (2009), p. 55.

interests as a group,[193] regardless of the uncertainties of these interests in detail.[194] This distinction of interest theory between the ability to be a right-holder and the capacity to enforce these rights, for instance judicially, is also reflected in a distinction made by *Boldizsár Nagy* between "legal personality" and "legal capacity": "The former expresses the fact that an entity is, or may be the bearer of international legal rights and duties, the latter that it is capable of acting in its own name exercizing [sic.] those rights and duties."[195] This is also consistent with the approach taken in this chapter, which strictly distinguishes between holding rights and enforcing rights: Before the subsequent section turns to the implementation of potential rights by means of representation (Sect. III), the present section first examines the legal personality of future generations as right-holders, thus, the existence of intergenerational rights (Sect. II). On a conceptional basis, two issues have been discussed: the existence of collective rights (Sect. 5.2.1.1) and the general argument against rights proliferation (Sect. 5.2.1.2).

#### 5.2.1.1 The Existence of Collective Rights

Conceptionally, *Edith Brown Weiss* did not consider intergenerational rights to be "rights possessed by individuals. Rather they are generational rights, which can only be usefully conceived at a group level."[196] Group rights are rights "possessed by a group qua group rather than by its members severally."[197] In this sense, intergenerational rights are held collectively by each future generation towards the present generation.[198] The notion of group rights constitutes another counter-argument against the aforementioned non-existence argument[199] as well as the non-identity problem.[200]

Further, the idea of collective rights of every future generation is equally embedded in the notion of planetary trust.[201] Comparable to a charitable trust that does not require identifiable beneficiaries,[202] future generations as groups of individuals

[193] Brown Weiss (1989), p. 96; Lawrence (2012), pp. 38–39. In favour of conceiving rights of future generations as individual rights, see Tremmel (2009), pp. 61–63.

[194] On the minimum certainty in this regard, see UNSG (2013), para. 22.

[195] Nagy (1998), pp. 57–60. See also Brown Weiss (1989), pp. 96–97; Redgwell (1999), p. 84.

[196] Brown Weiss (1989), p. 96. See also UNSG (2013), para. 22; Hiskes (2005), pp. 1356–1357; Brown Weiss (2021a), para. 13.

[197] Jones (2022), Sect. 1. See also Wenzel (2011), para. 2.

[198] Malhotra (1998), p. 42; Brown Weiss (2010), p. 109.

[199] See already *supra* in Sect. 3.2.2.

[200] Brown Weiss (1989), p. 96; Brown Weiss (1990), pp. 205–206. See also Woods (2016), pp. 297–301. On the potential conflict between rights of future generations and the non-identity problem, see Gosseries (2004), p. 10.

[201] In detail, see *supra* in Sect. 2.2.1.3.

[202] Restatement (Third) of Trusts § 28 (2003), p. 13.

would constitute adequate beneficiaries of the planetary trust;[203] they hold equitable rights under this trust.[204] In this planetary trust, "[w]hen a future generation becomes the living generation, its members acquire individual rights and obligations that are rooted in the relationship that all generations share with each other for the natural system."[205] Every new present generation thus remains beneficiary of the planetary resources in an individualised sense, but turns into a trustee of the planetary trust at the same time.[206] These rights and duties remain embedded in the temporal relationship of intergenerational equity.[207] The advantage of this combination of a trusteeship model with collective rights was fittingly described by *Bradley Bobertz* in 1987:

> The value of [Brown Weiss'] trusteeship model is that it offers an analytic structure to intergenerational justice that is not chained to an individualistic definition of human nature. The planetary trust benefits all humanity. Unlike rights theory, charitable trust law does not require the existence of identifiable individuals; [...] By discussing our obligations to posterity in terms of humanity's common planetary heritage, [Brown Weiss] escapes the contradictions of the individualistic approaches. This represents an important step, because the development of nonindividualistic [sic.] legal categories may enable us to better fulfill our intuitive feelings of responsibility and concern for the future.[208]

Notwithstanding this differentiation between individualistic rights-based approaches and intergenerational rights, the idea of group rights is not new to international law.[209] Collective rights have become a part of international human rights law as part of the so-called "third generation rights",[210] often also "solidarity rights".[211] In the 1970s and 1980s, the UNESCO addressed the emergence of such solidarity rights at several occasions.[212] So far, group rights have been recognised with regard to peoples as right-holders of the right to self-determination,[213] and they have developed more and more with regard to minorities and Indigenous peoples[214] as right-

[203] Brown Weiss (1984b), pp. 505–506.

[204] Ibid., p. 506.

[205] Brown Weiss (1997), p. 91. See also Brown Weiss (1989), p. 98.

[206] Brown Weiss (1984b), pp. 504–505, 507; Brown Weiss (1989), p. 17.

[207] Brown Weiss (2010), p. 109; Brown Weiss (1992), p. 77.

[208] Bobertz (1987), pp. 188–189.

[209] In general, on group rights, see Jones (2022).

[210] Introducing this term, see Vašák (1977). See also Marks (1981); Hassan (1983); Vašák (1984). For a critical assessment of this categorisation into generations, see Alston (1982); Wellman (2000).

[211] Minnerop-Röben et al. (2018), paras. 1–3.

[212] See Alston (1982), pp. 310–312. See also NGO-UNESCO Standing Committee – Working Group on the Teaching of Human Rights (1980).

[213] Wenzel (2011), para. 5. See, e.g., *International Covenant on Civil and Political Rights* (ICCPR), adopted 16 December 1966, entered into force 23 March 1976, 999 UNTS 171, Art. 1(1); *International Covenant on Economic, Social and Cultural Rights* (ICESCR), adopted 16 December 1966, entered into force 3 January 1976, 999 UNTS 171, Art. 1(1).

[214] On the writing style for writing about "Indigenous" people and communities, see Younging (2018).

holders.[215] This extension of right-holders in international human rights law accompanied the continuous expansion of the structures of international law in the last century, which generally included the emergence of new actors on the international plane.[216] Certain scepticism existed and still exists due to the potential conflicts between group rights and individual human rights.[217] However, these conflicts can be solved on a case-by-case basis without having to deny the existence of group rights altogether.[218]

Some commentators have criticised the inadequacy of collective rights in general, as they would not fit into the traditional framework of human rights as individual rights.[219] For instance, *Paul Barresi* claimed that a rights-based approach to intergenerational equity was not sufficiently based on Western legal and religious traditions,[220] contrary to what *Brown Weiss* had assumed in her work.[221] Since the main responsibility for effectively addressing intergenerational problems was on developed States, rules of intergenerational equity necessarily had to be consistent with the Western world view and ethics.[222] This last argument is typical for a mainly individualistic perspective on human rights, which was often criticised due to its Eurocentric bias.[223] Generally, the primarily individualistic approach to human rights law could be problematic in view of global cultural diversity. *Makau Mutua* stated in this regard:

> Another problem of the liberal tradition, which has been inherited by the human rights movement, is its unrelenting focus on individualism. […] The human rights corpus views the individual as the center of the moral universe, and therefore denigrates communities, collectives, and group rights. […] This is a particularly serious problem in areas of the world where group and community rights are deeply embedded both in the cultures of the peoples, and exacerbated by the multinational nature of the post-colonial state.[224]

This is why the idea of solidarity rights has particularly developed during the 1970s in the context of third world States and their independency.[225] So-called "Third World Approaches to International Law" ('TWAIL') have analysed and criticised

---

[215] Wenzel (2011), paras. 6–13.

[216] See, e.g., Brown Weiss (2000), p. 346; Sands (2001), pp. 543–556.

[217] Freeman (1995), p. 34. See also Jones (2022), Sects. 7–9.

[218] Wenzel (2011), paras. 14–20.

[219] Donnelly (2003), p. 25. See also Barresi (1997); Minnerop-Röben et al. (2018), paras. 21, 24; Jakab (2021), pp. 186–187; Jones (2022), Sect. 9. For one of the earliest critiques, see Waldron (1987), pp. 313–320.

[220] Barresi (1997), pp. 63–68 with reference to the historian's analysis of White (1967). *Barresi* rather considered concerns for future generations to be merely evolution-based: Barresi (1997), pp. 70–75.

[221] Brown Weiss (1989), pp. 18–19.

[222] Wright (1988), p. 74; Barresi (1997), pp. 63–65.

[223] Weston (1984), p. 266; Minnerop-Röben et al. (2018), para. 2; Theilen (2021), p. 848. Cf. also Francioni (2010), pp. 54–55.

[224] Mutua (2008), p. 1029.

[225] Minnerop-Röben et al. (2018), para. 38.

the Eurocentric and postcolonial focus of international law on Western liberal traditions,[226] including the focus on individual human rights.[227] In contrast to this Western liberal focus, the idea of solidarity rights in international law is related to communitarian philosophical concepts of justice, which also positioned the individual within a broader community instead of focussing on individualistic perspectives.[228] Consistently, several human rights regimes of the global South contained collective solidarity rights from the beginning,[229] such as the right to development,[230] the right to peace and security,[231] or the right to a healthy environment.[232] The communitarian perspective is particularly obvious in regard to the African Charter on Human and Peoples' Rights ('Banjul Charter'), as can already be deduced from the charter's title.[233] Regardless of the exact legal status these several solidarity rights might possess, protecting vulnerable groups through group rights is not foreign to international law.[234] The rights-based doctrine of intergenerational equity can build on existing structures of human rights law.[235] Consequently, the rights of future generations are conceptionally possible;[236] both with regard to an interest theory of rights and with regard to the conception as group rights of future generations as a collective.

[226] On TWAIL generally, see Mutua (2000); Chimni (2003); González Hauck et al. (2024), pp. 79–83. See also Frankenberg (2010), para. 31.

[227] Mutua (2000), p. 37 with further references; Mutua (2008), p. 1029. Arguing in favour of a "mild relativism" of human rights law, see Peters and Askin (2020), pp. 13–14.

[228] De-Shalit (1995), pp. 14–15; Thompson (2009), pp. 26, 28. Cf. also Wenar (2020), Sect. 7.1. In more detail, see *supra* in Sect. 3.3.4.

[229] For an overview, see Minnerop-Röben et al. (2018), paras. 4–5; Wenzel (2011), paras. 11–13.

[230] See, e.g., *African Charter on Human and Peoples' Rights* (Banjul Charter), adopted 17 June 1981, entered into force 21 October 1986, 1520 UNTS 217, Art. 22; *Revised Arab Charter on Human Rights* (Revised Arab Charter), adopted 22 May 2004, entered into force 15 March 2008, 12 International Human Rights Reports 893, Art. 37.

[231] Art. 23 of the Banjul Charter.

[232] See, e.g., Art. 24 of the Banjul Charter; *Additional Protocol to the American Convention on Human Rights in the Area of Economic, Social and Cultural Rights* (Protocol of San Salvador), adopted 17 November 1988, entered into force 16 November 1999, OAS TS N° 69; Art. 38 of the Revised Arab Charter. This environmental right is assessed in more detail *infra* in Section 5.2.2.2; as to the inconsistent terminology see also *infra* note 322.

[233] See Francioni (2010), pp. 51–52. See also *infra* notes 331–337.

[234] Wenzel (2011), para. 19. For a philosophical assessment of the differences between a group rights approach and an individualistic approach to rights of future generations, see Woods (2016).

[235] Cf. also Brown Weiss (2021a), para. 13.

[236] Schrijver (2009), p. 61; Riley (2016), pp. 62–63.

#### 5.2.1.2 The Argument Against Rights Proliferation

Nonetheless, there is another conceptional question concerning the rights-based approach to intergenerational equity: Why should intergenerational equity be rights-based at all—what would be the advantages, and what would be potential disadvantages or dangers? These questions are often discussed from a negative perspective; that means they are put forward in order to refuse new rights-based approaches that go beyond the traditional realm of human rights law.

It is important to illustrate the main reasons why concepts such as intergenerational equity tend to be framed in a rights-based form. As demonstrated, legal duties can exist independently of corresponding rights and would then be owed to the international community in general.[237] Although such obligations can also have a driving force for the obliged entities, a rights-based approach adds important components to the legal obligation.[238] First, conferring a right to a person elevates the interest of that person above mere preferences.[239] Second, rights enjoy a certain authority in relation to other considerations, even though they are not necessarily absolute in nature.[240] They have to be taken into account in any moral discussion of new policies, e.g., in the environmental realm.[241] As *John Merrills* put it: "not only must the right always be considered but very good reasons will be needed for denying it effect".[242] They are thereby often considered to be superior to other legal concerns and interests.[243] Third, while obligations can be owed to an abstract entity (e.g., society or humanity), a right always adds a specific right-holder to the corresponding duty.[244] The respective right-holder becomes a privileged player in the moral discussion.[245] This puts a stronger legal value on the enforcement of the duty since the potential right-holders will be encouraged to protest, or even demand through judicial proceedings that their rights be protected.[246] Thereby, a crucial moral force is added to the simple legal obligation.[247] Comparably, the Human Rights Committee treated an alleged violation of future generations' rights as an

[237] See *supra* notes 167–168.

[238] Brown Weiss (2010), p. 109; Brown Weiss (1992), pp. 78–79.

[239] Merrills (2010), p. 666.

[240] Dworkin (1978), p. 92; Brown Weiss (1989), p. 101; Burchardt (2012), p. 207. Cf. Campbell (2017), Sect. 2.

[241] Nickel (1993), p. 283; Merrills (1998), p. 26; Merrills (2010), p. 666.

[242] Merrills (1998), p. 27 with reference to Dworkin (1978), p. 92.

[243] Cf. also Theilen (2021), pp. 849–850 with further references.

[244] Cf. Brown Weiss (1989), p. 101.

[245] Merrills (1998), p. 26.

[246] Brown Weiss (1989), p. 101; Nickel (1993), p. 283.

[247] Brown Weiss (1989), p. 101; Brown Weiss (2010), p. 109; Popović (1996), pp. 496–498.

"expression of concern purporting to put into due perspective the importance of the matter raised in the communication".[248] This additional force plays an important role in legal and moral arguments, and the transformative power of new rights is a key effect of development in changing societies.[249]

Therefore, it is comprehensible why intergenerational equity could profit from a stronger concretisation and implementation in international law if it were to be framed as a concept of rights of future generations. However, there are some general objections to a so-called proliferation of human rights, or a rights expansionism respectively. These notions describe the "perception that there are 'many' human rights, and that the corpus of human rights covers an extremely broad range of subject-matters".[250] Commentators have raised these concerns on human rights proliferation for the last decades in several contexts.[251] They argued, *inter alia*, that the expansion of human rights had contributed to an increasing populist backlash against human rights law in general.[252] Some commentators have explicitly criticised the expansionist resort to rights-approaches in the context of environmental protection.[253] One core argument of the opponents of rights proliferation is the inflation or devaluation argument: "that positing too many human rights will lead to a devaluation of human rights as a whole".[254] In a similar mindset, *Raphael Aguiling Pangalangan* explicitly raised the inflation argument against the notion of intergenerational rights of future generations:

> Perhaps unbeknownst to the intergenerational justice advocate, to champion the rights of future generations may very well weaken the human rights movement today. It runs the risk of undoing the recognition of fundamental rights and revert to a teleological approach by deriving its value from the outcome pursued rather than the source from which it springs.[255]

He concluded that "intergenerational responsibility is incompatible with the philosophical foundations of human rights." [256]

[248] Human Rights Committee, *E.H.P. v. Canada,* Decision, 27 October 1982, UN Doc. CCPR/C/OP/1 at 20 (1984), para. 8. The Committee did not have to resolve the issue of admissibility on behalf of future generations since the plaintiffs based their complaint as well on the rights of living individuals, see *infra* in Sect. 5.3.3.3.2.

[249] Merrills (2010), p. 668. Cf. also Marks (1981), p. 439; Hassan (1983), pp. 72–73; Gearty (2010), p. 20.

[250] On a terminological distinction between "proliferation", "inflation" and "overreach", see Theilen (2021), pp. 834–835.

[251] See, e.g., Klein (2013), pp. 125–128; Posner (2014), p. 91; Dudai (2017), p. 18; Hannum (2019); Tasioulas (2019). Cf. also Alston (1984), p. 609. For an overview of these concerns, see Theilen (2021), pp. 834–838.

[252] Tasioulas (2019), pp. 1170–1171.

[253] See, e.g., Handl (1992), pp. 138–139; Nickel (1993), p. 282; Merrills (2010), pp. 668–669; Aguiling Pangalangan (2020).

[254] Theilen (2021), p. 834. Cf. also Alston (1982), pp. 317–318.

[255] Aguiling Pangalangan (2020).

[256] Ibid.

Since an overambitious rights expansionism could actually risk a successive dilution of the human rights system, it is indeed important to distinguish between actual human rights and mere human interests.[257] However, the general criticism raised by the aforementioned commentators is not convincing in its totality. First, as *Verena Kahl* elaborated, there is a difference between mere rhetoric references to human rights law and legalistic approaches.[258] Only the rhetoric use of human rights language would trigger the mentioned risk of rights inflation at all, so that these objections cannot exclude proper legalistic approaches.[259] Such a legalistic approach to intergenerational equity would have to follow certain criteria for the development of human rights,[260] such as proposed by the UNGA in 1986.[261] Second, as *Lorna McGregor* demonstrated, there is also a distinction "between the creation of entirely new legal rights and the implementation of existing rights, through the articulation of how they apply to particular groups or new contexts".[262] In case of the latter, *McGregor* suggested that arguments of overexpansion should not prevent the future development and adaptation of existing human rights law to current challenges.[263] Regarding intergenerational equity, the pronunciation of planetary rights does not necessarily constitute an attempt to create new rights, but it could also be understood as the temporal extension of existing human rights, *inter alia*, the right to a healthy environment, to new right-holders, i.e. future generations.[264]

Third, beyond these arguments, *Jens Theilen* offered a deconstruction of the inflation objection in general,[265] which demonstrated the formal emptiness of the objection and illustrated that it is largely based on a certain conservative and Eurocentric mindset without consistent legal reasoning.[266] Instead of offering clear and future-based criteria for the determination of (new) human rights, the inflation argument only pretends to have a solution by artificially distinguishing between real and supposed rights.[267] Due to the (neo-)liberal preferences behind this

[257] See, e.g., Kahl (2022a), p. 176 with references to Tasioulas (2019), pp. 1179–1195; Hannum (2019), p. 157.

[258] Kahl (2022a), p. 163.

[259] See ibid., pp. 177–178.

[260] Ibid., p. 177. See also Alston (1984), pp. 614–617.

[261] UNGA (1986), para. 4.

[262] McGregor (2019), p. 1295.

[263] Ibid., pp. 1294–1300.

[264] Brown Weiss (2021a), para. 15. See also *infra* notes 302–796, 342–353.

[265] Theilen (2021). *Theilen* did not generally reject any criticism of human rights overexpansion, see ibid., p. 835.

[266] *Theilen* framed the inflation argument as a "form of gatekeeping", see ibid., p. 844. Cf. also Buchanan (2013), p. 289; McGregor (2019), p. 1297.

[267] Theilen (2021), pp. 841–843.

distinction,[268] primarily civil and political rights are considered "core of rights",[269] which have to be protected against the devaluation by an overexpansion.[270] In contrast, the inclusion of other rights into the realm of human rights law is understood as an "artificial inflation"[271] without clarifying what exactly would be artificial. Instead, most socio-economic rights of the second generation[272] as well as solidarity or group rights are then considered "as subordinate and potentially threatening in how they differ from civil and political rights".[273] This critique is related to the aforementioned TWAIL critique of Eurocentric perspectives on human rights law.[274]

Overall, the foregoing counter-arguments illustrated that the general critique of human rights proliferation and human rights inflation should not be taken too seriously as far as they constitute an instrument to constrain any future development of human rights law without offering consistent and objective criteria for these restrictions. Human rights law has always been the source of progressive development in accordance with the societal needs and changing circumstances.[275] *Theilen* explicitly argued in support of an open-minded "mindset of wonder" with regard to the development of human rights law instead of constraining this development by incoherent gatekeeping.[276] In the context of human rights and environmental protection, *Conor Gearty* stated fittingly:

> And if we can expand our horizons to include an imaginative leap beyond the living into the realm of the billions of as yet unborn (indeed not-yet-conceived) humans of the future, we will be able to see that here is a vast category of the powerless who demand our attention. Our empathy with the other is one of our finest attributes and it is through the language of human rights that it finds a highly effective because universal form of contemporary expression.[277]

There is no conceptional obstacle that would prevent the evolution of (human) rights of future generations, or the extension of existing human rights to future generations as new group of right-holders respectively. This does not yet mean that such rights of

[268] As to his terminological understanding of liberalism and neoliberalism, see ibid., 833 (at footnote 14).

[269] Ignatieff (2003), pp. 89–90.

[270] Theilen (2021), pp. 846–847.

[271] Cf. Alston (1982), p. 315.

[272] See *supra* note 210.

[273] Theilen (2021), pp. 847–848.

[274] See *supra* notes 226–228. Defending the traditional approach of human rights law and arguing for less "hypercriticism" by human rights academics, see Bennoune (2019), p. 1215.

[275] Alston (1982), p. 321; Bennoune (2019), pp. 1212, 1234–1235; Kahl (2022a), pp. 176–177.

[276] Theilen (2021), pp. 850–854. The utopian aspirations invoked by *Theilen* point to a general transformative approach that aims at "rethinking international law" on a way to utopia, see briefly *infra* in Sect. 7.3.2.

[277] Gearty (2010), p. 22. Cf. also Francioni (2010), p. 55 who argued "for a more imaginative and courageous jurisprudence which takes into consideration the collective dimension of human rights affected by environmental degradation".

future generations actually exist in current international law, but that their development would be conceptionally possible. Neither the non-existence argument nor the rights' character as potential group rights argue against their possibility. The foregoing illustrations have further refuted the common objection of human rights proliferation. Based on these findings, the next section turns to the assessment of international law—and whether future generations are actually right-holders in the current legal regime.

### 5.2.2 *Status of Future Generations as Right-Holders Under International Law*

Most commentators who criticised the concept of rights of future generations have limited their observations to conceptional arguments, whereas the following section examines the legal basis for such rights in current international law. While the general conception of intergenerational equity does not require the existence of planetary rights, the specific doctrine of *Edith Brown Weiss* is based on a two-sided legal relationship of planetary rights and planetary duties.[278] The planetary rights mirror the three basic principles of intergenerational equity.[279] They encompass the "basic right to live on a planet with as good environmental quality and natural and cultural resource diversity as previous generations had and the right to have equitable access to the benefits and use of these resources."[280] The following sub-sections address, first, the references to "rights" of future generations in international law generally and human rights law in particular (Sect. 5.2.2.1). Second, they focus on the relationship between future generations and a human right to a healthy environment (Sect. 5.2.2.2).

#### 5.2.2.1 Rights of Future Generations in General International Law and Human Rights Law

As demonstrated in detail in Chap. 4, there is not much evidence of the specific doctrine in treaty and customary international law;[281] there is much less for rights of future generatio ns.[282] Among the various treaties with intergenerational elements,

---

[278] Brown Weiss (1989), pp. 95–117. See also Brown Weiss (2020), pp. 286–287.

[279] In detail, see already *supra* in Sect. 2.2.1.4.

[280] Brown Weiss (1989), p. 104. With comparable wording, see also ibid., p. 95: "They are the rights which each generation has to receive the planet in no worse condition than that of the previous generation, to inherit comparable diversity in the natural and cultural resource bases, and to have equitable access to the use and benefits of the legacy."

[281] See *supra* in Sects. 4.2.1 and 4.2.2.2.

[282] For instance, regarding the GPE, see Brown Weiss (2019), pp. 56–57.

only the Aarhus Convention and the Escazú Agreement contained explicit references to "the right of every person of present *and* future generations to live in an environment adequate to his or her health and well-being [...]" (emphasis added).[283] However, the actual relevance of these references for a rights-based approach to intergenerational equity remained unclear due to the mainly procedural nature of the two agreements.[284] Similarly, most international documents that formed the basis for the general conception of intergenerational equity remained silent on the issue of rights.[285] In 2002, the ILA took a rights-based approach in its New Delhi Declaration by referring to the "right of future generations to enjoy a fair level of the common patrimony".[286]

Several civil society initiatives also built on a rights-based approach to intergenerational equity.[287] The latest such initiative culminated in the Maastricht Principles on the Rights of Future Generations from February 2023.[288] The title, the preamble as well as the several principles explicitly mirror this rights-language. The Maastricht Principles generally envisage to extend the existing human rights regime to future generations[289]—arguing that none of the existing human rights treaties "contains a temporal limitation or limits rights to the present time".[290] Further, they define as legal basis for the respective human rights:

> a) International law in its various forms which recognizes human rights for all people, without limiting these rights to present generations;
>
> b) International law in its various forms that explicitly or implicitly recognize obligations and responsibilities towards future generations, and seek to ensure intergenerational equity; and
>
> c) General principles of law, as reflected in laws, norms, customs and values of States and peoples from all global regions and belief systems that recognize obligations and responsibilities towards future generations, or that are and will continue to be relevant to the protection of the human rights of all, without limiting them to present generations.[291]

[283] *Convention on Access to Information, Public Participation in Decision-making and Access to Justice in Environmental Matters* (Aarhus Convention), adopted 25 June 1998, entered into force 30 October 2001, 2161 UNTS 447, Art. 1. Cf. also *Regional Agreement on Access to Information, Public Participation and Justice in Environmental Matters in Latin America and the Caribbean* (Escazú Agreement), adopted 4 March 2018, entered into force 22 April 2021.

[284] In favour of a recognition of these rights, see Ebbesson et al. (2014), p. 30. Rejecting such a recognition in the Aarhus Convention, see Epiney et al. (2018), pp. 92–93. See already *supra* in Sect. 4.2.1 [notes 178–188].

[285] See already *supra* in Sect. 4.2.2.

[286] ILA Committee on Legal Aspects of Sustainable Development (2002), paras. 2.1–2.3. See also Cordonier Segger (2021a), pp. 63–65.

[287] Cousteau (1991), Art. 1; Lepage and Drafting Committee (2015), Art. VIII, XI.

[288] Liebenberg et al. (2023). See already *supra* in Sect. 2.1.1.5.

[289] On this connection, see also *infra* notes 298–313.

[290] Liebenberg et al. (2023), Preamble.

[291] Ibid., Principle 2.

Several other provisions specify the relation between intragenerational and intergenerational human rights.[292] Consequently, the parts on the intergenerational State obligations (to respect, to protect and to fulfil) are inherently based on the premise of accepted human rights of future generations.[293] However, so far, the Maastricht Principles remain a mere civil society project without any normative capacity or influence on State behaviour.[294]

Beyond this, international case law has been comparably silent on a rights-based approach. While most relevant decisions focused on the general conception of intergenerational equity, some individual opinions have explicitly argued in favour of rights of future generations.[295] In 1993, *Judge Weeramantry* elaborated on a "notion of equity", which included the "respect for the rights of future generations", and which he considered part of "principles whose fuller implementations have yet to be woven into the fabric of international law".[296] Three years later, *Weeramantry* explained in a dissenting opinion:

> It is to be noted in this context that the rights of future generations have passed the stage when they were merely an embryonic right struggling for recognition. They have woven themselves into international law through major treaties, through juristic opinion [...].[297]

However, the remaining case law on the global level does not seem to reflect this progressive assumption. The existing *national* case law referring to rights of future generations is examined in more detail below with respect to the potential implementation of such rights.[298] At this point, the current analysis must turn to international human rights law. There is an indivisible interconnection between human

---

[292] Ibid., Principles 5, 7.

[293] Ibid., Principles 16–21.

[294] See already *supra* in Sect. 4.2.2.2.

[295] ICJ, *Maritime Delimitation in the Area between Greenland and Jan Mayen (Denmark v. Norway),* Separate Opinion of Judge Weeramantry, 14 June 1993, ICJ Reports 1993, 211, para. 240; ICJ, *Request for an Examination of the Situation in Accordance with Paragraph 63 of the Court's Judgment of 20 December 1974 in the Nuclear Tests (New Zealand v. France) Case,* Dissenting Opinion of Judge Weeramantry, 22 September 1995, ICJ Reports 1995, 317, p. 341; ICJ, *Legality of the Threat or Use of Nuclear Weapons,* Dissenting Opinion of Judge Weeramantry, 8 July 1996, ICJ Reports 1996, 429, pp. 455–456; ICJ, *Gabčíkovo-Nagymaros Project (Hungary v. Slovakia),* Separate Opinion of Vice-President Weeramantry, 25 September 1997, ICJ Reports 1997, 88, p. 110; ICJ, *Pulp Mills on the River Uruguay (Argentina v. Uruguay),* Separate Opinion of Judge Cançado Trindade, 20 April 2010, ICJ Reports 2010, 125, para. 122. ICJ, *Obligations concerning Negotiations Relating to Cessation of the Nuclear Arms Race and to Nuclear Disarmament (Marshall Islands v. United Kingdom),* Dissenting Opinion of Judge Cançado Trindade, 5 October 2016, ICJ Reports 2016, 907, paras. 184–185. See also Brown Weiss (1997), p. 95; Molinari (2015), pp. 151–152.

[296] *Maritime Delimitation in the Area* (Separate Opinion of Judge Weeramantry), *supra* note 295, para. 240.

[297] *Nuclear Weapons* (Dissenting Opinion of Judge Weeramantry), *supra* note 295, p. 455.

[298] See *infra* in Sect. 5.3.3.3.3.

rights and the protection of the environment,[299] which is broadly recognised today in international law.[300] As the Independent Expert on the issue of human rights obligations relating to the enjoyment of a safe, clean, healthy and sustainable environment, *John Knox*, put it:

> Human rights are grounded in respect for fundamental human attributes such as dignity, equality and liberty. The realization of these attributes depends on an environment that allows them to flourish. [...] Human rights and environmental protection are inherently interdependent.[301]

This interdependence is also visible with regard to the relationship between intergenerational equity and the human rights regime. *Brown Weiss* understood the planetary rights of future generations to be part of international human rights law.[302] As formulated in the Goa Guidelines on Intergenerational Equity, "[t]here is a complementarity between recognized human rights and the proposed intergenerational rights".[303] Particular economic and social rights, such as the rights to food or to water, would hence be addressed not only to present but also to future generations.[304] This is reflected in the respective General Comments of the Committee on Economic, Social and Cultural Rights ('CESCR'), which explicitly stated that these rights must be guaranteed for present and future generations.[305] Beyond these specific rights, traditional human rights have also been reinterpreted at several occasions in order to incorporate standards of environmental quality and protection.[306] This "greening of human rights"[307] has been increasingly applied by different international human rights bodies, including the European Court of Human Rights ('ECtHR') and the IACHR;[308] it is an imminent example of the dynamic character of human rights law.[309] The greening particularly concerned the right to

---

[299] This connection becomes also relevant in regard to the evolutionary character of international environmental law, see *infra* in Sect. 6.2.4.

[300] For a very early reference, see already UNGA (1968). Further, see, e.g., UNCED (1992a), Principle 1; UN Economic and Social Council (ECOSOC), Commission on Human Rights (1994); Human Rights Council (2009), para. 18; Human Rights Council (2018); UNGA (2019); *The Environment and Human Rights* (Advisory Opinion), *supra* note 114, paras. 47–55. In more detail on this relationship, see also Anton and Shelton (2011); Boyle (2012).

[301] Human Rights Council (2012), para. 10.

[302] Brown Weiss (2021a), para. 14. In this sense, see also the idea of the Maastricht Principles: Liebenberg et al. (2023), Preamble, Principle 2.

[303] Brown Weiss et al. (1988).

[304] Brown Weiss (2021a), para. 14.

[305] Committee on Economic, Social and Cultural Rights (1999), para. 7; CESCR (2003), para. 11.

[306] For an overview, see, e.g., Taylor (1998), pp. 338–343; Savaresi (2023), paras. 3–10.

[307] This notion was introduced by *Alan Boyle*, see, e.g., Boyle (1998); Boyle (2012), p. 614.

[308] For an overview of the ECtHR case law, see European Court of Human Rights (ECtHR) (2022); Vöneky and Beck (2022), pp. 212–227. For an overview of the IACHR case law, see *The Environment and Human Rights* (Advisory Opinion), *supra* note 114, paras. 66–68.

[309] This dynamic or evolutionary character of human rights law is addressed in more detail *infra* in Sect. 6.2.3.

life[310] and the right to respect for private and family life.[311] In this context, General Comment No. 36 of the Human Rights Committee ('HRC') on the right to life is important, as the HRC stated on the connection between the right to life and the environment: "Environmental degradation, climate change and unsustainable development constitute some of the most pressing and serious threats to the ability of present *and future* generations to enjoy the right to life" (emphasis added).[312] In two subsequent decisions, the HRC confirmed this interrelation between the right to life and environmental degradation,[313] recalling the ability of present and future generations to enjoy that right.[314]

Recently, the UN Committee on the Rights of the Child ('CRC') prepared a draft for a general comment on children's rights and the environment with a special focus on climate change.[315] According to the draft's objectives, the general comment aims at shedding light "on the societal, legal, and other implications of concepts such as [...], 'future generations' 'intergenerational equity' etc" in the context of rights of the child.[316] On 22 August 2023, the CRC published its General Comment No. 26, which contains one paragraph titled "Intergenerational equity and future generations".[317] However, the CRC eventually missed the opportunity to engage with the relevant issues of intergenerational equity. It left important questions unanswered, and particularly, did not engage with the aspect of rights of future generations or their relationship with currently living children.[318]

Another important intergenerational aspect of human rights can be found in the jurisprudence of the IACHR concerning the rights of Indigenous communities.[319] In

---

[310] See, e.g., ECtHR, *Case of Öneryildiz v. Turkey,* Judgment, 30 November 2004, ECHR 2004-XII 1-153; ECtHR, *Case of Budayeva and others v. Russia,* Judgment, 20 March 2008, ECHR 2008-II 167; IACHR, *Yakye Axa Indigenous Community v. Paraguay (Merits, Reparations and Costs),* Judgment, 17 June 2005, OEA Series C No. 125, para. 163; Inter-American Commission on Human Rights, *Kuna Indigenous People of Madungandi and Embera Indigenous People of Bayano and their Members v. Panama,* Report, 30 November 2012, IAComHR Report N° 125/12, Case 12.354, paras. 233–234.

[311] See, e.g., ECtHR, *Case of López Ostra v. Spain,* Judgment, 9 December 1994, ECHR Series A no. 303-C; ECtHR, *Case of Hatton and others v. the United Kingdom,* Grand Chamber Judgment, 8 July 2003, ECHR 2003–VIII 189, paras. 96–104; ECtHR, *Case of Fadeyeva v. Russia,* Judgment, 9 June 2005, ECHR 2005-IV 255. In detail, see Vöneky and Beck (2022), pp. 214–223.

[312] HRC (2019), p. 62.

[313] HRC, *Portillo Cáceres v. Paraguay,* Decision, 25 July 2019, UN Doc. CCPR/C/126/D/2751/2016; HRC, *Ioane Teitiota v. New Zealand,* Decision, 24 October 2019, UN Doc. CCPR/C/127/D/2728/2016. See also Le Moli (2020); Reeh (2020).

[314] *Teitiota v. New Zealand* (Decision), *supra* note 313, para. 9.4. On the more recent decision in *Billy et al. v. Australia*, see *infra* in Sect. 5.3.3.3.2, notes 797–802.

[315] On the initial draft, see Committee on the Rights of the Child (CRC) (2021).

[316] Ibid., Concept note. On the connection between rights of future generations and children's rights, see also Nolan (2022). and *infra* in Sects. 5.3.3.2.1 and 5.3.3.3.2.

[317] CRC (2023), para. 11.

[318] For the detailed criciticism in this regard, see Nolan (2023).

[319] See Brown Weiss (2021a), para. 34.

the *Mayagna Awas Tingni Community* decision, the IACHR elaborated on the Indigenous communities' relations to their land:

> Among indigenous peoples there is a communitarian tradition regarding a communal form of collective property of the land, in the sense that ownership of the land is not centered on an individual but rather on the group and its community. [...] For indigenous communities, relations to the land are not merely a matter of possession and production but a material and spiritual element which they must fully enjoy, even to preserve their cultural legacy and transmit it to future generations.[320]

A joint separate opinion further elaborated on this intergenerational relationship of Indigenous communities, which extended their land rights to the past and to the future alike.[321]

#### 5.2.2.2 The Human Right to a Healthy Environment and Future Generations

Beyond these "greened" traditional human rights and the Indigenous communities' understanding of land rights, several developments point to the existence or the emergence of a new right to a healthy, clean, safe, favourable, ecologically balanced, ecologically sound, viable, sustainable, adequate and/or wholesome environment—from hereon called a "right to a healthy environment".[322] In light of some attempts of codification,[323] it is much disputed whether this right exists on a global, customary level.[324] Most recently, the draft GPE proposal had envisaged to incorporate this right into a legally binding document.[325] In 2021, the Human Rights Council adopted a resolution that recognised the "right to a clean, healthy and sustainable

[320] IACHR, *Mayagna (Sumo) Awas Tingni Community v. Nicaragua (Merits, Reparations and Costs),* Judgment, 31 August 2001, OEA Series C No. 79, para. 149. See also *Yakye Axa Indigenous Community v. Paraguay* (Judgment), *supra* note 310, para. 131.

[321] IACHR, *Mayagna (Sumo) Awas Tingni Community v. Nicaragua (Merits, Reparations and Costs),* Joint Separate Opinion of Judges Cançado Trindade, Pacheco Gómez and Abreu Burelli, 31 August 2001, OEA Series C No. 79, paras. 9–10 (at footnote 6). See also Keenan (2017).

[322] The terminology in this regard is inconsistent and depends on the legal source, see Vöneky and Beck (2022), p. 206. For an overview of different denominations, see, e.g., Human Rights Council (2012), paras. 12–13. Beyond the developments on a right to a healthy environment, the number of proposals for a right to a safe climate increased in the last years in light of an aggravating climate crisis, see, e.g., Lewis (2018), p. 202; Jegede (2020); Kahl (2022a).

[323] See, e.g., ECOSOC, Commission on Human Rights (1994), Annex I, para. 2; Human Rights Council (2018), Annex, Framework Principle 1. See also Vöneky and Beck (2022), pp. 201–205.

[324] Arguing in favour, see Sands (1989), pp. 394–396, 416; Nickel (1993), p. 295; Popović (1996), p. 603; Lenzerini (2002), p. 84; Boyle (2012). Emphasising the non-existence (yet) of such a right, see Gibson (1990), p. 10; Handl (1992), pp. 120–122; Nanda and Pring (2013), pp. 32, 620–621; Francioni and Quirico (2016), p. 155; Vöneky and Beck (2022), pp. 205–206. Differentiating, see Rodriguez-Rivera (2001), pp. 41–45; Proelß (2024), p. 659.

[325] International Group of Experts for the Pact (2017), Art. 1. In more detail, see *supra* in Sect. 2.1.1.5.

environment as a human right".[326] In July 2022, the UNGA also recognised this right in a non-binding resolution.[327] Although these proposals and resolutions have not been incorporated into a legally binding document so far, the recent recognition by the UNGA can contribute to a universal acceptance of such a right.[328] Since the question of the right's legal status largely exceeds the scope of the present work, it is left to the analysis of other commentators.[329] The following observations thus focus on the interrelation between this potential (future) human right and the planetary rights of future generations.

Most pertinent developments in this regard have occurred on the regional human rights level.[330] The first regional codification of such an autonomous environmental human right was the Banjul Charter, which entered into force in 1986.[331] Article 24 of the Banjul Charter stated that "[a]ll peoples have the right to a general satisfactory environment favorable to their development." In 2001, the African Commission on Human and Peoples' Rights ('ACHPR') decided for the first and only time on Article 24 of the Banjul Charter in its *Ogoniland* decision, in which the Nigerian government was accused to have caused environmental degradation and health problems among the Ogoni People by means of the State's oil production.[332] The ACHPR's decision established positive obligations of the States to protect their citizens from environmental degradation,[333] and it has been considered unique with regard to the collective right to a healthy environment.[334] Although neither the Banjul Charter nor the ACHPR made explicit reference to future generations, the links to intergenerational equity become clear considering the specific tension the ACHPR had to decide on: Article 24 itself incorporates the link between the right to a healthy environment and the right to development, which is itself protected in Article 22 of the Banjul Charter.[335] As the ACHPR did not consider that the right to development takes precedence over the right to a healthy environment, the concept of sustainable development can be seen as "a promising route towards reconciling the tensions inhabiting the linkages" between these two rights of the Banjul Charter.[336] In this sense, the needs of future generations play an essential role in limiting

326 Human Rights Council (2021a), para. 1.

327 UNGA (2022), para. 1.

328 See United Nations Environment Programme (UNEP) (2022).

329 See, e.g., Savaresi (2023), paras. 14–21; Boyd (2019).

330 For some examples on national case law referring to a right to a healthy environment of future generations, see Garofalo (2022). See further *infra* in Sect. 5.3.3.3.

331 Art. 24 of the Banjul Charter.

332 African Commission on Human and Peoples' Rights, *Social and Economic Rights Action Center (SERAC) and Center for Economic and Social Rights (CESR) v. Nigeria (Ogoniland case)*, Decision on Communication, 27 October 2001, Retrieved January 3, 2025, from http://hrlibrary.umn.edu/africa/comcases/155-96.html, para. 1.

333 Ibid., paras. 52–54.

334 Francioni (2010), pp. 51–52; Vöneky and Beck (2022), pp. 233–234.

335 See also Scholtz (2015), p. 407; Vöneky and Beck (2022), p. 233.

336 Scholtz (2015), p. 411 with reference to Cançado Trindade (1992), pp. 43–44.

the scope of the right to development, so that the Banjul Charter incorporates a mechanism that promotes both intergenerational and intra-generational equity.[337] From this, it could be concluded that Article 24 of the Banjul Charter implicitly also covers future generations as part of the collective of right-holders.[338]

More pertinently, in 2017, the IACHR took the opportunity in an advisory opinion to elaborate on the right to a healthy environment,[339] as enshrined in Article 11(1) of the Additional Protocol to the ACHR in the Area of Economic, Social and Cultural Rights ('Protocol of San Salvador').[340] Circumventing the problematic lack of proper justiciability of Article 11(1) of the Protocol of San Salvador,[341] the court elaborated in detail on the status and contents of the right as well as its contribution to the protection of all components of the environment.[342] Most importantly for the present context, the IACHR stated:

> The human right to a healthy environment has been understood as a right that has both individual and also collective connotations. In its collective dimension, the right to a healthy environment constitutes a universal value that is owed to both present and future generations. [...], a healthy environment is a fundamental right for the existence of humankind.[343]

The IACHR thus considered that the right to a healthy environment was owed both to present and to future generations.[344] But the court went even beyond this extension of the right to future generations; it also explicitly pointed out:

> [A]s an autonomous right, the right to a healthy environment, unlike other rights, protects the components of the environment, such as forests, rivers and seas, as legal interests in themselves, even in the absence of the certainty or evidence of a risk to individuals. This means that it protects nature and the environment, not only because of the benefits they provide to humanity or the effects that their degradation may have on other human rights,

---

[337] Scholtz (2015), pp. 411–413.

[338] On the communitarian perspective of the Banjul Charter, see already *supra* notes 225–233.

[339] *The Environment and Human Rights* (Advisory Opinion), *supra* note 114, paras. 56–64. See already *supra* in Sect. 4.2.2.2.

[340] Art. 11(1) of the Protocol of San Salvador.

[341] See IACHR, *The Environment and Human Rights (Requested by the Republic of Colombia)*, Concurring Opinion of Judge Sierra Porto, 15 November 2017, Retrieved January 3, 2025, from https://www.corteidh.or.cr/docs/opiniones/seriea_23_ing.pdf, para. 11; IACHR, *The Environment and Human Rights (Requested by the Republic of Colombia)*, Concurring Opinion of Judge Vio Grossi, 15 November 2017, Retrieved January 3, 2025, from https://www.corteidh.or.cr/docs/opiniones/seriea_23_ing.pdf, para. 3; Patarroyo Ramírez (2020); Benz and Kahl (2021), pp. 204–215.

[342] *The Environment and Human Rights* (Advisory Opinion), *supra* note 114, paras. 56–63. See also Kahl (2019), pp. 116–117; Vöneky and Beck (2022), p. 237.

[343] *The Environment and Human Rights* (Advisory Opinion), *supra* note 114, para. 59.

[344] See also Brown Weiss (2021a), para. 15; Kahl (2019), p. 116. Building on this aspect, see also on the currently pending advisory proceeding before the IACHR, *infra* in Sect. 5.3.3.1.

> […], but because of their importance to the other living organisms with which we share the planet that also merit protection in their own right. […][345]

This extensive understanding of the right to a healthy environment also departed from a merely anthropocentric perspective and could be considered to add an ecocentric component to human rights law.[346] In 2020, the IACHR confirmed this extensive understanding in its first contentious decision on the matter in the context of individual claims by several Indigenous communities.[347] Although the court did not again explicitly refer to future generations in this case, as it was not relevant, the aforementioned relation between land rights of Indigenous communities and future generations[348] potentially played a role in this case,[349] at least in two individual opinions.[350] All in all, the Protocol of San Salvador could thus be considered an indication of an upcoming rights-based approach to intergenerational equity.

At the Council of Europe level, there is no codified right to a healthy environment yet,[351] but a recent initiative aims at anchoring such a right within the Council of Europe framework.[352] Article 1 of the draft additional protocol to the European Convention for the Protection of Human Rights and Fundamental Freedoms ('ECHR') stipulates that "'the right to a safe, clean, healthy and sustainable environment' means the right of present and future generations to live in a non-degraded, viable and decent environment that is conducive to their health, development and well-being".[353]

---

[345] *The Environment and Human Rights* (Advisory Opinion), *supra* note 114, para. 62 with reference to International Union for Conservation of Nature and Natural Resources (IUCN) and World Commission on Environmental Law (2016), Principles 1, 2.

[346] See Feria-Tinta and Milnes (2016), pp. 72–74; Kahl (2019), pp. 116–117; Tigre and Urzola (2021). This partly refutes the initial criticism of the anthropocentric bias of international human rights law, see *supra* notes 177–184.

[347] IACHR, *Indigenous Communities of the Lhaka Honhat Association (Our Land) v. Argentina,* Judgment (Merits, Reparations and Costs), 6 February 2020, OEA Series C No. 400, para. 203. See also Tigre (2020); Benz and Kahl (2021).

[348] See Brown Weiss (2021a), para. 34 as well as *supra* notes 319–321.

[349] For instance, assuming that the IACHR decision was also based on the impacts that a harm can have on the "enjoyment of rights by future generations", cf. Patarroyo Ramírez (2020).

[350] IACHR, *Indigenous Communities of the Lhaka Honhat Association (Our Land) v. Argentina,* Separate Opinion of Judge Mac-Gregor Poisot, 6 February 2020, OEA Series C No. 400, para. 11; IACHR, *Indigenous Communities of the Lhaka Honhat Association (Our Land) v. Argentina,* Partially Dissenting Opinion of Judge Pérez Manrique, 6 February 2020, OEA Series C No. 400, para. 13.

[351] See Vöneky and Beck (2022), p. 213. For new developments, see Council of Europe, Steering Committee for Human Rights (2022).

[352] Council of Europe, Parliamentary Assembly (2021a, 2021b). The Committee of Ministers of the Council of Europe confirmed these parliamentary approaches and recommended to the member States to "actively consider recognising at the national level this right as a human right […]", see Council of Europe, Committee of Ministers (2022).

[353] Council of Europe, Parliamentary Assembly (2021a), Appendix, Art. 1.

As announced, the present work cannot comprehensively answer the question of legal status of a right to a healthy environment at the current state. This right definitely exists at some regional levels and there is much evidence that it is at least emerging on the international level.[354] In case of its emergence in the (near) future, this environmental right could equally encompass future generations as new right-holders. According to *Brown Weiss*: "A right to environment would implicitly include rights of both present and future generations."[355]

#### 5.2.2.3 Interim Conclusion

There has been some support for the connection of rights of future generations and existing or emerging human rights law.[356] *Richard Hiskes* even considered that the extension of environmental rights to future generations would further strengthen the claim for a human right to a healthy environment of the present generation.[357] *Verena Kahl* recently elaborated a complex proposal for a right to a safe climate, building on the inherent interconnectedness of climate change and human rights.[358] In this proposal, she turned, *inter alia*, to future generations as right-holders of such a right and assessed a variety of judicial and academic approaches to the legal personhood of future generations.[359] In the end, her proposal argues for a "holistic and rights-based approach to the intertemporal relationship between present and future generations of all species, based on the protection of the environment, [...] and ideas of intergenerational and, in a poly-lithic understanding of generation, interspecies justice".[360] She derived her proposal for a right to a safe climate, *inter alia*, from a holistic extension of the common concern of humankind[361] to "common concerns of present and future generations of allkind".[362]

Other commentators have rejected the existence of a rights-based approach to intergenerational equity at the present time,[363] even in the context of international

[354] See, e.g., Human Rights Council (2018).

[355] Brown Weiss (2021a), para. 15; Brown Weiss (2019), p. 57. Cf. also Brown Weiss (1989), p. 117.

[356] See Shelton (1991), pp. 133–134; Lenzerini (2002), p. 84; Hiskes (2005), pp. 1351–1356; Lewis (2018), p. 243; Popović (1996), p. 512. Cf. also Collins (2007), pp. 128–129; Tremmel (2009), pp. 60–61; Burchardt (2012), pp. 205–207; Boyd (2019), p. 36.

[357] Hiskes (2005), pp. 1351–1356.

[358] Kahl (2025) (Fortcoming).

[359] Ibid., pp. 476–502.

[360] Ibid., p. 499.

[361] On this concept's effects on the representation of future generations, see also *infra* in Sect. 5.3.3.2.2.

[362] Kahl (2025) (Forthcoming), pp. 549, 620.

[363] See, e.g., Boyle and Redgwell (2021), p. 122.

human rights law.[364] However, most rejections of such a right have not been consistently articulated, as they are often rather based on the aforementioned conceptional obstacles, such as non-existence, lack of collective rights or the proliferation argument.[365]

Based on the very few instances of treaties, soft law documents, international case law and the more common intergenerational dimensions in human rights law,[366] the current status of rights of future generations is not yet clearly detectable. It definitely has developed in the last decades and years. In 1989, *Brown Weiss* considered planetary obligations and rights to be "in the formative stage".[367] In 1992, *Raghunandan Pathak* stated that "the existing concept of a right-duty relationship will, in this context, have to be developed further to accommodate the case of rights of future generations."[368] Comparably, in 1998, *Ajai Malhotra* observed:

> Future generations cannot presently be regarded *stricto sensu* as a subject of international law; yet, given the rapid evolution of international law in recent decades, the possibility remains that they may well acquire such recognition at some future stage.[369]

Since then, the discussion of new right-holders has also turned to animals or entire ecosystems,[370] the relationship between human rights and environmental law has changed and the right to a healthy environment has increasingly gained contours on the regional and even on the global level. Nonetheless, the existing proponents of a rights-based approach to intergenerational equity do not necessarily claim that respective rights of future generations would *already* be accepted under current international law. Even *Brown Weiss* admitted in a recent work that "whether [intergenerational equity] conveys rights as well as responsibilities is not well established."[371] This illustrates that the concept of intergenerational equity still is in a constant state of evolution, which has not reached the full legal status of the rights-based specific doctrine of intergenerational equity yet.

---

[364] Merrills (2010), pp. 669–672; Vöneky and Beck (2022), pp. 275–277. Cf. also Michallet (2018), pp. 154–155 who also denied the existence of a right to the environment for present generations.

[365] See *supra* in Sect. 5.2.1.

[366] See also OHCHR (2021), pp. 57–58.

[367] Brown Weiss (1989), p. 103.

[368] Pathak (1992), p. 227.

[369] Malhotra (1998), p. 42. See also Bobertz (1987), p. 187.

[370] See *supra* notes 177–178.

[371] Brown Weiss (2019), p. 56. Cf. also Brown Weiss (2010), p. 114; Brown Weiss (2021a), para. 13.

### 5.2.3 Summary

The concept of intergenerational equity as a rights-based approach presupposes the existence of planetary duties as well as planetary rights of future generations. The foregoing analysis has illustrated two dimensions of these potential planetary rights.

First, several conceptional objections against a rights-based approach to intergenerational equity have been raised, but none of these objections are convincing. While the non-existence argument had already been addressed earlier, rights of future generations can be understood as collective rights—a concept that is long accepted in international human rights law. A general rejection of collective rights is only comprehensible from a Eurocentric, purely libertarian perspective. The same is true with regard to overzealous arguments against rights proliferation, if such arguments are used as a general means to constrain any future development of human rights law. As international human rights law has always contributed to the progressive development of international law, there are no compelling conceptional hindrances for a rights-based approach to intergenerational equity.

The second dimension refers to the actual legal existence of intergenerational rights in international law. Although it is conceptionally possible that future generations become right-holders as a collective in the (near) future, the current legal regime does not effectively accept such rights at this stage. The future development of international environmental law and of the concept of intergenerational equity will demonstrate whether this rights-based approach will become true anytime soon.

## 5.3 Institutional Implementation of Intergenerational Equity

The third open issue on the structural dimension of intergenerational equity concerns the institutional mechanisms of implementation of intergenerational obligations and/or rights. Implementation includes the most adequate form of representation for future generations as well as the most adequate institutional framework for this implementation. Since future generations encompass all unborn (i.e., non-existent) human beings[372] who cannot advocate or enforce their interests themselves today, the existing legal framework naturally suffers from a "presentist bias"[373]:

> We borrow environmental capital from future generations with no intention or prospect of repaying. They may damn us for our spendthrift ways, but they can never collect on our debt to them. We act as we do because we can get away with it: future generations do not vote; they have no political or financial power; they cannot challenge our decisions.[374]

[372] See *supra* in Sect. 2.2.1.2.2.

[373] See Boston (2016), p. 45.

[374] WCED (1987), Introduction para. 25.

To solve this bias and to overcome this "voicelessness" of future generations,[375] it is necessary to address potential frameworks concerning the representation of future generations.[376] Institutional implementation of intergenerational equity refers both to the representation of future generations in the course of policy-making and to their representation in judicial and quasi-judicial proceedings.[377] The following sections first elaborate on the understanding of "representation" in this context as well as on the potential limits and necessities of this representation (Sect. 5.3.1). Secondly, the analysis turns to the dimension of policy-making in the interests of future generations (Sect. 5.3.2), before addressing representation of future generations on different levels of judicial and quasi-judicial proceedings (Sect. 5.3.3).

### *5.3.1 Conceptional Arguments Against the Representation of Future Generations*

The foregoing section has already clarified the distinction between *having* rights, thus, being a right-holder, and *enforcing* these rights. According to the will theory of rights, which lacks this distinction, subjects must be able to enforce or waive their rights in order to be considered right-holders.[378] This confusion of notions has been dismissed above by adhering to an interest theory of rights (i.e., holding rights does not depend on the proper capacity to invoke them).[379] Vice versa, representation of future generations does not require the existence of actual rights of future generations under international law. As any institutional body of representation could either represent the rights or, more broadly, the interests of future generations, the following analysis does not necessarily depend on the potential future acceptance of future generations as right-holders. It is sufficient that common minimum interests of future generations as a collective can be identified today,[380] so that the representation and implementation of these interests is possible.[381] For this reason, the following sections use the notion of representation interchangeably with respect to "interests" or "rights" of future generations—without implying the existence of the latter.

---

[375] Niehaus and Davies (2021), p. 230.

[376] See Brown Weiss (1989), pp. 120–126. On a broader approach to "implementation strategies", see ibid., pp. 119–165; Brown Weiss (2021b), pp. 23–26.

[377] Redgwell (1999), pp. 84–85; Brown Weiss (2010), p. 110.

[378] See, e.g., Kramer (2013), pp. 248–249. In more detail, see *supra* in Sect. 3.2.2.

[379] See, e.g., Brown Weiss (1989), pp. 96–97; Nagy (1998), p. 57; Redgwell (1999), p. 84.

[380] See, e.g., UNSG (2013), para. 22.

[381] See Brown Weiss (2021b), pp. 26–27.

At this point, two connected arguments are often raised against the representation of future generations. First, representation of future generations in current policy-making would be undemocratic as it would impose a rule of future persons on the present generation although these future generations are not part of the sovereign power.[382] Second, since future generations are not capable to designate their representatives themselves, their representation would generally be impossible.[383] Both arguments can be addressed jointly as they concern the question what exactly is understood as (democratic) representation in the context of environmental governance.[384] While there is a broad range of political science literature on the representation of future generations, the present book focuses on a brief overview of the essential notions, which are relevant for the proper legal understanding.[385]

The first argument might already be problematic in the context of international environmental law, as it assumes a universal acceptance of democratic minimum standards on the international level.[386] However, international law is not *per se* a democratic regime,[387] and there is no universally accepted international right to democracy or to democratic governance,[388] although there are developments towards more people-orientated governance at the international level.[389] Therefore, the issue of democratic legitimacy of a global representative of future generations could even be neglected. Notwithstanding this, the issue of representation can also be relevant at the national level, as illustrated below,[390] so that a potential lack of democratic legitimacy has been discussed in literature. Democracy is a system of government, which embodies the ideal of political power based on the will of the people.[391] According to modern political theory, democratic governance requires that "all affected by collective decisions should have an opportunity to influence the outcome" (the "all affected principle").[392] Consequently, only those decisions are democratically legitimate and valid, to which all possibly affected persons (i.e., the *demos*)[393] have equal access and can equally contribute.[394]

---

[382] Cf. Arneson (2003), pp. 123–124; Beckman (2013), pp. 777–779. Illustrating the problem from different angles, see also Ekardt (2021a), pp. 374–386.

[383] Cf. Rosenkranz (1986), pp. 73–75; Supanich (1992), pp. 97–98; Merrills (1998), pp. 32–33; Beckerman (2006), p. 60.

[384] Generally on different concepts of democratic theory, see Shapiro (2009), pp. 10–33.

[385] In more detail on the political science discourse, see, e.g., Eckersley (2000); Beckman (2015); Boston (2016); Rose (2017).

[386] In detail, see Boutros-Ghali (1996), pp. 25–51; Kumm (2004), pp. 913–915; Besson (2011), pp. 383–384.

[387] States are the main actors, not the people as sovereigns of democracy, see Kumm (2004), p. 915.

[388] In detail, see Ehm (2013); Besson (2020); Boysen (2020).

[389] See, e.g., Boutros-Ghali (1996), pp. 29–51; Kumm (2004), pp. 917–927.

[390] See *infra* in Sects. 5.3.2.1 and 5.3.3.3.3.

[391] Boutros-Ghali (1996), p. 1.

[392] Urbinati and Warren (2008), p. 395. with further references.

[393] Rose (2017), p. 33.

[394] Habermas (1992), p. 370. See also Burgers (2020a), pp. 200–202.

At the same time, a representation of future generations in today's decision-making would only be democratically legitimate if future generations constituted part of these affected groups. Some commentators understood affectedness in a purely legalistic sense, meaning that "the decisions made by governments and legislatures define the entitlements, duties and benefits that apply to the subjects as a matter of law".[395] Only the persons within the legal authority of a decision, those subjected by this decision, would be democratically entitled to influence it.[396] *Ludvig Beckman* denied this with regard to future generations and stressed that future persons will never be legally bound by today's legislation as they could always change it at their own will.[397] Therefore, they would not be (legally) affected by current decision-making, which is why they must not be represented today as part of the *demos*. Otherwise, democratic legitimacy would be impaired, since this "will reduce the ability of 'the people' to rule itself democratically by introducing an asymmetry between rulers (the living and the unborn) and ruled (the living)."[398]

This strictly legalistic application of the all affected principle is neither the only nor its predominant understanding.[399] On the contrary, most democratic theorists, particularly in the context of future generations' representation,[400] understood affectedness in a causal sense in the context of democratic participation.[401] This means that "the claim to a democratic say [...] rests on the causal principle of having a pertinent affected interest".[402] This second understanding of the principle is linked to models of deliberative democracy and discourse ethics, as shaped for instance by *Jürgen Habermas*.[403] According to deliberative democracy theories:

> [C]ollectively binding decisions should, ideally, be made on the basis of a rational and impartial discourse [...] where all the affected parties (or their representatives) have the opportunity to participate and present critical arguments for and against the proposals that have been put forward.[404]

---

395 Beckman (2013), p. 779. Cf. also Näsström (2011).

396 Beckman (2013), p. 779. See also Burgers (2020a), pp. 203–204.

397 Beckman (2013), pp. 781–786 with references to Hobbes (1651/1651), p. 139; Rousseau (1762/1968), p. 69. In contrast, stressing the constitutional constraints on future generations by present law-making, see Thompson (2005), pp. 250–254; Rose (2017), pp. 37–39.

398 Beckman (2013), p. 787. At the same time, *Beckman* did not exclude the democratically legitimate role of ombudspersons for future generations, see Beckman and Uggla (2016), pp. 121–124. In more detail on ombudspersons, see *infra* notes 457–458.

399 Rose (2017), p. 35.

400 Ibid., p. 39.

401 See, e.g., Dobson (1996), p. 124; Eckersley (2000), p. 118; Goodin (2007), pp. 49–62.

402 Shapiro (2009), p. 52. For an exhaustive analysis of different versions of the "all affected interests" principle, see Goodin (2007), pp. 52–62.

403 Habermas (1992), pp. 349–398. According to *Robyn Eckersley*, deliberative democracy is characterised by unconstrained dialogue, inclusiveness and social learning: Eckersley (2000), pp. 120–123.

404 Ekeli (2005), p. 433.

Since there is no doubt that future human beings will be significantly affected by present decision-making in the realm of environmental policy, the inclusion of future generations into the democratic process would be justified on basis of the all affected principle in this deliberative democracy understanding.[405] In this sense, *Robyn Eckersley* framed the relevant approach as "democracy-*for*-the-affected" (emphasis added),[406] and *Kristian Ekeli* stipulated that "at least democratic decisions that significantly bear upon the lives of posterity cannot be regarded as legitimate unless future people have been given a voice in the decision making process".[407] This approach to include all affected groups and their interests in the decision-making process is also based on the concept of equal human dignity of all human beings, living today or in the future.[408] At the same time, it is consistent with the theory of justice presented by *John Rawls*,[409] which demands as one requirement of justice the maintenance of effective and just institutions—a requirement that can be easily applied to the intergenerational realm.[410] However, current decision-making processes often suffer from an extreme "presentist bias" with a short-term perspective only to the next election by existing voters.[411] As the direct participation of future generations in the deliberation process is not possible, their necessary inclusion within the all affected persons principle can only be achieved by means of representation.[412]

This leads to the second argument raised against representation: the fact that future generations cannot designate their representatives in the present themselves.[413] Within the framework of deliberative democracy, a broader understanding of representation has been developed, which "places legitimacy of representation not in the authorization by the constituency, but rather in the acceptability of the representative claim with the audience".[414] This kind of representation leaves open how exactly the representative is chosen: elected by the principal or appointed and

---

[405] Dobson (1996), pp. 131–135; Eckersley (2000), p. 118; Ekeli (2005); Thompson (2005), p. 247; Johnson (2007); Tremmel (2015), pp. 214–215, 219–220; Rose (2017), p. 41. In contrast, rejecting the requirement to include future generations into the deliberation process, see Unnerstall (1999), pp. 301–302; Jensen (2015), pp. 538–541. See also in contrast Heyward (2008), pp. 631–635. who argued that this understanding of deliberative democracy suffered from the effects of the non-identity problem. According to *Bernice Bovenkerk*, the non-identity problem can be overcome with deliberative democracy, see Bovenkerk (2015), pp. 503–508.

[406] Eckersley (2000), p. 119.

[407] Ekeli (2005), p. 443.

[408] See Boutros-Ghali (1996), p. 27; Dobson (1996), p. 135; Beyleveld et al. (2015), p. 550.

[409] *Clare Heyward* offered a Rawlsian approach as more appropriate alternative to deliberative democracy, see Heyward (2008), pp. 635–639.

[410] See already *supra* in Sect. 3.3.3.2.

[411] Kavka and Warren (1983), p. 21; Ekeli (2005), p. 431; Boston (2016), pp. 3–44.

[412] Several conceptional proposals for political representation of future generations have been made, see, e.g., Wood (2004); Ekeli (2005); Thompson (2005), pp. 256–259; Goodin (2007), p. 55.

[413] See *supra* note 383.

[414] Burgers (2020a), p. 204.

accepted by a broader audience.[415] For instance, according to an understanding developed by *Andrew Rehfeld*, representation means that a representative is "acting on behalf of a person or thing being represented (the 'representee') in relation to a particular function, which is accepted by a particular audience".[416] This audience would be the "relevant group of people who must recognise a claimant as a representative".[417] This kind of representation is not foreign to legal systems as can be seen with regard to the representation of vulnerable persons or persons with legal incapacity, whose representation is often based on legal authority rather than on the representees' consent or decision.[418] Similarly, representation in the context of future generations is understood in this sense in the following sections, and it goes beyond mere representation by elected representatives.[419] Delegation by the representees themselves (i.e., future generations) is not necessary.[420] Instead, it is sufficient that the relevant "audience" in the respective context recognises the representative's authority, if the accepted representative can at least make reasonable assumptions with respect to future generations' basic interests.[421] According to *Brown Weiss*, for the representation of future generations, it is "essential to define their interests and to have consensus on the basic underlying elements of [intergenerational equity]".[422] As has been illustrated above, uncertainties on the exact identities and interests of future persons do not preclude a philosophical or legal concept of intergenerational equity.[423] To the opposite, the knowledge today of essential basic interests of future generations[424] is sufficient to legitimise the appointment of respective representatives for future generations in the sense of the aforementioned understanding of representation.[425]

These elaborations on a deliberative democracy understanding of political representation offer an adequate framework for intergenerational equity. In order to include all affected persons in the deliberation process of environmental policies today, institutional mechanisms for the representation of future generations at

---

[415] Dobson (1996), p. 126 with reference to Birch (1971), p. 15.

[416] Rehfeld (2006), p. 5.

[417] Ibid. See also Saward (2010); Karnein (2016), pp. 93–94.

[418] See Rosenkranz (1986), pp. 74–80; Lawrence and Köhler (2017), pp. 653–654 (at footnote 46).

[419] Burgers (2020a), pp. 203–205. See also Lawrence and Köhler (2017), pp. 651–652. In contrast, *Morten Fibieger Byskov* and *Keith Hyams* argued in favour of a "hypothetical acceptance criterion" and derived "epistemic similarity" and "motivation" as two derivate criteria for the representation of future generations, see Fibieger Byskov and Hyams (2022).

[420] Lawrence and Köhler (2017), p. 652.

[421] Ibid., pp. 652–654.

[422] Brown Weiss (2010), p. 110.

[423] See *supra* in Sect. 3.2.4. Arguing that exactly this lack of knowledge prevents a form of representation, see Supanich (1992), pp. 97–98.

[424] UNSG (2013), para. 22.

[425] Brown Weiss (2010), p. 110; Redgwell (1999), pp. 96–97.

different levels arc important and also compatible with ideas of democratic legitimacy.[426] Consequently, the following section first addresses these existing or emerging institutional frameworks in the context of environmental policy-making (2), before turning to the representation of future generations in judicial implementation of intergenerational equity (3).

## 5.3.2 *Representation of Future Generations in Policy-Making*

The idea of "giving a voice to posterity"[427] refers primarily to the dimension of policy- and decision-making. With regard to the representation of future generations in this policy dimension, international environmental policy-making plays an important role, but there is also a widespread practice of representative institutions at the national level.[428] *Brown Weiss* stated that representatives of future generations "could be established at different levels – international, regional, national, or local – as appropriate".[429] While the national and local level would not have the same significance as a global representative might have for an international implementation of intergenerational equity, both approaches must be assessed in order to fully understand the mechanisms of implementation. Since the national representation of future generations is more developed today than representation at the international level, the next section first turns to the national level (Sect. 5.3.2.1), before addressing the international representation of future generations in policy-making (Sect. 5.3.2.2).

### 5.3.2.1 Institutional Representation of Future Generations by National Bodies

The concept of intergenerational equity has been codified in national constitutions and legislation in several ways and in many States world-wide.[430] These provisions range from abstract principles or obligations[431] to explicit recognition of rights of

---

[426] On the links between deliberative democracy and climate change litigation, see Niehaus (2023), pp. 224–226.

[427] Ekeli (2005).

[428] On the different levels of representation, see Nagy (1998), p. 62.

[429] Brown Weiss (1989), p. 124. For an overview of institutional initiatives in 1989, see ibid., pp. 148–152.

[430] Araújo and Koessler (2022).

[431] See, e.g., *Basic Law for the Federal Republic of Germany* (Basic Law of Germany), adopted 8 May 1949, entered into force 23 May 1949, Bundesgesetzblatt I (1949) S. 1; *Constitution of the Federative Republic of Brazil* (DELETE), adopted 5 October 1988, entered into force 5 October 1988.

future generations.[432] An exhaustive assessment of these domestic norms and their differences goes beyond the scope of this analysis and it has been addressed in other works.[433] Instead, the analysis focuses on some institutional mechanisms at the national level, which aim at the promotion of intergenerational equity and envisage to put intergenerational concerns in the centre of public conscience and policy-making.[434] The amount of these domestic institutions has increased in the last three decades although they still remain few in number.[435] They include consultative governmental bodies, ombudspersons as well as parliamentary committees.[436] Different institutions exist or existed in France (1993–1995),[437] in Finland (since 1993),[438] in Israel (2001–2007),[439] in Germany (since 2004),[440] in Hungary (since 2008),[441] in Tunisia (since 2014),[442] in Wales (since 2016),[443] and in several other States.[444] Beyond these existing bodies, there have been further suggestions for the establishment of comparable institutions, including respective model law propositions.[445] At the regional level, there have also been attempts to establish a Committee

[432] See, e.g., *Constitution of the Kingdom of Norway* (Constitution of Norway), adopted 16 May 1814, entered into force 17 May 1814; *Constitution of the Republic of Malawi* adopted 16 May 1994, entered into force 18 May 1995.

[433] See, e.g., UNSG (2013), paras. 37–38; Tremmel (2006), pp. 203–205; Collins (2007), pp. 130–131; Weston and Bach (2009), pp. 29–30, 39–40.

[434] For an overview, see UNSG (2013), paras. 39–48; Pearce (2012), pp. 4–5; Brown Weiss (2021a), paras. 49–51; Brown Weiss (2021b), pp. 30–32.

[435] Brown Weiss (2021a), para. 49.

[436] On the different potential mandates, see *infra* notes 449–459.

[437] On the Council for the Rights of Future Generations, see Prime Minister of France (1999); Brown Weiss (2010), p. 110. On a more recent proposal to establish a new institution, see Gaillard (2011), paras. 639–640.

[438] On the Parliamentary Committee for the Future, see UNSG (2013), para. 41; Brown Weiss (2021a), para. 51.

[439] On the Commission for Future Generations, see UNSG (2013), para. 43.

[440] On the Parliamentary Advisory Council on Sustainable Development, see Brown Weiss (2021b), p. 31; Reimer (2021).

[441] On the Parliamentary Commissioner for Future Generations, see Ambrusné (2010); Szabó (2021); Göpel and Pearce (2018), pp. 8–9.

[442] On the Authority for Sustainable Development and the Rights of Future Generations, see Brown Weiss (2021a), para. 50.

[443] On the Future Generations Commissioner for Wales, see Brown Weiss (2021b), p. 32; Netherwood and Flynn (2021). Between 2011 and 2016, Wales already had a Commissioner for Sustainable Futures, see UNSG (2013), para. 45.

[444] For an overview of comparable institutions in Canada, Malta, New Zealand and Sweden, see, e.g., Pearce (2012), pp. 4–5. For a detailed analysis of different national institutions, see Cordonier Segger et al. (2021), Chaps. 18–28.

[445] See, e.g., International Human Rights Clinic at Harvard Law School and Science and Environmental Health Network (2008, § 501(3), (4)); Weston and Bach (2009), p. 84. For an early proposition in the USA, see Allen (1994), pp. 739–741.

for Future Generations within the Council of Europe[446] as well as an EU Guardian for Future Generations,[447] so far without success.[448]

The existing national bodies are diverse in their powers as well as in their organisational structure.[449] For instance, the Hungarian Parliamentary Commissioner (or Ombudsperson) for Future Generations was established to protect the constitutional right to a healthy environment.[450] It had broad review and advisory functions, but it also had the power to receive and investigate complaints by citizens on environmental matters.[451] In 2012, the position of the Commissioner was integrated into the Office of the Commissioner for Fundamental Rights as a new Deputy Commissioner.[452] Despite this institutional reform, its main tasks and powers have not decreased, so that the Deputy Commissioner can still participate in investigations even *ex officio* and can propose to the Commissioner for Fundamental Rights to initiate proceedings before the Constitutional Court in matters concerning future generations.[453]

Despite some differences in their powers and their institutional framework, most representative institutions remained limited to an advisory and consultative function, and they are primarily involved in decision-making rather than in judicial enforcement of specific rights.[454] Therefore, they do not encompass all potential powers included in *Brown Weiss'* proposal of efficient representation.[455] *Brown Weiss* had suggested monitoring, review and advisory powers for the legislative as well as certain judicial enforcement powers of these representatives.[456] This form of representation would constitute an "ombudsperson", that means an "independent official that acts as a representative of public interests, scrutinising governmental administration and actions, performing an evaluative function, and seeking to ensure legality and fairness in public administration".[457] The ombudsperson would also be mandated to receive and investigate individual complaints concerning violations of future generations' interests.[458] Beyond this, "guardians" for future generations could be appointed to intervene in litigation to advocate for the best interests of

---

[446] Council of Europe (2003).

[447] Nesbit and Illés (2015). For further suggestions on the EU level, see Fülöp (2021), p. 152.

[448] Brown Weiss (2021b), p. 32.

[449] Anstee-Wedderburn (2014), p. 53. See also González-Ricoy and Rey (2019), pp. 6–9.

[450] See *Fundamental Law of Hungary* adopted 18 April 2011, entered into force 1 January 2012.

[451] UNSG (2013), para. 44; Anstee-Wedderburn (2014), p. 53.

[452] See Göpel and Pearce (2018), pp. 8–9; Brown Weiss (2021b), pp. 31–32.

[453] Göpel and Pearce (2018), p. 9; Brown Weiss (2021b), pp. 31–32.

[454] Brown Weiss (2010), pp. 110–111; Anstee-Wedderburn (2014), p. 53.

[455] Brown Weiss (1989), pp. 124–126.

[456] See Anstee-Wedderburn (2014), pp. 52–53.

[457] See ibid. with reference to Garner (2009), p. 1196.

[458] Cf. Fabbricotti and Venturini (2019), para. 2.

future generations.[459] The Hungarian Commissioner constitutes the only exception, which fills some of these judicial functions.[460]

Regardless of these differences, the national institutions should fulfil a certain degree of legitimacy, independence from national governments and transparency in their work.[461] *Brown Weiss* suggested six criteria national institutions for future generations should address: access, competence and credibility, efficiency, effectiveness and accountability.[462] For instance, credibility of an institution would include transparency in its activities as well as the institution's independence of any forces, which would prefer other special interests to those interests of future generations.[463] *Sándor Fülöp*, himself a former Hungarian ombudsman for future generations, summarised the following common features and values of future generations institutions:

> (1) long-termism rather than short-termism, intergenerational solidarity [...]; (2) system thinking, integration, multilevel (global, regional, national and local) and multidisciplinary networking; and (3) independence and legitimacy ensuing from, *inter alia*, transparency, accountability, accessibility and effectiveness.[464]

However, any attempts of standardisation of institutions for future generations have failed so far. Despite broad recognition of and advocacy for such institutions in legal and political science scholarship,[465] all existing institutions are solely based on national provisions without an overarching international framework. Several proposals have envisaged the codification of an international legal obligation to establish national ombudspersons; most of these proposals were voiced in the run-up to the Rio+20 conference in 2012.[466] However, neither the outcome document of Rio +20 contained the suggested obligation,[467] nor has there been any subsequent

---

[459] See Brown Weiss (1984a), pp. 278–279; International Human Rights Clinic at Harvard Law School and Science and Environmental Health Network (2008, § 501(3), (4)). On the differences, see also Fülöp (2021), p. 153.

[460] For a recent case brought by the Commissioner before the Constitutional Court of Hungary, see Brown Weiss (2021a), para. 42. See also *infra* in Sect. 5.3.3.3.3.2.

[461] Pearce (2012), pp. 5–6; Vincent (2012); Fülöp (2016), p. 207.

[462] Brown Weiss (2021b), pp. 28–30.

[463] Ibid., pp. 28–29.

[464] Fülöp (2021), p. 155. Further, on common tasks and functions of these institutions, see ibid., pp. 155–156.

[465] Apart from *Edith Brown Weiss* (Brown Weiss 2010, pp. 110–112), see, e.g., Wood (1996), pp. 302–305); Ekeli (2005); Beckman and Uggla (2016); Ekardt (2021a), pp. 386, 422. See also International Human Rights Clinic at Harvard Law School and Science and Environmental Health Network (2008).

[466] See, e.g., *Opinion of the European Economic and Social Committee on the 'Communication from the Commission to the European Parliament, the Council, the European Economic and Social Committee and the Committee of the Regions: Rio+20: Towards the Green Economy and Better Governance'—The Contribution of European Organised Civil Society* adopted 22 September 2011, EU OJ C 376, 102–109, COM(2011) 363 final; World Future Council et al. (2012), Part B. For further references, see Anstee-Wedderburn (2014), p. 55 (at footnotes 127–130).

[467] Ibid., pp. 58–59 In more detail, see *infra* in Sect. 5.3.2.3.

codification of such an obligation.[468] Consequently, the existing national bodies remain singular and they are only relevant for their respective national contexts. They are neither numerous enough to amount to a universal State practice indicating customary international law,[469] nor did they result from a pre-existing international legal obligation. Nonetheless, the existing national structures could serve as examples for the establishment of a global form of representation of future generations, as is assessed in the following section.

#### 5.3.2.2 Institutional Representation by a Global Representative for Future Generations

In 1972, the UNEP was founded in order "to safeguard and enhance the environment for the benefit of present and future generations".[470] Despite its strong role in the global protection of the environment, the institution was never conceived as a representative organ for future generations.[471] While *Brown Weiss* suggested the establishment of a global institution for future generations from the beginning of her works,[472] the first initiative for a global representative for future generations at the political level dates back to the run-up of the Rio Conference. The Government of Malta proposed the establishment of a "Guardian for Future Generations" at the international level.[473] However, the international community did not take up this proposal, and the idea of a global representative only received more attention in the context of the preparations of the Rio+20 conference, two decades later.[474] Legal scholarship has further developed this idea.[475]

The establishment of a "High Commissioner for Future Generations" would promote the interests of future generations in the policy-making processes of governments, international organisations and businesses by playing an important advocacy role for these interests.[476] It would be able to create a counterweight to the general tendency of States to focus only on short-term self-interests and it would

---

[468] Cf. ibid., 59 (at footnote 153); Brown Weiss (2021b), pp. 30–32.

[469] In more detail, see *supra* in Sect. 4.2.2.

[470] UNGA (1972), Preamble. Cf. also Fülöp (2021), p. 160.

[471] On the current and future role of the UNEP, see Ivanova (2020).

[472] Brown Weiss (1989), pp. 148–152.

[473] Preparatory Committee for the United Nations Conference on Environment and Development (1992), paras. 8–15. See also Leigh (1992), p. 152; Borg (1998), p. 140.

[474] Anstee-Wedderburn (2014), pp. 56–58. See *infra* notes 495–504.

[475] Aquilina (1998); Bruce (1998); Macdonald (1998); Rao (1998); Stone (1998); Pearce (2012); Fülöp (2016). Most recently, see also Caney (2022). For further assessments, see several chapters in González-Ricoy and Gosseries (2016). Critical of such an ombudsperson, see Fitzmaurice (2008), pp. 225–226.

[476] UNSG (2013), para. 56; Beyleveld et al. (2015).

thereby contribute to a better implementation of States' intergenerational obligations.[477] Comparable to the national level, a global representative institution could also be commissioned with different functions and powers.[478] Inspiration could be sought from existing examples of High Commissioners at the international level,[479] even from some Special Rapporteurs,[480] as well as from national institutions representing the interests of future generations.[481] While some commentators would confer only soft powers to such an office in order not to interfere too much with State sovereignty,[482] others argued in favour of a more ambitious approach and demanded that the commissioner ought to participate in international decision-making processes, and that it should be equipped with a variety of governance and cooperation functions.[483] For instance, the office could be inspired by examples of existing UN Special Rapporteurs who intervened during the negotiations of the Paris Agreement to voice their concern on the impact of climate change on human rights.[484] Some commentators even argued that a representative of future generations should incorporate a reporting system or the possibility to lodge individual complaints to that office.[485] The representative institution could also be allocated procedural powers, which would allow it to lodge complaints on behalf of future generations in cases, in which intergenerational obligations are violated.[486] These procedural powers could also include the possibility to file *amicus curiae* briefs before international or regional judicial and quasi-judicial bodies, as some of the existing UN Special Rapporteurs already did.[487]

Eventually, the institutional incorporation of a representative of future generations would depend on its exact powers and functions.[488] In any case, independence is necessary for the proper exercise of its functions.[489] Most proponents of a global

[477] See Nagy (1988), p. 321; Pearce (2012), pp. 2–3; Ward (2012), pp. 3–5.

[478] For an overview of possible functions, see Fülöp (2021), pp. 155–156.

[479] For instance, referring to the UN High Commissioner for Refugees or the UN High Commissioner for Human Rights, see UNSG (2013), para. 57; Macdonald (1998), pp. 153–154; Ward (2012), p. 9.

[480] See recently Ganesan (2022).

[481] UNSG (2013), paras. 58–59.

[482] Ibid., paras. 65–67; Macdonald (1998), p. 157; Anstee-Wedderburn (2014), pp. 59, 68–69; Beckman and Uggla (2016), pp. 124–131.

[483] Brown Weiss (1989), pp. 125–126; Pearce (2012), pp. 6–8; Ward (2012), pp. 15–16; Fülöp (2016), pp. 197–204.

[484] OHCHR (2014).

[485] Brown Weiss (1989), p. 125; Pearce (2012), p. 7; Fülöp (2016), pp. 204–206. For recent examples of complaints submitted to several Special Rapporteurs, see, e.g., CCLD (2020d-today); CCLD (2021a-today); Vöneky and Beck (2022), p. 260.

[486] Brown Weiss (1989), p. 125; Stone (1998), p. 71.

[487] See Ganesan (2022). On the representative function of *amicus curiae* briefs, see *infra* in Sect. 5.3.3.2.3 and Sect. 5.3.3.3, notes 773, 849.

[488] Cf. Brown Weiss (2010), pp. 112–113.

[489] Stone (1998), pp. 69–70; Pearce (2012), pp. 6, 8; Fülöp (2021), p. 155.

representative agreed that its infrastructure should somehow be integrated within the UN system, since the United Nations' mission includes "the vision of a better tomorrow and planning for future generations", which are "among the driving values of the Organization."[490] Another possibility would be the creation of a new UN standing body.[491] Some proposals even suggested to separate the representative's functions completely from the UN system and to create a new international body or to confer the task of representation to an NGO.[492] The representation of future generations could also be attributed to different guardians for distinct areas of law or it could be associated with different area-specific organisations.[493]

As mentioned, the proposals for the establishment of a High Commissioner for Future Generations were taken up in the run-up of the Rio+20 conference in 2012. Several stakeholders called for the establishment of such an office, not only at the national,[494] but also at the international level.[495] For instance, the 'World Future Council' and the 'Foundation for Democracy and Sustainable Development' argued in favour of an institution with stronger commitments whose mission it should be "to promote and protect the interests of future generations in the context of the imperative to meet the needs of the present without compromising the ability of future generations to meet their own needs".[496] The initiative suggested a strong advocate for the interests and needs of future generations with an agenda-setting role and which was more than a mere "talking shop".[497] It should have the competence to contribute in developing the international legal framework, and the stakeholders proposed several powers and responsibilities for this purpose.[498] Further, the High Commissioner should have the possibility to look into submissions of several actors with regard to intergenerational equity.[499] It was conceived as an independent office within the UN.[500]

Instead of taking up any of the ambitious proposals, the Zero Draft of the Rio+20 Conference outcome document chose a softened formulation.[501] In the draft's paragraph 57, the States would have agreed to "further consider the establishment

---

[490] UNSG (2013), para. 56. See also Rao (1998), p. 147; Pearce (2012), p. 8.

[491] Rao (1998), p. 147.

[492] Stone (1998), p. 69. On the role of NGOs in the representation of future generations, see also *infra* in Sect. 5.3.3.3.1.

[493] Ibid., pp. 69–70.

[494] See *supra* note 466.

[495] In addition to the references in note 466, see also UNGA (2011); Rio+20 Working Group (2011); Ward et al. (2012). For further references, see Anstee-Wedderburn (2014), p. 56.

[496] Ward et al. (2012), p. 1. In more detail, see Ward (2012).

[497] Ward et al. (2012), pp. 1–2.

[498] Ibid.

[499] Ibid., p. 3.

[500] Ibid.

[501] As to the critical reception of the adopted version, see Anstee-Wedderburn (2014), p. 58 (at footnotes 145–148).

of an Ombudsperson, or High Commissioner for Future Generations, to promote sustainable development".[502] Although this was already much weaker than proposed, even *this* wording did not make it into the final conference outcome document. A number of States were afraid that a High Commissioner with broad suggested powers and competences could heavily interfere in their sovereignty and national development, so that their objections resulted in the omission of this call for a global representative for future generations.[503] The only reference to future generations in the outcome document is contained in paragraph 86: "We will also consider the need for promoting intergenerational solidarity for the achievement of sustainable development, taking into account the needs of future generations, including by inviting the Secretary-General *to present a report* on this issue".[504]

Subsequently, in its report of 2013,[505] the Secretary-General suggested the creation of a high commissioner for future generations that could have the following powers:

> (a) The high commissioner could act as an advocate for intergenerational solidarity through interactions with Member States and other stakeholders, as well as across United Nations entities and specialized agencies;
>
> (b) Such an office could undertake research and foster expertise on policy practices to enhance intergenerational solidarity in the context of sustainable development at the international, regional, national and subnational levels and disseminate such expertise, as deemed appropriate;
>
> (c) The office could, at the request [of the UN], offer advice on the implementation of existing intergovernmental commitments to enhance the rights and address the needs of future generations;
>
> (d) The office could, upon request, also offer its support and advice, including to individual Member States, on best practices and on policy measures to enhance intergenerational solidarity.[506]

The report stressed that such a commissioner would not create any reporting obligations or complaints procedures.[507] Alternatively, a UNSG special envoy for future generations could be established, which would also advocate the needs of future generations by raising awareness, promoting best practices in policy-making and annually reporting to the UNGA.[508]

Despite these recommendations and subsequent calls for the establishment of a global representative institution,[509] the international community has not

[502] Bureau of the Preparatory Process for the UNCSD (2012), para. 57.

[503] Mehrishi (2012); Kemp (2012); Anstee-Wedderburn (2014), pp. 58–59 with further references.

[504] UNGA (2012), para. 86.

[505] In more detail, see already *supra* in Sect. 2.1.1.4.

[506] , para. 63.

[507] Ibid., para. 64.

[508] Ibid., para. 65.

[509] See, e.g., Le Blanc and Roehrl (2012), p. 15; Conference of Model Institutions for a Sustainable Future (2014), para. 2; EC (2018), para. 25. Most recently, see, e.g., Stockholm+50 Youth Assembly (2022), p. 10.

implemented any of these suggestions as of today. The establishment of the High-Level Political Forum on Sustainable Development has been the only institutional novelty at the Rio+20 Conference.[510] Since 2013, the HLPFSD acted as a "guardian of the sustainable development agenda",[511] but its mandate does not explicitly refer to future generations or intergenerational equity.[512] Generally, the HLPFSD has so far not considered any institutional arrangements as suggested in the UNSG Report and it is far from taking up the role of a High Commissioner for Future Generations itself.[513] Even more recently, the UN Human Rights Council adopted a resolution establishing the mandate of a new Special Rapporteur on the promotion and protection of human rights in the context of climate change;[514] but again its functions and powers do not refer to future generations at all.[515]

Consequently, it can be summarised that there is no global representative institution for future generations *de lege lata* as of today. Despite various attempts over the last decades to establish such an institution, future generations still have no voice in the process of international environmental policy-making. They are dependent on the good will of the policy-makers of the present generation and on the existing intergenerational obligations that arise from the general conception of intergenerational equity. However, they are not represented by a proper institution in the deliberation process of environmental policies, as would be required according to the all affected principle.

#### 5.3.2.3 Summary

On the level of policy-making, the foregoing analysis has shown that representation of future generations still is fragmented and lacks universal recognition. Despite various proposals and international initiatives, States have not agreed on any institutional form of representation yet. Instead, some occasional examples of national representative institutions exist that differ in their function, powers and exact institutional frameworks. In the run-up to the Rio+20 conference, it was suggested to implement an international obligation to establish national ombudspersons for future generations, but Sates preferred to leave this decision to their discretion. Furthermore, none of the attempts to establish a global High Commissioner for Future Generations have been successful. Comparable institutional reforms, such as the creation of the HLPFSD, cannot be considered to implement a representation

[510] UNGA (2012), paras. 84–86; UNGA (2013a).

[511] UNGA (2013b), para. 8. On the links between intergenerational equity and sustainable development, see *supra* in Sect. 2.3.1.

[512] UNGA (2013a). For some vague references in its work to future generations, see *supra* in Sect. 2.1.1.4 [note 99].

[513] Anstee-Wedderburn (2014), p. 60 (at footnote 162).

[514] Human Rights Council (2021b).

[515] On the importance of the new Special Rapporteur, see Savaresi (2021b).

mechanism for future generations in policy-making. Therefore, *Edith Brown Weiss'* idea to establish representative institutions at different levels[516] has remained a hypothetical suggestion so far, and future generations still have no universal voice in policy-making.

### 5.3.3 Representation of Future Generations in Judicial Proceedings

Besides representation in the policy-making processes of international law, future generations and their interests must and could also be represented in the context of judicial implementation. If the duty-bearers of intergenerational equity violate their planetary duties, this violation should be subject to judicial review at some level. Again, the main question is which institutional frameworks might already exist or could be envisaged in the future for an effective implementation and enforcement of intergenerational equity. As of today, there is no universal international judicial system for the implementation of environmental obligations.[517] Current international law provides for different frameworks for the judicial implementation of international environmental law. Before addressing these different frameworks, some common challenges of all of these proceedings are characterised in an overview (Sect. 5.3.3.1). The most adequate institutional framework for intergenerational equity depends, *inter alia*, on the respective duty-bearers, on the one hand, and on the potential representatives for future generations, on the other hand. As States have been identified as the primary duty-bearers of intergenerational obligations,[518] the main parts of the following sub-sections address judicial frameworks, in which States are the defendants. First and foremost, this concerns the level of inter-State disputes, thus, judicial proceedings between States before international judiciary (and quasi-judiciary) bodies, such as the ICJ (Sect. 5.3.3.2). Beyond this, individual complaints procedures have become increasingly important in international law, particularly in international human rights law, but also in environmental law. Therefore, the third sub-section turns to judicial and quasi-judicial frameworks of individual complaints procedures against States (Sect. 5.3.3.3)—on the international, regional as well as national level. In this context, individuals or other civil society actors could serve as representatives of future generations' interests. As far as private corporations could become duty-bearers of intergenerational equity under international law, the fourth sub-section briefly addresses few instances of case law with corporations as defendants (Sect. 5.3.3.4).

---

[516] Brown Weiss (1989), p. 124.

[517] Beyerlin and Grote Stoutenburg (2013), para. 96. On the role of the draft GPE to introduce such a system, see Parejo Navajas and Lobel (2018), p. 50.

[518] See *supra* in Sect. 5.1.1.

#### 5.3.3.1 Common Challenges of Judicial Implementation in Environmental Law

Regardless of whether a dispute on intergenerational questions takes place on the inter-State level or in individual complaints procedures, and regardless of whether it is a proceeding against a State or against a corporation, two problems generally influence any form of judicial proceeding dealing with environmental issues: causation (Sect. 5.3.3.1.1) and separation of powers (Sect. 5.3.3.1.2). These common challenges to environmental litigation are briefly addressed in the following. Since they not only concern the representation of future generations but (international) environmental law in general, the present book does not focus on them in detail.

##### 5.3.3.1.1 Causation

First, many environmental proceedings address environmental damage that has been caused to the respective plaintiffs or the environment in general. In these cases, the existence of a causal link is required between the potentially illegal conduct and the relevant damage. Causation is particularly relevant in the context of climate litigation,[519] or more generally with regard to long-term and complex effects of environmental degradation.[520] The standards of proof of causation differ depending on the respective liability regime.[521] Issues of causation play a crucial role with regard to civil liability before national courts. [522] They are more difficult to resolve in claims against private corporations than in claims against States.[523] However, causation is also a necessary requirement in the law of State responsibility, according to Articles 31 and 36 of the ARSIWA, if a State sues another State for compensation for environmental harm caused by a violation of international law.[524]

Particularly in the context of climate change, it will often be difficult to assess, which State's or corporation's behaviour resulted in which specific damage.[525] Damage and violations unfold their effect in transboundary and even global settings

[519] On the notion of "climate litigation", see *infra* note 782.

[520] In more detail, see Kehrer (2009), pp. 228–331; Rumpf (2019), pp. 154–157; Pfrommer et al. (2019). See also several contributions in Faure and Peeters (2011).

[521] De La Fayette (2010), pp. 325–326.

[522] See, e.g., US District Court for the Northern District of California, Oakland Division, *Native Village of Kivalina and City of Kivalina v. ExxonMobil Corporation* et al., Judgment, 30 September 2009, 663 F.Supp.2d 863; Regional Court of Essen, *Lliuya v. RWE,* Judgment, 15 December 2016, 2017 ZUR 370.

[523] Lambooy and Palm (2016), p. 333.

[524] See ILC (2001b), Art. 31 para. 10; Schmalenbach (2022b), pp. 351–352. With regard to damage caused by climate change, see Verheyen (2005).

[525] Van Dijk (2011), p. 219; Dellinger (2016), p. 1589; Douhan (2019), para. 32.

so that it will almost be impossible to attribute a certain damage in the future to a certain behaviour of a certain State or private corporation today.[526] For this reason, some national courts have already dismissed climate litigation cases as inadmissible.[527] Although liability processes largely differ in their specific approach to causation,[528] claims are more likely to be successful if there is a more obvious causal link between the defendants' actions and the occurred environmental damage.[529] In this context, the burden of proof in a specific regime is particularly relevant.[530] If it is for the claimant to prove the factual basis of causation, the aforementioned challenges will often lead to insurmountable obstacles.[531] Cumulative contribution of several actors to climate change-related effects constitutes a main problem in this regard.[532]

For these reasons, commentators and plaintiffs involved in environmental (particularly climate) litigation have brought forward new suggestions to solve the challenge of causation.[533] For instance, *Richard Tol* and *Roda Verheyen* suggested a distinction between "specific causation" and "general causation"; the latter would address causality "between an activity and the general outcome", as it can be established in the context of climate change.[534] With regard to multiple contributors to environmental damage, theories of proportionate liability or market share liability have been proposed, depending on the measurable contribution of the polluters.[535] Such proportionate attribution would at least allow for liability of the major polluters.[536] Further, several commentators suggested a reversal of the burden of proof in relation to the factual basis of causation.[537] For instance, the Institut de Droit International ('IDI') stated that it can be sufficient to establish "presumptions of causality relating to hazardous activities or cumulative damage or long-standing

---

[526] Dellinger (2016), p. 1589; Verheyen and Zengerling (2016), p. 438; Saxler et al. (2015), p. 132. If a plurality of actors has contributed with different acts to a certain damage, causation for the damage must be assessed for each actor's behaviour separately, see ILC (2001b), Art. 47 para. 8.

[527] See, e.g., *US District Court, Kivalina* (Judgment), *supra* note 522, pp. 880–881; *Regional Court of Essen, Lliuya* (Judgment), *supra* note 522, paras. 40–46.

[528] On the issue of liability for environmental damage, see already *supra* in Sect. 5.1.2.2.

[529] Lambooy and Palm (2016), p. 333 with regard to Federal High Court of Nigeria in the Benin Judicial Division, *Gbemre v. Shell Petroleum Development Company Nigeria Ltd.* et al., Judgment, 14 November 2005, (2005) African Human Rights Law Reports 151.

[530] Kehrer (2009), pp. 247–248.

[531] Ibid., 266 with further references.

[532] Rumpf (2019), p. 156.

[533] For more details, see Kehrer (2009), pp. 264–330. See also Saxler et al. (2015), pp. 131–132.

[534] Tol and Verheyen (2004), p. 1112.

[535] Van Dijk (2011), p. 220; Kehrer (2009), pp. 320–324. See also UNEP (2017), pp. 19–22 with further references.

[536] Van Dijk (2011), p. 220; Rumpf (2019), p. 156; Toft (2020), pp. 13–14.

[537] ILA Committee on Legal Aspects of Sustainable Development (2002), para. 4.2; Verheyen (2005), p. 262; Kehrer (2009), pp. 265–268. Rejecting such a reversal, see *Activities in the Area* (Advisory Opinion), *supra* note 41, para. 182; van Dijk (2011), p. 220.

damages not attributable to a single entity but to a sector or type of activity".[538] Generally, increasing knowledge on attribution science will facilitate issues of causation in the future.[539]

Although the propositions differ in detail, most commentators agree that a more appropriate approach to causation with regard to climate change and comparable environmental degradation is necessary.[540] Despite the existing unsuccessful cases, some courts have addressed causation more progressively.[541] Moreover, most judicial proceedings addressing intergenerational equity are forward-looking rather than backward-looking, thus, they address the defendants' obligations in the future instead of the harm done in the past.[542] Consequently, problems of causation are not *per se* frustrating judicial proceedings on behalf of future generations.

#### 5.3.3.1.2 Separation of Powers

Second, litigation in the context of environmental degradation often constitutes a separation of powers issue, as there is a certain risk that the judiciary might interfere with the political sphere.[543] Separation of powers requires the separate branches of government, the legislative, executive and judiciary, to act within the authority granted to them by the respective constitution.[544] Although it primarily applies to democratic societies, it is also relevant in non-constitutional systems with regard to specific policy-making powers granted to the respective branches of government.[545] A similar constraint exists on the international level as far as international courts and tribunals (e.g., the ICJ) have to distinguish between progressive development of law in their jurisprudence and actual legislation.[546] The ICJ stated as follows: "As is implied by [Article 38 of the ICJ Statute], the Court is not a legislative body. Its duty is to apply the law as it finds it, not to make it."[547]

Again, climate litigation constitutes a predominant example that raises certain problems with respect to separation of powers,[548] sometimes called the "political

538 Institut de Droit International (IDI) (1997), Art. 7.

539 Cf. Pfrommer et al. (2019). On the current stage of attribution science, see Chen et al. (2021), pp. 204–206.

540 See Kehrer (2009), pp. 299, 330; van Dijk (2011), pp. 220–221; Dellinger (2018), pp. 530, 546; Rumpf (2019), pp. 149–150, 156–157.

541 See *infra* notes 1106–1107.

542 For this distinction with respect to private corporations, see Toft (2020).

543 See Payandeh (2021), pp. 76–77 with further references.

544 UNEP (2020), p. 40.

545 UNEP (2017), p. 30.

546 See Pellet (2011), p. 1074.

547 ICJ, *South West Africa, Second Phase (Ethiopia v. South Africa; Liberia v. South Africa),* Judgment, 18 July 1966, ICJ Reports 1966, 6, para. 89.

548 In general, see Payandeh (2021) who also referred to related challenges of courts in the context of climate litigation, see ibid., pp. 78–80. See also Burgers (2020b).

question doctrine".[549] The role of courts in the context of climate change has thus played an important role in many climate litigation cases in the USA,[550] but also in other jurisdictions.[551] Particularly in the USA, the invocation of the political question doctrine by the defendant State was often successful and resulted in the dismissal of climate cases.[552] While the application and relevance of the political question doctrine depends on the exact separation between the powers in the respective domestic regimes,[553] some commentators criticised that recent court decisions have unduly interfered in the law-making powers of the legislative and executive branches.[554]

Certainly, the judiciary has to adhere to certain limits of its powers when engaging in litigation on environmental law. A court must respect the other branches' discretion in policy-making,[555] and it must not act *ultra vires* of its own competences by entering into the realm of politics.[556] However, separation of powers does not mean that there cannot be any overlaps between the different powers at all. Instead, the judiciary has a role to play in the control of the other branches of government.[557] Courts are authorised to adjudicate on the legislative's and executive's compliance with climate protection obligations as well as with higher-ranking constitutional and human rights provisions: "In declaring that the executive or the legislature violated these obligations, courts do not illegitimately engage in politics."[558] For the inter-State level, the ICJ pointed out on several occasions that "the fact that [a] question has political aspects [...] does not suffice to deprive it of its character as a 'legal question'".[559]

Furthermore, courts can at least assess whether the State has adhered to a certain minimum threshold, which can result from constitutional or international climate

---

549 Payandeh (2021), p. 73.

550 UNEP (2017), p. 30. For instance, in the *Juliana case,* see US Court of Appeals for the ninth Circuit, *Juliana v. United States,* Opinion, 17 January 2020, 947 F.3d 1159, 1171–1172, 1175.

551 UNEP (2020), p. 40; Aidun (2020); Eckes (2021a); Niehaus (2021). With regard to the Dutch *Urgenda* decision, see Hague District Court, *Urgenda Foundation v. The State of the Netherlands,* Judgment, 24 June 2015, European Case Law Identifier ECLI:NL:RBDHA:2015:7196, paras. 4.92–4.102. With regard to the German *Neubauer* decision, see *infra* note 1035.

552 In more detail on the *Juliana* case, see *infra* note 1010. See also *US District Court, Kivalina* (Judgment), *supra* note 522, pp. 871–877; *US Court of Appeals, Juliana* (Opinion), *supra* note 550, 1171–1172, 1175.

553 Cf. Payandeh (2021), pp. 72–76. On the differences between US and Dutch law, see Lambooy and Palm (2016), pp. 333–334.

554 See, e.g., Bergkamp (2015); Wegener (2019).

555 Spijkers (2018), p. 333; Payandeh (2021), p. 77.

556 Wegener (2019), pp. 142–144.

557 Collins (2017).

558 Payandeh (2021), p. 77. See also Spijkers (2021), p. 254.

559 *Nuclear Weapons* (Advisory Opinion), *supra* note 30, para. 13. See also ICJ, *Legal Consequences of the Construction of a Wall in the Occupied Palestinian Territory,* Advisory Opinion, 9 July 2004, ICJ Reports 2004, 136, para. 41; Bodansky (2017), p. 704.

law.[560] *Laura Burgers* elaborated in detail on the necessities of such a judicial involvement in climate protection: due to the "constitutionalization of the environment" and the fact that it constitutes a prerequisite for democracy, courts would necessarily have to contribute to the protection of the environment.[561] Such a corrective role of the judiciary is even more important with regard to the representation of interests that would otherwise not be heard in the policy-making process.[562] Courts thus offer a potential framework, which can attenuate the "voicelessness"[563] of future generations in decision-making,[564] a problem that has been underlined in the foregoing sections. Referring to *Burgers'* approach, *Daniel Bertram* suggested another interesting perspective on the role of the judiciary in future-oriented cases. He proposed to introduce a jurisdictional criterion that would restrain the "extratemporal jurisdiction" of courts in order to delimit their legitimate authority vis-à-vis the other powers.[565] This jurisdictional criterion would limit courts to decide only about cases that touch upon the "preservation of democratic choice".[566]

Overall, and regardless of the exact limitations and criteria imposed by the separation of powers doctrine, the following sections assume that the partly political nature of many intergenerational problems does not necessarily hinder successful proceedings before judicial and quasi-judicial bodies. Instead, the judiciary certainly will play a role, besides other actors, in the resolution of intergenerational equity-related disputes on behalf of future generations.

#### 5.3.3.2 Representation in Inter-State Proceedings

Traditionally, international judicial proceedings take place on an inter-State level before international courts and tribunals. This includes contentious as well as advisory proceedings, where provided.[567] In the foregoing chapters, several instances of international case law have already been presented in general,[568] regarding the legal nature of intergenerational equity,[569] or regarding the status of future generations as right-holders.[570] The following sub-sections do not revise these

[560] See Burgers (2022). See also *infra* notes 1137–1138. More critical, see Payandeh (2021), p. 77.

[561] Burgers (2020b), pp. 69–75.

[562] Slobodian (2020), p. 582; Niehaus (2021), pp. 249–250. Cf. also Eckes (2021b).

[563] Niehaus and Davies (2021), p. 230.

[564] Niehaus (2021), pp. 249–250. See also Abate (2020), pp. 43–96.

[565] Bertram (2022).

[566] Ibid. *Bertram* offered a first proposal how to operationalise extratemporal jurisdiction, which could be elaborated further.

[567] See, e.g., *Charter of the United Nations* (UN Charter), adopted 26 June 1945, entered into force 24 October 1945, 1 UNTS XVI, Art. 96.

[568] See *supra* in Sect. 2.1.2.

[569] See *supra* in Chap. 4.

[570] See *supra* in Sect. 5.2.2.

decisions comprehensively, but focus on those proceedings, in which some form of representation of future generations has been indicated. Three different types of representatives are addressed one after the other. International courts and tribunals could themselves be considered guardians or trustees of the interests of future generations (Sect. 5.3.3.2.1), or States could assume this role of representatives of future generations as primary subject of international law (Sect. 5.3.3.2.2). Eventually, some commentators suggested to grant this representative position to third parties within inter-State proceedings (Sect. 5.3.3.2.3).

##### 5.3.3.2.1 International Courts and Tribunals as Guardians for Future Generations

As has been indicated above, the actual references of the ICJ to intergenerational equity remained scarce and the Court considered intergenerational equity only one aspect to take into account beside others.[571] However, the aforementioned separate and dissenting opinions in these cases offered more insights into the potential representation of future generations' interests. Particularly, *Judge Weeramantry* took several opportunities to illustrate the special role he conferred to the judiciary in the context of sustainable development and intergenerational equity.[572] In the context of France's nuclear testing and the long-term impact of radioactive by-products, the ICJ stated in 1995:

> In a matter of which it is duly seised [sic.], this Court must regard itself as a trustee of those [intergenerational] rights in the sense that a domestic court is a trustee of the interests of an infant unable to speak for itself. If this Court is charged with administering international law, and if this principle [of intergenerational equity] is building itself into the corpus of international law, or has already done so, this principle is one which must inevitably be a concern of this Court.[573]

*Judge Weeramantry* confirmed this idea of the Court as a guardian of future generations' rights or interests 1 year later, in his dissenting opinion to the *Nuclear Weapons Advisory Opinion*:

> This Court, as the principal judicial organ of the United Nations, empowered to state and apply international law with an authority matched by no other tribunal must, in its jurisprudence, pay due recognition to the rights of future generations. If there is any tribunal that can recognize and protect their interests under the law, it is this Court.[574]

---

[571] See Fitzmaurice (2008), p. 225.

[572] See Voigt (2009), pp. 183–184.

[573] *Nuclear Tests 1995* (Dissenting Opinion of Judge Weeramantry), *supra* note 295, p. 341. Agreeing, see ICJ, *Request for an Examination of the Situation in Accordance with Paragraph 63 of the Court's Judgment of 20 December 1974 in the Nuclear Tests (New Zealand v. France) Case,* Dissenting Opinion of Judge Sir Geoffrey Palmer, 22 September 1995, ICJ Reports 1995, 381.

[574] *Nuclear Weapons* (Dissenting Opinion of Judge Weeramantry), *supra* note 295, 454–455.

While these passages had the most explicit wording in this regard, two other separate opinions also stressed the particular role the ICJ should have taken in the protection of intergenerational equity.[575] In this role as a trustee or guardian of the interests of future generations, the respective courts or tribunals could assume "a particular responsibility to ensure the balanced hearing of powerful and not so powerful or even voiceless interests, i.e. where the interest of generations unborn [...] are involved".[576]

The role of the ICJ and other international courts and tribunals becomes increasingly important, as some commentators have recently discussed these courts' and tribunals' impact in the realm of international climate litigation.[577] The unconventional approach to consider the respective court a guardian or trustee for future generations is particularly interesting in the context of advisory opinions. While the IACHR has already issued a relevant advisory opinion in 2017, in which it referred to the right to a healthy environment of future generations,[578] it did not consider itself a guardian of these future generations.[579] More recently, a new advisory proceeding has been initiated by Chile and Colombia before the IACHR on State obligations for responding to the climate emergency.[580] Although intergenerational aspects will probably play a role in the court's assessment of the respective human rights obligations, the issue of rights of *future* generations is not included in the questions' scope;[581] even less with view to their representation. Nonetheless, the upcoming advisory opinion will certainly play a decisive role in the further development of the interrelation of human rights and climate change.[582]

More pertinently, there have been several suggestions to initiate an advisory opinion before the ICJ, which would include questions of intergenerational equity and strengthen the role of future generations in international jurisprudence.[583] In 2011, the Pacific island nation of Palau planned to organise a majority in the UNGA to seek an advisory opinion from the ICJ on the legal responsibilities of States in the

[575] *Gabčíkovo-Nagymaros Project* (Separate Opinion of Vice-President Weeramantry), *supra* note 295, 109–110; *Pulp Mills* (Separate Opinion of Judge Cançado Trindade), *supra* note 295, paras. 114–124.

[576] Voigt (2009), p. 184. See also Fitzmaurice (2008), p. 225; Lawrence and Köhler (2017), pp. 653–654, 665.

[577] See, e.g., Verheyen and Zengerling (2016); Bodansky (2017); Wewerinke-Singh et al. (2021).

[578] *The Environment and Human Rights* (Advisory Opinion), *supra* note 114, para. 59.

[579] In detail on the relevance of this advisory opinion, see *supra* in Sect. 5.2.2.2.

[580] IACHR, *Climate Emergency and Human Rights,* Request for an Advisory Opinion, 9 January 2023, Retrieved January 3, 2025, from https://climatecasechart.com/non-us-case/request-for-an-advisory-opinion-on-the-scope-of-the-state-obligations-for-responding-to-the-climate-emergency/. For an overview, see CCLD (2023b-today).

[581] Kahl (2023).

[582] Ibid. See also Auz and Viveros-Uehara (2023). Due to this book's editorial deadline in January 2025, the actual findings of the IACHR from summer 2025 will have to be analysed and discussed on another occasion and in another place.

[583] Generally, see Boisson de Chazournes (2002); Sands (2016), pp. 25–28; Bodansky (2017), pp. 689–690; Lawrence and Köhler (2017), pp. 655–661; Dellinger (2018), pp. 548–549; Wewerinke-Singh et al. (2021), pp. 403–413.

context of climate change.[584] Although this initiative was not successful,[585] there have been new attempts in the last years, e.g., a request by the International Union for Conservation of Nature in 2016.[586] In December 2022, the Commission of Small Island States on Climate Change and International Law requested an advisory opinion from the ITLOS on climate change-related obligations emanating from UNCLOS.[587] However, intergenerational equity did not play a relevant role in the proceedings and the rendered opinion rendered in May 2024.[588]

Most promisingly, a recent initiative emerged in 2019 from a group of law students in the South Pacific, which evolved into a global initiative of the 'World's Youth for Climate Justice' that aims at "bring[ing] climate justice to the [ICJ]".[589] They suggested submitting the following broad and ambitious legal question to the ICJ: "What are the obligations of states under international law to protect the rights of present and future generations against the adverse effects of climate change?"[590] Since 2019, the Republic of Vanuatu has supported the initiative,[591] and in September 2021, the State announced to initiate this advisory opinion in the UNGA session in 2022/2023.[592] Recently, the proponents of an advisory proceeding have gained more supporters among various States—e.g., Australia as one major polluter.[593]

While the initiative World's Youth for Climate Justice advocated for an ambitious and broad legal question,[594] other commentators cautioned for a more careful wording, which does not touch upon too sensitive political issues.[595] *Peter Lawrence* and *Lukas Köhler* stressed that an advisory opinion in the context of climate change could "valuably highlight the inevitable impact of unrestrained climate change on the human rights of current and future generations and help in ramping

[584] See UN News (2011); Verheyen and Zengerling (2016), p. 427.

[585] Wewerinke-Singh et al. (2021), p. 406.

[586] IUCN (2016).

[587] For an overview, see CCLD (2022-2024b).

[588] ITLOS, *Request for an Advisory Opinion submitted by the Commission of Small Island States on Climate Change and International Law (COSIS),* Advisory Opinion, 21 May 2024, Retrieved January 3, 2025, from https://www.itlos.org/en/main/cases/list-of-cases/request-for-an-advisory-opinion-submitted-by-the-commission-of-small-island-states-on-climate-change-and-international-law-request-for-advisory-opinion-submitted-to-the-tribunal/

[589] In detail, see Schnakenberg et al. (2022). See also Brown Weiss (2021a), para. 33. On the role of youth initiatives for future generations, see *infra* in Sect. 5.3.3.3.2.

[590] Schnakenberg et al. (2022), p. 27.

[591] Wewerinke-Singh et al. (2021), p. 406.

[592] Burton (2021). In detail on this initiative, see Mayer (2023).

[593] Australia has voiced its support in the course of the 51st Pacific Islands Forum, see Pacific Islands Forum (2022), paras. 44–46. In more detail on the initiative's progress, see also Gunia (2022).

[594] Schnakenberg et al. (2022), pp. 27–28. Cf. also Sands (2016).

[595] See Bodansky (2017), pp. 708–709; Wewerinke-Singh et al. (2021), p. 410.

up pressure on governments."[596] According to *Philippe Sands*, the ICJ would also contribute to "developments of an international public consciousness on matters of global concern".[597] Beyond the necessary clarification and development of international environmental law, another advantage would be the potential harmonisation influence on subsequent national and regional case law on climate change.[598] Nonetheless, other authors questioned the added value of an advisory opinion on climate change as it would "at best put pressure on States [...], rather than directly cause them to reduce their emissions".[599]

Despite several political and diplomatic obstacles,[600] the ongoing efforts of the initiative finally culminated in a UNGA request for an Advisory Opinion in March 2023.[601] The UNGA requested an opinion on the following questions:

> (a) What are the obligations of States under international law to ensure the protection of the climate system and other parts of the environment from anthropogenic emissions of greenhouse gases for States and for present and future generations?
>
> (b) What are the legal consequences under these obligations for States where they, by their acts and omissions, have caused significant harm to the climate system and other parts of the environment, with respect to:
>
> (i) States, including, in particular, small island developing States, which due to their geographical circumstances and level of development, are injured or specially affected by or are particularly vulnerable to the adverse effects of climate change?
> (ii) Peoples and individuals of the present and future generations affected by the adverse effects of climate change?[602]

In the meantime, the ICJ has received 91 written statements by States, the highest number of written statements ever to have been filed in such advisory proceedings.[603] Additionally, several civil society actors like NGOs have also submitted written statements that might be considered by the Court.[604] From 2 to 13 December 2024, the Court held its public hearings, during which 96 States and 11 international organisations presented their oral statements.[605] It is beyond the scope of these

[596] Lawrence and Köhler (2017), p. 661.

[597] Sands (2016), p. 26. Cf. also Dellinger (2018), p. 549.

[598] Wewerinke-Singh et al. (2021), pp. 404–405. On this national case law, see *infra* in Sect. 5.3.3.3.3.

[599] Savaresi (2021a), pp. 387–390.

[600] Wewerinke-Singh et al. (2021), pp. 409–413; Savaresi et al. (2021).

[601] For an overview, see CCLD (2023a-today). Due to this book's editorial deadline in January 2025, the actual findings of the ICJ from summer 2025 will have to be analysed and discussed on another occasion and in another place

[602] ICJ, *Obligations of States in Respect of Climate Change*, UNGA Request for Advisory Opinion, 29 March 2023, UN Doc. A/RES/77/276.

[603] ICJ, *Obligations of States in Respect of Climate Change*, Press Release, 12 April 2024, Retrieved January 3, 2025, from https://www.icj-cij.org/sites/default/files/case-related/187/187-20240412-pre-01-00-en.pdf

[604] See CCLD (2023a-today). On the role of voluntary *amicus curiae* briefs before the ICJ, see *infra* in Sect. 5.3.3.2.3.

pre-publication additional remarks to review all of these statements in detail.[606] However, it should be mentioned that some of the NGO written statements have explicitly turned to the rights of future generations and the role of intergenerational equity in the questions before the ICJ.[607] Furthermore, several States addressed intergenerational equity and future generations—some of them in an explicit rights language, some only implicitly with references to the effects of climate change on future generations, again others rejecting the idea of rights of future generations at all.[608]

Compared to the initial question suggested by World's Youth for Climate Justice, the actual question put before the ICJ has been more nuanced.[609] Most importantly, it does not contain the explicit reference to "rights of present and future generations" anymore. Yet, question (a) still focuses on the State obligations for the protection of present and future generations and question (b) explicitly addresses the legal consequences of significant harm caused, *inter alia*, with respect to "peoples and individuals of the present and future generations". [610] Therefore, the legal questions on the climate protection obligations of States remains so inherently linked to intergenerational equity that the ICJ would certainly have to address the intergenerational aspects of these obligations.[611] This connection is also mirrored in the aforementioned submissions of the several NGOs as well as States.[612]

---

[605] For the verbatim records of the oral proceedings, see ICJ, *Obligations of States in Respect of Climate Change,* Verbatim Records, 2 December 2024, Retrieved January 3, 2025, from https://www.icj-cij.org/case/187/oral-proceedings

[606] The World's Youth for Climate Justice as initiator of the advisory proceedings has thoroughly observed the oral proceedings before the ICJ and commented on the various statements of States in December in their daily debriefs, see World's Youth for Climate Justice (2024).

[607] See, e.g., ICJ, *Obligations of States in Respect of Climate Change,* Written Statement by the Center for International Environmental Law (CIEL), Memorandum on the Rights of Future Generations, 20 March 2024, Retrieved January 3, 2025, from https://climatecasechart.com/non-us-case/request-for-an-advisory-opinion-on-the-obligations-of-states-with-respect-to-climate-change/; ICJ, *Obligations of States in Respect of Climate Change,* Written Statement by Greenpeace International, 21 March 2024, Retrieved January 3, 2025, from https://climatecasechart.com/non-us-case/request-for-an-advisory-opinion-on-the-obligations-of-states-with-respect-to-climate-change/; ICJ, *Obligations of States in Respect of Climate Change,* Written Statement by World's Youth for Climate Justice, 22 March 2024, Retrieved January 3, 2025, from https://climatecasechart.com/non-us-case/request-for-an-advisory-opinion-on-the-obligations-of-states-with-respect-to-climate-change/

[608] Explicitly referring to *rights* of future generations, e.g., Cameroon (3 December 2024), Liechtenstein (6 December 2024), Samoa and Senegal (both 11 December 2024); addressing intergenerational equity or future generations in general, e.g., the Philippines (3 December 2024), Ecuador and Spain (both 4 December 2024), Mexico (9 December 2024) and Peru (10 December 2024); rejecting the idea of rights of future generations at all, e.g., Germany (2 December 2024), Russia (4 December 2024) and Thailand (12 December 2024). For the exact oral statements, see *Climate Change Obligations* (Verbatim Records), *supra* note 605. and for respective summaries, see World's Youth for Climate Justice (2024), pp. 11, 25, 26, 41, 43, 67, 74, 89, 100–101, 113.

[609] Schnakenberg et al. (2022), p. 27.

[610] *Climate Change Obligations* (UNGA Request for Advisory Opinion), *supra* note 602.

The ICJ could again come close to its alleged role as a "trustee of those [intergenerational] rights".[613] It would be asked to interpret and apply the law not only with regard to current generations, but also to the effects on future generations. Despite the rephrased questions, the Court would not be prevented from also inferring an explicit protection of the rights of future generations.[614] Resort to an advisory opinion of the ICJ would then constitute a "means of promoting the common interest of human kind".[615]

However, this perspective on international courts and tribunals—particularly the ICJ—as guardians of the interests of future generations, let alone their representatives, is overall rather unusual.[616] Therefore, it is uncertain whether the ICJ would embrace this role at all.[617] Consequently, most conceptions of representation of future generations focus on the role of other actors rather than that of the courts themselves.

##### 5.3.3.2.2 States as Representatives of Future Generations

On the inter-State level of international adjudication, States would traditionally be the primary actors to exercise any representative function,[618] as they are the main subjects of public international law.[619] In this role, they have access to international adjudication in contentious cases, such as before the ICJ and the ITLOS.[620] Beside the ICJ and the ITLOS, any arbitral tribunal or court, the World Trade Organization ('WTO') dispute settlement bodies as well as regional human rights courts could constitute possible fora for intergenerational inter-State dispute settlement.[621] In detail, the possibility to invoke another State's responsibility for the violation of an international environmental law obligation before an international court depends

---

[611] See Schnakenberg et al. (2022), pp. 27, 47.

[612] *Climate Change Obligations* (Written Statement by the Center for International Environmental Law (CIEL), Memorandum on the Rights of Future Generations), *supra* note 607; World's Youth for Climate Justice (2024), pp. 100–101.

[613] *Nuclear Tests 1995* (Dissenting Opinion of Judge Weeramantry), *supra* note 295, p. 341.

[614] Tigre and Carrillo Bañuelos (2023).

[615] Boisson de Chazournes (2002), p. 107.

[616] For another interesting approach to conceive even national courts as "planetary stewards" in the context of climate litigation, see Kotzé (2021), pp. 1442–1443.

[617] Lawrence and Köhler (2017), pp. 655–656.

[618] Brown Weiss (1984a), pp. 273, 278; Brown Weiss (2010), p. 111.

[619] Crawford and Brownlie (2019), pp. 105–106.

[620] See *Statute of the International Court of Justice* (ICJ Statute), adopted 26 June 1945, entered into force 24 October 1945, 1 UNTS XVI, Art. 34(1); *United Nations Convention on the Law of the Sea* (UNCLOS), adopted 10 December 1982, entered into force 16 November 1994, 1833 UNTS 3, Art. 291.

[621] For an overview, see Verheyen and Zengerling (2016), pp. 421–438.

on various procedural questions, above all the issue of jurisdiction.[622] Before the ICJ, there are several procedural obstacles that could impede a contentious proceeding on environmental matters, such as the unlikeliness to agree on a special agreement or *compromis* in a specific environmental dispute (Article 36(1) of the ICJ Statute), the non-existence of applicable compromissory clauses (Article 36(1) of the ICJ Statute), of reciprocal optional clause declarations (Article 36(2), (3) of the ICJ Statute), or the use of extensive reservations *rationae materiae* to these declarations.[623] The following analysis does not further address these and other procedural obstacles, but it focuses on the question of legal representation of future generations by States in such disputes—provided that an international court has jurisdiction to decide on the matter.

As States remain the primary duty-bearers of intergenerational obligations, they definitely constitute appropriate respondents in international disputes. Beyond this, States could also assume the role as representatives for future generations or their interests as applicants in an inter-State judicial dispute. The following analysis examines whether States have already brought forward claims on behalf of future generations, and it assesses the potential circumstances for such a claim. In this context, not all of the aforementioned international jurisprudence with intergenerational aspects entails claims brought forward on behalf of future generations. Instead, it is a question of legal standing (i.e., the legal right to bring a claim) whether States are capable under current international law to invoke not only the violation of their proper rights but also those of future generations.[624] Generally, international law provides not only the possibility for States to invoke their own rights before an international court, but also to initiate proceedings on behalf of their nationals.[625] This invocation of third person rights within the regime of diplomatic protection constitutes a form of *parens patriae* standing in place of the State's own citizens;[626] it is an accepted notion in international dispute settlement.[627] In the context of intergenerational equity, *Edith Brown Weiss* and other commentators argued that States should also have standing to represent the interests of their future

---

[622] See Klein (2021), pp. 1042–1044; Schmalenbach (2022a), pp. 391–393, 398–400.

[623] In detail, see Wewerinke-Singh et al. (2021), pp. 398–402; Schmalenbach (2022a), pp. 398–400. In the context of environmental disputes, the "Connally reservation" as well as the "Vandenberg reservation" can often lead to a factual exclusion of the court's jurisdiction *rationae materiae*, see Schmalenbach (2022a), pp. 399–400.

[624] Brown Weiss (2010), p. 111; Lawrence (2012), p. 35.

[625] Crawford and Brownlie (2019), pp. 675–676; Kau (2024), p. 286.

[626] Breuer (2017), p. 324. See also Kau (2024), p. 286 (at footnote 381).

[627] See, e.g., ICJ, *Case concerning Military and Paramilitary Activities in and against Nicaragua (Nicaragua v. United States of America),* Judgment (Merits), 27 June 1986, ICJ Reports 1986, 14, p. 19; ICJ, *Application of the Convention on the Prevention and Punishment of the Crime of Genocide (Bosnia and Herzegovina v. Serbia and Montenegro),* Provisional Measures, Order, 8 April 1993, ICJ Reports 1993, 3, p. 7; ICJ, *Application of the International Convention on the Elimination of All Forms of Racial Discrimination (Georgia v. Russian Federation),* Preliminary Objections, Judgment, 1 April 2011, ICJ Reports 2011, 70, para. 16. On examples for non-nationals, see Gattini (2019), paras. 16, 19, 22.

nationals.[628] This would result from the conception of States as continuing entities, that means an intertemporal composite of their proper nationals in the past, the present and the future.[629] So far, only two cases indicated such an understanding of *parens patriae* standing for future nationals—at least they have been understood accordingly. Australia and New Zealand referred to the rights of "its people" in the *Nuclear Test* cases in order to point out France's violations of international law.[630] *Judge Weeramantry* interpreted:

> New Zealand's complaint that its rights are affected does not relate only to the rights of people presently in existence. The rights of the people of New Zealand include the rights of unborn posterity. Those are rights that a nation is entitled, and indeed obliged, to protect.[631]

More recently, *Lawrence* and *Köhler* suggested the example of "a Pacific island State [bringing] an action against a major greenhouse gas emitter State, in which the island State purported to bring the claim on behalf of the State's future generations, in addition to its existing citizens."[632] Such an initiative by Small Island Developing States ('SIDS') in inter-State litigation would fit the increasingly active role of SIDS in demanding more effective climate protection measures.[633] However, the introduction of such a contentious claim by SIDS seems currently unlikely as an alliance of Pacific island States has initiated advisory proceedings instead.[634]

Beyond this case of representation of future nationals, the assessment is much more complicated if a State attempted to represent *all* future generations in judicial proceedings. The first possible concept that comes to mind would be the possibility of *actio popularis* proceedings before an international court or tribunal, in which one State would "take legal action in vindication of a public interest".[635] The issue of *actio popularis* cannot be answered abstractly for general international law, since it depends on the respective judicial body.[636] While the ITLOS dispute resolution

---

[628] Brown Weiss (2010), p. 111. See also *Nuclear Tests 1995* (Dissenting Opinion of Judge Weeramantry), *supra* note 295, p. 341; Brown Weiss (1984a), p. 273; Lawrence and Köhler (2017), p. 655.

[629] Brown Weiss (1984a), p. 278.

[630] ICJ, *Request for the Indication of Interim Measures of Protection, Nuclear Tests Case (Australia v. France),* Request submitted by the Government of Australia, 9 May 1973, Retrieved January 3, 2025, from https://www.icj-cij.org/public/files/case-related/58/10725.pdf, p. 44. See also ICJ, *Request for the Indication of Interim Measures of Protection, Nuclear Tests Case (New Zealand v. France),* Order, 22 June 1973, ICJ Reports 1973,135, para. 23.

[631] *Nuclear Tests 1995* (Dissenting Opinion of Judge Weeramantry), *supra* note 295, p. 341. See also Brown Weiss (1984a), pp. 273–274.

[632] Lawrence and Köhler (2017), p. 655.

[633] See, e.g., Ronneberg (2016). On the role of climate change for SIDS, see, e.g., UNFCCC Secretariat (2005).

[634] See *supra* notes 584–593. On the level of individual complaints proceedings, see, however, *infra* notes 797–802, 806–808.

[635] *South West Africa, Second Phase* (Judgment), *supra* note 547, para. 88. See also Gattini (2019).

system theoretically offers possibilities of *actio popularis* claims,[637] the ICJ had explicitly rejected this possibility in its *South West Africa* case.[638] However, this restrictive procedural approach to ICJ jurisdiction has changed with the *Barcelona Traction* case and the subsequent development of the notion of *erga omnes* obligations.[639] In the latter decision, the ICJ made a distinction:

> between the obligations of a State towards the international community as a whole, and those arising vis-à-vis another State in the field of diplomatic protection. By their very nature the former are the concern of all States. In view of the importance of the rights involved, all States can be held to have a legal interest in their protection; they are obligations *erga omnes*.[640]

This notion of obligations *erga omnes* has later been codified in the ILC Articles on State Responsibility. While the general rule only grants *injured* States the right to invoke the responsibility of another State for an internationally wrongful act,[641] Article 48 of the ARSIWA introduced two possibilities of non-injured States to invoke the responsibility of another State:

> [...] if (a) the obligation breached is owed to a group of States including that State, and is established for the protection of a collective interest of the group; or (b) the obligation breached is owed to the international community as a whole.[642]

Article 48(1)(b) of the ARSIWA directly aimed at the implementation of the *Barcelona Traction* case law and was considered by the ILC to introduce a form of *actio popularis* in international law.[643] However, two questions must be answered in order to determine whether this concept of obligations *erga omnes* can pave the way for a representation of future generations by States. First, it is still controversial whether Article 48 of the ARSIWA actually was meant to introduce legal standing in every constellation of obligations *erga omnes*. Second, intergenerational equity would have to contain such obligations "owed to the international community as a whole".[644]

As to the first question, Article 48 of the ARSIWA only refers to the invocation of the responsibility of another State in certain circumstances—it does not explicitly envisage legal standing before an international court or tribunal.[645] The ICJ has so far been reluctant to grant legal standing for the invocation of obligations *erga omnes*

---

636 Gattini (2019), para. 69.

637 Ibid., paras. 23–26.

638 *South West Africa, Second Phase* (Judgment), *supra* note 547, para. 88. See also Brown Weiss (1984a), 278 (at footnote 88); Gattini (2019).

639 ICJ, *Barcelona Traction, Light and Power Company, Limited (Belgium v. Spain), Second Phase*, Judgment, 5 February 1970, ICJ Reports 1970, 3, para. 33. Generally, see Kammerhofer (2024).

640 *Barcelona Traction* (Judgment), *supra* note 639, para. 33.

641 Art. 42 of the ARSIWA.

642 Art. 48(1) of the ARSIWA.

643 ILC (1997), Art. 19 para. 10; ILC (2001b), p. 127, Art. 48 para. 8; Gattini (2019), paras. 6–7.

644 *Barcelona Traction* (Judgment), *supra* note 639, para. 33.

in general.[646] Instead, it accepted legal standing of a non-injured State in three instances,[647] in which it identified obligations *erga omnes partes*, meaning obligations of a specific treaty regime owed to all State parties of that treaty.[648] Similarly, the ITLOS stated in an advisory opinion that "[e]ach State Party may also be entitled to claim compensation in light of the *erga omnes* character of the obligations relating to preservation of the environment of the high seas and in the Area."[649] While these obligations *erga omnes partes* mirror the idea of Article 48(1)(a) of the ARSIWA,[650] the broader *erga omnes* obligations owed to the whole international community, as enshrined in Article 48(1)(b) of the ARSIWA, have not been the basis for legal standing before the ICJ so far.[651] For this reason, the invocation of State responsibility within the realm of international environmental law has also been rare as many environmental obligations protect global goods rather than only rights of individual States.[652]

Some commentators have criticised this reluctance and supported the understanding that Article 48(1)(b) grants an entitlement to invoke claims before judicial bodies.[653] In 2005, the IDI adopted a resolution on obligations *erga omnes*, in which it explicitly codified that—provided there is a sufficient jurisdictional link—a State to which an obligation *erga omnes* is owed "has standing to bring a claim to the [ICJ] or other international judicial institution in relation to a dispute concerning

---

[645] See, e.g., Hernández (2013); von Arnauld (2019), p. 126. In Article 48(2) of the ARSIWA, several claims the non-injured State can raise are listed, such as cessation and assurances of non-repetition.

[646] See Hernández (2013), pp. 47–49. Cf. ICJ, *East Timor (Portugal v. Australia),* Judgment, 30 June 1995, ICJ Reports 1995, 90, para. 29; Kammerhofer (2024), para. 10.

[647] ICJ, *Questions relating to the Obligation to Prosecute or Extradite (Belgium v. Senegal),* Judgment, 20 July 2012, ICJ Reports 2012, 422, paras. 66–70; ICJ, *Application of the Convention on the Prevention and Punishment of the Crime of Genocide (The Gambia v. Myanmar),* Preliminary Objections, Judgment, 22 July 2022, ICJ Reports 2022, 477, paras. 107–113. Implicitly, see also ICJ, *Whaling in the Antarctic (Australia v. Japan: New Zealand intervening),* Judgment, 31 March 2014, ICJ Reports 2014, 226, para. 56. See also Gattini (2019), paras. 20, 22 and *infra* notes 681–684.

[648] See *Obligation to Prosecute or Extradite* (Judgment), *supra* note 647, para. 68.

[649] *Activities in the Area* (Advisory Opinion), *supra* note 41, para. 180. See also Tanaka (2018), pp. 551–552.

[650] ILC (2001b), p. 126, Art. 48 para. 6; Gattini (2019), para. 6.

[651] Another important proceeding, in which obligations *erga omnes (partes)* have been invoked, was initiated in 2014 by the Marshall Islands against the United Kingdom: ICJ, *Obligations concerning Negotiations Relating to Cessation of the Nuclear Arms Race and to Nuclear Disarmament (Marshall Islands v. United Kingdom),* Preliminary Objections, Judgment, 5 October 2016, ICJ Reports 2016, 833. The ICJ rejected the claim during the preliminary objections phase due to the lack of a dispute between the parties, without considering the Marshall Island's standing based on obligations *erga omnes*, see Tanaka (2018), pp. 540–542.

[652] Beyerlin and Grote Stoutenburg (2013), para. 87. Generally on the particularities of enforcement in international environmental law, see ibid., para. 86.

[653] See Hernández (2013), pp. 57–58; von Arnauld (2019), pp. 126–127, 209, 244. For related suggestions, cf. also Gattini (2019), para. 22.

compliance with that obligation".[654] It remains to be seen if the Court will follow these suggestions in the future. If it maintains its restrictive approach to obligations *erga omnes*, the only justiciable option for States to represent the interests of future generations would be within a specific treaty regime, which incorporates intergenerational obligations. Most importantly, this could happen on the basis of the current climate protection regime, as intergenerational equity is enshrined both in the UNFCCC and in the Paris Agreement.[655] Yet, other international treaties could equally offer the basis for intergenerational obligations *erga omnes partes*.[656] On a customary basis and vis-à-vis the international community as a whole, it would not be possible according to current ICJ jurisprudence.

This leads to the second open question mentioned above—whether intergenerational equity contains such obligations *erga omnes* or *erga omnes partes* at all. Such obligations are collective in nature;[657] thus, they do not only protect the bilaterally owed interests of specific actors, but of the international community as a whole.[658] There is a certain interrelation between obligations *erga omnes* and the notion of peremptory norms of international law, *ius cogens*,[659] although they entail different legal consequences.[660] In its *Barcelona Traction* case, the ICJ identified a first list of acts from which obligations *erga omnes* derive: "from the outlawing of acts of aggression, and of genocide, as also from the principles and rules concerning the basic rights of the human person, including protection from slavery and racial discrimination."[661] Later, it added the right to self-determination and certain obligations of international humanitarian law as well as the prohibition of torture to the list.[662] The ILC explicitly stressed that the existing norms with *erga omnes* character

[654] IDI (2005), Art. 3.

[655] Art. 3(1) of the UNFCCC; *Paris Agreement* (Paris Agreement), adopted 12 December 2015, entered into force 4 November 2016, UN Doc. FCCC/CP/2015/L.9/Rev.1. See Boer (2021), p. 24; Cordonier Segger (2021b), pp. 740–741. Cf. also Savaresi (2021a), pp. 370–373.

[656] See, e.g., Art. 2(5)(c) of the UNECE Water Convention. In more detail, see *supra* in Sect. 4.2.1.

[657] ILC (2001b), p. 127, Art. 48 para. 10.

[658] *Barcelona Traction* (Judgment), *supra* note 639, para. 33.

[659] A peremptory norm of international law is "a norm accepted and recognized by the international community of States as a whole as a norm, from which no derogation is permitted and which can be modified only by a subsequent norm of general international law having the same character", see *Vienna Convention on the Law of Treaties* (VCLT), adopted 23 May 1969, entered into force 27 January 1980, 1155 UNTS 331, Art. 53.

[660] Beyerlin and Marauhn (2011), pp. 287–288; Kammerhofer (2024), paras. 17–21.

[661] *Barcelona Traction* (Judgment), *supra* note 639, para. 34.

are not exhaustive, but that "the scope of the concept will necessarily evolve over time".[663]

For this reason, it was often discussed whether and which norms of international environmental law could constitute obligations *erga omnes* or become peremptory norms of international law.[664] Since most norms of international environmental law aim at the protection of global environmental goods, their fulfilment is typically in the interest of the whole international community.[665] Originally, the ILC had envisaged to introduce the notion of international crimes in its Draft Articles on State Responsibility, as opposed to international delicts; this classification was mainly inspired by the recognition of peremptory norms of international law.[666] These international crimes would have included "a serious breach of an international obligation of essential importance for the safeguarding and preservation of the human environment".[667] Since this classification was not maintained in the final Draft Articles on State Responsibility in 2001, it must be doubted that environmental norms were considered *ius cogens* norms at that time.[668]

However, voices in favour of accepting international environmental law norms as *ius cogens* norms, or as obligations *erga omnes* respectively, increased in the last two decades.[669] They mainly referred to those norms of international environmental law that protect the global commons beyond national jurisdiction.[670] A strong argument lies in the concept of common concern of humankind, which has become part of international environmental law in the last decades.[671] Many environmental treaties and other documents referred to humankind or its common concern and interests.[672] The conception of the environment or certain environmental goods as

---

[662] *East Timor* (Judgment), *supra* note 646, para. 29; *Wall in Palestine* (Advisory Opinion), *supra* note 559, paras. 155–157 with reference to *Nuclear Weapons* (Advisory Opinion), *supra* note 30, para. 79. See also *Obligation to Prosecute or Extradite* (Judgment), *supra* note 647, para. 68. On the right to self-determination of the Palestinian people, see recently ICJ, *Legal Consequences Arising from the Policies and Practices of Israel in the Occupied Palestinian Territory, Including East Jerusalem,* Advisory Opinion, 19 July 2024, Retrieved January 3, 2025, from https://www.icj-cij.org/case/186/advisory-opinions, paras. 232, 274.

[663] ILC (2001b), p. 127, Art. 48 para. 9.

[664] See, e.g., Kornicker Uhlmann (1998); Brown Weiss (2002), pp. 804–805; Beyerlin and Grote Stoutenburg (2013), para. 87.

[665] See Bilder (1982), p. 198; Redgwell (1999), pp. 125–126; Lenzerini (2002), p. 65; Beyerlin and Marauhn (2011), p. 288.

[666] ILC (1997), Art. 19 paras. 15–16; Beyerlin and Marauhn (2011), p. 287.

[667] ILC (1997), Art. 19(3)(d).

[668] Beyerlin and Marauhn (2011), p. 287.

[669] See, e.g., Biermann (1996), p. 451; Shelton (2009), pp. 83, 86); Brown Weiss (2010), p. 111; Francioni (2012), pp. 455–458; Mégret (2013), pp. 63–64. See already Brown Weiss (1989), pp. 121–122.

[670] Cf. Ohlhoff (2003), p. 160. With regard to the protection of the marine environment, see, e.g., ILC (2001b), p. 127, Art. 48 para. 10. With regard to the no-harm rule, see Kornicker Uhlmann (1998), pp. 123–124.

[671] In detail, see *supra* in Sect. 2.3.3.

the common concern of humankind supports the idea of obligations that are owed to the international community as a whole.[673] For instance, *Francesco Francioni* suggested the "conceptualization and the legal treatment of the natural environment as a 'public good' to be administered in the interest of all and of the generations to come".[674] Furthermore, the common concern idea can also be applied to the concept of intergenerational equity in particular. As illustrated in detail in Chap. 2, the concept of common concern of humankind has significant intergenerational elements,[675] and it is related to intergenerational equity, which contains obligations towards future generations of humankind.[676] One can consistently conclude that the planetary obligations of intergenerational equity constitute obligations *erga omnes* that are owed to the international community as a whole, including future generations of humankind.[677] Interestingly, Article 48(1)(b) of the ARSIWA explicitly leaves out the words "of States" with regard to the "international community as a whole".[678] This understanding of the international community thus is broader than the "international community of States" used in other contexts.[679] It can include other potential subjects of international law, for instance future generations.[680]

Some of the more recent jurisprudence could be interpreted to favour an extension of *erga omnes* effects to certain environmental obligations. In 2014, the ICJ had to decide on the lawfulness of Japan's whaling programme under the Whaling Convention of 1946, which permitted the killing of whales for purposes of scientific research.[681] Australia had invoked Japan's responsibility although it was not injured itself by Japan's programme; it relied on the common legal interest of the international community.[682] Japan did not contest Australia's standing and the ICJ did not explicitly address the issue of *ius standi* in its decision. However, the Court implicitly accepted that Australia was entitled to invoke Japan's obligations *erga omnes partes*.[683] As the ICJ stated, these obligations must be interpreted in light of the convention's Preamble, which recognised "the interest of the nations of the world in

672 See, e.g., Cançado Trindade (2020), p. 339 with further references.

673 See Brunnée (2005), p. 25; Shelton (2009), p. 86; Boyle and Harrison (2013), pp. 258–259. With regard to climate protection, see, e.g., Fitzmaurice (2010), pp. 1020–1021; Soltau (2016). Cf. also Wewerinke-Singh et al. (2021), pp. 396–397.

674 Francioni (2012), p. 455.

675 Proelß and Haake (2017), p. 191.

676 Brunnée (2010), p. 566; Brown Weiss (2021a), para. 19; Cançado Trindade (2020), p. 339.

677 See *supra* note 669.

678 ILC (2001b), p. 84, Art. 25 para. 18.

679 See Art. 53 of the VCLT.

680 Brown Weiss (2002), p. 804. Cf. also Nagy (1988), p. 321.

681 *International Convention for the Regulation of Whaling* (Whaling Convention), adopted 2 December 1946, entered into force 10 November 1948, 161 UNTS 72, Art. VIII(1).

682 See Tanaka (2018), pp. 535–538; Meguro (2020), p. 937 with further references.

683 See Boyle and Harrison (2013), p. 260; Schmalenbach (2017a), p. 279; Meguro (2020), p. 937; Klein (2021), p. 1045.

safeguarding for future generations the great natural resources represented by the whale stocks".[684]

Although the decision has been rendered with respect to a specific treaty regime, the intergenerational component of the relevant treaty obligation is obvious.[685] From a substantive perspective, it is thus not clear why the obligations to preserve the natural resources of the planet for the benefit of future generations, as enshrined in the concept of intergenerational equity, should not equally be considered obligations *erga omnes*, even if they result from customary international law instead of treaty law.[686] A consistent application of this jurisprudence to other environmental obligations, often linked to intergenerational concerns, could thus lead to an upgrading and shaping of the notion of obligations *erga omnes*; it might offer certain opportunities in international environmental law.[687] For instance, *Judge Dugard* elaborated in a dissenting opinion in 2018 that "[t]he obligation not to engage in wrongful deforestation that results in the release of carbon into the atmosphere and the loss of gas sequestration services is certainly an obligation *erga omnes*."[688] As illustrated above, intergenerational equity would constitute another fitting example of obligations owed to the international community as a whole. In this case, a non-injured State could invoke the violation of intergenerational obligations pursuant to Article 48(1)(b) of the ARSIWA and would thereby act as a representative of future generations[689]—provided the ICJ will accept, in the future, obligations *erga omnes* as a basis for legal standing regardless of a specific treaty regime.[690]

In a more recent decision in *La Oroya v. Peru* from November 2023, the IACHR suggested to treat obligations of environmental protection as *ius cogens* norms:

> It is difficult to imagine international obligations of greater significance than those that protect the environment against unlawful or arbitrary conduct that causes serious, extensive, long-lasting and irreversible damage to the environment in a scenario of climate crisis that threatens the survival of species. In view of the above, international protection of the environment requires progressive recognition of the prohibition of this type of conduct as a peremptory norm (ius cogens) that gains the recognition of the international community as a whole as a norm from which no derogation is permitted. [...] In this sense, guaranteeing the interest of both present and future generations and the preservation of the environment against its radical degradation is fundamental for the survival of humanity.[691]

---

[684] See *Whaling in the Antarctic* (Judgment), *supra* note 647, para. 56.

[685] On intergenerational equity in the Whaling Convention, see already *supra* in Sect. 2.1.1.

[686] Cf. Schmalenbach (2017a), p. 279.

[687] Meguro (2020), pp. 937–938.

[688] ICJ, *Certain Activities Carried Out by Nicaragua in the Border Area (Costa Rica v. Nicaragua), Compensation,* Dissenting Opinion of Judge Ad Hoc Dugard, 2 February 2018, ICJ Reports 2018, 119, para. 35. See also Bendel (2019); Klein (2021), pp. 1051–1052.

[689] Brown Weiss (1984a), pp. 274–278; Brown Weiss (2010), p. 111. In general, see Beyerlin and Marauhn (2011), p. 363.

[690] See *supra* notes 647–648.

[691] IACHR, *Inhabitants of La Oroya v. Peru (Preliminary Objections, Merits, Reparations and Costs),* Judgment, 27 November 2023, OEA Series C No. 511, para. 129. (unofficial translation by climaterightsdatabase.com). For an overview, see Climate Rights Litigation Database (2021-2023).

Although this decision does not refer to *erga omnes (partes)* obligations, the reasoning for the suggested recognition as *ius cogens* norm might also be transferred to an argument for representation of (intergenerational) environmental rights by all State parties to a respective human rights treaty.

However, this path is not predetermined yet, as some developments rather indicate the contrary. In 2019, the ILC Special Rapporteur on peremptory norms of general international law concluded with respect to *ius cogens* that norms of international environmental law have not reached the status of *ius cogens* yet, or obligations *erga omnes* respectively, despite their importance for the international community.[692] Similarly, the 2021 ILC Draft Guidelines on the Protection of the Atmosphere acknowledged in its Preamble that the atmosphere was "essential for sustaining life on Earth, human health and welfare, and aquatic and terrestrial ecosystems", but explicitly rejected that the concept of common concern of humankind with regard to the atmosphere would entail any obligations *erga omnes* in the context of the guidelines.[693] This illustrates that it apparently does not suffice that a protected good constitutes a common concern of the international community, if it is not established on a case-by-case basis that this concern actually triggers a legal interest of any non-injured State to invoke this interest.[694] Other commentators have raised comparable objections; for instance, they pointed to the lack of acceptance of environmental obligations *erga omnes*.[695] Others generally questioned the adequacy of mechanisms of State responsibility and contentious litigation for the resolution of environmental disputes over common goods.[696]

So far, the *Whaling in the Antarctic* case remained the only case, in which *erga omnes* obligations played a role in environmental matters. The aforementioned *Nuclear Test* cases have remained the only instances, in which the applicants invoked violations of future individuals—but only of their future nationals.[697] At this stage, it seems unlikely that international courts and tribunals, particularly the ICJ, will overcome their procedural limits with regard to non-injured States that claim to represent the international community regarding environmental obligations *erga omnes*.[698] In international environmental law, States have a preference for international negotiation or at least alternative and treaty-specific non-compliance procedures instead of choosing the more confrontative means of international

[692] ILC (2019), para. 136.

[693] ILC (2021), pp. 15–16, Preamble para. 3.

[694] Cf. Beyerlin and Marauhn (2011), p. 363.

[695] Brunnée (2005), p. 32; Brunnée (2018), p. 174. Cf. also Meguro (2020), pp. 945–948.

[696] Simma (1989), pp. 299, 314; Redgwell (1999), p. 126 (at footnote 50); Fitzmaurice (2008), p. 228; Sands (2016), p. 28. See also Tanaka (2018), p. 543. Arguing against the inadequacy argument, see Brown Weiss (2002), p. 805.

[697] See *supra* notes 630–631.

[698] Concerning climate litigation, see Meguro (2020).

litigation.[699] All in all, despite some advantages of contentious litigation,[700] representation of future generations by an individual State in a judicial contentious proceeding is rather improbable in the near future. The currently suggested advisory proceedings might be more successful at this point.

##### 5.3.3.2.3 *Amicus Curiae* Representation of Future Generations

Apart from international courts and tribunals themselves and States as primary actors, non-State actors could play a representative role for future generations in inter-State judicial proceedings.[701] Although non-State actors have no access to these courts and tribunals as parties themselves,[702] they could play a role as intervening parties under certain circumstances illustrated below. Contrary to representation by States, this approach would not include the complicated procedural limits in contentious litigation regarding legal standing and *erga omnes* obligations. At the same time, representation by non-State actors would not be limited to contentious litigation but could equally play a role in advisory proceedings.[703]

The involvement of *amicus curiae* briefs in the proceedings before international courts and tribunals could allow for representation by non-State actors, such as international organisations or non-governmental organisations.[704] Traditionally, *amici curiae* (i.e., friends of the court) are neutral bystanders who do not have an own interest in a specific case but who bring to the attention of the court matters of fact and law in areas of their knowledge and on their own initiative.[705] This kind of *amicus curiae* participation in proceedings thus differs from third-party intervention by other (interested) States.[706] *Amici curiae* can also be appointed by the court to "present legal arguments which are otherwise unaddressed or unrepresented by the parties"[707]—a perfectly fitting description for a potential representative of unborn future generations. At the same time, future generations would not be represented by one of the involved parties in a dispute; this could be considered an advantage for

[699] Boyle and Harrison (2013), pp. 261–262; Schmalenbach (2022a), p. 383. See also Okowa (2010), p. 317; Lawrence and Köhler (2017), p. 656.

[700] See Nedeski et al. (2020).

[701] On the role of non-State actors in individual complaints procedures, see *infra* in Sect. 5.3.3.3.1.

[702] Art. 34(1) of the VCLT.

[703] Generally, see Zengerling (2013), pp. 174–179.

[704] Brown Weiss (2010), p. 112; Lawrence and Köhler (2017), pp. 661–664; Niehaus (2023), pp. 310–314.

[705] Krislov (1963), p. 694. Generally on the role of *amici curiae*, see Chinkin and MacKenzie (2002), pp. 136–139.

[706] Sands and MacKenzie (2008), para. 2.

[707] Chinkin and MacKenzie (2002), p. 136.

their effective representation because courts might receive these neutral interventions more readily.[708]

While some national law systems regularly include the possibilities of *amicus curiae* briefs,[709] the situation before international courts and tribunals depends on the respective procedural rules.[710] The procedural rules of the ICJ do not explicitly refer to the option of *amicus curiae* briefs, but certain provisions could provide for a legal basis for such non-State participation. With regard to contentious proceedings, Article 34(2) of the ICJ Statute allows for the request of information by public international organisations.[711] With regard to advisory proceedings, Article 66(2) of the ICJ Statute contains a similar provision referring to international organisations.[712] Further, apart from taking into consideration information furnished by *amicus* submissions, the Court can also entrust any organisation to carry out an inquiry or to give an expert opinion according to Article 50 of the ICJ Statute.[713] Although the ICJ has these procedural tools to include *amicus curiae* briefs in its proceedings,[714] it has only done so with regard to the submissions of governmental international organisations.[715] While submissions by governmental international organisations have been very limited in contentious cases,[716] more examples exist in advisory proceedings.[717]

Neither the wording of Article 34(2) of the ICJ Statute nor of Articles 66(2) and 50 of the ICJ Statute excludes non-governmental organisations from offering *amicus curiae* briefs.[718] However, the Rules of Court of the ICJ limit the Court's possibilities to request *amicus curiae* briefs in contentious proceedings to governmental international organisations alone.[719] Further, the Court issued Practice Directions in 2004 that stipulated that information submitted by NGOs in advisory proceedings does not become part of the case record, but will be "placed in a designated location in the Peace Palace" and can be "referred to by States and intergovernmental organizations" in their written and oral statements.[720] This was in line with the

[708] See Duffy (2018), p. 262.

[709] See, e.g., Shelton (1994), pp. 616–619.

[710] Varella (2013), pp. 43–53; Sands and MacKenzie (2008), paras. 3–28.

[711] See also *Rules of Court of the International Court of Justice* (Rules of Court), adopted 14 April 1978, entered into force 1 July 1978.

[712] Sands and MacKenzie (2008), paras. 6–10. On a recent decision of the ICJ to authorise the IUCN in an advisory proceeding, see Garrido Alvez (2023).

[713] On the ICJ's reluctant use of this possibility in science-related cases, see ICJ, *Pulp Mills on the River Uruguay (Argentina v. Uruguay),* Joint Dissenting Opinion of Judges Al-Khasawneh and Simma, 20 April 2010, ICJ Reports 2010, 108, pp. 112–115; Mbengue (2018).

[714] Sands (2016), p. 33; Lawrence and Köhler (2017), p. 664. Cf. also Cassese (2012b), p. 249.

[715] Lawrence and Köhler (2017), pp. 662–663; Sands and MacKenzie (2008), para. 9.

[716] Chinkin and MacKenzie (2002), pp. 141–143.

[717] Ibid., pp. 143–145.

[718] Lawrence and Köhler (2017), p. 664; Sands and MacKenzie (2008), para. 8.

[719] Art. 69(4) of the Rules of Court.

[720] ICJ (last updated 2023, Direction XII).

foregoing practice of the ICJ, which excluded NGO submissions on several occasions.[721] Overall, the ICJ has been reluctant to involve NGOs in its proceedings so far.[722] The ITLOS took a similarly restrictive approach in its *Activities in the Area Advisory Opinion* from 2011 when it informed two requesting NGOs about the Registrar's decision to post their *amicus curiae* briefs on the ITLOS website without adding them to the case file.[723] Thus, the consideration of an *amicus curiae* brief before an international court or tribunal depends a lot on the respective body's discretion.[724]

Some commentators criticised this restrictive approach of international courts and tribunals.[725] For instance, *Antonio Cassese* suggested a more open inclusion of *amici curiae* in the proceedings of contentious as well as advisory jurisdiction—explicitly not only for governmental organisations but also for NGOs.[726] He offered three reasons for this proposition:

> First, the Court would in no way abdicate its function to rule on existing law, for ultimately it could ignore or disregard the *amici curiae* briefs. Secondly, allowing *amici curiae* briefs would mean opening up to the international society at large, heeding the exigencies in the field of law emanating from that society, and stimulating the interest of both international civil society and intergovernmental actors in making the rule of law prevail in international relations. Thirdly, the experience of other tribunals shows that resort to *amici curiae* may prove of momentous assistance to courts [...][727]

For the same reasons, *amicus curiae* participation would assist the judges in their duty to promote intergenerational justice by introducing the perspective and interests of future generations in international judicial proceedings.[728] If the courts and tribunals were to take a more progressive approach towards NGO participation, as suggested, *inter alia*, by *Cassese*,[729] certain standards for NGO representation would be necessary in order to ensure a transparent consideration of interests as well as

---

721 See Chinkin and MacKenzie (2002), pp. 140–141 (at footnote 18); Valencia-Ospina (2005), pp. 231–232; Sands and MacKenzie (2008), para. 8, all with references to ICJ, *Legal Consequences for States of the Continued Presence of South Africa in Namibia (South West Africa) notwithstanding Security Council Resolution 276 (1970),* Advisory Opinion, 21 June 1971, ICJ Reports 1971, 16; *Nuclear Weapons* (Advisory Opinion), *supra* note 30.

722 Shelton (1994), pp. 619–628; Chinkin and MacKenzie (2002), pp. 140–141 (at footnote 18).

723 *Activities in the Area* (Advisory Opinion), *supra* note 41, paras. 13–14. See also Sands (2016), p. 27.

724 Chinkin and MacKenzie (2002), p. 139; Sands and MacKenzie (2008), paras. 3–5.

725 See, e.g., Shelton (1994).

726 Cassese (2012b), pp. 243–244.

727 Ibid.

728 Lawrence and Köhler (2017), p. 664.

729 See also Sands (2016), p. 33; Lawrence and Köhler (2017), p. 664. With regard to international climate litigation, cf. also Wewerinke-Singh et al. (2021), pp. 409–410. Even more progressive towards a stronger introduction of individuals before the ICJ, see Salam (2019), pp. 216–217.

legitimate representation.[730] However, it could also be promising to primarily allow *amicus curiae* briefs from governmental international organisations, specific organs or at least mandate holders within intergovernmental organisations in order to represent the interests of future generations.[731] This would rather be in accordance with the aforementioned narrow approach of the ICJ towards *amicus curiae* intervention. At the same time, it could perfectly be combined with the existing proposals for a High Commissioner for Future Generations as far as the latter would be mandated with corresponding procedural powers.[732] Several UN Special Rapporteurs have used such *amicus curiae* briefs already to intervene in international, regional and national court proceedings with links to human rights and the environment, but not on the inter-State level so far.[733] In case of an increasing practice of such *amici curiae*, this mechanism could become an important tool for representing the unaddressed interests of absent right-holders or other affected groups.[734]

#### 5.3.3.2.4 Summary

Overall, representation of future generations on the inter-State level has remained fragmentary so far. Although intergenerational equity sometimes played a role in international jurisprudence, there is no uniform and institutionalised procedure how the interests of future generations can be represented before international courts and tribunals. While procedural rules differ from court to court, some general observations can be made. First, States as primary actors on the inter-State level could play a role invoking not only their proper interests vis-à-vis other States, but also invoking the rights or interests of future generations. This could either be possible for their own future nationals or even for the international community as a whole, including future generations, based on obligations *erga omnes*. While the former might be conceivable without much objections, the latter faces some procedural obstacles, such as the restrictive approach of the ICJ to the concept of obligations *erga omnes*.

---

[730] Brown Weiss (2010), p. 112; Lawrence and Köhler (2017), p. 664. Cf. also Chinkin and MacKenzie (2002), pp. 138, 161–162.

[731] Lawrence and Köhler (2017), pp. 661–662.

[732] Ibid., p. 662. On the proposals as well as the procedural powers, see already *supra* in Sect. 5.3.2.2, note 487.

[733] See, e.g., ECtHR, *Duarte Agostinho and others v. Portugal and 32 other States,* Amicus Brief by UN Special Rapporteur on human rights and the environment (David R. Boyd) and UN Special Rapporteur on toxics and human rights (Marcos A. Orellana), 4 May 2021, Retrieved January 3, 2025, from https://climatecasechart.com/non-us-case/youth-for-climate-justice-v-austria-et-al/; CRC, *Sacchi* et al. *v. Argentina* et al., Amicus curiae briefs by UN Special Rapporteurs on human rights and the environment (David R. Boyd and John H. Knox), 1 September 2021, Retrieved January 3, 2025, from https://climatecasechart.com/non-us-case/sacchi-et-al-v-argentina-et-al/. See also Ganesan (2022). For the individual claims procedures, see *infra* in Sect. 5.3.3.3.

[734] For a positive perspective on such *amicus curiae* interventions, see Ploton and Montes de Oca (2022).

Both paths have not been explicitly tested by States on behalf of future generations as of today.

Second, international courts and tribunals themselves have sometimes been considered guardians or trustees of public interests, including the interests of future generations. This conception could be more promising than the idea of States acting as representatives, although it is potentially a rather symbolic form of representation. Due to the lack of representation of future generations in policy-making, this role of courts would also be consistent with the notion of separation of powers on the international level. It is particularly fitting in the context of advisory proceedings as the court acts as principal interpreter of international law. The recent attempt to initiate an advisory opinion on climate change obligations constitutes an opportunity to test this form of representation on the inter-State level.

Finally, and connected to this advisory jurisdiction, third-party interventions by neutral non-State actors could also be an adequate form of representation for the interests of future generations. The acceptance of *amicus curiae* briefs in international court proceedings could be a way forward in this regard. Despite the narrow understanding of international courts and tribunals so far, their procedural rules would generally allow for *amicus curiae* interventions. Although the current practice of inter-State proceedings does not offer a consistent institutional framework for effective intergenerational representation, the existing legal regime is not entirely hostile in regard of several of the aforementioned procedural possibilities. These can thus be seen as starting points for future developments of intergenerational equity.

#### 5.3.3.3 Representation in Proceedings of Civil Society Actors Against States

Besides these inter-State judicial frameworks, individual complaints procedures could be another option for the implementation of intergenerational equity. In the following, individual complaints procedures refer to any judicial dispute settlement mechanism as well as quasi-judicial frameworks for individual complaints, in which individuals and other civil society actors are entitled to invoke the responsibility of a State for breaches of international law, regardless of whether it is an international, a regional or even a national (quasi-)judicial framework. As of today, no environmental court or other body allows for specifically invoking violations of international environmental law by individuals. Even less, no specific and explicit regime exists to invoke the violation of intergenerational equity on behalf of future generations. Therefore, the following analysis turns to the several levels of existing individual claims procedures before judicial and quasi-judicial bodies in order to assess their relevance for the implementation of intergenerational equity. These are mainly bodies in the context of international human rights law,[735] and include, for instance,

[735] On the relevance of human rights law for intergenerational equity, see *supra* in Sect. 5.2.2.

the HRC or the CRC as well as regional bodies like the ECtHR, the IACHR or the ACHPR.[736]

Beyond these traditional international and regional fora, individual complaints procedures within national judicial systems could equally play a decisive role with regard to the concept of intergenerational equity under international law.[737] National case law can constitute part of State practice for the determination of customary international law if the national jurisprudence contributes to the development of law or at least indirectly influences the behaviour and practice of other State organs.[738] Further, Article 38(1)(d) of the ICJ Statute is not limited to international judicial decisions as subsidiary means for the determination of international law, but national decisions can also have value for this determination of law.[739] As illustrated below, national case law also plays a decisive role for the judicial practice in the context of environmental litigation worldwide, since existing decisions influence courts from other States, so that there is a transnational judicial discourse, particularly with regard to climate change litigation.[740] As far as some of the examined decisions are not directly based on norms of international law, they still interact with international law in the form of judicial internalisation.[741]

Before turning to the existing case law, the first sub-section addresses some preliminary questions related to the relevant actors, the forms of representation and the importance of human rights and climate change adjudication (Sect. 5.3.3.3.1). Then, two sub-sections structure the diverse instances of intergenerational equity case law in order to give an overview of potential institutional representative frameworks. First, the few relevant proceedings before international and regional bodies are analysed (Sect. 5.3.3.3.2). The last sub-section turns to the much wider field of national litigation, in which claimants have explicitly or implicitly referred to the representation of future generations (Sect. 5.3.3.3.3).

#### 5.3.3.3.1 Preliminary Remarks

With respect to the claimants assessed in this section, "civil society" can be understood in a broad sense, as it is not a legal term of art.[742] While civil society actors are most often defined in contrast to governmental as well as business actors,[743] the

[736] Generally, see, e.g., Kau (2024), pp. 329–351. For an overview of human rights bodies and environmental protection, see also Stephens (2009), pp. 310–321.

[737] For a comprehensive analysis, see Slobodian (2020).

[738] Crawford and Brownlie (2019), p. 38; von Arnauld (2019), p. 108.

[739] Crawford and Brownlie (2019), pp. 38–39.

[740] See, e.g., Dellinger (2018); Paiement (2020); Peel and Markey-Towler (2021); Bertram (2023), p. 130.

[741] See Koh (1997), p. 2657. See also briefly *infra* in Sect. 7.3.4.2.2 [note 402].

[742] Staberock (2011), para. 4.

[743] Ibid., para. 5 Consequently, civil society actors do not include national public institutions or organs with procedural rights, which have already been briefly addressed *supra* in Sect. 5.3.2.1.

present analysis not only encompasses collectives but also individual complainants who raise proper complaints or support other individual complainants. Many of the analysed individual complaints procedures have been initiated by groups of individuals, often by children,[744] but NGOs certainly played and play an important role in past and current litigation.[745] This new role of NGOs in international law can generally be observed in the last decades.[746] On the one hand, they have an increasing influence on international agenda-setting and law-making,[747] particularly in international human rights as well as environmental law.[748] They participate in international negotiations, support international organisations and contribute to the implementation of international law.[749]

On the other hand, NGOs also have an influence on the judicial field as they increasingly participate in litigation against States.[750] Particularly in international environmental law, important documents, such as the Rio Declaration and the Agenda 21, underlined the importance of including civil society organisation in administrative and judicial proceedings.[751] While an analysis of the overall role of NGOs in environmental law judicial proceedings would exceed the scope of the present analysis, other commentators have addressed this issue in more detail.[752] However, their increasing impact as well as their independence from State sovereignty constitute an immense opportunity to strengthen the achievement of international community interests in the international legal system.[753] This could specifically qualify them to fill the vacant agency for future generations and their interests, so that some commentators have argued in favour of this representative role of NGOs.[754] Their main advantage is their higher degree of independence vis-à-vis States, which are likely to give priority to their current economic or political interests.[755] Similarly, a newly-created international entity might also be limited by

---

[744] On the particular role of children and youth in this regard, see *infra* notes 829, 833–838, 865–869.

[745] See, e.g., van Dijk (2011), p. 210; Niehaus (2023), p. 292.

[746] See, e.g., Charnovitz (2006); Staberock (2011), paras. 25–38.

[747] Albin (1999); Varella (2013), pp. 17–30; Staberock (2011), paras. 25–28. For an instructive analysis of the influence of civil society actors, see Niehaus and Davies (2021), pp. 231–236.

[748] Hobe (2019); Fuchs (2009); Bodansky (2019), pp. 17–18; Brown Weiss (2011), pp. 21–22. With regard to international environmental law, this important role of civil society actors was already underlined in the Agenda 21, see UNCED (1992b), Chap. 27.

[749] See Varella (2013), pp. 17–30. The role of "Northern NGOs" from industrialised States can also be seen critical, see Scholtz (2007).

[750] Varella (2013), pp. 31–62; Fuchs (2009), paras. 54–69; Verheyen and Pabsch (2021). With regard to proceedings against private corporations, see *infra* in Sect. 5.3.3.4.

[751] UNCED (1992a), Principle 10; UNCED (1992b), para. 8.18. See also Fuchs (2009), para. 63.

[752] See, e.g., Zengerling (2013); Niehaus (2023), pp. 291–310.

[753] See Sands (1998), pp. 89–90; Cassese (2012a), pp. 682–683.

[754] Rosenkranz (1986), pp. 113–114; Sands (1998), pp. 89–90; Mensah (2008), pp. 808–809; Gaillard (2011), paras. 641–655; Lawrence (2016); Pirjatanniemi (2016), pp. 18–22.

[755] Rosenkranz (1986), p. 97.

certain political or diplomatic restraints, as it will always be accountable to and financed by the States that have established it.[756] In contrast, civil society actors generally are not restrained by these interests.[757]

At the same time, there are also certain disadvantages and dangers in conferring a representative function to civil society actors. Representation by NGOs raises problems of legitimacy and accountability.[758] As long as there is no official and institutionalised procedure, anyone could claim to represent the interests of future generations.[759] However, as illustrated above,[760] the representative must (and can) not be chosen by the representee in the current context, so that a strict form of (democratic) legitimacy would not be necessary.[761] In order to resolve these conflicts, *Joshua Rosenkranz* suggested court-appointed representatives for future generations based on a set of predetermined criteria.[762] As long as their legitimacy to act as representatives is not mandatorily determined by international law, their role remains subject to the good-will of the respective judicial body to a certain degree.[763]

As far as civil society actors appear in individual complaints procedures, they primarily have two procedural possibilities to represent future generations (i.e., to act on their behalf in the proceedings).[764] First, they can initiate these proceedings themselves, invoking the violation of not only their proper rights or interests but also those of future generations. Second, they can attempt to assist the courts as *amici curiae*. With regard to their proper initiatives, as far as they are granted legal standing to speak also on behalf of future generations, this could amount to an explicit representation of these rights or interests.[765] In many cases of environmental protection before courts and tribunals, legal standing requires an individual interest or an injury suffered by the person or a member of the group who are suing.[766] For this reason, international and national judicial bodies have regularly rejected *actio*

---

[756] Stone (1998), p. 69; Sands (1998), pp. 89–90.

[757] Rosenkranz (1986), pp. 97, 112–113.

[758] Stone (1998), p. 71; Merrills (1998), pp. 32–33; Niehaus (2023), pp. 305–310.

[759] Beckerman (2006), p. 60. Cf. Spijkers (2020).

[760] See already *supra* in Sect. 5.3.1.

[761] Lawrence and Köhler (2017), p. 652. *Nelly Stromquist* even assumed that "it is not a question of representation but rather of expression that gives NGOs the legitimacy to voice the needs of the oppressed and marginalized", see Stromquist (1998), p. 63.

[762] Rosenkranz (1986), pp. 98–102. Cf. also Allen (1994), p. 739. See also *infra* note 774.

[763] With regard to the policy process, cf. Marquez (2016), pp. 468–469.

[764] Cf. Fuchs (2009), para. 54. Categorising into three different approaches to representation of future generations, see Slobodian (2020), p. 576.

[765] Hadjiargyrou (2016), pp. 265–266; Michallet (2018), p. 157.

[766] UNEP (2020), pp. 37–39. With regard to US law, see Bobertz (1987), pp. 172–176.

*popularis* claims brought on behalf of general interests such as the environment.[767] As *Thomas Mensah* described it:

> It is still the case that in most instances the courts will follow the traditional doctrine that requires complainants to demonstrate some interest that pertains to themselves, as opposed to the general community, before they can be accorded standing to bring suit. However, some other courts have been more flexible in this and are willing to recognize the *locus standi* of applicants who are able to show a 'substantial or genuine' interest in the matter in issue.[768]

Potential representatives of future generations have similarly to cope with these restrictive procedural hurdles,[769] as is illustrated below. At the same time, the understanding of "representation" in the present book does explicitly not depend on the existence of actual subjective rights of future generations, so that representation must be understood in a broader sense than "legal standing", which is often based on individual rights.[770]

With regard to the role of NGOs as *amici curiae*, they can raise matters of fact and law in the context of intergenerational equity that would otherwise remain unrepresented.[771] While this procedural possibility has already been assessed on the inter-State level,[772] many individual complaints procedures—internationally and nationally—are much more open to *amicus curiae* participation of NGOs than in inter-State proceedings.[773] This intervention as non-party to a dispute could also offer more leeway to the respective courts and institutions to accept these NGOs as actual representatives if they fulfil certain predetermined criteria.[774] Nonetheless, most of the following examples refer to the direct initiation of judicial proceedings by civil society actors.[775]

---

[767] For human rights law, see, e.g., HRC, *Brun v. France,* Decision, 23 November 2006, UN Doc. CCPR/C/88/D/1453/2006, para. 6.3. See also Court of First Instance of the European Communities, *Greenpeace and others v. Commission,* Order, 9 August 1995, European Case Law Identifier ECLI: EU:T:1995:147, paras. 59–65; Court of Justice of the European Union, *Greenpeace and others v. Commission,* Judgment, 2 April 1998, European Case Law Identifier ECLI:EU:C:1998:153, paras. 29–34; Albers (2018), pp. 131–132; Verheyen and Pabsch (2021), pp. 516–524; Kelleher (2021), pp. 144–145.

[768] Mensah (2008), p. 808.

[769] See Redgwell (1999), p. 98. On general barriers to representation of future generations, see also Allen (1994), pp. 729–733.

[770] See already *supra* in Sect. 5.3.1, notes 380–381. With regard to a recent German case, see *infra* note 1051.

[771] Generally, see Chinkin and MacKenzie (2002), pp. 136–139.

[772] See *supra* in Sect. 5.3.3.2.3.

[773] Shelton (1994), pp. 630–642; Chinkin and MacKenzie (2002), pp. 145–149; Sands and MacKenzie (2008), paras. 15–18; Ploton and Montes de Oca (2022). On a proposal for United States national courts, see Allen (1994), p. 739.

[774] See *supra* note 762.

[775] On some examples of *amicus curiae* briefs, see *infra* notes 849–850.

Due to the indivisible interconnection between human rights and the protection of the environment,[776] human rights adjudication is naturally still the predominant forum for environmental litigation on the international, regional and national level.[777] This connection is even more obvious with regard to intergenerational equity,[778] as far as rights of future generations are understood as an intertemporal extension of the current human rights regime to the future.[779] However, not all analysed intergenerational cases are based on traditional human rights constellations.[780] Further, another development has reinforced the recourse to environmental litigation, also in the interest of future generations: climate litigation.[781] The UNEP defined climate change litigation "to include cases that raise material issues of law or fact relating to climate change mitigation, adaptation, or the science of climate change [and which] are brought before a range of administrative, judicial, and other adjudicatory bodies."[782] Although it could be said that climate litigation automatically concerns intergenerational issues due to the intergenerational character of most changes to the climatic system,[783] not all climate litigation cases actually involve the *representation* of future generations. Consequently, the present work does not offer a comprehensive analysis of all existing climate litigation cases. Considering the more than 1.300 climate law suits in the USA and more than 400 law suits in other jurisdictions worldwide,[784] this would definitely go beyond the scope of this book.[785] Particularly, the several other problematic issues of climate litigation, such as (extra-territorial) jurisdiction, causation or local remedies rules are also excluded from the present work.[786] Furthermore, not all relevant case law on intergenerational equity falls within the scope of climate litigation strictly speaking, but it also covers other categories like natural resources, pollution or challenges to mineral exploitation.[787]

Most importantly, the following sections do not intend to exhaustively address the entire existing case law on intergenerational equity in general. *Edith Brown Weiss* distinguished between two purposes of judicial references to intergenerational equity: "The first is for procedural matters, such as to grant standing to children as

[776] See, e.g., Human Rights Council (2012), para. 10 as well as in detail *supra* in Sect. 5.2.2.1.

[777] Cf. Meguro (2020), pp. 938–941.

[778] See Slobodian (2020), pp. 583–585.

[779] See, e.g., Brown Weiss et al. (1988).

[780] Cf. UNEP (2020), pp. 17–27.

[781] Generally, see Spentzou (2021).

[782] UNEP (2020), p. 6. See also UNEP (2017), p. 10; Setzer and Higham (2021), pp. 8–9.

[783] Cf. Niehaus (2021), pp. 249–250; Niehaus and Davies (2021), p. 241.

[784] These numbers are based on the entries of the Sabin Center for Climate Change Law at Columbia Law School (2007-2024). See also Setzer and Higham (2021), p. 8.

[785] For a more thorough analysis, see, e.g., Setzer and Vanhala (2019); Alogna et al. (2021); Kahl and Weller (2021); Savaresi and Setzer (2022); Saiger (2022).

[786] For some remarks on causation, see already *supra* in Sect. 5.3.3.1.1.

[787] Brown Weiss (2021a), para. 36.

representativc of future generations or to toll a statute of limitations for actions that cause significant harm to future generations. The second use is for its substantive content."[788] While some important substantive aspects have already been addressed in other sections above, [789] the following analysis focuses on those proceedings that can be considered to raise claims on behalf of future generations.[790] Some of these cases explicitly invoked the representation of future generations, others only did implicitly. While some of these explicit or implicit invocations of future generations are still pending, others have already been decided in the last years. Notwithstanding the different procedural stages of the relevant cases, they are both examined in the following section with regard to their potential to implement a form of judicial representation of future generations before international, regional and national courts and (quasi-)judiciary bodies. In some of the decided cases, the courts rejected the claimants' invocation of rights of future generations or they did not address this issue at all if it was not necessary for the resolution of the dispute. All of these instances are analysed here in order to evaluate the actual and potential impact of these forms of litigation for the establishment of a representative framework of intergenerational equity. Nonetheless, it is important to note that the success of a climate litigation or human rights litigation case does not only depend on the acceptance or non-acceptance of the respective claims by the courts. Rather, many instances of strategic litigation in these fields also have large impacts on the respective policy-makers and the public opinion even in case of a procedural loss.[791]

In order to structure the diverse instances of intergenerational equity case law and to get an overview of potential institutional representative frameworks, the next sub-section analyses the few relevant proceedings before international and regional judicial and quasi-judicial bodies (bb). The third sub-section then turns to the field of relevant national litigation (cc).

#### 5.3.3.3.2 International and Regional Level

For a long time, proceedings before international judicial and quasi-judicial bodies have remained scarce with regard to intergenerational equity and future generations. In 1982, the HRC had to decide a case, in which a communication was submitted not only on behalf of its authors, but also on behalf of future generations.[792] However,

[788] Ibid.

[789] Regarding the concept's legal status, see *supra* in Sect. 4.2.2; regarding the rights of future generations, see *supra* in Sect. 5.2.2. Further, in overview, see already *supra* in Sect. 2.1.2.

[790] For a systematic overview of relevant proceedings, see also Bertram (2023). For an overview of national case law on intergenerational equity in general, see, e.g., Hadjiargyrou (2016), pp. 264–268; Brown Weiss (2021a), paras. 36–48; Ramlogan (2011), pp. 222–230.

[791] See Setzer and Higham (2021), pp. 18–20 with further references; Duffy (2018), pp. 37–49, 63–69; Magraw (2020); Peel and Markey-Towler (2021), pp. 1496–1498. Cf. also Niehaus and Davies (2021), p. 236.

[792] *E.H.P. v. Canada* (Decision), *supra* note 248.

the Committee omitted to answer the question whether the right to life in Article 6 of the ICCPR in connection with environmental dangers can be invoked on behalf of future generations because the issue was not decisive for the case at hand.[793] Instead, the Committee treated the reference to future generations in a rhetorical way, "as an expression of concern purporting to put into due perspective the importance of the matter raised in the communication."[794] Based on more recent developments, the HRC clarified in its General Comment No. 36 that environmental degradation and climate change constituted serious threats "to the ability of present and future generations to enjoy the right to life".[795]

Notwithstanding this, recent case law of the Committee did not build on this intergenerational aspect of the right to life. While the HRC repeated this stipulation in its *Teitiota v. New Zealand* decision in 2019, it did not address the issue of standing for invoking the dangers for future generations.[796] Similarly, the right to life did not play an important role in the recent decision in *Billy et al. v. Australia* from 2022, as the HRC denied a violation of Article 6 of the ICCPR.[797] Since the complainants did not explicitly claim to act on behalf of future generations,[798] the Committee did not have to decide on this issue either. However, it found, *inter alia*, a violation of Article 27 of the ICCPR that guarantees certain cultural rights to Indigenous communities.[799] The HRC stated in this regard:

> [The] State party's failure to adopt timely adequate adaptation measures to protect the authors' collective ability to maintain their traditional way of life, to transmit to their children and future generations their culture and traditions and use of land and sea resources discloses a violation of the State party's positive obligation to protect the authors' right to enjoy their minority culture.[800]

Further, the Committee obliged Australia to establish *long-term* adaptation measures in order to prevent similar violations in the future.[801] Although this decision thus has obvious intergenerational elements,[802] its actual significance for the judicial *representation* of future generations before the HRC remains limited due to the lack of invocation in this regard.

---

[793] Ibid., para. 8(a). See also Vöneky and Beck (2022), p. 209.

[794] *E.H.P. v. Canada* (Decision), *supra* note 248, para. 8(a).

[795] HRC (2019), p. 62.

[796] *Teitiota v. New Zealand* (Decision), *supra* note 313, para. 9.4.

[797] HRC, *Daniel Billy et al. v. Australia,* Decision, 22 September 2022, UN Doc. CCPR/C/135/D/3624/2019, paras. 8.3–8.8. Critical of this rejection, see Kahl (2022b).

[798] HRC, *Daniel Billy et al. v. Australia,* Complaint, 13 May 2019, Retrieved January 3, 2025, from https://climatecasechart.com/non-us-case/petition-of-torres-strait-islanders-to-the-united-nations-human-rights-committee-alleging-violations-stemming-from-australias-inaction-on-climate-change/

[799] *Billy et al. v. Australia* (Decision), *supra* note 797, paras. 8.13–8.14. Generally, see CCLD (2019-2022).

[800] *Billy et al. v. Australia* (Decision), *supra* note 797, para. 8.14.

[801] Ibid., para. 11.

[802] On the relevance for intergenerational climate litigation, see Bertram (2023), pp. 132, 140, 144.

Regional human rights bodies have also only reluctantly referred to future generations in cases of Indigenous rights. For instance, the IACHR has avoided to address the issue of representation of future generations by Indigenous communities in the past,[803] despite their specific relationship with past and future generations.[804] This is remarkable since Indigenous communities constitute "transgenerational groups", which would be particularly well-suited to represent their future people.[805] For this reason, *Daniel Bertram* considered cultural rights of Indigenous communities to constitute "an auspicious resource for intergenerational litigation" with a "relatively small, clearly defined number of individuals and collectives" as beneficiaries.[806] In *Billy et al.*, the complainants were also part of inhabitants of an SIDS, thus, they belonged to the communities most affected by the negative impacts of climate change.[807] This particular affectedness and common experiences of the adverse effects of climate change could further speak in favour of an adequate representation of future generations by Indigenous people and inhabitants of SIDS.[808] The important role that Indigenous people and communities could play in the implementation of intergenerational obligations is also reflected in a separate opinion in the *Mayagna Awas Tingni Community* decision that elaborated on the intertemporal relationship of Indigenous communities with their land.[809] This

[803] *Mayagna Awas Tingni Community v. Nicaragua* (Judgment), *supra* note 320, para. 149. For the African context, see also *Ogoniland Case* (Decision on Communication), *supra* note 332, para. 67. There would also have been an opportunity to decide on this matter in one of the first attempts of climate litigation in the inter-American human rights system: In 2005, several Inuit organisations raised a petition against the USA before the IAComHR for violations resulting from global warming, see IAComHR, *Petition to the Inter-American Commission on Human Rights Seeking Relief from Violations Resulting from Global Warming Caused by Acts and Omissions of the United States (Submitted by Sheila Watt-Cloutier, with the Support of the Inuit Circumpolar Conference, on Behalf of All Inuit of the Arctic Regions of the United States and Canada,* Petition, 7 December 2005, Retrieved January 3, 2025, from https://climatecasechart.com/non-us-case/petition-to-the-inter-american-commission-on-human-rights-seeking-relief-from-violations-resulting-from-global-warming-caused-by-acts-and-omissions-of-the-united-states/. The Commission did not decide on the petition because it considered it not to provide sufficient information to establish a violation of relevant rights, see IAComHR, *Petition to the Inter-American Commission on Human Rights Seeking Relief from Violations Resulting from Global Warming Caused by Acts and Omissions of the United States (Submitted by Sheila Watt-Cloutier, with the Support of the Inuit Circumpolar Conference, on Behalf of All Inuit of the Arctic Regions of the United States and Canada,* Decision on Inadmissibility, 16 November 2006, Retrieved January 3, 2025, from https://climatecasechart.com/non-us-case/petition-to-the-inter-american-commission-on-human-rights-seeking-relief-from-violations-resulting-from-global-warming-caused-by-acts-and-omissions-of-the-united-states/

[804] Spentzou (2021), pp. 173–177. See already *supra* in Sect. 5.2.2, notes 319–321.

[805] Slobodian (2020), pp. 579–580. On the communitarian approach behind such transgenerational communities, see *supra* in Sect. 3.3.4.

[806] Bertram (2023), pp. 132, 140. See also Liebenberg et al. (2023), Principles 11, 12.

[807] On the role of SIDS in the context of advisory proceedings before the ICJ, see already *supra* notes 632–634.

[808] Fibieger Byskov and Hyams (2022), pp. 204–207.

[809] *Mayagna Awas Tingni Community v. Nicaragua* (Joint Separate Opinion of Judges Cançado Trindade, Pacheco Gómez and Abreu Burelli), *supra* note 321, paras. 8–10.

relationship could be understood to encompass representation for past as well as future generations.[810] In another separate opinion, *Judge Cançado Trindade* went even further and stipulated:

> Thus, I believe that the big challenge for legal writers who belong to the new generations lies in conceiving and formulating the conceptual construction of the legal representation of humanity as a whole (encompassing both present and future generations), seeking to consolidate its international juridical personality, against the backdrop of the new *jus gentium* of our times.[811]

In its recent decision in *La Oroya v. Peru* from November 2023, the IACHR referred to future generations on the sidelines of the decision.[812] It linked the precautionary principle to the duty of States "to preserve the environment in order to allow future generations opportunities for development and viability of human life".[813] With reference to intergenerational equity, the IACHR further confirmed its previous statements that the right to a healthy environment aims at protecting the interests of present and future generations alike.[814] In this context, it explicitly referred not only to the CRC General Comment No. 26,[815] but also to the more elaborate Maastricht Principles on the Human Rights of Future Generations.[816] Yet, it linked the principle of intergenerational equity only to the (future) rights of children and did eventually not take into consideration *unborn* future generations. Despite this reluctance, *Kahl* and *Rodriguez-Orúe* considered that the *La Oroya* decision could "could lead to new landmark developments for future-oriented claims in the Court's following case law".[817]

Even within the inter-American human rights system, these careful attempts to establish a form of representation for future generations constitute suggestions for future development rather than a description of the current procedural regimes. With regard to the European human rights system, the jurisprudence of the ECtHR is even less open to any kind of *actio popularis* proceedings on behalf of a wider group of persons and insisted on the requirement of an actual victim status.[818] *Peter Lawrence*

[810] For a currently pending example in New Zealand, see Waitangi Tribunal, New Zealand, *Mataatua District Maori Council v. New Zealand,* Application, 4 July 2017, Retrieved January 3, 2025, from https://climatecasechart.com/non-us-case/mataatua-district-maori-council-v-new-zealand/, para. 72.

[811] IACHR, *Sawhoyamaxa Indigenous Community v. Paraguay (Merits, Reparations and Costs),* Separate Opinion of Judge Cançado Trindade, 29 March 2006, OEA Series C No. 125, para. 34.

[812] *La Oroya v. Brazil* (Judgment), *supra* note 691. See also V. Kahl and Rodriguez-Orúe (2024).

[813] *La Oroya v. Brazil* (Judgment), *supra* note 691, para. 128.

[814] Ibid., para. 141.

[815] CRC (2023), para. 11. On this General Comment, see already *supra* notes 317–318.

[816] Liebenberg et al. (2023), Principle 7.

[817] Kahl and Rodriguez-Orúe (2024).

[818] Generally, see Gattini (2019), paras. 44–51.

observed that this strict requirement of victim status posed an obstacle to the representation of future generations within the European human rights system;[819] additionally to the requirement of temporal imminence.[820] These limits in some judicial systems are also illustrated by a recent climate litigation decision of the CJEU. In the *People's Climate Case*, persons from several States brought an action before the EU courts against several EU law acts and claimed that these acts violated higher ranking EU law, including the EU Charter of Fundamental Rights as well as the UNFCCC and the Paris Agreement.[821] Although the plaintiffs did not claim to invoke the rights of future generations but only the violation of their own fundamental rights, the CJEU even rejected this claim based on a very restrictive understanding of the EU procedural rules of standing.[822] According to the CJEU, legal standing is only conferred to persons who can establish that they are individually concerned by the contested legal acts, meaning that these acts distinguished them individually from other persons.[823] The representation of future generations would thus be incompatible with this restrictive regime under EU law.[824] In a parallel proceeding, the CJEU even understood the invocation of future generations to indicate the lack of legal standing:

> Furthermore, [the plaintiffs] themselves acknowledge that the protection and regulation of the environment is something which affects 'everyone in both current and future generations', a statement which is difficult to deny and which militates against the notion of individual concern.[825]

However, this procedural approach constitutes an extremely strict standing requirement. Such procedural constraints do not seem to reduce the efforts of climate litigation on the international and regional level, as two more recent cases illustrate. First, 16 children from different States filed a petition with the CRC in 2019,[826] invoking a violation of their rights under the UN Convention on the Rights of the

---

[819] Lawrence (2016), p. 34 with reference to: European Commission on Human Rights, *Noel Narvii Tauira and 18 others v. France,* Decision on the admissibility, 4 December 1995, Retrieved January 3, 2025, from https://hudoc.echr.coe.int/eng?i=001-87173, pp. 130–131.

[820] Bell-James and Collins (2022).

[821] For an overview, see CCLD (2018b).

[822] CJEU, *Carvalho and Others v Parliament and Council (People's Climate Case),* Judgment, 25 March 2021, European Case Law Identifier ECLI:EU:C:2021:252, paras. 37–50. See also CJEU, *Sabo and Others v Parliament and Council (EU Biomass Case),* Order, 14 January 2021, European Case Law Identifier ECLI:EU:C:2021:24, paras. 24–30.

[823] *People's Climate Case* (Judgment), *supra* note 822, para. 40. For some critical remarks, see, e.g., Krämer (2019); Winter (2020); Hornkohl (2021).

[824] Dörr (2022), p. 306.

[825] Court of Justice of the European Union, General Court, *Sabo and Others v Parliament and Council (EU Biomass Case),* Order, 6 May 2020, European Case Law Identifier ECLI:EU:T:2020:179, para. 30.

[826] CRC, *Sacchi* et al. *v. Argentina* et al., Petition, 23 September 2019, Retrieved January 3, 2025, from https://climatecasechart.com/non-us-case/sacchi-et-al-v-argentina-et-al/. For an overview, see CCLD (2019-2021).

Child by Argentina, Brazil, France, Germany and Turkey (*Sacchi* case).[827] Second, six Portuguese youth filed a complaint against 33 Council of Europe States before the ECtHR in 2020, in which they invoked several human rights violations due to the States' insufficient action on climate change (*Duarte Agostinho* case).[828] Both proceedings have in common that they have been initiated by young persons who primarily invoked the violation of their proper rights because they will be affected more by the effects of climate change.[829] These cases thus have an inherent intergenerational component in the sense of a conflict between the living older and younger generations.[830] The aforementioned *Billy et al.* case before the HRC was not directly initiated by children, but the complainants acted, *inter alia*, on behalf of their six children.[831] Although the present book does not focus on this understanding of "generations",[832] the two proceedings in *Sacchi* and *Duarte Agostinho* have important significance for the representation of future generations.

On the one hand, the substantive link between the protection of living children's rights and the consideration of the needs and interests of future generations is obvious.[833] On the other hand, and even more important in the current context, children and youth increasingly take an active role today in fighting for their rights as well as for environmental protection,[834] particularly with respect to climate change.[835] Children are taking not only political and activist means to achieve more respect for their rights and interests, but they are also raising complaints before judicial and quasi-judicial bodies to contest insufficient public actions to combat

[827] *Convention on the Rights of the Child* (Child Rights Convention), adopted 20 November 1989, entered into force 2 September 1990, 1577 UNTS 3, Art. 3, 6, 24, 30.

[828] ECtHR, *Duarte Agostinho and others v. Portugal and 32 other States,* Complaint, 2 September 2020, Retrieved January 3, 2025, from https://climatecasechart.com/non-us-case/youth-for-climate-justice-v-austria-et-al/. For an overview, see CCLD (2020-2024b).

[829] For a comparative analysis, see Lewis (2021).

[830] With regard to *Duarte Agostinho* and the ECHR, see Sandvig et al. (2021). Cf. also Donger (2022), p. 274.

[831] *Billy et al. v. Australia* (Decision), *supra* note 797, para. 1.1. They also invoked explicit violations of children rights (Art. 24 of the ICCPR), which the HRC did not address though, see ibid., paras. 3.7, 10.

[832] See *supra* in Sect. 2.2.1.2.2.

[833] UNSG (2013), paras. 49–50; Human Rights Council (2018), para. 68. Cf. also Atapattu (2019); Ippolito (2022), p. 26.

[834] UNSG (2013), paras. 51–52. In more detail, see also Pitts (2021). Most recently, see, e.g., Stockholm+50 Youth Assembly (2022). The HLPFSD recently acknowledged the role of young people as "critical agents of change and torchbearers of the 2030 Agenda for current and future generations", see ECOSOC (2022), para. 115.

[835] See Arts (2019); Lewis (2021); Gasparri et al. (2021); Donger (2022).

climate change and environmental degradation.[836] They generally make clear that this insufficient action endangers their lives already in the present.[837] Beyond this, these youth-led complaints either explicitly invoke the rights or interests of future generations and claim to speak on their behalf, or they are implicitly considered to encompass a representation of unborn generations.[838]

In the *Sacchi* petition before the CRC, intergenerational equity and the interests of future generations have explicitly been mentioned by the petitioners.[839] They invoked the respondents' obligation "to ensure intergenerational justice for children and posterity"[840] as well as the imminent risk and danger not only for themselves but also for future generations.[841] While the CRC took note of these claims in its decision,[842] it only accepted the petitioners' proper victim status under the Convention,[843] but it did not answer whether it considered the authors of the petition to act on behalf of future generations. This silence on the question of standing for future generations is typical for many judicial and quasi-judicial bodies if they consider it sufficient to decide the matter on the plaintiffs' proper legal standing.[844] Although the CRC accepted its jurisdiction as well as the legal standing of the petitioners, it eventually dismissed the petition as inadmissible because its authors had not exhausted domestic remedies before addressing the committee.[845] Therefore, the decision brought no further insights on the exact substantive relationship between the rights of the children and the legal position of future (i.e., unborn) generations.

The second proceeding in *Duarte Agostinho* before the ECtHR was initiated in 2020 by several youth plaintiffs.[846] Contrary to the *Sacchi* case, the only reference in the *Duarte Agostinho* complaint to the "concept of intergenerational equity" is much more abstract and cannot necessarily be seen as an intended representation of future,

---

[836] Bakker (2021a), p. 6; Niehaus and Davies (2021), p. 237; Daly (2022); Gradoni and Mantovani (2022). Cf. also Brown Weiss (2021b), pp. 36–38.

[837] Daly (2022), p. 21.

[838] Desmet (2019), p. 194; Gubbay and Wenzler (2021), p. 346; Gasparri et al. (2021), p. 99; Parker et al. (2022), p. 67; Bertram (2023), pp. 140–141. *Jacqueline Peel* and *Rebekkah Markey-Towler* considered this combination of the interests of children and future generations to constitute a strategic ingredient to select plaintiffs with "a compelling story", see Peel and Markey-Towler (2021), pp. 1487–1489.

[839] *Sacchi v. Argentina* et al. (Petition), *supra* note 826, paras. 28, 176, 193, 257–259, 303.

[840] Ibid., para. 176.

[841] Ibid., paras. 257–258.

[842] CRC, *Sacchi* et al. *v. Argentina* et al., Decision, 22 September 2021, UN Doc. CRC/C/88/D/107/2019, paras. 3.3, 3.7.

[843] Ibid., paras. 9.13–9.14.

[844] See already *supra* note 793.

[845] Ibid., 9.15–9.20. For a critical assessment of this dismissal, see, e.g., Gradoni and Mantovani (2022). For a positive assessment of the overall decision and on its impacts on climate litigation, see Nolan (2021).

[846] On the current state of the proceedings, see CCLD (2020-2024b).

unborn, generations.[847] This is in line with the aforementioned strict requirement of a victim status in the European human rights system.[848] Interestingly, in both proceedings, several public and civil society actors have submitted *amicus curiae* briefs to assist in the determination of the legal questions at hand—particularly the UN Special Rapporteur on human rights and the environment.[849] While the briefs did not address explicit representation for future generations either, their interventions illustrate the important role a global representative of future generations could play by actively introducing their interests in similar judicial and quasi-judicial proceedings.[850] Before this decision, the ECtHR has not dealt with a case explicitly addressing the rights, even less the standing, of future generations.[851] In its decision in April 2024, the ECtHR did not embrace the opportunity to do so either.[852] Instead, it dismissed the case as inadmissible for non-exhaustion of domestic remedies and lack of jurisdiction with regard to all respondent States but Portugal.[853] With regard to victim status, it explicitly abstained from examining the applicants' victim status;[854] it thereby did not consider intergenerational aspects at all.[855]

However, the ECtHR issued another interesting decision on 9 April 2024 with regard to the aspects of victim status and intergenerational equity: the *Klimaseniorinnen* case.[856] First, the court acknowledged that "policies to combat climate change inevitably involve issues of social accommodation and

---

[847] *Duarte Agostinho v. Portugal* et al. (Complaint), *supra* note 828, para. 8.

[848] See *supra* notes 818–819.

[849] See *Sacchi v. Argentina* et al. (Amicus curiae briefs by UN Special Rapporteurs on human rights and the environment (David R. Boyd and John H. Knox)), *supra* note 733; *Duarte Agostinho v. Portugal* et al. (Amicus Brief by UN Special Rapporteur on human rights and the environment (David R. Boyd) and UN Special Rapporteur on toxics and human rights (Marcos A. Orellana)), *supra* note 733. See also ECtHR, *Duarte Agostinho and others v. Portugal and 32 other States,* Amicus Brief by the European Commissioner for Human Rights, 5 May 2021, Retrieved January 3, 2025, from https://climatecasechart.com/non-us-case/youth-for-climate-justice-v-austria-et-al/

[850] See Ploton and Montes de Oca (2022). See already *supra* in Sects. 5.3.2.2 and 5.3.3.2.3.

[851] Albers (2018), p. 139; Peters (2021), pp. 165, 189; Keller and Heri (2022), pp. 13–14. For a comparable proceeding, see *infra* note 926.

[852] ECtHR, *Duarte Agostinho and others v. Portugal and 32 other States,* Judgment, 9 April 2024, Retrieved January 3, 2025, from https://hudoc.echr.coe.int/eng?i=001-233261

[853] Ibid., paras. 214, 227.

[854] Ibid., paras. 229–230.

[855] In another recent complaint against the UK, the claimants incidentally raise issues of intergenerational equity and refer to the interests of future generations "who do not have a voice or vote", see ECtHR, *Plan B.Earth and Others v United Kingdom,* Application, 11 July 2022, Retrieved January 3, 2025, from https://climatecasechart.com/non-us-case/plan-bearth-and-others-v-united-kingdom/, paras. 13, 15, 38. The claimants already implicitly mentioned future generations in the national proceedings before the High Court of Justice, see High Court of Justice, *Plan B Earth and Others v. Prime Minister,* Complaint, 1 May 2021, Retrieved January 3, 2025, from https://climatecasechart.com/non-us-case/plan-b-earth-and-others-v-prime-minister/, para. 39. The case was dismissed as inadmissible in January 2023; for details, see CCLD (2022-2023).

[856] ECtHR, *Verein Klimaseniorinnen Schweiz* et al. *v. Switzerland,* Judgment, 9 April 2024, Retrieved January 3, 2025, from https://hudoc.echr.coe.int/eng?i=001-233206

intergenerational burdensharing, both in regard to different generations of those currently living and in regard to future generations".[857] Second, the aforementioned strict requirements for victim status[858] have been confirmed and complemented with regard to the specifics of climate change cases.[859] In this context, the ECtHR rejected the victim status of the four individual complainants that raised the human rights violations alongside the association Klimaseniorinnen.[860] This would equally hinder the victim status of future generations before the ECtHR. Yet, the third interesting aspect in this context is most important for the representation of future generations: The court developed a very nuanced approach to the standing of associations in climate change-related cases.[861] It found, *inter alia*, that "collective action through associations or other interest groups may be one of the only means through which the voice of those at a distinct representational disadvantage can be heard and through which they can seek to influence the relevant decision-making processes".[862] Based on its newly-established criteria,[863] it concluded with regard to Klimaseniorinnen that "[i]t acts not only in the interest of its members, but also in the interest of the general public and future generations, with the aim of ensuring effective climate protection".[864] Consequently, the recent case law of the ECtHR can be considered a step towards the representation of future generations via the instrumentarium of NGOs.

Beyond these cases, youth-led litigation increases on all levels, as can be seen in the initiative for an advisory opinion before the ICJ,[865] in the aforementioned proceedings before the CRC and the ECtHR, but also in several national proceedings in the last years.[866] Some commentators even considered that every youth-led climate litigation constitutes at the same time a claim for the implementation of intergenerational equity,[867] arguing that "the rights of future generations are intrinsically linked to today's youth because youth understand more than any group that decisions today shape the wellbeing of generations tomorrow".[868] According to *Francesca Ippolito*, the protection of "future rights and future generations through 'immediate' action [...] would avoid the critical procedural profiles connected to the

---

[857] Ibid., paras. 410, 419–420.

[858] See *supra* notes 818–819.

[859] *Klimaseniorinnen v. Switzerland* (Judgment), supra note 856, paras. 465–472, 478–488.

[860] Ibid., paras. 527–535.

[861] Ibid., paras. 489–503.

[862] Ibid., para. 489.

[863] Ibid., para. 499.

[864] Ibid., para. 521.

[865] See *supra* notes 589–590. See also Gradoni and Mantovani (2022).

[866] For a first example, see already Republic of Philippines Supreme Court, *Oposa v. Factoran,* Decision, 30 July 1993, 33 International Legal Materials 173–206. In more detail, see *infra* notes 883–885.

[867] Parker et al. (2022), p. 67.

[868] Ibid., p. 79.

so far limited judicial recognition of the principle of inter-generational equity by international tribunals".[869] In contrast, *Aoife Nolan* addressed the interrelation between children's rights and the rights of unborn future generations in more detail and underlined the risks in equating them.[870] Although there are certainly some overlaps, she illustrated the differences and pointed out some unanswered issues with regard to the protection of future generations within international human rights law.[871] Despite these challenges, it is obvious that the young generation, in combination with the aforementioned role of NGOs, plays a decisive part in the further development of international human rights and environmental law and its implementation before courts on all levels. Several other proceedings on climate-change and other related issues could be added to the list.[872] It remains to be seen whether and how exactly this role will also shape an institutional framework of representation of future generations before the judiciary.

On the international and regional level, the attempts remained scarce and often abstract so far—if the respective bodies addressed standing for future generations at all. Although most of these courts have shown a certain openness towards environmental matters, the options for intergenerational representation are still limited.[873] If human rights litigation ought to become part in the implementation of intergenerational equity, certain reforms seem necessary.[874] Potentially, the international framework could be inspired in the future by the many examples of national litigation, which are addressed in the next sub-section.

##### 5.3.3.3.3 National Level

First and foremost, legal standing to bring a claim on the national level depends on the particular national procedural systems.[875] Since the procedural rules would never *explicitly* accept legal standing for future generations, the possibility to act on their behalf mostly emerges from a judicial interpretation of the existing general rules of standing.[876] Not all jurisprudence on intergenerational equity and sustainable development constitutes an acceptance of the representation of future generations.[877] The case law concerning intergenerational issues has increased with the phenomenon of

---

[869] Ippolito (2022), p. 20. Cf. also Atapattu (2019), p. 168.

[870] Nolan (2022). Cf. also Bertram (2023), p. 141.

[871] Nolan (2022), with further references.

[872] See, e.g., currently pending complaints before several UN Special Rapporteurs: CCLD (2020d-today).

[873] Lawrence (2016), pp. 33–36.

[874] Rosenkranz (1986), pp. 113–114; Lawrence (2016), p. 36; Pirjatanniemi (2016), pp. 18–22; Düwell and Bos (2016), p. 243.

[875] Michallet (2018), p. 157.

[876] Cf. ibid.

[877] Brown Weiss (2020), pp. 293–307.

climate litigation, particularly on the national level.[878] Of course, implementation of intergenerational equity can also be achieved on the national level without explicit representation. Nonetheless, the following section structures the existing case law in order to assess how national courts could form an institutional framework for the representation of future generations in judicial proceedings. First, it addresses the few instances, in which courts have *explicitly* accepted a claim brought on behalf of future generations (Sect. 5.3.3.3.3.1). Second, most of the completed case law avoided to decide on this issue as it was considered not decisive for the respective case (Sect. 5.3.3.3.3.2). Some of these latter cases could nonetheless be interpreted to *implicitly* accept representation, at least in an informal way. On the contrary, only few cases explicitly rejected the representation of future generations for procedural reasons. Eventually, the last sub-section gives an outlook with regard to some pending cases, which are also based on the representation of future generations and their interests (Sect. 5.3.3.3.3.3).

#### *5.3.3.3.3.1 Explicit Recognition of Representation*

The representation of future generations was explicitly addressed and accepted in the cases *Oposa v. Factoran*, (Sect. 5.3.3.3.3.1.1), *Urgenda* (Sect. 5.3.3.3.3.1.2), *People v. Arctic Oil* (Sect. 5.3.3.3.3.1.3) and *Future Generations v. Colombia* (Sect. 5.3.3.3.3.1.4).

##### *5.3.3.3.3.1.1 Oposa v. Factoran*

In 1993, the Philippines Supreme Court decided the famous *Oposa v. Factoran* case—the most important national case, always cited as a manifest implementation of the concept of intergenerational equity.[879] Beyond the substantive significance for intergenerational equity, the decision also explicitly accepted the claimants' legal standing to act on behalf of future generations:

> Petitioners minors assert that they represent their generation as well as generations yet unborn. We find no difficulty in ruling that they can, for themselves, for others of their generation and for the succeeding generations, file a class suit.[880]

The court read the petitioners' intergenerational claim in connection with a constitutional right to a healthful environment, [881] which again illustrates the links between these two matters.[882] The explicit recognition of the petitioners' standing on behalf of future generations is remarkable as the court would not have needed to accept this intergenerational representation in order to be able to decide on the matter. As in

[878] González-Ricoy and Rey (2019), pp. 4–5.

[879] *Oposa v. Factoran* (Decision), *supra* note 866. In general, see Manguiat and Yu (2003) as well as already *supra* in Sect. 2.1.2.

[880] *Oposa v. Factoran* (Decision), *supra* note 866, p. 185.

[881] Ibid. See also Fitzmaurice (2012), p. 101.

[882] See already *supra* in Sect. 5.2.2.2.

many cases, the claimants did not *exclusively* base their claim on the intergenerational aspect, but also invoked their own rights, which would have sufficed for a decision on the merits. In contrast to many other courts, as illustrated below, the Philippines Supreme Court did not take the easy way out as it did not avoid the issue of standing for future generations although it could have done so. Interestingly, the proceeding was initiated by a group of Philippine children in a class action that sought to stop the cutting of remaining national forests by government licensees. Thus, the judicial fight for intergenerational justice was again led by young persons who took an active role in the protection not only of their proper interests but also of the interests of future generations.[883] The Supreme Court's findings could even be interpreted in a way that obliges children of the present generation to take action also on behalf of future generations in order to fulfil their proper intergenerational obligations to protect the equitable access of future generations to the natural resource base.[884] Several of the more recent climate litigation proceedings are based on claims of the young generation;[885] often they can also be considered to defend not only interests of the current young generation, but also implicitly or explicitly of future, yet unborn generations.[886]

Despite its widely positive reception in legal scholarship,[887] some commentators criticised the *Oposa* decision for its merely symbolic character and denied its actual impact on environmental protection for future generations in and outside the Philippines.[888] This scepticism is at least justified with regard to the factual consequences of the decision in the Philippines as it did not affect the government's subsequent practice in respect of the timber licenses.[889] *Vaughan Lowe* concluded that the alleged representation of unborn generations could "scarcely be more than a rhetorical device".[890] This would mirror the approach the HRC had taken in its 1982 decision in *E.H.P. v. Canada.*[891] However, this criticism ignored the actual impacts the *Oposa* decision had in the following years on judicial proceedings, as it was

---

[883] In more detail on youth-led judicial initiatives in general, see *supra* notes 833–838, 867–869.

[884] See Gaillard (2011), para. 655.

[885] For details on some of these cases, see *infra* notes 932–940 (*Future Generations v. Colombia*); 968–970 (*Pandey v. India*); 997–1006 (*Juliana v. USA*); 1059–1061 (*Neubauer v. Germany*). For other examples, see, e.g., CCLD (2020-2024a); CCLD (2020-2022); Cameron and Weyman (2022).

[886] See *supra* notes 867–869.

[887] See, e.g., Allen (1994); Manguiat and Yu (2003), pp. 492–494; Brown Weiss (2010), pp. 111–112; Gaillard (2011), para. 655.

[888] See, e.g., Lowe (1999), pp. 27–28; Gatmaytan (2003); Redgwell (2016), p. 197.

[889] Gatmaytan (2003), pp. 466–468.

[890] Lowe (1999), p. 27.

[891] *E.H.P. v. Canada* (Decision), *supra* note 248, para. 8(a). See already *supra* notes 792–794.

regularly pleaded in several other jurisdictions ever since,[892] and it is still invoked in proceedings today.[893] *Maria Manguiat* and *Vicente Yu* therefore concluded that

> The Supreme Court's statement in *Oposa* relating to intergenerational equity and the standing of petitioners therein should be seen not merely as *obiter dictum*. It should also be seen as an authoritative and ultimately precedent-setting statement that has significantly advanced the meaning and scope of the constitutional right to a balanced and healthful ecology in ways that may be directly meaningful and useful for present generations in relation to their environmental duty to future generations. Indeed, the Supreme Court's discussion on intergenerational equity in *Oposa* was clear and directly addressed the issue of standing, and therefore should not be summarily dismissed as being without legal value.[894]

The *Oposa* decision has so far remained the most prominent and progressive decision that granted standing to civil society actors on behalf of future generations. However, many other decisions have also contributed to the role of future generations and their representation in judicial disputes.

##### *5.3.3.3.3.1.2 Urgenda v. The Netherlands*

The second important proceeding is more recent and forms part of increasing climate litigation. In the famous *Urgenda* case, a Dutch environmental group, together with 900 Dutch citizens, had initiated proceedings against the Dutch government in order to require it to strengthen its proper climate mitigation activities.[895] The plaintiffs based their claims, *inter alia*, on violations of their human rights under the ECHR.[896] Between 2015 and 2019, three Dutch courts decided on the complaint, and the Dutch Supreme Court upheld the preceding decisions and found in favour of the complainants. It obliged the Dutch State to reduce its greenhouse gas emissions by the end of 2020 by at least 25% compared to 1990 due to the risk of dangerous climate change that could have a severe impact on the lives and welfare of the Dutch residents.[897]

Much has been written about all three of these ground-breaking decisions and their enormous significance and impacts on Dutch law as well as climate litigation worldwide.[898] The aim of this book is not to repeat these manifold observations, but

---

[892] See, e.g., Manguiat and Yu (2003), pp. 489–492; Hadjiargyrou (2016), pp. 266–268 as well as *infra* notes 963–965, 969, 1021.

[893] Most recently, see National Green Tribunal at Principal Bench, New Delhi, *Ridhima Pandey v. India,* Petition, 25 March 2017, Retrieved January 3, 2025, from https://climatecasechart.com/non-us-case/pandey-v-india/, p. 46.

[894] Manguiat and Yu (2003), pp. 493–494.

[895] For an overview, see CCLD (2015-2020).

[896] *Convention for the Protection of Human Rights and Fundamental Freedoms* (ECHR), adopted 4 November 1950, entered into force 3 September 1953, 213 UNTS 221, Art. 2, 8.

[897] Supreme Court of the Netherlands, *The State of the Netherlands v. Urgenda Foundation,* Judgment, 20 December 2019, 59 International Legal Materials 4.

[898] See, e.g., Spijkers (2018); Spier (2020); Backes and van der Veen (2020); Bakker (2021b); van der Veen (2021); Wewerinke-Singh and McCoach (2021). For a critical assessment, see, e.g., Bergkamp (2015).

to focus on the decisions' significance for the judicial representation of future generations. The Urgenda association based its legal standing under Dutch law on its by-laws, which aim at a "sustainable society" and which allowed it to invoke the collective legal interests of current as well as future generations. The association argued that this interest is not only idealistic, but that it also legally aims at giving a voice to future generations.[899] The District Court of The Hague accepted these arguments and stated on Urgenda's standing:

> The term 'sustainable society' also has an intergenerational dimension, which is expressed in the definition of 'sustainability' in the Brundtland Report [...]. In defending the right of not just the current but also the future generations to availability of natural resources and a safe and healthy living environment, it also strives for the interest of a sustainable society.[900]

Consequently, the District Court explicitly considered Urgenda to act as representative for future generations—of Dutch as well as foreign nationals.[901] *Laura Burgers* underlined the significance of this decision's inclusiveness towards future generations, as it constituted "an instance of 'genuine' representation, where *rights* of future generations are invoked" (emphasis in the original).[902] While the Dutch State had not objected to the representation of future Dutch nationals by Urgenda at first instance,[903] it did object on appeal.[904] The Court of Appeal of the Hague upheld the District Court's decision, but its findings on the issue of standing differed slightly:

> It is not disputed between the parties that the claim of Urgenda, insofar as acting on behalf of the current generation of Dutch nationals against the emission of greenhouse gases on Dutch territory, is admissible. However, the State argued, as understood by the Court, that Urgenda cannot act on behalf of future generations of Dutch nationals nor of current and future generations of foreigners. The State does not have an interest in this ground of appeal, because Urgenda's claim is already admissible insofar as Urgenda acts on behalf of the interests of the current generation of Dutch nationals and individuals subject to the State's jurisdiction within the meaning of Article 1 [of the] ECHR, respectively. After all, it is without a doubt plausible that the current generation of Dutch nationals, in particular but not limited to the younger individuals in this group, will have to deal with the adverse effects of climate change in their lifetime if global emissions of greenhouse gases are not adequately reduced. Therefore, the Court does not have to consider the questions raised by the State in this ground of appeal.[905]

[899] See Burgers (2020a), p. 209.

[900] *Hague District Court, Urgenda* (Judgment), *supra* note 551, para. 4.8 (court translation).

[901] Loth (2016), pp. 13, 21–22; Albers (2018), pp. 139–140; Loth (2018), p. 339; Spijkers (2018), pp. 312, 331; Burgers (2020a), pp. 213, 217–218. See also briefly Tabau and Cournil (2015), p. 227; Verschuuren (2017), p. 15.

[902] Burgers (2020a), p. 217.

[903] *Hague District Court, Urgenda* (Judgment), *supra* note 551, para. 4.5; Burgers (2020a), p. 217.

[904] Hague Court of Appeal, *The State of the Netherlands v. Urgenda Foundation,* Judgment, 9 October 2018, European Case Law Identifier ECLI:NL:GHDHA:2018:2610, para. 37; Burgers (2020a), p. 233.

[905] *Hague Court of Appeal, Urgenda* (Judgment), *supra* note 904, 37 (court translation).

Similarly, the Dutch Supreme Court did not address the standing of Urgenda on behalf of future generations in its decision but endorsed the Court of Appeal's focus on the effects for current generations that were also represented by Urgenda.[906] Both courts considered the representation of future generations to be irrelevant for the resolution of the specific dispute, as Urgenda's invocation of the present generation's interests was sufficient.[907] Most commentators deduced from this that the higher courts rejected any representation of future generations and of current and future generations of people living abroad.[908] However, *Burgers* correctly pointed out that "the Court of Appeal *neither* said that such [standing] would *not* be possible" (emphasis in the original).[909] Instead, the higher courts' focus on current generations would be explicable by the mere fact that they considered the adverse effects of climate change to be sufficiently grave to endanger the lives of present generations.[910] *Burgers* continued:

> Does this therefore mean that the Court of Appeal contributes less to the empowerment of future generations in European private law than the District Court, in terms of rendering the public sphere more normatively legitimate and politically effective for them? Formally speaking, perhaps. Yet what really happened in this case is what will always happen with temporal boundaries to legal-political systems: at a certain point, these boundaries move towards you, as you grow older in time, and before you know it you are at the other side of that boundary. The Court therefore needed not to grapple with the complicated theoretical complications of representing future generations.[911]

Interestingly enough, the Court of Appeal nonetheless addressed some theoretical issues of representation by rejecting the Dutch State's arguments that Urgenda's alleged interest would be too large to be represented before a court: "[a class action] does not have to concern the interests of a clearly defined group of others. It may also concern the interests of an indeterminable, very large group of individuals."[912] Although this did not explicitly refer to future generations, the argument offers some assistance for potential representation of unborn generations in future litigation.[913]

All in all, the Dutch decisions in *Urgenda* can be interpreted in favour of judicial representation of future generations before national courts. While this representation by a Dutch NGO was only possible due to the progressive Dutch procedural law on public interest litigation,[914] the decision has had immense impacts on climate

---

[906] *Dutch Supreme Court, Urgenda* (Judgment), *supra* note 897, para. 4.7.

[907] Burgers and Staal (2018), p. 228; Mayer (2019), p. 176; Wewerinke-Singh and McCoach (2021), pp. 7–8. Cf. Brown Weiss (2021a), para. 44.

[908] See, e.g., Roy and Woerdman (2016), p. 170; Backes and van der Veen (2020), p. 308; Nollkaemper (2021), Sect. 1. Cf. also Wewerinke-Singh and McCoach (2021), pp. 7–8.

[909] Burgers (2020a), p. 234.

[910] Ibid., p. 236. See also Daly (2022), p. 21.

[911] Burgers (2020a), p. 236.

[912] *Hague Court of Appeal, Urgenda* (Judgment), *supra* note 904, 38 (court translation).

[913] Cf. Burgers (2020a), p. 234.

[914] See Spijkers (2020).

litigation worldwide, so that its inclusiveness towards future generations—first explicitly, then at least implicitly—is able to inspire further litigation on behalf, or at least in the direct interest, of future generations.[915]

### *5.3.3.3.3.1.3 People v. Arctic Oil*

The case *People v. Arctic Oil* in Norway is another recent proceeding, which could be considered to strengthen judicial representation of future generations.[916] The plaintiffs claimed a violation of a constitutional provision by the Norwegian government's issuing of oil and gas licences for deep-sea extraction.[917] This constitutional provision provides:

> Every person has the right to an environment that is conducive to health and to a natural environment whose productivity and diversity are maintained. Natural resources shall be managed on the basis of comprehensive long-term considerations that will safeguard this right for future generations as well.[918]

The plaintiffs sued not only on behalf of present citizens but also for the protection of future generations.[919] The Norwegian courts dismissed the claims on the merits since they considered the effects between the issuance of licenses and future greenhouse gas emissions to be too uncertain.[920] However, they affirmed the substantive rights-nature of Article 112 of the Norwegian Constitution, which guaranteed a healthy environment to every person of present and future generations.[921] While the Oslo District Court did not address the representation issue in its decision,[922] the Borgarting Court of Appeals referred to the second sentence of the constitutional provision and stated that "[t]he fact that the right is to be safeguarded across generations has an aspect of the concern for democracy, in that future

---

[915] For some cases in other jurisdictions, which have been inspired by *Urgenda*, see *infra* notes 971–973.

[916] For an overview, see CCLD (2016-2020).

[917] Oslo District Court, *Greenpeace Nordic Ass'n and Nature and Youth v. Ministry of Petroleum and Energy (People v. Arctic Oil),* Plaintiff's Petition, 18 October 2016, Retrieved January 3, 2025, from https://climatecasechart.com/non-us-case/greenpeace-nordic-assn-and-nature-youth-v-norway-ministry-of-petroleum-and-energy/. See also Dellinger (2018), p. 540.

[918] Art. 112 of the Constitution of Norway.

[919] *Oslo District Court, People v. Arctic Oil* (Plaintiff's Petition), *supra* note 917, 4, 41–42, 45–46. See also Burgers (2020a), p. 228.

[920] See, e.g., Oslo District Court, *Greenpeace Nordic Ass'n and Nature and Youth v. Ministry of Petroleum and Energy (People v. Arctic Oil),* Judgment, 4 January 2018, Retrieved January 3, 2025, from https://climatecasechart.com/non-us-case/greenpeace-nordic-assn-and-nature-youth-v-norway-ministry-of-petroleum-and-energy/; Borgarting Court of Appeal, *Greenpeace Nordic Ass'n and Nature and Youth v. Ministry of Petroleum and Energy (People v. Arctic Oil),* Judgment, 23 January 2020, Retrieved January 3, 2025, from https://climatecasechart.com/non-us-case/greenpeace-nordic-assn-and-nature-youth-v-norway-ministry-of-petroleum-and-energy/

[921] See Burgers (2020a), p. 230.

[922] Ibid., p. 232. However, on the principle of solidarity across generations, see *Oslo District Court, People v. Arctic Oil* (Judgment), *supra* note 920, p. 20.

generations cannot influence today's political processes".[923] Then, the court of appeal confirmed the substantive character of this rights provision.[924] It is exactly this voiceless position of future generations that constitutes the basis for any representative claim, so that the appeal decision must be understood to acknowledge the association's standing to represent future generations.[925] Since the complaints have been rejected in all instances for other reasons, the plaintiffs issued an application in 2021 before the ECtHR against the Norwegian government.[926] Interestingly, they did not only refer to intergenerational equity,[927] but two of the applicants explicitly argued:

> Applicants 7–8 also represent the interests of future generations. The Court has accepted the rights of NGOs to act on behalf of vulnerable individuals to protect the rights under Articles 2 and 8 [of the ECHR] in situations where the individual is deceased. The Applicants respectfully allege that the same considerations apply to generations unborn, especially in light of Applicant 7–8's involvement in the domestic proceedings where their standing was accepted.[928]

This pending proceeding must be envisaged in connection with the aforementioned recent climate change case law of the ECtHR, particularly the *Duarte Agostinho* case and the *Klimaseniorinnen* case;[929] it could certainly further elaborate the issue of representation of future generations before domestic courts and regional human rights bodies.[930]

#### *5.3.3.3.3.1.4 Future Generations v. Colombia*

Beside these progressive findings in *Urgenda* and *People v. Arctic Oil*, a third recent climate litigation case merits a proper analysis with respect to the representation of future generations: the case *Future Generations v. Colombia*.[931] Comparable to the aforementioned proceedings, a Colombian NGO, 'Dejusticia', and several young plaintiffs initiated the complaint against Colombian public bodies to enforce their environmental rights. Comparable to the *Oposa* case, the Colombian constitutional complaint also dealt with the insufficient reduction of deforestation in the Colombian Amazon. Beyond the telling name of the case, it contains several interesting aspects

---

[923] *Borgarting Court of Appeal, People v. Arctic Oil* (Judgment), *supra* note 920, 18 (court translation).

[924] Ibid., p. 18.

[925] Burgers (2020a), pp. 232, 255.

[926] ECtHR, *Greenpeace Nordic and Others v. Norway,* Complaint, 15 June 2021, Retrieved January 3, 2025, from https://climatecasechart.com/non-us-case/greenpeace-nordic-assn-v-ministry-of-petroleum-and-energy-ecthr/

[927] Ibid., para. 48.

[928] Ibid., para. 40.

[929] See *supra* notes 846–864.

[930] For information on the current stage of the proceeding, see CCLD (2021b-today).

[931] For an overview, see CCLD (2018a). For another interesting analysis, see Niehaus (2023), pp. 352–357.

with regard to judicial representation of future generations. First, the plaintiffs explicitly based their complaint on the principle of intergenerational equity, among others.[932] They considered themselves to be part of a future generation: "we are the generation that will face the greatest consequences of climate change. This allows us to affirm that we are a future generation, because in the future scenario 2041-2070 we have hope of being alive."[933] Therefore, they chose the special procedural remedy of *tutela*, which can be used to protect fundamental rights, including their proper rights.[934] This seems to build on a different understanding of "future generations" than established in this book,[935] as the complaint includes the living younger generation within its understanding of future generations.[936] However, their arguments referred to several general documents of international environmental law on intergenerational equity, such as the Brundtland Report.[937] Further, the plaintiffs explicitly referred to the Colombian legal system, which would allegedly recognise the existence of future generations as right-holders.[938] The representation of future generations by the plaintiff's action of *tutela* was more directly pointed out in the *amicus brief* from *James Hansen*, a leading climate scientist, who stated, *inter alia*, that the court "should deem that by and through Plaintiffs the rights of future generations of Colombians may be represented" and who referred to the "Plaintiffs, and the future generations for which they ineluctably must stand [...]".[939] This is in line with the aforementioned interconnection between youth-led litigation and the representation of (unborn) future generations.[940]

Second, the Supreme Court's decision can be described as a "milestone in environmental and future generations' rights protection".[941] In April 2018, less than 3 months after the complaint, the Supreme Court reversed the unfavourable lower court decision, confirmed the plaintiffs' claims and ordered the Colombian authorities to formulate action plans to counteract the deforestation in the Amazon as well as to construct an "intergenerational pact for the life of the Colombian

[932] Supreme Court of Colombia, *Future Generations v. Ministry of the Environment and Others*, Complaint, 29 January 2018, Retrieved January 3, 2025, from https://climatecasechart.com/non-us-case/future-generation-v-ministry-environment-others/, pp. 4, 80.

[933] Ibid., 4 (own translation with the support of Deepl.com).

[934] See Parker et al. (2022), p. 77 (at footnote 62).

[935] See *supra* in Sect. 2.2.1.2.2.

[936] *Future Generations v. Colombia* (Complaint), *supra* note 932, pp. 63–64.

[937] Ibid., pp. 64–65.

[938] Ibid., p. 65.

[939] Supreme Court of Colombia, *Future Generations v. Ministry of the Environment and Others*, Amicus Brief from Dr. James E. Hansen, 16 March 2018, Retrieved January 3, 2025, from https://climatecasechart.com/non-us-case/future-generation-v-ministry-environment-others/

[940] Parker et al. (2022), p. 79. See also *supra* notes 867–869.

[941] Acosta Alvarado and Rivas-Ramirez (2018). Cf. also Spentzou (2021), p. 169.

Amazon".[942] The court did not only mention the foundations of intergenerational equity,[943] it also explicitly referred to the "environmental rights of future generations" at several occasions.[944] It elaborated:

> The environmental rights of future generations are based on the (i) ethical duty of the solidarity of the species [...]. The first is explained by the fact that natural resources are shared by all inhabitants of Planet Earth, and by their descendants or future generations who do not yet materially hold them, but who are [...], addressees, and owners of them [...].[945]

This conception of rights of future generations within the concept of intergenerational equity resembles the specific understanding of *Brown Weiss'* doctrine and its conception of a planetary trust between all generations.[946] Further, the court did not only consider the living young generation to be protected, but also *unborn* future generations, as it stipulated:

> In terms of intergenerational equity, the transgression is obvious [due to the forecast of temperature increase]; future generations, including children who brought this action, will be directly affected, unless we presently reduce the deforestation rate to zero.[947]

These references of the Supreme Court, which partly went beyond what was explicitly claimed by the plaintiffs, illustrate the acceptance of rights of future generations as well as the procedural possibility for them to be represented by the currently living young generation.[948] *Joana Setzer* and *Lisa Benjamin* observed:

> With regard to standing, the decision applied the same constitutional provisions used for the protection of the environment for current generations, but this time to protect future generations, thereby substantially expanding the limits of such rights.[949]

Third, the Colombian decision demonstrates another particularity, which distinguishes it from the legal argumentation in the aforementioned Dutch and Norwegian proceedings. The former were based on mainly anthropocentric concepts of rights protection and operated within the procedural constraints of their proper European procedural systems. In contrast, the decision of the Colombian Supreme Court

[942] Supreme Court of Colombia, *Future Generations v. Ministry of the Environment and Others,* Decision, 5 April 2018, Retrieved January 3, 2025, from https://climatecasechart.com/non-us-case/future-generation-v-ministry-environment-others/, 47–49 (unofficial translation by Dejusticia).

[943] Ibid., 19–20, 37.

[944] Ibid., 19, 21 (own translation with the support of Deepl.com).

[945] Ibid., 19–20 (own translation with the support of Deepl.com).

[946] Brown Weiss (2021a), para. 8.

[947] *Future Generations v. Colombia* (Decision), *supra* note 942, 37 (own translation with the support of Deepl.com). See also Brown Weiss (2021a), para. 41.

[948] Acosta Alvarado and Rivas-Ramirez (2018), p. 524; Savaresi and Auz (2019), pp. 251–253; Setzer and Benjamin (2020), p. 92; Niehaus (2022); Garofalo (2022). Cf. also Parker et al. (2022), p. 79.

[949] Setzer and Benjamin (2020), p. 92.

reflects a more ecocentric approach to climate litigation and a rights-approach, which is not only based on individual fundamental rights but also on collective rights.[950] The court stated:

> This conception is the main essence on which the concept of the intrinsic value of the environment is based: respect for oneself implies, in itself, 'respect for the part of oneself that is composed of nature, and of which future generations will, in turn, be a part'.[951]

Consequently, the court also declared the Amazon a subject of rights, which is entitled to protection, conservation, maintenance and restoration,[952] as the Colombian Constitutional Court had already done with regard to the Atrato River in another decision.[953] This rights-based understanding with respect to a natural ecosystem gained an intergenerational component as the court ordered the Colombian State to construct an "intergenerational pact for the life of the Colombian Amazon".[954] These decisions are in line with the increasing developments of rights of nature in different legal systems in the Global South,[955] often grounded in Indigenous philosophies.[956] The decisions further illustrate how a more ecocentric approach to intergenerational issues could look like, if it focused on the interdependences between human beings, nonhuman animals and the ecosystem in general.[957] At the same time, such rights of nature approaches would face several obstacles in many European States due to the aforementioned individualistic conception of rights.[958] Although climate litigation in the Global North thus generally was not inspired by these more ecocentric approaches of courts in the Global South,[959] a truly transnational dialogue between the different legal systems would contribute to a further development of global environmental litigation with truly cosmopolitan decisions, which could include future generations as well as other species and nature itself in its protection.[960]

[950] *Future Generations v. Colombia* (Decision), *supra* note 942, pp. 20–21. See Niehaus (2022); Garofalo (2022).

[951] *Future Generations v. Colombia* (Decision), *supra* note 942, 21 (own translation with the support of Deepl.com).

[952] Ibid., pp. 45–46.

[953] In this *Atrato River Decision*, the Colombian Constitutional Court also argued with the protection of future generations and promoted an ecocentric approach to environmental rights, see CCLD (2015-2016).

[954] *Future Generations v. Colombia* (Decision), *supra* note 942, 46, 49 (unofficial translation by Dejusticia). See also Niehaus and Davies (2021), pp. 244–245; Slobodian (2020), p. 586.

[955] In more detail, see Burdon and Williams (2016); Tabios Hillebrecht and Berros (2017).

[956] See Tănăsescu (2020).

[957] On these ecocentric approaches, see already *supra* in Sect. 2.2.1.2.1.

[958] Schimmöller (2020). Cf. also Kauffman and Martin (2018).

[959] See Gellinsky and Fuchs (2021).

[960] See Niehaus (2022). On the links between intergenerational and nature-based arguments, see Lawrence (2022). For some pending cases in South American States, see *infra* notes 1082–1089.

##### *5.3.3.3.3.2 Potential Implicit Approaches to Representation*

The foregoing cases, which explicitly recognised the representation of future generations before national courts in one way or the other, have remained the exception in global environmental litigation. Although the complaints, in which the interests of future generations were explicitly or implicitly invoked, have increased in the last decades and years,[961] most proceedings on intergenerational equity lacked a sufficiently clear answer on genuine representation of future generations.

In 1996, the Supreme Court of Bangladesh rejected the petitioner's reliance on the *Oposa* jurisprudence in *Farooque v. Bangladesh.*[962] However, this constituted a rare example of explicit rejection of legal standing for future generations. For instance, several courts in India[963] and in Pakistan[964] referred to intergenerational equity or to future generations, but without actually addressing the issue of legal standing.[965] The Supreme Court of Pakistan stated in a recent decision:

> The great silent majority of future generations is rendered powerless and needs a voice. This Court should be mindful that its decisions also adjudicate upon the rights of the future generations of this country. It is important to question ourselves; how will the future generations look back on us and what legacy we leave for them?[966]

[961] Generally, see, e.g., Brown Weiss (2021a), paras. 36–48; Burgers (2020a), pp. 207–259.

[962] Supreme Court of Bangladesh, *Farooque vs. Government of Bangladesh,* Decision, 25 July 1996, 1 BLC (AD) (1996) 189. See also Manguiat and Yu (2003), p. 494; Fitzmaurice (2004), p. 191; Mensah (2008), p. 807.

[963] See, e.g., Calcutta High Court, *People United for Better Living v. State of West Bengal,* Order, 24 September 1992, 97 CWN 142, para. 2; Supreme Court of India, *Goa Foundation v. Union of India & Ors,* Judgment, 21 April 2014, 435 SCC 2012, paras. 68, 77–78, 86, 88.5, 88.10. See also Molinari (2015), pp. 145–146 with further references; Brown Weiss (2021a), para. 40; Scholtz (2021), pp. 342–343.

[964] Lahore High Court, Lahore Judicial Department, *Asghar Leghari v. Federation of Pakistan,* Judgment, 25 January 2018, Retrieved January 3, 2025, from https://climatecasechart.com/non-us-case/ashgar-leghari-v-federation-of-pakistan/, para. 12; Lahore High Court, Lahore Judicial Department, *Sheikh Asim Farooq v. Federation of Pakistan etc.,* Judgment, 30 August 2019, Retrieved January 3, 2025, from https://climatecasechart.com/non-us-case/sheikh-asim-farooq-v-federation-of-pakistan-etc/, paras. 5, 29; Supreme Court of Pakistan, *D. G. Khan Cement Company Ltd. v. Government of Punjab,* Judgment, 15 April 2021, Retrieved January 3, 2025, from https://climatecasechart.com/non-us-case/d-g-khan-cement-company-v-government-of-punjab/, para. 19. See also Dellinger (2018), pp. 538–539; Brown Weiss (2021a), para. 46.

[965] For an overview, see Hadjiargyrou (2016), pp. 266–267. who considered that "the concept of intergenerational equity is merely invoked to stress the gravity of environmental concerns and not exercised in its entirety as [Edith Brown Weiss] envisages it […]".

[966] *Khan Cement v. Pakistan* (Judgment), *supra* note 964, para. 19. See also Mensink (2022); Bertram (2023), pp. 135–136.

Sometimes, the representation of future generations' interests was linked to the public trust doctrine in its intergenerational dimension.[967] In the recent proceeding of *Pandey v. India*, the petitioners had explicitly based their claim on the right to a healthy environment of "the entire class of children and future generations",[968] referring both to the principle of intergenerational equity and to the *Oposa* jurisprudence.[969] The national court dismissed the petition for other reasons, again without addressing representation of future generations.[970]

Inspired by the Dutch *Urgenda* proceedings, the Belgian environmental NGO 'ASBL Klimaatzaak' challenged the Belgian State's insufficient approach of reducing greenhouse gas emissions.[971] The NGO based its claim on its by-laws, which stipulated its aim "to protect current and future generations from [hu]man-made climate change and biodiversity loss".[972] Contrary to Urgenda, the Belgian association did not explicitly invoke standing from these by-laws; it did "not 'talk for' but 'talk about' unborn future generations".[973] Nevertheless, this case constitutes a part of the many children-rights-based proceedings of the last years.[974] The Court of First Instance decided partly in favour of the plaintiffs in 2021, as it found the Belgian State to be in breach of its duty of care for insufficient climate protection. Yet, it did not address the issue of standing on behalf of future generations at all.[975] In 2016, a Swedish court rendered a comparable decision, which did not touch upon the representation of future generations despite the plaintiffs' representative claim.[976]

---

967 ILC (2021), p. 19 (at footnote 46) with further references; Razzaque (2001). Cf. e.g., Supreme Court of India, *Vellore Citizens Welfare Forum vs Union Of India & Ors,* Judgment, 28 August 1996, 1996 5 SCR 241. On the emergence of public trust claims in future climate litigation in China, see Zhou and Qin (2021), p. 264. In more detail on the relevance of the public trust doctrine, see *infra* notes 989–996.

968 *Pandey v. India* (Petition), *supra* note 893, p. 25.

969 Ibid., 3, 25, 43, 46. See also Chaturvedi (2021), pp. 1465, 1469.

970 See CCLD (2017-2019).

971 See CCLD (2014-2023); Dellinger (2018), pp. 536–537; Burgers (2020a), pp. 218–223.

972 Brussels Court of First Instance, *ASBL Klimaatzaak v. Belgian State* et al., Judgment, 17 June 2021, Retrieved January 3, 2025, from https://climatecasechart.com/non-us-case/vzw-klimaatzaak-v-kingdom-of-belgium-et-al/, p. 54 (unofficial translation with the support of Deepl.com). Similarly, a French NGO—*Notre affaire à tous*—based its climate litigation case on comparable association by-laws, see Torre-Schaub (2021), pp. 130–135. Cf. also Epstein and Deckert (2021), p. 360. In this role, the NGO also acted as *amicus curiae* before the French Constitutional Council in another proceeding, see French Constitutional Council, *In Re Climate Resilience Bill,* Amicus curiae brief by Notre Affaire à Tous Association, 15 October 2019, Retrieved January 3, 2025, from http://climatecasechart.com/non-us-case/external-contribution-to-the-french-constitutional-council/, p. 2.

973 Burgers (2020a), p. 222.

974 Ibid. See already *supra* notes 833–838.

975 *ASBL Klimaatzaak v. Belgium* (Judgment), *supra* note 972. The subsequent decision of the Court of Appeal of Brussels did not address this issue of standing either: Court of Appeal of Brussels, *Klimaatzaak* et al. *v. Belgian State* et al., Judgment, 30 November 2023, Retrieved January 3, 2025, from https://climatecasechart.com/non-us-case/vzw-klimaatzaak-v-kingdom-of-belgium-et-al/

976 In detail, see Burgers (2020a), pp. 224–227.

In 2020, the Constitutional Court of Hungary decided on a case brought by the Hungarian Parliamentary Commissioner for Future Generations in the context of protection of natural resources for future generations.[977] Formally, this case was not initiated by a civil society actor; instead, it constitutes a rare exception of formal representation by a public national entity with the power to initiate litigation on behalf of future generations.[978]

In the following, two judicial developments are presented in more detail, which did neither explicitly confirm nor reject legal standing for future generations, but their impact for intergenerational litigation cannot be underestimated: the status in US litigation, and particularly the *Juliana v. United States* case (Sect. 5.3.3.3.3.2.1), as well as the recent German case law in *Neubauer* et al. (Sect. 5.3.3.3.3.2.2).

###### *5.3.3.3.3.2.1 Litigation in the USA and Juliana v. United States*

The first important development took place in United States case law over the last years. Environmental and climate litigation generally is much more common in the USA with more than 1.300 climate change-related proceedings in total.[979] As within other jurisdictions, legal standing often is a problematic issue in these cases that address common goods such as the protection of the environment.[980] As *Bradley Bobertz* stated regarding intergenerational equity in US law, certain conceptual frustration "results from an individualized conception of rights and injuries", which also influenced the traditional standing doctrine.[981] In this context, the *Sierra Club* case offers interesting insights.[982] In this case, the Sierra Club, a US conservation organisation, brought suit against construction permits that had been granted to Walt Disney Enterprises for constructions in the Sequoia National Park. The plaintiffs argued that these constructions "would destroy or otherwise adversely affect the scenery, natural and historic objects and wildlife of the park, and would impair the enjoyment of the park for future generations."[983] After the district court had first affirmed standing for the NGO, the Supreme Court rejected the plaintiffs' standing to sue due to a strict understanding of the "injury in fact" requirement.[984] It thereby rejected to confer "standing upon organizations that have demonstrated 'an organizational interest in the problem' of environmental [...] protection".[985] However, two of the dissenting judges in this case argued for "an imaginative expansion

977 See Brown Weiss (2021a), para. 42.

978 See already *supra* in Sect. 5.3.2.1, notes 458–460.

979 Setzer and Higham (2021), p. 10.

980 Cf. Hodas (2018).

981 Bobertz (1987), p. 172. See also Mensah (2008), p. 806.

982 In detail, see Bobertz (1987), pp. 172–175.

983 US Supreme Court, *Sierra Club v. Morton,* Judgment, 19 April 1972, 405 U.S. 727, p. 734.

984 Ibid., pp. 740–741. On the general requirements of legal standing in the USA, see Farber (2021), pp. 239–241.

985 *Sierra Club* (Judgment), *supra* note 983, pp. 738–739.

of our traditional concepts of standing in order to enable an organization such as the Sierra Club [...] to litigate environmental issues".[986] Several commentators have elaborated on possible ways of intergenerational standing in US environmental law.[987] The increasing politicisation of the judicial landscape generally complicates to predict future judicial approaches to the standing doctrine in the context of climate litigation and future generations.[988]

In this context, public trust claims constitute an important form of litigation for the representation of future generations.[989] The public trust doctrine is part of domestic law in the USA and obliges the government to "act as a trustee and hold certain resources, such as water and/or property in trust for its citizens".[990] Beyond this basic understanding, it encompasses the "responsibility of the government, as trustee, to protect [these resources] from harm and ensure their use for the public and future generations".[991] This book does not analyse the US public trust doctrine in detail,[992] but the parallels to *Brown Weiss'* concept of an intergenerational trust become obvious and have already been illustrated above.[993] As early as 1971, a US district court extended the legal standing of an NGO in a public trust claim and included "generations yet unborn" in the members of the respective class action who have been granted standing.[994] While this case did not serve as precedent for the representation of future generations,[995] public trust litigation has become more popular in the last decade as several cases in all US States have been initiated by the organisation 'Our Children's Trust', which invoked the governmental duty to preserve natural resources for the benefit of current and future generations.[996]

With regard to legal standing for future generations, the recent proceedings in *Juliana v. United States* constitute the most important climate litigation case in the

---

[986] Ibid., 755, 757 (Dissenting Opinions of Justice Brennan and Justice Blackmun). Comparing these opinions with the *Farooque v. Bangladesh* and the *Oposa* case, see Mensah (2008), pp. 807–808.

[987] Rosenkranz (1986); Allen (1994); Just (1996).

[988] Farber (2021), pp. 238, 240.

[989] Niehaus and Davies (2021), pp. 243–244; Slobodian (2020), pp. 580–582. For some climate-related public trust proceedings, see CCLD (2011-2024). See also Montgomery (2021), pp. 342–345; UNEP (2017), pp. 23–25.

[990] Nguyen (2017), p. 354.

[991] Bosselmann (2020), p. 55. See also Nguyen (2017), pp. 354–355; Michallet (2018), p. 154.

[992] Generally, see Sax (1970).

[993] Brown Weiss (1984b); Redgwell (2016), p. 191; Collins (2017), pp. 315–319; Slobodian (2020), p. 582. See *supra* in Sect. 2.2.1.3.

[994] US District Court for the District of New Jersey, *Cape May County Chapter, Inc., Izaak Walton League of America v. Tito Macchia* et al., Judgment, 16 June 1971, 329 F.Supp. 504, p. 514. Questioning this case's value as precedent, see Bobertz (1987), p. 172 (at footnote 47).

[995] For some further public trust case law, see Redgwell (2016), pp. 191–192.

[996] See Lawrence (2016), p. 31; Laielli (2021), p. 1152 as well as *supra* note 989. For a recent complaint that is built on the public trust doctrine, see CCLD (2022-2024a). For public trust litigation in other States, see, e.g., CCLD (2012-today); CCLD (2016b-today) as well as *supra* note 967.

USA.[997] A group of plaintiffs, mainly children, had filed a lawsuit in 2015 against the federal government of the USA and asserted that the government violated their constitutional rights to life, liberty and property by causing dangerous carbon dioxide concentrations. They also argued that the government has violated its obligation to protect essential natural resources under the public trust doctrine.[998] Apart from the children and an NGO, "Future Generations" were explicitly listed as plaintiffs, represented by "their Guardian *Dr. James Hansen*".[999] The complaint invoked their "legal right to inherit well-stewarded public trust resources and to legal protection of their fundamental rights".[1000] The developments in the *Juliana* proceeding are ambiguous with regard to its impact on climate litigation in general and the representation of future generations in particular.[1001] The case occupied three different courts as the US government attempted several procedural steps to avoid a ruling on the substantive matter; the government argued before a District Court, a Court of Appeals and the Supreme Court that the plaintiffs lacked standing and, thus, it sought a dismissal of the case.[1002] Among this procedural back and forth, two decisions are of particular importance, even though in quite opposite ways.

In 2016, the plaintiffs were granted legal standing before the District Court of Oregon despite the government's objections.[1003] *Judge Aiken's* order confirmed that the plaintiffs met all of the traditional standing requirements under US law and denied the government's motion to dismiss.[1004] Although the order further elaborated broadly on the plaintiffs' possibility to bring a public trust claim and on its intergenerational elements,[1005] the Judge pointed out, in an *obiter dictum*, that it was not decisive for the present case to decide on the standing of future generations, since the other plaintiffs undoubtedly had standing to sue.[1006] The order concluded:

> This lawsuit may be groundbreaking, but that fact does not alter the legal standards governing the motions to dismiss. Indeed, the seriousness of plaintiffs' allegations underscores how vitally important it is for this Court to apply those standards carefully and

---

[997] For an overview, see CCLD (2015a-today). For another interesting analysis, see Niehaus (2023), pp. 344–352.

[998] US District Court for the District of Oregon, ninth Circuit, *Juliana v. United States,* Complaint, 12 August 2015, Retrieved January 3, 2025, from http://climatecasechart.com/case/juliana-v-united-states/

[999] Ibid., para. 92. See also US District Court for the District of Oregon, ninth Circuit, *Juliana v. United States,* Expert Report of James E. Hansen, 28 June 2018, Retrieved January 3, 2025, from http://climatecasechart.com/case/juliana-v-united-states/, pp. 1, 5.

[1000] *US District Court, Juliana* (Complaint), *supra* note 998, para. 92.

[1001] In overview, see Farber (2021), pp. 249–250.

[1002] "Juliana v. United States" (2021), p. 1931 (at footnote 24).

[1003] US District Court for the District of Oregon, ninth Circuit, *Juliana v. United States,* Opinion and Order, 10 November 2016, 217 F. Supp. 3d 1224.

[1004] Ibid., pp. 1242–1248.

[1005] Ibid., 1252–1262, particularly 1260.

[1006] Ibid., 1248 (at footnote 5).

> correctly. Federal courts too often have been cautious and overly deferential in the arena of environmental law, and the world has suffered for it.[1007]

The second relevant decision was issued by the Court of Appeals for the ninth Circuit in 2020 after an interlocutory appeal of the US government.[1008] While the Court of Appeals found that the plaintiffs met the injury and the causation requirements,[1009] it rejected the third requirement, redressability, on separation of powers reasons.[1010] This conservative approach to legal standing complicates the representation of future generations based on a public trust even though, once again, the court did not directly address future generations. The Court of Appeals decision was not rendered unanimously, but *Judge Staton* adopted a much-noticed dissenting opinion.[1011] Underlining the irreversibility of the potential damage for future generations,[1012] *Staton* found that the remedies sought by the plaintiffs met the redressability requirement so that they would have standing.[1013] She concluded:

> The denial of an individual, constitutional right – though grievous and harmful – can be corrected in the future, even if it takes 91 years. And that possibility provides hope for future generations. Where is the hope in today's decision?[1014]

Despite these promising pronunciations of *Judge Aiken* of the District Court and *Judge Staton* of the Court of Appeals, the proceedings could thus be considered to have failed in the end as they have never reached the merits of the case.[1015] On the

---

[1007] Ibid., p. 1262.

[1008] *US Court of Appeals, Juliana* (Opinion), *supra* note 550. See also Montgomery (2021), pp. 346–353.

[1009] *US Court of Appeals, Juliana* (Opinion), *supra* note 550, pp. 1168–1169.

[1010] Ibid., 1171–1172, 1175: "There is much to recommend the adoption of a comprehensive scheme to decrease fossil fuel emissions and combat climate change, […]. But it is beyond the power of an Article III court to order, design, supervise, or implement the plaintiffs' requested remedial plan. As the opinions of their experts make plain, any effective plan would necessarily require a host of complex policy decisions entrusted, for better or worse, to the wisdom and discretion of the executive and legislative branches." While the district court had also been sensible to the issue, it came to a different conclusion; that it would be allowed "to direct defendants to ameliorate plaintiffs' injuries but limit its ability to specify precisely how to do so", see *US District Court, Juliana* (Opinion and Order), *supra* note 1003, p. 1241. For some general remarks on separation of powers, see already *supra* in Sect. 5.3.3.1.2.

[1011] US Court of Appeals for the ninth Circuit, *Juliana v. United States,* Dissenting Opinion of Judge Staton, 17 January 2020, 947 F.3d 1175.

[1012] Ibid., p. 1176.

[1013] Ibid., p. 1182.

[1014] Ibid., p. 1191. See also Slobodian (2020), pp. 588–589.

[1015] A motion for rehearing *en banc* before the Court of Appeal had been denied in 2021, see US Court of Appeals for the ninth Circuit, *Juliana v. United States,* Order, Rehearing en banc denied, 10 February 2021, 986 F.3d 1295. Afterwards, the plaintiffs amended their complaint before the district court in order to seek declaratory relief, after having failed in settling the dispute with the new Biden-Harris administration, cf. Montgomery (2021), p. 354. Until today, the proceeding is ongoing, again before the three different courts due to procedural reasons. Currently, it is pending before the Supreme Court with the plaintiffs' petition for a writ of mandamus filed in September 2024. In more detail, see CCLD (2015a-today).

procedural level, it remains difficult for plaintiffs, even more so for future generations, to invoke their constitutional rights in the USA with regard to insufficient governmental climate change policies.[1016] Proponents of a strict separation of powers doctrine have welcomed the decision of the Court of Appeals.[1017] Nonetheless, the ambiguity of the *Juliana* case's impact should not be underestimated. Some commentators have underlined the many positive effects of the decisions in *Juliana*.[1018] The whole proceeding definitely contributed to a large publicity and sensibility towards the topic, including more than 25 *amicus briefs* that had been filed before the courts.[1019] This publicity, combined with the judicial self-restraint to address federal climate policy, could encourage environmental activists and civil society to turn even more actively to the policy-makers.[1020] In this sense, *Judge Aiken's* order can be used as convincing argument that "the right to a climate system capable of sustaining human life is fundamental to a free and ordered society [...]".[1021] It is also important to note that the respective courts did not dismiss the plaintiffs' arguments on the merits—to the contrary, the judges unequivocally endorsed the plaintiffs' extensive scientific reasoning and stated:[1022]

> Reluctantly, we conclude that such relief is beyond our constitutional power. Rather, the plaintiffs' impressive case for redress must be presented to the political branches of government.[1023]

In the context of future generations, the courts avoided to explicitly address the issue of representation, like many other courts.[1024] Nonetheless, the progressive approach to the traditional standing doctrine in the District Court illustrates that some US domestic courts are ready to endorse new solutions to public interest litigation in the context of environmental protection and climate change. Quite recently, a settlement agreement between the parties in a Hawaiian public trust litigation case explicitly acknowledged that the State's public trust obligations exist "for the benefit of present and future generations".[1025] Furthermore, the inherent connection between the

---

[1016] Mintz (2020), p. 204. With regard to the Supreme Court, see also Farber (2021), p. 250.

[1017] Wegener (2019), pp. 134–136.

[1018] Farber (2021), p. 250; Kempf (2021), pp. 1025–1039; Montgomery (2021), p. 355; Niehaus (2021), pp. 243, 250; Spentzou (2021), p. 170. See also Mintz (2020), pp. 203–204.

[1019] Niehaus (2021), pp. 243–244.

[1020] See Levy (2019), pp. 505–506; Kempf (2021), pp. 1035–1039. On the important interrelation between strategic litigation and climate activism, see Schönberger (2021).

[1021] *US District Court, Juliana* (Opinion and Order), *supra* note 1003, p. 1250. with explicit reference to *Oposa v. Factoran* (Decision), *supra* note 866, pp. 187–188. On the positive impact of this decision, see Montgomery (2021), p. 355.

[1022] Aidun (2020); Mintz (2020), p. 203.

[1023] *US Court of Appeals, Juliana* (Opinion), *supra* note 550, p. 1165.

[1024] Slobodian (2020), p. 577. See already *supra* notes 963–965, 973, 976.

[1025] Circuit Court of the First Circuit of the State of Hawai'i, *Navahine F. v. Hawai'i Department of Transportation,* Settlement Agreement, 17 May 2024, Retrieved January 3, 2025, from https://climatecasechart.com/case/navahine-f-v-hawaii-department-of-transportation/

public trust doctrine and the concept of intergenerational equity has been illustrated in the *Juliana* case[1026]—as well as in other jurisdictions.[1027] Therefore, some commentators have deduced from the *Juliana* decisions that so-called "atmospheric trust litigation" can still bring promising results in the future.[1028] If plaintiffs invoked the protection of the atmosphere as a trust asset under the public trust doctrine, they would thereby automatically act on behalf of present as well as future generations.[1029] More generally, future US climate litigation efforts could always refer to *Judge Staton's* dissenting opinion, which declared on the role of the judiciary in climate protection:

> The majority portrays any relief we can offer as just a drop in the bucket. [...] But we are perilously close to an overflowing bucket. These final drops matter. A lot. Properly framed, a court order – even one that merely postpones the day when remedial measures become insufficiently effective – would likely have a real impact on preventing the impending cataclysm.[1030]

##### *5.3.3.3.3.2.2 Neubauer et al. v. Germany*

Another important decision on intergenerational equity was rendered in 2021 by the Federal Constitutional Court of Germany in *Neubauer* et al.[1031] Between 2018 and 2020, a number of plaintiffs, including youth plaintiffs, foreign nationals from Nepal and Bangladesh and two environmental NGOs, have raised four constitutional complaints claiming that the German Climate Protection Law[1032] violated several fundamental rights under the German constitution ('Basic Law').[1033] The Federal Constitutional Court ruled in favour of the plaintiffs and declared parts of the German Climate Protection Law to be unconstitutional as the legislator did not proportionally distribute the necessary greenhouse gas reduction burdens over time; the legislator was obliged "to safeguard fundamental freedom over time and to spread the opportunities associated with freedom proportionately across generations".[1034] The court's exact findings were innovative as it did not use a reasoning

[1026] Laielli (2021), pp. 1152, 1170.

[1027] ILC (2021), p. 19 (at footnote 46). See also *supra* note 967.

[1028] Wood and Woodward (2016); Nguyen (2017), pp. 353–357; Schneider (2017); Couch (2020). Cf. also Kempf (2021), p. 1039.

[1029] Nguyen (2017), pp. 355–357; Schneider (2017), pp. 61–62; Couch (2020), pp. 226–232.

[1030] *US Court of Appeals, Juliana* (Dissenting Opinion of Judge Staton), *supra* note 1011, p. 1182.

[1031] Federal Constitutional Court of Germany, *Climate Change (Neubauer* et al.*)*, Order, 24 March 2021, 74 (2021) NJW 1723–1751.

[1032] *German Climate Protection Law* (DELETE), adopted 12 December 2019, entered into force 18 December 2019, Bundesgesetzblatt I (2019), S. 2513.

[1033] Basic Law of Germany. For an overview of the proceeding, see CCLD (2018c).

[1034] *Neubauer* et al. (Order), *supra* note 1031, para. 183 (court translation).

based on constitutional duties to protect, (e.g., the right to life).[1035] Instead, it turned to an intertemporal understanding of fundamental freedoms: if the State did not act accordingly to guarantee an intertemporally proportionate burden-sharing with regard to carbon dioxide emissions, this inaction would result in a disproportionate distribution of fundamental freedoms among generations.[1036] Although the decision was primarily based on German constitutional law, it contained important international components. The court not only based many assumptions on the international climate protection regime and findings of the IPCC,[1037] but it also stressed the constitutional obligation for the German State to contribute to international cooperation for the resolution of the climate crisis.[1038] The present work focuses on a few relevant observations with respect to the protection of future generations in the *Neubauer* et al. decision.[1039]

According to the relevant constitutional provision, the German State is explicitly obliged to protect the natural foundations of life "mindful also of its responsibility towards future generations".[1040] Although the Basic Law as well as the constitutional jurisprudence thus incorporate intergenerational equity into German constitutional law,[1041] the court has underlined that this provision does not confer any subjective rights to anyone.[1042] Some of the plaintiffs had invoked a subjective "right to a future consistent with human dignity",[1043] but the court did not answer whether such a right exists in the German constitution.[1044] Furthermore, the court explicitly clarified that it does not consider future generations right-holders under the German constitution:

> The duty to afford protection against risks to life and health can also establish a duty to protect future generations. [...] However, this duty to afford intergenerational protection has

1035 Ibid., paras. 143–181. With regard to duties to protect, the court adopted a very restrictive approach and considered the federal legislator to have a large margin of appreciation, based on the separation of powers, see ibid., para. 152. This margin of appreciation also resulted in the rejection of the foreign plaintiffs' claims from Nepal and Bangladesh, see ibid., paras. 173–181., which was already criticised elsewhere, see Kahl and Bustami (2021); Buser (2021b); Niehaus (2022).

1036 *Neubauer* et al. (Order), *supra* note 1031, paras. 183, 192.

1037 Ibid., paras. 204, 210–212.

1038 Ibid., paras. 199–204.

1039 For a more general analysis, see, e.g., Aust (2022).

1040 Art. 20a of the Basic Law of Germany.

1041 Buser (2021a), p. 1417; Kotzé (2021), p. 1440.

1042 *Neubauer* et al. (Order), *supra* note 1031, para. 112.

1043 Also "right to a humane future", see Federal Constitutional Court of Germany, *Climate Change (Neubauer* et al.*)*, Complaint, 6 February 2020, Retrieved January 3, 2025, from https://climatecasechart.com/non-us-case/neubauer-et-al-v-germany/, p. 105 (unofficial translation).

1044 *Neubauer* et al. (Order), *supra* note 1031, para. 113.

> a solely objective dimension because future generations – either as a whole or as the sum of individuals not yet born – do not yet carry any fundamental rights in the present [...].[1045]

Since German procedural constitutional law is rather strict with regard to legal standing of individuals and excludes any form of *actio popularis* petitions,[1046] none of the plaintiffs did explicitly invoke any rights of or representation for future generations:

> The complainants are not asserting the rights of unborn persons or even of entire future generations, neither of whom enjoy subjective fundamental rights [...]. Rather, the complainants are invoking their own fundamental rights.[1047]

For comparable procedural reasons, the court dismissed the complaints of the two environmental NGOs acting as "advocates of nature" as inadmissible because the associations lacked standing to lodge such a constitutional complaint.[1048] Although the decision of the court seemingly rejected any form of intergenerational standing for future generations, a proper analysis must come to a more differentiated result. On the one hand, it is obvious that the German court rejected the idea that future *unborn* generations could be right-holders today.[1049] *Andreas Buser* fittingly observed that the innovative intertemporal duty only protected "the fundamental rights of *living* generations *in the future*" (emphasis added).[1050]

On the other hand, this does not hinder any form of representation of the interests of future generations in general. Three observations can be made on this issue. First, it is reminded that the current analysis does not understand "representation" as irrevocably intertwined with the notion of rights. A representative of future generations could either represent their rights or, more broadly, their interests in general, so that it is not necessary to accept rights of future generations in order to allow for their representation.[1051] Consequently, the court's assessment that future generations could not have subjective rights did not automatically constitute a rejection of their representation.

Second, the Federal Constitutional Court did not have to decide on the question whether the plaintiffs had standing on behalf of future generations as none of them had actually decided to invoke such an intergenerational standing.[1052] Nonetheless, the court addressed both of these questions together (representation and subjective rights), as it obviously automatically linked the legal standing on behalf of future

[1045] Ibid., para. 146 (court translation).

[1046] Ibid., para. 110. According to *Andreas Buser*, the court implicitly accepted "a global *actio popularis*" in its decision, see Buser (2021a), pp. 1412–1413.

[1047] *Neubauer* et al. (Order), *supra* note 1031, para. 109 (court translation).

[1048] Ibid., paras. 136–137 (court translation). See also Aust (2022), p. 152.

[1049] *Neubauer* et al. (Order), *supra* note 1031, paras. 109, 146. See also Krämer-Hoppe (2021), p. 1400; Kotzé (2021), p. 1440; Vöneky and Beck (2022), pp. 276–277; Nguyen (2021); Aust (2022), p. 153.

[1050] Buser (2021a), p. 1410.

[1051] See *supra* notes 380–381 and note 770.

[1052] See *Neubauer* et al. (Order), *supra* note 1031, para. 109.

generations with the latter's subjective rights—an approach that is based on the strict procedural requirement in German law that standing to sue requires a subjective and individual right.[1053] Formally, the court thus rejected representation of future generations before a German court, if one equates legal standing to sue with the possibility to represent the interests of future generations. At a second glance, a less formal perspective speaks in favour of a strong intergenerational dimension of the decision—also with respect to *unborn* future generations. The Federal Constitutional Court underlined the objectively justiciable nature of the intergenerational obligations in the German Basic Law several times—there is a clear duty of the State towards future generations.[1054] Further, with regard to its innovative approach to the "intertemporal guarantees of freedom",[1055] the court clarified that it was aware of the fact that future generations have no voice in the democratic political process:

> In Art. 20a [of the Basic Law], environmental protection is elevated to a matter of constitutional significance because the democratic political process is organised along more short-term lines based on election cycles, placing it at a structural risk of being less responsive to tackling the ecological issues that need to be pursued over the long term. It is also because future generations – those who will be most affected – naturally have no voice of their own in shaping the current political agenda.[1056]

Beyond the strict requirement of legal standing—which is not open to a formal representation of future generations before German courts—one could still conclude that the "ground-breaking"[1057] decision and its innovative intertemporal approach to Article 20a of the Basic Law offer an implicit form of constitutionalised representation of future generations' interests in the democratic process.[1058]

This leads to the third important observation. While the intergenerational focus of the decision clearly addressed the relationship between the older generation and the younger living generation,[1059] it has been illustrated above that youth-led climate litigation often has a future-oriented perspective that also protects and represents the interests of *unborn* future generations.[1060] Although the court was certainly inspired by other climate litigation cases worldwide, including youth-led litigation,[1061] it unfortunately failed to draw inspiration from jurisdictions in the Global South, which sometimes have been more explicitly future-oriented, such as the Colombian

---

[1053] Ibid., para. 110. Cf. Nguyen (2021).

[1054] *Neubauer* et al. (Order), *supra* note 1031, paras. 146, 148, 205.

[1055] Ibid., para. 183 (court translation).

[1056] Ibid., para. 206 (court translation). See also *Borgarting Court of Appeal, People v. Arctic Oil* (Judgment), *supra* note 920, p. 18; Goldmann (2021).

[1057] Spier (2021).

[1058] Cf. also Biermann (2021); Bäumler (2021).

[1059] *Neubauer* et al. (Order), *supra* note 1031, para. 109; Krämer-Hoppe (2021), p. 1400.

[1060] See *supra* notes 833–838, 867–869.

[1061] *Neubauer* et al. (Order), *supra* note 1031, paras. 121, 157, 161, 202., e.g., with references to the *Urgenda* and *Juliana* cases.

*Future Generations* case.[1062] However, the German court deduced a principle of intergenerational proportionality from the German constitution:

> [O]ne generation must not be allowed to consume large portions of the CO2 budget while bearing a relatively minor share of the reduction effort, if this would involve leaving subsequent generations with a drastic reduction burden and expose their lives to serious losses of freedom [...].[1063]

Although this was primarily applied to the living younger generation, the wording does not exclude future unborn generations from its scope of protection. Even if this protection is not based on a fundamental *right* of future generations, this understanding of intergenerational equity as a proportional distribution of opportunities across generations[1064] became justiciable by the currently living youth,[1065] also in the interest of future generations. Overall, the Federal Constitutional Court's decision can certainly not be invoked as an example for the explicit representation of future generations; but neither can it be interpreted as a clear-cut rejection of such representation. Regardless of the obvious procedural limits in German law, the interests of future generations witnessed a strengthening in the intertemporal approach to fundamental rights protection. In the sense of such future-oriented climate litigation, it is worth mentioning that several follow-up complaints have been raised before the Federal Constitutional Court in 2023 and 2024 due to a recent (weakening) amendment of the German Climate Protection Law. One of these complaints, raised by more than 54.000 individuals and two NGOs, is explicitly labelled as "Future Lawsuit" ("Zukunftsklage")—whereas it again primarily builds on the future of the *living* younger generation.[1066]

#### *5.3.3.3.3.3 An Outlook on Pending Case Law*

The foregoing analysis has illustrated that only few cases exist that explicitly addressed and recognised the legal standing of current plaintiffs to represent the rights or interests of future generations. Apart from the straight-forward wording in *Oposa*, some of the decisions in the *Urgenda*, *People v. Arctic Oil* and the *Future Generations* cases must be interpreted in the sense of allowing representation of future generations in today's judicial proceedings. Most other relevant domestic proceedings have not been as explicit, but the respective courts rather remained silent on the issue of standing on behalf of future generations as far as they considered it unnecessary to resolve this question.[1067] While some of them could

[1062] See *supra* notes 955–960. On the criticism, see also Gellinsky and Fuchs (2021); Mührel (2021); Niehaus (2022).

[1063] *Neubauer* et al. (Order), *supra* note 1031, para. 192 (court translation).

[1064] On a comparison between the court's reasoning and *John Rawls'* theory of distributive justice, see Berkemann (2021), pp. 712–713.

[1065] Cf. Bäumler (2021); Rath and Benner (2021); Buser (2021a), p. 1417.

[1066] For an overview, see Climate Rights Litigation Database (2024-today).

[1067] Burgers (2020a), p. 266.

be considered to implicitly accept such standing or representation, others are ambiguous and do not provide guidance in this question. The immense procedural and substantive differences between the jurisdictional systems do not facilitate a coherent answer to the question either.

Notwithstanding this, the existing domestic case law is promising with regard to the representation of future generations.[1068] Transnational discourse on different paths of environmental and climate litigation can increase the case law on intergenerational representation, depending on what plaintiffs will invoke in the future. In Spain, two similar proceedings were initiated by *Greenpeace* before the Supreme Court of Spain in 2020 and 2021; both of which are based, *inter alia*, on intergenerational equity as well as the rights of future generations.[1069] The complaints contain several references to climate litigation in other States.[1070] In the meantime, the Supreme Court decided one of the cases and dismissed the claims made by Greenpeace—yet, it did not refer to the question of intergenerational equity.[1071] In Pakistan, two currently pending climate cases have been explicitly filed on behalf of the plaintiffs "as well as on behalf of future generation and youth of Pakistan".[1072] Although both cases are still pending,[1073] in *Ali v. Pakistan*, the Supreme Court of Pakistan has already overruled a registrar's objection concerning the representation of future generations.[1074]

In 2019, another youth-led case was filed before a Canadian federal court in *La Rose v. Her Majesty the Queen.*[1075] The complaint was based on the public trust doctrine and it explicitly raised "issues that transcend the interests of the plaintiffs and clearly impact all children and youth, present and future generations".[1076] The plaintiffs further argued that "it is not reasonable to expect other children or youth to

---

1068 Cf. ibid., pp. 260–268.

1069 See, e.g., Supreme Court of Spain, *Greenpeace v. Spain,* Complaint, 15 December 2020, Retrieved January 3, 2025, from https://climatecasechart.com/non-us-case/greenpeace-v-spain/, pp. 149–153. For an overview, see CCLD (2020-2023).

1070 *Greenpeace v. Spain* (Complaint), *supra* note 1069, 132, 137, 151.

1071 Supreme Court of Spain, *Greenpeace v. Spain,* Judgment, 20 June 2023, Retrieved January 3, 2025, from https://climatecasechart.com/non-us-case/greenpeace-v-spain/

1072 Lahore High Court, Lahore Judicial Department, *Maria Khan v. Federation of Pakistan,* Order, 15 February 2019, Retrieved January 3, 2025, from https://climatecasechart.com/non-us-case/maria-khan-et-al-v-federation-of-pakistan-et-al/, p. 1. See also Supreme Court of Pakistan, *Rabab Ali v. Federation of Pakistan,* Petition, 1 April 2016, Retrieved January 3, 2025, from https://climatecasechart.com/non-us-case/ali-v-federation-of-pakistan-2/, p. 4.

1073 For an overview, see CCLD (2018-2019); CCLD (2016a-today).

1074 See Albers (2018), p. 140.

1075 Federal Court of Canada, *La Rose* et al. *v. Her Majesty the Queen of Canada* et al., Complaint, 25 October 2019, Retrieved January 3, 2025, from https://climatecasechart.com/non-us-case/la-rose-v-her-majesty-the-queen/. Generally, on youth-led climate litigation in Canada, see Cameron and Weyman (2022).

1076 *La Rose v. Canada* (Complaint), *supra* note 1075, para. 27(a).

have to bring their own claims and it is impossible that those of future generations can do so now".[1077] While the complaint was dismissed in the first instance for lack of public interest standing, the court did not specifically address the representation of future generations.[1078] In the meantime, the Court of Appeal has reversed the first instance court's dismissal and decided that the case can go to trial.[1079] However, the court explicitly rejected the plaintiffs' claim based on the public trust doctrine: It did not find sufficient precedent in Canadian law to substantiate the "trust-like duty to protect public resources in the way that the youth appellants desire".[1080]

Last but not least, several pending proceedings before Latin American courts illustrate the future-oriented and ecocentric legal regimes,[1081] which have already resulted in the progressive Colombian decision in *Future Generations*.[1082] In Argentina, at least two cases with intergenerational aspects are currently pending before different courts.[1083] Apart from several references to intergenerational equity and future generations, one of the complaints argued, *inter alia*:

> It is therefore in this approach that we say that future generations are a subject of collective rights, non-existent at present, but trans-temporally and trans-spatially *represented* subjects. They are holders of rights, they are creditors of the present generations, who, by virtue of the principle of intergenerational equity, [...], must transmit to them a patrimonial volume of assets equivalent to that which they received. (emphasis added)[1084]

Further, at least three cases before Brazilian courts also demonstrate a strong intergenerational component.[1085] *Carlotta Garofalo* observed with regard to Latin American climate litigation that "the intergenerational dimension of the environmental right [to a healthy environment] emerged in multiple instances" and in Brazil, this was "facilitated by the direct recognition of 'the duty to defend and preserve the environment for present and future generations' in the [Brazilian] Constitution".[1086] Consequently, in *PSB v. Brazil*, the plaintiffs invoked a fundamental right of both present and future generations and highlighted "its clear intergenerational

[1077] Ibid., para. 27(c).

[1078] Federal Court of Canada, *La Rose* et al. *v. Her Majesty the Queen of Canada* et al., Order, 27 October 2020, 2020 FC 1008.

[1079] Federal Court of Appeal of Canada, *La Rose* et al. *v. His Majesty the King of Canada* et al., Judgment, 13 December 2023, 2023 FCA 241.

[1080] Ibid., paras. 62, 122. For more details on the pending proceeding, see CCLD (2019b-today).

[1081] Garofalo (2022). Cf. also Niehaus (2022).

[1082] Cf. also with references to a Chilean court that accepted the invocation of a constitutional right on behalf of future generations: Lenzerini (2002), p. 84; González-Ricoy and Rey (2019), p. 4.

[1083] For overviews of these proceedings, see CCLD (2020a-today); CCLD (2022b-today).

[1084] Supreme Court of Argentina, *Asociación Civil por la Justicia Ambiental v. Province of Entre Ríos,* et al. *(Delta del Paraná),* Complaint, 2 July 2020, Retrieved January 3, 2025, from https://climatecasechart.com/non-us-case/asociacion-civil-por-la-justicia-ambiental-v-province-of-entre-rios-et-al/, p. 8 (own translation with the support of Deepl.com).

[1085] For overviews of these proceedings, see CCLD (2020c-today); CCLD (2020b-today); CCLD (2022a-today).

[1086] Garofalo (2022).

characteristic".[1087] In *IAS v. Brazil*, the plaintiffs raised a "transindividual and intergenerational legal claim" and sought the recognition of a "right to an ecologically balanced environment for present and future generations".[1088] In an interlocutory order, the regional court already stated:

> Environmental litigation to safeguard life, livelihoods and health, as well as litigation on behalf of future generations is still a novelty here. However, we do recognize that this new environmental litigation is fundamental, for it promotes not only legal and governmental measures, but also the consciousness and culture of society itself, which will become increasingly concerned with promoting sustainable development. And it is of the utmost importance that courts, when faced with such litigation, do not treat it as an ordinary lawsuit, with ordinary parties. It is increasingly necessary to analyze the theoretical support offered by philosophical and sociological considerations, in addition to international agreements that propose considerations in relation to intergenerational litigation, as well as the decisions already issued by the courts in this area, such as the *Urgenda* decision.[1089]

#### 5.3.3.3.4 Summary

From the restrictive *E.H.P. v. Canada* decision of the HRC in 1982 to the youth-led *Sacchi* case, in which representation of future generations was left unanswered in 2021; from the progressive *Oposa* judgment in 1993 to the rather reserved German *Neubauer* decision in 2021; from an explicit acknowledgement of representation in the first *Urgenda* and *Juliana* decisions to the ecocentric finding on the intergenerational claims of *Future Generations* in Colombia—climate litigation offers a broad variety of results for the representative judicial claim on behalf of future generations. These results differ between the international, the regional and the national level. They also differ from region to region and from jurisdiction to jurisdiction, depending on the respective jurisdictional cultures and the procedural legal systems. Although there is obviously no uniform answer to the totality of these jurisdictions, the following general observations can be deduced from the foregoing analysis of international, regional and national litigation of civil society actors against States.

First, under public international law strictly speaking, there is no universal institutional system of representation of future generations and their interests before international or regional courts with individual complaints procedures. As far as

---

[1087] Federal Supreme Court of Brazil, *Partido Socialista Brasileiro (PSB)* et al. *v. Brazil,* Application, 11 November 2020, Retrieved January 3, 2025, from https://climatecasechart.com/non-us-case/brazilian-socialist-party-and-others-v-brazil/, para. 233 (unofficial translation). See also ibid., paras. 231–233, 440.

[1088] Federal Regional Court of the fourth Region, *Institute of Amazonian Studies (IAS) v. Brazil,* Complaint, 8 October 2020, Retrieved January 3, 2025, from https://climatecasechart.com/non-us-case/institute-of-amazonian-studies-v-brazil/, pp. 35, 40 (unofficial translation).

[1089] Federal Regional Court of the fourth Region, *Institute of Amazonian Studies (IAS) v. Brazil,* Order, 20 August 2021, Retrieved January 3, 2025, from https://climatecasechart.com/non-us-case/institute-of-amazonian-studies-v-brazil/, p. 8 (court translation).

regional human rights bodies have addressed environmental questions with intergenerational aspects, they did generally not address the representation issue. Some plaintiffs have attempted to explicitly or implicitly raise the interests of future generations in their stead, but the respective bodies have preferred to remain superficial or silent on this question. Mostly, they considered it sufficient to decide the matter on the basis of the plaintiffs' proper legal standing. It seems unlikely that this reluctance will decrease before these regional courts, particularly due to their procedural constraints, but there are still cases pending in the context of (intergenerational) climate litigation.

Second, the national level offers much more insight on possibilities of intergenerational representation before the judiciary. Some courts have been bolder and more avant-garde in recognising the respective plaintiffs' standing on behalf of future generations. These recognitions range from explicit acceptance of the representation (*Oposa;* District Court in *Urgenda*; *People v. Arctic Oil*; *Future Generations*) to more careful reasoning that could be interpreted as an implicit recognition (e.g., *Juliana*; *Neubauer*; *Pandey v. India*; *ASBL Klimaatzaak*). However, most courts, including the latter, also preferred to remain silent on the issue if they were able to decide the cases with regard to the plaintiffs' own standing. So far, the (youth) plaintiffs always also invoked their proper rights and the respective NGOs were either supported in their claims by individual plaintiffs or they had standing in public interest litigation with regard to general environmental interests. Nonetheless, it is obvious that many jurisdictions have shown a certain openness to intergenerational litigation, either in a more abstract, symbolic way or in the context of public trust litigation, which contains strong intergenerational elements. These national proceedings do not establish a universal institutional framework, which would oblige States under international law to allow for judiciary representation of future generations. Yet, the development is promising as transnational judicial dialogue has already led to mutual inspiration by the courts. Furthermore, these decisions interact with the international legal system in the form of judicial internalisation, which can have a decisive impact on the future development of international law strictly speaking.[1090] The increasing phenomenon of climate litigation offers more test cases in the future—and more and more of them are also invoking the rights and interests of future (unborn) generations.

Third, three main actors who attempt to represent future generations can be identified both on the regional and on the national level. Environmental NGOs play an important role as their statutory goals often not only include the protection of environmental goods in general, but explicitly aim at the protection of current as well as future generations from the impacts of environmental degradation. These statutory goals qualify them as representatives of future generations despite the aforementioned problems of accountability and legitimacy. The second relevant actors are members of Indigenous communities and/or inhabitants of SIDS that are most affected by impacts of climate change already today. Despite their potential for

[1090] See briefly *infra* note in Sect. 7.3.4.2.2 [note 402].

intergenerational representation, they have not explicitly claimed to act on behalf of future generations so far. The third important actor is the currently living younger generation—children and youth. While they do not form part of "future generations" as understood in this book, they obviously have a strong connection to these unborn future generations, particularly since generations overlap temporally. Furthermore, the interests of the youth and of future generations often resemble each other or coincide so that they can represent their proper rights and interests simultaneously with the interests of future generations. Youth-led litigation increased in the last years and most plaintiffs invoking standing or representation of future generations have been members of the younger generation. As *Lydia Slobodian* stated:

> By telling a story of children and young people fighting in the courts to preserve their future, raising the profile of climate cases, and increasing public awareness of future generations' rights, intergenerational equity in climate litigation is itself a source of hope.[1091]

Overall, the existing case law on intergenerational equity on the international and national level still lacks a coherent and systematic framework for the judicial representation of future generations. Despite the common threads of intergenerational litigation, this incoherence illustrates the non-binding character of the specific doctrine of intergenerational equity, which would require appropriate frameworks of implementation on the institutional, operative level. So far, the fragmentary, partly non-existent nature of implementation mechanisms on the international, regional and national level could reflect the more general conception of intergenerational equity to take into consideration the needs of future generations. Beyond an abstract consideration, the existing operative framework does not assist in the implementation of intergenerational equity as a legal norm.

#### 5.3.3.4 Representation in Proceedings Against Corporations

Besides judicial proceedings of individuals against States, litigation against private corporations could be considered another framework for the indirect implementation of intergenerational equity. This framework depends on the identification of corporations as duty-bearers of intergenerational equity. As elaborated, corporations are generally no subjects of international law apart from certain limited areas.[1092] With regard to international environmental law, corporations are not directly bound by any international obligations. Instead, States can be obliged to hold private actors accountable for causing environmental damage under due diligence obligations or specific civil liability regimes in environmental agreements.[1093] Consequently, most environmental obligations of private corporations emanate from national liability regimes. For this reason, any implementation of environmental obligations can only

[1091] Slobodian (2020), p. 589.

[1092] See *supra* in Sect. 5.1.2.2.

[1093] Muchlinski (2014), paras. 44–46.

take place on the national level where the respective victims could sue the responsible corporations for compensation.[1094] While it is not necessary that future generations are right-holders in order to be represented before courts, it would be necessary to conceive private corporations as fitting duty-bearers of intergenerational equity in order to consider them adequate defendants in judicial proceedings. Since this is not the case with regard to international law and intergenerational obligations, representation of future generations in judicial proceedings against corporations does not constitute a very promising path at this time.[1095] Nonetheless, there are some interesting developments in this context, which are briefly described in the following.

The relevance of climate change litigation for the implementation of intergenerational equity has already been illustrated in the foregoing sections. Beyond the demonstrated case law against States, climate litigation against private corporations has increased in the last years, most of it against fossil fuel companies.[1096] This form of climate litigation addresses the civil liability of private corporations under the respective national liability regimes.[1097] The cases are often based on national tort law as well as public or private nuisance claims.[1098] Proceedings against the private sector include cases against Carbon Majors, high emitting corporations or projects as well as financial markets cases.[1099] Most of these proceedings have been initiated in the USA,[1100] but as of today, more than 80 cases exist in other States.[1101]

Among the most relevant US proceedings, a US district court dismissed a claim of native Alaskans in 2009 seeking compensation from oil companies for impacts of climate change on their village *Kivalina*.[1102] The court dismissed the claim on grounds of the political question doctrine and due to lack of a sufficient causal link to establish standing.[1103] In Germany, the proceeding in the case *Lliuya v. RWE* is pending before the Higher Regional Court of Hamm.[1104] Therein, a Peruvian farmer argued that Germany's biggest electricity producer, RWE, had knowingly contributed to climate change by emitting substantial volumes of greenhouse gases. Thus,

[1094] Douhan (2019), para. 27.

[1095] Spentzou (2021), pp. 177–178.

[1096] See UNEP (2020), pp. 22–23; Setzer and Higham (2021), pp. 27–31. For a comprehensive analysis, see also Rumpf (2022).

[1097] See Faure and Peeters (2011), pp. 165–254 with several contributions; Lambooy and Palm (2016), pp. 324–332.

[1098] Dellinger (2018), pp. 528–533. See also UNEP (2017), pp. 34–36.

[1099] For a classification, see Setzer and Higham (2021), p. 28.

[1100] UNEP (2017), p. 34.

[1101] See CCLD (n.d.).

[1102] CCLD (2008-2013); Lambooy and Palm (2016), pp. 324–328.

[1103] *US District Court, Kivalina* (Judgment), *supra* note 522, pp. 871–881. On these issues, see in more detail *supra* in Sect. 5.3.3.1.

[1104] See CCLD (2015b-today); Rumpf (2019).

RWE would be under a duty to compensate him with regard to a portion of the expenses that were necessary to establish sufficient flood protections. After the first instance court dismissed the complaint for similar reasons of causation as in *Kivalina*,[1105] the Higher Regional Court of Hamm affirmed the appeal's admissibility and issued an order to take evidence on the risks and effects of climate change on the plaintiff's home and on RWE's contribution to that risk.[1106] Although the court has not adjudicated on the merits yet, it recognised that a private company could potentially be held liable for damage related to climate change—a promising development in law with regard to climate change litigation against private actors.[1107] Other cases against corporations have been decided or are pending in the USA,[1108] in the UK,[1109] in France,[1110] in Germany,[1111] and in many other States.[1112] In the USA, several public actors, such as larger cities, have raised public nuisance suits against fossil fuel companies.[1113] Despite their increasing relevance in climate litigation efforts, these cases against corporations remained backward-looking and addressed environmental harms that have been done in the past.[1114] In such civil liability cases, the claimants must demonstrate that they suffered an actual damage; they aim at compensation for damage done to existing individuals.[1115] This renders the representation of future generations in this type of proceedings difficult and unlikely.[1116] Consequently, none of these complaints were filed on behalf of future generations.[1117]

However, as far as complaints against private corporations are forward-looking and address positive duties to refrain from certain harmful activities *in the future*,[1118] they could theoretically include intergenerational duties as well as explicit or implicit representation,[1119] at least on the national level. In 2005, the plaintiffs in *Gbemre v. Shell* successfully challenged the practice of gas flaring in the Niger Delta by oil

[1105] *Regional Court of Essen, Lliuya* (Judgment), *supra* note 522, pp. 371–372.

[1106] Higher Regional Court of Hamm, *Lliuya v. RWE,* Order, 30 November 2017, 2018 ZUR 118, p. 119.

[1107] Rumpf (2019), p. 151. See also Wagner and Arntz (2021), pp. 410–411.

[1108] See Kosolapova (2011).

[1109] See Varvastian and Kalunga (2020).

[1110] See CCLD (2019-2024).

[1111] See Deutsche Umwelthilfe e.V. (2022). Generally, see Weller et al. (2021).

[1112] See *supra* note 1101.

[1113] Dellinger (2018), pp. 532–533. For some examples, see CCLD (2004-2011); CCLD (2018d).

[1114] Cf. Toft (2020), pp. 11–17.

[1115] Douhan (2019), paras. 15–16. See also Lambooy and Palm (2016), pp. 325–326.

[1116] Cf. van Dijk (2011), pp. 211–212; Spentzou (2021), pp. 177–181.

[1117] With regard to *Lliuya v. RWE* in Germany as well as *Notre Affaire à Tous v. Total* in France, see Burgers (2020a), pp. 223, 259.

[1118] Toft (2020), p. 17; Drugmand (2021).

[1119] Cf. Toft (2020), p. 26.

and gas companies before the Federal High Court of Nigeria.[1120] The court found that the defendant had an obligation to refrain from violating the claimants' human rights by environmental damage.[1121] Although the complaint did not explicitly mention future generations, the plaintiff was considered a representative "for himself and for each and every member of the Iweherekan Community in Delta State of Nigeria".[1122] In light of the immense pollution and environmental degradation in the Niger Delta, the existing interventions of the judiciary could be seen as a "ray of hope" to implement intergenerational equity and intergenerational rights against the harmful activities of private and governmental actors.[1123]

In Germany, the currently pending proceedings against several producers of automobiles build on the Federal Constitutional Court's findings in the *Neubauer* decision.[1124] Based on German tort law, the plaintiffs argued that the automobile producers failed to clearly and irreversibly commit to phase out the sale of cars with internal combustion engines, thereby violating their right to climate protection and the rights and freedoms of future generations.[1125] In light of the Constitutional Court's decision and the illustrations above, these claims are primarily based on the future infringements of the younger generation's rights, so that unborn future generations are not explicitly mentioned in the complaints.[1126]

In contrast, the ground-breaking *Urgenda* decision seems to have triggered another promising intergenerational case against a private corporation in the Netherlands. In 2019, several NGOs and more than 17.000 individual plaintiffs have initiated a proceeding against the Dutch energy producer Royal Dutch Shell.[1127] As illustrated regarding the identification of duty-bearers,[1128] the Dutch district court in *Milieudefensie v. Shell* ruled that Shell was obliged to reduce its greenhouse gas emissions by 45% by 2030,[1129] based, *inter alia*, on the corporation's international human rights obligations as incorporated in the UN Guiding Principles.[1130] Beyond these observations on the legal obligations of private corporations,[1131] the same District Court as in the first *Urgenda* decision clarified an important aspect on the representation of future generations:

[1120] *Gbemre v. Shell* (Judgment), *supra* note 529. See also Lambooy and Palm (2016), pp. 328–332.

[1121] *Gbemre v. Shell* (Judgment), *supra* note 529, paras. 4–6.

[1122] Ibid., paras. 1, 5. See also Lambooy and Palm (2016), p. 329.

[1123] Faga and Uchechukwu (2019), p. 204.

[1124] Deutsche Umwelthilfe e.V. (2022). See *supra* in Sect. 5.3.3.3.3.2.2.

[1125] See, e.g., CCLD (2021c-today).

[1126] See *supra* notes 1059–1065.

[1127] Hague District Court, *Vereniging Milieudefensie* et al. *v. Royal Dutch Shell plc.*, Summons, 5 April 2019, Retrieved January 3, 2025, from https://climatecasechart.com/non-us-case/milieudefensie-et-al-v-royal-dutch-shell-plc/

[1128] See *supra* notes 140–153.

[1129] *Hague District Court, Milieudefensie v. Shell* (Judgment), *supra* note 141, para. 5.3.

[1130] Ibid., paras. 4.4.9–4.4.21.

[1131] On two comparable proceedings against Shell, see Spentzou (2021), pp. 180–181.

> The court is of the opinion that the interests of current and future generations of the world's population, as served principally with the class actions, is not suitable for bundling. Although the entire world population is served by curbing dangerous climate change, there are huge differences in the time and manner in which the global population at various locations will be affected by global warming caused by $CO_2$ emissions. Therefore, this principal interest does not meet the requirement of 'similar interest' under Book 3 Section 305a Dutch Civil Code.
>
> However, the interests of current and future generations of Dutch residents and [...] of the inhabitants of the Wadden Sea area, [...], are suitable for bundling [...]. The collective claims are therefore declared not allowable insofar as they serve the interest of the world's population, except for the interest of Dutch residents and the inhabitants of the Wadden region.[1132]

The court thus again accepted a genuine representation of future generations of Dutch nationals by the plaintiff organisation, although the representation of current nationals would have been sufficient to render the complaint admissible.[1133] At the same time, it rejected standing on behalf of (present and) future generations of the world's population, as it considered the interests of different regions of the world to be too diverse to be represented by Milieudefensie and the other plaintiffs.[1134] Similar to *Urgenda*, the district court based this finding on the NGO's by-laws, which included the goal of sustainability.[1135] Several of the NGOs had also explicitly claimed to represent not only the interests of the present but also of future generations in general.[1136] *Laura Burgers* analysed the court's decision and positioned it within the theoretical philosophical debate on representation of future generations.[1137] She further deduced a "minimum principle" as solution to the theoretical problems of representation: despite the uncertainty on future generations' exact standpoints and the impossibility of their authorisation, the irreversible impacts of climate change on their mere existence allow judicially enforcing at least a minimum level of existence guaranteed by human rights.[1138]

As noted with regard to *Urgenda*, the future-oriented approach in *Milieudefensie* is primarily a consequence of the openness of Dutch law to public interest litigation.[1139] The important innovation of the recent decision consists in its extension to proceedings against private corporations. In 2011, *Chris van Dijk* still considered

---

[1132] *Hague District Court, Milieudefensie v. Shell* (Judgment), *supra* note 141, paras. 4.2.3–4.2.4 (court translation).

[1133] Spijkers (2021), pp. 243–244; Weller and Tran (2021), p. 344; Hösli (2021), p. 207; Burgers (2022).

[1134] See Weller and Tran (2021), p. 344; Peel and Markey-Towler (2021), p. 1488; Macchi and Zeben (2021), p. 410; Nollkaemper (2021).

[1135] Burgers (2022).

[1136] *Hague District Court, Milieudefensie v. Shell* (Summons), *supra* note 1127, paras. 285–295. In more detail, see Burgers (2020a), pp. 237–242.

[1137] Burgers (2022).

[1138] Ibid.

[1139] See Spijkers (2020).

proceedings against corporations on behalf of future generations as unlikely under Dutch law due to the necessary requirement of a damage that has already been suffered.[1140] However, the "forward-looking"[1141] character of the claims in *Milieudefensie* allowed for a more progressive approach, which included the interests of future generations. According to *Otto Spijkers*, "the ruling must be regarded as the next logical step in the legal history of the global phenomenon of climate litigation."[1142] Its success constitutes an important extension of judicial representation of future generations, at least on the national level and for the respective future nationals.

While the Hague Court of Appeal overturned the district court's decision in November 2024,[1143] it confirmed the latter's findings with regard to the representation of present and future generations of Dutch citizens.[1144] On Milieudefensie's standing, it found:

> These proceedings relate to the protection of individual citizens in the Netherlands and the Wadden Sea region from dangerous climate change. Although dangerous climate change will not have the same consequences for everyone, those consequences are to a large extent similar for everyone in the Netherlands and the Wadden Sea region. In terms of territory, this is a relatively limited area and the consequences of climate change will be more or less the same in that limited area. The interests of citizens in the Netherlands and the Wadden Sea region to be protected are therefore sufficiently similar and are suitable for pooling in these proceedings. […].[1145]

Therefore, the dismissal of Milieudefensie's claims by the appeals court does not impact the courts' findings on the representation of future generations of at least national citizens in proceedings against private corporations—irrespective of a potential decision by the Dutch Supreme Court in this case.

Another forward-looking attempt to hold private actors accountable was initiated in the Philippines—decided 30 years after the important *Oposa* decision. As illustrated above,[1146] the Philippines' Commission on Human Rights was asked in a petition to assess the responsibility of the 50 Carbon Majors for human rights violations resulting from the impacts of climate change.[1147] The plaintiffs based

[1140] Van Dijk (2011), pp. 211–212.

[1141] Toft (2020), p. 17.

[1142] Spijkers (2021), p. 255.

[1143] For an overview, see CCLD (2019a-today). See already *supra* in Sect. 5.1.2.2, note 148.

[1144] *Hague Court of Appeal, Milieudefensie v. Shell* (Judgment), *supra* note 148, paras. 6.2–6.4. In the appeal proceedings, Milieudefensie had argued that "it could have been concluded [that they] could also act on behalf of the public interest of current and future generations *of other countries* than the Netherlands" due to the "serious consequences [of climate change] for all people on earth" (emphasis added): Hague Court of Appeal, *Vereniging Milieudefensie* et al. *v. Royal Dutch Shell plc.,* Statement of Defence on Appeal, 18 October 2022, Retrieved January 3, 2025, from https://climatecasechart.com/non-us-case/milieudefensie-et-al-v-royal-dutch-shell-plc/. Yet, this argument was rejected by the appeals court in line with the district court, see *Hague Court of Appeal, Milieudefensie v. Shell* (Judgment), *supra* note 148, para. 6.2.

[1145] Ibid., para. 6.4.

[1146] See already *supra* notes 154–162.

[1147] For an overview, see CCLD (2015-2022).

their argumentation, *inter alia*, on intergenerational equity as well as on the findings in *Oposa*.[1148] In its final report, the Commission elaborated, *inter alia*, on the rights of future generations and intergenerational equity.[1149] Its observations on the role of business enterprises in the context of climate change are comparable to the Dutch district court's findings. The Commission also interpreted the UN Guiding Principles in accordance with "the *Oposa* Doctrine of 'intergenerational responsibility'."[1150] While the plaintiffs did not allege that they formally represented future generations, the focus on intergenerational aspects of both the petition and the report illustrates how the interests of future generations can be at least indirectly invoked—even vis-à-vis private corporations. Therefore, the Commission's intergenerational focus is in line with the fundamental decision in *Oposa v. Factoran* 30 years ago. It remains to be seen whether this example is again ahead of the times like *Oposa*, or whether other national bodies will follow this progressive approach to the responsibility of private corporations.

All in all, proceedings of individuals and NGOs against private corporations as well the latter's obligations under intergenerational equity remain scarce. Most of them are based on the respective civil liability regimes. Due to the lack of legal personality of private corporations under international law, as of today, it becomes difficult to assess whether and how far these few instances will have an influence on the international concept of intergenerational equity and its implementation. While certain rays of hope exist, for instance in the Netherlands and the Philippines, these rare exceptions constitute instances of national jurisprudence that goes beyond the explicit international regime of intergenerational equity.

### *5.3.4 Summary*

The foregoing sections on the institutional implementation of intergenerational equity have illustrated a fragmented picture instead of a uniform and coherent framework. The observations are based on a deliberative democracy understanding of "representation" that does not require the authorisation by the represented, but only the acceptance of the role of the representative by a particular audience.[1151] In the context of intergenerational equity, representation could happen in two dimensions. First, the interests of future generations could get a voice on the different levels of policy-making. There are some examples of domestic institutions, such as ombudspersons for future generations. However, their institutional settings and

[1148] *Carbon Majors for Human Rights Violations* (Petition), *supra* note 154, 6, 21, 30.

[1149] *Carbon Majors for Human Rights Violations* (Final Report), *supra* note 158, pp. 67–69; *Carbon Majors for Human Rights Violations* (Memorandum), *supra* note 157, paras. 8.51, 8.63, 8.65.

[1150] Ibid., para. 6.9.

[1151] Rehfeld (2006), p. 5.

powers differ from one State to the other and none of them are based on an international legal obligation to establish according institutions. In the last decades, several suggestions have been made on the creation of international law that requires either the establishment of national ombudspersons or of a global representative for future generations. The attempts to establish a High Commissioner for Future Generations, particularly during the Rio+20 conference, have been without success until today due to the objections of leading States. Institutions such as UNEP or the HLPFSD cannot be considered actual representatives of future generations, as their scope of work does not aim at implementing intergenerational equity *per se*. Consequently, as of today, future generations are not coherently represented in environmental policy-making, neither on the international nor on the national level. Future generations still have no universal voice in policy-making, but it remains to be seen whether future attempts might be more successful.

Second, intergenerational equity can be implemented in judicial fora, in which the interests of future generations could be represented. The relevant frameworks are even more fragmented than in policy-making. On the one hand, inter-State proceedings could be a fitting framework for representation. While States could act as representatives on the basis of *parens patriae* standing or *erga omnes (partes)* obligations, there has not been a single case, in which a State had invoked standing on behalf of future generations. Further, proposals to achieve representation for future generations by the means of *amicus curiae* briefs have not yet been transformed into practice, although they would be feasible under most procedural rules. Eventually, international courts themselves, particularly the ICJ, have sometimes been considered adequate representatives or trustees for future generations, although this constitutes a rather informal form of representation. Recent attempts to initiate an advisory opinion on climate change before the ICJ could further shape this judicial role in the near future. So far, the existing inter-State case law does not offer examples of genuine representation.

On the other hand, judicial and quasi-judicial proceedings of individuals and NGOs have demonstrated much more and diverse instances of potential representation for future generations. Although the number of proceedings against corporations has increased in the last years, only few instances actually refer to future generations or intergenerational equity. Most case law exists in proceedings against States. The case law before international or regional (human rights) bodies has remained scarce and does not offer much insight on a comprehensive representation of future generations on the international level strictly speaking. The national level is more fruitful for this analysis, although the success of suits on behalf of future generations differs largely from case to case. Common challenges of causation and the separation of powers doctrine complicated the cases for representatives of future generations. Further, most courts avoided to explicitly articulate on the issue of standing on behalf of future generations, as the question was so far not decisive in the proceedings. However, the analysed case law shows that civil society actors, particularly NGOs, Indigenous communities and young persons, are willing to advocate the interests of posterity. Some of these cases have been successful with regard to the explicit or implicit representation of future generations, and more and more proceedings are pending that raise the interests of future generations before the judiciary.

All in all, the institutional implementation of intergenerational equity is still fragmented. While there are increasing efforts to better represent future generations in policy-making and in judicial implementation, the current system still constitutes a piecemeal approach without internationally binding mechanisms. This fragmented system weakens the implementation not only of the specific doctrine but also of the general conception of intergenerational equity. Consequently, it seems obvious that future reform of the legal system is necessary in order to support an efficient and coherent implementation of intergenerational equity.[1152] Nonetheless, the existing approaches to representation on the national and international level can certainly offer fitting starting points for this future development and they already contribute to a refinement of the upcoming implementation system. Again, in the words of *Judge Staton*:

> [We] are perilously close to an overflowing bucket. These final drops matter. A lot. Properly framed, a court order – even one that merely postpones the day when remedial measures become insufficiently effective – would likely have a real impact on preventing the impending cataclysm.[1153]

## 5.4 Conclusion and Need for Further Analysis

This chapter has illustrated the potential duty-bearers, the right-holders and the institutional implementation frameworks of intergenerational equity. Although the open issues remain unanswered to a large extent, some clarifying observations can be made. Due to the current operative structures of international environmental law, States remain the primary duty-bearers of intergenerational obligations. Individuals and private corporations have increasingly been suggested as additional duty-bearers, but they are not directly obliged vis-à-vis future generations as of today.

The question of right-holders consists of two elements. First, the diverse conceptional objections to rights of future generations can be overcome and do not hinder a rights-based theory of intergenerational equity. Future generations could thus conceptionally become right-holders. Second, the current international legal system confers no rights to future generations yet, despite singular developments in case law, particularly before national courts. Future generations are no holders of legal rights under current international law.

The operational implementation framework of intergenerational equity is the most complex open issue. Based on a deliberative democracy understanding of representation, the chapter has first turned to representation in policy-making, before

[1152] The possibilities and likelihood of this future legal change is addressed *infra* in Sect. 7.3.3 and 7.3.4.

[1153] *US Court of Appeals, Juliana* (Dissenting Opinion of Judge Staton), *supra* note 1011, p. 1182.

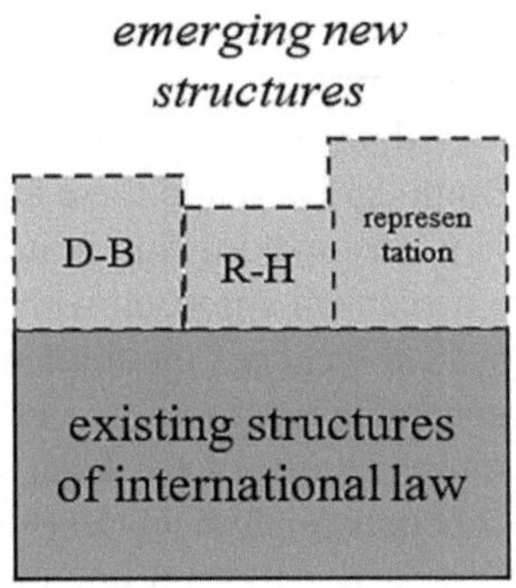


**Fig. 5.1** Emerging Operational Structures of Intergenerational Equity

addressing representation in judicial proceedings on different levels. The result is a fragmented and incoherent picture of singular instances of representation, particularly on the national level. However, several existing mechanisms have been touched upon, which point to potential developments in the future.

The foregoing sections have thus tried to answer the open issues of duty-bearers, right-holders and representation from a *de lege lata* perspective while illustrating certain emerging developments that could constitute an operational framework of intergenerational equity *de lege ferenda*. It has become clear that the structural mechanisms that govern intergenerational equity are constantly developing and that there is no obvious answer to the open issues. While Chap. 4 has already demonstrated the emerging character of the specific doctrine of intergenerational equity vis-à-vis the general conception, the issues of duty-bearers ('D-B'), right-holders ('R-H') and representation are comparably emerging, as Fig. 5.1 visualises.[1154]

The structural issues are subject to further legal development in the future. At this point, the legal analysis of the *status quo* would normally end with unsatisfying answers. The general conception of intergenerational equity remains too abstract as a principle to effectively hinder States from behaviour that has disastrous impacts on future generations. Since the specific doctrine does not yet constitute part of customary international law, it cannot contribute to a more future-oriented State behaviour. At the same time, it is obvious that the existing structures of implementation do not effectively respond to the current intergenerational challenges either. The present legal regime of intergenerational equity is not sufficient to prevent further human-made environmental degradations with long-term intergenerational impacts. Despite the long-standing historical development and systemic embeddedness of intergenerational equity (Chap. 2), despite the philosophical foundations of the concept (Chap. 3) and despite the legally binding character of the general conception of intergenerational equity as a legal principle (Chap. 4), the international

[1154] This illustration builds on Fig. 4.1, see *supra* in Sect. 4.3. The growing columns on top of the existing structures of international law represent the different open issues discussed in this chapter: the potential duty-bearers, right-holders and the frameworks of representation. As these structures are emerging (or not) at different speed and in different intensity, the columns have different heights. Chapter 7 takes this illustration up again for further development, see *infra* in Sect. 7.3.4.3.

community is far away from acting in a long-term manner that is conform with the idea of fairness between generations.

Therefore, this book turns away from a merely positivist assessment up to this point, and turns to an analysis of intergenerational equity *de lege ferenda* in the following chapters, thus, to the law "as it ought to be".[1155] However, it does not elaborate this law from scratch, but it builds on two important aspects. First, the foregoing analysis of the two manifestations of intergenerational equity as well as the structural developments constitute a fitting starting point for further elaborations. Second, the emerging character of these aspects of intergenerational equity triggers an important perspective that has not been taken into account with regard to intergenerational equity so far: an intertemporal perspective.[1156]

## References

Abate, R. (2020). *Climate change and the voiceless: Protecting future generations, wildlife, and natural resources*. Cambridge University Press. https://doi.org/10.1017/9781108647076

Acosta Alvarado, P. A., & Rivas-Ramirez, D. (2018). A milestone in environmental and future generations' rights protection: Recent legal developments before the Colombian Supreme Court. *Journal of Environmental Law, 30*(3), 519–526. https://doi.org/10.1093/jel/eqyO24

Aguiling Pangalangan, R. L. (2020, April 16). Ageless rights, intergenerational responsibilities: are human rights future-proof? *Cambridge International Law Journal Blog*. Retrieved January 3, 2025, from http://cilj.co.uk/2020/04/16/ageless-rights-intergenerational-responsibilities-are-human-rights-future-proof/

Aidun, H. (2020, March 13). Juliana in the world: Comparing the ninth circuit's decision to foreign rights-based climate litigation. *Climate Law Blog*. Retrieved January 3, 2025, from https://blogs.law.columbia.edu/climatechange/2020/03/13/juliana-in-the-world-comparing-the-ninth-circuits-decision-to-foreign-rights-based-climate-litigation/

Albers, J. H. (2018). Human rights and climate change: Protecting the right to life of individuals of present and future generations. *Security and Human Rights, 28*(1–4), 113–144. https://doi.org/10.1163/18750230-02801009

Albin, C. (1999). Can NGOs enhance the effectiveness of international negotiation? *International Negotiation, 4*(3), 371–387. https://doi.org/10.1163/15718069920848534

Allen, T. (1994). The Philippine children's case: Recognizing legal standing for future generations. *Georgetown International Environmental Law Review, 6*, 713–741.

Alogna, I., Bakker, C., & Gauci, J.-P. (Eds.). (2021). *Climate change litigation: Global perspectives*. Brill Nijhoff.

Alston, P. (1982). A third generation of solidarity rights: Progressive development or obfuscation of international human rights law? *Netherlands International Law Review, 29*(3), 307–322. https://doi.org/10.1017/S0165070X00012882

Alston, P. (1984). Conjuring up new human rights: A proposal for quality control. *American Journal of International Law, 78*(3), 607–621.

Ambos, K. (2021, June 29). Protecting the environment through international criminal law? *EJIL: Talk!* Retrieved January 3, 2025, from https://www.ejiltalk.org/protecting-the-environment-through-international-criminal-law/

[1155] Lachenmann (2012), para. 4.

[1156] The only reference to intertemporal law by *Brown Weiss* correctly points to the difference between both notions, see Brown Weiss (2021a), para. 19.

Ambrusné, É. T. (2010). The parliamentary commissioner for future generations of Hungary and his impact. *Intergenerational Justice Review, 5*(1), 18–24. https://doi.org/10.24357/IGJR.5.1.470

Anstee-Wedderburn, J. (2014). Giving a voice to future generations: Intergenerational equity, representative of generations to come, and the challenge of planetary rights. *Australian Journal of Environmental Law, 1*(1), 37–70.

Anton, D. K., & Shelton, D. (2011). *Environmental protection and human rights*. Cambridge University Press. https://doi.org/10.1017/CBO9780511974571

Aquilina, K. (1998). The relevance of UNCED to a guardian for future generations. In E. Agius & S. Busuttil (Eds.), *Future generations and international law: Proceedings of the international experts' meeting held by the future generations programme at the foundation for international studies, University of Malta* (Vol. 10, pp. 117–126). Earthscan Publications Ltd..

Araújo, R., & Koessler, L. (2022, August 12). The rise of the constitutional protection of future generations. *Verfassungsblog*. Retrieved January 3, 2025, from https://verfassungsblog.de/the-rise-of-the-constitutional-protection-of-future-generations/

Arneson, R. J. (2003). Defending the purely instrumental account of democratic legitimacy. *Journal of Political Philosophy, 11*(1), 122–132. https://doi.org/10.1111/1467-9760.00170

Arts, K. (2019). Children's rights and climate change. In C. Fenton-Glynn (Ed.), *Children's rights and sustainable development: Interpreting the UNCRC for future generations* (Vol. 10, pp. 216–235). Cambridge University Press.

Atapattu, S. A. (2019). Intergenerational equity and children's rights: The role of sustainable development and justice. In C. Fenton-Glynn (Ed.), *Children's rights and sustainable development: Interpreting the UNCRC for future generations* (Vol. 8, pp. 167–191). Cambridge University Press. https://doi.org/10.1017/9781108140348.008

Aust, H. P. (2022). Climate protection act case, order of the first senate. *American Journal of International Law, 116*(1), 150–157. https://doi.org/10.1017/ajil.2021.74

Austin, J. (1873). *Lectures on jurisprudence*. Henry Holt and Company.

Auz, J., & Viveros-Uehara, T. (2023, March 2). Another advisory opinion on the climate emergency? The added value of the Inter-American Court of Human Rights. *EJIL: Talk!* Retrieved October 10, 2024, from https://www.ejiltalk.org/another-advisory-opinion-on-the-climate-emergency-the-added-value-of-the-inter-american-court-of-human-rights/

Backes, C. W., & van der Veen, G. A. (2020). Urgenda: The final judgment of the Dutch Supreme Court. *Journal for European Environmental and Planning Law, 17*(3), 307–321.

Bakker, C. (2021a). Baptism of fire? The first climate case before the UN Committee on the Rights of the Child. *Questions of International Law, Zoom-in, 77*, 5–25.

Bakker, C. (2021b). Climate change litigation in The Netherlands: The Urgenda case and beyond. In I. Alogna, C. Bakker, & J.-P. Gauci (Eds.), *Climate change litigation: Global perspectives* (Vol. 9, pp. 199–224). Brill Nijhoff.

Barresi, P. A. (1997). Beyond fairness to future generations: An intragenerational alternative to intergenerational equity in the international environmental arena. *Tulane Environmental Law Journal, 11*(1), 59–88.

Bäumler, J. (2021, June 8). Sustainable development made justiciable: The German Constitutional Court's climate ruling on intra- and inter-generational equity. *EJIL: Talk!* Retrieved January 3, 2025, from https://www.ejiltalk.org/sustainable-development-made-justiciable-the-german-constitutional-courts-climate-ruling-on-intra-and-inter-generational-equity/

Beckerman, W. (2004). Intergenerational justice. *Intergenerational Justice Review, 2*, 1–5.

Beckerman, W. (2006). The impossibility of a theory of intergenerational justice. In J. C. Tremmel (Ed.), *Handbook of intergenerational justice* (Vol. 3, pp. 53–71). Edward Elgar Publishing.

Beckman, L. (2013). Democracy and future generations: Should the unborn have a voice? In J.-C. Merle (Ed.), *Spheres of global justice: Volume 2: Fair distribution—Global economic, social and intergenerational justice* (Vol. 62, pp. 775–788). Springer. https://doi.org/10.1007/978-94-007-5998-5_62

Beckman, L. (2015). Political representation of future generations and collective responsibility. *Jurisprudence, 6*(3), 516–534. https://doi.org/10.1080/20403313.2015.1065641

Beckman, L., & Uggla, F. (2016). An ombudsman for future generations: Legitimate and effective? In I. González-Ricoy & A. Gosseries (Eds.), *Institutions for future generations* (Vol. 7, 1st ed., pp. 117–134). Oxford University Press.

Bell-James, J., & Collins, B. (2022). Human rights and climate change litigation: Should temporal imminence form part of positive rights obligations? *Journal of Human Rights and the Environment, 13*(1), 212–237. https://doi.org/10.4337/jhre.2022.01.09

Bendel, J. (2019, December 6). Bringing deforestation before an International Court? *EJIL: Talk!* Retrieved January 3, 2025, from https://www.ejiltalk.org/bringing-deforestation-before-an-international-court/

Bennoune, K. (2019). In defense of human rights. *Vanderbilt Journal of Transnational Law, 52*(5), 1209–1236.

Benz, E., & Kahl, V. (2021). Das Urteil im Fall Lhaka Honhat: Die Ausweitung der Direkten Justiziabilität von DESCA und die Unerfüllte Hoffnung der Konkretisierung des Rechts auf eine Gesunde Umwelt. *Archiv Des Völkerrechts, 59*(2), 199. https://doi.org/10.1628/avr-2021-0011

Bergkamp, L. (2015). A Dutch Court's "revolutionary" climate policy judgment: The perversion of judicial power, the state's duties of care, and science. *Journal for European Environmental and Planning Law, 12*(3–4), 241–263. https://doi.org/10.1163/18760104-01204002

Berkemann, J. (2021). "Freiheitschancen Über die Generationen" (Art. 20a GG): Intertemporaler Klimaschutz im Paradigmenwechsel. *Die Öffentliche Verwaltung (DÖV), 74*(16), 701–715.

Bernet Kempers, E. (2022). Transition rather than revolution: The gradual road towards animal legal personhood through the legislature. *Transnational Environmental Law, FirstView, 1–22.* https://doi.org/10.1017/S2047102522000139

Bertram, D. (2022, August 15). Extratemporal jurisdiction test: When should courts address harm to the future? *Verfassungsblog*. Retrieved January 3, 2025, from https://verfassungsblog.de/extratemporal-jurisdiction/

Bertram, D. (2023). "For you will (still) be here tomorrow": The many lives of intergenerational equity. *Transnational Environmental Law, 12*(1), 121–149.

Besson, S. (2011). Sovereignty, international law and democracy. *European Journal of International Law, 22*(2), 373–387. https://doi.org/10.1093/ejil/chr029

Besson, S. (2020). The human right to democracy in international law: Coming to moral terms with an equivocal legal practice. In A. von Arnauld, K. von der Decken, & M. Susi (Eds.), *The Cambridge handbook of new human rights: Recognition, novelty, rhetoric* (Vol. 37, pp. 481–489). Cambridge University Press.

Beyerlin, U. (2010). Different types of norms in international environmental law policies, principles, and rules. In D. Bodansky, J. Brunnée, & E. Hey (Eds.), *The Oxford handbook of international environmental law* (Vol. 18, 1st ed., pp. 425–448). Oxford University Press.

Beyerlin, U., & Grote Stoutenburg, J. (2013). Environment, international protection. In A. Peters & R. Wolfrum (Eds.), *Max Planck encyclopedia of public international law*. Oxford University Press. (Article last updated December 2013).

Beyerlin, U., & Marauhn, T. (2011). *International environmental law*. Hart Publishing.

Beyleveld, D., Düwell, M., & Spahn, A. (2015). Why and how should we represent future generations in policymaking? *Jurisprudence, 6*(3), 549–566. https://doi.org/10.1080/20403313.2015.1065642

Bialek, J. (2019). Evaluating the zero draft on a UN treaty on business and human rights: What does it regulate and how likely is its adoption by states? *Goettingen Journal of International Law, 9*(3), 501–536.

Bielefeldt, H. (2021). Moving beyond anthropocentrism? Human rights and the charge of speciesism. *Human Rights Quarterly, 43*(3), 515–537. https://doi.org/10.1353/hrq.2021.0038

Biermann, F. (1996). "Common concern for humankind": The emergence of a new concept of international environmental law. *Archiv Des Völkerrechts, 34*, 426–481.

Biermann, F. (2021, April 30). Germany's climate law ruled unconstitutional: First reflections. *Global Sustainability Governance Blog*. Retrieved January 3, 2025, from https://www.frankbiermann.org/post/germany-s-climate-law-ruled-unconstitutional-first-reflections

Bilder, R. B. (1982). The present legal and political situation in Antarctica. In J. I. Charney (Ed.), *The new nationalism and the use of common spaces: Issues in marine pollution and the exploitation of Antarctica* (pp. 167–205). Allanheld Osmun.

Birch, A. H. (1971). *Representation*. Palgrave Macmillan. https://doi.org/10.1007/978-1-349-01044-8

Bobertz, B. C. (1987). Toward a better understanding of intergenerational justice. *Buffalo Law Review, 36*(1), 165–192.

Bodansky, D. (2017). The role of the international court of justice in addressing climate change: Some preliminary reflections. *Arizona State Law Journal, 49*, 689–712.

Bodansky, D. (2019). Top 10 developments in international environmental law. *Yearbook of International Environmental Law, 30*(1), 3–21. https://doi.org/10.2139/ssrn.3644557

Boer, B. (2021). The preamble. In G. van Calster & L. Reins (Eds.), *Paris agreement on climate change: A commentary* (pp. 5–32). Edward Elgar Publishing.

Boisson de Chazournes, L. (2002). Advisory opinions and the furtherance of the common interest of humankind. In L. Boisson de Chazournes, C. P. R. Romano, & R. MacKenzie (Eds.), *International organizations and international dispute settlement: Trends and prospects* (Vol. 6, pp. 105–118). Transnational Publishers, Inc.

Borg, S. (1998). Guarding intergenerational rights over natural resources. In E. Agius & S. Busuttil (Eds.), *Future generations and international law: Proceedings of the international experts' meeting held by the future generations programme at the foundation for international studies, University of Malta* (Vol. 11, pp. 127–141). Earthscan Publications Ltd..

Bosselmann, K. (2009). Environmental ethics. In A. Peters & R. Wolfrum (Eds.), *Max Planck encyclopedia of public international law*. Oxford University Press. (Article last updated January 2009).

Bosselmann, K. (2020). Environmental trusteeship and state sovereignty: Can they be reconciled? *Transnational Legal Theory, 11*(1–2), 47–61. https://doi.org/10.1080/20414005.2020.1757862

Boston, J. (2016). *Governing for the future: Designing democratic institutions for a better tomorrow* (1st ed.). Emerald Group Publishing Limited.

Boutros-Ghali, B. (1996). *An agenda for democratization*. United Nations Publication.

Bovenkerk, B. (2015). Public deliberation and the inclusion of future generations. *Jurisprudence, 6*(3), 496–515. https://doi.org/10.1080/20403313.2015.1065643

Boyd, D. (2019). A right to a healthy and sustainable environment. In Y. Aguila & J. E. Viñuales (Eds.), *A global pact for the environment: Legal foundations* (Vol. 2, pp. 30–36). Cambridge Centre for Environment, Energy and Natural Resource Governance (C-EENRG).

Boyle, A. E. (1998). The role of international human rights law in the protection of the environment. In A. E. Boyle & M. R. Anderson (Eds.), *Human rights approaches to environmental protection* (Vol. 3, pp. 43–65). Clarendon Press.

Boyle, A. E. (2012). Human rights and the environment: Where next? *European Journal of International Law, 23*(3), 613–642. https://doi.org/10.1093/ejil/chs016

Boyle, A. E., & Harrison, J. (2013). Judicial settlement of international environmental disputes: Current problems. *Journal of International Dispute Settlement, 4*(2), 245–276. https://doi.org/10.1093/jnlids/idt011

Boyle, A. E., & Redgwell, C. (2021). *Birnie, Boyle, and Redgwell's international law and the environment* (4th ed.). Oxford University Press.

Boysen, S. (2020). Remnants of a constitutional moment: The right to democracy in international law. In A. von Arnauld, K. von der Decken, & M. Susi (Eds.), *The Cambridge handbook of new human rights: Recognition, novelty, rhetoric* (Vol. 36, pp. 465–480). Cambridge University Press. https://doi.org/10.1017/9781108676106.037

Brandt, R. B. (1983). The concept of a moral right and its function. *The Journal of Philosophy, 80*(1), 29–45. https://doi.org/10.2307/2026285

Breuer, M. (2017). Das Rechtsfolgenregime des Diplomatischen Schutzes unter dem Einfluss der Menschenrechte. *Archiv Des Völkerrechts, 55*(3), 324–348. https://doi.org/10.1628/000389217X15039930483447

Brown Weiss, E. (1984a). Conservation and equity between generations. In T. Buergenthal (Ed.), *Contemporary issues in international law: Essays in honor of Louis B. Sohn* (pp. 245–289). Engel.

Brown Weiss, E. (1984b). The planetary trust: Conservation and intergenerational equity. *Ecology Law Quarterly, 11*, 495–582.

Brown Weiss, E. (1989). *In fairness to future generations: International law, common patrimony, and intergenerational equity*. Transnational Publishers, Inc.

Brown Weiss, E. (1990). Our rights and obligations to future generations for the environment. *American Journal of International Law, 84*(1), 198–207. https://doi.org/10.2307/2203020

Brown Weiss, E. (1992). Intergenerational equity and rights of future generations. In A. A. Cançado Trindade & E. Brown Weiss (Eds.), *Derechos humanos, desarrollo sustentable y medio ambiente: Human rights, sustainable development and the environment* (pp. 71–81). Banco Interamericano de Desarrollo.

Brown Weiss, E. (1997). A reply to Barresi's "beyond fairness to future generations". *Tulane Environmental Law Journal, 11*(1), 89–97.

Brown Weiss, E. (2000). The rise or the fall of international law? *Fordham Law Review, 69*(2), 345–372.

Brown Weiss, E. (2002). Invoking state responsibility in the twenty-first century. *American Journal of International Law, 96*, 798–816.

Brown Weiss, E. (2010). Implementing intergenerational equity. In M. Fitzmaurice, D. Ong, & P. Merkouris (Eds.), *Research handbook on international environmental law* (Vol. 5, pp. 100–116). Edward Elgar Publishing.

Brown Weiss, E. (2011). The evolution of international environmental law. *Japanese Yearbook of International Law, 54*, 1–27.

Brown Weiss, E. (2019). Intergenerational equity. In Y. Aguila & J. E. Viñuales (Eds.), *A global pact for the environment: Legal foundations* (Vol. 5, pp. 51–58). Cambridge Centre for Environment, Energy and Natural Resource Governance (C-EENRG).

Brown Weiss, E. (2020). *Establishing norms in a kaleidoscopic world*. Brill Nijhoff.

Brown Weiss, E. (2021a). Intergenerational equity. In A. Peters & R. Wolfrum (Eds.), *Max Planck encyclopedia of public international law*. Oxford University Press. (Article last updated April 2021).

Brown Weiss, E. (2021b). The theoretical framework for international legal principles of intergenerational equity and implementation through national institutions. In M.-C. Cordonier Segger, M. Szabó, & A. R. Harrington (Eds.), *Intergenerational justice in sustainable development treaty implementation: Advancing future generations rights through national institutions* (Vol. 2, pp. 16–43). Cambridge University Press.

Brown Weiss, E., Cançado Trindade, A. A., Kiss, A., Peng Cheng, L., Ploman, E. W., & Pathak, R. S. (1988, February 15). Goa guidelines on intergenerational equity: Statement of the United Nations University project on "international law, common patrimony and intergenerational equity". *United Nations University Project*. Retrieved January 3, 2025, from http://goenchimati.org/the-goa-guidelines-on-intergenerational-equity/

Bruce, M. (1998). A draft instrument establishing the role of a guardian. In E. Agius & S. Busuttil (Eds.), *Future generations and international law: Proceedings of the international experts' meeting held by the future generations programme at the foundation for international studies, University of Malta* (Vol. 14, pp. 163–165). Earthscan Publications Ltd..

Brunnée, J. (2005). International legal accountability through the lens of the law of state responsibility. *Netherlands Yearbook of International Law, 36*, 21–38. https://doi.org/10.1017/S0167676805000218

Brunnée, J. (2010). Common areas, common heritage, and common concern. In D. Bodansky, J. Brunnée, & E. Hey (Eds.), *The Oxford handbook of international environmental law* (Vol. 23, 1st ed., pp. 550–572). Oxford University Press.

Brunnée, J. (2018). International environmental law and community interests: Procedural aspects. In E. Benvenisti, G. Nolte, & K. Yalin-Mor (Eds.), *Community interests across international law* (Vol. 9, pp. 151–175). Oxford University Press.

Buchanan, A. E. (2013). *The heart of human rights*. Oxford University Press.

Burchardt, D. (2012). Zukünftige Generationen—Träger Kollektiver Rechte? In Junge Wissenschaft im Öffentlichen Recht e.V (Ed.), *Kollektivität—Öffentliches Recht zwischen Gruppeninteressen und Gemeinwohl: 52. Assistententagung Öffentliches Recht* (pp. 187–209). Nomos.

Burdon, P. D., & Williams, C. (2016). Rights of nature: A constructive analysis. In D. E. Fisher (Ed.), *Research handbook on fundamental concepts of environmental law* (Vol. 8, pp. 196–218). Edward Elgar Publishing.

Bureau of the Preparatory Process for the UNCSD. (2012, January 10). The future we want—Zero draft of the outcome document. *UN conference on sustainable development*. Retrieved January 3, 2025, from https://www.researchgate.net/publication/330443876_The_Future_We_Want_-_Zero_Draft_of_the_Outcome_Document

Burgers, L. (2020a). *Justitia, the people's power and mother earth: Democratic legitimacy of judicial law-making in European private law cases on climate change*. Ipskamp Printing.

Burgers, L. (2020b). Should judges make climate change law? *Transnational Environmental Law, 9*(1), 55–75. https://doi.org/10.1017/S2047102519000360

Burgers, L. (2022, January 19). The minimum principle: Future generations in the climate case against Royal Dutch Shell. *Völkerrechtsblog*. Retrieved January 3, 2025, from https://voelkerrechtsblog.org/the-minimum-principle/

Burgers, L., & Staal, T. (2018). Climate action as positive human rights obligation: The appeals judgment in Urgenda v The Netherlands. *Netherlands Yearbook of International Law, 49*, 223–244.

Burton, M. (2021, September 25). Vanuatu to push international court for climate change opinion. *REUTERS*. Retrieved January 3, 2025, from https://www.reuters.com/world/asia-pacific/vanuatu-push-international-court-climate-change-opinion-2021-09-25/

Buser, A. (2021a). Of carbon budgets, factual uncertainties, and intergenerational equity: The German Constitutional Court's climate decision. *German Law Journal, 22*(8), 1409–1422. https://doi.org/10.1017/glj.2021.81

Buser, A. (2021b, April 30). Die Freiheit der Zukunft: Zum Klima-Beschluss des Bundesverfassungsgerichts. *Verfassungsblog*. Retrieved January 3, 2025, from https://verfassungsblog.de/die-freiheit-der-zukunft/

Bustami, A., & Hecken, M.-C. (2021). Perspectives for a new international crime against the environment: International criminal responsibility for environmental degradation under the Rome Statute. *Goettingen Journal of International Law, 11*(1), 145–189.

Cameron, C., & Weyman, R. (2022). Recent youth-led and rights-based climate change litigation in Canada: Reconciling justiciability, charter claims and procedural choices. *Journal of Environmental Law, 34*(1), 195–207. https://doi.org/10.1093/jel/eqab026

Campbell, K. (2017). Legal rights. In E. N. Zalta (Ed.), *The Stanford encyclopedia of philosophy*. ISSN 1095-5054. Retrieved January 3, 2025, from https://plato.stanford.edu/archives/win2022/entries/legal-rights/. (Article last updated November 2017)

Cançado Trindade, A. A. (1992). Environment and development: Formulation and implementation of the right to development as a human right. In A. A. Cançado Trindade & E. Brown Weiss (Eds.), *Derechos Humanos, Desarrollo Sustentable y Medio Ambiente: Human rights, sustainable development and the environment* (pp. 39–70). Banco Interamericano de Desarrollo.

Cançado Trindade, A. A. (2020). *International law for humankind: Towards a new jus gentium* (3rd ed.). Brill Nijhoff.

Caney, S. (2022). Global climate governance, short-termism, and the vulnerability of future generations. *Ethics and International Affairs, 36*(2), 137–155. https://doi.org/10.1017/S0892679422000181

Cassese, A. (2012a). Gathering up the main threads. In A. Cassese (Ed.), *Realizing utopia: The future of international law* (Vol. 48, 1st ed., pp. 645–684). Oxford University Press.

Cassese, A. (2012b). The international court of justice: It is high time to restyle the respected old lady. In A. Cassese (Ed.), *Realizing utopia: The future of international law* (Vol. 19, 1st ed., pp. 239–249). Oxford University Press.

Charnovitz, S. (2006). Nongovernmental organizations and international law. *American Journal of International Law, 100*(2), 348–372.

Chaturvedi, E. (2021). Climate change litigation: Indian perspective. *German Law Journal, 22*(8), 1459–1470. https://doi.org/10.1017/glj.2021.85

Chen, D., Rojas, M., Samset, B. H., Cobb, K., Diongue-Niang, A., Edwards, P., Emori, S., Faria, S. H., Hawkins, E., Hope, P., Huybrechts, P., Meinshausen, M., Mustafa, S., Plattner, G.-K., & Treguier, A. M. (2021). Framing, context and methods. In V. Masson-Delmotte et al. (Eds.), *Climate change 2021—The physical science basis: Working group I contribution to the IPCC sixth assessment report* (pp. 147–286). IPCC. Retrieved January 3, 2025, from https://www.ipcc.ch/report/ar6/wg1/downloads/report/IPCC_AR6_WGI_Chapter01.pdf

Chimni, B. (2003). Third world approaches to international law: A manifesto. In A. Anghie, B. Chimni, K. Mickelson, & O. C. Okafor (Eds.), *The third world and international order: Law, politics and globalization* (pp. 47–73). Martinus Nijhoff Publishers.

Chinkin, C., & MacKenzie, R. (2002). Intergovernmental organizations as "friends of the court". In L. Boisson de Chazournes, C. P. R. Romano, & R. MacKenzie (Eds.), *International organizations and international dispute settlement: Trends and prospects* (Vol. 8, pp. 135–164). Transnational Publishers, Inc.

Chiussi Curzi, L., & Malafosse, C. (2022). A public international law outlook on business and human rights. *International Community Law Review, 24*(1–2), 11–35. https://doi.org/10.1163/18719732-bja10070

Clapham, A. (2010). The role of the individual in international law. *European Journal of International Law, 21*(1), 25–30. https://doi.org/10.1093/ejil/chq001

Climate Change Litigation Databases. (n.d.). *Non-US climate change litigation: Suits against corporations*. Sabin Center for Climate Change Law at Columbia Law School. Retrieved January 3, 2025, from http://climatecasechart.com/non-us-case-category/corporations/

Climate Change Litigation Databases. (2004-2011). *American Electric Power Co. v. Connecticut*. Sabin Center for Climate Change Law at Columbia Law School. Retrieved January 3, 2025, from http://climatecasechart.com/case/american-electric-power-co-v-connecticut/

Climate Change Litigation Databases. (2008-2013). *Native village of Kivalina v. ExxonMobil Corp*. Sabin Center for Climate Change Law at Columbia Law School. Retrieved January 3, 2025, from http://climatecasechart.com/case/native-village-of-kivalina-v-exxonmobil-corp/

Climate Change Litigation Databases. (2011-2024). *U.S. climate change litigation: Public trust claims. Sabin Center for Climate Change Law at Columbia Law School*. Retrieved January 3, 2025, from http://climatecasechart.com/case-category/public-trust-claims/

Climate Change Litigation Databases. (2012-today). *Mbabazi and Others v. the Attorney General and National Environmental Management Authority*. Sabin Center for Climate Change Law at Columbia Law School. Retrieved January 3, 2025, from http://climatecasechart.com/non-us-case/mbabazi-et-al-v-attorney-general-et-al/

Climate Change Litigation Databases. (2014-2023). *VZW Klimaatzaak v. Kingdom of Belgium & Others*. Sabin Center for Climate Change Law at Columbia Law School. Retrieved January 3, 2025, from http://climatecasechart.com/non-us-case/vzw-klimaatzaak-v-kingdom-of-belgium-et-al/

Climate Change Litigation Databases. (2015-2016). *Atrato River Decision T-622/16 of November 10, 2016* (Sentencia T-622/16 de Noviembre 10, 2016). Sabin Center for Climate Change Law at Columbia Law School. Retrieved January 3, 2025, from http://climatecasechart.com/non-us-case/atrato-river-decision-t-622-16-of-november-10-2016/

Climate Change Litigation Databases. (2015-2022). *In re Greenpeace Southeast Asia and Others* (Commission on Human Rights of the Republic of the Philippines). Sabin Center for Climate

Change Law at Columbia Law School. Retrieved January 3, 2025, from http://climatecasechart.com/non-us-case/in-re-greenpeace-southeast-asia-et-al/

Climate Change Litigation Databases. (2015a-today). *Juliana v. United States*. Sabin Center for Climate Change Law at Columbia Law School. Retrieved January 3, 2025, from http://climatecasechart.com/case/juliana-v-united-states/

Climate Change Litigation Databases. (2015b-today). *Lliuya v. RWE AG*. Sabin Center for Climate Change Law at Columbia Law School. Retrieved January 3, 2025, from http://climatecasechart.com/non-us-case/lliuya-v-rwe-ag/

Climate Change Litigation Databases. (2015-2020). *Urgenda Foundation v. State of the Netherlands*. Sabin Center for Climate Change Law at Columbia Law School. Retrieved January 3, 2025, from http://climatecasechart.com/non-us-case/urgenda-foundation-v-kingdom-of-the-netherlands/

Climate Change Litigation Databases. (2016-2020). *Greenpeace Nordic Ass'n and Nature and Youth v. Ministry of Petroleum and Energy (People v. Arctic Oil)*. Sabin Center for Climate Change Law at Columbia Law School. Retrieved January 3, 2025, from http://climatecasechart.com/non-us-case/greenpeace-nordic-assn-and-nature-youth-v-norway-ministry-of-petroleum-and-energy/

Climate Change Litigation Databases. (2016a-today). *Ali v. Federation of Pakistan*. Sabin Center for Climate Change Law at Columbia Law School. Retrieved January 3, 2025, from http://climatecasechart.com/non-us-case/ali-v-federation-of-pakistan-2/

Climate Change Litigation Databases. (2016b-today). *Mataatua District Maori Council v. New Zealand*. Sabin Center for Climate Change Law at Columbia Law School. Retrieved January 3, 2025, from http://climatecasechart.com/non-us-case/mataatua-district-maori-council-v-new-zealand/

Climate Change Litigation Databases. (2017-2019). *Pandey v. India*. Sabin Center for Climate Change Law at Columbia Law School. Retrieved January 3, 2025, from http://climatecasechart.com/non-us-case/pandey-v-india/

Climate Change Litigation Databases. (2018a). *Future Generations v. Ministry of the Environment and Others (Demanda Generaciones Futuras v. Minambiente)*. Sabin Center for Climate Change Law at Columbia Law School. Retrieved January 3, 2025, from http://climatecasechart.com/non-us-case/future-generation-v-ministry-environment-others/

Climate Change Litigation Databases. (2018-2019). *Maria Khan et al. v. Federation of Pakistan et al.* Sabin Center for Climate Change Law at Columbia Law School. Retrieved January 3, 2025, from http://climatecasechart.com/non-us-case/maria-khan-et-al-v-federation-of-pakistan-et-al/

Climate Change Litigation Databases. (2018b). Armando Ferrão Carvalho and Others v. the European Parliament and the Council: The People's Climate Case. *Sabin Center for Climate Change Law at Columbia Law School*. 2018-2021a. Retrieved January 3, 2025, from http://climatecasechart.com/non-us-case/armando-ferrao-carvalho-and-others-v-the-european-parliament-and-the-council/

Climate Change Litigation Databases. (2018c). *City of New York v. BP p.l.c.* Sabin Center for Climate Change Law at Columbia Law School. Retrieved January 3, 2025, from http://climatecasechart.com/case/city-new-york-v-bp-plc/

Climate Change Litigation Databases. (2018d). *Neubauer et al. v. Germany*. Sabin Center for Climate Change Law at Columbia Law School. Retrieved January 3, 2025, from http://climatecasechart.com/non-us-case/neubauer-et-al-v-germany/

Climate Change Litigation Databases. (2019-2021). *Sacchi et al. v. Argentina et al.* Sabin Center for Climate Change Law at Columbia Law School. Retrieved January 3, 2025, from http://climatecasechart.com/non-us-case/sacchi-et-al-v-argentina-et-al/

Climate Change Litigation Databases. (2019-2022). *Daniel Billy and others v Australia (Torres Strait Islanders Petition). Sabin Center for Climate Change Law at Columbia Law School.* Retrieved January 3, 2025, from http://climatecasechart.com/non-us-case/petition-of-torres-strait-islanders-to-the-united-nations-human-rights-committee-alleging-violations-stemming-from-australias-inaction-on-climate-change/

Climate Change Litigation Databases. (2019-2024). *Notre Affaire à Tous and Others v. Total*. Sabin Center for Climate Change Law at Columbia Law School. Retrieved January 3, 2025, from http://climatecasechart.com/non-us-case/notre-affaire-a-tous-and-others-v-total/

Climate Change Litigation Databases. (2019a-today). *Milieudefensie et al. v. Royal Dutch Shell plc*. Sabin Center for Climate Change Law at Columbia Law School. Retrieved January 3, 2025, from http://climatecasechart.com/non-us-case/milieudefensie-et-al-v-royal-dutch-shell-plc/

Climate Change Litigation Databases. (2019b-today). *La Rose v. Her Majesty the Queen*. Sabin Center for Climate Change Law at Columbia Law School. Retrieved January 3, 2025, from http://climatecasechart.com/non-us-case/la-rose-v-her-majesty-the-queen/

Climate Change Litigation Databases. (2020-2022). *Sharma and others v. Minister for the Environment*. Sabin Center for Climate Change Law at Columbia Law School. Retrieved January 3, 2025, from http://climatecasechart.com/non-us-case/raj-seppings-v-ley/

Climate Change Litigation Databases. (2020-2023). *Greenpeace v. Spain*. Sabin Center for Climate Change Law at Columbia Law School. Retrieved January 3, 2025, from http://climatecasechart.com/non-us-case/greenpeace-v-spain/

Climate Change Litigation Databases. (2020-2024a). *Do-Hyun Kim et al. v. South Korea*. Sabin Center for Climate Change Law at Columbia Law School. Retrieved January 3, 2025, from http://climatecasechart.com/non-us-case/kim-yujin-et-al-v-south-korea/

Climate Change Litigation Databases. (2020-2024b). *Duarte Agostinho and Others v. Portugal and 32 Other States*. Sabin Center for Climate Change Law at Columbia Law School. Retrieved January 3, 2025, from http://climatecasechart.com/non-us-case/youth-for-climate-justice-v-austria-et-al/

Climate Change Litigation Databases. (2020a-today). *Asociación Civil por la Justicia Ambiental v. Province of Entre Ríos, et al. (Delta del Paraná Case)*. Sabin Center for Climate Change Law at Columbia Law School. Retrieved January 3, 2025, from http://climatecasechart.com/non-us-case/asociacion-civil-por-la-justicia-ambiental-v-province-of-entre-rios-et-al/

Climate Change Litigation Databases. (2020b-today). *Institute of Amazonian Studies v. Brazil*. Sabin Center for Climate Change Law at Columbia Law School. Retrieved January 3, 2025, from http://climatecasechart.com/non-us-case/institute-of-amazonian-studies-v-brazil/

Climate Change Litigation Databases. (2020c-today). *PSB et al. v. Brazil (on Deforestation and Human Rights)*. Sabin Center for Climate Change Law at Columbia Law School. Retrieved January 3, 2025, from http://climatecasechart.com/non-us-case/brazilian-socialist-party-and-others-v-brazil/

Climate Change Litigation Databases. (2020d-today). *Rights of indigenous people in addressing climate-forced displacement*. Sabin Center for Climate Change Law at Columbia Law School. Retrieved January 3, 2025, from http://climatecasechart.com/non-us-case/rights-of-indigenous-people-in-addressing-climate-forced-displacement/

Climate Change Litigation Databases. (2021a-today). *Environmental Justice Australia (EJA) v. Australia*. Sabin Center for Climate Change Law at Columbia Law School. Retrieved January 3, 2025, from http://climatecasechart.com/non-us-case/environmental-justice-australia-eja-v-australia/

Climate Change Litigation Databases. (2021b-today). *Greenpeace Nordic Ass'n v. Ministry of Petroleum and Energy (ECtHR)*. Sabin Center for Climate Change Law at Columbia Law School. Retrieved January 3, 2025, from http://climatecasechart.com/non-us-case/greenpeace-nordic-assn-v-ministry-of-petroleum-and-energy-ecthr/

Climate Change Litigation Databases. (2021c-today). *Kaiser, et al. v. Volkswagen AG*. Sabin Center for Climate Change Law at Columbia Law School. Retrieved January 3, 2025, from http://climatecasechart.com/non-us-case/kaiser-et-al-v-volkswagen-ag/

Climate Change Litigation Databases. (2022-2023). *Plan B. Earth and Others v. the United Kingdom*. Sabin Center for Climate Change Law at Columbia Law School. Retrieved January 3, 2025, from http://climatecasechart.com/non-us-case/plan-bearth-and-others-v-united-kingdom/

Climate Change Litigation Databases. (2022-2024a). *Navahine F. v. Hawai'i Department of Transportation*. Sabin Center for Climate Change Law at Columbia Law School. Retrieved January 3, 2025, from http://climatecasechart.com/case/navahine-f-v-hawaii-department-of-transportation/

Climate Change Litigation Databases. (2022-2024b). *Request for an advisory opinion submitted by the Commission of Small Island States on Climate Change and International Law*. Sabin Center for Climate Change Law at Columbia Law School. Retrieved January 3, 2025, from https://climatecasechart.com/non-us-case/18416/

Climate Change Litigation Databases. (2022a-today). *Conectas Direitos Humanos v. BNDES and BNDESPAR*. Sabin Center for Climate Change Law at Columbia Law School. Retrieved January 3, 2025, from http://climatecasechart.com/non-us-case/conectas-direitos-humanos-v-bndes-and-bndespar/

Climate Change Litigation Databases. (2022b-today). *Greenpeace Argentina et. al., v. Argentina et. al: "Fundación Greenpeace Argentina y Ots. v. Estado Nacional y Ots."*. Sabin Center for Climate Change Law at Columbia Law School. Retrieved January 3, 2025, from http://climatecasechart.com/non-us-case/greenpeace-argentina-et-al-v-argentina-et-al/

Climate Change Litigation Databases. (2023a-today). *Request for an advisory opinion on the obligations of states with respect to climate change*. Sabin Center for Climate Change Law at Columbia Law School. Retrieved January 3, 2025, from https://climatecasechart.com/non-us-case/request-for-an-advisory-opinion-on-the-obligations-of-states-with-respect-to-climate-change/

Climate Change Litigation Databases. (2023b-today). *Request for an advisory opinion on the scope of the state obligations for responding to the climate emergency*. Sabin Center for Climate Change Law at Columbia Law School. Retrieved January 3, 2025, from https://climatecasechart.com/non-us-case/request-for-an-advisory-opinion-on-the-scope-of-the-state-obligations-for-responding-to-the-climate-emergency/

Climate Rights Litigation Database. (2021-2023). *Inhabitants of La Oroya v Peru*. Climate Rights and Remedies Project of the University of Zurich. Retrieved January 3, 2025, from https://climaterightsdatabase.com/2024/03/26/inhabitants-of-la-oroya-v-peru/

Climate Rights Litigation Database. (2024-today). *"Zukunftsklage" (Greenpeace and ors. v. Germany): Neubauer II/Steinmetz III*. Climate Rights and Remedies Project of the University of Zurich. Retrieved January 3, 2025, from https://climaterightsdatabase.com/2024/06/27/zukunftsklage-greenpeace-and-germanwatch-and-ors-v-germany/

Collins, L. M. (2007). Revisiting the doctrine of intergenerational equity in global environmental governance. *Dalhousie Law Journal, 30*(1), 73–134.

Collins, L. M. (2017). Judging the anthropocene: Transformative adjudication in the anthropocene epoch. In L. J. Kotzé (Ed.), *Environmental law and governance for the anthropocene* (Vol. 14, pp. 309–327). Hart Publishing.

Committee on Economic, Social and Cultural Rights. (1999, May 12). *General Comment No. 12 (2002): The Right to Adequate Food (Art. 11 of the ICESCR)*. UN Doc. E/C.12/1999/5.

Committee on Economic, Social and Cultural Rights. (2003, January 20). *General Comment No. 15 (2002): The Right to Water (Arts. 11 and 12 of the ICESCR)*. UN Doc. E/C.12/2002/11.

Committee on the Rights of the Child. (2021, December 9). Draft General Comment No. 26 on Children's Rights and the Environment with a Special Focus on Climate Change—Concept Note. Retrieved January 3, 2025, from https://www.ohchr.org/en/treaty-bodies/crc/concept-note-general-comment-childrens-rights-and-environment-special-focus-climate-change

Committee on the Rights of the Child. (2023, August 22). *General Comment No. 26: Children's rights and the environment, with a special focus on climate change*. UN Doc. CRC/C/GC/26.

Conference of Model Institutions for a Sustainable Future. (2014, April 26). *Budapest Memorandum: Signed by the Participants of the Conference of Model Institutions for a Sustainable Future Held in Budapest, 24–26 April 2014*. Retrieved January 3, 2025, from https://www.kas.de/c/document_library/get_file?uuid=60b5569a-ef44-96f2-7ed9-aa18d3ea2449&groupId=264621

Cordonier Segger, M.-C. (2021a). International treaty law and policy for future generations. In M.-C. Cordonier Segger, M. Szabó, & A. R. Harrington (Eds.), *Intergenerational justice in sustainable development treaty implementation: Advancing future generations rights through national institutions* (Vol. 3, pp. 47–67). Cambridge University Press.

Cordonier Segger, M.-C. (2021b). Intergenerational justice in the Paris agreement on climate change. In M.-C. Cordonier Segger, M. Szabó, & A. R. Harrington (Eds.), *Intergenerational justice in sustainable development treaty implementation: Advancing future generations rights through national institutions* (Vol. 37, pp. 731–753). Cambridge University Press.

Cordonier Segger, M.-C., Szabó, M., & Harrington, A. R. (Eds.). (2021). *Intergenerational justice in sustainable development treaty implementation: Advancing future generations rights through national institutions*. Cambridge University Press.

Couch, K. (2020). After Juliana: A proposal for the next atmospheric trust litigation strategy. *William and Mary Environmental Law and Policy Review, 45*(1), 219–246.

Council of Europe. (2003, January 22). *Setting up a Committee for Future Generations: Motion for a Resolution*. Doc. 9668.

Council of Europe, Committee of Ministers. (2022, September 27). *Human rights and the protection of the environment*. Recommendation CM/Rec(2022)20.

Council of Europe, Parliamentary Assembly. (2021a, September 29). *Anchoring the Right to a Healthy Environment: Need for Enhanced Action by the Council of Europe*. Recommendation 2211 (2021).

Council of Europe, Parliamentary Assembly. (2021b, September 29). *Anchoring the right to a healthy environment: Need for enhanced action by the Council of Europe*. Resolution 2396 (2021).

Council of Europe, Steering Committee for Human Rights. (2022). *Environment and human rights (CDDH-ENV): Website*. Council of Europe. Retrieved January 3, 2025, from https://www.coe.int/en/web/human-rights-intergovernmental-cooperation/environment-and-human-rights

Cousteau, J.-Y. (1991). *A bill of rights for future generations: Draft general assembly resolution*. Cousteau Society. Retrieved January 3, 2025, from https://archivos.juridicas.unam.mx/www/bjv/libros/8/3635/12.pdf

Crawford, J. (2006). State responsibility. In A. Peters & R. Wolfrum (Eds.), *Max Planck encyclopedia of public international law*. Oxford University Press. (Article last updated September 2006).

Crawford, J., & Brownlie, I. (2019). *Brownlie's principles of public international law* (9th ed.). Oxford University Press.

D'Amato, A. (1990). Do we owe a duty to future generations to preserve the global environment? *American Journal of International Law, 84*, 190–198.

Daly, A. (2022). Climate competence: Youth climate activism and its impact on international human rights law. *Human Rights Law Review, 22*, 1–24.

de George, R. (1981). The environment, rights, and future generations. In E. Partridge (Ed.), *Responsibilities to future generations: Environmental ethics* (pp. 157–166). Prometheus Books.

de La Fayette, L. A. (2010). International liability for damage to the environment. In M. Fitzmaurice, D. Ong, & P. Merkouris (Eds.), *Research handbook on international environmental law* (Vol. 16, pp. 320–360). Edward Elgar Publishing.

Dellinger, M. (2016). An "act of god"? Rethinking contractual impracticability in an era of anthropogenic climate change. *Hastings Law Journal, 67*(6), 1551–1620.

Dellinger, M. (2018). See you in court: Around the world in eight climate change lawsuits. *William and Mary Environmental Law and Policy Review, 42*(2), 525–551.

De-Shalit, A. (1995). *Why posterity matters: Environmental policies and future generations*. Routledge Taylor & Francis Group.

Desmet, E. (2019). Children's rights and the environmental dimension of sustainable development. In C. Fenton-Glynn (Ed.), *Children's rights and sustainable development: Interpreting the UNCRC for future generations* (Vol. 9, pp. 192–215). Cambridge University Press.

Deutsche Umwelthilfe e.V. (2022, March 24). Die Klagen der Deutschen Umwelthilfe gegen BMW und Mercedes-Benz: Background Paper. Retrieved January 3, 2025, from https://www.duh.de/fileadmin/user_upload/download/Projektinformation/Verkehr/Klimaklage_Verkehr/DUH-Hintergrund-Papier_Unternehmensklagen.pdf

Dobson, A. (1996). Representative democracy and the environment. In W. M. Lafferty & J. Meadowcroft (Eds.), *Democracy and the environment: Problems and prospects* (Vol. 7, pp. 124–139). Edward Elgar Publishing.

Donger, E. (2022). Children and youth in strategic climate litigation: Advancing rights through legal argument and legal mobilization. *Transnational Environmental Law, 11*(2), 263–289. https://doi.org/10.1017/S2047102522000218

Donnelly, J. (2003). *Universal human rights in theory and practice* (2nd ed.). Cornell University Press.

Dörr, O. (2022). State responsibility for climate change under EU and German law. In E. Schulev-Steindl et al. (Eds.), *Climate change, responsibility and liability* (1st ed., pp. 299–311). Nomos.

Douhan, A. (2019). Liability for environmental damage. In A. Peters & R. Wolfrum (Eds.), *Max Planck encyclopedia of public international law*. Oxford University Press. (Article last updated March 2019).

Drugmand, D. (2021, December). *The rise in forward-looking corporate climate cases: From Shell to Santos*. Center for International Environmental Law. Retrieved January 3, 2025, from https://www.ciel.org/rise-in-forward-looking-corporate-climate-cases/

Dudai, R. (2017). Human rights in the populist era: Mourn then (re)organize. *Journal of Human Rights Practice, 9*(1), 16–21. https://doi.org/10.1093/jhuman/hux005

Duffy, H. (2018). *Strategic human rights litigation: Understanding and maximising impact*. Bloomsbury Publishing PLC.

Dupuy, P.-M., & Viñuales, J. E. (2018). *International environmental law* (2nd ed.). Cambridge University Press.

Düwell, M., & Bos, G. (2016). Human rights and future people: Possibilities of argumentation. *Journal of Human Rights, 15*(2), 231–250.

Dworkin, R. (1978). *Taking rights seriously*. Harvard University Press.

Ebbesson, J., Gaugitsch, H., Jendrośka, J., Marshall, F., & Stec, S. (2014). *The Aarhus Convention: An implementation guide* (2nd ed.). United Nations Publication.

Eckersley, R. (2000). Deliberative democracy, ecological representation and risk: Towards a democracy of the affected. In M. Saward (Ed.), *Democratic innovation: Deliberation, representation, and association* (Vol. 9, pp. 117–132). Routledge Taylor & Francis Group.

Eckes, C. (2021a, May 10). Separation of powers in climate cases: Comparing cases in Germany and The Netherlands. *Verfassungsblog*. Retrieved January 3, 2025, from https://verfassungsblog.de/separation-of-powers-in-climate-cases/

Eckes, C. (2021b, June 15). The courts strike back: The shell case in light of separation of powers. *Verfassungsblog*. Retrieved January 3, 2025, from https://verfassungsblog.de/the-courts-strike-back/

Ehm, F. (2013). *Das völkerrechtliche Demokratiegebot: Eine Untersuchung zur schwindenden Wertneutralität des Völkerrechts gegenüber den staatlichen Binnenstrukturen*. Mohr Siebeck.

Ekardt, F. (2021a). *Theorie der Nachhaltigkeit: Ethische, Rechtliche, Politische und Transformative Zugänge—Am Beispiel von Klimawandel, Ressourcenknappheit und Welthandel* (2nd ed.). Nomos. https://doi.org/10.5771/9783845254593

Ekardt, F. (2021b, June 9). Shell's climate obligation: Climate, civil courts, human rights, and balance of powers. *Verfassungsblog*. Retrieved January 3, 2025, from https://verfassungsblog.de/shells-climate-obligation/

Ekeli, K. S. (2005). Giving a voice to posterity: Deliberative democracy and representation of future people. *Journal of Agricultural and Environmental Ethics, 18*(5), 429–450. https://doi.org/10.1007/s10806-005-7048-z

Epiney, A., Diezig, S., Pirker, B., & Reitemeyer, S. (2018). *Aarhus-Konvention: Handkommentar*. Nomos; Manz; Helbing & Lichtenhahn.

Epstein, R. A., & Deckert, K. (2021). Climate change litigation in France. In W. Kahl & M.-P. Weller (Eds.), *Climate change litigation: A handbook* (pp. 336–362). C.H. Beck; Nomos.

European Commission. (2018, September 24). *Political declaration adopted at the Nelson Mandela Peace Summit: Statement*. European Union (EU). Retrieved January 3, 2025, from https://ec.europa.eu/commission/presscorner/detail/en/STATEMENT_18_5885

European Commission. (2020-2022). *Sustainable corporate governance: Public consultation*. European Union (EU). Retrieved January 3, 2025, from https://ec.europa.eu/info/law/better-regulation/have-your-say/initiatives/12548-Sustainable-corporate-governance_en

European Court of Human Rights. (2022, July). Environment and the European Convention on Human Rights: Factsheet. Retrieved January 3, 2025, from https://www.echr.coe.int/documents/fs_environment_eng.pdf

Evaristus, O. (2007). The U.N. global compact and accountability of transnational corporations: Separating myth from realities. *Florida Journal of International Law, 19*(1), 1–38.

Fabbricotti, A., & Venturini, C. (2019). Ombudsperson. In A. Peters & R. Wolfrum (Eds.), *Max Planck encyclopedia of public international law*. Oxford University Press. (Article last updated July 2019).

Faga, H. P., & Uchechukwu, U. (2019). Oil exploration, environmental degradation, and future generations in The Niger Delta: Options for enforcement of intergenerational rights and sustainable development through legal and judicial activism. *Journal of Environmental Law and Litigation, 34*, 185–218.

Farber, D. (2021). Climate change litigation in the United States. In W. Kahl & M.-P. Weller (Eds.), *Climate change litigation: A handbook* (pp. 237–252). C.H. Beck; Nomos.

Faure, M., & Peeters, M. (Eds.). (2011). *Climate change liability*. Edward Elgar Publishing.

Feinberg, J. (1974). The rights of animals and unborn generations. In W. Blackstone (Ed.), *Philosophy and environmental crisis* (pp. 43–68). University of Georgia Press.

Feria-Tinta, M., & Milnes, S. C. (2016). The rise of environmental law in international dispute resolution: The inter-American court of human rights issues a landmark advisory opinion on the environment and human rights. *Yearbook of International Environmental Law, 27*, 64–81. https://doi.org/10.1093/yiel/yvy004

Fibieger Byskov, M., & Hyams, K. (2022). Who should represent future generations in climate planning? *Ethics and International Affairs, 36*(2), 199–214. https://doi.org/10.1017/S0892679422000168

Fitzmaurice, M. (2004). The international court of justice and the environment. *Non-State Actors and International Law, 4*(3), 173–197. https://doi.org/10.1163/1571807042794645

Fitzmaurice, M. (2008). Intergenerational equity revisited. In I. Buffard, J. Crawford, A. Pellet, & S. Wittich (Eds.), *International law between universalism and fragmentation: Festschrift in honour of Gerhard Hafner* (Vol. 11, pp. 195–229). Martinus Nijhoff Publishers.

Fitzmaurice, M. (2010). International responsibility and liability. In D. Bodansky, J. Brunnée, & E. Hey (Eds.), *The Oxford handbook of international environmental law* (Vol. 44, 1st ed., pp. 1011–1034). Oxford University Press.

Fitzmaurice, M. (2012). Some reflections on legal and philosophical foundations of international environmental law. *Polish Yearbook of International Law, 32*, 89–110.

Francioni, F. (2010). International human rights in an environmental horizon. *European Journal of International Law, 21*(1), 41–55. https://doi.org/10.1093/ejil/chq019

Francioni, F. (2012). Realism, utopia, and the future of international environmental law. In A. Cassese (Ed.), *Realizing utopia: The future of international law* (Vol. 34, 1st ed., pp. 442–460). Oxford University Press.

Francioni, F., & Quirico, O. (2016). Untying the gordian knot: Towards the human right to a climatically sustainable environment? In O. Quirico & M. Boumghar (Eds.), *Climate change and human rights: An international and comparative law perspective* (pp. 133–155). Routledge Taylor & Francis Group.

Frankenberg, G. (2010). Critical theory. In A. Peters & R. Wolfrum (Eds.), *Max Planck encyclopedia of public international law*. Oxford University Press. (Article last updated October 2010).

Freeman, M. D. A. (1995). Are there collective human rights? *Political Studies, 43*(1), 25–40. https://doi.org/10.1111/j.1467-9248.1995.tb01734.x

Fuchs, C. (2009). Environment, role of non-governmental organizations. In A. Peters & R. Wolfrum (Eds.), *Max Planck encyclopedia of public international law*. Oxford University Press. (Article last updated March 2009).

Fülöp, S. (2016). The institutional representation of future generations. In G. Bos & M. Düwell (Eds.), *Human rights and sustainability: Moral responsibilities for the future* (Vol. 15, pp. 195–211). Routledge Taylor & Francis Group.

Fülöp, S. (2021). Future generations institutions to implement international obligations towards future generations. In M.-C. Cordonier Segger, M. Szabó, & A. R. Harrington (Eds.), *Intergenerational justice in sustainable development treaty implementation: Advancing future generations rights through national institutions* (Vol. 7, pp. 137–161). Cambridge University Press.

Gaillard, É. (2011). *Générations Futures et Droit Privé: Vers un Droit des Générations Futures*. LGDJ Lextenso Éditions.

Gaillard, É. (2012). Des Crimes Contre L'Humanité Aux Crimes Contre les Générations Futures: Vers une Transposition du Concept Ethique de Responsabilité Transgénérationnelle en Droit Pénal International? *McGill International Journal of Sustainable Development Law & Policy, 7*(2), 180–202.

Ganesan, P. (2022, April 11). UN Human Rights Council appoints new UN special rapporteur on human rights and climate change. *Climate Rights Blog*. Retrieved January 3, 2025, from https://climaterightsdatabase.com/2022/04/11/un-human-rights-council-appoints-new-un-special-rapporteur-on-human-rights-and-climate-change-2/

Garner, B. A. (Ed.). (2009). *Black's law dictionary* (9th ed.). West.

Garofalo, C. (2022, March 24). As the lungs of the earth dry out, climate litigation heats up: Can rights-based strategies become a valid tool for the protection of the Amazon Forest? *Verfassungsblog*. Retrieved January 3, 2025, from https://verfassungsblog.de/as-the-lung-of-the-earth-dries-out-climate-litigation-heats-up/

Garrido Alvez, D. B. (2023, July 27). The Concept of International Organizations in the practice of the International Court of Justice. *EJIL: Talk!* Retrieved December 30, 2024, from https://www.ejiltalk.org/the-concept-of-international-organization-in-the-practice-of-the-international-court-of-justice/

Gasparri, G., El Omrani, O., Hinton, R., Imbago, D., Lakhani, H., Mohan, A., Yeung, W., & Bustreo, F. (2021). Children, adolescents, and youth pioneering a human rights-based approach to climate change. *Health and Human Rights Journal, 23*(2), 95–108.

Gatmaytan, D. B. (2003). The illusion of intergenerational equity: Oposa v. Factoran as pyrrhic victory. *Georgetown International Environmental Law Review, 15*(3), 457–485.

Gattini, A. (2019). Actio popularis. In A. Peters & R. Wolfrum (Eds.), *Max Planck encyclopedia of public international law*. Oxford University Press. (Article last updated February 2019).

Gearty, C. A. (2010). Do human rights help or hinder environmental protection? *Journal of Human Rights and the Environment, 1*(1), 7–22.

Gellinsky, K., & Fuchs, M.-C. (2021, May 26). Bitte noch mehr: Rechtsprechungsdialog im Karlsruher Klimabeschluss. *Verfassungsblog*. Retrieved January 3, 2025, from https://verfassungsblog.de/bitte-noch-mehr/

Giabardo, C. V. (2024, December 17). Corporate climate responsibility after "Milieudefensie vs. Shell" Court of Appeal Decision. *EJIL: Talk!* Retrieved January 3, 2025, from https://www.ejiltalk.org/corporate-climate-responsibility-after-milieudefensie-vs-shell-court-of-appeal-decision/

Gibson, N. (1990). The right to a clean environment. *Saskatchewan Law Review, 54*(1), 5–18.

Goldmann, M. (2021, April 30). Judges for future: The climate action judgment as a postcolonial turn in constitutional law? *Verfassungsblog*. Retrieved January 3, 2025, from https://verfassungsblog.de/judges-for-future/

González Hauck, S., Kahl, V., Etkin, B., Green, A., Paige, T. P., & Bagchi, K. (2024). Approaches. In S. González Hauck, R. Kunz, & M. Milas (Eds.), *Public international law: A multi-perspective approch* (Vol. 3, 1st ed., pp. 63–108). Routledge.

González-Ricoy, I., & Gosseries, A. (Eds.). (2016). *Institutions for future generations* (1st ed.). Oxford University Press.

González-Ricoy, I., & Rey, F. (2019). Enfranchising the future: Climate justice and the representation of future generations. *Wiley Interdisciplinary Reviews: Climate Change, 10*(5), e598. https://doi.org/10.1002/wcc.598

Goodin, R. E. (2007). Enfranchising all affected interests, and its alternatives. *Philosophy and Public Affairs, 35*(1), 40–68. https://doi.org/10.1111/j.1088-4963.2007.00098.x

Göpel, M., & Pearce, C. (2018, March). *Guarding our future: How to include future generations in policy making*. World Future Council. Retrieved January 3, 2025, from https://www.worldfuturecouncil.org/wp-content/uploads/2018/07/brochure_guarding2018b.pdf

Gorski, S. (2013). Individuals in international law. In A. Peters & R. Wolfrum (Eds.), *Max Planck encyclopedia of public international law*. Oxford University Press. (Article last updated August 2013).

Gosseries, A. (2004). Constitutionalizing future rights? *Intergenerational Justice Review, 2*, 10–11.

Gradoni, L., & Mantovani, M. (2022, March 24). No kidding! Mapping youth-led climate change litigation across the North-South divide. *Verfassungsblog*. Retrieved January 3, 2025, from https://verfassungsblog.de/no-kidding/

Gubbay, I., & Wenzler, C. (2021). Intergenerational climate change litigation: The first climate communication to the UN Committee on the Rights of the Child. In I. Alogna, C. Bakker, & J.-P. Gauci (Eds.), *Climate change litigation: Global perspectives* (Vol. 15, pp. 343–365). Brill Nijhoff.

Gunia, A. (2022, July 18). Pacific island nations are bringing their climate justice fight to the World's Highest Court. *Time*. Retrieved January 3, 2025, from https://time.com/6197027/pacific-island-nations-vanuatu-climate-change/

Habermas, J. (1992). *Faktizität und Geltung: Beiträge zur Diskurstheorie des Rechts und des demokratischen Rechtsstaats* (1st ed.). Suhrkamp.

Hadjiargyrou, Z. (2016). A conceptual and practical evaluation of intergenerational equity in international environmental law. *International Community Law Review, 18*, 248–277.

Handl, G. (1992). Human rights and the protection of the environment: A mildly revisionist view. In A. A. Cançado Trindade & E. Brown Weiss (Eds.), *Derechos Humanos, Desarrollo Sustentable y Medio Ambiente: Human rights, sustainable development and the environment* (p. 117). Banco Interamericano de Desarrollo.

Hannum, H. (2019). *Rescuing human rights: A radically moderate approach*. Cambridge University Press.

Hassan, F. (1983). Solidarity rights: Progressive evolution of international human rights law. *New York Law School Human Rights Annual, 1*, 51–74.

Heller, K. J. (2021, June 23). Skeptical thoughts on the proposed crime of "ecocide" (that isn't). *OpinioJuris*. Retrieved January 3, 2025, from https://opiniojuris.org/2021/06/23/skeptical-thoughts-on-the-proposed-crime-of-ecocide-that-isnt/

Hernández, G. I. (2013). A reluctant guardian: The international court of justice and the concept of 'international community'. *British Yearbook of International Law, 83*(1), 13–60. https://doi.org/10.1093/bybil/brt003

Heyward, C. (2008). Can the all-affected principle include future persons? Green deliberative democracy and the non-identity problem. *Environmental Politics, 17*(4), 625–643. https://doi.org/10.1080/09644010802193591

Higgins, P. (2016). *Eradicating ecocide: Laws and governance to prevent the destruction of our planet* (2nd ed.). Shepheard-Walwyn.

Higgins, R. (1995). *Problems and process: International law and how we use it*. (Reprint). Clarendon Press.

Hilson, C. (2024, November 15). Into reverse gear: Shell v Milieudefensie and the non-regression principle. *Verfassungsblog*. Retrieved January 3, 2025, from https://verfassungsblog.de/shell-milieudefensie-non-retrogression/

Hiskes, R. P. (2005). The right to a green future: Human rights, environmentalism, and intergenerational justice. *Human Rights Quarterly, 27*(4), 1346–1364.

Hobbes, T. (1651). *Leviathan: Or the matter, forme, & power of a commonwealth ecclasiasticall and civil*. Printed for Andrew Crooke. (Original work published 1651).

Hobe, S. (2019). Human rights, role of non-governmental organizations. In A. Peters & R. Wolfrum (Eds.), *Max Planck encyclopedia of public international law*. Oxford University Press. (Article last updated May 2019).

Hodas, D. (2018). Us climate change adjudication: The epic journey from a petition for rulemaking to national greenhouse gas regulation. In C. Voigt & Z. Makuch (Eds.), *Courts and the environment* (Vol. 15, pp. 345–368). Edward Elgar Publishing.

Hohfeld, W. N. (1913). Some fundamental legal conceptions as applied in judicial reasoning. *Yale Law Journal, 23*(1), 16–59. https://doi.org/10.2307/786270

Hornkohl, L. (2021, April 6). The CJEU dismissed the people's climate case as inadmissible: The limit of plaumann is plaumann. *European Law Blog*. Retrieved January 3, 2025, from https://www.europeanlawblog.eu/pub/the-cjeu-dismissed-the-peoples-climate-case-as-inadmissible-the-limit-of-plaumann-is-plaumann/release/1

Hösli, A. (2021). Milieudefensie et al. v. Shell: A tipping point in climate change litigation against corporations? *Climate Law, 11*(2), 195–209. https://doi.org/10.1163/18786561-11020005

Human Rights Committee. (2019, September 3). *General Comment No. 36: Article 6: right to life*. UN Doc. CCPR/C/GC/36.

Human Rights Council. (2009, January 15). *Report of the Office of the UN High Commissioner for Human Rights on the Relationship Between Climate Change and Human Rights*. UN Doc. A/HRC/10/61.

Human Rights Council. (2011, March 21). *Report of the Special Representative of the Secretary-General on the issue of human rights and transnational corporations and other business enterprises – UN Guiding Principles on Business and Human Rights: Implementing the United Nations "Protect, Respect and Remedy" Framework*, by J. Ruggie. UN Doc. A/HRC/17/31.

Human Rights Council. (2012, December 24). *Report of the Independent Expert on the issue of human rights obligations relating to the enjoyment of a safe, clean, healthy and sustainable environment*, by J. H. Knox. UN Doc. A/HRC/22/43.

Human Rights Council. (2014, July 14). *Elaboration of an international legally binding instrument on transnational corporations and other business enterprises with respect to human rights*. UN Doc. A/HRC/RES/26/9.

Human Rights Council. (2018, January 24). *Report of the Special Rapporteur on the issue of human rights obligations relating to the enjoyment of a safe, clean, healthy and sustainable environment*, by J. H. Knox. UN Doc. A/HRC/37/59.

Human Rights Council. (2021a, October 8). *The human right to a clean, healthy and sustainable environment*. UN Doc. A/HRC/RES/48/13.

Human Rights Council. (2021b, October 8). *Mandate of the special rapporteur on the promotion and protection of human rights in the context of climate change*. UN Doc. A/HRC/RES/48/14.

Human Rights Council. (2021c, August 17). *Open-Ended Intergovernmental Working Group on Transnational Corporations and Other Business Enterprises with respect to Human Rights: Legally Binding Instrument to Regulate, in International Human Rights Law, the Activities of Transnational Corporations and Other Business Enterprises (Third Revised Draft)*. Retrieved January 3, 2025, from https://www.ohchr.org/Documents/HRBodies/HRCouncil/WGTransCorp/Session6/LBI3rdDRAFT.pdf

Ignatieff, M. (2003). Human rights as idolatry. In M. Ignatieff & A. Gutmann (Eds.), *Human rights as politics and idolatry* (3rd ed., pp. 53–100). Princeton University Press.

Ijalaye, D. A. (1978). *The extension of corporate personality in international law*. Oceana Publications, Inc; A. W. Sijthoff.

ILA Committee on Legal Aspects of Sustainable Development. (2002, April 6). *New Delhi declaration of principles of international law relating to sustainable development: Resolution 3/2002*. International Law Association. Retrieved January 3, 2025, from https://www.ila-hq.org/en_GB/documents/conference-resolution-english-new-delhi-2002-3

Independent Expert Panel for the Legal Definition of Ecocide (Ed.) (2021, June). *Proposal for the legal definition of ecocide: Commentary and core text*. Stop Ecocide Foundation. Retrieved January 3, 2025, from https://www.stopecocide.earth/legal-definition-of-ecocide

Institut de Droit International. (1997, September 4). Responsibility and liability under international law for environmental damage. Retrieved January 3, 2025, from https://www.idi-iil.org/app/uploads/2017/06/1997_str_03_en.pdf

Institut de Droit International. (2005, August 27). Obligations and rights erga omnes in international law. Retrieved January 3, 2025, from https://www.idi-iil.org/app/uploads/2017/06/2005_kra_01_en.pdf

International Council on Human Rights. (2002). *Beyond voluntarism: Human rights and the developing international legal obligations of companies*. International Council on Human Rights Policy.

International Court of Justice. (2023). Practice directions of the international court of justice. Last updated 24 October 2023. Retrieved January 3, 2025, from https://www.icj-cij.org/en/practice-directions

International Group of Experts for the Pact. (2017, June). Draft Global Pact for the Environment. *Global Pact for the Environment*. Retrieved January 3, 2025, from https://globalpactenvironment.org/en/documents-en/the-pact-text/

International Human Rights Clinic at Harvard Law School, & Science and Environmental Health Network. (2008, November). *An environmental right for future generations: Model state constitutional provisions & model statute*. Harvard Law School. Retrieved January 3, 2025, from http://static1.squarespace.com/static/5ad8bb3336099bd6ed7b022a/5b5606108290855de08a94fb/5b5606028290855de08a9283/1532364290776/Model-State-Constitutional-Provision-and-Model-Statute.pdf

International Law Commission. (1975, May–July). *Report of the ILC on the Work of its 27th Session, 5 May-25 July 1975 – Official Records of the General Assembly, 30th Session, Supplement No. 10*. UN Doc. A/10010/Rev.1.

International Law Commission. (1995, May–July). *Report of the ILC on the Work of its 47th Session, 2 May-21 July 1995 – Official Records of the General Assembly, 50th Session, Supplement No. 10*. UN Doc. A/50/10.

International Law Commission. (1996a). *Draft Code of Crimes against the Peace and Security of Mankind with commentaries*. UN Doc. A/51/10.

International Law Commission. (1996b, March 27). *Document on Crimes Against the Environment*, by C. Tomuschat. UN Doc. ILC(XLVIII)/DC/CRD.3.

International Law Commission. (1997, January). *Draft articles on state responsibility with commentaries thereto*. UN Doc. A/CN.4/SER.4/1976/Add. 1.

International Law Commission. (2001a). *Draft articles on prevention of transboundary harm from hazardous activities, with commentaries*. UN Doc. A/56/10, 144–170.

International Law Commission. (2001b). *Draft articles on the responsibility of states for internationally wrongful acts, with commentaries*. UN Doc. A/56/10, 20–143.

International Law Commission. (2006). *Draft principles on the allocation of loss in the case of transboundary harm arising out of hazardous activities, with commentaries*. UN Doc. A/61/10.

International Law Commission. (2019, January 31). *Fourth Report by the Special Rapporteur on Peremptory Norms of General International Law (jus cogens)*, by D. Tladi. UN Doc. A/CN.4/727.

International Law Commission. (2021). *Draft Guidelines on the Protection of the Atmosphere, with Commentaries thereto*. UN Doc. A/76/10.

International Union for Conservation of Nature and Natural Resources. (2016, September 10). *Request for an advisory opinion of the International Court of Justice on the principle of sustainable development in view of the needs of future generations*. WCC-2016-Res-079-EN.
International Union for Conservation of Nature and Natural Resources, & World Commission on Environmental Law. (2016, April). IUCN world declaration on the environmental rule of law. Retrieved January 3, 2025, from https://www.iucncongress2020.org/sites/www.iucncongress2020.org/files/sessions/uploads/english_world_declaration_on_the_environmental_rule_of_law_final.pdf
Ippolito, F. (2022). The best interests of the child: Another string to the environmental and climate protection bow? *Questions of International Law, Zoom-out, 89*, 7–27.
Ivanova, M. (2020). Fighting fire with a thermometer? Environmental efforts of the United Nations. *Ethics and International Affairs, 34*(3), 339–349. https://doi.org/10.1017/S0892679420000404
Jakab, A. (2021). Sustainability in European constitutional law. In M.-C. Cordonier Segger, M. Szabó, & A. R. Harrington (Eds.), *Intergenerational justice in sustainable development treaty implementation: Advancing future generations rights through national institutions* (Vol. 8, pp. 166–200). Cambridge University Press.
Jegede, A. O. (2020). Arguing the right to a safe climate under the UN human rights system. *International Human Rights Law Review, 9*(2), 184–212. https://doi.org/10.1163/22131035-00902001
Jensen, K. K. (2015). Future generations in democracy: Representation or consideration? *Jurisprudence, 6*(3), 535–548. https://doi.org/10.1080/20403313.2015.1065649
Jodoin, S. (2010, August 15). Crimes against future generations: A new approach to ending impunity for serious violations of economic, social, and cultural rights and international environmental law. *A WFC & CISDL Legal Working Paper*. Retrieved January 3, 2025, from https://www.worldfuturecouncil.org/wp-content/uploads/2016/01/WFC_CISDL_2010_Crimes_against_Future_Generations.pdf
Jodoin, S., & Saito, Y. (2011). Crimes against future generations: Harnessing the potential of individual criminal accountability for global sustainability. *McGill International Journal of Sustainable Development Law & Policy, 7*(2), 115–155. https://doi.org/10.2139/ssrn.2942145
Johnson, G. F. (2007). Discursive democracy in the transgenerational context and a precautionary turn in public reasoning. *Contemporary Political Theory, 6*(1), 67–85. https://doi.org/10.1057/palgrave.cpt.9300253
Jones, P. (2022). Group rights. In E. N. Zalta (Ed.), *The Stanford encyclopedia of philosophy*. ISSN 1095-5054. Retrieved January 3, 2025, from https://plato.stanford.edu/entries/rights-group/. (Article last updated August 2022)
Juliana v. United States. (2021). Ninth circuit holds that developing and supervising plan to mitigate anthropogenic climate change would exceed remedial powers of article III court. *Harvard Law Review, 134*(5), 1929–1936.
Just, R. A. (1996). Intergenerational standing under the endangered species act: Giving back the right to biodiversity after Lujan v. Defenders of Wildlife. *Tulane Law Review, 71*, 597–633.
Kahl, V. (2019). Ökologische Revolution am Interamerikanischen Gerichtshof für Menschenrechte: Besprechung des Rechtsgutachtens Nr. 23 “Umwelt und Menschenrechte” (OC-23/17). *Zeitschrift Für Europäisches Umwelt- Und Planungsrecht, 17*(2), 110–131.
Kahl, V. (2022a). A human right to climate protection: Necessary protection or human rights proliferation? *Netherlands Quarterly of Human Rights, 40*(2), 158–179.
Kahl, V. (2022b, October 3). Rising before sinking: The UN Human Rights Committee’s landmark decision in Daniel Billy et al. v. Australia. *Verfassungsblog*. Retrieved January 3, 2025, from https://verfassungsblog.de/rising-before-sinking/
Kahl, V. (2023, March 10). Warming Up: The Chilean and Colombian Request for an Inter-American Advisory Opinion on the Climate Emergency and Human Rights. *Verfassungsblog*. Retrieved January 3, 2025, from https://verfassungsblog.de/warming-up/
Kahl, V. (2025, Fortcoming). *The right to a safe climate: Leading human rights law into the anthropocene* [Dissertation]. Universität Hamburg.

Kahl, V., & Bustami, A. (2021, May 7). Auf den Zweiten Blick: BVerfG zwischen Innovativem Klimarechtsschutz und Pflicht Ohne Schutz? *JuWissBlog*. Retrieved January 3, 2025, from https://www.juwiss.de/46-2021/

Kahl, V., & Rodriguez-Orúe, J. D. (2024, May 16). Upgrading environmental rights: La Oroya and its significance for a safer climate. *Verfassungsblog*. Retrieved January 3, 2025, from https://verfassungsblog.de/upgrading-environmental-rights/

Kahl, W., & Weller, M.-P. (Eds.). (2021). *Climate change litigation: A handbook*. C.H. Beck; Nomos.

Kammerhofer, J. (2024). Obligations erga omnes. In A. Peters & R. Wolfrum (Eds.), *Max Planck encyclopedia of public international law*. Oxford University Press. (Article last updated February 2024).

Kampourakis, I. (2019). Csr and social rights: Juxtaposing societal constitutionalism and rights-based approaches imposing human rights obligations on corporations. *Goettingen Journal of International Law, 9*(3), 537–569. https://doi.org/10.3249/1868-1581-9-3-kampourakis

Karnein, A. (2016). Can we represent future generations? In I. González-Ricoy & A. Gosseries (Eds.), *Institutions for future generations* (Vol. 5, 1st ed., pp. 83–97). Oxford University Press.

Karska, E. (2021). Drafting an international legally binding instrument on business and human rights. *International Community Law Review, 23*(5), 466–485. https://doi.org/10.1163/18719732-23050004

Kau, M. (2024). Der Staat und der Einzelne als Völkerrechtssubjekte. In A. Proelß (Ed.), *Völkerrecht* (Vol. 3, 9th ed., pp. 199–385). De Gruyter.

Kauffman, C. M., & Martin, P. L. (2018). Constructing rights of nature norms in the US, Ecuador, and New Zealand. *Global Environmental Politics, 18*(4), 43–62. https://doi.org/10.1162/glep_a_00481

Kavka, G. S., & Warren, V. (1983). Political representation for future generations. In R. Elliot (Ed.), *Environmental philosophy: A collection of readings* (pp. 20–39). University of Queensland Press.

Keenan, A. (2017). Sustainable development priorities in the inter-american human rights system. In M.-C. Cordonier Segger & C. G. Weeramantry (Eds.), *Sustainable development principles in the decisions of international courts and tribunals: 1992–2012* (Vol. 21, pp. 491–514). Routledge Taylor & Francis Group.

Kees, A. (2011). Responsibility of states for private actors. In A. Peters & R. Wolfrum (Eds.), *Max Planck encyclopedia of public international law*. Oxford University Press. (Article last updated March 2011).

Kehrer, F. (2009). *Staatenverantwortlichkeit und Meeresspiegelanstieg*. Lang.

Kelleher, O. (2021). A critical appraisal of friends of the irish environment v. government of Ireland. *Review of European, Comparative and International Environmental Law, 30*(1), 138–146. https://doi.org/10.1111/reel.12367

Keller, H., & Heri, C. (2022). The future is now: Climate cases before the ECtHR. *Nordic Journal of Human Rights, 40*, 1–22.

Kelsen, H. (1969). *Pure theory of law*. University of California Press.

Kemp, L. (2012, August 5). Reviewing Rio: Lessons for the future. *The ANU Rio+20 Project*. Retrieved January 3, 2025, from http://anurio20.blogspot.com/2012/08/reviewing-rio-lessons-for-future.html

Kempf, C. N. (2021). Why did so many do so little? Movement building and climate change litigation in the time of Juliana v. United States. *Texas Law Review, 99*(5), 1005–1040.

Klein, E. (2013). Menschenrechtsinflation? In D. Hanschel (Ed.), *Mensch und Recht: Festschrift für Eibe Riedel zum 70. Geburtstag* (pp. 117–129). Duncker & Humblot.

Klein, N. (2021). International environmental law disputes before international courts and tribunals. In L. Rajamani & J. Peel (Eds.), *The Oxford handbook of international environmental law* (Vol. 60, 2nd ed., pp. 1038–1053). Oxford University Press.

Koh, H. H. (1997). Why do nations obey international law? *Yale Law Journal, 106*, 2599–2659.

Koivurova, T., & Singh, K. (2022). Due diligence. In A. Peters & R. Wolfrum (Eds.), *Max Planck encyclopedia of public international law*. Oxford University Press. (Article last updated August 2022).

Kornicker Uhlmann, E. M. (1998). State community interests, jus gogens and protection of the global environment: Developing criteria for peremptory norms. *Georgetown International Environmental Law Review, 11*(1), 101–136.

Kosolapova, E. (2011). Liability for climate change-related damage in domestic courts: Claims for compensation in the USA. In M. Faure & M. Peeters (Eds.), *Climate change liability* (Vol. 8, pp. 189–205). Edward Elgar Publishing.

Kotzé, L. J. (2021). Neubauer et al. versus Germany: Planetary climate litigation for the anthropocene? German Law Journal, 22(8), 1423–1444. doi: https://doi.org/10.1017/glj.2021.87.

Krajewski, M. (2021, October). Analysis of the third draft of the UN Treaty on Business and Human Rights. Coopération Internationale pour le Développement et la Solidarité. Retrieved January 3, 2025, from https://www.cidse.org/2021/10/20/analysis-of-the-third-draft-of-the-un-treaty-on-business-and-human-rights/

Kramer, M. H. (2013). Some doubts about alternatives to the interest theory of rights. *Ethics, 123*(2), 245–263. https://doi.org/10.1086/668705

Krämer, L. (2019). Climate change, human rights and access to justice. *Journal for European Environmental and Planning Law, 16*(1), 21–34.

Krämer-Hoppe, R. (2021). The climate protection order of the federal constitutional court of Germany and the north-south divide. *German Law Journal, 22*(8), 1393–1408. https://doi.org/10.1017/glj.2021.84

Krislov, S. (1963). The amicus curiae brief: From friendship to advocacy. *Yale Law Journal, 72*(4), 694–721.

Kumm, M. (2004). The legitimacy of international law: A constitutionalist framework of analysis. *European Journal of International Law, 15*(5), 907–931. https://doi.org/10.1093/ejil/15.5.907

Lachenmann, F. (2012). Legal positivism. In R. Wolfrum (Ed.), *The Max Planck encyclopedia of public international law*. Oxford University Press.

Laielli, L. (2021). Bolstering Juliana: Enforceability of environmental claims through international treaty obligations in U.S. Courts. *St. Mary's Law Journal, 52*(4), 1149–1180.

Lambooy, T., & Palm, H. (2016). Challenging the human rights responsibility of states and private corporations for climate change in domestic jurisdictions. In O. Quirico & M. Boumghar (Eds.), *Climate change and human rights: An international and comparative law perspective* (pp. 307–335). Routledge Taylor & Francis Group.

Lawrence, P. (2012). Justice for future generations: Environment discourses, international law and climate change. In B. Jessup & K. Rubenstein (Eds.), *Environmental discourses in public and international law* (pp. 23–46). Cambridge University Press.

Lawrence, P. (2016). An atmospheric trust to protect the environment for future generations? Reform options for human rights law. In G. Bos & M. Düwell (Eds.), *Human rights and sustainability: Moral responsibilities for the future* (Vol. 3, pp. 25–39). Routledge Taylor & Francis Group.

Lawrence, P. (2022). Justifying representation of future generations and nature: Contradictory or mutually supporting values? *Transnational Environmental Law, 11*, 1–27. https://doi.org/10.1017/S2047102522000176

Lawrence, P., & Köhler, L. (2017). Representation of future generations through international climate litigation: A normative framework. *German Yearbook of International Law, 60*, 640–667.

Le Blanc, D., & Roehrl, A. (2012, May). Back to our common future: sustainable development in the 21st century (SD21) project (summary for policymakers). UN Department of Economic and Social Affairs. Retrieved January 3, 2025, from https://sustainabledevelopment.un.org/content/documents/UN-DESA_Back_Common_Future_En.pdf

Le Moli, G. (2020). The human rights committee, environmental protection and the right to life. *International and Comparative Law Quarterly, 69*(3), 735–752. https://doi.org/10.1017/S0020589320000123

Legal Tribune Online. (2024, November 12). Berufungsinstanz hebt historisches Klimaurteil auf: Shell muss CO2-Aus-stoß doch nicht senken. Retrieved January 3, 2025, from https://www.lto.de/recht/nachrichten/n/klimaschutz-shell-berufungsinstanz-den-haag-umweltvoelkerrecht

Leigh, K. (1992). Liability for damage to the global commons. *Australian Year Book of International Law, 14*, 129–156.

Lenzerini, F. (2002). The interplay between environmental protection and human and peoples' rights in international law. *African Yearbook of International Law, 10*(1), 63–108. https://doi.org/10.1163/22116176-90000102

Lepage, C., & Drafting Committee (2015, September 25). Universal Declaration of Humankind Rights: Draft Presented Under the Aegis of Corinne Lepage, Commissioned by the President of the French Republic. *Alliance DDHU* 2022. Retrieved January 3, 2025, from https://ddhu.org/la-declaration/

Levy, N. (2019). Juliana and the political generativity of climate litigation. *Harvard Environmental Law Review, 43*(2), 479–506.

Lewis, B. (2018). *Environmental human rights and climate change: Current status and future prospects*. Springer. https://doi.org/10.1007/978-981-13-1960-0

Lewis, B. (2021). Children's human rights-based climate litigation at the frontiers of environmental and children's rights. *Nordic Journal of Human Rights, 39*(2), 180–203.

Liebenberg, S., Khalfan, A., Kothari, M., Muffett, C., Sepúlveda Carmona, M., Venne-Manyfingers, S., & Wewerinke-Singh, M. (2023, February 3). *Maastricht principles on the human rights of future generations*. Maastricht University. Retrieved January 3, 2025, from https://www.rightsoffuturegenerations.org/the-principles

López Latorre, A. F. (2020). In defence of direct obligations for businesses under international human rights law. *Business and Human Rights Journal, 5*(1), 56–83. https://doi.org/10.1017/bhj.2019.27

Loth, M. A. (2016). Climate change liability after all: A Dutch landmark case. *Tilburg Law Review, 21*(1), 5–30.

Loth, M. A. (2018). Too big to trial? Lessons from the Urgenda case. *Uniform Law Review, 23*(2), 336–353. https://doi.org/10.1093/ulr/uny015

Lowe, V. (1999). Sustainable development and unsustainable arguments. In A. E. Boyle & D. A. C. Freestone (Eds.), *International law and sustainable development: Past achievements and future challenges* (pp. 19–37). Oxford University Press.

Macchi, C. (2021). The climate change dimension of business and human rights: The gradual consolidation of a concept of "climate due diligence". *Business and Human Rights Journal, 6*(1), 93–119. https://doi.org/10.1017/bhj.2020.25

Macchi, C., & Zeben, J. (2021). Business and human rights implications of climate change litigation: Milieudefensie et al. v Royal Dutch Shell. *Review of European, Comparative and International Environmental Law, 30*(3), 409–415. https://doi.org/10.1111/reel.12416

Macdonald, R. S. J. (1998). Future generations: Searching for a system of protection. In E. Agius & S. Busuttil (Eds.), *Future generations and international law: Proceedings of the international experts' meeting held by the future generations programme at the foundation for international studies, University of Malta* (Vol. 13, pp. 149–159). Earthscan Publications Ltd..

Magraw, D. B. (2020). From the Inuit petition to the Teitiota case: Human rights and success in climate litigation. *Proceedings of the ASIL Annual Meeting, 114*, 86. https://doi.org/10.1017/amp.2021.12

Malhotra, A. (1998). A commentary on the status of future generations as a subject of international law. In E. Agius & S. Busuttil (Eds.), *Future generations and international law: Proceedings of the international experts' meeting held by the future generations programme at the foundation for international studies, University of Malta* (Vol. 5, pp. 39–50). Earthscan Publications Ltd..

Manguiat, M. S. Z., & Yu, V. P. B. (2003). Maximizing the value of Oposa v. Factoran. *Georgetown International Environmental Law Review, 15*(3), 487–496.
Marks, S. (1981). Emerging human rights: A new generation for the 1980s. *Rutgers Law Review, 33*(2), 435–453.
Marquez, L. M. M. (2016). The relevance of organizational structure to NGOs' approaches to the policy process. *International Journal of Voluntary and Nonprofit Organizations, 27*(1), 465–486. https://doi.org/10.1007/s11266-015-9555-5
Mayer, B. (2019, October 9). The State of The Netherlands v. Urgenda Foundation: Ruling of the court of appeal of the Hague. *Transnational Environmental Law, 8*(1), 167–192.
Mayer, B. (2023). International advisory proceedings on climate change. *Michigan Journal of International Law, 44*(1), 41–115.
Mbengue, M. M. (2018). Experts: International court of justice (ICJ). In A. Peters & R. Wolfrum (Eds.), *Max Planck encyclopedia of public international law*. Oxford University Press. (Article last updated October 2018).
McCorquodale, R. (2018). The individual and the international legal system. In M. D. Evans (Ed.), *International law* (Vol. 10, 5th ed., pp. 259–285). Oxford University Press.
McGregor, L. (2019). Looking to the future: The scope, value and operationalization of international human rights law. *Vanderbilt Journal of Transnational Law, 52*(5), 1281–1314.
Mégret, F. (2013). The case for a general international crime against the environment. In M.-C. Cordonier Segger & S. Jodoin (Eds.), *Sustainable development, international criminal justice, and treaty implementation* (pp. 50–70). Cambridge University Press. https://doi.org/10.1017/CBO9781139507561.006
Mégret, F. (2015). Offences against future generations: A critical look at the Jodoin/Saito proposal and a suggestion for future thought. *McGill International Journal of Sustainable Development Law & Policy, 7*(2), 157. https://doi.org/10.2139/ssrn.2942145
Meguro, M. (2020). Litigating climate change through international law: Obligations strategy and rights strategy. *Leiden Journal of International Law, 33*(4), 933–951. https://doi.org/10.1017/S0922156520000473
Mehrishi, M. (2012, January 25). *Comments by Mrs. Mira Mehrishi, Additional Secretary, Ministry of Environment, on the Zero Draft "The Future We Want"*. Ministry of Environment, Government of India. Retrieved January 3, 2025, from https://www.pminewyork.gov.in/pdf/uploadpdf/75799ind2033.pdf
Mensah, T. A. (2008). Using judicial bodies for the implementation and enforcement of international environmental law. In I. Buffard, J. Crawford, A. Pellet, & S. Wittich (Eds.), *International law between universalism and fragmentation: Festschrift in honour of Gerhard Hafner* (Vol. 40, pp. 797–815). Martinus Nijhoff Publishers.
Mensink, E. (2022, August 29). Intergenerational justice: From courtroom to politics? *Völkerrechtsblog*. Retrieved January 3, 2025, from https://voelkerrechtsblog.org/intergenerational-justice-from-courtroom-to-politics/
Merrills, J. G. (1998). Environmental protection and human rights: Conceptual aspects. In A. E. Boyle & M. R. Anderson (Eds.), *Human rights approaches to environmental protection* (Vol. 2, pp. 25–41). Clarendon Press.
Merrills, J. G. (2010). Environmental rights. In D. Bodansky, J. Brunnée, & E. Hey (Eds.), *The Oxford handbook of international environmental law* (Vol. 28, 1st ed., pp. 663–680). Oxford University Press. https://doi.org/10.1093/oxfordhb/9780199552153.013.0028
Michallet, I. (2018). Equity and the interests of future generations. In L. Krämer & E. Orlando (Eds.), *Principles of environmental law* (pp. 150–160). Edward Elgar Publishing.
Minnerop-Röben, P., Roht-Arriaza, N., & Aminzadeh, S. C. (2018). Solidarity rights (development, peace, environment, humanitarian assistance). In A. Peters & R. Wolfrum (Eds.), *Max Planck encyclopedia of public international law*. Oxford University Press. (Article last updated February 2018).

Mintz, J. A. (2020). They threw up their hands: Observations on the US ninth circuit court of appeals' unsatisfying opinion in Juliana v United States. *Journal of Energy and Natural Resources Law, 38*(2), 201–204. https://doi.org/10.1080/02646811.2020.1743516

Molinari, C. (2015). Principle 3. In J. E. Viñuales (Ed.), *The Rio declaration on environment and development: A commentary* (1st ed., pp. 139–156). Oxford University Press.

Montgomery, W. (2021). Juliana v. United States: The ninth circuit's opening salvo for a new era of climate litigation. *Tulane Environmental Law Journal, 34*(2), 341–356.

Muchlinski, P. T. (2014). Corporations in international law. In A. Peters & R. Wolfrum (Eds.), *Max Planck encyclopedia of public international law*. Oxford University Press. (Article last updated June 2014).

MühGrel, J. (2021, May 3). All that glitters is not gold: The German Constitutional Court's climate ruling and the protection of persons beyond german territory against climate change impacts. *Völkerrechtsblog*. Retrieved January 3, 2025, from https://voelkerrechtsblog.org/de/all-that-glitters-is-not-gold/

Mutua, M. (2000). What is TWAIL? *Proceedings of the ASIL Annual Meeting, 94*(5–8), 31–38.

Mutua, M. (2008). Human rights and powerlessness: Pathologies of choice and substance. *Buffalo Law Review, 56*(4), 1027–1034.

Mwanza, R. (2018). Enhancing accountability for environmental damage under international law: Ecocide as a legal fulfilment of ecological integrity. *Melbourne Journal of International Law, 19*, 1–28.

Nagy, B. (1988). Common heritage of mankind: The status of future generations. *Proceedings on the Law of Outer Space, 31*, 319–325.

Nagy, B. (1998). Speaking without a voice. In E. Agius & S. Busuttil (Eds.), *Future generations and international law: Proceedings of the international experts' meeting held by the future generations programme at the foundation for international studies, University of Malta* (Vol. 6, pp. 51–64). Earthscan Publications Ltd..

Nanda, V. P., & Pring, G. (Eds.). (2013). *International environmental law for the 21st century* (2nd ed.). Martinus Nijhoff Publishers.

Nässtrӧm, S. (2011). The challenge of the all-affected principle. *Political Studies, 59*(1), 116–134. https://doi.org/10.1111/j.1467-9248.2010.00845.x

Nedeski, N., Sparks, T., & Hernández, G. I. (2020, April 30). Judging climate change obligations: Can the world court rise to the ocasion? Part II: What role for international adjudication? *Völkerrechtsblog*. Retrieved January 3, 2025, from https://voelkerrechtsblog.org/judging-climate-change-obligations-can-the-world-court-raise-the-occasion-2/

Nesbit, M., & Illés, A. (2015, September). Establishing an EU "guardian for future generations": Report and recommendations for the world future council. Institute for European Environmental Policy. Retrieved January 3, 2025, from https://ieep.eu/publications/establishing-an-eu-guardian-for-future-generations/

Netherwood, A., & Flynn, A. (2021). Welsh commissioner for sustainable futures. In M.-C. Cordonier Segger, M. Szabó, & A. R. Harrington (Eds.), *Intergenerational justice in sustainable development treaty implementation: Advancing future generations rights through national institutions* (Vol. 22, pp. 411–433). Cambridge University Press.

NGO-UNESCO Standing Committee – Working Group on the Teaching of Human Rights. (1980, July 9). *The rights of solidarity: An attempt at conceptual analysis*. UN Doc. SS.80/CONF.806/6.

Nguyen, N. (2021, May 7). Klimaschutz vs. Individualrechtsschutz: Wie Sich das BVerfG um Ausgleich Bemüht. *JuWissBlog*. Retrieved January 3, 2025, from https://www.juwiss.de/45-2021/

Nguyen, Y. (2017). Constitutional protection for future generations from climate change. *Hastings Constitutional Law Quarterly, 44*(3), 347–370.

Nickel, J. W. (1993). The human right to a safe environment: Philosophical perspectives on its scope and justification. *Yale Journal of International Law, 18*(1), 281–296.

Nickel, J. W. (2024). Human rights. In E. N. Zalta (Ed.), *The Stanford encyclopedia of philosophy*. ISSN 1095-5054. Retrieved January 3, 2025, from https://plato.stanford.edu/entries/rights-human/. (Article last updated May 2024)

Niehaus, M. (2021). Gerichte gegen Gesetzgeber? Der Klimawandel in den Gerichtssälen. In B. Huggins et al. (Eds.), *Zugang zu Recht: 61. JTÖR Münster 2021* (pp. 241–260). Nomos.

Niehaus, M. (2022, March 23). Protecting whose children? The rights of future generations in the courts of Germany and Colombia. *Verfassungsblog*. Retrieved January 3, 2025, from https://verfassungsblog.de/protecting-whose-children/

Niehaus, M. (2023). *Global climate constitutionalism "from below"*. Springer.

Niehaus, M., & Davies, K. J. (2021). Voices for the voiceless: Climate protection from the streets to the courts. *Journal of Human Rights and the Environment, 12*(2), 228–253. https://doi.org/10.4337/jhre.2021.02.04

Nolan, A. (2021, October 20). Children's rights and climate change at the UN Committee on the Rights of the Child: Pragmatism and Principle in Sacchi v Argentina. *EJIL: Talk!* Retrieved January 3, 2025, from https://www.ejiltalk.org/childrens-rights-and-climate-change-at-the-un-committee-on-the-rights-of-the-child-pragmatism-and-principle-in-sacchi-v-argentina/

Nolan, A. (2022, May 26). The children are the future – or not? Exploring the complexities of the relationship between the rights of children and future generations. *EJIL: Talk!* Retrieved January 3, 2025, from https://www.ejiltalk.org/the-children-are-the-future-or-not-exploring-the-complexities-of-the-relationship-between-the-rights-of-children-and-future-generations/

Nolan, A. (2023, September 11). General comment no. 26 on children and the environment: A milestone in international human rights law? *EJIL: Talk!* Retrieved October 10, 2024, from https://www.ejiltalk.org/general-comment-no-26-on-children-and-the-environment-a-milestone-in-international-human-rights-law/

Nollkaemper, A. (2006). Responsibility of transnational corporations in international environmental law: Three perspectives. In G. Winter (Ed.), *Multilevel governance of global environmental change: Perspectives from science, sociology and the law* (Vol. 7, pp. 179–199). Cambridge University Press.

Nollkaemper, A. (2021, May 28). Shell's responsibility for climate change: An international law perspective on a groundbreaking judgment. *Verfassungsblog*. Retrieved January 3, 2025, from https://verfassungsblog.de/shells-responsibility-for-climate-change/

Nollkaemper, A. (2024, November 12). Lessons of a landmark lost: The judgment of the Hague Court of Appeal in Shell v Milieudefensie. *Verfassungsblog*. Retrieved January 3, 2025, from https://verfassungsblog.de/shell-milieudefensie-climate-litigation/

Norton, B. G. (1982). Environmental ethics and the rights of future generations. *Environmental Ethics, 4*(4), 319–337. https://doi.org/10.5840/enviroethics1982444

O'Brien, E. (2021, June 11). An international crime of "ecocide": What's the story? *EJIL: Talk!* Retrieved January 3, 2025, from https://www.ejiltalk.org/an-international-crime-of-ecocide-whats-the-story/

Office of the High Commissioner for Human Rights. (2014, October 17). A New climate change agreement must include human rights protection for all: An open letter from special procedures mandate-holders of the human rights council to the state parties to the UNFCCC on the occasion of the meeting of the ad hoc working group on the Durban platform for enhanced action in Bonn (20–25 October 2014). Retrieved January 3, 2025, from https://www.ohchr.org/sites/default/files/Documents/HRBodies/SP/SP_To_UNFCCC.pdf

Office of the High Commissioner for Human Rights. (2015). Understanding human rights and climate change: Submission of the OHCHR to the 21st conference of the parties to the UNFCCC. Retrieved January 3, 2025, from https://www.uncclearn.org/resources/library/understanding-human-rights-and-climate-change/

Office of the High Commissioner for Human Rights. (2021, September). Frequently asked questions on human rights and climate change: Fact sheet no. 38. Retrieved January 3, 2025, from https://www.ohchr.org/en/publications/fact-sheets/fact-sheet-no-38-frequently-asked-questions-human-rights-and-climate

Ohlhoff, S. (2003). *Methoden der Konfliktbewältigung bei Grenzüberschreitenden Umweltproblemen im Wandel: Überwindung der Grenzen Herkömmlicher Streitbeilegung durch Systeminterne Flexibilität und Systemexterne Innovation*. Springer.

Okowa, P. (2010). Responsibility for environmental damage. In M. Fitzmaurice, D. Ong, & P. Merkouris (Eds.), *Research handbook on international environmental law* (Vol. 15, pp. 303–319). Edward Elgar Publishing.

Organisation for Economic Co-operation and Development. (2011). OECD guidelines for multinational enterprises: 2011 edition. Retrieved January 3, 2025, from https://www.oecd.org/en/publications/oecd-guidelines-for-multinational-enterprises_9789264115415-en.html

Organisation for Economic Co-operation and Development. (2023). OECD guidelines for multinational enterprises: 2023 Edition. Retrieved January 3, 2025, from https://www.oecd.org/en/publications/oecd-guidelines-for-multinational-enterprises-on-responsible-business-conduct_81f92357-en.html

Pacific Islands Forum. (2022, July 18). Report: Communique of the 51st Pacific Islands forum leaders meeting (Suva, Fiji, 11–14 July 2022). Retrieved January 3, 2025, from https://forumsec.org/publications/report-communique-51st-pacific-islands-forum-leaders-meeting

Paiement, P. (2020). Urgent agenda: How climate litigation builds transnational narratives. *Transnational Legal Theory, 11*(1–2), 121–143. https://doi.org/10.1080/20414005.2020.1772617

Paiement, P. (2024, November 15). Towards a Bundle of Duties: Shell v Milieudefensie confirms major developments in climate change liability. *Verfassungsblog*. Retrieved January 3, 2025, from https://verfassungsblog.de/shell-milieudefensie-climate-obligations/

Parejo Navajas, T., & Lobel, N. (2018). Framing the global pact for the environment: Why it's needed, what it does, and how it does it. *Fordham Environmental Law Review, 30*(1), 32–62.

Parker, L., Mestre, J., Jodoin, S., & Wewerinke-Singh, M. (2022). When the kids put climate change on trial: Youth-focused rights-based climate litigation around the world. *Journal of Human Rights and the Environment, 13*(1), 64–89. https://doi.org/10.4337/jhre.2022.01.03

Patarroyo Ramírez, P. A. (2020, May 11). Justiciability of "implicit" rights: Developments on the right to a healthy environment at the Inter-American Court of Human Rights. *EJIL: Talk!*. Retrieved January 3, 2025, from https://www.ejiltalk.org/justiciability-of-implicit-rights-developments-on-the-right-to-a-healthy-environment-at-the-inter-american-court-of-human-rights/

Pathak, R. S. (1992). The human rights system as a conceptual framework for environmental law. In E. Brown Weiss (Ed.), *Environmental change and international law: New challenges and dimensions* (Vol. 8, pp. 205–243). United Nations University Press.

Payandeh, M. (2021). The role of courts in climate protection and the separation of powers. In W. Kahl & M.-P. Weller (Eds.), *Climate change litigation: A handbook* (pp. 62–80). C.H. Beck; Nomos.

Pearce, C. (2012, May). *Ombudspersons for future generations: A proposal for Rio+20: Bringing intergenerational justice into the heart of policy-making*. UN Environment Programme. Retrieved January 3, 2025, from https://wedocs.unep.org/20.500.11822/7444

Peel, J., & Markey-Towler, R. (2021). Recipe for success? Lessons for strategic climate litigation from the Sharma, Neubauer, and Shell cases. *German Law Journal, 22*(8), 1484–1498. https://doi.org/10.1017/glj.2021.83

Pellet, A. (2011). Shaping the future of international law: The role of the world court in law-making. In M. H. Arsanjani, J. Cogan, R. Sloane, & S. Wiessner (Eds.), *Looking to the future: Essays on international law in honor of W. Michael Reisman* (Vol. 51, pp. 1065–1083). Martinus Nijhoff Publishers.

Perry-Kessaris, A. (2010). Corporate liability for environmental harm. In M. Fitzmaurice, D. Ong, & P. Merkouris (Eds.), *Research handbook on international environmental law* (pp. 361–376). Edward Elgar Publishing.

Peters, A., & Askin, E. (2020). Der Internationale Menschenrechtsschutz in Zeiten von Postglobalismus und Populismus. *MPIL Research Paper Series No. 13*. Retrieved January 3, 2025, from https://ssrn.com/abstract=3590257

Peters, B. (2021). Zur Anwendbarkeit der Europäischen Menschenrechtskonvention in Umwelt- und Klimaschutzfragen. *Archiv Des Völkerrechts, 59*(2), 164–198. https://doi.org/10.1628/avr-2021-0010

Pezzot, R., & Graf, J.-P. (2022, February 3). Ecocide – Legal revolution or symbolism? *Völkerrechtsblog*. Retrieved January 3, 2025, from https://voelkerrechtsblog.org/ecocide-legal-revolution-or-symbolism/

Pfrommer, T., Goeschl, T., Proelss, A., Carrier, M., Lenhard, J., Martin, H., Niemeier, U., & Schmidt, H. (2019). Establishing causation in climate litigation: Admissibility and reliability. *Climatic Change, 152*(1), 67–84. https://doi.org/10.1007/s10584-018-2362-4

Pietrzykowski, T. (2020). Animal rights. In A. von Arnauld, K. von der Decken, & M. Susi (Eds.), *The Cambridge handbook of new human rights: Recognition, novelty, rhetoric* (Vol. 18, pp. 243–252). Cambridge University Press. https://doi.org/10.1017/9781108676106.019

Pirjatanniemi, E. (2016). Greening human rights law: A focus on the european convention on human rights. In G. Bos & M. Düwell (Eds.), *Human rights and sustainability: Moral responsibilities for the future* (Vol. 2, pp. 11–24). Routledge Taylor & Francis Group.

Pisillo Mazzeschi, R. (1991). Forms of international responsibility for environmental harm. In F. Francioni (Ed.), *International responsibility for environmental harm* (Vol. 2, pp. 15–35). Graham & Trotman.

Pitts, J. (2021). Are we giving the voice of the future a word in the present? In M.-C. Cordonier Segger, M. Szabó, & A. R. Harrington (Eds.), *Intergenerational justice in sustainable development treaty implementation: Advancing future generations rights through national institutions* (Vol. 13, pp. 254–265). Cambridge University Press.

Ploton, V., & Montes de Oca, J. U. (2022, April 18). "Friends of the Court" Making the most of amicus curiae with UN treaty bodies. *EJIL: Talk!* Retrieved January 3, 2025, from https://www.ejiltalk.org/friends-of-the-court-making-the-most-of-amicus-curiae-with-un-treaty-bodies/

Popović, N. A. (1996). In pursuit of environmental human rights: Commentary on the draft declaration of principles on human rights and the environment. *Columbia Human Rights Law Review, 27*(3), 487–604.

Portmann, R. (2010). *Legal personality in international law*. Cambridge University Press. https://doi.org/10.1017/CBO9780511779848

Posner, E. A. (2014). *The twilight of human rights law*. Oxford University Press.

Preparatory Committee for the United Nations Conference on Environment and Development. (1992, February 21). *Principles on general rights and obligations, proposal and comments submitted by the delegation of Malta*. UN Doc. A/CONF.151/PC/WG.III/L.8/Rev.1/Add.2.

Pribytkova, E. (2020). What global human rights obligations do we have? *Chicago Journal of International Law, 20*(2), 384–449.

Prime Minister of France. (1999, July 15). *Réponse du Premier ministre à la Question écrite n° 17086 de M. Serge Mathieu (Bilan des activités du Conseil pour les droits des générations futures)*. JO Sénat du 15/07/1999, 2407.

Proelß, A. (2022). Prinzipien des Internationalen Umweltrechts. In A. Proelß (Ed.), *Internationales Umweltrecht* (Vol. 3, 2nd ed., pp. 95–150). De Gruyter.

Proelß, A. (2024). Raum und Umwelt im Völkerrecht. In A. Proelß (Ed.), *Völkerrecht* (Vol. 5, 9th ed., pp. 553–697). De Gruyter.

Proelß, A., & Haake, C. (2017). Gemeinschaftsräume in der Entwicklung: Von der Res Communis Omnium zum Common Heritage of Mankind. In A. von Arnauld (Ed.), *Völkerrechtsgeschichte (n): Historische narrative und Konzepte im Wandel* (pp. 171–192). Duncker & Humblot.

Ramlogan, R. (2011). *Sustainable development: Towards a judicial interpretation*. Martinus Nijhoff Publishers.

Rao, G. (1998). The United Nations as a guardian for future generations. In E. Agius & S. Busuttil (Eds.), *Future generations and international law: Proceedings of the international experts' meeting held by the future generations programme at the foundation for international studies, University of Malta* (Vol. 11, pp. 143–148). Earthscan Publications Ltd..

Rath, K., & Benner, M. (2021, May 7). Ein Grundrecht auf Generationengerechtigkeit? Die Relevanz des Klimaschutz-Beschlusses des Bundesverfassungsgerichts für Andere Rechtsgebiete mit Intergenerationaler Bedeutung. *Verfassungsblog*. Retrieved January 3, 2025, from https://verfassungsblog.de/ein-grundrecht-auf-generationengerechtigkeit/

Rauxloh, R. (2011). The role of international criminal law in environmental protection. In F. N. Botchway (Ed.), *Natural resource investment and Africa's development* (pp. 423–461). Edward Elgar Publishing.

Raz, J. (1984). Legal rights. *Oxford Journal of Legal Studies, 4*(1), 1–21. https://doi.org/10.1093/ojls/4.1.1

Razzaque, J. (2001). Application of public trust doctrine in Indian environmental cases. *Journal of Environmental Law, 13*, 221–234.

Redgwell, C. (1998). Life, the universe and everything: A critique of anthropocentric rights. In A. E. Boyle & M. R. Anderson (Eds.), *Human rights approaches to environmental protection* (Vol. 4, pp. 71–87). Clarendon Press.

Redgwell, C. (1999). *Intergenerational trusts and environmental protection*. Juris.

Redgwell, C. (2016). Principles and emerging norms in international law: Intra- and inter-generational equity. In C. P. Carlarne, K. R. Gray, & R. Tarasofsky (Eds.), *The Oxford handbook of international climate change law* (Vol. 9, 1st ed., pp. 185–201). Oxford University Press.

Reeh, G. (2020, February 18). Climate change in the Human Rights Committee. *EJIL: Talk!* Retrieved January 3, 2025, from https://www.ejiltalk.org/climate-change-in-the-human-rights-committee/

Rehfeld, A. (2006). Towards a general theory of political representation. *The Journal of Politics, 68*(1), 1–21. https://doi.org/10.1111/j.1468-2508.2006.00365.x

Reimer, F. (2021). Institutions for a sustainable future: The German Parliamentary Advisory Council on Sustainable Development. In M.-C. Cordonier Segger, M. Szabó, & A. R. Harrington (Eds.), *Intergenerational justice in sustainable development treaty implementation: Advancing future generations rights through national institutions* (Vol. 20, pp. 374–394). Cambridge University Press.

Restatement (Third) of Foreign Relations Law § 601 (1987).

Restatement (Third) of Trusts § 28 (2003).

Riddell, A. (2016). Human rights responsibility of private corporations for climate change? The state as a catalyst for compliance. In O. Quirico & M. Boumghar (Eds.), *Climate change and human rights: An international and comparative law perspective* (pp. 53–67). Routledge Taylor & Francis Group.

Riley, S. (2016). International human rights and duties to future generations: The role of an international constitution. In G. Bos & M. Düwell (Eds.), *Human rights and sustainability: Moral responsibilities for the future* (Vol. 5, pp. 53–66). Routledge Taylor & Francis Group.

Rio+20 Working Group. (2011, October 28). Rio+20: Open challenge paper. *Alliance for Future Generations*. Retrieved January 3, 2025, from http://www.if.org.uk/wp-content/uploads/2012/04/AFG-Rio+20-challenge-paper-final.pdf

Rodriguez-Rivera, L. E. (2001). Is the human right to environment recognized under international law: It depends on the source. *Colorado Journal of International Environmental Law and Policy, 12*(1), 1–46.

Ronneberg, E. (2016). Small islands and the big issue: Climate change and the role of the alliance of small Island states. In C. P. Carlarne, K. R. Gray, & R. Tarasofsky (Eds.), *The Oxford handbook of international climate change law* (Vol. 34, 1st ed., pp. 761–776). Oxford University Press.

Rose, M. (2017). *Zukünftige Generationen in der Heutigen Demokratie: Theorie und Praxis der Proxy-Repräsentation*. Springer.

Rosenkranz, E. J. (1986). A ghost of christmas yet to come: Standing to sue for future generations. *Journal of Law and Technology, 1*, 67–114.

Rosini, M. (2022). From CSR to HRDD: An overview of approaches, initiatives and measures adopted by the European Union. *International Community Law Review, 24*(1–2), 57–78.

Rousseau, J.-J. (1968). *The social contract* (1st ed.). Penguin Books. (Original work published 1762).

Roy, S., & Woerdman, E. (2016). Situating Urgenda v The Netherlands within comparative climate change litigation. *Journal of Energy and Natural Resources Law, 34*(2), 165–189.

Rumpf, M. (2019). Der Klimawandel als Zunehmendes Haftungsrisiko für "Carbon Majors": Saul A. Lliuya v. RWE im Kontext der Internationalen Climate Change Litigation. *Zeitschrift Für Europäisches Umwelt- Und Planungsrecht, 17*(2), 145–158.

Rumpf, M. (2022). Climate change litigation and the private sector: Assessing the liability risk for multinational corporations and the way forward for strategic litigation. In E. Schulev-Steindl et al. (Eds.), *Climate change, responsibility and liability* (1st ed., pp. 441–490). Nomos.

Sabin Center for Climate Change Law at Columbia Law School. (2007-2024). Climate change litigation databases. Retrieved January 3, 2025, from http://climatecasechart.com/

Saiger, A.-J. (2022). *Nationale Gerichte im Klimaschutzvölkerrecht: Eine rechtsvergleichende Untersuchung zum Pariser Übereinkommen* [1 Online-Ressource (355 Seiten)]. Nomos. https://doi.org/10.5771/9783748934653.

Salam, N. (2019). Reflections on international law in changing times: 60th anniversary symposium, Harvard Law School, March 9, 2019. *Harvard International Law Journal, 60*(2), 201–217.

Sands, P. (1989). The environment, community and international law. *Harvard International Law Journal, 30*(2), 393–420.

Sands, P. (1998). Protecting future generations: Precedents and practicalities. In E. Agius & S. Busuttil (Eds.), *Future generations and international law: Proceedings of the international experts' meeting held by the future generations programme at the foundation for international studies, University of Malta* (Vol. 8, pp. 83–91). Earthscan Publications Ltd..

Sands, P. (2001). Turtles and torturers: The transformation of international law. *New York University Journal of International Law and Policy, 33*, 527–559.

Sands, P. (2016). Climate change and the rule of law: Adjudicating the future in international law. *Journal of Environmental Law, 28*(1), 19–35. https://doi.org/10.1093/jel/eqw005

Sands, P., & MacKenzie, R. (2008). International court and tribunals, amicus curiae. In A. Peters & R. Wolfrum (Eds.), *Max Planck encyclopedia of public international law*. Oxford University Press. (Article last updated January 2008).

Sands, P., Peel, J., & Fabra, A. (2018). *Principles of international environmental law* (4th ed.). Cambridge University Press.

Sandvig, J., Dawson, P., & Tjelmeland, M. (2021, June 23). Can the ECHR encompass the transnational and intertemporal dimensions of climate harm? *EJIL: Talk!* Retrieved January 3, 2025, from https://www.ejiltalk.org/can-the-echr-encompass-the-transnational-and-intertemporal-dimensions-of-climate-harm/

Savaresi, A. (2021a). Inter-state climate change litigation: "Neither a chimera nor a panacea". In I. Alogna, C. Bakker, & J.-P. Gauci (Eds.), *Climate change litigation: Global perspectives* (Vol. 16, pp. 366–392). Brill Nijhoff.

Savaresi, A. (2021b, October 12). The UN HRC recognizes the right to a healthy environment and appoints a new special rapporteur on human rights and climate change: What does it all mean? *EJIL: Talk!*. Retrieved January 3, 2025, from https://www.ejiltalk.org/the-un-hrc-recognizes-the-right-to-a-healthy-environment-and-appoints-a-new-special-rapporteur-on-human-rights-and-climate-change-what-does-it-all-mean/

Savaresi, A. (2023). Environment and human rights. In A. Peters & R. Wolfrum (Eds.), *Max Planck encyclopedia of public international law*. Oxford University Press. (Article last updated December 2023).

Savaresi, A., & Auz, J. (2019). Climate change litigation and human rights: Pushing the boundaries. *Climate Law, 9*(3), 244–262.

Savaresi, A., Kulovesi, K., & van Asselt, H. (2021, December 17). Beyond COP26: Time for an advisory opinion on climate change? *EJIL: Talk!* Retrieved January 3, 2025, from https://www.ejiltalk.org/beyond-cop26-time-for-an-advisory-opinion-on-climate-change/

Savaresi, A., & Setzer, J. (2022). Rights-based litigation in the climate emergency: Mapping the landscape and new knowledge frontiers. *Journal of Human Rights and the Environment, 13*(1), 7–34. https://doi.org/10.4337/jhre.2022.0002

Saward, M. (2010). *The representative claim*. Oxford University Press. https://doi.org/10.1093/acprof:oso/9780199579389.001.0001

Sax, J. L. (1970). The public trust doctrine in natural resource law: Effective judicial intervention. *Michigan Law Review, 68*(3), 471–566. https://doi.org/10.2307/1287556

Saxler, B., Siegfried, J., & Proelss, A. (2015). International liability for transboundary damage arising from stratospheric aerosol injections. *Law, Innovation and Technology, 7*(1), 112–147. https://doi.org/10.1080/17579961.2015.1052645

Schimmöller, L. (2020). Paving the way for rights of nature in Germany: Lessons learnt from legal reform in New Zealand and Ecuador. *Transnational Environmental Law, 9*(3), 569–592. https://doi.org/10.1017/S2047102520000126

Schmalenbach, K. (2017a). Friedliche Streitbeilegung. In A. Proelß (Ed.), *Internationales Umweltrecht* (Vol. 8, pp. 243–282). De Gruyter.

Schmalenbach, K. (2017b). Verantwortlichkeit und Haftung. In A. Proelß (Ed.), *Internationales Umweltrecht* (Vol. 7, pp. 211–282). De Gruyter.

Schmalenbach, K. (2022a). Friedliche Streitbeilegung. In A. Proelß (Ed.), *Internationales Umweltrecht* (Vol. 8, 2nd ed., pp. 373–421). De Gruyter.

Schmalenbach, K. (2022b). Verantwortlichkeit und Haftung. In A. Proelß (Ed.), *Internationales Umweltrecht* (Vol. 7, 2nd ed., pp. 329–372). De Gruyter.

Schnakenberg, J., Fleming, A., Ukhorskiy, D., Shetye, A., & Baars, L. (2022). Human rights in the face of the climate crisis: A youth-led initiative to bring climate justice to the International Court of Justice. *World's Youth for Climate Justice*. Retrieved January 3, 2025, from https://static1.squarespace.com/static/5f063a0c8f53b604aed84729/t/638f9ee73dfbf63abd0cc021/1670356715298/Second+Edition+Legal+Report.pdf

Schneider, M. (2017). Where Juliana went wrong: Applying the public trust doctrine to climate change adaptation at the state level. *Environmental Law and Policy Journal, 41*(1), 47–68.

Scholtz, W. (2007). Northern NGOs, Southern NGOs and international environmental law: The common interest of humankind is the interest of northern mankind! *South African Yearbook of International Law, 32*, 247–260.

Scholtz, W. (2015). Human rights and the environment in the African Union context. In A. Grear & L. J. Kotzé (Eds.), *Research handbook on human rights and the environment* (Vol. 19, pp. 401–423). Edward Elgar Publishing.

Scholtz, W. (2021). Equity. In L. Rajamani & J. Peel (Eds.), *The Oxford handbook of international environmental law* (Vol. 20, 2nd ed., pp. 335–349). Oxford University Press.

Schönberger, P. (2021, May 17). Germany's "fair share" of climate change jurisprudence. *Völkerrechtsblog*. Retrieved January 3, 2025, from https://voelkerrechtsblog.org/de/germanys-fair-share-of-climate-change-jurisprudence/

Schrijver, N. J. (2009). After us, the deluge? The position of future generations of humankind in international environmental law. In M. A. R. M. Salih (Ed.), *Climate change and sustainable development: New challenges for poverty reduction* (Vol. 4, pp. 59–78). Edward Elgar Publishing.

Seidl-Hohenvelden, I. (1987). *Corporations in and under international law*. Cambridge University Press.

Setzer, J., & Benjamin, L. (2020). Climate litigation in the global south: Constraints and innovations. *Transnational Environmental Law, 9*(1), 77–101. https://doi.org/10.1017/S2047102519000268

Setzer, J., & Higham, C. (2021). *Global trends in climate litigation: 2021 snapshot - Policy report*. Grantham Research Institute on Climate Change and the Environment and Centre for Climate Change Economics and Policy, London School of Economics and Political Science.

Setzer, J., & Vanhala, L. C. (2019). Climate change litigation: A review of research on courts and litigants in climate governance. *Wiley Interdisciplinary Reviews: Climate Change, 10*(3), 1–19.

Shapiro, I. (2009). *The state of democratic theory* (3rd ed.). Princeton University Press.

Shelton, D. (1991). Human rights, environmental rights and the right to the environment. *Stanford Journal of International Law, 28*(1), 103–138.

Shelton, D. (1994). The participation of nongovernmental organizations in international judicial proceedings. *American Journal of International Law, 88*(4), 611–642. https://doi.org/10.2307/2204133

Shelton, D. (2009). Common concern of humanity. *Environmental Policy and Law, 39*(2), 83–86.

Simma, B. (1989). International crimes: Injury and countermeasures: Comments on part 2 of the ILC work on state responsibility. In A. Cassese, J. H. H. Weiler, & M. Spinedi (Eds.), *International crimes of state: A critical analysis of the ILC's draft article 19 on state responsibility* (pp. 283–316). De Gruyter.

Slobodian, L. (2020). Defending the future: Intergenerational equity in climate litigation. *Georgetown Environmental Law Review, 32*(3), 569–590.

Soltau, F. (2016). Common concern of humankind. In C. P. Carlarne, K. R. Gray, & R. Tarasofsky (Eds.), *The Oxford handbook of international climate change law* (Vol. 10, 1st ed., pp. 202–212). Oxford University Press.

Spentzou, D. (2021). Climate change litigation as a means to address intergenerational equity and climate change. *Queen Mary Law Journal, 2*, 153–183. https://doi.org/10.26494/QMLJ3944

Spier, J. (2020). 'The "strongest" climate ruling yet': The Dutch Supreme Court's urgenda judgment. *Netherlands International Law Review, 67*(2), 319–391. https://doi.org/10.1007/s40802-020-00172-5

Spier, J. (2021, May 10). Guest commentary: A ground-breaking judgment in Germany. *Climate Law Blog*. Retrieved January 3, 2025, from https://blogs.law.columbia.edu/climatechange/2021/05/10/guest-commentary-a-ground-breaking-judgment-in-germany/

Spijkers, O. (2018). The Urgenda case: A successful example of public interest litigation for the protection of the environment? In C. Voigt & Z. Makuch (Eds.), *Courts and the environment* (Vol. 14, pp. 305–344). Edward Elgar Publishing.

Spijkers, O. (2020, March 6). Public interest litigation before domestic courts in The Netherlands on the basis of international law: Article 3:305a Dutch Civil Code. *EJIL: Talk!* Retrieved January 3, 2025, from https://www.ejiltalk.org/public-interest-litigation-before-domestic-courts-in-the-netherlands-on-the-basis-of-international-law-article-3305a-dutch-civil-code/

Spijkers, O. (2021). Friends of the earth Netherlands (Milieudefensie) v Royal Dutch Shell. *Chinese Journal of Environmental Law, 5*(2), 237–256. https://doi.org/10.1163/24686042-12340073

Staberock, G. (2011). Civil society. In A. Peters & R. Wolfrum (Eds.), *Max Planck encyclopedia of public international law*. Oxford University Press. (Article last updated March 2011).

Stawasz, A., & Sebo, J. (2022, August 19). Bridging legal longtermism and animal law. *Verfassungsblog*. Retrieved January 3, 2025, from https://verfassungsblog.de/bridging-legal-longtermism-and-animal-law/

Steiner, H., & Vallentyne, P. (2009). Libertarian theories of intergenerational justice. In A. Gosseries & L. H. Meyer (Eds.), *Intergenerational justice* (Vol. 2, pp. 50–76). Oxford University Press.

Stephens, T. (2009). *International courts and environmental protection*. Cambridge University Press. https://doi.org/10.1017/CBO9780511576034

Stockholm+50 Youth Assembly. (2022, May). Stockholm+50 global youth policy paper: Third official version. Retrieved January 3, 2025, from https://www.sparkblue.org/content/stockholm-50-global-youth-policy-paper

Stone, C. D. (1972). Should trees have standing? Toward legal rights for natural objects. *Southern California Law Review, 45*, 450–501.

Stone, C. D. (1998). Safeguarding future generations. In E. Agius & S. Busuttil (Eds.), *Future generations and international law: Proceedings of the international experts' meeting held by the future generations programme at the foundation for international studies, University of Malta* (Vol. 7, pp. 65–79). Earthscan Publications Ltd..

Stop Ecocide Foundation. (n.d.). *Stop ecocide international: Breaking news and press releases*. Retrieved January 3, 2025, from https://www.stopecocide.earth/press-releases

Stromquist, N. P. (1998). NGOs in a new paradigm of civil society. *Current Issues in Comparative Education, 1*(1), 62–67.

Stucki, S. (2020). Towards a theory of legal animal rights: Simple and fundamental rights. *Oxford Journal of Legal Studies, 40*(3), 533–560.

Supanich, G. P. (1992). The legal basis of intergenerational responsibility: An alternative view—The sense of intergenerational identity. *Yearbook of International Environmental Law, 3*(1), 94–107. https://doi.org/10.1093/yiel/3.1.94

Szabó, M. (2021). Intergenerational justice under international treaty law: The obligations of the state to future generations and the example of the Hungarian ombudsman for future generations. In M.-C. Cordonier Segger, M. Szabó, & A. R. Harrington (Eds.), *Intergenerational justice in sustainable development treaty implementation: Advancing future generations rights through national institutions* (Vol. 4, pp. 68–98). Cambridge University Press.

Tabau, A.-S., & Cournil, C. (2015). New perspectives for climate justice: District Court of the Hague, 24 June 2015, Urgenda Foundation versus The Netherlands. *Journal for European Environmental and Planning Law, 12*, 221–240.

Tabios Hillebrecht, A. L., & Berros, M. V. (2017). *Can nature have rights? Legal and political insights*. Rachel Carson Center for Environment and Society. https://doi.org/10.5282/RCC/8164

Tanaka, Y. (2018). Reflections on locus standi in response to a breach of obligations erga omnes partes: A comparative analysis of the whaling in the Antarctic and South China Sea cases. *Law and Practice of International Courts and Tribunals, 17*(3), 527–554.

Tănăsescu, M. (2020). Rights of nature, legal personality, and indigenous philosophies. *Transnational Environmental Law, 9*(3), 429–453. https://doi.org/10.1017/S2047102520000217

Tasioulas, J. (2019). Saving human rights from human rights law. *Vanderbilt Journal of Transnational Law, 52*(5), 1167–1208.

Taylor, P. E. (1998). From environmental to ecological human rights: New dynamic in international law. *Georgetown International Environmental Law Review, 10*(2), 309–398.

Theilen, J. T. (2021). The inflation of human rights: A deconstruction. *Leiden Journal of International Law, 34*(4), 831–854. https://doi.org/10.1017/S0922156521000297

Thompson, D. F. (2005). Democracy in time: Popular sovereignty and temporal representation. *Constellations, 12*(2), 245–261. https://doi.org/10.1111/j.1351-0487.2005.00414.x

Thompson, J. (2009). Identity and obligation in a transgenerational polity. In A. Gosseries & L. H. Meyer (Eds.), *Intergenerational justice* (Vol. 1, pp. 25–49). Oxford University Press. https://doi.org/10.1093/acprof:oso/9780199282951.003.0002

Tigre, M. A. (2020, June 2). Inter-American Court of human rights recognizes the right to a healthy environment. *ASIL Insights*. Retrieved January 3, 2025, from https://www.asil.org/insights/volume/24/issue/14/inter-american-court-human-rights-recognizes-right-healthy-environment

Tigre, M. A., & Carrillo Bañuelos, J. A. (2023, March 29). The ICJ's advisory opinion on climate change: What happens now? *Climate Law Blog*. Retrieved January 3, 2025, from https://blogs.law.columbia.edu/climatechange/2023/03/29/the-icjs-advisory-opinion-on-climate-change-what-happens-now/

Tigre, M. A., & Urzola, N. (2021). The 2017 inter-American court's advisory opinion: Changing the paradigm for international environmental law in the anthropocene. *Journal of Human Rights and the Environment, 12*(1), 24–50. https://doi.org/10.4337/jhre.2021.01.02

Toft, K. H. (2020). Climate change as a business and human rights issue: A proposal for a moral typology. *Business and Human Rights Journal, 5*(1), 1–27. https://doi.org/10.1017/bhj.2019.22

Tol, R. S., & Verheyen, R. (2004). State responsibility and compensation for climate change damages: A legal and economic assessment. *Energy Policy, 32*(9), 1109–1130. https://doi.org/10.1016/S0301-4215(03)00075-2

Tomuschat, C. (2010). The responsibility of other entities: Private individuals. In J. Crawford (Ed.), *The law of international responsibility* (Vol. 23.1, pp. 317–329). Oxford University Press.

Torre-Schaub, M. (2021). Climate change litigation in France: New perspectives and trends. In I. Alogna, C. Bakker, & J.-P. Gauci (Eds.), *Climate change litigation: Global perspectives* (Vol. 6). Brill Nijhoff.

Tremmel, J. C. (2006). Establishing intergenerational justice in national constitutions. In J. C. Tremmel (Ed.), *Handbook of intergenerational justice*. Edward Elgar Publishing.

Tremmel, J. C. (2009). *A theory of intergenerational justice*. Earthscan Publications Ltd. https://doi.org/10.4324/9781849774369

Tremmel, J. C. (2015). Parliaments and future generations: The four-power model. In D. Birnbacher & M. Thorseth (Eds.), *The politics of sustainability: Philosophical perspectives* (Vol. 12, pp. 212–233). Routledge Taylor & Francis Group.

Turner, S. J., & Bright, C. (2022). From "due diligence" to "adequate redress": Towards compulsory human rights and environmental insurance for companies? *International Community Law Review, 24*, 145–165. https://doi.org/10.1163/18719732-12341487

UN Conference on Environment and Development. (1992a). *Rio declaration on environment and development*. UN Doc. A/CONF.151/26 (Vol. I).

UN Conference on Environment and Development. (1992b, June). *Agenda 21*. UN Doc. A/CONF.151/26 (Vol. II).

UNFCCC Secretariat. (2005, January). Climate change, small island developing states. Retrieved January 3, 2025, from https://unfccc.int/resource/docs/publications/cc_sids.pdf

United Nations. (1972, June 16). *Declaration of the United Nations conference on the human environment*. UN Doc. A/Conf.48/14/Rev. 1 (1973).

United Nations Economic and Social Council (ECOSOC). (2022, August 15). *Ministerial Declaration of the High-Level Segment of the 2022 Session of the Economic and Social Council and the 2022 High-Level Political Forum on Sustainable Development, Convened Under the Auspices of the Council, on the Theme "Building Back Better from the Coronavirus Disease (COVID-19) While Advancing the Full Implementation of the 2030 Agenda for Sustainable Development"*. UN Doc. E/HLS/2022/1.

United Nations Economic and Social Council (ECOSOC), Commission on Human Rights. (1994, July 6). *Final Report by the Special Rapporteur on Human Rights and the Environment*, by F. Z. Ksentini. UN Doc. E/CN.4/Sub.2/1994/9.

United Nations Educational, Scientific and Cultural Organization. (1997, November 12). *Declaration on the responsibilities of the present generations towards future generations*. UNESCO Doc. 29/C Resolution 44.

United Nations Environment Programme. (2017). *The status of climate change litigation: A global review*. UN Environment Programme.

United Nations Environment Programme. (2020). *Global climate litigation report: 2020 status review*. UN Environment Programme.

United Nations Environment Programme. (2022, July 28). In historic move, UN declares healthy environment a human right. Retrieved January 3, 2025, from https://www.unep.org/news-and-stories/story/historic-move-un-declares-healthy-environment-human-right

United Nations General Assembly. (1968, December 3). *Problems of the Human Environment*. UN Doc. A/RES/2398(XXIII).

United Nations General Assembly. (1972, December 15). *Institutional and financial arrangements for international environmental cooperation*. UN Doc. A/RES/2997(XXVII).

United Nations General Assembly. (1980, October 30). *Historical responsibility of states for the preservation of nature for present and future generations*. UN Doc. A/RES/35/8.

United Nations General Assembly. (1982, October 28). *World charter for nature*. UN Doc. A/RES/37/7.

United Nations General Assembly. (1986, December 4). *Setting international standards in the field of human rights*. UN Doc. A/RES/41/120.

United Nations General Assembly. (2002, January 28). *Responsibility of states for internationally wrongful acts*. UN Doc. A/RES/56/83.

United Nations General Assembly. (2006, December 18). *Allocation of loss in the case of transboundary harm arising out of hazardous activities*. UN Doc. A/RES/61/36.

United Nations General Assembly. (2011, October 7). *Declaration Adopted at the Sixty-Fourth Annual Conference of the Department of Public Information for Non-Governmental Organizations (Bonn, Germany, 3–5 September 2011) – Letter Dated 7 October 2011 from the Permanent Representative of Germany to the UN Addressed to the President of the General Assembly*. UN Doc. A/66/750.

United Nations General Assembly. (2012, July 27). *The future we want*. UN Doc. A/RES/66/288.

United Nations General Assembly. (2013a, August 23). *Format and organizational aspects of the high-level political forum on sustainable development. Resolution adopted by the General Assembly on 9 July 2013*. UN Doc. A/RES/67/290.

United Nations General Assembly. (2013b, November 13). *Summary of the first meeting of the high-level political forum on sustainable development*. UN Doc. A/68/588.

United Nations General Assembly. (2015, October 21). *Transforming our world: The 2030 agenda for sustainable development*. UN Doc. A/RES/70/1.

United Nations General Assembly. (2019, July 15). *Report of the special rapporteur on the issue of human rights obligations relating to the enjoyment of a safe, clean, healthy and sustainable environment*, by D. Boyd. UN Doc. A/74/161.

United Nations General Assembly. (2022, July 28). *The human right to a clean, healthy and sustainable environment*. UN Doc. A/RES/76/300.

UN Global Compact. (2000). The ten principles of the UN global compact. Retrieved January 3, 2025, from https://www.unglobalcompact.org/what-is-gc/mission/principles

UN News. (2011, September 22). *Palau seeks UN world court opinion on damage caused by greenhouse gases*. Retrieved January 3, 2025, from https://news.un.org/en/story/2011/09/388202

United Nations Secretary-General. (2013, August 15). *Intergenerational solidarity and the needs of future generations, report of the Secretary-General*. UN Doc. A/68/322.

UN Sub-Commission on the Promotion and Protection of Human Rights. (2003, August 13). *Norms on the responsibilities of transnational corporations and other business enterprises with regard to human rights*. UN Doc. E/CN.4/Sub.2/2003/12/Rev.2 (2003).

Unnerstall, H. (1999). *Rechte zukünftiger Generationen*. Königshausen & Neumann.

Urbinati, N., & Warren, M. E. (2008). The concept of representation in contemporary democratic theory. *Annual Review of Political Science, 11*(1), 387–412. https://doi.org/10.1146/annurev.polisci.11.053006.190533

Valencia-Ospina, E. (2005). Non-governmental organizations and the international court of justice. In T. Treves (Ed.), *Civil society, international courts and compliance bodies* (Vol. 16, pp. 227–232). Asser.

van der Veen, G. A. (2021). Climate change litigation in The Netherlands: The Urgenda case and beyond. In W. Kahl & M.-P. Weller (Eds.), *Climate change litigation: A handbook* (pp. 363–377). C.H. Beck; Nomos.

van Dijk, C. (2011). Civil liability for global warming in The Netherlands. In M. Faure & M. Peeters (Eds.), *Climate change liability* (Vol. 9, pp. 206–226). Edward Elgar Publishing.

Varella, M. D. (2013). The role of non-governmental organizations in international environmental law. *SSRN Electronic Journal*. Online publication 21 March 2013. https://doi.org/10.2139/ssrn.2237677.

Varvastian, S., & Kalunga, F. (2020). Transnational corporate liability for environmental damage and climate change: Reassessing access to justice after Vedanta v. Lungowe. *Transnational Environmental Law, 9*(2), 323–345. https://doi.org/10.1017/S2047102520000138

Vašák, K. (1977). A thirty-year struggle: The sustained efforts to give force of law to the universal declaration of human rights. *UNESCO Courier, 11*, 29–30.

Vašák, K. (1984). Pour une Troisième Génération des Droits de l'Homme. In C. Swinarski (Ed.), *Etudes et Essais Sur Le Droit International Humanitaire et Sur Les Principes de la Croix-Rouge: En l'Honneur de Jean Pictet* (Vol. LXVII, pp. 837–850). Martinus Nijhoff Publishers.

Verheyen, R. (2005). *Climate change damage and international law: Prevention, duties and state responsibility*. Martinus Nijhoff Publishers.

Verheyen, R., & Pabsch, S. (2021). The role of non-governmental organizations for climate change litigation. In W. Kahl & M.-P. Weller (Eds.), *Climate change litigation: A handbook* (pp. 507–531). C.H. Beck; Nomos.

Verheyen, R., & Zengerling, C. (2016). International dispute settlement. In C. P. Carlarne, K. R. Gray, & R. Tarasofsky (Eds.), *The Oxford handbook of international climate change law* (Vol. 19, 1st ed., pp. 417–440). Oxford University Press.

Verschuuren, J. (2017). The role of sustainable development and the associated principles of environmental law and governance in the anthropocene. In L. J. Kotzé (Ed.), *Environmental law and governance for the anthropocene* (Vol. 1, pp. 3–29). Hart Publishing.

Vincent, A. (2012). Ombudspersons for future generations: Bringing intergenerational justice into the heart of policymaking. *UN Chronicle*. Retrieved January 3, 2025, from https://www.un.org/en/chronicle/article/ombudspersons-future-generations-bringing-intergenerational-justice-heart-policymaking

Voigt, C. (2009). *Sustainable development as a principle of international law: Resolving conflicts between climate measures and WTO law*. Martinus Nijhoff Publishers. https://doi.org/10.1163/ej.9789004166974.i-428

von Arnauld, A. (2019). *Völkerrecht* (4th ed.). C.F. Müller.

Vöneky, S., & Beck, F. (2022). Umweltschutz und Menschenrechte. In A. Proelß (Ed.), *Internationales Umweltrecht* (Vol. 5, 2nd ed., pp. 191–286). De Gruyter.

Wagner, G., & Arntz, A. (2021). Liability for climate damages under the German law of torts. In W. Kahl & M.-P. Weller (Eds.), *Climate change litigation: A handbook* (pp. 405–428). C.H. Beck; Nomos.

Waldron, J. (1987). Can communal goods be human rights? *European Journal of Sociology, 28*(2), 296–322. https://doi.org/10.1017/S0003975600005518

Ward, H. (2012, March). *Committing to the future we want: A high commissioner for future generations at Rio+20* (Discussion Paper). Foundation for Democracy and Sustainable Development; World Future Council. Retrieved January 3, 2025, from http://www.fdsd.org/wp-content/uploads/2014/11/Committing-to-the-future-we-want-main-report.pdf

Ward, H., Roderick, P., & Pearce, C. (2012, February 14). *The mandate of a UN high commissioner for future generations*. World Future Council; Foundation for Democracy and Sustainable Development. Retrieved January 3, 2025, from https://www.fdsd.org/wp-content/uploads/2014/11/UN-High-Commissioner-for-FGs-mandate.pdf

Wegener, B. W. (2019). Urgenda – World rescue by court order? The "climate justice"-movement tests the limits of legal protection. *Journal for European Environmental and Planning Law, 16*(2), 125–147.

Weller, M.-P., Nasse, J.-M., & Nasse, L. (2021). Climate change litigation in Germany. In W. Kahl & M.-P. Weller (Eds.), *Climate change litigation: A handbook* (pp. 378–404). C.H. Beck; Nomos.

Weller, M.-P., & Tran, M.-L. (2021). Milieudefensie et al. vs Shell: Auswirkungen für Klimaklagen Gegen Deutsche Unternehmen. *Zeitschrift Für Europäisches Umwelt- Und Planungsrecht, 19*(4), 342–356.

Wellman, C. (2000). Solidarity, the individual and human rights. *Human Rights Quarterly, 22*(3), 639–657.

Wenar, L. (2020). Rights. In E. N. Zalta (Ed.), *The Stanford encyclopedia of philosophy*. ISSN 1095-5054. Retrieved January 3, 2025, from https://plato.stanford.edu/entries/rights/. (Article last updated February 2020)

Wenzel, N. (2011). Group rights. In A. Peters & R. Wolfrum (Eds.), *Max Planck encyclopedia of public international law*. Oxford University Press. (Article last updated January 2011).

Weston, B. H. (1984). Human rights. *Human Rights Quarterly, 6*(3), 257–283.

Weston, B. H., & Bach, T. (2009). *Recalibrating the law of humans with the laws of nature: Climate change, human rights, and intergenerational justice*. Vermont Law School.

Wewerinke-Singh, M., Aguon, J., & Hunter, J. (2021). Bringing climate change before the international court of justice: Prospects for contentious cases and advisory opinions. In I. Alogna, C. Bakker, & J.-P. Gauci (Eds.), *Climate change litigation: Global perspectives* (Vol. 17, pp. 393–414). Brill Nijhoff.

Wewerinke-Singh, M., & McCoach, A. (2021). The State of The Netherlands v Urgenda Foundation: Distilling best practice and lessons learnt for future rights-based climate litigation. *Review of European, Comparative and International Environmental Law, 30*, 1–9. https://doi.org/10.1111/reel.12388

White, L. (1967). The historical roots of our ecological crisis. *Science, 155*, 1203–1207.

Winter, C., Schuett, J., Martínez, E., van Arsdale, S., Araújo, R., Hollman, N., Sebo, J., Stawasz, A., O'Keefe, C., & Rotola, G. (2021, January). Legal priorities research: A research agenda. *Legal Priorities Project*. Retrieved January 3, 2025, from https://papers.ssrn.com/sol3/papers.cfm?abstract_id=3931256.

Winter, G. (2020). Armando Carvalho and Others v. EU: Invoking human rights and the Paris agreement for better climate protection legislation. *Transnational Environmental Law, 9*(1), 137–164. https://doi.org/10.1017/S2047102520000072

Wolfe, K. (2003). Greening the international human rights sphere: Environmental rights and the draft declaration of principles on human rights and the environment. *Review of Current Law and Law Reform, 9*(1), 45–58.

Wood, J. C. (1996). Intergenerational equity and climate change. *Georgetown International Environmental Law Review, 8*, 293–332.

Wood, M. C., & Woodward, C. W., IV. (2016). Atmospheric trust litigation and the constitutional right to a healthy climate system: Judicial recognition at last. *Washington Journal of Environmental Law and Policy, 6*(2), 634–684.

Wood, P. M. (2004). Intergenerational justice and curtailments on the discretionary powers of governments. *Environmental Ethics, 26*(4), 411–428. https://doi.org/10.5840/enviroethics20042646

Woods, K. (2016). The rights of (future) humans qua humans. *Journal of Human Rights, 15*(2), 291–306. https://doi.org/10.1080/14754835.2015.1106310

World Commission on Environment and Development. (1987). *Report of the World Commission on Environment and Development: Our common future (Brundtland Report)* (1987). UN Doc. A/42/427 Annex.

World Future Council, Intergenerational Foundation, Planetary Boundaries Initiative, & Foundation for Democracy and Sustainable Development. (2012, August 28). HC 172 outcomes of The UN Rio +20 earth summit: Written evidence submitted by alliance for future generations. *Alliance for Future Generations*. Retrieved January 3, 2025, from https://publications.parliament.uk/pa/cm201213/cmselect/cmenvaud/writev/172/m02.htm

World Summit on Sustainable Development. (2002, September 4). *Johannesburg declaration on sustainable development*. UN Doc. A/CONF.199/20.

World's Youth for Climate Justice. (2024, December 2). *Historic climate hearings at the International Court of Justice: Daily debriefs compendium*. Retrieved January 3, 2025, from https://www.wy4cj.org/icjao-oral-hearings-debrief

Wright, J. C. (1988). *Future generations and the environment*. Centre for Resource Management.

Younging, G. (2018). *Elements of indigenous style: A guide for writing by and about indigenous peoples*. Brush Education.

Zengerling, C. (2013). *Greening international jurisprudence: Environmental NGOs before international courts, tribunals, and compliance committees*. Martinus Nijhoff Publishers.

Zhou, C., & Qin, T. (2021). Prospects for climate change litigation in China. In I. Alogna, C. Bakker, & J.-P. Gauci (Eds.), *Climate change litigation: Global perspectives* (Vol. 11, pp. 244–268). Brill Nijhoff.

# Part II
# Intertemporal Law

The second part of this book illustrates that the temporal dimension of intergenerational equity calls for an intertemporal assessment of the concept. The so-called "doctrine of intertemporal law" constitutes an important method to adequately assess the temporally relevant legal regime for the assessment of a legal norm. This intertemporal assessment can assist in answering the open issues and the general relevance of emerging developments with respect to intergenerational equity. First, Chapter 6 illustrates the relevant aspects of the existing doctrine of intertemporal law. Then, the present author develops a modification of this doctrine to the context of intergenerational equity in Chapter 7 in order to adequately answer the question which legal regime is temporally applicable to the analysis of intergenerational equity today.

# Chapter 6
# The Existing Doctrine of Intertemporal Law

Due to the evolutionary interrelation between the two manifestations of intergenerational equity, legal change over time is an important issue in the context of intergenerational relations. The relationship between time and law is complex and touches upon a broad variety of issues.[1] For the scope of this book, not all of them are relevant for the intertemporal analysis of environmental norms. The core issue is the so-called "doctrine of intertemporal law",[2] which addresses the delimitation of the temporal sphere of application of a norm.[3] The content of legal norms can and often will evolve over time, either due to different interpretations or because of changes in the systemic framework. Thus, whenever applying a principle or rule of international law, which arose in the past, to circumstances in the present, the question arises as to whether the old or the current law is to be applied.[4] While in some legal disputes the intertemporal law doctrine has also been applied to the evolution of facts and scientific knowledge that may influence the content of a legal rule over time,[5] the present work primarily focuses on the evolution of law. In this

---

[1]For some exemplary issues in the context of public international law, see Higgins (1997); Tomuschat (2022); d'Aspremont (2022); McNeilly and Warwick (2022); Polackova van der Ploeg et al. (2022). See also Brown Weiss (1989), pp. 28–34.

[2]Synonymously, the terms "theory", "principle" or "rule" of intertemporal law, or "of intertemporality" are used. This book exclusively uses the most common denomination "doctrine of intertemporal law", in order to not further engage in the concept's normative capacity. On synonyms, see Kotzur (2008, para. 5).

[3]Institut de Droit International (IDI) (1975), Preamble; Kotzur (2008), para. 1.

[4]Permanent Court of Arbitration, *Island of Palmas Case (United States v. The Netherlands)*, Arbitral Award, 4 April 1928, RIAA II (1928), 829, p. 845; Kotzur (2008), para. 1; D'Amato (1992), p. 1234.

[5]See International Court of Justice, *Request for an Examination of the Situation in Accordance with Paragraph 63 of the Court's Judgment of 20 December 1974 in the Nuclear Tests (New Zealand v. France) Case,* Dissenting Opinion of Judge Weeramantry, 22 September 1995, ICJ Reports 1995, 317, pp. 339–341; Merkouris (2015), pp. 132–133.



A. Bustami, *The Legal Relationship between Present and Future Generations*,
https://doi.org/10.1007/978-3-032-03345-1_6

sense, the doctrine of intertemporal law serves as a method to determine the temporally applicable *lex lata*.

Since questions regarding the intertemporal application of norms exist in all domestic legal systems, the doctrine has sometimes been referred to as a general principle of law in the sense of Article 38(1)(c) of the ICJ Statute.[6] However, its particular manifestation in international law amounts to a rule of customary international law, supported by general State practice and *opinio iuris* and confirmed by jurisprudence.[7] The doctrine has so far mainly been considered with regard to territorial disputes and issues of treaty interpretation.[8] Although it generally applies to all norms of public international law that involve questions of temporal application,[9] its exact contours are still underdeveloped beyond these specific areas.[10] Intertemporal law operates between two legal values: On the one hand, legal stability governs international relations to guarantee legal certainty and the international rule of law.[11] On the other hand, law must be sufficiently flexible and open to progress of human life and society.[12] A clearly shaped doctrine of intertemporal law must resolve this sometimes dichotomous relation.[13]

For the first time, arbitrator *Max Huber* explicitly formulated the doctrine of intertemporal law in the *Island of Palmas* award of 1928.[14] The arbitrator had to decide whether the Island of Palmas formed a part of the territory belonging to the USA or the Netherlands. According to *Huber*, "a juridical fact must be appreciated in the light of the law contemporary with it, and not of the law in force at the time when a dispute in regard to it arises or falls to be settled".[15] This main aspect of intertemporal law has subsequently often been referred to as the "principle of contemporaneity".[16] This principle was further specified by *Huber* as he distinguished between the creation of a right—to which the principle of contemporaneity applied—and its "existence [...], in other words its continued manifestation, [which] shall follow the conditions required by the evolution of law".[17]

---

[6] Kotzur (2008), para. 5.

[7] Ibid. For its manifestation in international jurisprudence, see the following analysis.

[8] Li (2018), pp. 369–385; Kotzur (2008), paras. 2–3.

[9] D'Amato (1992), p. 1234; Elias (1980), pp. 285–286; Kotzur (2008), para. 2.

[10] Wheatley (2021), pp. 488–489. Some of these lacunae are addressed in more detail below, see *infra* in Sect. 7.2.1.

[11] For the international rule of law, see Chesterman (2007), paras. 37–46.

[12] ICJ, *Request for Interpretation of the Judgment of 15 June 1962 in the Case concerning the Temple of Preah Vihear (Cambodia v. Thailand) (Cambodia v. Thailand),* Separate opinion of Judge Cançado Trindade, 18 July 2011, ICJ Reports 2011, 566, para. 13; IDI (1975), Preamble; Thacher (1987), p. 136; Kotzur (2008), para. 4. See also Cassese (2012), p. xviii.

[13] Li (2018), pp. 383–385.

[14] *Island of Palmas* (Arbitral Award), *supra* note 4.

[15] Ibid., p. 845.

[16] D'Amato (1992), p. 1234; Inagaki (2015), p. 128. In this context, the term "principle" is not used in a technical sense as in Sect. 4.1.1.

[17] *Island of Palmas* (Arbitral Award), *supra* note 4, p. 845.

Following this twofold approach, the doctrine of intertemporal law encompasses contemporaneity as well as considerations of subsequent developments.[18] In order to fully understand the doctrine of intertemporal law, as it is applied today by international courts and tribunals, these two aspects must be assessed separately. As such, the next section addresses the main component of contemporaneity, which remains the starting point of every intertemporal assessment (Sect. 6.1). Then, different versions of the so-called "evolutionary" approaches that have developed in international law are assessed in the second section of this chapter (Sect. 6.2).

## 6.1 The Principle of Contemporaneity

In 1975, the IDI proclaimed in its resolution on intertemporal law:

> Unless otherwise indicated, the temporal sphere of application of any norm of public international law shall be determined in accordance with the general principle of law by which any fact, action or situation must be assessed in the light of the rules of law that are contemporaneous with it.[19]

According to this main rule of intertemporal law, the law "contemporary" with the relevant facts should be the temporal reference point. Although jurisprudence and academic literature have not always used consistent terminology,[20] the present author understands "contemporaneity" to refer to the time in the past and not the time of an arising dispute or its settlement; following the reasoning of the *Island of Palmas* award.[21] This element of intertemporal law has also been incorporated in the Articles on State Responsibility as Article 13 clarifies that a State is only in breach of an international obligation if "the State is bound by the obligation in question at the time the act occurs".[22] It is generally applicable to all international obligations,[23] although there are two main areas, in which the principle of contemporaneity has played an important role.

---

[18] ICJ, *Land and Maritime Boundary between Cameroon and Nigeria (Cameroon v. Nigeria: Equatorial Guinea intervening),* Separate Opinion of Judge Al-Khasawneh, 10 October 2002, ICJ Reports 2002, 492, para. 13; International Law Commission (2006), paras. 475–477; Fitzmaurice (2008), p. 104; Tanaka (2010), pp. 115–116. For a more restrictive understanding of "intertemporal law", see D'Amato (1992), p. 1235.

[19] IDI (1975), Article 1.

[20] See, e.g., Stec (1999), p. 367 (at footnote 180); Boisson de Chazournes and Mbengue (2017), p. 443. Some commentators considered contemporaneity to be tantamount to "non-retroactivity" as the core element of intertemporal law, see D'Amato (1992), p. 1235. Non-retroactivity in international law primarily refers to the application of treaties, see Rodas (1973); Kotzur (2008), paras. 3, 8, so that the current analysis only mentions issues of retroactivity where necessary for reasons of delimitation, see *infra* notes 37, 101.

[21] *Island of Palmas* (Arbitral Award), *supra* note 4, p. 845; Fitzmaurice (1953), p. 5.

[22] International Law Commission (2001), Art. 13 para. 1. For a thought-provocative assessment of the inter-temporality in the law of international responsibility, see d'Aspremont (2022) who established a theory on international responsibility as serial, linear and two-directional time travel.

[23] ILC (2001), Art. 13 para. 6. For further examples of application, see generally ibid., Art. 13 paras. 2–4.

Disputes over territorial titles have been the first field of application, such as in the *Island of Palmas* case itself. In earlier case law on territorial disputes, arbitral bodies had already relied on contemporaneity as the leading rule to establish the temporally applicable law.[24] Further, the principle of contemporaneity was applied by the ICJ on various occasions regarding the creation of territorial titles,[25] although it has never explicitly established its understanding of intertemporal law.[26] In any case, the first element of intertemporal law requires the courts and tribunals to positively ascertain the legal regime at the historical moment in the past.[27] This task suffers from uncertainties and can be susceptible to errors and to certain temporal or Eurocentric biases.[28] These challenges regarding the ascertainment of the law in the past are not addressed in this book.

Beyond territorial disputes, the principle of contemporaneity has often played a role in the application of a treaty that was concluded in the distant past.[29] First, this concerns the validity of treaties concluded in the past, which would be invalid under the legal rules at the time when the dispute arises.[30] The VCLT includes certain conditions under which a treaty concluded in the past might be invalid due to changes of law or circumstances that took place until the present.[31] Apart from these exceptions, a treaty remains valid according to the principle of contemporaneity.[32] The ICJ applied this first aspect of *Huber's* doctrine to the validity of a treaty in its *Right of Passage* case in 1960.[33]

Second, the first component of the intertemporal law doctrine is also applicable in the context of treaty interpretation.[34] At the beginning of the drafting process of the VCLT, the drafters intended to include a direct reference to the doctrine of

---

[24] Arbitral Tribunal, *Award regarding the Boundary between the Colony of British Guiana and the United States of Venezuela,* Arbitral Award, 3 October 1899, RIAA XXVIII (2007), 331, p. 338; PCA, *Grisbådarna Case,* Arbitral Award, 23 October 1909, RIAA XI (1961), 147, p. 159.

[25] ICJ, *Minquiers and Ecrehos (France v. United Kingdom),* Judgment, 17 November 1953, ICJ Reports 1953, 47, p. 56; ICJ, *Temple of Preah Vihear (Cambodia v. Thailand),* Judgment, 15 June 1962, ICJ Reports 1962, 6, pp. 16–22; ICJ, *Western Sahara,* Advisory Opinion, 16 October 1975, ICJ Reports 1975, 12, para. 77. On the *Minquiers and Ecrehos* case, see also Fitzmaurice (1953), pp. 7–8.

[26] See Wheatley (2021), p. 498.

[27] Martin (2021), p. 89.

[28] In more detail, see ibid., pp. 86–99 who reconceptualised the assumptions of intertemporal law with regard to the ascertainment of legal norms in the past. For another critical assessment, see also von Arnauld (2021).

[29] Jennings et al. (1992), pp. 1281–1282; D'Amato (1992), p. 1234; Kotzur (2008), para. 3.

[30] Akhtar-Khavari (2003), paras. 8–13.

[31] *Vienna Convention on the Law of Treaties* (VCLT), adopted 23 May 1969, entered into force 27 January 1980, 1155 UNTS 331, Art. 53, 61 and 62.

[32] Akhtar-Khavari (2003), paras. 10–12.

[33] ICJ, *Right of Passage over Indian Territory Case (Portugal v. India),* Judgment (Merits), 12 April 1960, ICJ Reports 1960, 6, 37.

[34] See ILC (2013), para. 54; Fitzmaurice (1957), pp. 225–226; Elias (1980), pp. 300–301; M. Fitzmaurice (2008), p. 112; Bjorge (2014), p. 142; Kotzur (2008), para. 11. *Ulf Linderfalk* is

intertemporal law.[35] However, the initial draft Article 56 was removed from subsequent drafts, so that the VCLT does not include a direct reference to intertemporal law.[36] Questions of intertemporal delimitation were completely left to the general rules of treaty interpretation in Articles 31, 32 of the VCLT,[37] and to the provision on non-retroactivity of treaties in Article 28 of the VCLT.[38] The principle of contemporaneity could be understood as a special application of the interpretative rule based on the "ordinary meaning to be given to the terms of the treaty in their context" in Article 31(1) of the VCLT, that means the "context in which the terms occur".[39] Contemporaneity is also strongly linked to interpretative efforts to detect the contracting parties' original intentions.[40] This was pointed out during the VCLT drafting process[41] as well as in international case law.[42]

In 1953, the ICJ applied a contemporaneous approach to interpretation in its *US Nationals in Morocco* case.[43] The scope of the jurisdictional clauses of the relevant treaties depended on the meaning of the word "dispute" therein. According to the Court, in order to determine this meaning, "it is necessary to take into account the meaning of the word 'dispute' at the times when the two treaties were concluded".[44] The ICJ made similar recourse to the time of the relevant treaties' conclusion in other

---

more critical and underlined that the doctrine of intertemporal law and the rules of treaty interpretation serve different purposes, see Linderfalk (2008), pp. 116–117.

[35] ILC (1964b), pp. 8–9, Art. 56.

[36] Merkouris (2015), pp. 135–136. For some criticism of the originally proposed article, see ILC (1964a), pp. 33–34.

[37] ILC (2018), Conclusion 8 para. 3; Higgins (1997), p. 518; Inagaki (2015), p. 129; Merkouris (2015), pp. 137–139. See also *infra* Sect. 6.2.1.

[38] See Kotzur (2008), para. 8 and *supra* note 19.

[39] G. G. Fitzmaurice (1957), p. 226. See also Kotzur (2008), para. 8.

[40] IDI (1975), paras. 3–4.

[41] ILC (1966), p. 199, para. 9. One of the ILC members underlined that "the intention of the parties should be controlling": ILC (1964a), p. 34.

[42] ICJ, *South West Africa, Second Phase (Ethiopia v. South Africa; Liberia v. South Africa),* Judgment, 18 July 1966, ICJ Reports 1966, 6, para. 16; ICJ, *Dispute regarding Navigational and Related Rights (Costa Rica v. Nicaragua),* Judgment, 13 July 2009, ICJ Reports 2009, 213, para. 63.

[43] ICJ, *Rights of United States Nationals in Morocco Case (France v. United States of America),* Judgment, 27 August 1952, ICJ Reports 1952, 176.

[44] Ibid., p. 189.

judgments,[45] at least as a starting point for treaty interpretation.[46] Arbitral bodies have also based their reasoning on the law and meaning of terms at the time of a treaty's conclusion[47]—as well as legal scholarship that underlined the relevance of the practice and circumstances at this time in the past.[48]

Overall, contemporaneity constitutes the main component of intertemporal law and it operates in accordance with the concept of legal certainty.[49] As *Gerald Fitzmaurice* stated with regard to contemporaneous treaty interpretation:

> Not to take account of contemporary practice and circumstances, and to interpret such treaties according to modern concepts, would often amount to importing into them provisions they never really contained, and imposing on the parties obligations they never actually assumed.[50]

[45] *South West Africa, Second Phase* (Judgment), *supra* note 42, paras. 16, 89. Most of these disputes arose with regard to territorial delimitations in treaties, see *Temple of Preah Vihear 1962* (Judgment), *supra* note 25, 16–22, 33–35; ICJ, *Kasikili/Sedudu Island (Botswana v. Namibia),* Judgment, 13 December 1999, ICJ Reports 1999, 1045, paras. 21, 25; ICJ, *Land and Maritime Boundary between Cameroon and Nigeria (Cameroon v. Nigeria: Equatorial Guinea intervening),* Judgment, 10 October 2002, ICJ Reports 2002, 303, para. 59. These treaty interpretation cases faced the same challenges of proper ascertainment of the law of the past, see *supra* notes 26–27 as well as Martin (2021), pp. 15–18, 45–46 with reference to the *Land and Maritime Boundary* case between Cameroon and Nigeria.

[46] *Navigational and Related Rights* (Judgment), *supra* note 42, para. 63. Cf. Jennings et al. (1992), p. 1282.

[47] PCA, *North Atlantic Coast Fisheries Case (Great Britain v. United States),* Arbitral Award, 7 September 1910, RIAA XI (1910), 167, p. 196; Commission of Arbitration, *The Ambatielos Claim (Greece v. United Kingdom of Great Britain and Northern Ireland),* Arbitral Award, 6 March 1956, RIAA XII (1956), 83, p. 108; Arbitral Tribunal, *Case concerning the delimitation of the maritime boundary between Guinea and Guinea-Bissau,* Ad Hoc Arbitration Tribunal Award, 14 February 1985, RIAA XIX (1985), 149, para. 39; Eritrea-Ethiopia Boundary Commission, *Decision Regarding Delimitation of the Border between Eritrea and Ethiopia,* Arbitral Award, 13 April 2002, RIAA XXV (2002), 83, para. 3.5. For an example before the CJEU, see Higgins (1996), p. 180.

[48] Tanaka (2013), pp. 154–155; G. G. Fitzmaurice (1957), pp. 208, 226 with reference to ICJ, *Minquiers and Ecrehos (France v. United Kingdom),* Individual Opinion of Judge Levi Carneiro, 17 November 1953, ICJ Reports 1953, 85, p. 91; *Ambatielos Claim* (Arbitral Award), *supra* note 47, p. 108. See also ILC (2018), Conclusion 8, para. 6 (at footnotes 330–333) with further references as well as Jennings et al. (1992), p. 1282; Merkouris (2015), p. 130, fn. 44; Crawford and Brownlie (2019), p. 367.

[49] IDI (1975), preamble; Thacher (1987), p. 136; Kotzur (2008), para. 4.

[50] G. G. Fitzmaurice (1957), p. 226.

## 6.2 Evolutionary Approaches as Exceptions to Contemporaneity

Notwithstanding the value of legal certainty, the doctrine of intertemporal law goes beyond a static consideration of past times when the relevant act occurred.[51] In the *Island of Palmas* case, the doctrine's second element was formulated as follows: "[T]he existence of the right, in other words its continued manifestation, shall follow the conditions required by the evolution of law".[52] Therefore, changes and evolutions that take place in the aftermath of the emergence of a specific norm must be taken into consideration under certain circumstances.

This second element has remained controversial until today.[53] It was considered to have been wrongly interpreted,[54] and to be "highly disturbing"[55] due to the legal uncertainty it caused. *Anthony D'Amato* considered it to be completely contradictory to the first element, which is why it should be understood restrictively.[56] Other commentators referred to the complementarity between the first element's focus on contemporaneity and the second element's extension to subsequent developments.[57] The relevance of evolutionary approaches to intertemporal law would be a logical consequence of "a dynamic understanding of international law in accordance with the changing international society rather than [...] a static interpretation of rules".[58] In his separate opinion in the *Land and Maritime Boundary* case, *Judge Al-Khasawneh* made clear that the doctrine of intertemporal law requires the interpreter "to enquire into the quality of the juridical act in the light not only of the alleged practice but in the light of the totality of the law [relating to the relevant legal issue]".[59] The ARSIWA did not explicitly incorporate this second element into Article 13, but the ILC clarified in its commentaries that the principle in Article 13 "does not entail that treaty provisions are to be interpreted as if frozen in time" and that "[t]he evolutionary interpretation of treaty provisions is permissible in certain cases [...]".[60]

---

[51] *Land and Maritime Boundary* (Separate Opinion of Judge Al-Khasawneh), *supra* note 18, para. 13.

[52] *Island of Palmas* (Arbitral Award), *supra* note 4, p. 845.

[53] See, e.g., Jessup (1928); Lauterpacht (1933), pp. 283–284; Higgins (1997), pp. 515–516; D'Amato (1992), p. 1235; Harris and Sivakumaran (2015), para. 5–013.

[54] Higgins (1997), p. 516. On the different interpretations of the award, see Wheatley (2021), p. 488.

[55] Jessup (1928), p. 740.

[56] D'Amato (1992), p. 1235. Cf. also Higgins (1997), p. 516.

[57] *Land and Maritime Boundary* (Separate Opinion of Judge Al-Khasawneh), *supra* note 18, paras. 13–17; Elias (1980), pp. 291, 305; Khan (2007), p. 169. Cf. Jennings et al. (1992), p. 1282.

[58] Khan (2007), p. 169. See also *Temple of Preah Vihear 2011* (Separate opinion of Judge Cançado Trindade), *supra* note 12, paras. 12–13; Elias (1980), p. 291.

[59] *Land and Maritime Boundary* (Separate Opinion of Judge Al-Khasawneh), *supra* note 18, para. 12.

[60] ILC (2001), Art. 13 para. 9.

The controversies regarding the second element of the intertemporal law doctrine surfaced again in a recent advisory opinion of the ICJ in the *Chagos Archipelago* proceeding.[61] The ICJ had been asked by the UNGA to clarify the legal status of the Chagos archipelago in the Indian Ocean. The archipelago had been detached from Mauritius by the UK as administering power in 1965, before Mauritius became independent in 1968. One of the issues in that case was the existence of the right of peoples to self-determination at the relevant time.[62] Although the ICJ did not explicitly mention the intertemporal law doctrine,[63] its argumentation addressed the question of the temporally applicable law:

> The Court is of the view that, while its determination of the applicable law must focus on the period from 1965 to 1968, this will not prevent it, particularly when customary rules are at issue, from considering the evolution of the law on self-determination since the adoption of the [UN Charter and a resolution of 1960]. Indeed, State practice and *opinio juris*, […], are consolidated and confirmed gradually over time.[64]

These observations could point to a classic understanding of the first element of intertemporal law, contemporaneity, as the ICJ would apply the law contemporary with the relevant acts between 1965 and 1968. However, the Court continued that it "may also rely on legal instruments which postdate the period in question, when those instruments confirm or interpret pre-existing rules or principles."[65] In this sense, it took into account not only the 1960 UNGA Resolution,[66] but also the post-dating 'Friendly-Relations Declaration' from 1970.[67] While the Court formally still determined the law contemporary to the relevant facts in the past,[68] it introduced an evolutionary element into its assessment, which required looking at change in customary international law over time.[69] *Steven Wheatley* summarised this new intertemporal law element of the ICJ as follows:

> [T]wo apparently conflicting propositions can be true: that the International Court of Justice would not have recognised a customary right of peoples to self-determination in the late 1960s, and would have found the detachment of the Chagos Archipelago to be lawful at the time; and that the ICJ could, with the benefit of hindsight, identify the 1960 Declaration as the defining moment in the crystallisation of the self-determination norm, and therefore conclude that the detachment was unlawful *at that time* (emphasis in the original).[70]

---

[61] ICJ, *Legal Consequences of the Separation of the Chagos Archipelago from Mauritius in 1965*, Advisory Opinion, 25 February 2019, ICJ Reports 2019, 95.

[62] In more detail, see Pavlopoulos (2021).

[63] Wheatley (2021), p. 498.

[64] *Chagos Archipelago* (Advisory Opinion), *supra* note 61, para. 142.

[65] Ibid., para. 143.

[66] United Nations General Assembly (1960). See *Chagos Archipelago* (Advisory Opinion), *supra* note 61, paras. 150–152.

[67] UNGA (1970). See *Chagos Archipelago* (Advisory Opinion), *supra* note 61, para. 155.

[68] Cf. Ghimisi (2019), p. 104.

[69] For a detailed analysis of the Court's intertemporal law understanding, see Wheatley (2021), pp. 498–507.

[70] Ibid., pp. 502–503.

This advisory opinion has remained oddly uncommented upon considering its implications for intertemporal law.[71] For *Wheatley*, the difference between the UK's arguments and the Court's findings resulted from "conflicting understandings of the second branch of the intertemporal law doctrine",[72] that means the evolutionary element. This might be true in the sense that the Court added an evolutionary element to the principle of contemporaneity, but at the same time, it was still a contemporaneous perspective on the law applicable at the time of the relevant acts. The Court did not embrace an entirely evolutionary approach by applying the right to self-determination "as it stands today".[73] Instead, it only adapted the perspective from which the applicable contemporaneous law is determined; this perspective would be the "privileged position of 'now' […] with the benefit of hindsight".[74] From this privileged perspective, it still determined the law contemporaneous at the relevant time in the past.[75] The *Chagos Archipelago* advisory opinion further remained an exception in two respects: It is one of the few instances, in which an evolutionary element became relevant in the context of a territorial dispute,[76] although some of the separate opinions in the *Western Sahara* advisory opinion expressed support for a more progressive approach.[77] Further, the second component of the intertemporal law doctrine was rarely applied in the context of customary international law norms, but mostly in the context of "evolutionary (treaty) interpretation".[78] This is why the following sub-sections focus on these different forms of evolutionary interpretation that have developed since the *Island of Palmas* findings, and the author gets back to the advisory opinion and its value for the proposed intertemporal approach in Chap. 7 below.[79]

First, the relevant provisions in Articles 31, 32 of the VCLT are assessed (Sect. 6.2.1). Beyond these general rules, two main approaches have developed in case law, which are illustrated successively: the "generic term" approach of the ICJ often starts with the original intention of the parties (Sect. 6.2.2), while the "living instrument" approach is based on an object and purpose interpretation (Sect. 6.2.3).[80] Finally, the

---

[71] For some brief comments, see, e.g., Gurmessa (2019), pp. 202–204; Allen (2020), pp. 208–210.

[72] Wheatley (2021), p. 500. See also Allen (2020), p. 208.

[73] This was argued for instance by Cyprus during the proceedings, see ICJ, *Legal Consequences of the Separation of the Chagos Archipelago from Mauritius in 1965,* Written Statement by the Republic of Cyprus, 11 May 2018, retrieved 3 January 2025, from https://www.icj-cij.org/public/files/case-related/169/169-20180511-WRI-01-00-EN.pdf, para. 9. Cf. also Allen (2020), p. 209.

[74] Wheatley (2021), p. 505.

[75] Ibid. For some additional remarks on *Wheatley's* approach, see Gurmendi (2021).

[76] Mostly, these were resolved based on the principle of contemporaneity, see *supra* notes 23–24.

[77] See McWhinney (1984), pp. 190–192 with further references.

[78] The terms "evolutionary interpretation", "evolutive interpretation" and "dynamic interpretation" are often used interchangeably, sometimes with slight differences, see Djeffal (2019), p. 22 (at footnote 8). Cf. also Merkouris (2015), p. 131 with further references. For a general working definition for evolutionary interpretation, see Bjorge (2018), p. 191.

[79] See *infra* in Sect. 7.3.3.1.

[80] Inagaki (2015), pp. 135–139.

interpretation of international environmental treaties is examined in greater depth since the relevant cases are sometimes considered to constitute a new category of evolutionary approach (Sect. 6.2.4).

### 6.2.1 Evolutionary Interpretation Under Articles 31(3) and 32 of the VCLT

As illustrated above, the VCLT remains silent on any explicit form of evolutionary interpretation.[81] Nonetheless, some of the general rules on treaty interpretation are relevant in the context of intertemporal law, particularly Article 31(3) of the VCLT. Besides the aforementioned rules of Article 31(1), based on the ordinary meaning and the parties' intentions, Article 31(3) of the VCLT refers to subsequent practice and any rules of international law applicable between the parties.[82] In 2018, the ILC adopted its 'Draft Conclusions on Subsequent Agreements and Subsequent Practice in Relation to the Interpretation of Treaties'.[83] Conclusion 8 stipulates:

> [S]ubsequent agreements and subsequent practice [...] may assist in determining whether or not the presumed intention of the parties upon the conclusion of the treaty was to give a term used a meaning which is capable of evolving over time.[84]

The conclusion avoided taking a position on whether contemporaneity to the treaty's conclusion or an evolutionary understanding of the treaty's terms should be predominant.[85] Instead, it objectively referred to the means of interpretation in Article 31(3) of the VCLT.[86] These dynamic means of interpretation can confirm either that a specific term is to be interpreted in a contemporaneous way, or that it is to be understood in an evolutive sense.[87] The ILC Fragmentation Report of 2006 took a comparable approach and preferred to indicate some relevant comments when

---

[81] See *supra* notes 33–40.

[82] From 2008 to 2018, the ILC addressed the intertemporal aspects of treaty interpretation, cf. ILC (2008-2018): First, a study group examined the topic 'Treaties over Time': ILC (2009), paras. 220–226. The study group issued three reports on the topic (see Nolte (2013b), part 5.), before the ILC changed the work format in 2012 and appointed *Georg Nolte* as Special Rapporteur for the topic 'Subsequent Agreements and Subsequent Practice in Relation to the Interpretation of Treaties', see ILC (2012), para. 227.

[83] ILC (2018).

[84] Ibid., Conclusion 8.

[85] Dupuy (2011), p. 127.

[86] ILC (2018), Conclusion 8 para. 4: Therein, the Commission also referred to "any other means of treaty interpretation".

[87] Merkouris (2015), p. 139; Dörr (2018), paras. 107–108; Djeffal (2019), p. 33. For a strict application of Article 31(3)(c) of the VCLT in an intertemporal context, see PCA, *Dispute Concerning Access to Information Under Article 9 of the OSPAR Convention between Ireland and the United Kingdom of Great Britain and Northern Ireland,* Final Award, 2 July 2003, RIAA XXIII (2003), 59, paras. 101–103.

*applying* Article 31(3) of the VCLT instead of formulating a specific intertemporal rule, "[b]ecause it seems pointless to try to set any general and abstract preference between the past and the present".[88]

In the *Navigational and Related Rights* case, the ICJ explicitly identified two distinct situations, in which a term's meaning can change:

> On the one hand, the subsequent practice of the parties, within the meaning of Article 31(3) (b) [of the VCLT], can result in a departure from the original intent on the basis of a tacit agreement between the parties. On the other hand, there are situations in which the parties' intent upon conclusion of the treaty was, or may be presumed to have been, to give the terms used [...] a meaning or content capable of evolving [...].[89]

This indicates that the notion of "evolutionary interpretation" can go beyond the scope of Article 31(3) of the VCLT on subsequent agreements and subsequent practice.[90] Yet, other commentators have underlined the limits that Article 31 VCLT would impose on any form of evolutionary interpretation.[91] For instance, *Judge Bedjaoui* stressed in a separate opinion that the intention of the parties was the decisive starting point for any interpretation and "that the general rule governing the interpretation of a treaty remains that set out in Article 31 [of the VCLT]."[92]

Beyond this, evolutionary interpretation could be considered as a supplementary means of interpretation under Article 32 of the VCLT,[93] although this is not supported by international jurisprudence so far. *Osamu Inagaki* pointed out that Article 32 of the VCLT can only be invoked if certain conditions are met[94]:

> in order to confirm the meaning resulting from the application of Article 31, or to determine the meaning when the interpretation according to Article 31 (a) leaves the meaning ambiguous or obscure; or (b) leads to a result which is manifestly absurd or unreasonable.

Overall, the relation between the general rules of treaty interpretation in Articles 31, 32 of the VCLT and evolutionary approaches is ambiguous and controversial. It goes beyond the scope of the present work to offer a comprehensive analysis of this complex relationship and the exact contours of evolutionary interpretation in all

---

[88] ILC (2006), para. 478. See also *infra* notes 102, 114 and 138.

[89] *Navigational and Related Rights* (Judgment), *supra* note 42, para. 64.

[90] Dupuy (2011), p. 127; Inagaki (2015), pp. 130–131; Fitzmaurice (2020), p. 26. Implicitly, see also ICJ, *Gabčíkovo-Nagymaros Project (Hungary v. Slovakia),* Separate Opinion of Vice-President Weeramantry, 25 September 1997, ICJ Reports 1997, 88, p. 114. As to an opposite understanding, see ILC (2018), Conclusion 8 para. 12; Bjorge (2014), pp. 76–139. For a more detailed distinction between Article 31(3) of the VCLT and evolutionary interpretation, see *infra* notes 160–166.

[91] ICJ, *Gabčíkovo-Nagymaros Project (Hungary v. Slovakia),* Separate Opinion of Judge Bedjaoui, 25 September 1997, ICJ Reports 1997, 120, paras. 6–8; Mileva and Fortuna (2019), pp. 138–139.

[92] *Gabčíkovo-Nagymaros Project* (Separate Opinion of Judge Bedjaoui), *supra* note 91, paras. 7, 18.

[93] ILC (2013), para. 118, Draft Conclusion 3 § 3; Jennings et al. (1992), pp. 1277, 1280; Inagaki (2015), p. 143. Cf. also Killander (2010), pp. 149–150; Villiger (2009), Art. 32 para. 5.

[94] Inagaki (2015), p. 143.

contexts.[95] At the very least, it must be acknowledged that the VCLT rules provide neither specific guidance on how the different components—ordinary meaning, intention, object and purpose—interrelate with each other and with evolutionary interpretation, nor on their respective weight in the interpretation process.[96] *Oliver Dörr* pointed out that "the dynamic approach to the interpretation of treaties must be distinguished from the use of dynamic means of interpretation".[97]

In international case law, two main approaches to evolutionary interpretation have developed. This case law was sometimes based on Article 31(3) of the VCLT,[98] and many commentators attributed the decisions to the general rules of treaty interpretation.[99] However, some of these cases partly developed autonomous approaches, as demonstrated in the next sections. Regardless of whether one considers the following evolutionary approaches to be included in the general regime of Article 31 of the VCLT or to constitute (partly) independent rules, the VCLT rules are not exhaustive and, therefore, other approaches could supplement them.[100] These supplementary rules would have to be compatible with the general rules of the VCLT[101] as well as with the limits of non-retroactivity.[102] Both evolutionary approaches of treaty interpretation—based on generic terms and on the treaty's object and purpose—in principle fulfil these requirements.

### 6.2.2 *Evolutionary Interpretation Due to the Generic Nature of a Term*

The first category of evolutionary interpretation approaches in jurisprudence is based on the interpretation of a "generic term" in a treaty. A generic term is "a known legal term, whose content the parties expected would change through time".[103] The

[95] For such a detailed analysis, see Bjorge (2014).

[96] Arato (2018), pp. 217–218.

[97] Dörr (2018), para. 27.

[98] See *Gabčíkovo-Nagymaros Project* (Separate Opinion of Judge Bedjaoui), *supra* note 91, para. 18.

[99] See Christoffersen (2009), p. 61; Killander (2010), p. 146; Dörr (2018), para. 104; Djeffal (2019), p. 28.

[100] Dörr (2018), para. 32.

[101] *Gabčíkovo-Nagymaros Project* (Separate Opinion of Judge Bedjaoui), *supra* note 91, paras. 6–8; Merkouris (2015), p. 150; Bjorge (2018).

[102] International Centre for Settlement of Investment Disputes, *Mondev International Ltd. v. United States of America,* Award, 11 October 2002, ICSID Case No. ARB(AF)/99/2 (NAFTA), para. 70; Merkouris (2015), pp. 147, 150. See also *supra* note 19. However, on the limits of non-retroactivity apart from criminal law, see von Arnauld (2021), pp. 417–418.

[103] ICJ, *Kasikili/Sedudu Island (Botswana v. Namibia),* Declaration of Judge Higgins, 13 December 1999, ICJ Reports 1999, 1113, para. 2. Cf. also ILC (2006), para. 478; Merkouris (2015), pp. 141–142.

utilisation of such a generic term in a treaty requires the term's evolutionary interpretation. In the *Aegean Sea Continental Shelf* decision, the ICJ analysed that the expression "the territorial status of Greece" was used as a generic term and consequently held that the "presumption necessarily arises that its meaning was intended to follow the evolution of the law and to correspond with the meaning attached to the expression by the law in force at any given time".[104]

Two conclusions can be drawn from this approach: On the one hand, the ICJ based its findings primarily on the parties' original intention, or at least what it considered to be their presumed intention.[105] It undertook some effort in its reasoning to make an accurate assessment of the parties' original intention.[106] This intention at the time of the treaty's conclusion could have pointed both to an evolutionary understanding of the relevant terms and to a static understanding in the sense of contemporaneity.[107] The focus on the parties' intention has been shared by many commentators.[108] For instance, *Eirik Bjorge* concluded that "evolutionary interpretation is inexorably linked to the objectivized intention of the parties".[109] On the other hand, the Court considered the terms in question from a broader perspective, including their general meaning at the time of the treaty's conclusion.[110] Thereby, it deduced the relevant term's generic character also from the "nature of the word 'status' itself"[111] rather than only from the parties' clear-cut intention.[112]

The earlier *Namibia Advisory Opinion* of 1971 illustrates the extent to which the Court was willing to base its interpretation on the presumed generic meaning of a term rather than on the obvious intentions of the parties.[113] After confirming contemporaneity as the default rule,[114] the Court explicitly stated as an alternative that "the fact that the concepts [...] were not static, but were by definition evolutionary" had to be taken into account.[115] It understood the relevant terms to be evolutionary in nature, which is why the parties "must consequently be deemed to

[104] ICJ, *Aegean Sea Continental Shelf Case (Greece v. Turkey),* Judgment, 19 December 1978, ICJ Reports 1978, 3, para. 77.

[105] Akhtar-Khavari (2003), paras. 18–20; Inagaki (2015), pp. 135–137; Merkouris (2015), p. 143, fn. 124. In so far, there are parallels to the VCLT's approach in order to assess the parties' presumed intention: ILC (2018), Conclusion 8.

[106] See Fitzmaurice (2008), p. 106 with reference to Thirlway (1990), p. 135.

[107] Merkouris (2015), p. 144. For some examples of the latter, see already *supra* notes 41–46.

[108] Bjorge (2014), pp. 76–139 with further references.

[109] Ibid., p. 139.

[110] Elias (1980), pp. 296–301; ILC (2018), Conclusion 8 para. 11.

[111] *Aegean Sea Continental Shelf* (Judgment), *supra* note 104, para. 75.

[112] Akhtar-Khavari (2003), para. 21.

[113] Generally on the ICJ's practice between static and evolutionary treaty interpretation, see Djeffal (2015), pp. 214–271.

[114] Critical, see Bjorge (2014), pp. 123–125.

[115] ICJ, *Legal Consequences for States of the Continued Presence of South Africa in Namibia (South West Africa) notwithstanding Security Council Resolution 276 (1970),* Advisory Opinion, 21 June 1971, ICJ Reports 1971, 16, para. 53. See also ILC (2006), para. 478 (at footnote 678).

have accepted them as such".[116] Additionally, it stated that "an international instrument has to be interpreted and applied within the framework of the entire legal system prevailing at the time of the interpretation".[117] While some commentators welcomed this progressive kind of generic term interpretation beyond the parties' primary intention,[118] others heavily criticised the Court for departing from the original intention approach.[119] *Panos Merkouris* argued that the generic term approach must eventually be based on the intention of the parties.[120]

Generally, international judicial bodies have taken a flexible approach in using different means of interpretation for the assessment of the parties' intention, or what the respective body considered to be their *presumed* intention.[121] Several other decisions of the ICJ[122] as well as of other courts and tribunals[123] have regularly referred to a term's generic nature in its interpretation.[124] The evolutionary character of generic term interpretation can thus be understood as an approach that is ostensibly based on the parties' original intention, but which often recurs to the presumed

---

[116] *Namibia* (Advisory Opinion), *supra* note 115, para. 53. According to *Eirik Bjorge*, this finding was based on the principle of good faith, see Bjorge (2014), p. 75.

[117] *Namibia* (Advisory Opinion), *supra* note 115, para. 53.

[118] McWhinney (1984), p. 199. This endorsement followed, *inter alia*, from a more criticised precedent ruling of the Court on a similar matter: *South West Africa, Second Phase* (Judgment), *supra* note 42. See McWhinney (1984), pp. 184–185. In a dissenting opinion to this earlier judgment, *Judge Tanaka* already proposed a dynamic interpretation of the relevant obligations, see ICJ, *South West Africa, Second Phase (Ethiopia v. South Africa; Liberia v. South Africa),* Dissenting Opinion of Judge Tanaka, 18 July 1966, ICJ Reports 1966, 250, pp. 293–294. See also *infra* note 135.

[119] ICJ, *Legal Consequences for States of the Continued Presence of South Africa in Namibia (South West Africa) notwithstanding Security Council Resolution 276 (1970),* Dissenting Opinion of Judge Gerald Fitzmaurice, 21 June 1971, ICJ Reports 1971, 220, para. 85; *Kasikili/Sedudu Island* (Declaration of Judge Higgins), *supra* note 103, para. 4; ICJ, *Dispute regarding Navigational and Related Rights (Costa Rica v. Nicaragua),* Separate Opinion of Judge Skotnikov, 13 July 2009, ICJ Reports 2009, 283, paras. 5–6; Thirlway (1990), pp. 136–137; French (2006), p. 300. See also Akhtar-Khavari (2003), paras. 27–29; M. Fitzmaurice (2008), p. 118; Tanaka (2013), pp. 153, 159.

[120] Merkouris (2015), pp. 141–144. See also Bjorge (2014), pp. 127–130.

[121] Dupuy (2011), pp. 130–131.

[122] *Navigational and Related Rights* (Judgment), *supra* note 42, paras. 64–70; ICJ, *Pulp Mills on the River Uruguay (Argentina v. Uruguay),* Judgment, 20 April 2010, ICJ Reports 2010, 14, para. 204.

[123] World Trade Organization Appellate Body, *United States – Import Prohibition of Certain Shrimp and Shrimp Products,* Report of the Appellate Body, 12 October 1998, WTO Doc. WT/DS58/AB/R, paras. 127–130; PCA, *Award in the Arbitration regarding the Iron Rhine ("Ijzeren Rijn") Railway between the Kingdom of Belgium and the Kingdom of the Netherlands,* Arbitral Award, 24 May 2005, RIAA XXVII (2005), 35, para. 79; WTO Appellate Body, *China – Measures Affecting Trading Rights and Distribution Services for Certain Publications and Audiovisual Entertainment Products,* Report of the Appellate Body, 21 December 2009, WTO Doc. WT/DS363/AB/R, para. 369 (at footnote 681); International Tribunal for the Law of the Sea, *Responsibilities and obligations of States sponsoring persons and entities with respect to activities in the Area (Request for Advisory Opinion submitted to the Seabed Disputes Chamber),* Advisory Opinion, 1 February 2011, ITLOS Reports 2011, 10, paras. 117, 211.

[124] ILC (2018), Conclusion 8 paras. 11–12; Inagaki (2015), pp. 135–137.

intention as understood by the respective judicial body. Although this seems arbitrary and subject to the body's judicial discretion, it eventually is in accordance with the ILC's findings in its Draft Conclusion 8:

> [B]y using the phrase 'presumed intention', [draft conclusion 8] refers to the intention of the parties as determined through the application of the various means of interpretation [in Articles 31, 32 of the VCLT]. The 'presumed intention' is thus not a separately identifiable original will, and the *travaux préparatoires* are not the primary basis for determining the presumed intention of the parties [...]. And although interpretation must seek to identify the intention of the parties, this must be done by the interpreter on the basis of the means of interpretation that are available at the time of the act of interpretation and that include subsequent agreements and subsequent practice of parties to the treaty. The interpreter thus has to answer the question of whether parties can be presumed to have intended, upon the conclusion of the treaty, to give a term used a meaning that is capable of evolving over time.[125]

Overall, it becomes clear that evolutionary interpretation is often "inexorably linked to the objectivized intention of the parties".[126] For the purpose of the present analysis, it is not necessary to decide whether the original (presumed) intention is always the decisive factor or whether the following form of evolutionary interpretation constitutes an alternative approach. In any case, a second branch of jurisprudence has evolved on the issue of evolutionary interpretation. It focuses primarily on a treaty's object and purpose, which is assessed in more detail in the following sub-section.

### *6.2.3 Evolutionary Interpretation Based on a Treaty's Object and Purpose*

In some cases, the respective treaty's object and purpose has apparently played a more important role than the original intention of the parties.[127] Some commentators, for instance *Rosalyn Higgins*, rejected the stand-alone relevance of object and purpose and underlined the interplay of the different means of interpretation as "an application of a wider principle – intention of the parties, reflected by reference to the objects and purpose – that guides the law of treaties".[128] In the *RosInvest* jurisdiction award, the arbitral tribunal stated that human rights treaties "represent the very archetype of treaty instruments in which the Contracting Parties must have intended that the principles and concepts which they employed should be understood and

[125] ILC (2018), Conclusion 8 para. 9. See also Fitzmaurice (2020), pp. 26–27.

[126] Bjorge (2014), p. 139. who considered that this was always the case.

[127] French (2006), pp. 298–300; M. Fitzmaurice (2008), p. 117; Tanaka (2013), pp. 154–156; Inagaki (2015), pp. 137–139; Crawford and Brownlie (2019), pp. 365–366.

[128] Higgins (1996), p. 181. See also Bjorge (2014), pp. 118–120; Merkouris (2015), pp. 140–141; Arato (2018), pp. 212–215; Bjorge (2018).

applied in the light of developing social attitudes".[129] However, this coexistence is not always as harmonious, since a treaty's object and purpose may often develop independently from, or even contrary to,[130] the original intention.[131] *Matthias Herdegen* observed that "the teleological interpretation may easily become the vehicle for a dynamic interpretation of an agreement, which departs from the subjective intent of the parties".[132] Therefore, the evolutionary generic term interpretation can be distinguished from an approach, which is primarily based on the object and purpose, regardless of the parties' intention.[133]

For instance, the arbitral tribunal in the *Iron Rhine Railway* case took a teleological[134] approach when it stated that an "evolutive interpretation, which would ensure an application of the treaty that would be effective in terms of its object and purpose, will be preferred to a strict application of the intertemporal rule".[135] In his dissenting opinion to the *South West Africa* decision in 1966, *Judge Tanaka* already proposed an evolutionary interpretation, as he based his reasoning regarding South Africa's obligations on the fact that "the main purposes of the mandate system are ethical and humanitarian".[136] Even the Court's aforementioned *Namibia Advisory Opinion*[137] could fit into this category of treaties, which benefit from an evolutionary interpretation based on their object and purpose,[138] although this advisory opinion was often considered to follow a generic term approach. This last case illustrates that the boundaries are fluid between a purely teleological interpretation and a progressive generic term approach based on the parties' presumed intention.[139]

Some commentators suggested differentiating between the object and purpose of different *types* of treaties.[140] They distinguished between, on the one hand, limited bilateral treaties and, on the other hand, multilateral law-making or normative

[129] Arbitral Tribunal, *RosInvestCo UK Ltd. v. The Russian Federation,* Award on Jurisdiction, 1 October 2007, retrieved 3 January 2025, from https://www.italaw.com/sites/default/files/case-documents/ita0719.pdf, para. 39.

[130] Arato (2018), p. 207.

[131] See Sinclair (1984), p. 131; Fitzmaurice (2008), p. 132; Nolte (2020), pp. 6–7.

[132] Herdegen (2020), paras. 14–15.

[133] In contrast to this, *Eirik Bjorge* argued that all interpretation rules of the VCLT eventually serve the establishment of the parties' presumed or objectified intention, see Bjorge (2014), pp. 76–139; Bjorge (2018), pp. 203–204. Cf. also *RosInvest* (Award on Jurisdiction), *supra* note 129, para. 39.

[134] On the nuances between "teleological interpretation", "effectiveness" and "dynamic interpretation", see M. Fitzmaurice (2008), pp. 113–117; Klabbers (2006), paras. 17–20.

[135] *Iron Rhine Railway* (Arbitral Award), *supra* note 123, para. 80. See also Inagaki (2015), p. 137; Nolte (2020), p. 6. By "strict application of the intertemporal rule", the arbitral tribunal is referring to the principle of contemporaneity.

[136] *South West Africa, Second Phase* (Dissenting Opinion of Judge Tanaka), *supra* note 118, p. 294. Cf. also Arato (2018), pp. 209–210.

[137] *Namibia* (Advisory Opinion), *supra* note 115.

[138] Akhtar-Khavari (2003), paras. 25–26.

[139] See *supra* notes 118. Cf. also ILC (2006), para. 478.

[140] Herdegen (2020), para. 40.

treaties.[141] This suggestion was also reflected in *Gerald Fitzmaurice's* distinction between reciprocal (bilateral and multilateral) treaties and treaties with a "more absolute type of obligation", namely "integral" and "interdependent" treaties.[142] While the interpretation of reciprocal treaties would be more strictly limited by the parties' original intention and would often rely on contemporaneous interpretation, normative treaties would be more likely to be open to evolutionary interpretation due to their object and purpose.[143] These normative treaties would include constitutive instruments of international organisations[144] as well as human rights treaties.[145] As this differentiation was criticised as unfeasible,[146] it was neither taken up in the VCLT[147] nor by the ILC in recent codification attempts.[148] The present book addresses the criticism of this differentiation and a more fitting distinction, formulated by *Julian Arato*, in more detail below.[149] Regardless of the appropriateness of this differentiation, the analysis of the following case law illustrates that human rights treaties constitute a specific field of application for evolutionary interpretation based on the object and purpose.[150]

As the first human rights body, the ECtHR already stipulated in 1978 that the ECHR "comprises more than mere reciprocal engagements between contracting States".[151] The ECHR would rather create "over and above a network of mutual, bilateral undertakings, objective obligations".[152] This alleged special nature of human rights treaties[153] led the ECtHR in its *Tyrer v. UK* decision of 1978 to recall that the ECHR is a "living instrument" and would consequently be open to interpretation under present-day conditions.[154] This living instrument approach is now

[141] As to a comparable distinction, see Arato (2018), pp. 217–226.

[142] ILC (1958), para. 91. See also ILC (2006), para. 262.

[143] ILC (1964a), p. 36, para. 20; Sørensen (1973), pp. 15–16; Baade (1957), pp. 247–248; McWhinney (1984), p. 198; Bernhardt (1999), pp. 16–17, 21; M. Fitzmaurice (2008), pp. 117–118, 120; Dupuy (2011), pp. 131–132; Kolb (2016), pp. 158–165.

[144] Dupuy (2011), p. 133; Merkouris (2015), pp. 139–141; Herdegen (2020), paras. 41–44.

[145] Bernhardt (1999), pp. 16–17, 21–22; Herdegen (2020), paras. 45–46.

[146] See already Sørensen (1973), p. 16.

[147] See Crawford and Keene (2020), p. 938.

[148] ILC (2018), Conclusion 2 para. 15. See also Hamamoto (2020), pp. 76–77.

[149] See *infra* notes 252–261.

[150] ILC (2013), para. 63. In more detail, see also Crawford and Keene (2020), pp. 942–944. On the evolutionary character of human rights law, see already *supra* in Sect. 5.2.2. On the importance of the object and purpose for human rights jurisprudence, see Villiger (2009), Art. 31 para. 11.

[151] European Court of Human Rights, *Republic of Ireland v. the United Kingdom,* Judgment, 18 January 1978, Reports of Judgments and Decisions Series A no. 25, para. 239. In detail on the role of the ECtHR in evolutionary interpretation, see Djeffal (2015), pp. 272–342.

[152] *Ireland v. UK* (Judgment), *supra* note 151, para. 239. See also Nolte (2013a), pp. 244–245.

[153] Ibid., p. 302; Dörr (2018), para. 26. Critical of such a subject matter distinction, see Arato (2018), pp. 209–212; Christoffersen (2009), p. 61; in more detail *supra* in Sect. 6.2.4.2.

[154] ECtHR, *Case of Tyrer v. The United Kingdom,* Judgment, 25 April 1978, ECHR Series A no. 26, para. 31.

settled in the case law of the ECtHR[155]; it is not primarily based on the treaty parties' original intention.[156] Further, it differs from traditional approaches to interpretation by treating the whole Convention as a living instrument instead of focusing on specific treaty terms.[157]

For this reason, some commentators argued that the specialised interpretation regime of the ECHR differed from the general interpretation rules of the VCLT,[158] or that the ECtHR has at least partly developed more specific rules of interpretation beyond the VCLT.[159] Other commentators understood the general VCLT regime to be flexible and loose enough to encompass particular interpretation practices of specific treaty regimes.[160] The ECtHR often started with the general means of interpretation in the VCLT.[161] As *Georg Nolte* observed, none of the regional human rights tribunals "call[ed] into question the applicability of Article 31 of the VCLT as a point of departure and framework for their treaty interpretation".[162] However, certain particularities of genuine ECtHR jurisprudence exist in the context of its evolutionary interpretation approach.[163] When the ECtHR took into account subsequent developments after the conclusion of the Convention,[164] it did *not* limit these developments to those enshrined in Article 31(3) of the VCLT.[165] Instead, it referred to a broader variety of subsequent developments in law and practice.[166] This included developments of law beyond the scope of application between the decisive

---

[155] ECtHR, *Marckx v. Belgium,* Judgment, 13 June 1979, ECHR Series A no. 31, para. 41; ECtHR, *Case of Powell and Rayner v. the United Kingdom,* Judgment, 21 February 1990, ECHR Series A no. 172; ECtHR, *Case of Loizidou v. Turkey (Preliminary Objections),* Judgment, 23 March 1995, ECHR Series A no. 310, paras. 71–74; ECtHR, *Case of Christine Goodwin v. the United Kingdom,* Judgment, 11 July 2002, ECHR 2002-VI 1, para. 74; ECtHR, *Demir and Baykara v. Turkey,* Grand Chamber Judgment, 12 November 2008, ECHR 2008-V 333, para. 67. Critical of this expansive interpretation of human rights treaties, see Melchem (2009), pp. 945–946.

[156] M. Fitzmaurice (2008), p. 132; Inagaki (2015), p. 138; Nolte (2020), pp. 6–7.

[157] M. Fitzmaurice (2008), p. 121; Dörr (2018), para. 26. As to this "holistic approach", see, e.g., Fitzmaurice (2008), pp. 152–153.

[158] Craven (2000), p. 491; Letsas (2010), pp. 512, 514.

[159] Sinclair (1984), pp. 131–133; Cançado Trindade (2003), pp. 5–7; Fitzmaurice (2008), pp. 121–122, 151–152; Nolte (2013a), pp. 266–268.

[160] Killander (2010), pp. 146–150; Djeffal (2019), pp. 28, 31; Gardiner (2020), p. 486; Çali (2020), p. 505. Cf. also Arato (2012), p. 382; Crawford and Keene (2020), p. 940; Ulfstein (2020), p. 928.

[161] ECtHR, *Case of Golder v. the United Kingdom,* Judgment, 21 February 1975, ECHR Series A no. 18, paras. 29–36. See also ILC (2018), Conclusion 8 para. 14; Ulfstein (2020), pp. 918–919.

[162] Nolte (2013a), p. 302, Conclusion 2.

[163] Crawford and Keene (2020), pp. 942–944.

[164] Such subsequent circumstances can contain evolutions of law as well as evolutions of fact, see Merkouris (2015), pp. 132–133.

[165] Inagaki (2015), pp. 139–144. For a more restrictive approach, see *OSPAR Convention* (Final Award), *supra* note 87, paras. 101–103.

[166] Nolte (2013a), pp. 266–268. See also Ulfstein (2020), pp. 920–922. *Osamu Inagaki* pointed out that supplementary means of interpretation (Article 32 of the VCLT) could only become relevant under restrictive conditions, see Inagaki (2015), p. 143.

State parties.[167] The latter is generally not encompassed by Article 31(3) of the VCLT,[168] although some commentators considered the provision in a less restrictive way and argued that it allows the inclusion of law applicable only between some of the State parties.[169] In any case, it can be concluded that the ECtHR evolutionary approach "represents a step beyond the broadest construction generally put forth" of Article 31(3)(c) of the VCLT.[170]

The ECtHR's case law on evolutionary interpretation was met with criticism for deviating from the general rules of treaty interpretation.[171] For instance, *Geir Ulfstein* criticised that the ECtHR did not "distinguish clearly between evolutive interpretation based on Article 31(1), i.e. on the ECHR's object and purpose, and, on the other hand, such interpretation based on Article 31(3)(b) and 31(3)(c) [of the VCLT]".[172] *Christian Djeffal* offered a detailed set of variables, which illustrate ways of limiting and enhancing static or evolutive interpretations in ECtHR cases.[173] Despite this criticism, other human rights bodies have applied a comparably broad living instrument approach to their respective human rights treaties.[174] For instance, the HRC in *Judge v. Canada* stated that "the Covenant should be interpreted as a living instrument and the rights protected under it should be applied in context and in the light of present-day conditions."[175] The IACHR referred to the precedent jurisprudence of the ECtHR and clarified on several occasions:

> [H]uman rights treaties are living instruments whose interpretation must consider the changes over time and present-day conditions. [...] This Court, therefore, must adopt the proper approach to consider this question in the context of the evolution of the fundamental rights of the human person in contemporary international law.[176]

---

[167] See, e.g., *Marckx v. Belgium* (Judgment), *supra* note 155, para. 41; *Demir v. Turkey* (Grand Chamber Judgment), *supra* note 155, paras. 67, 103. See also Inagaki (2015), pp. 139–143. On the case law of the IACHR, cf. Merkouris (2015), p. 146 (at footnote 140).

[168] See Villiger (2009), Art. 31 paras. 15, 25; Inagaki (2015), pp. 141–142.

[169] See French (2006), p. 307; Dörr (2018), paras. 103–104.

[170] Arato (2012), p. 378. In more detail on the different understandings of Article 31(3)(c) of the VCLT, see ibid., pp. 377–382.

[171] ECtHR, *Case of National Union of Belgian Police v. Belgium,* Separate Opinion of Judge Sir Gerald Fitzmaurice, 27 October 1975, Reports of Judgments and Decisions Series A no. 19, para. 9; Fitzmaurice (1957), p. 208; Sinclair (1984), pp. 131–133; Warbrick (1990), p. 1080. Generally, on the relationship between evolutionary interpretation and Articles 31, 32 of the VCLT, see *supra* notes 89–91.

[172] Ulfstein (2020), p. 928.

[173] Djeffal (2015), pp. 338–342.

[174] ILC (2018), Conclusion 8 paras. 15–16; Merkouris (2015), p. 146 with further references.

[175] Human Rights Committee, *Roger Judge v. Canada,* Communication, 13 August 2003, UN Doc. CCPR/C/78/D/829/1998, para. 10.3.

[176] Inter-American Court of Human Rights, *The Right to Information on Consular Assistance in the Framework of the Guarantees of the Due Process of Law (Requested by the United Mexican States),* Advisory Opinion, 1 October 1999, OEA Series A No. 16, paras. 114–115. See also IACHR, *Juan Humberto Sánchez v. Honduras (Interpretation of the Judgment of Preliminary Objection, Merits, Reparations and Costs),* Judgment, 26 November 2003, OEA Series C No. 102, para. 56; IACHR,

In its 2017 Advisory Opinion on *The Environment and Human Rights*, the IACHR used this evolutionary approach to clarify that it must take into account "the principles, rights and obligations of international environmental law", which are part of the international *corpus iuris*, when interpreting the Inter-American human rights norms.[177] Interestingly, the IACHR explicitly stated that it considered this evolutionary approach to be "consequent with the general rules of interpretation [...] established by the [VCLT]".[178]

Ultimately, the scarce case law of the ICJ on human rights treaties does not offer more insight into the relationship between evolutionary interpretation and the VCLT.[179] While *James Crawford* and *Amelia Keene* argued that the ICJ "employs interpretive techniques seen in the human rights context as part of its arsenal for general interpretation",[180] the relevant case law is rather based on generic term interpretation.[181] The only potential (but implicit) exceptions, the *South West Africa* decision and the *Namibia Advisory Opinion*, have been assessed above.[182]

Regardless of whether one considers the human rights related cases to fall within the scope of Articles 31 and 32 of the VCLT or whether they constitute a more specific regime of treaty interpretation, the foregoing section has illustrated that the evolutionary approach differs from the generic term approach. While the latter is based primarily on the parties' original intention with regard to specific treaty *terms*, the former focuses on the treaty's object and purpose *as a whole*. The respective human rights bodies based their evolutionary living instrument interpretation on the allegedly normative or law-making character of human rights treaties. The following section now turns to another kind of multilateral treaty, namely environmental treaties, and assesses whether the existing case law allows for a comparable evolutionary approach.

---

*Case of the Ituango Massacres v. Colombia (Preliminary Objections, Merits, Reparations and Costs),* Judgment, 1 July 2006, retrieved 3 January 2025, from https://www.corteidh.or.cr/docs/casos/articulos/seriec_148_ing.pdf, para. 157; Arévalo Narváez and Patarroyo Ramírez (2016). For further references, see ILC (2018), Conclusion 8 para. 15; Merkouris (2015), p. 146 (at footnotes 135, 139).

[177] IACHR, *The Environment and Human Rights (Requested by the Republic of Colombia),* Advisory Opinion, 15 November 2017, retrieved 3 January 2025, from https://www.corteidh.or.cr/docs/opiniones/seriea_23_ing.pdf, para. 55. See also Mileva and Fortuna (2019), p. 134.

[178] *The Environment and Human Rights* (Advisory Opinion), *supra* note 177, para. 43. See already *The Right to Information on Consular Assistance* (Advisory Opinion), *supra* note 176, para. 114.

[179] For an overview, see Crawford and Keene (2020), pp. 940–942.

[180] Ibid., p. 947.

[181] See *supra* note 110 and *infra* in Sect. 7.2.2.1 [note 44] on *Aegean Sea Continental Shelf* (Judgment), *supra* note 104, paras. 75, 77.; *supra* notes 88, 121 on *Navigational and Related Rights* (Judgment), *supra* note 42, paras. 64–70.; *infra* notes 189–195 on *Pulp Mills* (Judgment), *supra* note 122. On the exception of the *Whaling in the Antarctic* case, see *infra* notes 202–207.

[182] See *supra* notes 135–138.

### 6.2.4 International Environmental Law as Subject Matter Reason for Evolutionary Interpretation?

Parallel to the aforementioned evolutionary approaches to treaty interpretation, some commentators have suggested forms of evolutionary interpretation for other regimes of international law. According to these approaches, the allegedly special nature of certain substantive treaty regimes requires the interpretation of these treaties in an evolutionary manner. This "subject matter" approach to evolutionary interpretation has already been briefly indicated above, but only with regard to human rights treaties.[183] It is also discussed in regard to environmental treaties.[184] *Nina Mileva* and *Marina Fortuna* took a comparable perspective when they analysed "environmental protection as an object of evolutionary interpretation".[185] In this context, the next sub-sections refer to the evolutionary approaches to environmental treaties, understood broadly as all treaties that include issues concerning the protection of the environment.[186] First, the existing case law on these evolutionary approaches is presented (Sect. 6.2.4.1). Second, it is assessed whether and how far these cases establish a new kind of evolutionary approach (Sect. 6.2.4.2). This analysis is decisive for the adaptation of intertemporal law to the environmental[187] concept of intergenerational equity.[188]

#### 6.2.4.1 Existing Case Law

In 2010, the ICJ issued the *Pulp Mills* decision, which addressed matters of international environmental law and contained important elements of evolutionary interpretation.[189] The Court had to interpret several environmental provisions in a treaty between Argentina and Uruguay on the rational utilisation of parts of the Uruguay River, *inter alia*, the parties' obligation "to protect and preserve the aquatic environment".[190] In this decision, the Court referred to its precedent case law on

---

[183] See *supra* notes 139–144.

[184] See, e.g., ILC (2006), p. 250.

[185] Mileva and Fortuna (2019), pp. 125–129. Their second research perspective turned to "environmental protection as a tool for evolutionary interpretation", see ibid., pp. 129–136, which partly correlates with the aforementioned human rights case law in the context of environmental protection, see *supra* note 176.

[186] See Tanaka (2010), p. 113; Mileva and Fortuna (2019).

[187] As demonstrated in detail above, the present book focuses on the environmental aspects of intergenerational equity, see *supra* in Sect. 2.2.1.1.

[188] See *infra* in Sect. 7.3.1.2.2.

[189] On this decision, see already *supra* in Sect. 4.1.2.

[190] See *Statute of the River Uruguay between the Government of the Eastern Republic of Uruguay and the Government of the Argentine Republic* (1975 Statute of the River Uruguay), adopted 26 February 1975, entered into force 18 September 1976, 1295 UNTS 331, Art. 41.

evolutionary interpretation,[191] particularly to the *Navigational and Related Rights* case, which was based on "the parties' intent upon conclusion of the treaty […] to give the terms used – or some of them – a meaning or content capable of evolving […]".[192] This evolutionary approach in the *Pulp Mills* decision thus built on the generic (i.e., evolutionary) meaning of the terms "obligation to protect and preserve".[193] Beyond this, *Judge Cançado Trindade's* separate opinion could be understood to suggest a subject matter evolutionary approach to the interpretation of environmental treaties.[194] *Mileva* and *Fortuna* also deduced from this decision that environmental protection would *per se* constitute "an object of evolutionary interpretation resulting from the evolution of law".[195] Yet, the Court itself remained silent on this topic.[196]

Comparably, the WTO Appellate Body's report on *Certain Shrimp and Shrimp Products* noted that "the generic term 'natural resources' in [the relevant provision] is not static in its content or reference but is rather 'by definition, evolutionary'".[197] The Appellate Body also referred to two ICJ cases that followed the generic term's evolutionary interpretation.[198] In contrast to *Pulp Mills*, this decision did not address a genuinely environmental treaty, but concerned a WTO trade dispute. However, the WTO Agreement's "objective of sustainable development"[199] transformed the genuine trade dispute into an environmental dispute on sustainable development,[200] so that one could also assume a subject matter-based evolutionary approach. At the same time, this specific case illustrates some of the difficulties of the subject matter approach, as demonstrated below.[201]

---

[191] *Pulp Mills* (Judgment), *supra* note 122, para. 204. See *supra* note 121.

[192] *Navigational and Related Rights* (Judgment), *supra* note 42, para. 64.

[193] *Pulp Mills* (Judgment), *supra* note 122, para. 204.

[194] ICJ, *Pulp Mills on the River Uruguay (Argentina v. Uruguay),* Separate Opinion of Judge Cançado Trindade, 20 April 2010, ICJ Reports 2010, 125, paras. 115–119. See also Arato (2018), pp. 207, 210.

[195] Mileva and Fortuna (2019), p. 127. They also elaborated on the evolutionary interpretation the ICJ would have reaffirmed in ICJ, *Certain Activities Carried Out by Nicaragua in the Border Area (Costa Rica v. Nicaragua) and Construction of a Road in Costa Rica along the San Juan River (Nicaragua v. Costa Rica),* Judgment, 16 December 2015, ICJ Reports 2015, 665, para. 104. see Mileva and Fortuna (2019), pp. 128–129.

[196] Cf. *Pulp Mills* (Separate Opinion of Judge Cançado Trindade), *supra* note 194, para. 116.

[197] *Certain Shrimp and Shrimp Products* (Report of the Appellate Body), *supra* note 123, para. 130. See also *supra* note 122.

[198] See references in ibid., 130 (at footnote 109). to *Namibia* (Dissenting Opinion of Judge Gerald Fitzmaurice), *supra* note 119; *Aegean Sea Continental Shelf* (Judgment), *supra* note 104.

[199] *Agreement Establishing the World Trade Organization* (WTO Agreement), adopted 15 April 1994, entered into force 1 January 1995, 33 ILM 1125, Preamble.

[200] Mbengue (2020), pp. 174–175.

[201] In detail, see *infra* in Sect. 6.2.4.2.

The *Whaling in the Antarctic* case from 2014 offered another example for a dispute based on an environmental treaty, the Whaling Convention.[202] The ICJ judgment did not dwell in detail on the question of evolutionary interpretation, it only observed that "[t]he functions conferred on the [International Whaling] Commission have made the Convention an evolving instrument".[203] At the same time, the Court rejected Australia's argument that the Whaling Convention would have evolved from a resource management system to an "increasingly conservation-oriented system".[204] *Yoshifumi Tanaka* concluded that the ICJ, on the one hand, seemingly rejected characterising the convention as a treaty on environmental protection, but on the other hand, put much weight on the conservation aspect, so that it accepted a "*de facto* transformation of the [Whaling Convention] into an environmental protection treaty".[205] Again, *Judge Cançado Trindade* elaborated further on the evolutionary character of the Whaling Convention in a whole section of his separate opinion.[206] He referred to the variety of international case law on evolutionary treaty interpretation,[207] and he suggested that the application and interpretation of the Whaling Convention by the majority judgment illustrated the convention's character as a "living instrument".[208] This evolving character would even have caused "with the passing of time, a move towards conservation of living marine resources as a common interest".[209] This would mean that the evolving character has led to a transformation of the Whaling Convention into an environmental treaty over time.[210] Overall, this analysis of the *Whaling in the Antarctic* case points to an evolutionary approach based on the relevant treaty's object and purpose as a whole instead of specific treaty provisions.

Finally, it is the ICJ's *Gabčíkovo-Nagymaros Project* case that constitutes the exemplary case for evolutionary interpretation of a treaty with direct links to environmental protection.[211] While the *Gabčíkovo-Nagymaros Project* decision has already been examined in this book regarding its implications for sustainable development and intergenerational equity,[212] this section focuses on the Court's

[202] *International Convention for the Regulation of Whaling* (Whaling Convention), adopted 2 December 1946, entered into force 10 November 1948, 161 UNTS 72. See already *supra* in Sect. 5.3.3.2.2.

[203] ICJ, *Whaling in the Antarctic (Australia v. Japan: New Zealand intervening),* Judgment, 31 March 2014, ICJ Reports 2014, 226, para. 45.

[204] See Tanaka (2018), p. 538.

[205] Ibid. See also Sakai (2016), pp. 317–318.

[206] ICJ, *Whaling in the Antarctic (Australia v. Japan: New Zealand intervening),* Separate Opinion of Judge Cançado Trindade, 31 March 2014, ICJ Reports 2014, 348, paras. 27–40.

[207] Ibid., paras. 29–32.

[208] Ibid., paras. 28, 33–37.

[209] Ibid., para. 71.

[210] See Tanaka (2018), p. 538 (at footnote 62).

[211] See, e.g., de Castro (1997), p. 26; Akhtar-Khavari (2003).

[212] See *supra* in Sects. 2.1.2, 4.1.2 and 4.2.2.

findings on treaty law and inter-temporality.[213] The Court had to consider Hungary's various arguments for its unilateral termination of the 1977 Treaty between Czech-oslovakia and Hungary.[214] Articles 15, 19 and 20 of said treaty were of particular relevance for the Court's assessment, as they provided for the protection of the water quality, the natural environment and fishing interests.[215] The ICJ examined whether Hungary was allowed to unilaterally terminate its treaty obligations and it found, *inter alia*, that "[b]y inserting these evolving provisions in the Treaty, the parties recognized the potential necessity to adapt the Project. Consequently, the Treaty is not static, and is open to adapt to emerging norms of international law."[216] The Court drew a comparable conclusion in regard to Hungary's allegations on a fundamental change of circumstances within the meaning of Article 62 of the VCLT:

> [N]ew developments in the state of environmental knowledge and of environmental law can [not] be said to have been completely unforeseen. […] [T]he formulation of Articles 15, 19 and 20 […] made it possible for the parties to take account of such developments and to apply them when implementing those treaty provisions.[217]

While the decision is often considered to be another example of the Court's approach to evolutionary interpretation, no consensus exists with regard to the exact foundation of the Court's approach.[218] It is not clear whether the Court adopted a form of generic term interpretation by considering the parties' presumed intention on the provisions in question, or whether it based its findings primarily on the object and purpose and particular nature of treaties addressing environmental issues.[219] *Mileva* and *Fortuna* argued that the decision "stands at the beginning of a sequence of interpretative episodes by the ICJ […] through the practice of evolutionary interpretation".[220]

When the Court referred to the "[not] completely unforeseen" developments of environmental knowledge and law,[221] and to the fact that the "parties recognized the potential necessity to adapt the project",[222] it implied a certain connection to the

---

[213] ICJ, *Gabčíkovo-Nagymaros Project (Hungary v. Slovakia),* Judgment, 25 September 1997, ICJ Reports 1997, 7, paras. 104, 111–115.

[214] *Treaty between the Hungarian People's Republic and the Czechoslovak Socialist Republic concerning the Construction and Operation of the Gabčíkovo-Nagymaros System of Locks* (1977 Treaty concerning the Gabčíkovo-Nagymaros System), entered into force 16 September 1977, 32 ILM 1247. On Hungary's argumentation, see *Gabčíkovo-Nagymaros Project* (Judgment), *supra* note 213, para. 92.

[215] Ibid., para. 18.

[216] Ibid., para. 112. Cf. Boyle (1997), p. 15.

[217] *Gabčíkovo-Nagymaros Project* (Judgment), *supra* note 213, para. 104.

[218] Stec and Eckstein (1997), pp. 47–48; Tanaka (2010), pp. 121–124; Tanzi (2020), pp. 234–237.

[219] M. Fitzmaurice (2008), pp. 108–111; Tanaka (2013), pp. 143–147. There are many more unclear issues concerning the consequences of such an evolutionary interpretation, see ibid., pp. 158–160.

[220] Mileva and Fortuna (2019), p. 126.

[221] *Gabčíkovo-Nagymaros Project* (Judgment), *supra* note 213, para. 104.

[222] Ibid., para. 112.

parties' original intention at the time of the conclusion of the treaty.[223] *Duncan French* noted that the Court's "implicit presumption is that, in light of the current importance placed upon environmental considerations, the parties could *not* have intended such obligations *not* to hold such a meaning" (emphasis in the original).[224] Similarly, two separate opinions emphasised that the parties' intentions can be presumed to have envisaged an evolutionary understanding of the relevant terms.[225] Therefore, the Court's decision was often considered to be part of its established jurisprudence on the evolutionary character of generic terms.[226] The terms "protection of nature", "quality of the water" and "fishing interests" would constitute said generic terms, which hence "made it possible for the parties to take account of such developments[...]".[227]

However, the ICJ did not thoroughly examine the parties' intention with regard to the relevant treaty provisions,[228] but instead based its reasoning on a mere presumption of these intentions as well as the terms' general evolutionary nature.[229] This is in line with the progressive approach to evolutionary interpretation based on the parties' presumed intention, which the Court already took in the aforementioned *Namibia Advisory Opinion*.[230]

Apart from the generic term approach, the Court's findings on the evolutionary interpretation of the 1977 Treaty could also be assessed from a teleological perspective, that means based on the treaty's object and purpose in general.[231] *Judge Weeramantry* examined the intertemporal aspects of the case in more detail in his separate opinion,[232] which arguably offers more insight into the legal reasoning behind the judgment.[233] It is noteworthy that *Weeramantry* found the VCLT to "offer very little guidance regarding this matter" since Article 31(3)(c) of the VCLT "scarcely covers this aspect with the degree of clarity requisite to so important a matter".[234] Further, he commented that the evolutionary approach in the majority

---

[223] French (2006), p. 297; Dupuy (2011), p. 130; Inagaki (2015), pp. 135–136.

[224] French (2006), p. 297.

[225] *Gabčíkovo-Nagymaros Project* (Separate Opinion of Vice-President Weeramantry), *supra* note 90, p. 113; *Gabčíkovo-Nagymaros Project* (Separate Opinion of Judge Bedjaoui), *supra* note 91, paras. 8, 17.

[226] Stec and Eckstein (1997), p. 48; Akhtar-Khavari (2003), para. 42.

[227] *Gabčíkovo-Nagymaros Project* (Judgment), *supra* note 213, para. 104.

[228] French (2006), p. 296; Tanaka (2013), p. 148.

[229] Akhtar-Khavari (2003), paras. 43–44 with reference to *Gabčíkovo-Nagymaros Project* (Judgment), *supra* note 213, para. 112. Cf. also de Castro (1997), p. 26.

[230] See *supra* notes 114–118.

[231] ILC (2006), para. 478 (at footnote 680); de Castro (1997), p. 26.

[232] *Gabčíkovo-Nagymaros Project* (Separate Opinion of Vice-President Weeramantry), *supra* note 90, pp. 111–115.

[233] Stec and Eckstein (1997), pp. 47, 49. Cf. also Sands (1999), p. 394.

[234] *Gabčíkovo-Nagymaros Project* (Separate Opinion of Vice-President Weeramantry), *supra* note 90, p. 114. On the VCLT's gap on intertemporal law in treaty interpretation, see *supra* notes 84–89.

judgment did not only result from the relevant provisions' generic nature,[235] but also from the particular nature of treaties dealing with projects that impact the environment.[236] Therefore, the parties' intention seems irrelevant for such an evolutionary interpretation.[237]

However, even if this was true, the reason for this evolutionary nature of environmental treaties did not become clear at first glance. There are at least two conclusions that could be drawn from *Judge Weeramantry's* observations. Either his reasoning was based on the inherent link of international environmental law to human rights or on the special subject matter of international environmental treaties. First, with regard to the inherent link of international environmental law to human rights,[238] *Weeramantry* stated:

> Environmental rights are human rights. Treaties that affect human rights cannot be applied in such a manner as to constitute a denial of human rights as understood at the time of their application. A Court cannot endorse actions which are a violation of human rights by the standards of their time merely because they are taken under a treaty which dates back to a period when such action was not a violation of human rights.[239]

He also referred to *Judge Tanaka's* dissenting opinion in *South West Africa* from 1966 and continued:

> The ethical and human rights related aspects of environmental law bring it within the category of law so essential to human welfare that we cannot apply to today's problems in this field the standards of yesterday.[240]

Further, *Weeramantry* referred to the aforementioned ECtHR case law,[241] particular the decision in *Tyrer v. UK*.[242] This underlines that he understood the relevant treaty to be linked to the exercise of human rights, thus becoming a living instrument that must be interpreted in the light of the evolutionary developments of international environmental law and sciences.[243]

---

[235] Ibid., p. 113.

[236] Ibid., pp. 113–114. Cf. also Boyle (1997), pp. 15–16; Tanaka (2010), p. 124.

[237] Akhtar-Khavari and Rothwell (1998), p. 527; Fitzmaurice (2000), p. 87; Akhtar-Khavari (2003), para. 59.

[238] See Stec and Eckstein (1997), p. 48; Stec (1999), p. 367; Akhtar-Khavari (2003), paras. 58, 65–66. In general on this link, see *supra* in Sect. 5.2.2 [notes 300–301].

[239] *Gabčíkovo-Nagymaros Project* (Separate Opinion of Vice-President Weeramantry), *supra* note 90, p. 114.

[240] Ibid., 114 with reference to *South West Africa, Second Phase* (Dissenting Opinion of Judge Tanaka), *supra* note 118, pp. 293–294. On the latter, see *supra* note 135.

[241] *Gabčíkovo-Nagymaros Project* (Separate Opinion of Vice-President Weeramantry), *supra* note 90, p. 115.

[242] *Tyrer v. UK* (Judgment), *supra* note 154, para. 31.

[243] Akhtar-Khavari (2003), paras. 65–66.

Second, some commentators argued that treaties addressing environmental concerns had an evolutive character themselves due to their special subject matter.[244] In this context, *Judge Weeramantry* found that "[e]nvironmental concerns are live and continuing concerns whenever the project under which they arise may have been inaugurated."[245] *Afhsin Akhtar-Khavari* deduced from the Court's findings that "evolving environmental law and scientific knowledge should have been integrated into the treaty relationship even if [the Court] had not interpreted [Articles 15, 19 and 20] in the way that it did."[246] Further, he concluded that "[i]t is not too far-fetched to argue that international environmental law principles, and particularly sustainable development, had expanded the scope of the Treaty's objectives."[247]

Comparably, *Yoshifumi Tanaka* found:

> [O]ne can argue that the safeguarding of the benefits for present and future generations is at the heart of environmental protection. Hence there appears to be scope to argue that in essence, inter-temporality is reflected in the object and purpose of environmental treaties. If this is the case, it can be reasonably presumed that environmental treaties include a mobile content by nature.[248]

#### 6.2.4.2 Analysis

All in all, the jurisprudence on environmental-related treaties is complex and open to interpretation. While the ICJ generally seemed to favour a generic term interpretation based on specific treaty provisions, separate opinions and other commentators also understood the existing case law from a more teleological perspective. According to them, the object and purpose of environmental treaties required these treaties to be interpreted in an evolutionary way due to their special nature as living instruments.[249] For instance, *Mileva* and *Fortuna* argued for such a subject matter-related particularity of environmental treaties, as they identified "a general

---

[244] This assertion is in accordance with other tendencies in international law-making that support the evolutionary nature of international environmental law in general. One example is the dynamic development of multilateral environmental agreements in the context of the decisions of its organs, cf. Fitzmaurice (2009), pp. 3–7. Further, some theoretical approaches to environmental law advocated for a more adaptive law-making with regard to environmental law in order to strengthen resilience of both social and ecological systems, cf. Garmestani et al. (2014), pp. 320–328.

[245] *Gabčíkovo-Nagymaros Project* (Separate Opinion of Vice-President Weeramantry), *supra* note 90, p. 114.

[246] Akhtar-Khavari (2003), para. 45 with reference to *Gabčíkovo-Nagymaros Project* (Judgment), *supra* note 213, para. 140.

[247] Akhtar-Khavari (2003), para. 47. Cf. Mbengue (2020), p. 173. See also *supra* notes 204, 209. Generally on the evolutive character of sustainable development, see Barral (2018), p. 107.

[248] Tanaka (2013), p. 156. See also ibid., pp. 174–175; Tanaka (2010), pp. 111, 124. *Yoshifumi Tanaka* (Tanaka (2013), pp. 157–158.) brought forward a similar argument with reference to *Iron Rhine Railway* (Arbitral Award), *supra* note 123, paras. 57–59.

[249] See, e.g., *Whaling in the Antarctic* (Separate Opinion of Judge Cançado Trindade), *supra* note 206, paras. 27–40; Kolb (2016), pp. 158–165.

forward-progressing development of environmental protection through the practice of evolutionary interpretation".[250]

At the same time, the differentiation between treaties based on their subject matter alone is neither convincing nor helpful.[251] In the ILC Fragmentation Report, the Study Group stated:

> [T]he characterizations ('trade law', 'environmental law') have no normative value *per se*. They are only informal labels that describe the instruments from the perspective of different interests or different policy objectives. Most international instruments may be described from various perspectives: a treaty dealing with trade may have significant human rights and environmental implications and vice versa.[252]

For comparable reasons, *Arato* criticised the considerable practical ambiguities and indeterminacy in assessing a treaty's general object and purpose in order to decide between contemporaneous and evolutionary interpretation.[253] He pointed out that "treaties can have multiple, and perhaps even divergent objects and purposes",[254] which he illustrated with reference to the WTO's *Certain Shrimp and Shrimp Products* case.[255] Instead, he offered a distinction that assists in evaluating whether evolutionary interpretation is persuasive and how to balance it with conflicting elements of interpretation under the VCLT.[256] This approach builds on the proposition offered by *Gerald Fitzmaurice* as Special Rapporteur to the Law of Treaties in 1958.[257] *Fitzmaurice* distinguished between treaty provisions of "ordinary treaties" with reciprocal relationships and treaties with so-called "integral" or "interdependent" (i.e., non-reciprocal) obligations.[258] Although this distinction was not introduced into the VCLT, several traces are left,[259] and the ILC Fragmentation Report explicitly referred to *Fitzmaurice's* original proposition.[260] There are also certain parallels to the notion of *erga omnes* and *erga omnes partes* obligations.[261]

---

[250] Mileva and Fortuna (2019), p. 139.

[251] Arato (2018), pp. 209–212; Hamamoto (2020), pp. 76–77.

[252] ILC (2006), para. 21. See also ibid., paras. 55, 117.

[253] Arato (2018), pp. 213–215. He referred to the illustrative example of the arbitral tribunal's object and purpose interpretation in the *Iron Rhine* case: *Iron Rhine Railway* (Arbitral Award), *supra* note 123, pp. 80–84. See *supra* note 134.

[254] Arato (2018), p. 213 with reference to Sinclair (1984), p. 130.

[255] *Certain Shrimp and Shrimp Products* (Report of the Appellate Body), *supra* note 123. See already *supra* notes 196–198.

[256] Arato (2018), pp. 208, 222.

[257] ILC (1958), para. 91. A similar distinction had already been introduced by *Fitzmaurice's* predecessor *Hersch Lauterpacht*: ILC (1954), p. 135. See already *supra* notes 141–142.

[258] Arato (2018), pp. 217–218.

[259] Ibid., pp. 220–221.

[260] ILC (2006), p. 250.

[261] Arato (2018), p. 221 with reference to ILC (2001), Art. 42(b), 48. See also *infra* note 269.

*Arato* pointed out that reciprocal treaty obligations are subject to the State parties' consent, thus, potentially to generic term interpretation based on the parties' intention. Treaties with "integral obligations" would result from the parties' agreement to create obligations that are no longer restricted by their continuous intentions.[262] The distinction also finds support in international case law that referred to exactly this type of integral obligations.[263] According to *Yukiya Hamamoto*, "different emphasis can be placed on various means of interpretation depending on treaty provisions" and "[t]he nature of rights and obligations arising from a specific treaty may affect the possible role of subsequent agreements and subsequent practice in their interpretation."[264] This focus on the nature of the relevant rights and obligations mirrors *Arato's* approach and offers more guidance than the reference to the (potentially arbitrarily chosen) subject matter of the treaty as a whole. This approach can help to "explain (and justify) the instincts of judges and arbitrators in singling out certain kinds of treaties as specially capable of autonomous evolution."[265]

In this sense, the apparent inconsistency in the aforementioned case law on evolutionary interpretation in environmental cases could be approached from this distinction. With regard to the non-reciprocal obligations in the Whaling Convention of 1946,[266] it can easily be understood from this perspective why evolutionary interpretation based on the object and purpose dominates in the *Whaling in the Antarctic* case.[267] However, even in treaties with typically reciprocal contractual relationships, evolutionary interpretation can become relevant, particularly on the basis of generic terms, which themselves express the parties' presumed intention to an evolutionary understanding. Thus, this generic term interpretation was decisive in the *Certain Shrimp and Shrimp Products* as well as in the *Pulp Mills* cases.[268]

Beyond these generic terms, the environmental obligations in the respective treaties[269] go beyond the reciprocal main regime of these treaties since the preservation and protection of certain natural resources is arguably also in the interest of

[262] Arato (2018), p. 223. See also *supra* note 142.

[263] *Ireland v. UK* (Judgment), *supra* note 151, para. 239; IACHR, *The Effect of Reservations on the Entry into Force of the American Convention on Human Rights (Arts. 74 and 75) (Requested by the Inter-American Commission on Human Rights),* Advisory Opinion, 24 September 1982, OEA Series A No. 2, para. 29; International Criminal Tribunal for the former Yugoslavia, *Prosecutor v. Kupreškić et al.,* Trial Judgment, 14 January 2000, retrieved 3 January 2025, from https://casebook.icrc.org/case-study/icty-prosecutor-v-kupreskic-et-al, paras. 517–518; *RosInvest* (Award on Jurisdiction), *supra* note 129, para. 40. See also Arato (2018), pp. 208, 224.

[264] Hamamoto (2020), pp. 76–77.

[265] Arato (2018), p. 224.

[266] See particularly Article VIII of the Whaling Convention.

[267] *Whaling in the Antarctic* (Separate Opinion of Judge Cançado Trindade), *supra* note 206, paras. 27–40.

[268] *Certain Shrimp and Shrimp Products* (Report of the Appellate Body), *supra* note 123, para. 130; *Pulp Mills* (Judgment), *supra* note 122, para. 204.

[269] See Art. 41 of the 1975 Statute of the River Uruguay; Art. 15, 19 and 20 of the 1977 Treaty concerning the Gabčíkovo-Nagymaros System.

the international community as a whole and not at the disposal of the contracting parties.[270] For this reason, commentators who argued in favour of an evolutionary interpretation due to the object and purpose are correct as far as they considered the respective treaty norms to allow for a dynamic incorporation of contemporary international environmental law into the obligations at hand. However, it is not so much the somewhat misguiding category of "environmental treaties" that requires evolutionary interpretation,[271] but the integral nature of most environmental obligations that introduce evolutionary elements into the respective treaties. In this sense, the Court observed in the *Gabčíkovo-Nagymaros Project* decision:

> By inserting these evolving provisions in the Treaty, the parties recognized the potential necessity to adapt the Project. Consequently, the Treaty is not static, and is open to adapt to emerging norms of international law. By means of Articles 15 and 19 [of the 1977 Treaty concerning the Gabčíkovo-Nagymaros System], new environmental norms can be incorporated in the Joint Contractual Plan.[272]

Despite the partly helpful distinction between different subject matters of treaties, there is no new evolutionary approach that would specifically apply to "environmental treaties". Yet, environmental obligations in treaties—regardless of the latter's nature as a whole—can trigger an evolutionary interpretation due to the integral nature of these obligations. This evolutionary approach either results from specific generic terms, based on the parties' original intention, or from the object and purpose of these provisions, which can turn the treaty to a dynamic, or "living", instrument that is to be interpreted in light of the evolution of law.

## 6.3 Summary and Conclusion

This chapter has highlighted the complex elements of the doctrine of intertemporal law and the interplay between them. The starting point for delimitation of the temporal sphere of application of a norm are the facts and the law contemporaneous with the creation of a specific international norm. This principle of contemporaneity points to a static understanding of the law that relies on stability and certainty of the legal system. It is the general rule of intertemporal law.

Nonetheless, jurisprudence has increasingly assessed dynamic subsequent developments of the law. The second element of intertemporal law thus requires the interpreter to assess the legal regime at the time of the application or interpretation of the relevant norm. This takes into account the dynamic character of the legal system, at least under certain circumstances. These evolutionary approaches have been particularly relevant in the context of treaty interpretation. While the general rules

[270] On the potential *erga omnes* character of many environmental obligations, see Brown Weiss (1989), pp. 121–122 as well as *supra* in Sect. 5.3.3.2.2.

[271] As argued, e.g., by Tanaka (2013), p. 156.

[272] *Gabčíkovo-Nagymaros Project* (Judgment), *supra* note 213, para. 112.

of interpretation, codified in Articles 31, 32 of the VCLT, provide some guidance in this process, they do not address *all* issues of intertemporal treaty interpretation in an exhaustive way. Instead, autonomous forms of evolutionary treaty interpretation have developed in the form of the generic term case law as well as even more progressive approaches on the basis of the respective treaty's object and purpose. Evolutionary approaches based on generic terms often start with the parties' original intention at the time of the treaty's conclusion. However, they have increasingly emancipated from the actual intentions by considering the parties' presumed intentions in a more flexible way. The second evolutionary approach, based on a treaty's object and purpose, is most common in international human rights jurisprudence in the form of the living instrument interpretation. Due to the specific nature of human rights treaties—or the integral nature of human rights obligations—, they have been interpreted to be open to evolutionary developments in the law. Eventually, these specific evolutionary approaches build on the VCLT rules, but they partly go beyond them and incorporate certain particularities.

Some arguments have been brought forward concerning subject matter-related approaches to evolutionary interpretation. In this context, human rights treaties and constitutive treaties of international organisations have been considered to fall, generally, within the object and purpose-based evolutionary interpretation. The same argument has been made in respect of environment-related treaties. However, instead of focusing on a treaty's label as an "environmental treaty", the existing case law points to a more nuanced distinction between different types of treaty *obligations*. As environmental protection obligations often contain either generic terms or are of an "integral" non-reciprocal character, they are able to incorporate subsequent developments of international environmental law into the respective treaty regime, regardless of the latter's general subject matter. All in all, evolutionary approaches to treaty interpretation can thus either be based on the parties' (presumed) intention or on the general object and purpose of the treaties concerned, which can often be deduced from the types of obligations included therein. Having outlined the elements of the existing doctrine of intertemporal law, the next chapter applies an intertemporal perspective to the concept of intergenerational equity.

## References

Akhtar-Khavari, A. (2003). The passage of time in international environmental disputes. *Murdoch University Electronic Journal of Law, 10*(4), 1–22.

Akhtar-Khavari, A., & Rothwell, D. R. (1998). The ICJ and the Danube Dam Case: A missed opportunity for international environmental law. *Melbourne University Law Review, 22*, 507.

Allen, S. (2020). Self-determination, the chagos advisory opinion and the chagossians. *International and Comparative Law Quarterly, 69*(1), 203–220. https://doi.org/10.1017/S0020589319000526

Arato, J. (2012). Constitutional transformation in the ECtHR: Strasbourg's expansive recourse to external rules of international law. *Brooklyn Journal of International Law, 37*(2), 349–387.

Arato, J. (2018). Accounting for difference in treaty interpretation over time. In A. Bianchi, D. Peat, & M. Windsor (Eds.), *Interpretation in international law* (Vol. 10, 1st ed., pp. 205–228). Oxford University Press.

Arévalo Narváez, C. E., & Patarroyo Ramírez, P. A. (2016). Treaties over time and human rights: A case law analysis of the inter-American court of human rights. *Anuario Colombiano De Derecho Internacional, 10*, 295–331. https://doi.org/10.12804/revistas.urosario.edu.co/acdi/a.5290

Baade, H. W. (1957). Intertemporales Völkerrecht. *German Yearbook of International Law, 7*(2), 229–256.

Barral, V. (2018). The principle of sustainable development. In L. Krämer & E. Orlando (Eds.), *Principles of environmental law* (pp. 103–114). Edward Elgar Publishing.

Bernhardt, R. (1999). Evolutive treaty interpretation: Especially of the European convention on human rights. *German Yearbook of International Law, 42*, 11–25.

Bjorge, E. (2014). *The evolutionary interpretation of treaties*. Oxford University Press.

Bjorge, E. (2018). The Vienna rules, evolutionary interpretation and the intentions of the parties. In A. Bianchi, D. Peat, & M. Windsor (Eds.), *Interpretation in international law* (Vol. 9, 1st ed., pp. 189–204). Oxford University Press.

Boisson de Chazournes, L., & Mbengue, M. M. (2017). Gabčíkovo-Nagymaros Project (Hungary/Slovakia) (1997). In C. Miles & E. Bjorge (Eds.), *Landmark cases in public international law* (Vol. 18, pp. 435–453). Bloomsbury Publishing PLC.

Boyle, A. E. (1997). The Gabčíkovo-Nagymaros Case: New law in old bottles. *Yearbook of International Environmental Law, 8*(1), 13–20. https://doi.org/10.1093/yiel/8.1.13

Brown Weiss, E. (1989). *In fairness to future generations: International law, common patrimony, and intergenerational equity*. Transnational Publishers, Inc.

Çali, B. (2020). Specialized rules of treaty interpretation: Human rights. In D. B. Hollis (Ed.), *The Oxford guide to treaties* (Vol. 21, 2nd ed., pp. 504–523). Oxford University Press.

Cançado Trindade, A. A. (2003). The developing case law of the inter-American court of human rights. *Human Rights Law Review, 3*(1), 1–25. https://doi.org/10.1093/hrlr/3.1.1

Cassese, A. (2012). Introduction. In A. Cassese (Ed.), *Realizing utopia: The future of international law* (Vol. 0, 1st ed., pp. xvii–xxii). Oxford University Press.

Chesterman, S. (2007). Rule of law. In A. Peters & R. Wolfrum (Eds.), *Max Planck encyclopedia of public international law*. Oxford University Press. (Article last updated July 2007).

Christoffersen, J. (2009). Impact on general principles of treaty interpretation. In M. T. Kamminga & M. Scheinin (Eds.), *The impact of human rights law on general international law* (Vol. 3, pp. 37–61). Oxford University Press.

Craven, M. (2000). Legal differentiation and the concept of the human rights treaty in international law. *European Journal of International Law, 11*(3), 489–519. https://doi.org/10.4324/9781315092492-13

Crawford, J., & Brownlie, I. (2019). *Brownlie's principles of public international law* (9th ed.). Oxford University Press.

Crawford, J., & Keene, A. (2020). Interpretation of the human rights treaties by the international court of justice. *The International Journal of Human Rights, 24*(7), 935–956. https://doi.org/10.1080/13642987.2019.1600509

D'Amato, A. (1992). International law, intertemporal problems. In R. Bernhardt & P. Macalister-Smith (Eds.), *Encyclopedia of public international law: Published under the auspices of the Max Planck Institute for comparative public law and international law* (pp. 1234–1236). Elsevier. (Article last updated January 1992).

d'Aspremont, J. (2022). Time travel in the law of international responsibility. In S. Besson (Ed.), *Theories of international responsibility law* (Vol. 11, pp. 252–277). Cambridge University Press.

de Castro, P. C. (1997). The judgment in the case concerning the Gabčíkovo-Nagymaros project: Positive signs for the evolution of international water law. *Yearbook of International Environmental Law, 8*(1), 21–31. https://doi.org/10.1093/yiel/8.1.21

Djeffal, C. (2015). *Static and evolutive treaty interpretation: A functional reconstruction*. Cambridge University Press.

Djeffal, C. (2019). An interpreter's guide to static and evolutive interpretations: Solving intertemporal problems according to the VCLT. In G. Abi-Saab, K. Keith, & G. Marceau (Eds.), *Evolutionary interpretation and international law* (Vol. 4, pp. 21–34). Hart Publishing.

Dörr, O. (2018). Article 31. In O. Dörr & K. Schmalenbach (Eds.), *Vienna convention on the law of treaties: A commentary* (2nd ed., pp. 559–616). Springer.

Dupuy, P.-M. (2011). Evolutionary interpretation of treaties: Between memory and prophecy. In E. Cannizzaro & M. H. Arsanjani (Eds.), *The law of treaties beyond the Vienna Convention* (Vol. 7, pp. 123–137). Oxford University Press.

Elias, T. O. (1980). The doctrine of intertemporal law. *American Journal of International Law, 74*(2), 285–307. https://doi.org/10.2307/2201503

Fitzmaurice, G. G. (1953). The law and procedure of the International Court of Justice, 1951-4: General principles and sources of law. *British Yearbook of International Law, 30*, 1–70.

Fitzmaurice, G. G. (1957). The law and procedure of the International Court of Justice 1951-4: Treaty interpretation and other treaty points. *British Yearbook of International Law, 33*, 203–293.

Fitzmaurice, J. (2000). The ruling of the International Court of Justice in the Gabcikovo-Nagymaros case: A critical analysis. *European Environmental Law Review, 9*(3), 80–88.

Fitzmaurice, M. (2008). Dynamic (evolutive) interpretation of treaties: Part I. *Hague Yearbook of International Law, 21*, 101–156.

Fitzmaurice, M. (2009). Dynamic (evolutive) interpretation of treaties: Part II. *Hague Yearbook of International Law, 22*, 3–31.

Fitzmaurice, M. (2020). Subsequent agreement and subsequent practice: Some reflections on the International Law Commission's draft conclusions. *International Community Law Review, 22*(1), 14–32. https://doi.org/10.1163/18719732-12341419

French, D. (2006). Treaty interpretation and the incorporation of extraneous legal rules. *International and Comparative Law Quarterly, 55*(2), 281–314.

Gardiner, R. K. (2020). The Vienna convention rules on treaty interpretation. In D. B. Hollis (Ed.), *The Oxford guide to treaties* (Vol. 19, 2nd ed., pp. 459–488). Oxford University Press.

Garmestani, A. S., Allen, C. R., Arnold, C. A., & Gunderson, L. H. (2014). Introduction: Social-ecological resilience and law. In A. S. Garmestani & C. R. Allen (Eds.), *Social-ecological resilience and law* (pp. 1–14). Columbia University Press.

Ghimisi, A. (2019). Recent developments of the right to self-determination before the international court of justice: The Chagos advisory opinion. *Journal of Research and Innovation for Sustainable Society, 1*(2), 101–106. https://doi.org/10.33727/JRISS.2019.2.13:101-106

Gurmendi, A. (2021, February 1). A few comments on "revisiting the doctrine of intertemporal law". *OpinioJuris*. Retrieved January 3, 2025, from http://opiniojuris.org/2021/02/01/a-few-comments-on-revisiting-the-doctrine-of-intertemporal-law/.

Gurmessa, A. F. (2019). Advisory opinion of the international court of justice on the case of Chagos Archipelago: A commentary. *Hawassa University Journal of Law, 3*, 191–216.

Hamamoto, Y. (2020). Possible limitations to the role of subsequent agreements and subsequent practice: Viewed from some state practices. *International Community Law Review, 22*(1), 61–83. https://doi.org/10.1163/18719732-12341421

Harris, D. J., & Sivakumaran, S. (2015). *Cases and materials on international law* (8th ed.). Sweet & Maxwell.

Herdegen, M. (2020). Interpretation in international law. In A. Peters & R. Wolfrum (Eds.), *Max Planck encyclopedia of public international law*. Oxford University Press. (Article last updated November 2020).

Higgins, R. (1996). Some observations on the inter-temporal rule in international law. In J. Makarczyk (Ed.), *Theory of international law at the threshold of the 21st century: Essays in honour of Krzysztof Skubiszewski* (pp. 173–181). Kluwer Law International.

Higgins, R. (1997). Time and the law: International perspectives on an old problem. *International and Comparative Law Quarterly, 46*(03), 501–520. https://doi.org/10.1017/S0020589300060784

Inagaki, O. (2015). Evolutionary interpretation of treaties re-examined: The two-stage reasoning. *Journal of International Cooperation Studies, 22*(2–3), 127–149.

Institut de Droit International. (1975, August 11). The intertemporal problem in public international law. Retrieved January 3, 2025, from https://www.idi-iil.org/app/uploads/2017/06/1975_wies_01_en.pdf

International Law Commission. (1954, July 8). *Second report by the special rapporteur on the law of treaties*, by H. Lauterpacht. UN Doc. A/CN.4/87.

International Law Commission. (1958, March 18). *Third report by the special rapporteur on the law of treaties*, by G. G. Fitzmaurice. UN Doc. A/CN.4/115.

International Law Commission. (1964a, May 11). *Summary records of the sixteenth session of the International Law Commission*. UN Doc. A/CN.4/SER.A/1964.

International Law Commission. (1964b, March–July). *Third report by the special rapporteur on the law of treaties*, by H. Waldock. UN Doc. A/CN.4/167.

International Law Commission. (1966, May 4). *Summary records of the eighteenth session of the International Law Commission*. UN Doc. A/CN.4/SER.A/1966.

International Law Commission. (2001). *Draft articles on the responsibility of States for Internationally Wrongful Acts, with commentaries*. UN Doc. A/56/10, 20–143.

International Law Commission. (2006, April 13). *Fragmentation of international law: Difficulties arising from the diversification and expansion of international law (Report of the Study Group of the ILC)*, by M. Koskenniemi. UN Doc. A/CN.4/L.682.

International Law Commission. (2008-2018). Subsequent agreements and subsequent practice in relation to interpretation of treaties: Analytical guide to the work of the International Law Commission. *United Nations* (UN). Retrieved January 3, 2025, from https://legal.un.org/ilc/guide/1_11.shtml.

International Law Commission. (2009, May–August). *Report of the ILC on the work of its 61st session, 4 May-5 June, 6 July-7 August 2009 – Chapter XII: Treaties over Time*. UN Doc. A/64/10.

International Law Commission. (2012, May–August). *Report of the ILC on the work of its 64th Session, 7 May–1 June, 2 July-3 August 2012 – Official Records of the General Assembly, 67th session, Supplement No. 10, Chapter X: Treaties over Time*. UN Doc. A/67/10, 77–80.

International Law Commission. (2013, March 19). *First report by the Special Rapporteur on Subsequent Agreements and Subsequent Practice in Relation to Treaty Interpretation*, by G. Nolte. UN Doc. A/CN.4/660.

International Law Commission. (2018). *Draft Conclusions on Subsequent Agreements and Subsequent Practice in Relation to the Interpretation of Treaties, with Commentaries*. UN Doc. A/73/10, 16–116.

Jennings, R., Watts, A., & Oppenheim, L. F. L. (Eds.). (1992). *Oppenheim's international law: Volume I peace* (9th ed.). Longman House.

Jessup, P. C. (1928). The Palmas Island Arbitration. *American Journal of International Law, 22*(4), 735–752. https://doi.org/10.2307/2188429

Khan, D.-E. (2007). Max Huber as Arbitrator: The Palmas (Miangas) case and other arbitrations. *European Journal of International Law, 18*(1), 145–170. https://doi.org/10.1093/ejil/chm011

Killander, M. (2010). Interpreting regional human rights treaties. *SUR International Journal on Human Rights, 7*(13), 145–169.

Klabbers, J. (2006). Treaties, object and purpose. In A. Peters & R. Wolfrum (Eds.), *Max Planck encyclopedia of public international law*. Oxford University Press. (Article last updated December 2006).

Kolb, R. (2016). *The law of treaties: An introduction*. Edward Elgar Publishing.

Kotzur, M. (2008). Intertemporal law. In A. Peters & R. Wolfrum (Eds.), *Max Planck encyclopedia of public international law*. Oxford University Press. (Article last updated April 2008).

Lauterpacht, H. (1933). *The function of law in the international community*. Clarendon Press.

Letsas, G. (2010). Strasbourg's interpretive ethic: Lessons for the international lawyer. *European Journal of International Law, 21*(3), 509–541. https://doi.org/10.1093/ejil/chq056

Li, Z. (2018). International intertemporal law. *California Western International Law Journal, 48*(2), 341–398.

Linderfalk, U. (2008). Doing the right thing for the right reason: Why dynamic or static approaches should be taken in the interpretation of treaties. *International Community Law Review, 10*(2), 109–141. https://doi.org/10.1163/187197308X311272

Martin, E. (2021). *The application of the doctrine of intertemporality in contentious proceedings*. Duncker & Humblot.

Mbengue, M. M. (2020). On sustainable development: A conversation with judge Weeramantry. In S. Forlati, M. M. Mbengue, & B. K. McGarry (Eds.), *The Gabčíkovo-Nagymaros Judgment and its contribution to the development of international law* (Vol. No. 12, pp. 166–192). Brill Nijhoff.

McNeilly, K., & Warwick, B. (Eds.). (2022). *The times and temporalities of international human rights law*. Hart Publishing.

McWhinney, E. (1984). The time dimension in international law, historical relativism and intertemporal law. In J. Makarczyk (Ed.), *Essays in international law in honour of Judge Manfred Lachs* (pp. 179–199). Martinus Nijhoff Publishers.

Melchem, K. (2009). Treaty bodies and the interpretation of human rights. *Vanderbilt Journal of Transnational Law, 42*, 905–947.

Merkouris, P. (2015). (Inter)temporal considerations in the interpretative process of the VCLT: Do treaties endure, perdure or exdure? In M. Ambrus & R. A. Wessel (Eds.), *Netherlands yearbook of international law 2014: Between pragmatism and predictability: Temporariness in international law* (Vol. 45, pp. 121–156). T.M.C. Asser Press. https://doi.org/10.1007/978-94-6265-060-2_6

Mileva, N., & Fortuna, M. (2019). Environmental protection as an object of and tool for evolutionary interpretation. In G. Abi-Saab, K. Keith, & G. Marceau (Eds.), *Evolutionary interpretation and international law* (Vol. 13, pp. 123–140). Hart Publishing.

Nolte, G. (2013a). Jurisprudence under special regimes relating to subsequent agreements and subsequent practice: Report 2. In G. Nolte (Ed.), *Treaties and subsequent practice* (Vol. 17, pp. 210–306). Oxford University Press.

Nolte, G. (Ed.). (2013b). *Treaties and subsequent practice*. Oxford University Press.

Nolte, G. (2020). Introductory note to the special issue of ICLR on the outcome of the ILC work on "Subsequent agreements and subsequent practice in relation to the interpretation of treaties". *International Community Law Review, 22*(1), 4–13. https://doi.org/10.1163/18719732-12341418

Pavlopoulos, N. (2021). Chagos (advisory opinion). In A. Peters & R. Wolfrum (Eds.), *Max Planck encyclopedia of public international law*. Oxford University Press. (Article last updated March 2021).

Polackova van der Ploeg, K., Pasquet, L., & Castellanos-Jankiewicz, L. (2022). *International law and time: Narratives and techniques*. Springer.

Rodas, J. G. (1973). The doctrine of non-retroactivity of international treaties. *Revista Da Faculdade De Direito, Universidade De São Paulo, 68*(2), 341–360. https://doi.org/10.11606/issn.2318-8235.v68i2p341-360

Sakai, H. (2016). After the whaling in the Antarctic Judgment: Its lessons and prospects from a Japanese perspective. In M. Fitzmaurice & D. Tamada (Eds.), *Whaling in the Antarctic: Significance and implications of the ICJ judgment* (Vol. No. 10, pp. 308–345). Brill Nijhoff.

Sands, P. (1999). International courts and the application of the concept of "sustainable development". *Max Planck United Nations Year Book, 3*, 389–405.

Sinclair, I. (1984). *The Vienna convention on the law of treaties* (2nd ed.). Manchester University Press.

Sørensen, M. (1973). Le Problème Dit du Droit Intertemporel Dans l'Ordre International: 11e Commission, Rapport Provisoire. *Institut de Droit International* (IDI). 1973. Retrieved January 3, 2025, from https://www.idi-iil.org/app/uploads/2017/05/4025-55-OCR.pdf.

Stec, S. (1999). Do two wrongs make a right? Adjudicating sustainable development in the Danube Dam Case. *Golden Gate University Law Review, 29*(3), 317–397.

Stec, S., & Eckstein, G. E. (1997). Of Solemn Oaths and obligations: The environmental impact of the ICJ's decision in the case concerning the Gabčíkovo-Nagymaros project. *Yearbook of International Environmental Law, 8*(1), 41–50. https://doi.org/10.1093/yiel/8.1.41

Tanaka, Y. (2010). Evolutive interpretation of treaties concerning environmental protection: The Gabčíkovo-Nagymaros project case revisited. In C. Henrichsen, J. E. Rytter, & S. Rønsholdt (Eds.), *Ret, Informatik og Samfund: Festskrift til Peter Blume* (1st ed., pp. 109–126). Jurist- og Økonomforbundets forlag.

Tanaka, Y. (2013). Reflections on time elements in the international law of the environment. *Zeitschrift Für Ausländisches Öffentliches Recht Und Völkerrecht, 73*, 139–175.

Tanaka, Y. (2018). Reflections on Locus Standi in response to a Breach of Obligations Erga Omnes Partes: A comparative analysis of the whaling in the Antarctic and South China Sea cases. *Law and Practice of International Courts and Tribunals, 17*(3), 527–554.

Tanzi, A. (2020). Concluding remarks: The legacy of a landmark case. In S. Forlati, M. M. Mbengue, & B. K. McGarry (Eds.), *The Gabčíkovo-Nagymaros Judgment and its contribution to the development of international law* (Vol. 15, pp. 229–243). Brill Nijhoff.

Thacher, P. S. (1987). Equity under change. *American Society of International Law Proceedings, 81*, 133–137.

Thirlway, H. W. A. (1990). The law and procedure of the International Court of Justice 1960-1989: Part one. *British Yearbook of International Law, 60*(1), 1–157. https://doi.org/10.1093/bybil/60.1.1

Tomuschat, C. (2022). Die Bedeutung der Zeit im Völkerrecht. *Archiv Des Völkerrechts, 60*, 1–22. https://doi.org/10.1628/avr-2022-0002

Ulfstein, G. (2020). Interpretation of the ECHR in light of the Vienna convention on the law of treaties. *The International Journal of Human Rights, 24*(7), 917–934. https://doi.org/10.1080/13642987.2019.1598055

United Nations General Assembly. (1960, December 14). *Declaration on the Granting of Independence to Colonial Countries and Peoples*. UN Doc. A/RES/1514 (XV).

United Nations General Assembly. (1970, October 24). *Declaration on Principles of International Law concerning Friendly Relations and Co-operation among States in accordance with the Charter of the United Nations*. UN Doc. A/RES/2625 (XXV).

Villiger, M. E. (2009). *Commentary on the 1969 Vienna convention on the law of treaties*. Martinus Nijhoff Publishers.

von Arnauld, A. (2021). How to illegalize past injustice: Reinterpreting the rules of intertemporality. *European Journal of International Law, 32*(2), 401–432.

Warbrick, C. (1990). Coherence and the European Court of Human Rights: The adjudicative background to the soering case. *Michigan Journal of International Law, 11*(4), 1073–1096.

Wheatley, S. (2021). Revisiting the doctrine of intertemporal law. *Oxford Journal of Legal Studies, 41*(2), 484–509. https://doi.org/10.1093/ojls/gqaa058

# Chapter 7
# Modification of the Doctrine of Intertemporal Law to Intergenerational Equity

The second research question of this book is which legal regime of intergenerational equity is temporally applicable for addressing the open issues of the intertemporal legal relationship between present and future generations. At this stage, the introductory thought experiment can be called to mind to reformulate the research question more simply: Which legal understanding of intergenerational equity would and should the representatives of the present generation and the High Commissioner for Intergenerational Relations base their answer on in their intertemporal confrontation in the year 2025?

At this point, it becomes important to recall that intergenerational equity is a constantly evolving concept. This is why the analysis in Part I of this book required both a positivist assessment *de lege lata* and a more open-minded perspective on the legal regime of intergenerational equity *de lege ferenda*. As Chaps. 2 to 4 of this book illustrated, the concept of intergenerational equity is evolving, first, with regard to its substantive contents—between the legally binding general conception as an abstract principle and the emerging specific doctrine of *Brown Weiss* that is based on planetary obligations and rights. Second, it is also evolving with regard to its underlying structures and institutional frameworks, as illustrated in Chap. 5. The *lex lata* assessment of Chaps. 2 to 5 has thus been complemented by potentially emerging developments of intergenerational equity *de lege ferenda*. The boundaries between the existing and the emerging manifestations of intergenerational equity are obviously fluid and not always easy to distinguish, as illustrated in more detail below.[1]

Due to these fluid boundaries between *lex lata* and *lex ferenda*, intertemporal law, including its evolutionary elements, constitutes an important and necessary doctrine to assess which legal regime is decisive for the present and future contents of intergenerational equity. However, the existing doctrine of intertemporal law has some flaws with respect to its application to intergenerational equity as the following

[1] See *infra* in Sect. 7.3.3.1.



A. Bustami, *The Legal Relationship between Present and Future Generations*,
https://doi.org/10.1007/978-3-032-03345-1_7

analysis demonstrates. Therefore, this last chapter before the Conclusion develops an adequate intertemporal perspective on intergenerational equity. First, the existing doctrine of intertemporal law, as illustrated in Chap. 6, is hypothetically applied to a future intergenerational dispute in order to test the doctrine's usefulness in this regard (Sect. 7.1). In a second step, it becomes clear that this unmodified application is unpersuasive and inappropriate for the temporal assessment of intergenerational equity (Sect. 7.2). Thus, the existing doctrine of intertemporal law needs to be modified in order to adequately fit the particularities of intergenerational equity as a customary norm. This chapter suggests such a modification in its third and final section (Sect. 7.3).

## 7.1 Hypothetical Application of the Unmodified Doctrine of Intertemporal Law to the Concept of Intergenerational Equity

According to the unmodified doctrine of intertemporal law, questions of temporal delimitation arise in case of a dispute between two parties regarding the meaning and content of a particular legal norm. Therefore, the issue of intertemporal law with regard to intergenerational equity is addressed on the basis of such a hypothetical dispute. This dispute would arise in the future if a respective 'future generation' claimed to be violated by the actions or failures of the 'present generation'.[2] In that future scenario, and leaving aside for a moment the factual difficulty of bringing future and present generation to the same table,[3] the question may arise which temporal legal regime is relevant to the application of intergenerational equity.

The following hypothetical scenario constitutes the basis for an unmodified intertemporal delimitation of intergenerational equity and it builds on the time travel thought experiment presented in the Introduction:[4] In the year 2100, representatives of the future generation ('generation X+80')[5] argue before an international court that the (present) generation of the early twenty-first century ('generation X') violated its obligations under the concept of intergenerational equity due to the actions and omissions in the first half of the twenty-first century. The competent court must

---

[2]In this hypothetical scenario, at the time of the dispute (in the future), the roles of these generations will have changed to the (then) present generation as a potential right-holder and the (then) past generation(s) as duty-bearers. Nonetheless, for reasons of comprehensibility, the terms 'future generation' and 'present generation' are used in the following sections. Further, the present tense is used to describe the actions and considerations in the future hypothetical scenario.

[3]As to this aspect, see *infra* in connection with note 61.

[4]For another thought-provocative conception of international (responsibility) law as time travel, see d'Aspremont (2022).

[5]The reasons for choosing the year 2100 for the purpose of illustration have been explained *supra* in Sect. 2.2.1.2.2. The reference to a 'generation X+80' constitutes an approximate denomination that points to the future generation of the year 2100.

decide whether there was such a violation of the applicable law. It is confronted with the complicated task to assess which legal regime is temporally applicable to the dispute at hand: the legal regime contemporaneous to the creation of the norm, or the legal regime that has evolved since that creation. Before illustrating the underlying differences, a preliminary question has to be answered with regard to the applicability of the doctrine of intertemporal law to intergenerational equity (Sect. 7.1.1). Subsequently, the analysis demonstrates which legal regime the principle of contemporaneity points to (Sect. 7.1.2), and which legal development is referred to by evolutionary approaches (Sect. 7.1.3).

### *7.1.1 Preliminary Observation: Applicability to Intergenerational Equity as a Norm*

Intertemporal law addresses the delimitation of the temporal sphere of a norm's application.[6] Although the doctrine has only been applied in some areas of international law so far, it is universally applicable to all norms of public international law.[7] Consequently, the respective court in the hypothetical scenario would only apply the doctrine of intertemporal law to the dispute, if intergenerational equity was a legal norm. This preliminary question can be answered with regard to the current legal status of the concept of intergenerational equity.

As demonstrated in detail in Chap. 4, two manifestations of intergenerational equity exist as of today in legal practice and academic discourse: the general conception of intergenerational equity (i.e., the need to take into account the interests of future generations),[8] and the elaborate doctrine of intergenerational equity, which is much more specific and includes intergenerational duties and rights.[9] Both manifestations have normative capacity as they have the capacity to directly influence the behaviour of their addressees, but in different ways: the general conception of intergenerational equity in the form of a legal principle, the doctrine of intergenerational equity as a legal rule, as far as its normative capacity is concerned.[10]

The legal status as legally binding norms of international law differs from one manifestation to the other. While the general conception of intergenerational equity is enshrined in several international treaties and constitutes a legal principle of customary international law, the elaborate doctrine of intergenerational equity lacks such a legally binding character. Although it is contained in some international

[6]Institut de Droit International (IDI) (1975, Preamble); Kotzur (2008, para. 1).

[7]D'Amato (1992), p. 1234; Elias (1980), pp. 285–286; Kotzur (2008, para. 2).

[8]See, e.g., Dupuy and Viñuales (2018), p. 92.

[9]See Brown Weiss (1989).

[10]See *supra* in Sect. 4.1.

documents and often referred to by jurisprudence, it can only be regarded as an emerging, not yet binding, norm of customary international law.[11]

However, this merely emerging character of the rule of intergenerational equity does not prevent a temporal assessment of the concept in general. Quite the opposite, the established legal status of the general conception of intergenerational equity constitutes a sufficient reference point for the doctrine of intertemporal law. Since this manifestation of intergenerational equity is a norm of international treaty law and customary international law, the court in the hypothetical scenario can assess which legal regime is temporally applicable to the intergenerational dispute. With regard to the concept of intergenerational equity more broadly, the general conception of intergenerational equity thus constitutes the starting point of the intertemporal analysis. Yet, in light of the transitional character of the two manifestations, it is possible that an evolutionary approach to the concept can reveal a change in the legal status of the specific doctrine, so that the latter could eventually also play a role in the assessment.[12]

### 7.1.2 Contemporaneity in the Context of Intergenerational Equity

Having observed this, the fictional intergenerational dispute in the year 2100 must be assessed based on the two elements of the (unmodified) doctrine of intertemporal law. According to the first element, the principle of contemporaneity, a legal norm must be assessed in light of the legal regime contemporaneous with the creation of the relevant norm.[13] Therefore, it is necessary to look at the creation of the concept of intergenerational equity.

The concept's historical development in international law began in the 1970s and advanced in the 1980s and 1990s.[14] For the several treaty regimes that incorporated the general conception of intergenerational equity,[15] the "time of creation" would be identical with their respective entries into force.[16] With regard to customary

[11] See *supra* in Sect. 4.2.

[12] On the transitional relationship, see already briefly *supra* in Sect. 2.3.1.2. The emergence of a more elaborate manifestation of intergenerational equity could even constitute the basis for the perspective assessment of future developments, as is demonstrated *infra* in Sect. 7.3.3.2.

[13] Permanent Court of Arbitration, *Island of Palmas Case (United States v. The Netherlands)*, Arbitral Award, 4 April 1928, RIAA II (1928), 829, p. 845.

[14] See, e.g., United Nations (1972, Principles 1, 2); World Commission on Environment and Development (1987, Chapter 2, para. 1); UN Conference on Environment and Development (1992, Principles 3, 21).

[15] In detail, see *supra* in Sect. 4.2.1.

[16] See, e.g., the 1970s for the *Convention Concerning the Protection of the World Cultural and Natural Heritage* (World Heritage Convention), adopted 16 November 1972, entered into force 17 December 1975, 1037 UNTS 151. and the 1990s for the UNFCCC and *Convention on the*

international law, most binding and non-binding documents that mentioned intergenerational equity and most evidence of its customary nature have emanated between the 1990s and today.[17] The general conception has thus achieved its customary status in the three decades since the 1990s, which would consequently mark the norm's "time of creation". Since the specific doctrine of intergenerational equity has not yet gained legally binding force in the first two decades of the twenty-first century, it would not be relevant at the level of contemporaneity.[18]

The first element of intertemporal law thus points to the legal regime of the first decades of the twenty-first century. This legal regime contains the general conception of intergenerational equity and would be the main basis for the resolution of any future dispute in the year 2100. In other words, the positivist analysis of intergenerational equity *de lege lata*, as presented above in Chaps. 2, 4 and 5, is the starting point for the delimitation of the temporal scope of the norm. Based solely on the principle of contemporaneity, the hypothetical intergenerational dispute would have to be solved based on this legal regime in the beginning of the twenty-first century.

### *7.1.3 Evolutionary Approaches to Intergenerational Equity*

Beyond this starting point, the doctrine of intertemporal law contains exceptions on how subsequent developments of law can become relevant for the delimitation of the temporal sphere of a norm: evolutionary approaches. Only if the conditions of an evolutionary approach are met in the hypothetical scenario, legal developments subsequent to the early decades of the twenty-first century would become relevant. If this is not the case, the only temporal legal regime relevant to the resolution of the hypothetical dispute would remain the law contemporaneous with the creation of intergenerational equity.

At this point, the reasons for these exceptions—"generic term" and "object and purpose" approaches—are not assessed in detail yet with regard to the hypothetical dispute, as they involve certain difficulties in the context of intergenerational equity.[19] Instead, for the time being, it suffices to assume that the court in the future dispute affirms such reasons for an evolutionary approach to intergenerational equity. Based on this assumption, the evolutionary component of intertemporal law would influence the temporally applicable legal regime. Instead of only focusing

*Protection and Use of Transboundary Watercourses and International Lakes* (UNECE Water Convention), adopted 17 March 1992, entered into force 6 October 1996, 1936 UNTS 269.

[17] In detail, see *supra* in Sect. 4.2.2.1.

[18] However, see below in the context of the modified doctrine of intertemporal law, *infra* in Sect. 7.3.3.2.

[19] On these difficulties, see *infra* in Sect. 7.2.1. On the proper assessment of both evolutionary approaches to intergenerational equity, see *infra* in Sect. 7.3.1.2.

on the time of creation of intergenerational equity, the dispute would have to be solved based on the legal developments since that time until the time of the dispute on the norm's application.[20] In the context of the hypothetical future dispute between generation X and generation X+80, the court would have to take into consideration the legal developments in exactly this time period: between the 2020s and the year 2100. Eventually, the legal regime temporally applicable to the intergenerational dispute would be the evolved regime at the time of its resolution in the year 2100.

## 7.2 Need for a Modification of Intertemporal Law to the Concept of Intergenerational Equity

At first glance, the foregoing application of intertemporal law to the hypothetical future scenario in the year 2100 seems perfectly adequate to determine the temporally applicable law. As far as one awaits the occurrence of a dispute in the future based on alleged violations of intergenerational equity, the existing doctrine of intertemporal law offers answers. However, several arguments contradict this conclusion and illustrate the lack of persuasiveness of an unmodified application of the doctrine to intergenerational equity and the need for an adequate modification. These arguments are demonstrated in the following sub-sections, before Sect. 7.3 turns to the modified doctrine of intertemporal law for the delimitation of the temporal scope of intergenerational equity.

The first argument results from the treaty-related particularities of evolutionary approaches, on the one hand, and the specific legal status of intergenerational equity as a customary norm, on the other hand (Sect. 7.2.1). The other two arguments are less formal, but constitute objections with regard to the substantive particularities of intergenerational equity. The subsequent section thus focuses on the intertemporal legal relationship between present and future generations, as this relationship largely differs from any other issue of international law that has been addressed by the doctrine of intertemporal law so far (Sect. 7.2.2) Then, the author demonstrates how the irreversibility and long-term effects of most violations of intergenerational obligations have a decisive impact on the potential resolution of disputes in the future. These irreversible impacts render it futile to apply the existing retrospective doctrine of intertemporal law to intergenerational disputes in the future (Sect. 7.2.3).

[20] See *Island of Palmas* (Arbitral Award), *supra* note 13, p. 845.

### 7.2.1 Evolutionary Approaches and Customary International Law

The first argument against an unmodified application of the existing doctrine of intertemporal law to intergenerational equity results from the legal status of the assessed norm. Generally, both elements of the doctrine of intertemporal law apply universally to *all* norms of international law,[21] regardless of the latter's legal status as treaty law or customary law. The universal idea behind intertemporal law is the balance between legal stability and the flexible development of the international legal system,[22] so that it retains its value and applicability with regard to all sources of international law. There is no reason why evolutionary approaches should not equally be relevant for the concept of intergenerational equity. Despite this universality of intertemporal law, most evolutionary approaches have developed in the context of treaty law and treaty interpretation. The generic term approach refers to treaty terms and assesses the intention (or presumed intention) of specific treaty parties as to the dynamic nature of certain terms.[23] Similarly, the object and purpose approach refers to the object and purpose of specific treaty terms or the treaty regime as a whole.[24] The same is true for the analysis on the evolutionary interpretation of treaties with links to environmental protection.[25]

With these observations in mind, the legal status of intergenerational equity becomes important. Although there are several international treaties that incorporate the general conception of intergenerational equity, they regulate specific fields of international environmental law and do not establish a universal norm of intergenerational equity.[26] Interestingly, the recent *Whaling in the Antarctic* case from 2014 constitutes an example for evolutionary treaty interpretation with regard to a treaty that itself contains an explicit reference to future generations in its Preamble.[27] However, the present book focuses on the analysis of the customary nature of intergenerational equity in order to examine a holistic and universally applicable norm, regardless of the specific treaty regime.[28] With regard to the close affiliation of evolutionary approaches to treaty interpretation, there is thus a significant gap between the customary nature of intergenerational equity, on the one hand,

---

[21] D'Amato (1992), p. 1234; Elias (1980), pp. 285–286; Kotzur (2008, para. 2).

[22] IDI (1975, Preamble); Kotzur (2008, para. 4).

[23] In detail, see *supra* in Sect. 6.2.2.

[24] In detail, see *supra* in Sect. 6.2.3.

[25] In detail, see *supra* in Sect. 6.2.4.

[26] See, e.g., *supra* note 16.

[27] International Court of Justice, *Whaling in the Antarctic (Australia v. Japan: New Zealand intervening),* Judgment, 31 March 2014, ICJ Reports 2014, 226, para. 56 with reference to *International Convention for the Regulation of Whaling* (Whaling Convention), adopted 2 December 1946, entered into force 10 November 1948, 161 UNTS 72, Preamble. For more details, see *supra* in Sect. 6.2.4.1.

[28] See already *supra* in Sect. 4.2.1.

and the main instances of application for evolutionary intertemporal law approaches, on the other hand.

In contrast to treaty law, customary international law has not been much discussed in the context of intertemporal law and evolutionary approaches. The *Chagos Archipelago* advisory opinion is one of the few judicial instances of discussion.[29] Although the passage of time plays an important role in the formation and development of customary international law,[30] this issue has not been debated a lot in international legal discourse.[31] For instance, the ILC mentioned the time element of customary international law only once in its 2018 'Draft Conclusions on Identification of Customary International Law' with regard to the establishment of State practice.[32] While clarifying that "some period of time must elapse for a general practice to emerge",[33] the Draft conclusions also explicitly stated:

> [...] the draft conclusions do not address, directly, the processes by which customary international law develops over time. Yet in practice identification cannot always be considered in isolation from formation; [...]. The draft conclusions thus inevitably refer in places to the formation of rules of customary international law. They do not, however, deal systematically with how such rules emerge, change, or terminate.[34]

This dynamic character explains that customary international law is continuously changing.[35] It is much more fluid than treaty regimes whose terms and provisions are more or less static and only occasionally subject to amendment. While the intertemporal perspective on treaty law always starts with contemporaneous interpretation, this nature of customary international law could actually speak in favour of a presumption for evolutionary perspectives as a starting point. Despite the obvious relevance of intertemporal law for changes in customary international law, there is no formulation of the doctrine that would adequately transfer intertemporal law's second element, evolutionary approaches, to the context of customary international law. Even the aforementioned *Chagos Archipelago* advisory opinion applied a progressive variation of the principle of contemporaneity, not so much an evolutionary approach *stricto sensu*.[36] This variation of contemporaneity does not fill the existing discrepancies between the doctrine of intertemporal law and the customary

---

[29] ICJ, *Legal Consequences of the Separation of the Chagos Archipelago from Mauritius in 1965,* Advisory Opinion, 25 February 2019, ICJ Reports 2019, 95. In more detail, see *supra* in Sect. 6.2.

[30] ICJ, *Dispute regarding Navigational and Related Rights (Costa Rica v. Nicaragua),* Separate Opinion of Judge Sepúlveda-Amor, 13 July 2009, ICJ Reports 2009, 273, para. 25; Wheatley (2021), pp. 489–491.

[31] Wheatley (2021), p. 489.

[32] International Law Commission (2018a, Conclusion 8(2)).

[33] Ibid., Conclusion 8, para. 9.

[34] Ibid., Conclusion 1, para. 5 See also ILC (2016, para. 16).

[35] Cf. Wheatley (2021), pp. 490–491.

[36] Ibid., p. 505 See also *supra* in Sect. 6.2.

nature of intergenerational equity, although it could still serve as a starting point for the suggested modification below.[37]

Consequently, the discrepancies are at least indicative of the inadequacy of an unmodified application to intergenerational equity. At this stage, the existing reasons for evolutionary approaches—generic terms and a treaty's object and purpose—are not *par for par* applicable to the customary law concept of intergenerational equity. This constitutes the first *methodological* obstacle for an unmodified application of the existing doctrine of intertemporal law. Any rule of intertemporal law for the consideration of intergenerational issues has necessarily to be adapted to the specific customary status of intergenerational equity.[38] Before elaborating this necessary modification, the following sub-sections illustrate two *substantive* reasons why the existing doctrine of intertemporal law is unpersuasive and inadequate for a proper resolution of intergenerational disputes.

### 7.2.2 *The Inherently Intertemporal Nature of Intergenerational Equity*

Intergenerational equity governs the "relationship that each generation has to other generations [...] in using the common patrimony of natural and cultural resources of our planet".[39] This intertemporal element plays an important role in the modified evolutionary assessment of the concept, illustrated below.[40] But it is also a reason of distinction between disputes on intergenerational equity and any other international legal relationship. This book illustrates this distinction by contrasting intergenerational equity to the main areas of application of intertemporal law, this means territorial boundary disputes and disputes concerning treaty interpretation (Sect. 7.2.2.1). Beyond this comparative reasoning, the same inherently intertemporal nature of intergenerational equity is supported from a philosophical perspective (Sect. 7.2.2.2).

#### 7.2.2.1 Differences Between Intergenerational Equity and Other Intertemporal Constellations

The delimitation of the temporal sphere of application of a norm usually arises in the context of a dispute, understood as a "disagreement on a point of law or fact, a conflict of legal views or interests between parties".[41] Therefore, the comparison

[37] See *infra* in Sect. 7.3.3.1.

[38] See *infra* in Sect. 7.3.1.2.

[39] Brown Weiss (1989), p. 21.

[40] See *infra* in Sect. 7.3.1.2.2.

[41] ICJ, *East Timor (Portugal v. Australia),* Judgment, 30 June 1995, ICJ Reports 1995, 90, para. 22.

between different applications of intertemporal law must address the underlying dispute situations. With regard to territorial titles, a dispute can arise between two States as to the affiliation of a certain part of territory. If this territory has allegedly been acquired by one State in the distant past (e.g., 100 years before the dispute arose), it must be determined which legal regime is applicable to the resolution of the dispute. This can either be the legal regime at the time of the decision of the dispute in the present (time X) or the legal regime at the time of the alleged acquisition in the past (time X-100). Since international law could have evolved during this period, the passage of time between the alleged acquisition in the past and the dispute in the present renders the matter intertemporal.[42] Although the dispute involves intertemporal issues, the actual legal relationship between the disputing parties is not intertemporal itself. Instead, the disputing parties always constitute contemporary States that are temporally fixed to a specific point in time: State A at time X is in dispute with State B at time X.

The same is true with regard to the second area of the doctrine of intertemporal law, namely treaty law and treaty interpretation. If a dispute arises today (time X) between two States as to the correct interpretation of certain terms in a treaty, which was concluded 100 years ago, the temporally applicable legal regime must be determined. This is an intertemporal question and, as shown, its resolution is quite complex: On the one hand, the principle of contemporaneity might point to the law at the time of the treaty's conclusion (time X-100).[43] On the other hand, evolutionary approaches can require the dispute to be solved on the basis of subsequent developments since time X-100 until time X in the present.[44] The intertemporal nature of this legal dispute results, first, from the time gap between treaty conclusion and treaty interpretation and, second, from certain trigger points for evolutionary interpretation in the treaty (generic terms or the object and purpose). However, the legal relationship underlying the dispute again remains a relationship at the specific time X between two contemporary States A and B at time X.

Further, human rights law merits a second look, since it constitutes the most common area for evolutionary interpretation. In most contemporary institutional frameworks, human rights disputes take place between individual complainants and a State that has allegedly violated the complainants' human rights.[45] Apart from the

---

[42]This was the case, e.g., in the *Island of Palmas* case (*Island of Palmas* (Arbitral Award), *supra* note 13, p. 845) or in the *Minquiers and Ecrehos* case (ICJ, *Minquiers and Ecrehos (France v. United Kingdom),* Judgment, 17 November 1953, ICJ Reports 1953, 47, p. 56).

[43]The time of a treaty's conclusion was decisive, e.g., in ICJ, *Rights of United States Nationals in Morocco Case (France v. United States of America),* Judgment, 27 August 1952, ICJ Reports 1952, 176, p. 189.

[44]The time of the interpretation of the treaty terms was decisive, e.g., in ICJ, *Aegean Sea Continental Shelf Case (Greece v. Turkey),* Judgment, 19 December 1978, ICJ Reports 1978, 3, para. 77.

[45]For the current illustration, constellations of inter-State disputes in human rights regimes are left out, see, e.g., Art. 33 of the ECHR. These inter-State human rights disputes would not differ from the foregoing example of treaty interpretation between State A and State B.

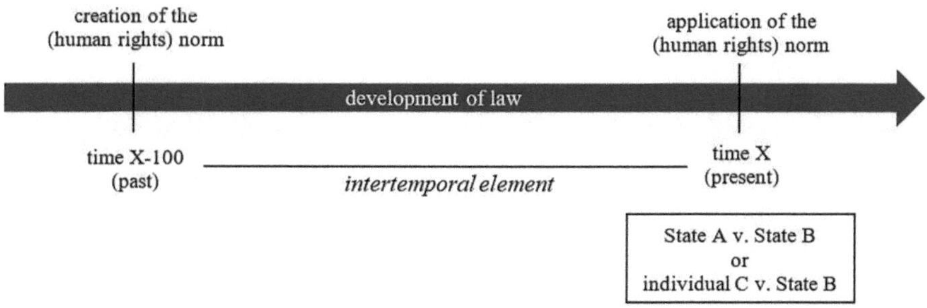


**Fig. 7.1** Intertemporal character of territorial boundary and (human rights) treaty disputes

fact that the disputing parties constitute different subjects of international law, the dispute is similar to any other treaty-related dispute as far as the temporal dimension is concerned. The court has to determine the temporally applicable law to the human rights treaty's interpretation in order to resolve the dispute. As demonstrated above, the "living instrument" character of human rights treaties establishes their particular intertemporal nature, so that evolutionary interpretation prevails over the principle of contemporaneity.[46] However, at second glance, this does not result in any changes concerning the temporal relationship between the parties of the dispute: Again, the obliged entity is State B at time X and the right-holder is an individual C existing at that similar time X. The following illustration (Fig. 7.1) reflects the intertemporal character in these main fields of application of the intertemporal law doctrine.

There is another aspect that could potentially stretch the temporal element of a dispute on treaty interpretation, including human rights disputes: There is an additional time gap in the scenario, if the act or omission that led to the alleged violation by a State occurred at a time X-20 whereas the effects of that act or omission materialise at a later stage (time X-10), and/or the respective dispute is resolved even later in the present (time X). However, this does not influence the intertemporal character of the dispute as a whole, which still emanates from the time gap between the treaty's conclusion at time X-100 and the decision of the dispute at time X. A time gap of a few years between the alleged act and the occurrence of its consequences, and/or between these consequences and a decision on a subsequent dispute, might pose additional temporal questions.[47] Yet, this time gap does not temporally extend the legal relationship at hand. State B would be the obliged entity that violated the legal position of State A or the human rights of an individual C at time X-20. Except for rare cases of State succession, the usual constellation would be that the same State B's conduct is challenged by State A or by individual C in a dispute a few years later (at time X). Similarly, State A or individual C are not only the entities whose rights have been violated at time X-20, but also the ones who are

[46] See *supra* in Sect. 6.2.3 [notes 154–155, 175–176].

[47] In more detail on the intertemporal element in the law of State responsibility, see d'Aspremont (2022), pp. 265–270.

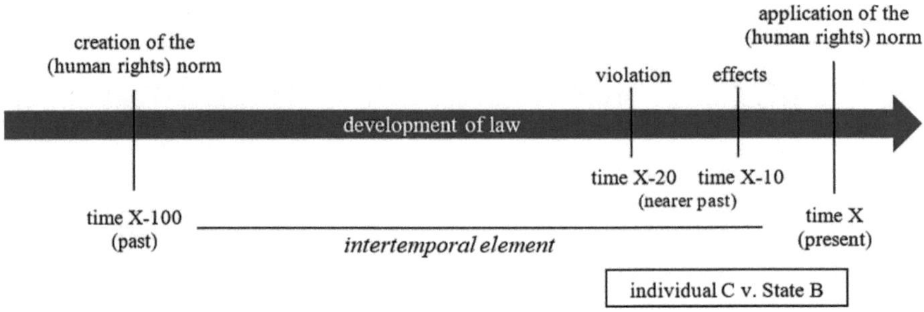


**Fig. 7.2** Intertemporal character of (human rights) disputes in case of temporal extension

claiming this violation in a subsequent dispute at time X after the violation's effects have occurred at time X-10 in the present. This additional complexity in the scenario is visualised in Fig. 7.2.

Due to the comparably short time span between the act or omission, the effects and the dispute, traditional treaty interpretation cases (e.g., in the context of human rights violations) usually concern contemporaneous disputing parties within the same present generation at time X. In contrast, intergenerational equity normally addresses relations over a *longer* time span. As the present author understands "future generations" in the sense of unborn generations,[48] the concept of intergenerational equity links entirely different generations with one another.[49] Its inherently intertemporal nature essentially differs from the kind of inter-temporality within traditional human rights scenarios. This can be illustrated with two intermediary examples: the human right to a healthy environment and the increasing rights-based climate litigation disputes. Intergenerational rights can be considered to constitute the temporal extension of a human right to a healthy environment to the future.[50] The IACHR even stated that it was owed both to present *and* future generations.[51] However, this right to a healthy environment, including its potentially intergenerational component, is precisely not an example for traditional human rights protection. There is a transition from the traditional human rights dimension to the intergenerational dimension. As soon as a human rights violation today creates long-term consequences in the distant future, and thereby extends over a longer period of time than in the aforementioned example,[52] it leaves the realm of

[48] In detail, see *supra* in Sect. 2.2.1.2.2.

[49] Cf. Brown Weiss (1989), p. 34.

[50] Ibid., p. 117; Brown Weiss (2019), p. 57. In more detail on this relation, see *supra* in Sect. 5.2.2.2.

[51] Inter-American Court of Human Rights, *The Environment and Human Rights (Requested by the Republic of Colombia),* Advisory Opinion, 15 November 2017, retrieved 3 January 2025, from https://www.corteidh.or.cr/docs/opiniones/seriea_23_ing.pdf, para. 59. See also Brown Weiss (1989), p. 117.

[52] "Long-term" in this context means a time period of more than 70 or 80 years, or even longer, so that it encompasses more than one generation in the sense of the present book (see *supra* in Sect. 2.

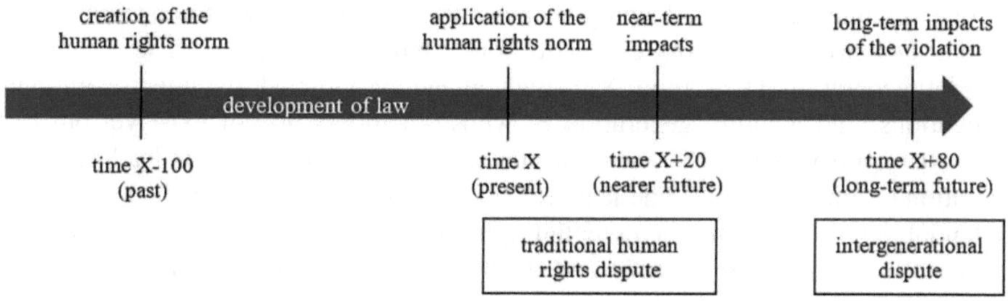


**Fig. 7.3** Distinction between the intertemporal character of human rights disputes and intergenerational disputes

traditional human rights law and becomes a matter of intergenerational equity that must be assessed differently.

The same delimitation can be applied to the context of rights-based climate litigation.[53] As far as claimants in climate litigation cases invoke the violation of their proper rights in the recent past or present (i.e., their own victim status), the case is built on a traditional human rights scenario, at least from a temporal perspective.[54] If they invoke the violation of their proper rights in the near future, the case can still be considered in the context of traditional human rights disputes, as far as the respective procedural mechanisms allow for the invocation of future violations.[55] However, if a climate litigation case aims at the protection of future generations from harm in the more distant future, the case becomes one of intergenerational equity, as has been illustrated in more detail in Chap. 5.[56] The more climate litigation aims at the prevention from long-term harm that exceeds the present generation of right-holders, the more it bursts the limits of traditional human rights disputes, particularly from the perspective of intertemporal law. For this reason, some commentators have criticised traditional human rights law to be inadequate to overcome challenges of climate change.[57] Although the boundaries between both illustrated scenarios can of course be fluid, the distinction can be based on the temporal dimension between violation and impacts. The following illustration (Fig. 7.3) displays this distinction.

2.1.2.2). The modified doctrine of intertemporal law below offers a more detailed explanation of the reference time of approximately 80 years, see *infra* in Sect. 7.3.2.

[53] In more detail on the relevance of rights-based climate litigation for intergenerational equity, see *supra* in Sect. 5.3.3.3.

[54] See, e.g., European Court of Human Rights, *Duarte Agostinho and others v. Portugal and 32 other States,* Complaint, 2 September 2020, retrieved 3 January 2025, from https://climatecasechart.com/non-us-case/youth-for-climate-justice-v-austria-et-al/.

[55] See, e.g., Federal Constitutional Court of Germany, *Climate Change (Neubauer et al.),* Order, 24 March 2021, 74 (2021) NJW 1723–1751.

[56] See, e.g., Supreme Court of Colombia, *Future Generations v. Ministry of the Environment and Others,* Decision, 5 April 2018, retrieved 3 January 2025, from https://climatecasechart.com/non-us-case/future-generation-v-ministry-environment-others/.

[57] See, e.g., Kahl (2022), pp. 173–175.

Overall, intergenerational equity always relates two parties with one another who are not contemporaneous but exist at different moments in time.[58] These can be a present generation D at time X, which allegedly violated its intergenerational obligations, and a future generation E, whose members do not exist yet but that will exist approximately 80 years after the alleged acts or omissions leading to the violation (at time X+80).[59] The legal relationship is temporally stretched so that the potential duty-bearers and the potential right-holders, or beneficiaries,[60] can technically not exist at the same time and much less be confronted in a legal dispute. Although the hypothetical scenario above has assumed that such a dispute could take place at time X+80, this was only for the purpose of illustration.[61] Indeed, State B as part of the present generation D at time X might not exist anymore at time X+80. If it does, it is much more difficult to hold State B accountable at time X+80 for the acts or omissions it was responsible for in its (then) distant past (at time X).[62] However, future generation E will claim that the present generation D as a whole (at time X) violated its intergenerational obligations, not State B alone. Although States are the only duty-bearers of intergenerational obligations under current international law,[63] the fiction of continuously existing State entities[64] does not change the legal relationship on which intergenerational disputes are based. Further, the potential victims of the violations of intergenerational equity, the members of future generation E, have not existed at time X when the violating acts or omissions occurred. Consequently, the opposing duty-bearers and right-holders remain *non*-contemporaries in this intertemporal legal relationship across generations. In addition to the time gap between the creation of intergenerational equity and the norm's application in a dispute (i.e., the first intertemporal factor), the inherently intertemporal legal relationship between generation D and generation E constitutes the second intertemporal factor in intergenerational disputes (see Fig. 7.4).

This crucial distinction to other intertemporal constellations in international law is one reason why the existing doctrine of intertemporal law is inadequate to properly solve intertemporal issues on intergenerational equity. These intertemporal particularities of the legal relationship between present and future generations are not only obvious from the foregoing comparisons. The inherently intertemporal nature of intergenerational equity is also *normatively* supported from an ethical-philosophical perspective, as illustrated in the next sub-section.

---

[58] See Brown Weiss (1989), p. 21.

[59] See *supra* note 5.

[60] On the difficulties of characterising future generations as right-holders, see *supra* in Sect. 5.2. In the following sections, the denomination as "right-holders" does not necessarily assume this characterisation.

[61] See *supra* in connection with note 3.

[62] Yet, there is a certain presumption for continuity of States, so that it will technically be the same legal entity; on the continuity of States, see Crawford and Brownlie (2019), pp. 123, 132, 412.

[63] See *supra* in Sect. 5.1.

[64] See also Brown Weiss (1989), p. 48. Critical with regard to States as reliable reference points for intergenerational time horizons, see Bertram (2023), pp. 27–28.

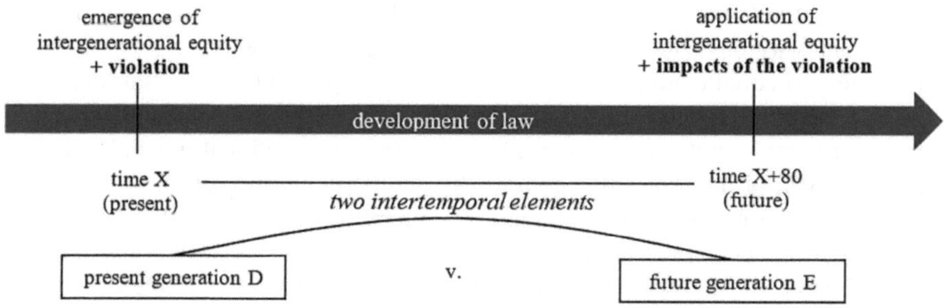


**Fig. 7.4** Inherently intertemporal nature of intergenerational disputes

#### 7.2.2.2 Intertemporal Nature from a Philosophical Perspective

In order to assess the inherently intertemporal nature of intergenerational relations from a philosophical perspective, the respective pre-legal foundations of intergenerational equity must be recalled. This particularly concerns social contract theories and communitarian approaches.[65] As demonstrated in Chap. 3, the principles of justice in *John Rawls'* thought experiment of the original position emanate from a hypothetical agreement between representatives of all deciding parties.[66] In the context of intergenerational justice, *Rawls* assumed that the representatives behind the veil of ignorance lack knowledge about certain information of their particular situation, such as information on gender, talents or disabilities, social status or the generation they are living in.[67] *Rawls* himself understood the original position not as an assembly of *all* generations, but as an assembly of all members of the same generation who do not know *which* generation they belong to, but who have to decide for all generations to come.[68] *Rawls'* conception of the original position is not compelling. In contrast, some commentators argued in favour of the original position as a general assembly, meaning a hypothetical gathering of "representatives of all past, present, and future generations [who] do not know which generation they belong to and will later live as".[69]

Both interpretations demonstrate that intergenerational equity addresses a legal relationship between generations and regulates a just distribution of resources over time. Although "[u]nborn future generations cannot agree to a social contract with current and past generations" and although "[t]ime travel is science fiction",[70] the thought experiment of a general assembly best serves as a visual illustration for the

---

[65] In more detail on these philosophical foundations, see *supra* in Sect. 3.3.3.2 and Sect. 3.3.4.2.

[66] Wenar (2021, Section 4.6).

[67] Rawls (1971/1999), pp. 118–119.

[68] Ibid., pp. 120–121; Rawls and Kelly (2001, para. 25.2).

[69] Tremmel (2013), pp. 485, 487–497. Cf. also Gosseries (2001), p. 312; Gardiner (2009), pp. 114–116.

[70] Solum (2001), p. 203.

intertemporal relationship between present and future generations. This thought experiment was envisaged by *Rawls* to establish the core principles of justice under fair and equal conditions. Transferred to the legal realm, these fair and equal conditions would be necessary to establish the substantive scope of the concept of intergenerational equity. Imagining all generations in a fictional general assembly behind the veil of ignorance, the complexity and particularities of intergenerational equity as a legal norm become obvious. The intertemporal relationship between all these "contractors"—present and future generations—necessarily must have an impact then on the determination of the temporally applicable legal regime.

A similar consideration can result from the communitarian foundations of intergenerational equity. According to *Edith Brown Weiss*, the legal relationship of intergenerational equity is based on a "partnership among all generations".[71] For communitarians, present and future generations form a transgenerational community with "lifetime-transcending interests", which is the moral reason for any obligations towards the future.[72] Although communitarian approaches explicitly rejected the idea of an intergenerational contract,[73] the idea of a transgenerational community of humanity *also* underlines the inherently intertemporal character of intergenerational equity.

Both these philosophical foundations allow for a change of perspective on the relevant legal regime of intergenerational equity. In other words: if intergenerational equity is based on the idea of a hypothetical contract between all generations, the provocative question could be: Why should the contents of intergenerational equity only be measured against the legal regime today, but not against future developments of law—although the latter will shape the legal understanding of the contracting future generations?[74] If intergenerational equity is also based on the idea of a transgenerational community of all generations, a comparable question arises: Why should the perspective of the living members of this community alone matter for the establishment of the community's legal norms? In both hypothetical scenarios, the legal interests and arguments of future generations would have to be taken into consideration alongside those of the present generation when it comes to the creation of a norm of intergenerational equity. This philosophical perspective further underlines the inherently intertemporal nature of intergenerational equity that calls for a modified doctrine of intertemporal law.

[71] Brown Weiss (1992), p. 73. See also Burke (1790/1986), p. 110.

[72] See, e.g., Thompson (2009). See also De-Shalit (1995), pp. 21–50.

[73] See, e.g., Makoff and Read (2017), pp. 242–249.

[74] Cf. also *infra* in note 122.

### 7.2.3 *The Irreversibility of Violations of Intergenerational Equity*

Another line of argument why a modified doctrine of intertemporal law is necessary builds on the irreversibility of most violations of intergenerational equity. In the aforementioned hypothetical dispute scenario between the present generation D (at time X) and a specific future generation E (at time X+80), the intertemporal questions are dealt with at a time when the effects of the violation have emanated in the meantime, in the year 2100. At that time, the present generation D has become a past generation and the future generation E has become the present generation. This means that the potential right-holder, generation E, would be expected to wait until the effects of generation D's acts arise in the distant future so that the violation of intergenerational obligations by the present (and in 2100 past) generation D could be challenged in a dispute in the future. The year 2100 would be considered the time of the dispute as well as the relevant time for assessing the temporally applicable legal regime. Existing (climate) litigation in which future harms are invoked do not refute this retrospective approach to intertemporal law. Most decisions are mainly based on occurred damage or on dangers in the nearer future. Beyond this, the cases in which damage in the distant future alone has been accepted by the courts remain scarce.[75] The retrospective view on intertemporal law is inherent in the traditional understanding of the doctrine that always relates the present to the past.[76]

However, intergenerational equity disputes conflict with a retrospective resolution of the temporal element. In *Judge Staton's* dissenting opinion in the *Juliana* proceeding, she observed:

> What sets this harm [caused by climate change] apart from all others is not just its magnitude, but its irreversibility. The devastation might look and feel somewhat different if future generations could simply pick up the pieces and restore the Nation. But plaintiffs' experts speak of a certain level of global warming as 'locking in' this catastrophic damage.[77]

This irreversible character does not only concern climate change but also other issues of intergenerational equity due to long-term degradations of the planet:

> irreversible losses of species diversity and of renewable resources such as soils and fish or costly environmental contamination [...]. [T]he present generation may trigger irreversible changes in the global climate system that will affect habitability in parts of the world.[78]

While this key observation was already made in the 1980s by *Brown Weiss*,[79] the irreversible character of intergenerational problems has become even more obvious today due to profound knowledge regarding the negative effects of climate change

---

[75] See *supra* in Sect. 7.3.3.

[76] Brown Weiss (1989), p. 30.

[77] US Court of Appeals for the 9th Circuit, *Juliana v. United States,* Dissenting Opinion of Judge Staton, 17 January 2020, 947 F.3d 1175, pp. 34–35.

[78] Brown Weiss (1989), p. 23.

[79] Ibid., pp. 6–11 See also Brown Weiss (2010), pp. 100–102, 114.

and environmental degradation in general.[80] In 2019, the President of the General Assembly warned that "only 11 years [were] left to prevent irreversible damage from climate change".[81] The time travel thought experiment in Chap. 1 has already visualised some of the potential irreversible impacts of the current environmental degradation.

In a more profound sense, every action is irreversible, as its reversal would never change history.[82] However, this is different with regard to many forms of environmental damage. These are irreversible in a more essential sense, that means the loss of certain environmental goods is final because something unique and irreplaceable will be lost.[83] The "changes do not revert if the forcing is removed, leaving a committed change to the system".[84] According to *Cass Sunstein*, this conception of irreversibility, which is typical for environmental damage, must be distinguished from a mere economic perspective, which is rather based on a cost-benefit analysis.[85] Climate change constitutes the most serious concern of irreversible damage.[86] Even if some greenhouse gas emissions may not literally be permanent but may gradually be cancelled out by planetary dynamics, they do so only over a time-scale of centuries.[87] In 2014, the IPCC stated:

> Many aspects of climate change and associated impacts will continue for centuries, even if anthropogenic emissions of greenhouse gases are stopped. The risks of abrupt or irreversible changes increase as the magnitude of the warming increases.[88]

The irreversible character of many effects of climate change is known today in detail,[89] for instance with regard to the weakening of the Atlantic meridional overturning, the collapse of the Greenland ice sheet, the permafrost carbon release and other effects.[90] Further, certain tipping points[91] have already been and can be exceeded soon. The exceedance of these tipping points can lead to abrupt changes in the global as well as regional ecosystems, reinforce further global warming and threaten the livelihood of many million people.[92] *Henry Shue* pointed out that

---

80 See, e.g., Gardiner (2006), pp. 150–152.

81 United Nations General Assembly (UNGA) (2019).

82 Buchanan (2011), p. 352.

83 Sunstein (2010), p. 237. Cf. also Buchanan (2009), p. 1262.

84 Lee et al. (2021), p. 630.

85 Buchanan (2011), pp. 351–352. In more detail on different conceptions of irreversibility: Sunstein (2010), pp. 230, 237–239.

86 Buchanan (2011), p. 350.

87 IPCC (2021), p. 21. See also Shue (2017), pp. 209, 210–212 with further references.

88 IPCC (2014, Summary for Policymakers, 8).

89 Most recently, see IPCC (2022), pp. 11, 21.

90 Lee et al. (2021), pp. 633–635. See also IPCC (2021), pp. 21–23.

91 Tipping points are "critical threshold[s] beyond which a system reorganizes, often abruptly and/or irreversibly", see Lee et al. (2021), p. 633. See already *supra* in Chap. 1 [note 30].

92 Potsdam Institute for Climate Impact Research (2024). See also Hoegh-Guldberg et al. (2018), pp. 262–264; Chen et al. (2021), pp. 202–203; Lee et al. (2021), pp. 633–634.

"passing the threshold for such a change is passing a point of no return".[93] The effects of these environmental degradations thus are irreversible by human beings for all practical purposes.[94] The same is true, for instance, in the context of biodiversity loss.[95]

From a legal perspective, irreversibility becomes relevant when considering possible remedies for the violation of international law. In an intergenerational dispute, these remedies could either be claimed today vis-à-vis the potential perpetrators of generation D, or they could be claimed in the future by generation E, which is why the international regime on reparation is briefly addressed in the following. Customary international law, as codified in Articles 34 to 37 of the ARSIWA, recognises three forms of reparation for injury caused by an internationally wrongful act: restitution, compensation and satisfaction.[96] Restitution aims at "the re-establishment of the situation which existed before occurrence of the wrongful act", as far as this restitution is not materially impossible.[97] In case of environmental damage, the ICJ has often directly turned to compensation pursuant to Article 36 of the ARSIWA instead of restitution due to the irreversible and long-lasting character of this damage; restitution was then considered to be impossible.[98] This one-sided focus on compensation was criticised by *Judge Cançado Trindade* in a separate opinion in 2018.[99] He considered compensation to be insufficient and argued for the need of non-pecuniary reparations in the context of environmental damage.[100] Nonetheless, the ICJ in that decision did not address restitution at all, but only dealt with potential compensation of the environmental damage at hand.[101]

When addressing compensation, it is not clear which forms of environmental damage are exactly encompassed by the general regime of State responsibility. A distinction is made between direct damage to the environment and indirect effects of environmental harm which might cause damage to persons and property.[102] Apart from some specific regimes, a general and legally binding definition of compensable

---

[93] Shue (2017), p. 210. See also Cassotta (2019), p. 67.

[94] Sunstein (2010), pp. 227–228; Shue (2017), p. 209. See also Buchanan (2011), pp. 351–352.

[95] See IPBES (2019), p. 10.

[96] See also Permanent Court of International Justice, *Case concerning the Factory at Chorzów (Germany v. Poland) (Claim for Indemnity),* Judgment (Merits), 13 September 1928, PCIJ Ser. A, No. 10.

[97] ICJ, *Pulp Mills on the River Uruguay (Argentina v. Uruguay),* Judgment, 20 April 2010, ICJ Reports 2010, 14, para. 273. See also Art. 35 of the ARSIWA.

[98] Fitzmaurice (2010), p. 1019; Schmalenbach (2022), pp. 349–350.

[99] ICJ, *Certain Activities Carried Out by Nicaragua in the Border Area (Costa Rica v. Nicaragua), Compensation,* Separate Opinion of Judge Cançado Trindade, 2 February 2018, ICJ Reports 2018, 61.

[100] Ibid., paras. 42–45, 59–65 with references to IDI (1997, Art. 24, 25).

[101] ICJ, *Certain Activities Carried Out by Nicaragua in the Border Area (Costa Rica v. Nicaragua), Compensation,* Judgment, 2 February 2018, ICJ Reports 2018, 15, para. 31. In more detail, see Tanaka (2021).

[102] Schmalenbach (2022), p. 350.

environmental damage does not exist yet. In 2008, the UNEP suggested in its 'Draft Guidelines for the Development of National Legislation on Liability' the following very wide definition:

> 'Environmental damage' means an adverse or negative effect on the environment that [...] (b) [is] significant which is to be determined on the basis of factors, such as: (i) [the] long-term or permanent change, to be understood as change that will not be redressed through natural recovery within an [sic.] reasonable period of time; (ii) [the] extent of the qualitative or quantitative changes that adversely or negatively affect the environment; (iii) [the] reduction or loss of the ability of the environment to provide goods and services either of a permanent nature or on a temporary basis; (iv) [the] extent of any adverse or negative effect/impact on human health; (v) [the] aesthetic, scientific, and recreational value of parks, wilderness areas, and other lands.[103]

The IDI also envisaged a broad understanding in a resolution from 1997, as it included "both economic loss and the costs of environmental reinstatement and rehabilitation",[104] and clarified that "the fact that environmental damage is irreparable or unquantifiable shall not result in exemption from compensation".[105] However, such a wide understanding has not become part of general international law.[106] Article 36(2) of the ARSIWA requires financial measurability for compensation under public international law whereas the loss of certain environmental resources is not financially measurable.[107] Consequently, while some forms of environmental damage may be compensable under the current law of State responsibility, the most serious and long-lasting effects of the present generation's environmentally harmful activities exceed the economically-driven logic of reparation.[108]

This combination of the irreversibility of many environmental damage and strict criteria for compensation generates a particularly striking problem for intergenerational equity since these long-lasting and irreversible effects often cause harm only over a longer time span. As long as long-term effects on flora, fauna and future human beings are not encompassed by the market-driven understanding of damage and reparation,[109] the existing legal framework of State responsibility lacks the capacity to sufficiently remedy violations of intergenerational obligations *today*. The following paradox illustrates this dilemma: On the one hand, if a claimant at time X attempted to confront a duty-bearer of intergenerational equity within the present generation D with this duty-bearer's violations of intergenerational obligations, no measurable and compensable damage to human beings or the environment has occurred so far, according to the existing law of State

[103] United Nations Environment Programme (2008, Guideline 3 para. 3).

[104] IDI (1997, Art. 24).

[105] Ibid., Art. 25. See also *Certain Activities Carried Out by Nicaragua, 2018* (Separate Opinion of Judge Cançado Trindade), *supra* note 99, para. 46.

[106] Schmalenbach (2022), p. 350.

[107] Scovazzi (2001), p. 65; Bowman (2002), pp. 42–43; Fitzmaurice (2010), p. 1019; Schmalenbach (2022), p. 351.

[108] Boyle (2002); Fitzmaurice (2010), pp. 1019–1020; Schmalenbach (2022), p. 351.

[109] Fitzmaurice (2010), pp. 1019–1020; Schmalenbach (2022), pp. 349–350.

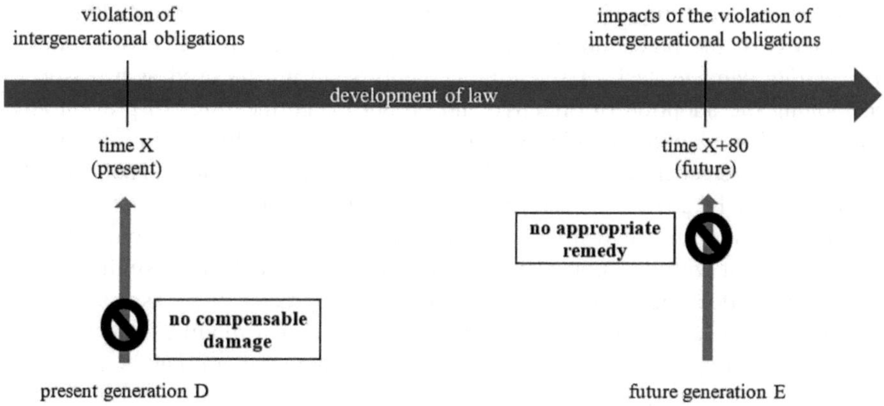


**Fig. 7.5** Irreversibility paradox in intergenerational disputes

responsibility.[110] There are no fitting remedies because the claimant would fail to present evidence of an existing measurable and compensable damage.

On the other hand, if the dispute is to be resolved at time X+80, when the intergenerational damage on the environment and human beings will have occurred, there will be a measurable and thus compensable damage. However, two other problems occur that render potential claims meaningless. First, the potential perpetrator and duty-bearer of intergenerational equity, the present generation D, will have become the past generation—a problem that has already been addressed above regarding the inherently intertemporal nature of intergenerational relations.[111] Second, with regard to reparation, the potential right-holders that have been harmed might be able to claim reparation of a specific damage, but the respondent to that claim will not be able to offer an appropriate remedy anymore, since the exceeded tipping points of the climatic system and the irreversible character of the damage could not be restituted or compensated anymore. Reparation in any form would be impossible, thus, future respondents of an intergenerational claim would lack any possibility to adhere to their responsibility.[112] Moreover, the environmental damage caused in the meantime might have become so disastrous that human and non-human life will be impossible, or subject to unthinkable and catastrophic circumstances on a planet hostile to life—leading to an irreversibility paradox. This paradox is visualised in Fig. 7.5.

[110] Already today, there is a lot of perceptible damage caused by climate change and other environmental degradations. However, strictly speaking, this damage does not arise from violations of intergenerational obligations since it technically concerns matters of *intra*-generational equity due to the specific understanding of "future generations" presented *supra* in Sect. 2.2.1.2.2. The present book thus focuses on the long-term effects that have not amounted to measurable damage today, see already *supra* note 52.

[111] See *supra* in Sect. 7.2.2.1.

[112] Cf. also Ekardt (2021), pp. 300–301.

So far, irreversibility of environmental damage has most often been addressed in the context of the precautionary approach: "[w]here there is a risk of serious or *irreversible* damage, lack of scientific certainty shall not be used as a reason for postponing the adoption of effective and proportionate measures to prevent environmental degradation" (emphasis added).[113] There is an obvious link to the protection of future generations, as the UNSG Report on intergenerational solidarity has already stated in 2013.[114] Therefore, some commentators argued in favour of a modified form of an irreversible harm precautionary principle that would combine risk assessment with decision-making under uncertainty and irreversibility.[115] The present book does not follow this precautionary approach in its assessment, but argues that the same reasons that militate in favour of a modified precautionary approach also require a modified understanding of intertemporal law in the context of intergenerational equity. The problem of "intergenerational buck-passing" leaves future generations with unsolvable intergenerational problems.[116] Instead of being trapped in this "intergenerational buck-passing, the resolution of the intertemporal dispute between present and future generations must be solved before irreversible damage is caused and compensation is not possible any longer. It cannot be sufficient to hide behind the theoretical inaptitude of current legal imagination.[117] Instead, the irreversibility of most violations of intergenerational equity requires the present generation to solve the intertemporal law assessment of the concept today by adopting a modified version of intertemporal law, which overcomes the futility of future dispute resolution. If the temporally applicable legal regime is thus determined *today* in order to resolve the intergenerational dispute, then the present generation D can react with reversible forms of remedies at time X to the compensable damage that will occur to future generation E at time X+80. The irreversibility paradox could be overcome by a new perspective on the intertemporal legal relationship, as illustrated in Fig. 7.6.

### 7.2.4 Interim Conclusion on the Need for a Modification

The delimitation of the temporally applicable law for intergenerational equity cannot be solely based on the existing doctrine of intertemporal law. The foregoing observations have illustrated that intergenerational equity requires the present generation

[113] See, e.g., UNCED (1992, Principle 15); International Group of Experts for the Pact (2017, Art. 6); *United Nations Framework Convention on Climate Change* (UNFCCC), adopted 9 May 1992, entered into force 21 March 1994, 1771 UNTS 107, Art. 3(3). In detail, see also Mbengue (2019), p. 74.

[114] United Nations Secretary-General (2013, para. 26). See also briefly *supra* in Sect. 2.3.

[115] Farrow (2004); Gardiner (2006), pp. 161–165; Sunstein (2010); Hartzell-Nichols (2019).

[116] Gardiner (2006).

[117] Ibid., 151, 166.

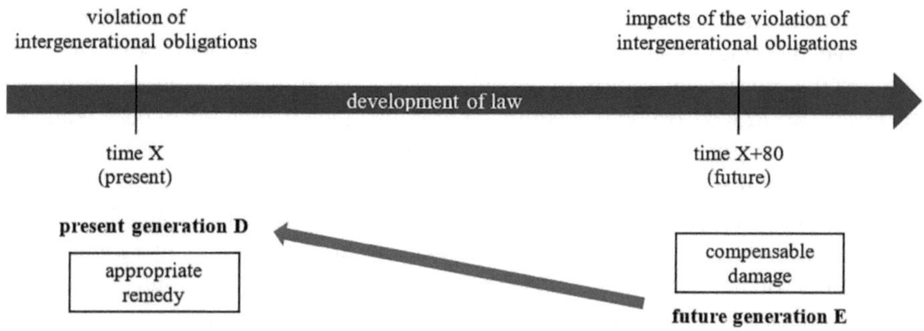


**Fig. 7.6** Intertemporal legal relationship to overcome the irreversibility paradox

to take another perspective on their legal relationship towards the future. The existing doctrine of intertemporal law does not adequately address the particular constellation of intergenerational relations. On a formal level, the customary legal status of intergenerational equity would already require an adapted version of the existing evolutionary, and treaty-related, approaches.

Beyond this methodological difficulty, other important particularities of intergenerational equity result in the inadequacy of an unmodified application of intertemporal law. To begin with, the intertemporal nature of intergenerational equity concerns a legal relationship that extends over time. This nature considerably differs from all other legal relationships, which traditionally oppose contemporaneous disputing parties of the same (present) generation. Intertemporal law normally becomes relevant in cases of a legal dispute in the present between legal actors in the present on a scenario that touches legal questions with links to the past and the present. In contrast, violations of intergenerational obligations address behaviour of legal actors in the present that causes effects in the (distant) future on legal actors in the future and which touches legal questions with links to the present and the future. Therefore, it is not persuasive to apply a traditional retrospective conception of intertemporal law to the delimitation of the temporal scope of intergenerational equity. It is not the time gap between a norm in the past and a dispute in the present that establishes the intertemporal nature of intergenerational equity. This intertemporal nature is established by the temporal non-contemporaneity between the duty-bearers and the beneficiaries of intergenerational equity.

This intertemporal character of intergenerational equity is also supported by philosophical perceptions of intergenerational justice, particularly *John Rawls'* social contract theory, but also communitarian approaches to justice. *Rawls'* idea of justice is based on principles that all affected representatives would agree to in the original position behind a veil of ignorance. This naturally requires asking which rules these representatives might have in mind when they decide on the principles of justice. In a hypothetical general assembly of all generations behind this veil of ignorance, it seems logical that not only the legal perceptions of the *present* generation would play a role, but that the equal and fair conditions of negotiation would also demand to take into consideration the legal perceptions of all future generations. These conceptional questions from a philosophical point of view challenge the traditional perspective on legal relationships. This point of view requires the present generation to consider legal developments, which have not yet occurred. As *Rawls'* original position only constitutes a thought experiment, one could easily argue that it could not change any actual legal assessment of intergenerational equity. However, his thought experiment must at least serve as a starting point for any further consideration of intergenerational equity in its legal manifestation.[118] International environmental law in general and intergenerational equity in particular are fundamentally based on principles of distributive justice so that they cannot be detached from their philosophical foundations.

Beside the intertemporal nature of intergenerational equity, the main characteristics of violations of intergenerational obligations also require a modification of intertemporal law. These violations have long-term and often irreversible effects that do not occur until decades later. The existing approach of intertemporal law would require to await the time X+80 in the future when the impacts of the violation have manifested in order to determine the applicable law to solve the intergenerational dispute. This hypothetical future application of intertemporal law leads to unsatisfactory results as there will be no appropriate remedy for the irreversible impacts of intergenerational problems.

Consequently, the perspective of intertemporal law must be modified in the context of intergenerational equity. Instead of leaving the determination to future courts or interpreters for the retrospective resolution of unsolvable future disputes, the temporally applicable law should be determined today. This requires a forward-looking approach to intertemporal law, which not only links the present to the past, but also extends the present to the future. The following section suggests some modifications of intertemporal law.

## 7.3 A Modified Doctrine of Intertemporal Law Applicable to the Customary Norm of Intergenerational Equity

The modified doctrine of intertemporal law should not be considered an entirely new conception but rather as a modification of the existing doctrine. There is no need to reinvent the wheel. Instead, it is a better option to identify starting points from the foregoing hypothetical application of the existing doctrine and to adapt them to the concept of intergenerational equity. This means that the dichotomous character of intertemporal law is also relevant in this modification. Both elements, the principle of contemporaneity and evolutionary approaches, determine the temporally applicable legal regime with regard to intergenerational equity, which is first addressed in the following sub-sections (Sect. 7.3.1). However, the necessary shift of perspective is the main challenge of a modified doctrine of intertemporal law. This section

[118] On the consequences of this starting point, see *infra* in Sect. 7.3.3.3.

describes this shift of perspective and compares the suggested approach to existing attempts to progressively shape the future development of international law (Sect. 7.3.2). Then, fitting starting points are identified that allow for certain predictions of the future development of intergenerational equity in particular (Sect. 7.3.3). Eventually, an outlook section elaborates on a potential framework to methodologically concretise these predictions of the future development of intergenerational equity (Sect. 7.3.4).

## *7.3.1 The Modified Components of Intertemporal Law*

Starting with the two pillars of intertemporal law, any modified doctrine would also build on contemporaneity and evolutionary approaches. Therefore, the next sub-sections first address the legal regime in the present, contemporaneous to the establishment of the customary norm of intergenerational equity (Sect. 7.3.1.1). While the application of evolutionary treaty interpretation has been skipped in the hypothetical case above,[119] the modified doctrine of intertemporal law would then have to establish adequate parameters for evolutionary approaches, which are not solely based on treaty interpretation ("generic term", "treaty's object and purpose"), but which can also be applied to the legal source of customary international law (Sect. 7.3.1.2).

### 7.3.1.1 Modified Version of Contemporaneity

Contemporaneity remains the primary point of departure for an intertemporal assessment and refers to the law contemporaneous to the norm's creation.[120] In the hypothetical dispute scenario above that takes place in the year 2100, intergenerational equity has already been assessed under the principle of contemporaneity. This analysis pointed to the creation of intergenerational equity in the (hypothetical) past of the beginning twenty-first century.[121] The modified version of contemporaneity does not change this result. The essential question remains at which time or time period the concept of intergenerational equity has evolved as a legal norm. This time would mark the legal regime contemporaneous to its creation.[122] With respect to the general conception of intergenerational equity, which

---

[119] See *supra* in Sect. 7.1.3.

[120] *Island of Palmas* (Arbitral Award), *supra* note 13, p. 845.

[121] See *supra* notes 14–18.

[122] From the point of view of an intergenerational legal relationship, it could even be argued that the criterion of "contemporaneity" in the sense of intertemporal law must be understood in a more complex way than merely referring to the creation of an emerging norm of intergenerational equity in the present. If one linked the contemporaneity criterion to the legal relationship instead, the criterion is stretched to its limits in the context of intergenerational relations since it is not even clear

constitutes the currently binding manifestation of the concept, its first roots can be traced back to the beginning of the twentieth century; it further developed in the 1970s and has become more relevant since the 1990s until today.[123] Consequently, the "time of creation" of intergenerational equity relates to the three decades since the 1990s when the norm emerged in the form of the general conception in customary international law. Since the specific doctrine of intergenerational equity has not gained legally binding force yet, it does not form part of the contemporaneous legal regime relevant at this point. However, the transitional relationship between the contemporaneous general conception and the more specific manifestation of intergenerational equity is still important within the modified doctrine of intertemporal law, as addressed below.[124]

More generally, the foregoing observations have already illustrated a first particularity of this modified doctrine with regard to the addressed customary norm. While treaty norms are established at a very specific time in the past, at the time of the respective treaty's conclusion, customary international law is a continuously evolving source that is not necessarily created at one specific moment, but emanates from continuing State practice and *opinio iuris*. No particular duration for these elements is necessary,[125] and "the passage of time of only a short period of time is not necessarily, or of itself, a bar to the formation of a new rule of customary international law".[126] Yet, at least a short period of time is necessary to establish the crucial extensive and virtually uniform practice.[127] Therefore, the modified version of contemporaneity in the context of customary international law always points to a more extended time of creation than with respect to a treaty norm. More specifically, this is the period at the beginning of the twenty-first century.[128]

It might seem more than obvious to address the current legal regime when analysing the contents of a legal principle such as intergenerational equity. For this reason, every assessment of intergenerational equity in scholarship and jurisprudence always turned to the contemporaneous legal regime. This reflects the traditional positivist approach to international law, which examines the law as it is—not

---

what "contemporaneous" would exactly mean due to the inherently intertemporal nature of this relationship, see *supra* in Sect. 7.2.2.1. Starting with the point of view of the present generation D, contemporaneity could relate to this potential duty-bearer at time X. However, taking as an example the potential beneficiary, future generation E, "contemporaneous" could equally refer to that time in the future (time X+80). See already *supra* note 74. However, this book does not follow up on this point of view in the following modifications.

[123] In detail, see *supra* in Sect. 4.2.2.1.

[124] See *infra* in Sect. 7.3.3.2.

[125] ILC (2018a, Conclusion 8(2)).

[126] ICJ, *North Sea Continental Shelf Cases (Germany v. Denmark; Germany v. Netherlands)*, Judgment (Merits), 20 February 1969, ICJ Reports 1969, 3, para. 74.

[127] The existence of "instant custom" is generally rejected, see ILC (2018a, Conclusion 8, para. 9) with reference to *North Sea Continental Shelf* (Judgment (Merits)), *supra* note 126, para. 74.

[128] See already *supra* in Sect. 7.1.2.

as it ought to be or as it will become.[129] For the same reason, this book has also started with this positivist approach in assessing the historical background, legal contents and the current legal nature of intergenerational equity in the first chapters. Even the extensive analysis of the open issues of intergenerational equity in Chap. 5 has served the purpose of distinguishing between the *lex lata* status of intergenerational equity today and the suggestions *de lege ferenda* with regard to the duty-bearers, right-holders and institutional frameworks of implementation. The transition between the law *de lege lata* and *de lege ferenda* often is not as clear-cut as the legal discourse might assume.[130] Applying the modified version of contemporaneity to intergenerational equity challenges this clear-cut distinction even more due to the continuous development of the concept in the present. Therefore, the contemporaneous perspective on intergenerational equity can only be considered the necessary point of departure of intertemporal law—which is followed by the more decisive step towards modified evolutionary approaches to intergenerational equity.

#### 7.3.1.2 Modified Evolutionary Approaches

The second element of intertemporal law requires turning to evolutionary approaches, that means taking into account the evolution of law subsequent to the norm's creation when assessing the temporally relevant content of intergenerational equity. The traditional evolutionary approaches of intertemporal law have so far mainly been applied to the interpretation of treaty regimes. Further, these approaches of evolutionary interpretation only applied under certain conditions (i.e., the existence of a generic term or the general evolutionary object and purpose of the respective treaty). As the present work primarily assesses the customary norm of intergenerational equity, the existing evolutionary approaches do not fit and they must be modified for the context of customary international law.

In the hypothetical application of the unmodified doctrine above, it has been assumed that the conditions of an evolutionary approach to intergenerational equity would be met. The relevant evolution of law pointed to the time period between the 2020s (or time X) and the hypothetical future dispute in the year 2100 (or time X +80).[131] The following sub-sections dismantle the mere *assumption* and have a closer look at adequately modified evolutionary approaches. Two aspects are relevant for this closer look: First, the generally more dynamic character of customary international law vis-à-vis treaty law has to be taken into account,[132] which means that evolutionary approaches might even face less strict requirements.[133] Second, the existing evolutionary approaches nonetheless serve as helpful starting points for the

[129] Lachenmann (2012, paras. 2–5).

[130] See also Virally (1988), p. 73; von Arnauld (2021). In more detail, see *infra* in Sect. 7.3.3.1.

[131] See *supra* in Sect. 7.1.3.

[132] Cf. ILC (2018a, Conclusion 8 para. 9).

[133] See already *supra* in Sect. 7.2.1.

following modification. However, the following sub-sections illustrate that the original generic term approach itself is inadequate in the context of customary norms (Sect. 7.3.1.2.1) whereas the evolutionary object and purpose approach can be appropriately modified for this context (Sect. 7.3.1.2.2).

#### 7.3.1.2.1 Inadequate Generic Term Approach

A stand-alone generic term approach would require that the concept of intergenerational equity contains legal terms "whose content the parties expected would change through time".[134] The problem of this approach is that the customary norm of intergenerational equity does not consist of any *written* generic terms comparable to specific treaty provisions. In order to find an adequate modification for unwritten norms of customary international law, the "generic term" approach could be analogously applied to the most common wordings of the concept of intergenerational equity. The general conception of intergenerational equity, as legally binding norm, is reflected in typical but varying formulations.[135] These formulations either involve the requirement to meet or to take into account the needs of future generations,[136] or their interests respectively;[137] or they refer to the responsibility of the present generation towards future generations,[138] sometimes linked to the requirement to protect the environment for the benefit of future generations.[139] The variety of wordings illustrates the difficulty of applying generic term approaches to a customary norm.

Additionally, the static or generic nature of a treaty provision would normally depend on the original intention of the treaty parties.[140] Instead of focusing on the intention of specific authors of the corresponding treaty term, it is unclear whose intention is relevant in the context of customary norms. Although reference to the

---

[134] ICJ, *Kasikili/Sedudu Island (Botswana v. Namibia),* Declaration of Judge Higgins, 13 December 1999, ICJ Reports 1999, 1113, para. 2.

[135] For a comprehensive analysis of the relevant documents, see *supra* in Sect. 4.2.2.1.

[136] See, e.g., "[to meet] the needs of the present without compromising the ability of future generations to meet their own needs" (WCED (1987, Chapter 2 para. 1)); or "to equitably meet developmental and environmental needs of present and future generations" (UNCED (1992, Principle 3)).

[137] See, e.g., "due regard shall be paid to the interests of present and future generations" (*Agreement Governing the Activities of States on the Moon and Other Celestial Bodies* (Moon Agreement), adopted 5 December 1979, entered into force 11 July 1984, 1363 UNTS 3, Art. 4). See also Dupuy and Viñuales (2018), p. 92.

[138] See, e.g., "solemn responsibility to protect and improve the environment for present and future generations" (UN (1972, Principle 1)); or "a dedication to future generation" (UNSG (2013, para. 3)). See also Collins (2007), p. 118.

[139] This formulation is particularly common in some of the treaty regimes that incorporate the general conception of intergenerational equity, see, e.g., Art. 3(1) of the UNFCCC.

[140] See Inagaki (2015), pp. 135–137.

intention-based element of *opinio iuris* could be a possible option,[141] there is a clear difference between generic terms in a written treaty text and the unwritten source of customary international law.[142] The intention of the concerned States is not explicitly articulated in the documents that reflect the general conception of intergenerational equity. In case of written treaty terms, their interpretation can at least be based on specific acts or statements in the course of the foregoing negotiations. For instance, judicial bodies can refer to the relevant *travaux préparatoires* in order to assess the intention of the treaty parties.[143] Even though the aforementioned common formulations of intergenerational equity can also be found in written soft law texts, these documents do not have the same authority on their own to be interpreted like treaty terms. Furthermore, the difficulties of clearly assessing the *opinio iuris* of States with regard to a customary norm of environmental law[144] are even amplified with regard to the evolutionary character of this norm. For these reasons, the analogous assessment of the actual intention of relevant States cannot give convincing and reliable answers as to the evolutionary quality of the corresponding terms.

At this stage, the broader perspective on generic terms comes into play. Rather than limiting themselves to the parties' obvious and primary intention, international courts and tribunals have demonstrated more flexibility as they resorted to an analysis of the *presumed* intention of the parties.[145] Regardless of the parties' obvious intention, the relevant notions could be evolutionary by nature so that they "must consequently be deemed to have [been] accepted [...] as such".[146] However, with respect to customary international law, the assessment of the presumed intention of all States that are bound by a norm becomes so vague and abstract that it is not distinguishable anymore from the evolutionary approach based on the object and purpose of a legal norm.[147] Therefore, it is more suitable to dismiss the distinction between generic term and object and purpose approaches in the context of the customary norm of intergenerational equity. The following modified evolutionary approach focuses on an assessment of the "object and purpose" of the concept, which can answer the question whether the general conception of intergenerational equity is to be understood as a static concept or whether it is subject to evolutionary

---

[141] On consent in treaty as well as in customary international law, see Brunnée (2022, paras. 1–4, 6–7, 16–17); Kämmerer (2024), pp. 69–70, 81, 90–94. Stressing that customary international law does not require consent in an intentional sense, see Pellet (2012), p. 819.

[142] Cf. Herdegen (2020, para. 63).

[143] See Dörr (2018, para. 111); Herdegen (2020, para. 16).

[144] See Dupuy (2010), pp. 450–454; Dupuy et al. (2021), pp. 389–392. In more detail on these difficulties, see already *supra* in Sect. 4.2.2.

[145] See ILC (2018b, Conclusion 8 paras. 11–12); Dupuy (2011), pp. 130–131. In more detail, see *supra* in Sect. 6.2.2 [notes 121–125].

[146] ICJ, *Legal Consequences for States of the Continued Presence of South Africa in Namibia (South West Africa) notwithstanding Security Council Resolution 276 (1970)*, Advisory Opinion, 21 June 1971, ICJ Reports 1971, 16, para. 53.

[147] See *infra* note 181.

developments. This approach would be identical with an underlying presumed intention of the States within their *opinio iuris*, as briefly illustrated below.

#### 7.3.1.2.2 Evolutionary Approach Based on the "Object and Purpose" of Intergenerational Equity

The evolutionary approaches based on a treaty's object and purpose can either point to a static or to a dynamic understanding of the treaty's provisions.[148] The notion of "object and purpose" is linked to treaties in the sense of the VCLT.[149] Jurisprudence on this evolutionary approach referred to the object and purpose of a treaty as a whole.[150] For instance, the "living instrument" approach of human rights bodies is also based on the nature of the respective human rights instruments in general.[151] Thus, these approaches require an overarching framework from which the object and purpose can be derived.[152]

In contrast to treaty interpretation, the evolutionary assessment of the customary manifestation of intergenerational equity cannot be based on a binding treaty text, which could be categorised as a "living instrument" based on its object and purpose. For this reason, evolutionary interpretation must be appropriately modified in order to analyse whether this customary norm could also contain a comparable object and purpose, and whether this object and purpose would justify an evolutionary approach to its temporal application. Generally, "object and purpose" is understood as a single notion without distinction between the object and the purpose.[153] Before the appearance of this notion, the same idea was sometimes discussed as the "spirit of a treaty".[154] It referred to the overall idea, the main aim or objective behind a treaty regime. The object and purpose approach is thus based on a norm's *telos* instead of its textual meaning alone.[155] Such a teleological observation of intergenerational equity could be possible despite the lack of a written treaty text.

Intergenerational equity limits the present generations' possibilities to meet their needs as it forbids them to "compromis[e] the ability of future generations to meet their own needs".[156] The overall idea behind the concept is the "environmental

---

[148] Fitzmaurice (2008), p. 117; Inagaki (2015), pp. 137–139.

[149] See Art. 31(1) of the VCLT. See also Klabbers (2006).

[150] See, e.g., PCA, *Award in the Arbitration regarding the Iron Rhine ("Ijzeren Rijn") Railway between the Kingdom of Belgium and the Kingdom of the Netherlands,* Arbitral Award, 24 May 2005, RIAA XXVII (2005), 35, para. 80. See also Klabbers (2006, para. 7).

[151] See, e.g., ECtHR, *Case of Tyrer v. The United Kingdom,* Judgment, 25 April 1978, ECHR Series A no. 26, para. 31. See also *supra* in Sect. 6.2.3.

[152] Cf. Klabbers (2006, para. 6).

[153] Ibid., para. 8.

[154] Ibid., para. 1.

[155] On the nuances between "object and purpose" and "teleological interpretation", see ibid., paras. 17–20; Fitzmaurice (2008), pp. 113–117; and already *supra* in Sect. 6.2.3.

[156] WCED (1987, Introduction para. 27, Chapter 2 para. 1).

responsibility towards thc future".[157] Intergenerational equity aims at shaping the relationship between present and future generations in the use and exploitation of the planetary resources.[158] Overall, its object and purpose could be identified as the balance between the needs of present and future generations in respect of the distribution of natural resources.[159] This object and purpose is comparable to the object and purpose of a treaty notion. If this object and purpose required an evolutionary understanding, intergenerational equity would be subjected to the developing temporal legal regime rather than a static understanding of contemporaneity.

As already demonstrated above, intergenerational equity profoundly differs from any other international legal relationship.[160] The evolutionary object and purpose of these other relationships emanates from the fact that a legal norm created in the past aimed at the regulation of legal disputes between disputing parties also in the future and adapted to the evolving legal circumstances of that future. For instance, the "living instruments" in human rights treaties aimed at regulating future human rights disputes in the context of the respective time. In contrast, intergenerational equity does not aim at the regulation of future disputes between future opposing parties. Instead, it extends the legal relationship between the opposing parties themselves (i.e., generations at different moments in time) from the present to the future across time (see Figs. 7.4 and 7.6). Intergenerational equity thus is inherently future-oriented.[161] According to *Virginie Barral*, the concept "by its nature demands the adoption of a long-term perspective".[162]

This long-term perspective of intergenerational equity requires a certain flexibility and openness to future developments of facts and law. The object and purpose to balance the actions of present and the needs of future generations cannot be achieved if the intergenerational obligations would be limited to a static understanding of the norm. New technology has increased the impact that the present generation's actions have on the interests and needs of future generations. New scientific findings have further increased the present generation's knowledge of these impacts and their consequences for future generations. These new developments necessarily change the factual basis for any legal relationship between present and future generations. They also immensely influence the legal meaning and scope as well as the importance of the present generation's obligation to take into account the interests of future generations. Former 'present generations' might have compromised the ability of former 'future generations' to meet their needs, but their limited or non-existent knowledge of these impacts led to reduced intergenerational obligations in the past. However, the developments of environmental science and law have not been

---

[157] Collins (2007), p. 118.

[158] Brown Weiss (1989), p. 21.

[159] See ibid., pp. 37–38; Hadjiargyrou (2016), pp. 257–258.

[160] On the inherently intertemporal nature of intergenerational equity, see *supra* in Sect. 7.2.2.

[161] Cf. Brown Weiss (1989), p. 34; Molinari (2015), pp. 140, 155.

[162] Barral (2012), p. 382.

unforeseen, but could have been expected to a certain degree.[163] Consequently, the content of intergenerational equity depends on the evolutionary development of factual knowledge and the corresponding legal regime.

These observations on the object and purpose of intergenerational equity as such are further supported by a broader perspective on the system, to which intergenerational equity belongs.[164] If one considers "object and purpose" to refer to an overarching idea behind a certain norm,[165] then the perspective on the overarching framework of international environmental law becomes important for the analysis. Some of the aforementioned particularities of international environmental law could assist in this analysis.[166] For instance, the evolutionary character of environmental norms played an important role in some environmental cases.[167] According to *Judge Cançado Trindade* in the *Whaling in the Antarctic* case, the evolving character of environmental conservation provisions even turned the Whaling Convention into a living instrument.[168] Within legal scholarship, *Yoshifumi Tanaka* observed that the protection of future generations would be "at the heart of environmental protection"[169] and:

> The interpretation and application of rules of international environmental law give rise [...] to inter-temporal issues since measures taken by public authorities of today may affect the living conditions of future generations. It can be argued that inter-temporality is an important element to be taken into account in the interpretation and application of rules of international environmental law.[170]

Other commentators made comparable comments with regard to sustainable development and common concern and common heritage of humankind.[171]

---

[163] Cf. ICJ, *Gabčíkovo-Nagymaros Project (Hungary v. Slovakia),* Judgment, 25 September 1997, ICJ Reports 1997, 7, para. 104.

[164] In general on the systemic framework of intergenerational equity, see *supra* in Sect. 2.3.

[165] With regard to treaty law, see Klabbers (2006, para. 6).

[166] See *supra* in Sect. 6.2.4.

[167] See, e.g., *Gabčíkovo-Nagymaros Project* (Judgment), *supra* note 163, para. 140; ICJ, *Gabčíkovo-Nagymaros Project (Hungary v. Slovakia),* Separate Opinion of Vice-President Weeramantry, 25 September 1997, ICJ Reports 1997, 88, p. 114; World Trade Organization Appellate Body, *United States – Import Prohibition of Certain Shrimp and Shrimp Products,* Report of the Appellate Body, 12 October 1998, WTO Doc. WT/DS58/AB/R, paras. 129–130. With regard to the *Gabčíkovo-Nagymaros Project* decision, some arguments of the ICJ rather referred to specific generic terms than to an overarching object and purpose, see *Gabčíkovo-Nagymaros Project* (Judgment), *supra* note 163, para. 104. However, there are even some parallels between these terms and the typical formulations of intergenerational equity that also aim at the protection of the environment for the benefit of future generations.

[168] ICJ, *Whaling in the Antarctic (Australia v. Japan: New Zealand intervening),* Separate Opinion of Judge Cançado Trindade, 31 March 2014, ICJ Reports 2014, 348, paras. 27–40; Kolb (2016), pp. 158–165; Mileva and Fortuna (2019), p. 139.

[169] Tanaka (2013), p. 156.

[170] Ibid., p. 175.

[171] Borg (1998), pp. 135, 137–138; Barral (2012), p. 382.

Notwithstanding this, a pure subject matter classification of environmental norms as evolutionary is not sufficient as an explanation for evolutionary approaches.[172] However, as suggested by *Julian Arato*, and explained in detail in Chap. 6 above,[173] the assessment of the nature of the relevant *obligations* can assist in determining the evolutionary character of intergenerational equity. According to *Arato*, the nature of obligations can be distinguished between traditional reciprocal obligations and integral non-reciprocal obligations.[174] Intergenerational relations are the archetype of integral obligations in international environmental law. First, they are entirely based on concepts of non-reciprocity, or at least only indirect forms of reciprocity.[175] Second, intergenerational equity is also archetypical in the sense that it is strongly linked to concepts like common heritage and common concern of humankind.[176] Intergenerational obligations are not owed to specific other States in a reciprocal manner but to the whole international community of future humanity.[177] Moreover, intergenerational equity can be considered a temporal extension of human rights to future human beings,[178] which further supports this integral nature of intergenerational obligations. All of these arguments speak in favour of an evolutionary understanding of the concept.

Consequently, the inherently intertemporal character of intergenerational equity does not only justify the modification of the intertemporal law doctrine in general, as demonstrated above.[179] It also points to the necessarily evolutionary object and purpose behind the concept that requires a "living" and dynamic process in order to adopt to a changing legal regime.[180] At this point, an argumentation analogous to the jurisprudential approach of "presumed intention" would come to the same conclusion:[181] Due to the future-oriented character of intergenerational equity, the concept "must consequently be deemed to have [been] accepted [...] as such".[182] As mentioned above, this generic term reference to the presumed intention is so vague in the context of customary international law that it is not actually linked to a measurable intent of the relevant States anymore. Therefore, this book suggests to reject the generic term approach with regard to intergenerational equity, and instead focuses on the analysis of an analogous object and purpose, which better fits the legal status of a customary norm.

---

[172] Arato (2018), pp. 209–212; Hamamoto (2020), pp. 76–77.

[173] See *supra* in Sect. 6.2.4.2.

[174] Arato (2018), pp. 217–218, 223.

[175] In detail on this issue, see *supra* in Sect. 3.2.3.

[176] Cançado Trindade (2020), pp. 344, 347; Borg (1998), p. 135. In more detail, see *supra* in Sect. 2.3.3.

[177] This is independent from the question of corresponding right-holders, see *supra* in Sect. 5.2.

[178] Brown Weiss (2021, para. 15); Hiskes (2005), pp. 1355–1356.

[179] See *supra* in Sect. 7.2.2.

[180] Thacher (1987), p. 136.

[181] See *supra* note 147.

[182] *Namibia* (Advisory Opinion), *supra* note 146, para. 53.

After the application of this modified evolutionary approach to intergenerational equity, a merely contemporaneous perspective would fail to recognise the concept's evolutionary nature and would be contra-intuitive to its temporally extended legal reference points. The temporally applicable legal regime of intergenerational equity must be determined not only according to the principle of contemporaneity, but primarily in an evolutionary manner.

### 7.3.2 *Shift of Perspective from Retrospective to Prospective Assessment*

So far, the modifications of the doctrine of intertemporal law for intergenerational equity were only cosmetic since they took the existing two elements as starting points and adapted them to the context of customary international law. The characterisation of intergenerational equity as an inherently intertemporal notion pointed to its evolutionary character that has to be interpreted and applied in light of the evolving legal regime. Beyond this, the main modification of the doctrine of intertemporal law follows from the two reasons mentioned above: the inherently intertemporal nature of intergenerational equity and the irreversibility of its violations. Instead of awaiting the future hypothetical disputes, the decisive time to determine the temporal sphere of application of the concept is today. The present generation must apply the doctrine of intertemporal law at time X with regard to its intertemporal relationship with the future.

At this stage, the foregoing analysis on the relevant evolution of law is recalled: An evolutionary approach to intergenerational equity points to the developments of law between the creation of intergenerational equity today (at time X) and the potential future effects on future generations (e.g., at time X+80, in the long-term future). As the current book suggests time X in the present as relevant time of the intertemporal law assessment, instead of the time of the future dispute,[183] the determination of the temporal sphere of application takes on a prospective character. It looks from the present to the future instead of the past.[184] This shift of perspective is consistent with the particular nature of intergenerational equity as *Brown Weiss* already observed in 1989:

> For purposes of this study on justice between generations [...], it is sufficient to note that an intertemporal dimension, which primarily relates the present to the past, already exists in many aspects of law in the traditions of public international law [...]. The proposed principles of equity between generations and the related set of planetary obligations and rights, which focus primarily on the relationship between present and future generations,

---

[183] The time of the future dispute was relevant in the hypothetical application above, see *supra* in Sect. 7.1.3.

[184] Cf. d'Aspremont (2022), p. 258 (at footnote 31) Generally, on the necessity of focusing more on the future in international (environmental) law, cf. Cassotta (2019), p. 66; Kotzé (2020), p. 94.

> extend the basic concern we already have with intertemporal problems, albeit for a longer time horizon.[185]

However, several challenges arise with this future-oriented application of intertemporal law. The lack of a clearly defined time period for the application of evolutionary approaches constitutes a first challenge. In the traditional retrospective doctrine of intertemporal law, it is unequivocal *which* legal developments have to be taken into consideration, since the choice of the applicable legal regime is taken from an *ex post* perspective, looking backwards from the end of the legal development. In order to resolve a dispute with intertemporal character, the deciding body has to consider the developments between a specific time in the past when the norm was established (e.g., time X-100) and a specific time in the present when the dispute arises (time X) (see Figs. 7.1 and 7.2).

In the modified doctrine applicable to intergenerational equity, only the first point in time is clearly defined—the time of the establishment of intergenerational equity as a legal norm (time X).[186] As the temporally applicable law must also be prospectively determined at time X, the second point in time, the time of the dispute, has not occurred yet. Future developments of international law will not end at some point, but international law will likely be subject to constant change in the future and from one generation to the other, as the future consists of a hypothetically endless succession of future generations without temporal restriction.[187] This creates an endless succession of temporally intertwined legal regimes, some of them newly emerging while others are fading. Consequently, it is not possible to determine *one* general future legal regime, which would constitute the reference point for the evolutionary approaches of the modified doctrine. Instead, with regard to every future time period, there is a different legal regime to consider. This means different evolutionary manifestations of intergenerational equity might occur at different points in time in the future.

For this reason, and for the purpose of illustration, the present book has focused since the beginning on a specific time period in the future (from time X to time X +80), or on a specific future generation in the year 2100 respectively. The evolutionary intertemporal assessment of intergenerational equity for all future legal regimes would certainly go beyond the scope of a single analysis. The year 2100 constitutes an appropriate reference time for two reasons, as illustrated in more detail in Chap. 2 above.[188] First, it is consistent with the understanding of "future generations" as "those generations that do not exist yet".[189] With regard to a global average life expectancy between 70 and 75 years,[190] and not beyond 89 years

185 Brown Weiss (1989), p. 34.

186 See *supra* in Sect. 7.3.1.1.

187 On this aspect and the corresponding uncertainties, see, e.g., Malhotra (1998), p. 41; Anstee-Wedderburn (2014), pp. 64–65. See also *supra* in Sect. 3.2.4.

188 See *supra* in Sect. 2.2.1.2.2.

189 Brown Weiss (2021, para. 4).

190 World Health Organization (WHO) (2019).

average in any State,[191] only very few and very young members of the present generation will still be alive in the year 2100. Second, this reference year does not point too far into the future, so that it allows at the same time overcoming some uncertainties with regard to the current generation's knowledge of the future. Current scientific research, particularly in the context of climate change, is increasingly accurate today in projecting and explaining the partly irreversible effects of the present generation's behaviour on the ecosystems in the future.[192] Most of these predictions also concern the time period until the end of the twenty-first century.

This more specific reference period facilitates the acceptance of a prospective intertemporal law assessment starting today and looking into the future. However, scientific progress in climate sciences does not facilitate predictions of future *law*. In contrast, the development of international law is not measurable in the same way as scientific changes in ecosystems. As law is in general human-made, particularly from a positivist perspective,[193] it does not follow scientific laws of nature.[194] Theoretically, the creators of international law, primarily States,[195] could decide tomorrow to establish a new international norm from scratch that did not originate in prior developments at all. From a positivist perspective, this norm would then become law without following any (quasi-)scientific process that could have been predicted beforehand.[196]

The prospective assessment of future developments of law could thus easily be regarded as a futile endeavour. Since lawyers are neither prophets nor fortune-tellers, it would be impossible for them, or at least presumptuous, to make any assumptions on the future legal regime 80 years from today. Notwithstanding this, the prediction of future developments of international law has been the research object of scholars for a long time. In international relations, "forecasting has always been a central aspiration".[197] But there have also been attempts of *legal* scholars to predict the future development of law. In 1921, *Lassa Oppenheim* offered certain observations on how the pressing problems of international law could be solved in the future.[198] Several other commentators have equally tried to make more or less ambitious predictions of the near and far future of international law.[199]

---

[191] Central Intelligence Agency (2022).

[192] See, e.g., Lee et al. (2021), pp. 570–612.

[193] Lachenmann (2012, para. 2).

[194] To a certain degree, the idea of natural law contradicts this observation, see Orakhelashvili (2007, paras. 1–3).

[195] Lachenmann (2012, paras. 29–36).

[196] Yet, this is generally not the reality of the development of law as the next section illustrates in more detail.

[197] Metternich et al. (2016). Cf. Choucri (1978).

[198] Oppenheim (1921), pp. 7–8. *Oppenheim* made clear that he did not attempt to "peer into the future with the eyes of prophecy".

[199] Black and Falk (1972); Macdonald et al. (1973); McDougal (1980), pp. 325–334; Sands (2001), pp. 543–556; Carmody (2002).

Other works have focused on developing progressive paths international law could or should take in the future.[200] For instance, *Antonio Cassese* edited a compilation of works in 2012[201] that identified major problems of current international law and started "imaginative thinking" on how to overcome these problems in order to shape the future of international law.[202] The 2017 Special Section of the *German Yearbook of International Law* on utopianism took a comparable approach as it aimed at "rethinking international law" in an attempt to shape its potential directions on the way to utopia.[203] Some of the contributions in this issue built on *Philip Allott's* methodology of a utopian legal order.[204] For *Allott*, an imaginative re-invention of the international legal system and its ideas constitutes the necessary engine for actual change in international legal structures.[205]

Beyond this, the idea of constitutionalisation of international law also makes certain assumptions on the development of the international legal system.[206] Although there are different schools of global constitutionalism,[207] constitutionalist approaches have in common that they consider modern international law to have developed a common normative basis with elements of typical constitutional law.[208] Comparable with the aforementioned utopian scenarios, international constitutionalism is an approach that "seek[s] to imagine an international constitutional ordering, and seek[s] to work towards that".[209] *Martti Koskenniemi* fittingly described global constitutionalism as a "mindset", which can assist in normatively strengthening universal values in international law.[210]

Finally, the idea of "reimagining"[211] international law is also widespread in today's international environmental law discourse. Most suggestions are based on the insight that humanity has entered a new epoch, the Anthropocene, in which humans are a decisive factor shaping the conditions of the planet and the

[200] Most recently, see also the edited contribution Popovski and Malhotra (2023).

[201] Cassese (2012c).

[202] Cassese (2012b), p. xxi. For one of these suggestions, see *infra* note 223.

[203] On the Special Section's approach, see Theilen et al. (2017), pp. 317–318.

[204] Allott (2017), pp. 209–232. See also Allott (1990/2001).

[205] Cryer et al. (2011), p. 57.

[206] A comprehensive analysis of constitutionalist approaches would exceed the scope of the present book. For an overall analysis, see Klabbers et al. (2009).

[207] Fassbender (2009), pp. 27–51 with further references.

[208] Kämmerer (2024), pp. 20–21. One of these elements is the notion of "international community", which has become a symbol for constitutionalist ideas, see Payandeh (2010), pp. 43–51; Paulus (2013, paras. 1–5, 18).

[209] Cryer et al. (2011), p. 52. Cf. also Peters (2012), p. 120.

[210] Koskenniemi (2007).

[211] See Stephens (2017).

environment.[212] For instance, the recent concept of Earth system law[213] rethinks environmental law alongside the four key characteristics of the Earth system: interconnectedness of the ecosystem, unpredictability, instability and complexity.[214] Thereby, Earth system law attempts to offer a new legal framework, which departs from the existing primacy of anthropocentrism and State sovereignty and moves towards the idea of integrity of the entire Earth system.[215] Similarly, according to *Brown Weiss*, concepts like the global commons and public goods have become increasingly important in the current Anthropocene epoch.[216] In order to establish fitting norms for the new "kaleidoscopic world"[217] of the Anthropocene,[218] *Brown Weiss* elaborated in detail on environmental concepts, such as the common heritage and common concern of humankind, sustainable development,[219] and particularly intergenerational equity.[220] *Sandra Cassotta* also argued for a paradigm shift in international environmental law and governance.[221] Future environmental law could shift towards an "untraditional system of law based on a non-state-centric vision" that is more flexible and proactive vis-à-vis current and future challenges.[222] These suggestions are similar to utopian approaches that suggest future legal frameworks *de lege ferenda*. A comparable future-oriented suggestion was made by *Francesco Francioni* in his utopian reimagination of international environmental law.[223]

Although these concepts, approaches and suggestions aim at predicting future developments of international law from different perspectives, they have two characteristics in common. Firstly, all of them assume that future developments of law *are* predictable to a certain degree. At the same time, secondly, they do not provide

[212] Cassotta (2019), pp. 54–58; Brown Weiss (2020), pp. 35–38, 100.

[213] Generally, on Earth system science and the particular concept of Earth system law, see Kim and Kotzé (2021), pp. 12–14. For another terminology, see Kotzé (2020), p. 78. On the links between constitutionalism and Earth system law, see Kotzé (2019a), p. 23.

[214] Kotzé (2020), pp. 77–78. See also Bosselmann (2017). On the key principles of the Anthropocene, see also Burdon (2020), pp. 35–37.

[215] Sessions (1974); Kotzé (2020), pp. 100–101; Bosselmann (2020), pp. 54–55. For a more differentiated and critical analysis, see Burdon (2020), pp. 37–42. Comparably, *Verena Kahl* puts forward a holistic approach to addressing climate change by means of a right to a safe climate and in order to "[lead] human rights law into the Anthropocene", see Kahl (2025 Forthcoming).

[216] Brown Weiss (2020), pp. 100–122.

[217] For an explanation of what *Brown Weiss* considers as the characteristics of this "kaleidoscopic world", see ibid., p. 23.

[218] Ibid., pp. 144–148.

[219] Ibid., pp. 179–196.

[220] Ibid., pp. 282–307.

[221] Cassotta (2019).

[222] Ibid., p. 66.

[223] Francioni (2012), p. 443. Comparably future-oriented, *Daniel Bertram* concluded in a recent work: "Only by wholeheartedly embracing this anticipatory function can scholarship uncover weaknesses and holes in the international legal fabric, shift perspectives, and regenerate the discourse over law's role in confronting our precarious existence", see Bertram (2023), p. 31.

for sufficient methodological justifications for their presumptions.[224] Some of them attempt to progressively shape new developments instead of describing current or actually predicting future developments based on a consistent methodology.[225] For instance, constitutionalisation attempts to give a normative explanation for the overall development of international law from coexistence over cooperation to an alleged constitutional order. But it is a normatively charged claim rather than an empirically descriptive perspective on the current or future status of international law.[226] Further, it does not offer an operational framework under which legal change in international law can be properly assessed. *Craig Eggett* summarised this criticism as follows:

> Overlooking or conflating the system's normative foundations has limited the extent to which global constitutionalism has precipitated real change in international law. Put differently, while attempting to redesign or reconceptualise the system, constitutionalist [sic] have failed to actually engage with the system.[227]

However, such a methodological framework to reliably predict future developments of international law would be necessary in the context of the suggested modified doctrine of intertemporal law. In order to shift the doctrine's focus from a present-past to a future-oriented perspective, a systematic approach to legal change is required. Such a methodological framework would build upon certain mechanisms of international legal change and systemise their interactions and developments.[228] Based on these mechanisms, the framework would allow making reasoned assumptions on the future development of intergenerational equity. In the end, it could become possible to take a prospective intertemporal perspective on intergenerational equity instead of only observing the evolutionary developments of law over time and of retrospectively applying them at a certain point in the future.

### 7.3.3 *Starting Points for the Prediction of Future Change Regarding Intergenerational Equity*

The customary norm of intergenerational equity constitutes a good example for legal changes that do not occur suddenly and from scratch, but result from ongoing and evolutionary processes in the international legal system. The following section thus first addresses the transitional period of customary norms in the process of legal

---

[224] See Sandholtz (2009), p. 4.

[225] With regard to a variety of international legal theories, see Diehl and Ku (2010), p. 15.

[226] See von Arnauld (2019), pp. 11–12; Kjeldgaard-Pedersen (2019), p. 283. See also Proelss (2006), p. 244; Peters (2012), pp. 119–120.

[227] Eggett (2019), p. 214.

[228] This book chooses such a methodological framework by *Paul Diehl* and *Charlotte Ku* below (*infra* in Sect. 7.3.4), see Diehl and Ku (2010). Of course, there might be other frameworks as fitting, e.g., elaborated by Krisch and Yildiz (2023); Sandholtz and Stiles (2009).

change by referring to recent commentators who have analysed this transitional period (Sect. 7.3.3.1). Then, the author turns to the two manifestations of intergenerational equity that exemplify this transitional period (Sect. 7.3.3.2). These observations already allow for a preliminary conclusion on the modified doctrine of intertemporal law for the assessment of intergenerational issues (Sect. 7.3.3.3).

#### 7.3.3.1 Period of Transition Between Old and New Norms of Customary International Law

As illustrated above, "time is [an] important element in the process of creation of customary international law".[229] The ILC in its 'Draft Conclusions on Identification of Customary International Law' also touched upon this relevance of time for the formation of a customary norm.[230] However, the focus of the ILC analysis lied on the identification of customary international law at "a particular time" and not on the processes of development of these norms.[231] This leaves a certain gap in the legal analysis as customary international law is not formed in a sudden instant,[232] but its elements, particularly State practice, must emerge over a certain period of time.[233] Often, some difficulties arise in the identification of the exact moment when a specific practice and *opinio iuris* have exceeded a critical threshold to establish a new customary norm.[234] Most strikingly, this evolutionary character of customary international law requires "a large number of States starting to follow a practice that is at variance with the normal practice [for] a new customary rule of general international law [to] eventually come into existence".[235] For this reason, *James Crawford* considered it to be impossible to identify the law on a specific day without looking at the formation period of a customary norm.[236]

While the ILC has omitted to address these difficulties, *Steven Wheatley* developed a convincing approach to the temporal assessment of customary international law, as he tried to "revisi[t] the doctrine of intertemporal law".[237] This approach is helpful for the application of the modified doctrine of intertemporal law to

[229] *Navigational and Related Rights* (Separate Opinion of Judge Sepúlveda-Amor), *supra* note 30, para. 25. Cf. also ICJ, *Request for Interpretation of the Judgment of 15 June 1962 in the Case concerning the Temple of Preah Vihear (Cambodia v. Thailand) (Cambodia v. Thailand),* Separate opinion of Judge Cançado Trindade, 18 July 2011, ICJ Reports 2011, 566, paras. 12–13. See *supra* in Sect. 7.2.1.

[230] ILC (2018a, Conclusion 1, para. 5). See also Wheatley (2021), pp. 489–491.

[231] ILC (2016, para. 16).

[232] Implicitly, see *North Sea Continental Shelf* (Judgment (Merits)), *supra* note 126, para. 74.

[233] ILC (2018a, Conclusion 8, para. 9).

[234] ILC (2016, para. 17).

[235] Fitzmaurice (1957), p. 113.

[236] Crawford (2014), pp. 81–82.

[237] Wheatley (2021).

intergenerational equity, which is why it is illustrated in the following. Beyond his analysis of the *Chagos Archipelago* advisory opinion,[238] *Wheatley* assessed in detail the passage of time in international law. After distinguishing between two ways of thinking about time,[239] he committed to the A-series theory of time.[240] According to this theory, the passage of time is real and customary norms evolve "from the future, through the present and on to the past".[241] This means that A-theorists accept that the law is continuously evolving and that every moment in time must be described in a "tensed" logic and language, meaning that something either *was*, *is* or *will be* the case.[242] For a legal norm, at a certain time, it can be said that it *will become* custom (future); later, it *is* a customary norm (present); and after further passage of time, it can be observed that the norm *was* part of customary international law (past). According to a tensed logic, every temporal statement on a certain moment in time is only true from the specific temporal point of view.[243] Consequently, two statements that apparently conflict with each other can be true at the same time, as *Wheatley* observed with respect to the ICJ's *Chagos Archipelago* advisory opinion.[244] This analysis makes him identify three periods of time in the temporal process of change of customary international law:

> (1) the period when there is consensus that the old rule must be applied; (2) a period of transition, when some [S]tate practice and *opinio juris* will support the old rule and some the new; and (3) the time when there is agreement that the new rule is to be applied.[245]

The period of transition is characterised by uncertainty as it is not clear yet whether the new norm will crystallise or not, whether the law will change or remain in the *status quo*.[246] In this transition period, a court would not be able to apply the new norm of customary international law before it has not actually crystallised and been accepted as new law.[247] The actual legal status of a customary norm is only achieved at moment (3) when there is sufficient State practice and *opinio iuris*. However, this is only true from the tensed perspective during the period of transition. In contrast, a court or other observer in the "privileged position of 'now'" might assess the same situation differently "with the benefit of hindsight".[248] Such a privileged observer

[238] See *supra* in Sect. 6.2.

[239] Wheatley (2021), pp. 492–494.

[240] Ibid., pp. 502–505.

[241] Ibid., p. 497. See also Allott (1999), p. 1.

[242] Wheatley (2021), p. 485.

[243] Ibid., p. 493.

[244] Ibid., pp. 502–503 See already *supra* in Sect. 6.2 [note 70].

[245] Ibid., p. 505.

[246] Ibid.

[247] See ICJ, *Fisheries Jurisdiction (United Kingdom v. Iceland),* Merits, Judgment, 25 July 1974, ICJ Reports 1974, 3, para. 40; PCA, *Dispute Concerning Access to Information Under Article 9 of the OSPAR Convention between Ireland and the United Kingdom of Great Britain and Northern Ireland,* Final Award, 2 July 2003, RIAA XXIII (2003), 59, paras. 101–103.

[248] Wheatley (2021), p. 505.

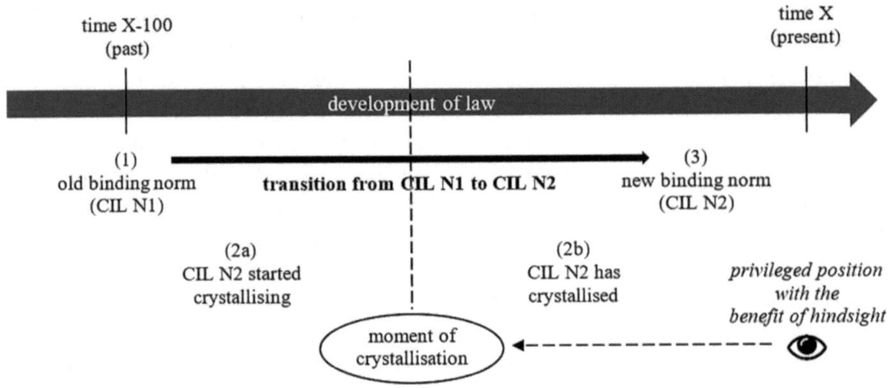


**Fig. 7.7** Transition of customary international law according to *Steven Wheatley*

would *retrospectively* know whether the emerging norm in the past has actually crystallised or whether the law has remained in the *status quo*.[249] From the privileged position of now, the transition period (2) can be split in two periods with different effects on the temporally applicable law:

> (2a) the period when the new rule was crystallising, but had not yet crystallised, when the old rule must still be applied; (2b) the period after the moment of crystallisation, but before the agreement on the existence of a new general practice accepted as law, when the new rule must now be applied.[250]

While moment (2a) refers to a time when there is still more evidence that speaks in favour of the old customary rule, the subsequent period (2b) changes this tendency as the law then leans towards the new customary norm that has crystallised. The moment between these two periods would be the decisive moment of change, the moment of crystallisation. After this moment, the new customary norm sufficiently crystallised to supersede the old norm, but it was not yet accepted as binding law until the subsequent moment (3).[251] This means that a court during the period of transition, even at moment (2b), would still have to apply the old rule. However, from the "privileged position of 'now'" and "with the benefit of hindsight", a court could retrospectively apply the new crystallising norm to the period (2b) after the moment of crystallisation.[252] This ongoing process of change also describes the transition of the law *de lege ferenda* to the law *de lege lata*; it demonstrates the fluid boundaries between these two artificially separated statuses.[253] The present author attempts to visualise this period of transition with Fig. 7.7.

---

[249] Ibid., pp. 505–506.

[250] Ibid., p. 506.

[251] Ibid., pp. 506–507.

[252] Ibid., p. 506.

[253] See Virally (1988), p. 73 as well as already *supra* in Sect. 7.3.1.1.

In reaction to *Wheatley's* article, *Alonso Gurmendi* added some interesting thoughts on this fluid distinction between the *lex lata* and the *lex ferenda* at a specific time in the past.[254] While he agreed on many points with *Wheatley*, he criticised that public international law at a specific point in time is not a "monolithic concept", but a continuous "discourse where various actors agree and disagree, contradict and complement each other".[255] This means that, in a period of transition in the past, there would not only be *one* clear-cut answer to the accepted law, but rather a set of different ideas and interpretations of the law that are accepted in parts or not. This would render the period of transition more blurred and more difficult to assess, even with the benefit of hindsight. Instead of focusing on *the one* true law at time X-100 during a period of transition, *Gurmendi* argued in favour of appreciating and understanding all of the different accepted interpretations of the law at that time.[256] Yet, he agreed with *Wheatley* as far as he also argued that the result of an intertemporal consideration of the law in the past can differ depending on the temporal position the observer takes.

*Andreas von Arnauld* elaborated a comparable reinterpretation of intertemporal law when assessing the legality of past injustice.[257] He built his conception upon a framework of *jurisgenesis*, this means a framework that also conceives of normative change as a continuous process.[258] Comparable to *Gurmendi*, he pointed out the controversial discussions on specific issues of law even in the past.[259] He argued in favour of taking into account these controversies in the intertemporal assessment:

> Where contemporaries already protested against cruel and inhumane practices by appealing to ethical standards that are the moral foundation of today's international legal rules, and where those protests actually contributed to an express illegalization of the conduct in question, so the *jurisgenetic* argument here goes, we might consider loosening the intertemporal strictures somewhat. Thus, we can feel entitled to extend the verdict of illegality to practices that had already been denounced by contemporaries whose protests contributed to bringing about the express illegalization of such practices.[260]

For *von Arnauld*, ethical and moral principles in international law constituted the necessary entry point for the emergence of new norms of international law.[261] These principles would also be the justification of why to consider contemporaneous controversies in an intertemporal assessment because they constituted part of the *lex lata* at that time.[262] At the same time, this illustrated the "blurring of the lines

[254] Gurmendi (2021).

[255] Ibid.

[256] Ibid.

[257] Von Arnauld (2021).

[258] Ibid., pp. 414–415 with reference to Cover (1983), p. 40.

[259] Von Arnauld (2021), pp. 409–410.

[260] Ibid., p. 415.

[261] Ibid., pp. 408–413.

[262] Ibid., pp. 415–416.

between *lex lata* and *lex ferenda*".[263] In the end, the ethical and moral principles would therefore lead to a loosening of the strict application of the traditional doctrine of intertemporal law.[264] Comparable to *Wheatley*, this means applying in the retrospective these upcoming changes of a legal norm during the analysed moment in the past while they were still emerging based on ethical and societal developments. This process of *jurisgenesis* and the controversial discussions leading to legal change in the past constitute not only an important aspect of *von Arnauld's* approach, but they also reflect *Gurmendi's* criticism of a monolithic conception of the law.[265] Both of these approaches fit *Wheatley's* idea of a transitional period in the development of customary international law, although the answer *Gurmendi* and *von Arnauld* would give as to the contemporaneous *lex lata* might not be as clear-cut as the answer given by *Wheatley*.[266]

Most importantly for the current context, all of these reinterpretations of intertemporal law focus on the assessment of the transition period between an old norm and a new norm of customary international law. They also have in common that they distinguish between the intertemporal law that would have been applied from the contemporaneous perspective *during* the transition period and the intertemporal law that must be applied from the privileged position of today, "with the benefit of hindsight".[267]

Getting back to the intertemporal assessment of the customary norm of intergenerational equity, this has two implications. If these findings were applied to the hypothetical dispute scenario in the year 2100, then the retrospective application of intertemporal law would allow profiting from the benefit of hindsight at time X+80. From this privileged position, it would be possible to determine and apply a potential new norm of intergenerational equity that would have had crystallised in the period of transition, at time X. However, *Wheatley*, *Gurmendi* and *von Arnauld* would *not* claim that this new norm would have to be applied at time X during the transition period; in contrast, a contemporaneous court at time X would have to apply the old norm until there is sufficient acceptance of the newly emerged norm.[268] Therefore, the aforementioned reinterpretations of intertemporal law do not address the shift of perspective that is necessary for the intertemporal approach to intergenerational equity. The next sub-section fills this lacuna by extending the idea of period of transition to the context of intergenerational equity.

---

[263] Ibid., p. 418.

[264] Ibid., pp. 417–418 *Von Arnauld* applied this reinterpretation of intertemporal law to the law of State responsibility and argued in favour of satisfaction as the most adequate form of reparation in case of historical injustice, in detail, see ibid., pp. 420–428.

[265] See ibid., p. 416.

[266] However, see the answer given to *Gurmendi's* blog post by *Jessica Dorsey* in *Wheatley's* name: Gurmendi (2021).

[267] Wheatley (2021), p. 505.

[268] See ibid., pp. 505–507.

#### 7.3.3.2 The Two Manifestations of Intergenerational Equity

The reinterpretations of intertemporal law elaborated by *Wheatley* and *von Arnauld* offer a useful perspective on the transitional character of legal changes in international law. The same transitional character can be observed with regard to the concept of intergenerational equity. As illustrated in detail in Chaps. 2, 4 and 5, intergenerational equity is far from static, but it consists of developing nuances that range from the established general conception to the more specific doctrine of intergenerational equity. These two manifestations of the general idea of fairness across generations offer a perfect example of the continued development of customary norms.

On one side of the spectrum, there is the general conception, which is enshrined in binding and non-binding documents and is part of customary international law. It constitutes the old and current norm of customary international law, the law *de lege lata* at time X—and the law contemporaneous to the creation of the norm, as envisaged by the traditional principle of contemporaneity. On the other side of the spectrum, there is the specific doctrine of intergenerational equity that consists of more sophisticated duties and that is built on the idea of rights of future generations as well as to more elaborated institutional frameworks of representation. The latter does not form part of the contemporarily binding customary international law, but it is an emerging norm.[269]

This emerging character of the doctrine points explicitly to the transitional period that intergenerational equity is going through. Today, at time X, there is not enough evidence of the existence of sufficient *opinio iuris* and State practice with regard to the specific doctrine of intergenerational equity, but there are first indications for emerging *opinio iuris* and State practice, as illustrated in Chap. 4. If the specific doctrine is accepted as binding international law in the near future, then it will have to be retrospectively applied in the context of evolutionary approaches from the hypothetical perspective at time X+80. Further, according to *Wheatley* and *von Arnauld*, if the specific doctrine is currently crystallising as new norm of intergenerational equity, then it will even have to be applied to any current dispute, but again only retrospectively, with the benefit of hindsight from time X+80. At that time, there will be enough knowledge about the actual crystallisation and the overcoming of the preceding *status quo*.[270] However, at time X, during the period of transition, the specific doctrine cannot be considered as relevant law *de lege lata* yet. According to the unmodified doctrine of intertemporal law, a court would not be allowed "to apply 'evolving international law and practice'" as it does not have the "authority to apply law in *statu nascendi*".[271]

[269] Molinari (2015), p. 155.

[270] See Wheatley (2021), pp. 505–506.

[271] *OSPAR Convention* (Final Award), *supra* note 247, paras. 101–103. See also *Fisheries Jurisdiction* (Merits, Judgment), *supra* note 247, para. 40.

At this stage, the necessary shift of perspective comes into play. While the traditional doctrine of intertemporal law is absolutely suitable for norms of public international law in general, the aforementioned particularities of intergenerational equity justify a deviation. The important findings on the transitional character of customary norms have thus to be reinterpreted again in the context of intergenerational problems. Due to the suggested modification of intertemporal law, the upcoming future changes of intergenerational equity must result in their *prospective* application to an intergenerational dispute at time X. Despite the ongoing transition and despite the lack of hindsight at time X, it is necessary and justified to anticipate the ongoing crystallisation of a new norm of intergenerational equity. Of course, there is no guarantee during the period of transition that the new norm of intergenerational equity will actually crystallise.[272] Yet, as *Catherine Redgwell* stated already in 1999, "a process of 'creeping intergenerationalisation' may be observed".[273] This "intergenerationalisation" comes along with a strong normative development of international environmental law in general.[274] As demonstrated in Chap. 4,[275] the emerging evidence with regard to the specific doctrine offers some indications for this transition of intergenerational equity.

Beyond this evidence of State practice and *opinio iuris*, the ethical-legal principles *von Arnauld* referred to offer an even more convincing indication for the actual change of intergenerational equity.[276] Comparable to the ethical requirements of humanity that led to the controversial discussion of colonial abuses in the nineteenth and twentieth century,[277] intergenerational equity is also based on essential moral and philosophical considerations.[278] Regardless of whether these considerations are based on utilitarian, libertarian, contractarian or communitarian approaches or whether they emanate from religious and cultural traditions, there is a universal ethical understanding that the present generation has a responsibility towards future generations.[279] From a strictly legal point of view, these ethical ideas have so far only been enshrined in the general conception of intergenerational equity. But the increasing knowledge about the present generation's impacts on the future has decisively changed the impact of ethical considerations of the future. Today, the public outrage vis-à-vis the intergenerational ignorance and the omissions of the present has gained a momentum. This can be seen with regard to global climate

[272] See Wheatley (2021), p. 505.

[273] Redgwell (1999), p. 126.

[274] Cf. Francioni (2012), pp. 444–447. On the systemic embeddedness of intergenerational equity, see *supra* in Sect. 2.3.

[275] See *supra* in Sect. 4.2.2.2.

[276] See von Arnauld (2021), pp. 408–413.

[277] Ibid., pp. 408–409.

[278] In detail, see *supra* in Chap. 3.

[279] UNSG (2013, para. 12); Brown Weiss (1989), pp. 18–21. More recently, the philosophical approach of "longtermism" also supports this concern for future generations, see, e.g., Winter et al. (2021), pp. 13–17, which is widely accepted among legal scholars, see Martínez and Winter (2022).

protests,[280] widespread climate litigation initiated by civil society actors,[281] the increasing objections of the most affected States against environmental degradation and their claims of a more ambitious climate protection world-wide.[282] The discourse of intergenerational problems is not only shaped by actors of legal professions but increasingly by political opposition of Green parties, criticism in the media pointing to the long-term effects of environmental degradation, the community of climate sciences and various civil society actors, such as environmental NGOs, human rights groups and representatives of the youth.[283] The ethical notions of intergenerational justice and the legal concept of intergenerational equity have thus started to overlap, which again illustrates the fluid boundaries[284] between the *lex lata* content of intergenerational equity and *lex ferenda* that is based on ethical-legal principles.

Despite the delimitations between intergenerational equity *de lege lata* and *de lege ferenda* in the foregoing chapters, the modified perspective on intertemporal law illustrates the difficulties of these strict distinctions. The legal regime of intergenerational equity is continuously evolving as can already be seen in the context of increasing intergenerational climate litigation. While the majority of State practice and *opinio iuris* today does not yet support the legal status of the specific doctrine of intergenerational equity,[285] many developments indicate that this prevailing perspective might soon prove to have been superseded by the emerging new norm of customary international law.[286] Consequently, the shift of perspective within the modified doctrine of intertemporal law requires anticipating the ongoing developments of intergenerational equity and justifies taking these developments into consideration today at time X, even without the benefit of hindsight. In contrast to *Wheatley's* approach, this observation results in an intertemporal shift of perspective with regard to intergenerational problems, as visualised in Fig. 7.8.[287]

---

[280] Luckner (2021), pp. 16–20.

[281] See *supra* in Sect. 5.3.3.3.

[282] See, e.g., UNGA (2015, para. 11). See also Gupta (2016); Ronneberg (2016).

[283] On the influences of these actors, see von Arnauld (2021), pp. 410–413. For some examples of civil society initiatives that attempted to incorporate stronger intergenerational obligations, see also *supra* in Sect. 4.2.2.2.

[284] See Wheatley (2021), p. 503; von Arnauld (2021), p. 418.

[285] See *supra* in Sect. 4.2.2.2.

[286] For an interesting perspective on *Judge Cançado Trindade* as minoritarian voice at the ICJ, see Gurmendi (2021).

[287] This illustration applies *Wheatley's* conceptualisation (see *supra* Fig. 7.7) to the two manifestations of intergenerational equity ('IGE N1' and 'IGE N2'), but with the elaborated shift of perspective. The exact "moment of crystallisation" is not as easy to determine from the non-privileged position without the benefit of hindsight, thus, the prospective approach cannot remove all doubts vis-à-vis the uncertainties of future legal developments; as to this, see *supra* in Sect. 7.3.3.3.

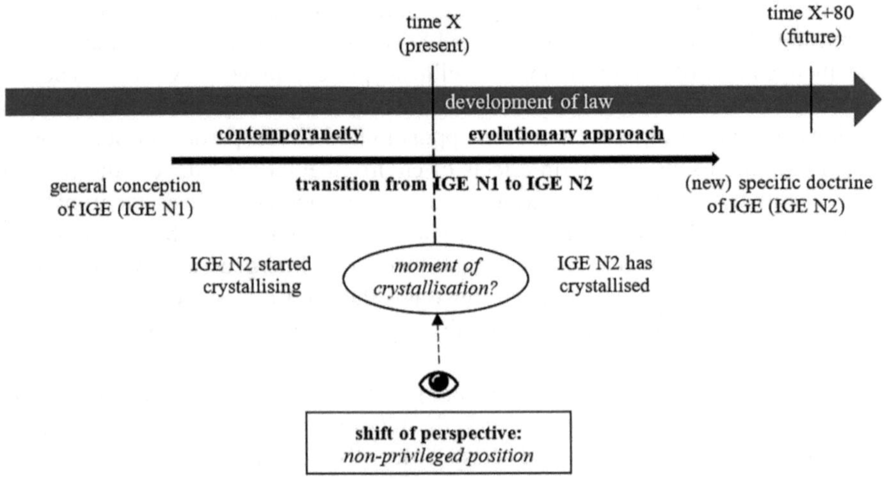


**Fig. 7.8** Transition of the customary norm of intergenerational equity and shift of perspective

#### 7.3.3.3 Interim Conclusion on the Modified Doctrine of Intertemporal Law

Anticipating and taking into consideration future developments of law—this suggestion is likely going to face criticism concerning its feasibility, since lawyers are neither prophets nor fortune-tellers, and they cannot actually travel through time. However, this objection does not change the foregoing analysis and its results, which point to the shift of perspective. It is necessary to assess the temporally applicable intergenerational obligations today in order to act accordingly instead of awaiting actual future disputes when the current violations have irreversibly materialised. At this stage, the findings of this book already offer two interim conclusions in order to overcome this initial criticism.

First, the acceptance of the logical shift of perspective might already be sufficient for an according change of mindset in the current legal discourse. Even if one considered the prediction of future developments of intergenerational equity to be impossible, it is the moment of reflection about the consequences of the modified doctrine that could already lead to a prospective approach to intertemporal law. According to the proposed modification, it is not sufficient to consider the temporally applicable law in the context of intergenerational obligations only from a retrospective angle. Instead, it is important that the members of the present generation are conscious about the relevance of future legal developments for the assessment of their obligations towards the future. If there is enough probability that the legal content of intergenerational equity will emerge in a more specific form, then this future emergence should already play a decisive role in the current legal discourse, regardless of the absolute certainty on its future bindingness. This change of mindset is also justified from an ethical-legal perspective, if one gets back to *John Rawls'* hypothetical original position. Behind the veil of ignorance, the legal perspective of the present generation would not take precedence over the legal perspective of any future generation. All perspectives must be taken into account in the original position. Only then, the philosophical-legal principles would constitute principles of justice. Applied to the introductory thought experiment with the time traveller from the year 2100, the present generation in the 2020s would also be required to accept the legal perspective from this time traveller, even if future developments of law would not have been accepted yet.[288] The suggested modified doctrine of intertemporal law would then constitute a discursive means of dealing with intergenerational conflicts in a metaphor of legal time travel.[289]

Beyond this metaphorical change of mindset, second, the foregoing analysis offered a more systematic incentive to reflect on probable future developments of intergenerational equity already today. This would not require predicting future international law from scratch. Instead, the anticipation of future change would build upon the transitional period between the general conception and the specific doctrine of intergenerational equity. The continuous evolution of the concept from one of its manifestations to the other constitutes a promising starting point for a prospective assessment of future law and facilitates the predictability of the concept's future developments. Thereby, it is not necessary to focus on the legal regime at a specific time in the future, but rather to anticipate whether intergenerational equity will undergo the transition from its old to a new manifestation in the near future. The reinterpretations of intertemporal law by *Wheatley* and *von Arnauld* constitute helpful frameworks that are complemented by the intergenerational shift of perspective. Based on the transitional character of the customary norm of intergenerational equity,[290] and justified by the latter's intertemporal particularities,[291] the aforementioned metaphorical change of mindset is thus supported by a more specific projection of likely future changes of intergenerational equity. Decision-makers and judges would have to be less fixated on the uncontroversial and accepted positive law in the present in the context of intergenerational constellations. They would also have to look at currently emerging developments of the concept and to be open to the prospective consideration of evolutions, even ahead of their final crystallisation. The analysis of the specific doctrine of intergenerational equity in Chaps. 2, 4 and 5 offers the necessary contours for these emerging developments.

Yet, the focus on the transitional period between the old and the new norm of intergenerational equity is still superficial as it does not assess the likelihood of the latter's crystallisation; it does not offer an overall systematic approach to future legal change. Therefore, the following section presents an overview of a possible

[288] This consideration is further illustrated in the Concluding Chapter below, see *infra* in Sect. 8.4.

[289] On international responsibility as a discursive means of time travel, see d'Aspremont (2022), p. 265. This discursive time travel could easily be extended from the present to the future, see ibid., 258 (at footnote 31).

[290] See *supra* in Sect. 7.3.3.1.

[291] See *supra* in Sect. 7.2.2 and Sect. 7.2.3.

framework to go beyond these first interim conclusions and to actually make some methodologically reasoned predictions on the future of intergenerational equity.

## *7.3.4 A Framework of the International Legal System for the Prediction of Legal Change*

In order to make reasoned assumptions on the future development of intergenerational equity, it is necessary to apply a convincing methodology that offers an analytical framework to understand and predict future changes of international law. *Paul Diehl* and *Charlotte Ku* established such a framework in their work 'The Dynamics of International Law' from 2010.[292] This framework allows understanding the development and advancement of international law.[293] It goes beyond the aforementioned utopian approaches of rethinking and reframing international law,[294] as those approaches either remained too descriptive of the existing legal order or they only prescriptively advocated what the law *should* be.[295] The following sub-sections of this chapter begin with describing the two subsystems of international law on which *Diehl* and *Ku's* framework is based (Sect. 7.3.4.1). Then, the interactions between these subsystems are illustrated (Sect. 7.3.4.2), as these interactions can assist in the prediction of future developments of intergenerational equity (Sect. 7.3.4.3).

### 7.3.4.1 Distinction Between the Normative and the Operating System of International Law

This section successively describes the two subsystems of international law as identified by *Diehl* and *Ku* in their framework, starting with the normative system (Sect. 7.3.4.1.1) before turning to the operating system (Sect. 7.3.4.1.2). The book briefly outlines their characteristics, distinguishes them from one another and points to the general evolutions within the subsystems of international law. It further exemplifies this framework by illustrating the normative and the operating system of intergenerational equity, before subsequently turning to the interaction between these two systems (Sect. 7.3.4.2).

---

292 Diehl and Ku (2010).

293 Ku and Diehl (2016), p. 52.

294 See *supra* in Sect. 7.3.2, notes 197–223.

295 See Diehl and Ku (2010), pp. 1–2, 4.

#### 7.3.4.1.1 Normative System

The normative system of international law "defines the acceptable standards for behavior in the international system".[296] It consists of the directive aspects of international law and identifies its substantive values and goals, which States have to comply with.[297] *Diehl* and *Ku* described the normative system as "quasi-legislative in character by mandating particular values and directing specific changes in [S] tate and other actors' behaviors".[298] These values and goals can be mirrored either in prescriptions or in proscriptions.[299] To be fully part of the normative system, they must constitute binding law in contrast to mere soft law.[300] Put differently, the substantive contents of international law, the material obligations and rights, constitute the normative system as understood by *Diehl* and *Ku*. Their characterisation of the normative system resembles *Herbert Hart's* "primary rules of law", meaning those substantive rules of a legal system that impose duties on actors to perform or abstain from actions.[301] The normative system thus answers the question *what* is owed by the actors of international law.

Mostly, the substantive contents of international law are contained in issue-specific standards for accepted behaviour.[302] These issue-specific norms include diverse areas as human rights provisions, prohibitions of environmentally harmful behaviour or of certain methods of warfare in humanitarian law, rules of international trade law and much more.[303] All of these norms form the normative system of international law. The normative system has expanded and developed in the last decades in two different ways. On the one hand, it has gained in scope within old areas of international law, such as the expansion of norms in international humanitarian law or the law of the sea.[304] On the other hand, new fields of international law have emerged and evolved in the last decades; for instance, human rights law and environmental law.[305] International environmental law is among the areas of

---

[296] Ibid., p. 43.

[297] Ku and Diehl (2016), pp. 32, 34.

[298] Diehl and Ku (2010), p. 42.

[299] Ibid.

[300] Ibid., 42, 52–53.

[301] Hart (2012), p. 81. On the parallels and distinctions between the normative system and *Hart's* primary rules, see *infra* notes 332–336.

[302] Diehl and Ku (2010), pp. 42–43.

[303] Cf. ibid., p. 43.

[304] Ibid., pp. 44–45.

[305] Ibid., pp. 45–46. See already Friedmann (1964), pp. 152–186. See also Sands (2001), pp. 548–552; Tomuschat (2011), pp. 335–336.

international law that has evolved most in the last century,[306] its modern contents having developed since the 1970s.[307]

The emergence of the concept of intergenerational equity since the 1970s constitutes one example for this expansion of the normative system. The normative system with regard to intergenerational equity can be identified more specifically by illustrating the substantive standards for accepted behaviour in this context—again distinguishing between the general conception and the specific doctrine of intergenerational equity. The general conception obliges its addressees "to take into account the interests of future generations"[308] and stipulates an "environmental responsibility towards the future".[309] As a component of sustainable development, the idea of fairness between generations constitutes an essential element of modern international environmental law.[310] Further, it has achieved normative capacity as a legal principle of international law;[311] and beyond that, it has also become part of binding international treaties and of customary international law.[312] Thereby, it is part of the normative elements of international law and strongly interwoven with other evolving notions, such as intra-generational equity or the common concern of humankind.

The legal status of the general conception of intergenerational equity is important because *Diehl* and *Ku* developed their theoretical framework primarily with regard to "hard law, namely rights and obligations that are accepted as legally binding by actors in the system".[313] Nonetheless, they conceded the overlaps between legal and non-legal norms in public international law and understood the international legal system as a permeable rather than a closed system,[314] which is consistent with the aforementioned fluid boundaries between *lex lata* and *lex ferenda*.[315] This means that non-legally binding concepts could, on the one hand, influence the evolution of the normative system,[316] and on the other hand, become legally binding norms over time if included in the sources of international law.[317]

Consequently, the more elaborate manifestation of intergenerational equity, *Brown Weiss'* doctrine, could become relevant within the normative system of

[306] Diehl and Ku (2010), pp. 45–46; Francioni (2012), pp. 444–447. For an overview, see, e.g., Brown Weiss (2011), pp. 22–24; Bodansky (2020), pp. 7–8; Rajamani and Peel (2021).

[307] See, e.g., Epiney (2022), p. 13. See already *supra* in Sect. 2.1.

[308] Dupuy and Viñuales (2018), p. 92.

[309] Collins (2007), p. 118.

[310] Dupuy and Viñuales (2018), p. 88.

[311] See *supra* in Sect. 4.1.3.

[312] See *supra* in Sect. 4.2.1 and Sect. 4.2.2.1.

[313] Diehl and Ku (2010), p. 52.

[314] Ibid., pp. 52–53.

[315] See *supra* note 263.

[316] Ibid., p. 53.

[317] However, to become legally binding norms, they must, first, have normative capacity, as illustrated *supra* in Sect. 4.1.

international law, as it has the normative capacity required to become part of international law in the form of either treaty law or a customary norm. The doctrine stipulates the obligation of present generations "to pass on the natural and cultural resources of the planet [to future generations] in no worse condition than received".[318] This obligation must be fulfilled by conservation of options of natural resources, conservation of their quality and conservation of equitable access to these resources.[319] As these substantive contents of intergenerational equity are not legally binding, they do not form part of the normative system of international law yet. However, in case of their emergence as treaty or customary law in the future, they would constitute part of the normative system as substantive norms, which are capable of imposing duties on the present generation to perform or abstain from certain actions.[320] This is in accordance with *Diehl* and *Ku's* understanding of international law as a permeable system. Overall, the book has thus addressed questions of the normative system of intergenerational equity particularly in Chap. 2 and Chap. 4 when analysing the legal content as well as the legal nature of the concept—this connection has already been implied at the end of Chap. 4.[321]

###### 7.3.4.1.2 Operating System

According to *Diehl* and *Ku*, the second subsystem of international law, the operating system, constitutes "the platform and structure to govern and to manage international relations".[322] The operating system answers, *inter alia*, the following questions:

> Who [...] are the authorized decision-makers in international law? Whose actions can bind not only the parties involved, but also others? How do we know that an authoritative decision has taken place? When does the resolution of a conflict or a dispute give rise to new law?[323]

The operating system can concern institutional issues, including the institutions and processes to enforce international law and to guarantee its compliance.[324] These institutions can operate at the global or at a regional level; they can operate in a generalist manner or deal with specific issues; they can be institutions for policy-making, bodies of dispute resolution or they can address other compliance mechanisms.[325]

---

[318] Brown Weiss (1989), pp. 37–38.

[319] Ibid., pp. 38–45.

[320] Cf. Hart (2012), p. 81.

[321] See *supra* Sect. 4.3 [note 378].

[322] Diehl and Ku (2010), p. 28.

[323] Ibid., p. 29.

[324] Ibid., 29, 35.

[325] Ibid., pp. 34–35.

Beside institutional matters, the operating system covers several non-institutional aspects,[326] which range from the distinction between different sources of law[327] to the identification of actors in the international legal system[328] to the determination of jurisdiction for dispute resolution.[329] For instance, the identification of actors constitutes an essential part of the operating system, as it helps to determine the subjects that can have rights and obligations under international law:[330]

> [A]ny legal operating system must specify its users. Those actors in the system are assigned roles in how the law is made, what rights are accorded to those actors, what obligations exist, and finally how, when, and by whom those rights and obligations can be exercised.[331]

While the normative system addresses *what* is owed by international actors, the operating system addresses *who* are the addressees of international obligations and rights and *how* these obligations and rights are to be fulfilled, respected and particularly implemented and enforced.

As mentioned above, the distinction between normative and operating system resembles *Hart's* distinction between primary and secondary rules of law.[332] The normative system is comparable to primary rules,[333] while the operating system resembles *Hart's* secondary rules of law, that means those rules that describe how primary rules might be "ascertained, introduced, eliminated, varied, and the fact of their violation conclusively determined".[334] Secondary rules encompass, *inter alia*, rules on the establishment of new substantive norms or on matters of jurisdiction, thus, they refer to the operative structures behind the substantive legal norms. However, as *Diehl* and *Ku* pointed out, their distinction and *Hart's* classification differs. While *Hart* considered secondary rules to be "parasitic" to the primary ones,[335] *Diehl* and *Ku's* framework confers a higher importance and independence to the operating system.[336] Notwithstanding these differences, the classification of the international legal system into normative elements (i.e., substantive rules and principles) and operative structures behind these norms can generally be found in the works of other scholars.[337] The distinction is comparably reflected in the traditional structure of many international law textbooks, as they distinguish between a general

326 See also Ku and Diehl (2016), pp. 32–33.

327 Diehl and Ku (2010), pp. 30–34.

328 Ibid., pp. 31–33.

329 Ibid., pp. 33–34.

330 Ibid., pp. 31–32.

331 Ibid., p. 32.

332 Hart (2012), p. 79. *Diehl* and *Ku* compared their framework to other related ideas in legal scholarship, see Diehl and Ku (2010), pp. 35–37, 43–44.

333 See *supra* note 301.

334 Hart (2012), p. 94.

335 Ibid., p. 81.

336 Diehl and Ku (2010), p. 37; Ku and Diehl (2016), p. 34.

337 See, e.g., Ellickson (1991); Tanzi (2011); Francioni (2012), pp. 454–455.

part on international law—comparable to the operating system—and issue-specific subject matters—comparable to the normative system.[338]

Parallel to the expansion of the normative system, the operating system has also evolved in the last decades. This evolution concerned the expansion of relevant actors (e.g., individuals as new subjects of international law),[339] the evolution of new institutional frameworks (e.g., the increasing relevance of international organisations and the growing number of international judicial bodies)[340] and the changing forms of law-making (e.g., the constantly growing number of new treaties and the increasing relevance of soft law).[341] Some of these evolutions of the operating system have also been of particular importance in the realm of international environmental law, such as the increasing role of soft law.[342]

In order to exemplify the operating system, the book further identifies the relevant structural elements with respect to intergenerational equity. While the normative system of intergenerational equity refers to the contents of the associated obligations, the operating system of intergenerational equity regulates the underlying structures that govern the functioning of the concept. As these structures particularly consist of the relevant actors and subjects as well as the institutional mechanisms,[343] it can be said that Chap. 5 has addressed the elements of the operating system of intergenerational equity:[344] Who are the potential duty-bearers that are bound by intergenerational obligations?[345] Who are the corresponding right-holders of intergenerational equity, if there are any?[346] How can intergenerational equity be efficiently implemented, how can the interests of future generations be represented and which institutional framework exists in order to provide such implementation?[347]

With regard to the general conception, these issues are crucial if the normative elements of intergenerational equity are to be translated into effective implementation. As the general conception does not explicitly raise these issues due to its very general character, it does not require *specific* forms of structures. This is different with regard to the specific doctrine of intergenerational equity as this doctrine is based on the idea of a planetary trust with intergenerational obligations and

338 Diehl and Ku (2010), p. 29. See, e.g., Evans (2018); von Arnauld (2019).

339 See also Mosler (1962); Friedmann (1964), pp. 67, 213–252; Sands (2001), pp. 543–548.

340 See also Friedmann (1964), pp. 275–295; Sands (2001), pp. 552–556.

341 Generally on these developments, see Diehl and Ku (2010), pp. 37–42. Cf. also Brown Weiss (2000), p. 346. On the changes in law-making and the role of soft law in international law, see Ku (2005), pp. 639–641; Pauwelyn et al. (2012).

342 Chinkin (2000), pp. 27–28.

343 Diehl and Ku (2010), pp. 29–35.

344 This connection has also already been implied at the end of Chap. 5, see *supra* in Sect. 5.4.

345 See *supra* in Sect. 5.1.

346 See *supra* in Sect. 5.2.

347 See *supra* in Sect. 5.3.

corresponding rights of future generations,[348] as well as on mechanisms of implementation and representation.[349] Therefore, the idea of future generations as right-holders and of an efficient representation of future generations are inherent elements of *Brown Weiss'* doctrine of intergenerational equity.

All of these questions have been difficult to assess and the answers have not always been clear-cut. There is neither consensus on the possibility of future generations to be right-holders nor on the identification of the respective duty-bearers. Particularly, the operating system does not provide for the "present generation" to be a subject of law, but at the same time, the current legal structures do not allow identifying singular entities apart from States and international organisations who would—in their totality—be considered as the obliged entity of intergenerational equity. With respect to the institutional framework, attempts to introduce a global institution of representation have been unsuccessful, just as the universal introduction of national ombudspersons. The analysis in Chap. 5 has further illustrated the fragmented instances of judicial representation of future generations, which do not amount to universal structures of implementation. Moreover, there is a continuous evolution with regard to all of these aspects. This demonstrates the immense relevance of the operating system for the assessment of intergenerational equity.

### 7.3.4.2 System Interaction

Beyond the mere classification of the international legal system into two subsystems, the relation and interaction between these two subsystems constitutes the most important and distinctive feature of *Diehl* and *Ku's* methodological framework. The present work briefly illustrates this relation between normative and operating system (Sect. 7.3.4.2.1), before turning to an overview of the main factors that influence system interaction and thereby favour or hinder legal change (Sect. 7.3.4.2.2). Although this book does not apply *Diehl* and *Ku's* framework to intergenerational equity in detail, the section ends with an outlook on how it *could* be used with a view to strengthening the intertemporal perspective on intergenerational equity (Sect. 7.3.4.3).

#### 7.3.4.2.1 The Relation Between Normative and Operating System

According to *Diehl* and *Ku*, international legal change is based on a complex and interconnected relation between the normative and the operating system, which can have a mutually reinforcing impact on one another.[350] Therefore, the balance

[348] Brown Weiss (1989), pp. 95–109.

[349] Ibid., pp. 119–158.

[350] Diehl and Ku (2010), pp. 50–52.

between both subsystems, the "degree to which the operating and normative systems are aligned", is important.[351] There are two forms of imbalance between normative and operating system:

> An imbalance would signify that some prescriptions or proscriptions [i.e., normative system] exist without the means to create necessary ancillary rules, monitor behavior, ensure compliance, and/or adjudicate disputes [i.e., operating system]. Such an imbalance would have critical consequences for the ability of international law to influence behavior. Less critical, but still indicative of imbalance, is when operating system procedures are above and beyond what is needed for the normative system. That is, operating system mechanisms exist in international law, but are not necessary or no longer correspond to the needs of the normative system.[352]

For *Diehl* and *Ku*, the imbalance between both subsystems is an essential element of the international legal system. In contrast, *balance* between the systems would be "neither necessary nor even likely".[353] This is an important difference between their framework of legal change and other traditional approaches that consider the substance and the structures of international law in a constant status of equilibrium.[354] Other commentators have elaborated comparable approaches to system interaction and imbalance, which also distinguish between structural changes and changes of norms of international law.[355] Although these approaches differ in detail, the comparable starting points support the ideas behind *Diehl* and *Ku's* methodology. The present book does not address these other approaches, but focuses on the framework offered by *Diehl* and *Ku.*

Since "it is unlikely that there are many points in time, if any, in which the two operating and normative systems are perfectly aligned",[356] the relationship between both subsystems is an important aspect of this framework of legal change. *Diehl* and *Ku* distinguished several normative-operating system configurations and thereby identified different situations of balance and imbalance in international law.[357] Most often, one subsystem lags behind the other and this imbalance can be either temporal or permanent.[358] The effects of imbalance between the subsystems can differ. If the operating system lags behind the developments of the normative system,[359] the most relevant and negative impact of this imbalance would be the ineffectiveness of the normative rules.[360] This also renders the implementation of the

[351] Ibid., p. 53.

[352] Ibid., p. 54.

[353] Ibid.

[354] See ibid., 49, 54.

[355] See, e.g., Cook (2004), pp. 98–99; Sandholtz (2009), p. 6; Stiles and Sandholtz (2009), pp. 325–330; Rauber (2018); Kleinlein (2018), pp. 6–9.

[356] Diehl and Ku (2010), p. 57.

[357] Ibid., pp. 55–57.

[358] Ibid., pp. 56–57.

[359] If the normative system lags behind the structures of the operating system, this is less grave, see ibid., p. 59.

[360] Ibid., pp. 57–58.

normative system by dispute resolution more difficult.[361] An underdeveloped operating system can also have the effect of slowing down further evolutions of the normative system if the underlying structures are insufficient.[362]

The two subsystems do not exist independently from each other, but they have reciprocal influence on one another.[363] Various factors within one system can either favour or hinder change in the other system and thereby achieve an equilibrium or not.[364] These factors are briefly illustrated in the next sub-section.

#### 7.3.4.2.2 Overview of the Main Factors for System Interaction

The extent to which one subsystem influences change in the other subsystem depends on several factors. The system interactions that are triggered by these factors constitute the core elements of the framework of legal change.[365] Although there is no automatism towards system equilibrium in international law,[366] *Diehl* and *Ku* considered that there is often a "self-regulating *tendency* in the interaction of the two systems toward equilibrium or balance" (emphasis added).[367]

Based on the foregoing observations on imbalance, two main system configurations are possible. On the one hand, the normative system could be further developed than the operating system. In this case, the influence of normative system change on the operating system is important.[368] On the other hand, the operating system influences the normative system as it can either nurture or limit change in the normative system, depending on whether the operating system is over- or underdeveloped.[369] Further, systemic imbalance can lead to certain *extra*-systemic adaptations with a view to filling lacuna within the operating system in case of a permanent imbalance.[370] This book provides only an overview of the factors that favour or hinder balance between the two systems; it focuses on the influences of the normative system on an underdeveloped operating system.

---

361 Ibid., p. 58.

362 Ibid., pp. 58–59.

363 In order to explain under which circumstances change in one system results in change of the other system or not, *Diehl* and *Ku* applied the punctuated equilibrium model by *Gary Goertz*, see Goertz (2003), and adopted it to their framework of legal change, see Diehl and Ku (2010), pp. 64–71.

364 Ibid., pp. 54–55. See also Cook (2004), p. 98.

365 Diehl and Ku (2010), pp. 70–71.

366 Ibid., 57–59, 60.

367 Ibid., p. 70.

368 Ibid., pp. 74–102.

369 Ibid., pp. 129–150.

370 Ibid., pp. 103–128.

According to *Diehl* and *Ku's* specific understanding of the international legal system as an evolutionary system,[371] the necessary conditions that must be met to cause change in the other subsystem can be both endogenous and exogenous.[372] Endogenous factors come from within the legal system itself, while exogenous factors influence the legal system from the outside.[373] These two dimensions are illustrated by the main conditions that can lead from normative system change to subsequent changes in the operating system. First, there must be necessity for change of the operating system, which is an endogenous factor. Second, a sufficient political shock must occur from the outside in order to trigger operating system change. If these two conditions are met, the operating system can follow the development of the normative system, if there is, third, no opposition to this change by leading States and if, fourth, domestic political and legal influences do not hinder this change.

(1) "Necessity for change" means that "the *status quo* [operating] system cannot handle the requirements placed upon it by the adoption of new normative standards".[374] There are three different cases of necessity in this context: insufficiency, incompatibility and ineffectiveness. In the case of insufficiency, the operating system does not possess relevant provisions at all to deal with the new rules or principles.[375] In the case of incompatibility, the operating system is even contrary to the new normative system (e.g., the potential contradictions between new international criminal law and sovereign immunity).[376] In the case of ineffectiveness, there are relevant operating mechanisms but these are not well designed to meet the challenges presented by the overdeveloped normative system.[377] In all of these cases, the operating system must necessarily change in order to give effect to the new normative standards.[378]
(2) Beside the necessity for change, the impetus of a "political shock" is required.[379] Political shocks constitute "dramatic changes in the international political environment".[380] They have in common that they are significant events and processes whose impact is felt in a large area of the world, and which are able to disrupt existing political perceptions while their effects can result in change in several possible directions.[381] They do not necessarily have to happen in a short period of time (e.g., wars or terrorist attacks), but they can also extend over a

[371] In more detail, see ibid., pp. 59–64.
[372] Ibid., 60, 70.
[373] Ibid., p. 70.
[374] Ibid., pp. 75–76
[375] Ibid., p. 77.
[376] Ibid., pp. 77–78.
[377] Ibid., p. 78.
[378] Ibid., p. 76.
[379] Ibid., pp. 79–81. Cf. Young (1989), p. 371.
[380] Diehl and Ku (2010), p. 79.
[381] Ibid., p. 68. For a comparable analysis in this regard, see also Sandholtz (2009), p. 11; Stiles and Sandholtz (2009), pp. 326–329.

longer time frame and accumulate to major political changes.[382] Further, political shocks can either trigger change within the normative and the operating system simultaneously or sequentially.[383] In the former case, there would be no imbalance between the systems since the change in the operating system *directly* follows the normative system change. It is thus only the latter case, which is relevant for the present book: If a political shock only leads to normative system change, the result is imbalance between the systems. The operating system change might then only be initiated by another political shock, possibly many years later than the one, which has originally led to the normative system change.[384]

Although necessity for change and political shocks constitute the two sufficient requirements of operating system change, two other endogenous factors may limit or hinder such change. While these latter factors do not need to be *actively* fulfilled for system change, their role in system imbalance can be decisive.[385]

(3) The "opposition of leading States"[386] is the first possible constraint. Contrary to hegemonic views of international law[387] and "realists" in international relations theory,[388] *Diehl* and *Ku* rejected the argument that legal change would mainly depend on powerful States' interests.[389] Their framework does not assume that these "leading States" have absolute power, as *Diehl* and *Ku* rejected these States' power to hinder the development of the *normative* system.[390] However, leading States could have an influence on the development of the *operating* system,[391] This influence does not confer to them the power to unilaterally determine the future development of the operating system, but only to block operating system change if this is in their interest.[392] They thereby remain essential key actors in the progressive development of the international legal system.

---

[382] Diehl and Ku (2010), pp. 67–68. See also Stiles and Sandholtz (2009), pp. 325–326. *Diehl* and *Ku* referred to the "amassing of scientific evidence on global warming" as one example for more gradual political shocks, see Diehl and Ku (2010), p. 68.

[383] Diehl and Ku (2010), p. 80. See also Siverson (1980).

[384] Diehl and Ku (2010), pp. 80–81.

[385] Ibid., 69, 81.

[386] *Diehl* and *Ku* did not explicitly define, which States they considered to be "leading States". They only underlined that the identification of the leading States depends on the relevant substantive issue areas concerned, see ibid., pp. 82–83.

[387] Keohane (1980). See also Goldsmith and Posner (2005), pp. 24–40.

[388] Slaughter and Hale (2013, para. 4). See also Antunes and Camisão (2017).

[389] Diehl and Ku (2010), pp. 81–82.

[390] Ibid., p. 83.

[391] Ibid. See also Sandholtz (2009), p. 13.

[392] Diehl and Ku (2010), pp. 83–84. Cf. Young (1989), p. 373; Ku (2005), p. 641. *Wayne Sandholtz* also distinguished between major States' power to make new rules and their ability to escape conviction after breaking the rules: Sandholtz (2009), pp. 13–14.

(4) Further, "domestic political and legal influences" can also hinder operating system change.[393] Domestic political concerns can affect the outcomes of the operating system as constraining factors since many norms of international law are not self-executing. These norms need to be incorporated into the national level, for instance, by providing national remedies, adapting jurisdictional rules, or changing the legal standing to bring claims.[394] Therefore, the incorporation can fail due to domestic opposition to a certain norm although the concerned State might have contributed to the norm's creation before.[395] Moreover, States can conduct "two-level" games[396] by first supporting the creation of an international norm and then blocking the necessary structural changes on the domestic level.[397]

Beyond these intra-systemic relations and influences between the normative and the operating system, *Diehl* and *Ku* clarified at various occasions that international law is not a closed system of normative and operating subsystems, but that it is also subject to external, or extra-systemic, influences.[398] In case of imbalance between the two systems, subsequent operating system change is not the only way to achieve effectiveness. Instead, system imbalance often leads to adaptations outside the inflexible processes of the operating system with a view to filling the latter's lacuna.[399] These adaptations are extra-systemic in two regards. First, they escape the explicit categories of operating and normative system; second, they are mostly extra-legal, as they are not directly linked to binding norms of international law.[400] *Diehl* and *Ku* identified four extra-systemic solutions to system imbalance: the increasing role of soft law; of NGOs[401] and transnational networks in the international system; legal internalisation[402] of international law; and other domestic legal

---

[393] Diehl and Ku (2010), p. 85.

[394] Ibid. Cf. also Ginsburg (2006).

[395] Diehl and Ku (2010), p. 86.

[396] See Evans et al. (1993).

[397] Diehl and Ku (2010), pp. 86–87.

[398] Ibid., p. 103.

[399] As to the inflexibility of institutional mechanisms of change, see also Cassese (2012a), p. 658.

[400] See Ku and Diehl (2006).

[401] See also *infra* note 419.

[402] Legal internalisation means that the reliance on international institutions of the operating system is replaced by domestic legal mechanisms, see Ku (2005), pp. 645–648; Diehl and Ku (2010), p. 114. Cf. also Koh (1997), p. 2657. There are some overlaps between extra-systemic legal internalisation and regular domestic political and legal implementation. However, the process of domestic implementation is a result of explicit operating system requirements on the international level, so that the aforementioned opposing political or legal influences (*supra* notes 393–397) constitute direct endogenous constraints of operating system change. On the contrary, if no explicit implementation of structures on the national level is demanded by the operating system, domestic systems could, nonetheless, react and adapt to the existing imbalance in international law between normative aspiration and operational structures, see Diehl and Ku (2010), p. 114.; cf. also Cassese

and political processes.[403] Consequently, implementation and effectiveness of the normative system do not always depend on the operating system alone, but gaps in the operating system can partly be addressed by such external mechanisms and actors.[404] These extra-systemic adaptations also strongly influence the exact direction of change in international law beside the previously presented factors for operating system change.[405]

Eventually, the interdependence between normative system and operating system change also materialises in the reverse direction as the operating system can nurture or limit change in the normative system. *Diehl* and *Ku* identified six ways how the operating system can influence the normative system.[406]

(1) The operating system can set the parameters of acceptability of normative system change.[407] This can occur, for instance, in the form of "constitutional limits" or hierarchy of norms, such as *ius cogens*.[408] But in the absence of constitutional principles,[409] limitations of acceptability can also be the result of judicial review.[410]
(2) The operating system clarifies the credible commitment of States to standards of the normative system.[411] For instance, the institutional structures of the operating system can have an important impact on the development of new international norms, as they "enhance the credibility of commitments by raising the costs of defection".[412]
(3) At the same time, the operating system must provide a certain flexibility to allow States to exit or modify existing elements of the normative system if they consider it necessary.[413] *Inflexibility* in the compliance mechanisms of international law might hinder the acceptance of States and prevent further normative system change since States will not be inclined to limit their sovereign leeway

(2012a), p. 677. These adaptations would then constitute extra-systemic factors that could only have indirect impacts on the further development of the international legal system.

[403] Ku and Diehl (2006); Diehl and Ku (2010), pp. 108–125.

[404] Diehl and Ku (2010), pp. 103–104, 125. See also Luhmann (1988), p. 22.

[405] Cf. Diehl and Ku (2010), pp. 78–79 with reference to Sandholtz (2009).

[406] Diehl and Ku (2008); Diehl and Ku (2010), pp. 133–149. On a different account of how the "conceptual foundations" of international law can restrain the development of the normative system of international environmental law, see Sparks (2020).

[407] Diehl and Ku (2010), pp. 133–136.

[408] Ibid., p. 133.

[409] On the limits of constitutionalisation in international law, see already *supra* in Sect. 7.3.2, notes 206–210.

[410] Diehl and Ku (2010), pp. 134–135.

[411] Ibid., pp. 136–138.

[412] Ibid., p. 136. Cf. also Young (1989), pp. 370–371; Helfer and Slaughter (2005), p. 931; Ku and Diehl (2016), pp. 33–34.

[413] Diehl and Ku (2010), pp. 138–140.

too much.[414] Therefore, an elaborated operating system can at the same time nurture or hinder progressive normative system development.[415]

(4) The specification of the rights and obligations of the relevant actors in international law (i.e., actor specification) can also have important impacts on the normative system.[416] The stronger the influence of different and new actors on law-making becomes, the greater is their potential impact on the substantive provisions of international law.[417] The increasing impact of various stakeholders, such as international organisations or NGOs on international law-making thus not only constitutes an extra-systemic adaptation,[418] but it can also influence future change of the normative system.[419]

(5) Forum specification means that the choice of a specific forum in the operating system can affect the normative outcome of a certain law-making process.[420] Forum specification is closely linked to actor specification since the forum influences the respective actors.[421] But the different agenda-setting powers in the different forums also directly influence the possible issues for new legal rules. Thereby, the chosen forum has an impact on the provisions that finally become law.[422]

(6) Finally, the operating system can, in specific cases, allow for direct law-making powers of other actors than States,[423] if States conferred law-making authority to international organisations (e.g., the EU).[424] This also has impacts on future change of the normative system.

The sophisticated analysis of system interaction offered by *Diehl* and *Ku* illustrates that change in international law is not arbitrary or unpredictable, but that it follows certain mechanisms and processes. In case of imbalance between the normative and the operating system of a specific norm of international law, change can occur in two directions. If the normative system is ahead of the operating system, necessity for change and political shocks are necessary to cause subsequent change of the operating system, while opposition of leading States and domestic influences can constrain this change. If the normative system lags behind, the aforementioned six elements of the operating system can influence whether and how the normative system will change. These elements include, *inter alia*, actor and forum specification

[414] Ibid.

[415] Cf. Sparks (2020).

[416] Diehl and Ku (2010), pp. 140–144.

[417] Ibid., p. 140.

[418] For NGOs, see already *supra* note 401.

[419] Ibid., pp. 141–144. On the increasing role of NGOs, see also Shelton (1994); Çakmak (2004), p. 102; Charnovitz (2006).

[420] Diehl and Ku (2010), pp. 144–147. Cf. also Sandholtz (2009), pp. 9–10.

[421] Diehl and Ku (2010), p. 145.

[422] Ibid., pp. 145–146.

[423] Ibid., pp. 147–149.

[424] See ibid., pp. 147–148.

as well as the degree of flexibility of the operating system. Besides these intra-systemic impacts, extra-systemic adaptations can occur in order to fill the lacuna of the systemic imbalance, for instance, in the form of an increasing role of soft law and of NGOs in the international arena.

#### 7.3.4.3 An Outlook: Application to Intergenerational Equity

*Diehl* and *Ku* illustrated their framework with the example of the genocide norm in international law.[425] However, they stressed that their illustration was not meant as a full test of their theory since this would go beyond the scope of any single study. Instead, they pointed out that a cumulative "series of studies across many components of the normative system would serve to be a test of our expectation that international law works dynamically and interactively [...]."[426] In the same spirit, the present author suggests to add the analysis of intergenerational equity to the "series of studies" initiated and encouraged by *Diehl* and *Ku*. If one applied their framework of international legal change to the normative and the operating system of intergenerational equity, this would allow for more sophisticated predictions on the latter's future development than with regard to the transitional character of the two manifestations of the concept.[427] For those who dare to engage more with a modified doctrine of intertemporal law that prospectively looks to the future, this framework permits to anticipate future developments of intergenerational equity beyond the two interim conclusions above.[428]

The following brief overview demonstrates that the normative and the operating system of intergenerational equity constitute a good example of the interactions between both systems. Specifically, the imbalance between both subsystems with regard to intergenerational equity is evident. To begin with, the general conception of intergenerational equity proclaims certain normative obligations of States with a view to protecting the interests of future generations. However, there is no universal and comprehensive structural framework that allows effectively implementing these obligations.

From a broader perspective, the subsystems of intergenerational equity are essentially connected to the general structures of international environmental law, particularly its many deficiencies.[429] *Francesco Francioni* identified these deficiencies to the point: On the one hand, there would be no consensus on the understanding of the "environment" as object of protection of international environmental law, so

[425] Ibid., p. 88.

[426] Ibid.

[427] See *supra* in Sect. 7.3.3.

[428] See *supra* in Sect. 7.3.3.3.

[429] For some possible institutional responses to the existing weaknesses, see Kiss (2005), pp. 576–584.

that its protection still remains elusive today.[430] Although the substantive developments of international environmental law have been extensive in the last decades,[431] some commentators criticised exactly this normative fragmentation due to its inability "to keep humanity from crossing or fast approaching planetary boundaries".[432] *Louis Kotzé* even considered international environmental law to generally "lack [...] normative ambition".[433]

On the other hand, *Francioni* pointed to the evident lack in enforcement mechanisms that is opposed to stronger institutional frameworks within the realms of human rights law and international economic law.[434] This lack of effective implementation is exemplary within the climate change regime,[435] but it is inherent in international environmental law as a whole.[436] *Francioni* considered this insufficient institutional framework "the true Achilles' heel of the present system of international environmental law."[437] Consequently, the latter's deficiencies result primarily from the imbalance between normative ambitions and operating system mechanisms. In this sense, the UNSG stated in its 2018 Report on the gaps in international environmental law:

> There are significant gaps and deficiencies with respect to the applicable principles of environmental law; the normative and *institutional* content of the sectoral regulatory regimes, as well as their articulation with environment-related regimes; the *governance structure* of international environmental law; and the *effective implementation* of, *compliance* with and *enforcement* of international environmental law (emphasis added).[438]

The same structural deficits exist with regard to the general conception of intergenerational equity. While its normative content establishes a legal principle of international law, it remains abstract and elusive to some extent. More importantly, there is even less clarity on its underlying operating system, which lacks the structures to implement any element of the general conception's normative content. As the operating system thus lags behind the aspirations of the normative system of intergenerational equity, this imbalance results in an ineffective implementation of

---

[430] Francioni (2012), p. 447.

[431] See already *supra* notes 306–307.

[432] Stephens (2017), pp. 34–47, 48. See also Kotzé (2019a), p. 16.

[433] Kotzé (2019b).

[434] Francioni (2012), pp. 447–449. According to *Francioni*, these asymmetries between strong enforcement of trade-related rules and non-existent institutional frameworks in international environmental law have contributed to the enormous institutional weaknesses of environmental law and have often resulted in even further distortion, see ibid., pp. 449–453. Cf. also Kotzé (2019a), pp. 16–17.

[435] Andresen (2021), pp. 994–997.

[436] See Beyerlin and Grote Stoutenburg (2013, paras. 85–96) Cf. also Cassotta (2019), pp. 63–66.

[437] Francioni (2012), p. 458. See also ibid., pp. 454–455.

[438] UNSG (2018, para. 100). On the report, see already *supra* in Sect. 2.1.1.5.

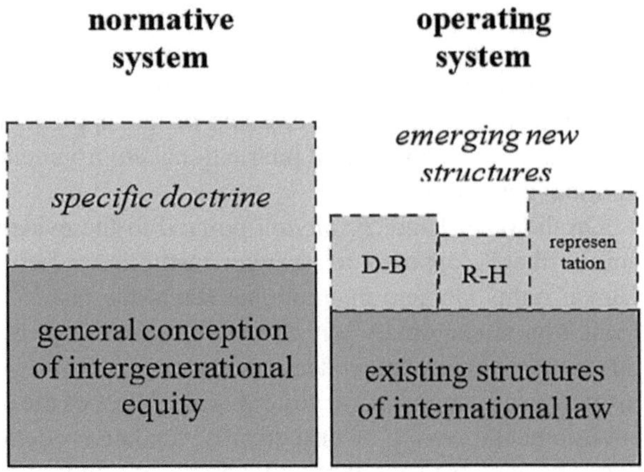


**Fig. 7.9** Normative and operating system of intergenerational equity

the normative system,[439] which can slow down further evolutions of the concept.[440]

The disparity between normative and operating system is even more evident with respect to the specific doctrine of intergenerational equity. The emerging rule of customary international law has not become part of the normative system yet. However, *Brown Weiss'* doctrine builds on the idea of an planetary trust with specific intergenerational duties of conservation and rights of future generations,[441] it further requires effective mechanisms of representation of future generations and their interests.[442] In contrast to the general conception of intergenerational equity, the substantive contents of the specific doctrine would thus explicitly require stronger and more sophisticated structures for its effective implementation. As illustrated, the existing operating system of international law does not offer these structures. Only States are considered duty-bearers of international environmental obligations, not the "present generation" as a whole. Future generations are currently not considered subjects of international law, so that they cannot be right-holders of a planetary trust within the meaning of *Brown Weiss'* doctrine. Furthermore, Chap. 5 has demonstrated in detail the fragmented and incomplete institutional mechanisms of intergenerational equity. The operating system elements that would be necessary to effectively implement the specific doctrine are only slowly emerging. Consequently, there is an even greater imbalance between the underdeveloped operating system and the normative system with regard to the specific doctrine of intergenerational equity. Figure 7.9 visualises the overall imbalance between the normative and the operating system of intergenerational equity, building on foregoing illustrations in Chaps. 4 (Fig. 4.1) and 5 (Fig. 5.1).

[439] Diehl and Ku (2010), pp. 57–58.

[440] Ibid., pp. 58–59.

[441] Brown Weiss (1989), pp. 95–109.

[442] Brown Weiss (2010), pp. 110–113.

In this overview of normative and operating system, both transitional processes within intergenerational equity become obvious. There is a transition between the general conception of intergenerational equity and the emerging specific doctrine. Further, the structures of international law with regard to intergenerational equity are also in a transitional process of change—between States as only duty-bearers ('D-B') and the acceptance of additional duty-bearers, between the non-existence of future generations and their potential acceptance as right-holders ('R-H') and between the existing fragmented framework and a potential coherent framework of representation. However, as the operating system still lags behind the more ambitious normative content of intergenerational equity, both subsystems remain in a status of imbalance. This imbalance is common, and even most likely, in the international legal system.[443] At the same time, the imbalance is neither perpetual nor unchangeable. Legal change in both subsystems often results from exactly this imbalance and the interrelated influences between normative and operating system. The foregoing sections have outlined the various influential factors that can lead to convergence of, and even equilibrium between, the two subsystems.

By understanding the interactions between the subsystems and applying this understanding to intergenerational equity, it would become possible to make assumptions on the future development of both the operating as well as the normative system of the norm. The interactions between the subsystems are reciprocal.[444] In case the aforementioned factors of system change are established, the normative system's ambitious claims could trigger further development of the operating system that is currently still lagging behind. Vice-versa, an evolving operating system of international law could subsequently trigger the decisive transition within the normative system, from the general conception to the specific doctrine of intergenerational equity.

While the exact application of *Diehl* and *Ku's* framework to the interactions within intergenerational equity requires further detailed research, this methodologically reasoned framework illustrates that the prediction of future legal change *is* possible to a certain degree. Although this prediction cannot assume absolute validity due to the future's uncertainty, it further assists in shaping a prospective intertemporal perspective on the evolutionary concept of intergenerational equity. A detailed assessment of intergenerational equity by means of *Diehl* and *Ku's* framework would constitute the adequate basis for the evolutionary approaches to intergenerational equity within the meaning of the modified doctrine of intertemporal law.

Of course, the application of this framework does not preclude the application of comparable or different frameworks that have been elaborated by other commentators on future legal change—for instance as recently presented in an edited book by *Nico Krisch* and *Ezgi Yildiz*.[445] Their book seeks to get "closer to an understanding

[443] Diehl and Ku (2010), p. 54.

[444] See ibid., pp. 64–71.

[445] Krisch and Yildiz (2023).

of how change happens in international law, and consequently of the factors that facilitate or hinder the reception of political transformations in the international legal order".[446] For this purpose, the book chapters look in more detail on strategies of change, forms of change and forces of change. However, it is beyond the scope of the present work to look into their analysis in more detail.

## 7.4 Conclusion of Chapter 7

This Chapter has elaborated a modification of intertemporal law in the context of intergenerational equity. For three reasons, it is necessary to modify the doctrine of intertemporal law to the particularities of intergenerational equity. First, the evolutionary approaches of the existing doctrine are primarily shaped for the interpretation of treaty norms. As the present book focuses on the *customary* character of intergenerational equity, this requires certain modifications to the legal status of customary international law. Second, the inherently intertemporal nature of intergenerational equity essentially differs from other intertemporal constellations of international law. Territorial disputes or traditional human rights disputes can be intertemporal with respect to the time gap between the creation of the norms and their later application. However, the underlying relationships are not intertemporal, as the involved parties of the disputes remain contemporaneous members of the same generation even though the respective norm might have been established in the past. As opposed to this, intergenerational equity establishes a legal relationship between the present and future generations that is extended over time. This extended legal relationship is also reflected in *John Rawls'* underlying philosophical image of a hypothetical original position, in which the principles of justice are established behind a veil of ignorance. The third reason for a modification of intertemporal law is the irreversibility of most intergenerational problems. It comes to nothing if it were necessary to await an intergenerational dispute in the future in order to retrospectively delimit the temporally applicable law. At that time in the future, the environmental damage will already have occurred, but the potential duty-bearer will not be able to remedy this damage appropriately due to the irreversibility of the disastrous effects of anthropogenic global warming and other intergenerational problems. Due to these conceptual particularities of intergenerational equity, a modification of the existing doctrine is necessary in order to determine the temporally applicable legal regime for the assessment of intergenerational equity today.

It was the main purpose of this chapter to establish such a modified doctrine of intertemporal law. Basically, the two elements of intertemporal law remain important even within this modification: first, the principle of contemporaneity, and second, evolutionary approaches. Contemporaneity points to the legal regime of intergenerational equity at the time of its creation, meaning the establishment of

[446] Ibid., p. 3.

intergenerational equity as a customary norm since the 1990s until today. The contemporaneous content of this norm would be the general conception of intergenerational equity—the need to take into account the interests of future generations.[447] Beyond contemporaneity, the existing evolutionary approaches would have to be adapted from mere tools of treaty interpretation to the assessment of customary norms. This results in a modified evolutionary approach that is primarily based on the "object and purpose" of intergenerational equity. Due to the dynamic character of this object and purpose, the evolutionary intertemporal assessment would turn to the subsequent developments of intergenerational equity since its creation. It would point to the application of the emerging specific doctrine of intergenerational equity, including potential planetary rights of future generations and institutional frameworks of representation.

Despite these formal parallels to the existing doctrine of intertemporal law, the decisive modification is the shift of perspective. While intertemporal law normally is an instrument that links the present to the past, it has to be extended from the present to the future in the context of intergenerational relations. In order not to wait for the effects of intergenerational violations to occur in the future, intertemporal law must become future-oriented. Instead of the traditional retrospective application, it must be modified in order to prospectively determine the temporally applicable legal regime today vis-à-vis the future. This requires to take into consideration future developments of intergenerational equity today.

Certainly, this prospective approach to intergenerational equity will face some criticism as lawyers will never be able to predict the future development of international law with certainty. Needless to say, this is not the claim of this book. But regardless of the legitimate objections to a prediction of future developments of law, the elaborated reasons for a necessary modification of intertemporal law remain valid. It is not persuasive to maintain the retrospective framework of intertemporal law with regard to intergenerational equity. For this reason, the present chapter has offered three possible outcomes for the modified intertemporal perspective on intergenerational equity. At the very least, the lack of persuasiveness of the retrospective doctrine in respect of intergenerational equity should trigger a change of mindset vis-à-vis intergenerational problems today. The legal relationship between the present and future generations is so inherently intertemporal and shaped by risks of irreversibility that the present generation would be required to consider the intertemporal perspective of future generations on the legal regime of the present. If the members of the present generation became conscious about this perspective of the potential right-holders, this might change the way they see their obligations towards future generations. It would lead to a prospective and proactive view on intergenerational equity instead of waiting for intergenerational disputes to arise and

[447] See, e.g., Dupuy and Viñuales (2018), p. 92.

to solve them retrospectively.[448] In the end, this would mean taking *Rawls'* idea of fair and equal conditions behind the veil of ignorance seriously. Only if the perspectives of all generations in the fictional original position are considered to the same degree, the resulting principles of intergenerational justice will actually constitute just and equal principles.

Beyond this abstract change of mindset in current international environmental law, it would also be possible to engage more substantially with the potential future developments of intergenerational equity. Based on the transitional character of intergenerational equity as a norm of customary international law, the two-fold manifestations of the concept offer an adequate starting point for such a cautious outlook on the future. Customary international law is often in a process of transition between old norms and new norms. Similarly, the concept of intergenerational equity is situated between its currently binding manifestation of the general conception and its emerging manifestation of a more specific doctrine, as presented in the works of *Brown Weiss*. Although it is not certain that the concept will develop into the specific doctrine, the continuous evolution of intergenerational equity and the increasing amount of evidence of the specific doctrine in international legal discourse speak in favour of the future development of the concept. The attempt of predicting this future development would thus build upon the transitional period between the general conception and the specific doctrine of intergenerational equity. This would also facilitate the assessment of the future generation's perspective on the current legal regime, as this assessment could be based on the contents of the specific doctrine of intergenerational equity. This includes the planetary duties as well as the emerging structures of future generations as right-holders and their institutional representation in policy-making and judicial proceedings. Consequently, decision-makers and judges would have to be less fixated on the accepted general conception of intergenerational equity as a legal principle. They would also have to become open to the prospective consideration of emerging developments of the concept. The specific doctrine would then already play a decisive role in today's decision-making and dispute resolution even ahead of its final crystallisation as legally binding norm.

While this Chapter has offered a first idea of the consequences of this modified intertemporal approach, the details of these consequences remain to be analysed in subsequent research. In this sense, the present work leaves some questions open on the practical implementation of the modified doctrine and it should be understood as an initial invitation to more detailed research. Notwithstanding this, the Concluding Chap. 8 offers a brief outlook on a potential practical application for decision-makers and judges.[449]

[448] More generally, *Sandra Cassotta* stated in this regard that "environmental law should develop as a proactive law rather than being reactive in order to face unpredictability […]", see Cassotta (2019), p. 66.

[449] See *infra* in the in Sect. 8.4.

Finally, it could be possible to apply a methodologically convincing framework for the prediction of future change in international law in order to make even more reliable assumptions on the future development of intergenerational equity. The present author does not consider the application of such a framework to be absolutely necessary for an intertemporal perspective on intergenerational equity, as illustrated with the two foregoing interim conclusions. Nonetheless, the framework of the international legal system by *Paul Diehl* and *Charlotte Ku* constitutes an appropriate analytical tool to engage in this assessment.[450] Their framework builds on the identification of two subsystems of international law: the normative and the operating system. While the normative system refers to the substantive values and goals that shape international legal obligations, the operating system contains the structures that govern international relations. The interactions and imbalances between these two subsystems determine the continuous and future development of international law, both in content and in structures. This chapter has only briefly sketched out the main ideas of *Diehl* and *Ku's* methodological framework without applying it in detail to the concept of intergenerational equity. However, a more detailed analysis of the interactions and conditions for system change between normative and operating system of intergenerational equity could make it possible to predict the future changes of the concept more specifically and with a higher probability. These predictions would then influence the present generation's legal obligations towards the future as they would have to be considered from an intertemporal perspective as part of the evolutionary approach. If, for instance, multinational corporations develop into proper subjects of international environmental law in the future, then they could already today be held responsible vis-à-vis future generations. If the evolutionary future development of intergenerational equity includes the acceptance of new right-holders, this development would already shape the legal relationship between present and future generations today. And if the further development of intergenerational equity points to a more institutionalised form of representation on the policy-making and/or the judicial level, then these institutional frameworks would already gain weight today.

This intertemporal and future-oriented perspective on intergenerational equity is neither easy nor unambiguous. It is challenging and it can carry legal uncertainty to some degree. Nevertheless, it is necessary and evident with regard to the intertemporal problems associated with intergenerational equity. The legal and just relationship between the present and future generations depends on such an evolutionary and prospective approach to intergenerational equity. While this future-oriented approach might seem unrealistic or utopian, *Pierre-Marie Dupuy* correctly stated: "Utopia is only reprehensible when it is a substitute for action, not when it inspires it."[451]

[450] Diehl and Ku (2010).

[451] Dupuy (2020).

## References


Allott, P. (1999). International law and the idea of history. *Journal of the History of International Law, 1*(1), 1–21.

Allott, P. (2001). *Eunomia: New order for a new world*. Oxford University Press. (Original work published 1990).

Allott, P. (2017). *Eutopia: New philosophy and new law for a troubled world*. Edward Elgar Publishing.

Andresen, S. (2021). Effectiveness. In L. Rajamani & J. Peel (Eds.), *The Oxford handbook of international environmental law* (Vol. 57, 2nd ed., pp. 988–1002). Oxford University Press.

Anstee-Wedderburn, J. (2014). Giving a voice to future generations: Intergenerational equity, representative of generations to come, and the challenge of planetary rights. *Australian Journal of Environmental Law, 1*(1), 37–70.

Antunes, S., & Camisão, I. (2017). Realism. In S. McGlinchey, R. Walters, & C. Scheinpflug (Eds.), *International relations theory* (Vol. 1, pp. 15–21). E-International Relations Publishing.

Arato, J. (2018). Accounting for difference in treaty interpretation over time. In A. Bianchi, D. Peat, & M. Windsor (Eds.), *Interpretation in international law* (Vol. 10, 1st ed., pp. 205–228). Oxford University Press.

Barral, V. (2012). Sustainable development in international law: Nature and operation of an evolutive legal norm. *European Journal of International Law, 23*(2), 377–400. https://doi.org/10.1093/ejil/chs016

Bertram, D. (2023). "For You Will (Still) Be Here Tomorrow": The many lives of intergenerational equity. *Transnational Environmental Law, 12*(1), 121–149.

Beyerlin, U., & Grote Stoutenburg, J. (2013). Environment, international protection. In A. Peters & R. Wolfrum (Eds.), *Max Planck Encyclopedia of Public International Law*. Oxford University Press. (Article last updated December 2013).

Black, C. E., & Falk, R. A. (Eds.). (1972). *The future of the international legal order: Volume 4: The structure of the international environment*. Princeton University Press. https://doi.org/10.1515/9781400873074

Bodansky, D. (2020). The role and limits of the international court of justice in international environmental law. In E. Carlos & K. Partlett (Eds.), *The Cambridge companion to the international court of justice*. Cambridge University Press.

Borg, S. (1998). Guarding intergenerational rights over natural resources. In E. Agius & S. Busuttil (Eds.), *Future generations and international law: Proceedings of the International Experts' Meeting Held by the Future Generations Programme at the Foundation for International Studies, University of Malta* (Vol. 11, pp. 127–141). Earthscan Publications Ltd..

Bosselmann, K. (2017). The imperative of ecological integrity: Conceptualising a fundamental legal norm for a new "world system" in the anthropocene. In L. J. Kotzé (Ed.), *Environmental law and governance for the anthropocene* (Vol. 11, pp. 241–265). Hart Publishing.

Bosselmann, K. (2020). Environmental trusteeship and state sovereignty: Can they be reconciled? *Transnational Legal Theory, 11*(1–2), 47–61. https://doi.org/10.1080/20414005.2020.1757862

Bowman, M. (2002). Biodiversity, intrinsic value, and the definition and valuation of environmental harm. In M. Bowman & A. E. Boyle (Eds.), *Environmental damage in international and comparative law: Problems of definition and valuation* (Vol. 4, 1st ed., pp. 41–62). Oxford University Press.

Boyle, A. E. (2002). Reparation for environmental damage in international law: Some preliminary problems. In M. Bowman & A. E. Boyle (Eds.), *Environmental damage in international and comparative law: Problems of definition and valuation* (Vol. 2, 1st ed., pp. 17–26). Oxford University Press.

Brown Weiss, E. (1989). *In fairness to future generations: International law, common patrimony, and intergenerational equity*. Transnational Publishers, Inc.

Brown Weiss, E. (1992). Intergenerational equity and rights of future generations. In A. A. Cançado Trindade & E. Brown Weiss (Eds.), *Derechos Humanos, Desarrollo Sustentable y Medio*

*Ambiente: Human rights, sustainable development and the environment* (pp. 71–81). Banco Interamericano de Desarrollo.

Brown Weiss, E. (2000). The rise or the fall of international law? *Fordham Law Review, 69*(2), 345–372.

Brown Weiss, E. (2010). Implementing intergenerational equity. In M. Fitzmaurice, D. Ong, & P. Merkouris (Eds.), *Research handbook on international environmental law* (Vol. 5, pp. 100–116). Edward Elgar Publishing.

Brown Weiss, E. (2011). The evolution of international environmental law. *Japanese Yearbook of International Law, 54*, 1–27.

Brown Weiss, E. (2019). Intergenerational equity. In Y. Aguila & J. E. Viñuales (Eds.), *A global pact for the environment: Legal foundations* (Vol. 5, pp. 51–58). Cambridge Centre for Environment, Energy and Natural Resource Governance (C-EENRG).

Brown Weiss, E. (2020). *Establishing norms in a kaleidoscopic world.* Brill Nijhoff.

Brown Weiss, E. (2021). Intergenerational equity. In A. Peters & R. Wolfrum (Eds.), *Max Planck Encyclopedia of Public International Law*. Oxford University Press. (Article last updated April 2021).

Brunnée, J. (2022). Consent. In A. Peters & R. Wolfrum (Eds.), *Max Planck Encyclopedia of Public International Law*. Oxford University Press. (Article last updated January 2022).

Buchanan, N. H. (2009). What do we owe future generations? *George Washington Law Review, 77*(5–6), 1237–1297.

Buchanan, N. H. (2011). What kind of environment do we owe future generations? *Lewis & Clark Law Review, 15*(2), 339–367.

Burdon, P. D. (2020). Ecological law in the anthropocene. *Transnational Legal Theory, 11*(1–2), 33–46. https://doi.org/10.1080/20414005.2020.1748483

Burke, E. (1986). *Reflections on the revolution in France: And on the proceedings in certain societies in London relative to that event* (1st ed.). Penguin Books. (Original work published 1790).

Çakmak, C. (2004). The role of Non-Governmental Organizations (NGOs) in the norm creation process in the field of human rights. *Turkish Journal of International Relations, 3*(1), 100–122.

Cançado Trindade, A. A. (2020). *International law for humankind: Towards a New Jus Gentium* (3rd ed.). Brill Nijhoff.

Carmody, C. (2002). A look back at looking forward: Ronald St. John Macdonald and the future of international law. *Canadian Yearbook of International Law, 40*, 323–343.

Cassese, A. (2012a). Gathering up the main threads. In A. Cassese (Ed.), *Realizing Utopia: The future of international law* (Vol. 48, 1st ed., pp. 645–684). Oxford University Press.

Cassese, A. (2012b). Introduction. In A. Cassese (Ed.), *Realizing Utopia: The future of international law* (1st ed., pp. xvii–xxii). Oxford University Press.

Cassese, A. (Ed.). (2012c). *Realizing Utopia: The future of international law* (1st ed.). Oxford University Press. https://doi.org/10.1093/acprof:oso/9780199691661.001.0001

Cassotta, S. (2019). The development of environmental law within a changing environmental governance context: Towards a new paradigm shift in the anthropocene era. *Yearbook of International Environmental Law, 30*(1), 54–67. https://doi.org/10.1093/yiel/yvaa071

Central Intelligence Agency. (2022). *The World Factbook: Life Expectancy at Birth*. 2022. Retrieved January 3, 2025, from https://www.cia.gov/the-world-factbook/field/life-expectancy-at-birth.

Charnovitz, S. (2006). Nongovernmental organizations and international law. *American Journal of International Law, 100*(2), 348–372.

Chen, D., Rojas, M., Samset, B. H., Cobb, K., Diongue-Niang, A., Edwards, P., Emori, S., Faria, S. H., Hawkins, E., Hope, P., Huybrechts, P., Meinshausen, M., Mustafa, S., Plattner, G.-K., & Treguier, A. M. (2021). Framing, context and methods. In IPCC, *Climate Change 2021 – The Physical Science Basis: Working Group I Contribution to the IPCC Sixth Assessment Report* (V. Masson-Delmotte et al. (Eds.)), pp. 147–286. Retrieved January 3, 2025, from https://www.ipcc.ch/report/ar6/wg1/downloads/report/IPCC_AR6_WGI_Chapter01.pdf.

Chinkin, C. (2000). Normative development in the international legal system. In D. Shelton (Ed.), *Commitment and compliance: The role of non-binding norms in the international legal system* (Vol. 1, pp. 21–42). Oxford University Press.

Choucri, N. (Ed.). (1978). *Forecasting in international relations: Theory, methods, problems, prospects*. Freeman.

Collins, L. M. (2007). Revisiting the doctrine of intergenerational equity in global environmental governance. *Dalhousie Law Journal, 30*(1), 73–134.

Cook, R. H. (2004). Dynamic content: The strategic contingency of international law. *Duke Journal of Comparative and International Law, 14*(1), 89–123.

Cover, R. M. (1983). Nomos and narrative. *Harvard Law Review, 97*(1), 1–68.

Crawford, J. (2014). *Chance, order, change: The course of international law; general course on public international law*. Martinus Nijhoff Publishers.

Crawford, J., & Brownlie, I. (2019). *Brownlie's principles of public international law* (9th ed.). Oxford University Press.

Cryer, R., Hervey, T., Sokhi-Bulley, B., & Bohm, A. (2011). *Research methodologies in EU and international law*. Hart Publishing.

D'Amato, A. (1992). International law, intertemporal problems. In R. Bernhardt & P. Macalister-Smith (Eds.), *Encyclopedia of public international law: Published Under the Auspices of the Max Planck Institute for Comparative Public Law and International Law* (pp. 1234–1236). Elsevier. (Article last updated January 1992).

d'Aspremont, J. (2022). Time travel in the law of international responsibility. In S. Besson (Ed.), *Theories of international responsibility law* (Vol. 11, pp. 252–277). Cambridge University Press.

De-Shalit, A. (1995). *Why posterity matters: Environmental policies and future generations.* Routledge Taylor & Francis Group.

Diehl, P. F., & Ku, C. (2008). Colouring within the lines: How the international legal operating system influences rule creation. *Global Society, 22*(3), 319–336. https://doi.org/10.1080/13600820802090470

Diehl, P. F., & Ku, C. (2010). *The dynamics of international law*. Cambridge University Press. https://doi.org/10.1017/CBO9780511817328

Dörr, O. (2018). Article 31. In O. Dörr & K. Schmalenbach (Eds.), *Vienna Convention on the Law of Treaties: A commentary* (2nd ed., pp. 559–616). Springer.

Dupuy, P.-M. (2010). Formation of customary international law and general principles. In D. Bodansky, J. Brunnée, & E. Hey (Eds.), *The Oxford handbook of international environmental law* (Vol. 19, 1st ed., pp. 449–466). Oxford University Press.

Dupuy, P.-M. (2011). Evolutionary interpretation of treaties: Between memory and prophecy. In E. Cannizzaro & M. H. Arsanjani (Eds.), *The Law of Treaties Beyond the Vienna Convention* (Vol. 7, pp. 123–137). Oxford University Press.

Dupuy, P.-M. (2020). Intergenerational reflections on international law: An essay from Pierre Marie Dupuy. *EJIL: Talk!* 31 January 2020. Retrieved January 3, 2025, from https://www.ejiltalk.org/intergenerational-reflections-on-international-law-an-essay-from-pierre-marie-dupuy/

Dupuy, P.-M., & Viñuales, J. E. (2018). *International environmental law* (2nd ed.). Cambridge University Press.

Dupuy, P.-M., Le Moli, G., & Viñuales, J. E. (2021). Customary international law and the environment. In L. Rajamani & J. Peel (Eds.), *The Oxford handbook of international environmental law* (Vol. 23, 2nd ed., pp. 385–401). Oxford University Press.

Eggett, C. (2019). The role of principles and general principles in the "constitutional processes" of international law. *Netherlands International Law Review, 66*(2), 197–217. https://doi.org/10.1007/s40802-019-00139-1

Ekardt, F. (2021). *Theorie der Nachhaltigkeit: Ethische, Rechtliche, Politische und Transformative Zugänge – Am Beispiel von Klimawandel, Ressourcenknappheit und Welthandel* (2nd ed.). Nomos. https://doi.org/10.5771/9783845254593

Elias, T. O. (1980). The doctrine of intertemporal law. *American Journal of International Law, 74*(2), 285–307. https://doi.org/10.2307/2201503
Ellickson, R. C. (1991). *Order without law: How neighbors settle disputes*. Harvard University Press.
Epiney, A. (2022). Gegenstand, Entwicklung, Quellen und Akteure des Internationalen Umweltrechts. In A. Proelß (Ed.), *Internationales Umweltrecht* (Vol. 1, 2nd ed., pp. 1–51). De Gruyter.
Evans, M. D. (Ed.). (2018). *International law* (5th ed.). Oxford University Press.
Evans, P. B., Jacobson, H. K., & Putnam, R. D. (Eds.). (1993). *Double-edged diplomacy: International bargaining and domestic politics*. University of California Press.
Farrow, S. (2004). Using risk assessment, benefit-cost analysis, and real options to implement a precautionary principle. *Risk Analysis, 24*(3), 727–735. https://doi.org/10.1111/j.0272-4332.2004.00471.x
Fassbender, B. (2009). *The United Nations Charter as the Constitution of the International Community*. Martinus Nijhoff Publishers. https://doi.org/10.1163/ej.9789004175105.i-216
Fitzmaurice, G. G. (1957). The general principles of international law considered from the standpoint of the rule of law. *Recueil Des Cours, 92*, 1–227.
Fitzmaurice, M. (2008). Dynamic (Evolutive) Interpretation of Treaties: Part I. *Hague Yearbook of International Law, 21*, 101–156.
Fitzmaurice, M. (2010). International responsibility and liability. In D. Bodansky, J. Brunnée, & E. Hey (Eds.), *The Oxford handbook of international environmental law* (Vol. 44, 1st ed., pp. 1011–1034). Oxford University Press.
Francioni, F. (2012). Realism, Utopia, and the future of international environmental law. In A. Cassese (Ed.), *Realizing Utopia: The future of international law* (Vol. 34, 1st ed., pp. 442–460). Oxford University Press.
Friedmann, W. (1964). *The changing structure of international law*. Columbia University Press.
Gardiner, S. M. (2006). Protecting future generations: Intergenerational buck-passing, theoretical ineptitude and a brief for a global core precautionary principle. In J. C. Tremmel (Ed.), *Handbook of intergenerational justice* (Vol. 8, pp. 148–169). Edward Elgar Publishing.
Gardiner, S. M. (2009). A contract on future generations? In A. Gosseries & L. H. Meyer (Eds.), *Intergenerational justice* (Vol. 3, pp. 77–118). Oxford University Press.
Ginsburg, T. (2006). Locking in democracy: Constitutions, commitment, and international law. *New York University Journal of International Law and Policy, 38*(4), 707–760.
Goertz, G. (2003). *International norms and decision making: A punctuated equilibrium model*. Rowman & Littlefield.
Goldsmith, J. L., & Posner, E. A. (2005). *The limits of international law*. Oxford University Press.
Gosseries, A. (2001). What do we owe the next generation(s). *Loyola of Los Angeles Law Review, 35*, 293–354.
Gupta, J. (2016). The least developed countries and climate change law. In C. P. Carlarne, K. R. Gray, & R. Tarasofsky (Eds.), *The Oxford handbook of international climate change law* (Vol. 33, 1st ed., pp. 740–756). Oxford University Press.
Gurmendi, A. (2021). A Few Comments on "Revisiting the Doctrine of Intertemporal Law". *OpinioJuris*. 1 February 2021. Retrieved January 3, 2025, from http://opiniojuris.org/2021/02/01/a-few-comments-on-revisiting-the-doctrine-of-intertemporal-law/
Hadjiargyrou, Z. (2016). A conceptual and practical evaluation of intergenerational equity in international environmental law. *International Community Law Review, 18*, 248–277.
Hamamoto, Y. (2020). Possible limitations to the role of subsequent agreements and subsequent practice: Viewed from some state practices. *International Community Law Review, 22*(1), 61–83. https://doi.org/10.1163/18719732-12341421
Hart, H. L. A. (2012). *The concept of law: (Edited by Leslie Green, Joseph Raz, and Penelope A. Bulloch)* (3rd ed.). Clarendon Press.
Hartzell-Nichols, L. (2019). *Climate of risk: Precautionary principles, catastrophes, and climate change*. Routledge Taylor & Francis Group.

Helfer, L. R., & Slaughter, A.-M. (2005). Why states create international tribunals: A response to professors Posner and Yoo. *California Law Review, 93*(3), 899–956.

Herdegen, M. (2020). Interpretation in international law. In A. Peters & R. Wolfrum (Eds.), *Max Planck Encyclopedia of Public International Law*. Oxford University Press. (Article last updated November 2020).

Hiskes, R. P. (2005). The right to a green future: Human rights, environmentalism, and intergenerational justice. *Human Rights Quarterly, 27*(4), 1346–1364.

Hoegh-Guldberg, O., Jacob, D., Taylor, M., Bindi, M., Brown, S., Camilloni, I., Diedhiou, A., Djalante, R., Ebi, K. L., Engelbrecht, F., Guiot, J., Hijoka, Y., Mehrotra, S., Payne, A., Seneviratne, S. I., Thomas, A., Warren, R., & Zhou, G. (2018). Impacts of 1.5°C of global warming on natural and human systems. In IPCC, *Global Warming of 1.5°C: An IPCC Special Report on the Impacts of Global Warming of 1.5°C Above Pre-Industrial Levels and Related Global Greenhouse Gas Emission Pathways, in the Context of Strengthening the Global Response to the Threat of Climate Change, Sustainable Development, and Efforts to Eradicate Poverty* (V. Masson-Delmotte et al. (Eds.)), pp. 175–311. Retrieved January 3, 2025, from https://www.ipcc.ch/sr15/.

Inagaki, O. (2015). Evolutionary interpretation of treaties re-examined: The two-stage reasoning. *Journal of International Cooperation Studies, 22*(2–3), 127–149.

Institut de Droit International. (1975). *The Intertemporal Problem in Public International Law*. 11 August 1975. Retrieved January 3, 2025, from https://www.idi-iil.org/app/uploads/2017/06/1975_wies_01_en.pdf.

Institut de Droit International. (1997). Responsibility and Liability Under International Law for Environmental Damage. 4 September 1997. Retrieved January 3, 2025, from https://www.idi-iil.org/app/uploads/2017/06/1997_str_03_en.pdf.

International Group of Experts for the Pact. (2017). Draft Global Pact for the Environment. *Global Pact for the Environment*. June 2017. Retrieved January 3, 2025, from https://globalpactenvironment.org/en/documents-en/the-pact-text/.

International Law Commission. (2016). *Fourth Report by the Special Rapporteur on Identification of Customary International Law*, by M. Wood (8 March 2016). UN Doc. A/CN.4/695.

International Law Commission. (2018a). *Draft Conclusions on Identification of Customary International Law, with Commentaries* (2018). UN Doc. A/73/10, 122-156.

International Law Commission. (2018b). *Draft Conclusions on Subsequent Agreements and Subsequent Practice in Relation to the Interpretation of Treaties, with Commentaries* (2018). UN Doc. A/73/10, 16-116.

IPBES. (2019). Summary for Policymakers. In Intergovernmental Platform on Biodiversity and Ecosystem Services, *Global Assessment Report on Biodiversity and Ecosystem Services* (E. S. Brondízio, J. Settele, S. Diaz & H. T. Ngo (Eds.)). Retrieved January 3, 2025, from https://ipbes.net/global-assessment

IPCC. (October 2014). *Climate Change 2014: Synthesis Report*. Contributions of Working Groups I, II and III to the Fifth Assessment Report of the Intergovernmental Panel on Climate Change (Core Writing Team, R. K. Pachauri & L. Meyer (Eds.)). Retrieved January 3, 2025, from https://www.ipcc.ch/report/ar5/syr/

IPCC. (2021). Summary for Policymakers. In IPCC, *Climate Change 2021 – The Physical Science Basis: Working Group I Contribution to the IPCC Sixth Assessment Report* (V. Masson-Delmotte et al. (Eds.)). Retrieved January 3, 2025, from https://www.ipcc.ch/report/ar6/wg1/downloads/report/IPCC_AR6_WGI_SPM.pdf.

IPCC. (2022). Summary for Policymakers. In IPCC, *Climate Change 2022 – Impacts, Adaptation and Vulnerability: Working Group II Contribution to the IPCC Sixth Assessment Report* (H.-O. Pörtner et al. (Eds.)), pp. 1–35. Retrieved January 3, 2025, from https://www.ipcc.ch/report/ar6/wg2/downloads/report/IPCC_AR6_WGII_SummaryForPolicymakers.pdf

Kahl, V. (2022). A human right to climate protection: Necessary protection or human rights proliferation? *Netherlands Quarterly of Human Rights, 40*(2), 158–179.

Kahl, V. (2025 Fortcoming). *The right to a safe climate: Leading human rights law into the anthropocene* [Dissertation]. Universität Hamburg, Hamburg.
Kämmerer, A. (2024). Begriff, Geschichte und Rechtsquellen des Völkerrechts. In A. Proelß (Ed.), *Völkerrecht* (Vol. 1, 9th ed., pp. 1–106). De Gruyter.
Keohane, R. O. (1980). The theory of hegemonic stability and changes in international economic regimes, 1967–1977. In O. R. Holsti, R. M. Siverson, & A. L. George (Eds.), *Change in the international system* (Vol. 6, pp. 131–162). Westview Press.
Kim, R. E., & Kotzé, L. J. (2021). Planetary boundaries at the intersection of earth system law, science and governance: A state-of-the-art review. *Review of European, Comparative and International Environmental Law, 30*(1), 3–15. https://doi.org/10.1111/reel.12367
Kiss, A. (2005). The legal ordering of environmental protection. In R. S. J. Macdonald & D. M. Johnston (Eds.), *Towards world constitutionalism: Issues in the legal ordering of the world community* (Vol. 21, pp. 567–584). Martinus Nijhoff Publishers.
Kjeldgaard-Pedersen, A. (2019). Global constitutionalism and the international legal personality of the individual. *Netherlands International Law Review, 66*(2), 271–286. https://doi.org/10.1007/s40802-019-00140-8
Klabbers, J. (2006). Treaties, object and purpose. In A. Peters & R. Wolfrum (Eds.), *Max Planck Encyclopedia of Public International Law*. Oxford University Press. (Article last updated December 2006).
Klabbers, J., Peters, A., & Ulfstein, G. (Eds.). (2009). *The constitutionalization of international law*. Oxford University Press.
Kleinlein, T. (2018). Matters of interpretation: How to conceptualize and evaluate change of norms and values in the international legal order. *KFG Working Paper Series No. 24*. December 2018. Retrieved January 3, 2025, from https://papers.ssrn.com/sol3/papers.cfm?abstract_id=3292051
Koh, H. H. (1997). Why do nations obey international law? *Yale Law Journal, 106*, 2599–2659.
Kolb, R. (2016). *The law of treaties: An introduction*. Edward Elgar Publishing.
Koskenniemi, M. (2007). Constitutionalism as mindset: Reflections on kantian themes about international law and globalization. *Theoretical Inquiries in Law, 8*(1), 9–36.
Kotzé, L. J. (2019a). A global environmental constitution for the anthropocene? *Transnational Environmental Law, 8*(1), 11–33. https://doi.org/10.1017/S2047102518000274
Kotzé, L. J. (2019b). International environmental law's lack of normative ambition: An opportunity for the global pact for the environment? *Journal for European Environmental and Planning Law, 16*(3), 213–236. https://doi.org/10.1163/18760104-01603002
Kotzé, L. J. (2020). Earth system law for the anthropocene: Rethinking environmental law alongside the earth system metaphor. *Transnational Legal Theory, 11*(1–2), 75–104. https://doi.org/10.1080/20414005.2020.1776556
Kotzur, M. (2008). Intertemporal law. In A. Peters & R. Wolfrum (Eds.), *Max Planck Encyclopedia of Public International Law*. Oxford University Press. (Article last updated April 2008).
Krisch, N., & Yildiz, E. (Eds.). (2023). *The many paths of change in international law*. Oxford University Press. https://doi.org/10.1093/oso/9780198877844.001.0001
Ku, C. (2005). Forging a multilayered system of global governance. In R. S. J. Macdonald & D. M. Johnston (Eds.), *Towards world constitutionalism: Issues in the legal ordering of the world community* (Vol. 23, pp. 631–651). Martinus Nijhoff Publishers.
Ku, C., & Diehl, P. F. (2006). Filling in the gaps: Extrasystemic mechanisms for addressing imbalances between the international legal operating system and the normative system. *Global Governance: A Review of Multilateralism and International Organizations, 12*, 161–183.
Ku, C., & Diehl, P. F. (2016). The primary effects of secondary rules: Institutions and multi-level governance. In M. Heupel & T. Reinold (Eds.), *The rule of law in global governance* (Vol. 2, pp. 29–57). Palgrave Macmillan.
Lachenmann, F. (2012). Legal positivism. In R. Wolfrum (Ed.), *The Max Planck Encyclopedia of Public International Law*. Oxford University Press.
Lee, J.-Y., Marotzke, J., Bala, G., Cao, L., Corti, S., Dunne, J. P., Engelbrecht, F., Fischer, E., Fyfe, J. C., Jones, C., Maycock, A., Mutemi, J., Ndiaye, O., Panickal, S., & Zhou, T. (2021). Future

global climate: Scenario-based projections and near-term information. In IPCC, *Climate Change 2021 – The Physical Science Basis: Working Group I Contribution to the IPCC Sixth Assessment Report* (V. Masson-Delmotte et al. (Eds.)), pp. 553–672. Retrieved January 3, 2025, from https://www.ipcc.ch/report/sixth-assessment-report-working-group-i/

Luckner, K. (2021). #WhoseLawIsItAnyway: How the Internet Augments Civil Society Participation in International Law Making. *MPIL Research Paper Series No. 15*. 2021. Retrieved January 3, 2025, from https://ssrn.com/abstract=3867227.

Luhmann, N. (1988). The unity of the legal system. In G. Teubner (Ed.), *Autopoietic law: A new approach to law and society* (Vol. 2, pp. 12–35). De Gruyter.

Macdonald, R. S. J., Morris, G. L., & Johnston, D. M. (1973). International Law and Society in the Year 2000. *Canadian Bar Review, 51*, 316–332. https://doi.org/10.1016/B978-1-85573-345-9.50005-4

Makoff, R., & Read, R. (2017). Beyond just justice: Creating space for a future-care ethic. *Philosophical Investigations, 40*(3), 223–256. https://doi.org/10.1111/phin.12138

Malhotra, A. (1998). A commentary on the status of future generations as a subject of international law. In E. Agius & S. Busuttil (Eds.), *Future generations and international law: Proceedings of the International Experts' Meeting Held by the Future Generations Programme at the Foundation for International Studies, University of Malta* (Vol. 5, pp. 39–50). Earthscan Publications Ltd.

Martínez, E., & Winter, C. (2022). Is legal longtermism common sense? *Verfassungsblog*. 9 August 2022. Retrieved January 3, 2025, from https://verfassungsblog.de/is-legal-longtermism-common-sense/.

Mbengue, M. M. (2019). Precaution. In Y. Aguila & J. E. Viñuales (Eds.), *A global pact for the environment: Legal foundations* (Vol. 8, pp. 73–78). Cambridge Centre for Environment, Energy and Natural Resource Governance (C-EENRG).

McDougal, M. S. (1980). International law and the future. *Mississippi Law Journal, 50*, 259–334.

Metternich, N. W., Gleditsch, K. S., & Dworschak, C. (2016). Forecasting in international relations. In C. J. Nolan (Ed.), *Oxford bibliographies*. Oxford University Press. https://doi.org/10.1093/obo/9780199743292-0179

Mileva, N., & Fortuna, M. (2019). Environmental protection as an object of and tool for evolutionary interpretation. In G. Abi-Saab, K. Keith, & G. Marceau (Eds.), *Evolutionary interpretation and international law* (Vol. 13, pp. 123–140). Hart Publishing.

Molinari, C. (2015). Principle 3. In J. E. Viñuales (Ed.), *The Rio Declaration on Environment and Development: A commentary* (1st ed., pp. 139–156). Oxford University Press.

Mosler, H. (1962). Die Erweiterung des Kreises der Völkerrechtssubjekte. *Zeitschrift Für Ausländisches Öffentliches Recht Und Völkerrecht, 22*, 1–48.

Oppenheim, L. F. L. (1921). *Future of international law*. Clarendon Press.

Orakhelashvili, A. (2007). Natural law and justice. In A. Peters & R. Wolfrum (Eds.), *Max Planck Encyclopedia of Public International Law*. Oxford University Press. (Article last updated August 2007).

Paulus, A. L. (2013). International community. In A. Peters & R. Wolfrum (Eds.), *Max Planck Encyclopedia of Public International Law*. Oxford University Press. (Article last updated March 2013).

Pauwelyn, J., Wessel, R. A., & Wouters, J. (2012). An introduction to informal international lawmaking. In J. Pauwelyn, R. A. Wessel, & J. Wouters (Eds.), *Informal international lawmaking* (pp. 1–10). Oxford University Press. https://doi.org/10.1093/acprof:oso/9780199658589.003.0001

Payandeh, M. (2010). *Internationales Gemeinschaftsrecht: Zur Herausbildung Gemeinschaftsrechtlicher Strukturen im Völkerrecht der Globalisierung*. Springer. https://doi.org/10.1007/978-3-642-13141-7

Pellet, A. (2012). Art. 38. In A. Zimmermann et al. (Eds.), *The Statute of the International Court of Justice: A commentary* (2nd ed., pp. 731–870). Oxford University Press.

Peters, A. (2012). Are we moving towards constitutionalization of the world community? In A. Cassese (Ed.), *Realizing Utopia: The future of international law* (Vol. 10, 1st ed., pp. 118–135). Oxford University Press.

Popovski, V., & Malhotra, A. (Eds.). (2023). *Reimagining the international legal order*. Routledge, Taylor & Francis Group.

Potsdam Institute for Climate Impact Research. (2024). *Tipping elements: The Achilles Heels of the Earth System*. 2024. Retrieved January 3, 2025, from https://www.pik-potsdam.de/en/output/infodesk/tipping-elements

Proelss, A. (2006). Die Internationale Gemeinschaft im Völkerrecht: Normative Realität, Konkrete Utopie oder "Academic Research Tool"? In J. Badura (Ed.), *Mondialisierungen: "Globalisierung" im Lichte transdisziplinärer Reflexionen* (pp. 233–252). transcript.

Rajamani, L., & Peel, J. (2021). Reflections on a decade of change in international environmental law. *Cambridge International Law Journal, 10*(1), 6–31. https://doi.org/10.4337/cilj.2021.01.01

Rauber, J. (2018). *Strukturwandel als Prinzipienwandel: Theoretische, Dogmatische und Methodische Bausteine eines Prinzipienmodells des Völkerrechts und seiner Dynamik*. Springer. https://doi.org/10.1007/978-3-662-55471-5

Rawls, J. (1999). *A theory of justice*. (Revised edn). Harvard University Press. (Original work published 1971).

Rawls, J., & Kelly, E. (2001). *Justice as fairness: A restatement* (2nd ed.). Harvard University Press.

Redgwell, C. (1999). *Intergenerational trusts and environmental protection*. Juris.

Ronneberg, E. (2016). Small islands and the big issue: Climate change and the role of the alliance of small island states. In C. P. Carlarne, K. R. Gray, & R. Tarasofsky (Eds.), *The Oxford handbook of international climate change law* (Vol. 34, 1st ed., pp. 761–776). Oxford University Press.

Sandholtz, W. (2009). Explaining international norm change. In W. Sandholtz & K. W. Stiles (Eds.), *International norms and cycles of change* (Vol. 1, pp. 1–26). Oxford University Press.

Sandholtz, W., & Stiles, K. W. (Eds.). (2009). *International norms and cycles of change*. Oxford University Press.

Sands, P. (2001). Turtles and torturers: The transformation of international law. *New York University Journal of International Law and Policy, 33*, 527–559.

Schmalenbach, K. (2022). Verantwortlichkeit und Haftung. In A. Proelß (Ed.), *Internationales Umweltrecht* (Vol. 7, 2nd ed., pp. 329–372). De Gruyter.

Scovazzi, T. (2001). State responsibility for environmental harm. *Yearbook of International Environmental Law, 12*(1), 43–67. https://doi.org/10.1093/yiel/12.1.43

Sessions, G. S. (1974). Anthropocentrism and the environmental crisis. *Humboldt Journal of Social Relations, 2*(1), 71–81.

Shelton, D. (1994). The participation of nongovernmental organizations in international judicial proceedings. *American Journal of International Law, 88*(4), 611–642. https://doi.org/10.2307/2204133

Shue, H. (2017). Climate dreaming: Negative emissions, risk transfer, and irreversibility. *Journal of Human Rights and the Environment, 8*(2), 203–216.

Siverson, R. M. (1980). War and change in the international system. In O. R. Holsti, R. M. Siverson, & A. L. George (Eds.), *Change in the international system* (Vol. 9, pp. 211–229). Westview Press.

Slaughter, A.-M., & Hale, T. (2013). International relations, principal theories. In A. Peters & R. Wolfrum (Eds.), *Max Planck Encyclopedia of Public International Law*. Oxford University Press. (Article last updated September 2013).

Solum, L. B. (2001). To Our children's children's children: The problems of intergenerational ethics. *Loyola of Los Angeles Law Review, 35*, 163–233.

Sparks, T. (2020). The place of the environment in state of nature discourses: Reassessing nature, property and sovereignty in the anthropocene. *MPIL Research Paper Series No. 10*. 2020. Retrieved January 3, 2025, from https://ssrn.com/abstract=3561671.

Stephens, T. (2017). Reimagining international environmental law in the anthropocene. In L. J. Kotzé (Ed.), *Environmental law and governance for the anthropocene* (Vol. 2, pp. 31–54). Hart Publishing.

Stiles, K. W., & Sandholtz, W. (2009). Cycles of international norm change. In W. Sandholtz & K. W. Stiles (Eds.), *International norms and cycles of change* (Vol. 12). Oxford University Press.

Sunstein, C. R. (2010). Irreversibility. *Law, Probability and Risk, 9*(3–4), 227–245. https://doi.org/10.1093/lpr/mgq010

Tanaka, Y. (2013). Reflections on time elements in the international law of the environment. *Zeitschrift Für Ausländisches Öffentliches Recht Und Völkerrecht, 73*, 139–175.

Tanaka, Y. (2021). Temporal elements in the valuation of environmental damage: Reflections on the Costa Rica v. Nicaragua Compensation Case before the International Court of Justice. *Nordic Journal of International Law, 90*, 257–291.

Tanzi, A. (2011). Remarks on sovereignty in the evolving constitutional features of the international community. In M. H. Arsanjani, J. Cogan, R. Sloane, & S. Wiessner (Eds.), *Looking to the future: Essays on International Law in Honor of W. Michael Reisman* (Vol. 17, pp. 299–322). Martinus Nijhoff Publishers.

Thacher, P. S. (1987). Equity under change. *American Society of International Law Proceedings, 81*, 133–137.

Theilen, J. T., Hassfurther, I., & Staff, W. (2017). Guest editors' introduction: Towards Utopia – Rethinking international law. *German Yearbook of International Law, 60*, 315–334.

Thompson, J. (2009). Identity and obligation in a transgenerational polity. In A. Gosseries & L. H. Meyer (Eds.), *Intergenerational justice* (Vol. 1, pp. 25–49). Oxford University Press. https://doi.org/10.1093/acprof:oso/9780199282951.003.0002

Tomuschat, C. (2011). International law as a coherent system: Unity or fragmentation? In M. H. Arsanjani, J. Cogan, R. Sloane, & S. Wiessner (Eds.), *Looking to the future: Essays on International Law in Honor of W. Michael Reisman* (Vol. 18, pp. 323–354). Martinus Nijhoff Publishers.

Tremmel, J. C. (2013). The convention of representatives of all generations under the "veil of ignorance". *Constellations, 20*(3), 483–502. https://doi.org/10.1111/1467-8675.12049

UN Conference on Environment and Development. (1992). *Rio Declaration on Environment and Development* (1992). UN Doc. A/CONF.151/26 (Vol. I).

United Nations. (1972). *Declaration of the United Nations Conference on the Human Environment* (16 June 1972). UN Doc. A/Conf.48/14/Rev. 1 (1973).

United Nations Environment Programme. (2008). *Fourth Programme for the Development and Periodic Review of Environmental Law. Note by Executive Director. Addendum: Draft Guidelines for the Development of National Legislation on Liability, Response Action and Compensation for Damage Caused by Activities Dangerous to the Environment* (26 November 2008). UN Doc. UNEP/GC.25/INF/15/Add.3.

United Nations General Assembly. (2015). *Follow-up to and Implementation of the SIDS Accelerated Modalities of Action (SAMOA) Pathway and the Mauritius Strategy for the Further Implementation of the Programme of Action for the Sustainable Development of Small Island Developing States* (22 December 2015). UN Doc. A/RES/70/202.

United Nations General Assembly. (2019). Only 11 Years Left to Prevent Irreversible Damage from Climate Change, Speakers Warn during General Assembly High-Level Meeting: Seventy-Third Session, High-Level Meeting on Climate and Sustainable Development. *General Assembly Meetings Coverage*. 28 March 2019. Retrieved January 3, 2025, from https://www.un.org/press/en/2019/ga12131.doc.htm

United Nations Secretary-General. (2013). *Intergenerational Solidarity and the Needs of Future Generations, Report of the Secretary-General* (15 August 2013). UN Doc. A/68/322.

United Nations Secretary-General. (2018). *Gaps in International Environmental Law and Environment-related Instruments: Towards a Global Pact for the Environment* (30 November 2018). UN Doc. A/73/419.

Virally, M. (1988). To what extent are the traditional categories of Lex Lata and Lex Ferenda Still Viable? Ii. Discussion A. Lex Lata and Lex Ferenda. In A. Cassese & J. H. H. Weiler (Eds.), *Change and stability in international law making* (pp. 66–101). De Gruyter.
von Arnauld, A. (2019). *Völkerrecht* (4th ed.). C.F. Müller.
von Arnauld, A. (2021). How to illegalize past injustice: Reinterpreting the rules of intertemporality. *European Journal of International Law, 32*(2), 401–432.
Wenar, L. (2021). John Rawls. In E. N. Zalta (Ed.). *The Stanford Encyclopedia of Philosophy.* ISSN 1095-5054. Retrieved January 3, 2025, from https://plato.stanford.edu/entries/rawls/. (Article last updated April 2021)
Wheatley, S. (2021). Revisiting the doctrine of intertemporal law. *Oxford Journal of Legal Studies, 41*(2), 484–509. https://doi.org/10.1093/ojls/gqaa058
Winter, C., Schuett, J., Martínez, E., van Arsdale, S., Araújo, R., Hollman, N., Sebo, J., Stawasz, A., O'Keefe, C., & Rotola, G. (2021). Legal priorities research: A research agenda. *Legal Priorities Project*. January 2021. Retrieved January 3, 2025, from https://papers.ssrn.com/sol3/papers.cfm?abstract_id=3931256.
World Commission on Environment and Development. (1987). *Report of the World Commission on Environment and Development: Our Common Future (Brundtland Report)* (1987). UN Doc. A/42/427 Annex.
World Health Organization. (2019). The Global Health Observatory: Global Health Estimates – Life Expectancy and Leading Causes of Death and Disability. 2019. Retrieved January 3, 2025, from https://www.who.int/data/gho/data/themes/mortality-and-global-health-estimates.
Young, O. R. (1989). The politics of international regime formation: Managing natural resources and the environment. *International Organization, 43*(3), 349–375. https://doi.org/10.1017/S0020818300032963

# Chapter 8
# Conclusion

Back to the time traveller from 2100 before the State representatives of the COP30 in 2025 in Brazil…

*"Why do you act in explicit violation of your responsibilities under the concept of intergenerational equity?", the High Commissioner for Intergenerational Relations asks the State representatives.*

*After a brief silence, these representatives begin to discuss the learnt information among each other. A loud commotion breaks out as many representatives have to process the magnitude of the negative impacts their action will have on future generations. At first, shock and consternation prevail as most representatives ask themselves* why *they actually acted as they did. An argument ensues about the moral failure they displayed by disregarding their descendants. After a while, the substance of the discussion changes as they search for excuses for their behaviour. They start to ask themselves whether and how they actually violated their* legal *responsibilities under the concept of intergenerational equity:*

*"But did we even violate any of our responsibilities?"*

*"There is no such thing as legal duties to conserve the planet for future generations!"*

*"Our development needs indeed to be sustainable – but that also includes our right to development!"*

*"And what about* intra-*generational equity? We must not forget the poorest of the present generation!"*

*"Why should we even care for any future generation? You should be glad that you have been born at all! How do we harm you? And anyway, what has the future ever done for us?"*

*"Intergenerational equity is not more than a vague policy goal and moral principle! Are we even bound by any legal obligation at all?"*

*"Who would be obliged anyway?"*

*"And future generations do not exist today – you have no right to blame us for our actions!"*



A. Bustami, *The Legal Relationship between Present and Future Generations*,
https://doi.org/10.1007/978-3-032-03345-1_8

*"How could we know what the interests of future generations will be? You are the first one who is actually authorised to represent them!"*

*It takes a while until the UNSG and the President of the COP30 succeed in calming the State representatives in their endless arguments and objections to the provocative reproach of the High Commissioner. The High Commissioner remains calm before she answers their objections with one counter-question: "From which point of view do you make all of these legal assumptions? To our opinion, the future generation of the year 2100, you* are *violating your obligations under intergenerational equity."*

Certainly, a verbal exchange between a time traveller from the future and State representatives at the COP30 would take a different course. However, the hypothetical objections and the last counter-question of the High Commissioner illustrate the two overarching research questions this book examined. First, it analysed the normative content and the structures of the legal concept of intergenerational equity as it exists today in international law. The book thus shed some light on the obscure and inconsistent perspectives on the concept. These perspectives are reflected in the fictional objections and questions of the State representatives above. Second, the book took an intertemporal perspective on the legal relationship between present and future generations by asking which legal regime should be temporally applicable to the assessment of the concept in general.

This last concluding chapter summarises the findings of the analysis as it contextualises them. Along the distinction between the normative and the operating system of intergenerational equity, the conclusion first addresses the normative aspects of the concept (Sect. 8.1), before illustrating the findings on the structural issues of intergenerational equity (Sect. 8.2). Then, the chapter turns to the modified intertemporal law perspective on the concept (Sect. 8.3). The conclusion eventually gives an outlook on unanswered aspects and potential future research building on the intertemporal perspective on intergenerational equity (Sect. 8.4).

## 8.1 Intergenerational Equity—A Concept of Many Colours

If it were unambiguously clear what to understand under "intergenerational equity", the answer to the question of the fictional High Commissioner for Intergenerational Relations could be easily given from the present generation's perspective. Part I of this book would not contain four chapters, but two brief chapters; the book could have directly focused on the intertemporal law perspective of Part II. Intergenerational equity is much more complex and has many colours. It is intertwined with other concepts of international environmental law, it is based on philosophical foundations of intergenerational justice and it is present in jurisprudence and legal scholarship, in treaty as well as in customary international law. With regard to the substantive contents and the legal nature of the concept, the following three delimitations summarise the initial findings of this analysis: Intergenerational equity operates within the historical development of international environmental law between the overarching concept of sustainable development and academic conceptualisation (Sect. 8.1.1). It constitutes a philosophical principle of justice as well as a concept of environmental law (Sect. 8.1.2) and it is more than a mere rhetorical device, partly in the form of a legally binding norm of international law (Sect. 8.1.3).

### 8.1.1 Between Historical and Systemic Context and Academic Conceptualisation

While the concern for future generations has ancient cultural and religious roots, the origins of the current understanding of intergenerational equity date back to the developments of international environmental law in the twentieth century. The most important developments in this regard have occurred since the 1970s, as shown in Chap. 2.[1] The Stockholm Declaration proclaimed the responsibility for future generations in general terms, whereas the Brundtland Report from 1987 offered the wording of intergenerational equity that is today considered the main meaning of the concept: "development that meets the needs of the present without compromising the ability of future generations to meet their own needs".[2] This report equally constitutes the hour of birth of sustainable development and illustrates the intertwined relationship of both concepts. Since that time, a broad variety of international legal and non-legal documents has reiterated this or comparable wordings as they stressed the responsibility of the present generation to protect the environment for future generations. The Rio Declaration in 1992, the UNGA Resolution 'The Future We Want' in 2012 as well as important environmental treaties (e.g., the UNFCCC, the UNECE Water Convention or the Aarhus Convention) constitute some important examples. International jurisprudence has also increasingly addressed concerns of intergenerational equity since the 1990s—for instance by the ICJ in its *Nuclear Weapons Advisory Opinion* and the *Gabčíkovo-Nagymaros Project* case. In the last three decades, intergenerational equity and the concern for future generations reappeared again and again in political and legal declarations (e.g., the UNESCO Declaration of 1997 and the ILA New Delhi Declaration of 2002), in the SDGs of 2015 and in individual opinions before the ICJ (e.g., the *Pulp Mills* case of 2010 and the *Whaling in the Antarctic* case of 2014). In 2013, the UNSG analysed the issue of "intergenerational solidarity" in a detailed report. The current developments in climate change law build upon the responsibility towards future generations. The most recent suggestions for a GPE as binding codification of environmental principle also contained a provision on intergenerational equity.

[1] See *supra* in Sect. 2.1.

[2] World Commission on Environment and Development (1987, Introduction, para. 27, Chapter 2, para. 1).

The complexity of intergenerational equity and its embeddedness within international environmental law is equally reflected in its interrelationship with other overlapping environmental concepts.[3] The notions of common heritage and common concern of humankind take comparably future-oriented perspectives, as the references to "humankind" encompass both present and future members of humanity. They constitute concepts that link environmental goods together across generations in order to preserve them for the future of humanity. This future-orientation is also inherent in the idea of a "heritage" of humankind.

The relationship of intergenerational equity with its ostensible counter-part *intra*-generational equity is more complicated. While intergenerational equity governs the fair and equitable distribution of natural resources between different generations, intra-generational equity is concerned with the just distribution of resources within the same generation among different members of this generation in different regions of the world. This is why some critics of the concept of intergenerational equity argued that it would be more important to focus on the just distribution between living members of the present generation than protecting unborn future generations. However, intergenerational and intra-generational equity do not exclude each other, but are strongly linked with one another. The concern for future generations is always subject to meeting the needs of the present generation, which requires a fair distribution of resources within the present generation. At the same time, this leads to differentiated degrees of obligation of different regions of the world in the context of intergenerational equity—mirrored in the concept of "common but differentiated responsibilities".

Furthermore, inter- and intra-generational equity complement each other as important components of the overarching concept of sustainable development. Sustainable development contains both dimensions of equity and balances them with each other. It requires balancing the needs of the present with the needs of future generations. This function of sustainable development illustrates the latter's character as an overarching meta-principle that unites several sub-concepts, such as intergenerational equity. The requirement to take into account the needs of future generations and to act in a way that does not compromise their ability to meet their own needs constitutes the intergenerational component of sustainable development and at the same time the core idea of intergenerational equity. For this reason, the Brundtland Report's wording is always considered the birth document of both sustainable development and intergenerational equity.

Parallel to these developments and systemic interrelations, international legal scholarship has attempted to conceptualise the concern for future generations within international environmental law since the 1980s.[4] Most prominently, the works of *Edith Brown Weiss* since her seminal work from 1989, 'In Fairness to Future Generations', have shaped the academic understanding of intergenerational equity. This understanding partly goes beyond the general obligation to take into

---

[3]See *supra* in Sect. 2.3.

[4]See *supra* in Sect. 2.2.

consideration the needs of future generations. *Brown Weiss* asserted an obligation "to pass on the natural and cultural resources of the planet in no worse condition than received".[5] This doctrine of intergenerational equity is further based on the idea of an intergenerational trust with future generations as beneficiaries and the present generation as both beneficiary and trustee of the trust. Three intergenerational duties of conservation result from this trust relationship: the duty to conserve the diversity of the natural resource base to offer future generations the same possibilities (conservation of options), the duty to maintain a quality of the environment in no worse condition than the present generation benefitted from (conservation of quality) and the duty to grant a non-discriminatory minimum level of access to the common natural resources to all members of the present and future generations (conservation of equitable access). These duties interact with each other, they build on the understanding of corresponding planetary rights of future generations and on the establishment of representative institutional frameworks on both the international and the national level.

Although *Brown Weiss* and other commentators based their analysis of intergenerational equity on the existing international references to future generations, their conceptualisation goes beyond the explicit wording and understandings of the concept in most international documents. For this reason, Chaps. 2 and 4 of this book pointed out and underlined an important distinction between different references to future generations and intergenerational equity.[6] Different documents, sources, cases and other legal actors can mean different concepts when referring to "intergenerational equity" or the interests of future generations more generally. This resulted in the first core observation of the book: there are at least two different manifestations of the overall concept of intergenerational equity today. These manifestations coexist and overlap, they constitute nuances on a spectrum that articulate the concern for the needs of future generations. On one side of the spectrum, a general conception of intergenerational equity reflects the Brundtland Report's obligation not to compromise the ability of future generations to meet their own needs. This general understanding has been shaped since the 1970s in international environmental law. It is general and rather abstract as it does not contain specific duties or rights and as it is not accompanied by more specific means of implementation. It can be summarised as the requirement to take into account the interests of future generations or as a general idea of environmental responsibility towards the future. This general conception of intergenerational equity is equivalent to the intergenerational component of sustainable development. On the other side of the spectrum, a more specific doctrine of intergenerational equity, as elaborated by *Brown Weiss* and other commentators, contains specific duties of conservation. This specific manifestation is built on the idea of planetary rights of future generations and on their representation in institutional frameworks. While the distinction between these two manifestations is unfortunately often ignored in legal scholarship

[5]Brown Weiss (1989), pp. 37–38.

[6]See *supra* in Sect. 2.3.1.2 and Chap. 4.

and case law, it is important since many controversies on intergenerational equity do not actually contest the contents of the general conception. Criticism rather addresses the characteristics of the more specific doctrine of intergenerational equity or even only specific components of the latter, such as the rights-based approach or the reasonableness of representation of future generations. Any reliable and comprehensive analysis of intergenerational equity today should thus differentiate between at least these two manifestations.

*Returning to the thought experiment, this first finding would allow the State representatives to specify their concerns for future generations in their answers to the High Commissioner: "There are at least two different understandings of 'intergenerational equity' – do you think we violated our obligation under the general conception or the conservation duties of the specific doctrine?"*

### *8.1.2 Between General Justice Principle and Environmental Law Concept*

The embeddedness of intergenerational equity is complex not only with regard to international environmental law but also with regard to its moral and philosophical foundations. The concern for future generations touches many aspects of human society, so that philosophers, politicians, economists and other disciplines have equally discussed questions of intergenerational equity and justice. The concern for future generations is further anchored in many cultures and regions worldwide and has ancient traditional and religious roots—from Indigenous concepts of the Earth to monotheistic religions, such as Christianity and Islam. While the detailed assessment of these extra-legal foundations is beyond the scope of this book, the various overlaps between morality, philosophy and law shape the colourful concept of intergenerational equity that constitutes a legal manifestation of distributive justice. Therefore, Chap. 3 examined the delimitations and parallels between the different realms. The philosophical discussions of "intergenerational justice" and the corresponding legal discussions have influenced each other in two respects. First, many critical objections to intergenerational equity in the legal realm are inseparably linked to the underlying philosophical objections to any theory of intergenerational justice.[7] Second, different philosophical approaches to intergenerational justice have shaped the current legal understandings of intergenerational equity.[8]

With regard to the criticism of intergenerational equity, many critical observers did not directly question the *legal* existence of intergenerational equity, but they questioned the *moral* value of future generations. For instance, proponents of the non-identity problem argue that the present generation could never actually harm future generations with their actions as the existence of future generations itself

---

[7] See *supra* in Sect. 3.2.

[8] See *supra* in Sect. 3.3.

generally depends on the activities of their ancestors. If the members of the present generation were to take different environmental policy decisions that are conform to their intergenerational obligations, this would necessarily cause different human beings to come into existence in the future compared to an alternative time line, in which they had not taken these policy decisions. Consequently, any theory of intergenerational justice would be illogical as the coming into existence in an environmentally degraded world would still be better than not coming into existence at all. This objection questions the possibility of moral obligations towards future human beings in general. Beside the non-identity problem, the legal discussions of rights of future generations are inherently linked to the conceptional objection of the non-existence argument, recalled further below.[9] Due to these overlaps between the legal discussion and the pre-legal foundations of intergenerational equity, it is important to address the differences between the two realms, but also to answer the philosophical questions before turning to an exhaustive legal assessment of intergenerational equity. If the philosophical objections were convincing, some of the legal issues could be pointless from the beginning. However, as Chap. 3 has demonstrated, all of these objections have been refuted by other philosophers. For instance, the non-identity problem can be overcome by several adapted views of morality and harm.

As far as the conceptional problems of intergenerational justice are overcome, there are different philosophical approaches to intergenerational justice that have been influential for the legal concept of intergenerational equity. The general conception of intergenerational equity was mainly inspired by distributive versions of libertarian thinking. While the first part of the Brundtland Report's wording ("development that meets the needs of the present") starts with a libertarian understanding of basic liberties for present human beings, the second part ("without compromising the ability of future generations to meet their own needs") limits these liberties in the form of an intergenerational Lockean proviso. The general conception of intergenerational equity is also mainly sufficientarian as it does not aim at an equal distribution of natural resources between all human beings of present and future generations. Based on this general conception, it is sufficient that future generations maintain the ability to fulfil their basic needs above a minimum threshold.

Beyond these influences of libertarian thinking, a more diverse set of philosophical approaches influenced the *specific* doctrine of *Brown Weiss*. Her works explicitly referred to *John Rawls'* contractualist theory of justice. According to *Rawls'* hypothetical thought experiment, the representatives of all members of society and of all generations come together in an "original position" behind a "veil of ignorance" that renders them ignorant of their own capabilities, social status and the generation they are born in.[10] From this original position with just and fair conditions for negotiations, *Rawls* deduced principles of justice, *inter alia*, a just savings

[9] See *infra* in Sect. 8.2.2, note 17.

[10] Rawls (1971/1999).

principle that enables future generations to meet at least their basic needs. Again, this approach is mainly sufficientarian. Beyond these sufficientarian elements, the specific doctrine of intergenerational equity also contains egalitarian elements (e.g., concerning the conservation of equal access to the natural resources). The specific manifestation of intergenerational equity has also been based on communitarian approaches to justice. The communitarian idea of an intergenerational community as a partnership between past, present and future generations is comparable to the notion of a planetary trust between present and future generations. These communitarian approaches also integrate many Indigenous perspectives on their relationship with past and future generations into the legal concept of intergenerational equity.

Chapter 3 did not take a stand on the different philosophical and cultural approaches to intergenerational justice. Instead, the second important contribution of this book consists in the clearer delimitation between legal and philosophical objections to intergenerational equity as well as in the illustration of the important parallels and influences between intergenerational equity and intergenerational justice. None of the philosophical objections to intergenerational justice convincingly hinder a legal concept of intergenerational equity. Further, the libertarian, contractualist and communitarian foundations of intergenerational equity play an important role in its legal understanding. Some of these philosophical perspectives have also assisted in the development of the modified doctrine of intertemporal law suggested in Chap. 7.[11]

*Returning to the thought experiment, these important considerations allow the State representatives to delimit their moral and their legal understanding of intergenerational equity in their answers to the High Commissioner: "Yes, we are morally obliged to take into account the needs of future generations. But this does not automatically mean that we are also legally bound by any intergenerational obligation."*

### 8.1.3 Between Rhetorical Device and Legally Binding Norm

The parallels and overlaps between the legal and the philosophical realms of intergenerational equity and justice render it more difficult to answer this latter question—whether the concern for future generations also has legal or merely moral value. Due to the uncertainties of delimitation, the concern for future generations and the notion of "intergenerational equity" are easily misused as a mainly rhetorical device, as a moral category of argumentation, but without legal meaning of any kind whatsoever. At the same time, it was also easy for critical commentators to reject any legal force and significance of intergenerational equity due to the concept's vagueness and the many inconsistencies in its understanding within

[11] See *supra* in Sect. 7.2.2.2.

international environmental law. For these reasons, it was important to analyse the different aspects of the legal nature of intergenerational equity in both its manifestations.

The legal nature of a concept consists of two separate aspects. First, a concept—in a non-technical meaning—could constitute a legal principle or a legal rule with the normative capacity to steer the behaviour of its addressees, or it could constitute a mere policy without such normative capacity. Second, the legal nature of a norm depends on its legal status, this means on its legally binding character as part of one of the sources of international law. With regard to both aspects of legal nature, the book distinguished between the two manifestations of intergenerational equity. As to the normative capacity of intergenerational equity, the general conception stipulates a normative goal for its addressees—the consideration of the interests of future generations—, which must be achieved to the greatest extent legally and factually possible. It thus has the normative capacity in the form of a legal principle. The specific doctrine of intergenerational equity goes beyond this general and abstract principle as it stipulates a more explicit obligation of the present generation to pass on the natural resources to future generations in no worse condition than received. It further includes three conservation duties that direct their addressees to act in specific ways. Thereby, the structure of the doctrine of intergenerational equity is much more sophisticated than that of the general conception; it stipulates more than a normative goal. The specific doctrine of intergenerational equity thus has normative capacity in the form of a legal rule of international law.

Beyond their normative capacity, manifestations of intergenerational equity also differ with regard to their legal status. The general conception is enshrined in many treaty regimes, such as the UNFCCC, the CBD or the Aarhus Convention. It also constitutes a norm of customary international law that has emerged since the 1990s and is today reflected in broad and universal State practice and *opinio iuris*. Despite its general character, the general conception is a legally binding principle of international environmental law that requires States to act accordingly in order to allow future generations to meet their own needs. In contrast to the general conception, the specific doctrine of intergenerational equity does not have this legally binding character. As of today, there are no treaties codifying the specific duties of conservation, as formulated by *Brown Weiss* since the 1980s. The GPE would have been the only potential exception, but the existing proposals have not resulted in an actual codification process so far. Moreover, current State practice and *opinio iuris* do not sufficiently reflect the existence of a specific doctrine within customary international law, although there are references to respective conservation duties in a few international documents. Similarly, most references to future generations do not include the notion of rights, but there is an increasing number of examples that explicitly invoke rights of future generations, particularly in soft law documents. For instance, the ILA New Delhi Declaration addresses some of the basic ideas of the specific doctrine of intergenerational equity. The UNESCO Declaration of 1997 is another example of a strong soft law document that speaks in favour of more specific intergenerational obligations that point towards the specific doctrine. Some of the separate and dissenting opinions before the ICJ in the last decades have equally elaborated in more detail on the content of intergenerational equity, including duties of conservation and the notion of rights. However, the existing examples do not establish a customary norm in the form of the specific doctrine of intergenerational equity yet, but they foreshadow the emergence of a more specific manifestation of the concept within customary international law.

The analysis in Chap. 4 demonstrated that intergenerational equity is more than a mere rhetorical device and more than a mere moral obligation. The concept of intergenerational equity has normative capacity and constitutes an actual legal norm in current international environmental law despite the distinctions in its manifestations. While the general conception of intergenerational equity is a legally binding principle in treaty as well as customary international law, the specific doctrine has the normative capacity of a legal rule, but it lacks the legally binding force as of today. Intergenerational obligations can steer the behaviour of States towards a more future-oriented way, but they only do so in the form of the general manifestation, as the specific doctrine still remains a mere scholarly conceptualisation. The distinction of the two manifestations' legal nature is essential as it allows distinguishing between the concept of intergenerational equity *de lege lata* and its potential changes *de lege ferenda*. Put differently, the general conception constitutes the *lex lata* manifestation of intergenerational equity, while the specific doctrine is a perspective for a *lex ferenda* development in the future.

*Returning to the thought experiment, these distinctions on the legal nature of intergenerational equity allow the State representatives to answer the last follow-up question regarding the legally binding effects of the concept in their answers to the High Commissioner: "We admit that intergenerational equity is not only a moral principle or soft policy goal, but also a legally binding principle. Yet, we are only bound by the general obligation to take into consideration the needs of future generations, not by any specific duties of conservation!"*

## 8.2 Intergenerational Equity—A Concept with Unanswered Questions

These observations on the substantive contents, the philosophical foundations and the legal nature of intergenerational equity already illustrate many of the concept's complexities. Beyond these aspects of the normative system of intergenerational equity, its operating system (i.e., the structural elements that govern intergenerational equity) is equally complex and some of these structures of intergenerational equity are still underexamined.[12] Chapter 5 of this book has therefore analysed three aspects regarding the operationalisation of intergenerational equity that remain still mostly unanswered in current legal discourse: the identification of the duty-bearers of intergenerational obligations (Sect. 8.2.1), the

[12] As to the distinction between normative and operating system, see in detail *supra* in Sect. 7.3.4.

characterisation of future generations as right-holders (Sect. 8.2.2) and the institutional forms of implementation and representation of the interests of future generations (Sect. 8.2.3). The findings of Chap. 5 further illustrate the emerging character of intergenerational equity between *lex lata* and *lex ferenda*. The concept's general manifestation requires less structural operationalisation than the more specific doctrine that constitutes a rights-based approach and builds on a representative framework for the needs of future generations.

### *8.2.1 States as the Primary Duty-Bearers of Intergenerational Equity*

Both the general conception and the specific doctrine of intergenerational equity contain obligations with a view to enabling future generations to meet their own needs. For the general conception, it is the obligation to take into account the needs of future generations in decision-making today; for the specific doctrine, there are three duties of conservation of natural resources with even more explicit sub-duties. With regard to these obligations, the primary structural question addresses the identification of duty-bearers: Who is obliged to fulfil these obligations? Rhetorically, the answer would be: "the present generation". The strictly positivist answer would rather be: "States". The actual answer to this legal question lies somewhere in-between.

The present generation itself, meaning the international community of humankind, is definitely no fitting subject of duties under current international law. However, if all members of the present generation were considered duty-bearers of intergenerational equity, as stated by *Brown Weiss*, this would include, *inter alia*, States, individuals and private corporations. The legal personhood and subjectivity of these actors under international law is partly controversial and complex. To begin with, individuals are only considered direct duty-bearers of international legal obligations in the domain of international criminal law. As of today, there is no international crime that would sanction individuals for the violation of environmental obligations with long-term effects. Proposals to introduce a crime of ecocide into the Rome Statute could point into this direction, but the *status quo* of international law does not accept individuals as duty-bearers of intergenerational obligations.[13]

The international legal personhood of private corporations is even more complex.[14] Apart from the realm of international investment law, their capacity as bearers of international legal obligations is very disputed, but it is intensely discussed in the domains of international human rights law and international environmental law, particularly with regard to transnational corporations. There have been some initiatives to increase the responsibility of transnational corporations for

[13] See *supra* in Sect. 5.1.2.1.

[14] See *supra* in Sect. 5.1.2.2.

their violations of human rights and environmental standards, such as the UN Guiding Principles or the UN Global Compact, but these documents constitute mere soft law documents and establish voluntary compliance mechanisms without legally binding character. There is no codified treaty regime for the international legal responsibility of private corporations and the few instances of progressive attempts and proposals are not sufficient to establish respective duties of corporations under customary international law. Generally, international law relies on an indirect responsibility of corporations via the intermediate level of national law. In some treaty regimes and recent codification proposals, State parties are obliged to take measures in order to guarantee the compliance to human rights and environmental standards by business corporations and to establish a domestic system of legal liability. However, this does not amount to a direct legal obligation of these corporations under international law, whereby they cannot be considered duty-bearers of international law as it stands.

This leaves the principal subjects of public international law, States, as potential duty-bearers of intergenerational equity.[15] States definitely are duty-bearers of international environmental law obligations in general, and of the legally binding general conception of intergenerational equity in particular—both under customary international law and the relevant treaty regimes. As duty-bearers, they are obliged to take into account the interests and needs of future generations in their own policy-making. However, their intergenerational obligations are not limited to their own activities that could have an impact on future generations, but they are also responsible for their omissions as far as they would have been obliged to take certain measures under a due diligence obligation. International environmental law requires States to ensure that activities within their territory do not cause environmental harm. This means that their intergenerational obligation also requires them to take certain measures to prevent activities of other actors within their territory from having negative long-term impacts on future generations. These measures include both legislative and administrative action in order to hinder private actors from such harmful activities. This due diligence dimension of intergenerational equity links the obligations of States to the activities of private corporations on their territory, as these corporations could consequently be obliged under *national* law to refrain from certain activities. Again, this does not make the private corporations themselves duty-bearers of intergenerational equity, but States remain the primary and only responsible duty-bearers under international law—potential future developments with regard to private corporations or individuals notwithstanding.

*Returning to the thought experiment, this identification of States as duty-bearers of intergenerational equity does not facilitate the confrontation with the High Commissioner for the State representatives. They would have to specify: "You cannot hold every member of our generation accountable for their intergenerational behaviour, but the States we represent are definitely obliged by the general conception of intergenerational equity."*

[15] See *supra* in Sect. 5.1.1.

### 8.2.2 The Potential of Future Generations to Become Right-Holders of Intergenerational Equity

In any case, the identification of the correct duty-bearers is not as disputed in the context of intergenerational equity as the question whether the concept establishes corresponding rights of future generations. This question encompasses two separate dimensions that are often inconsistently mixed up in legal scholarship: the conceptional possibility of future generations to be right-holders today and the legal attribution of intergenerational rights to future generations.

The conceptional doubts on a rights-based approach to intergenerational equity reject the idea of future generations to hold rights at all.[16] If future generations did not have the potential to become right-holders at all, any *legal* discussion on such rights would be moot from the beginning. The conceptional doubts are based either on philosophical considerations, on different understandings of theories of rights or on a general scepticism about the expansion of rights-based approaches. To begin with, the philosophical objections refer to the aforementioned non-existence argument, already illustrated in Chap. 3, that is simply based on the assumption that existence is a necessary prerequisite for having rights.[17] This assumption again builds on a will theory of rights that considers rights to give their holders actual control over the duty of other persons. Lacking the ability to exercise this control today, future generations would not be able to hold rights. In contrast, future generations could be considered potential right-holders from a perspective of an interest theory of rights, which only requires future generations to have interests today. For interest theorists, the non-existence of future generations does not hinder their capacity as right-holders. Beyond the non-existence argument, an interest theory of rights also assists in overcoming the common objection to rights of future generations linked to the rejection of collective rights.[18] In opposition to a purely Eurocentric and libertarian perspective on the primacy of individual human rights, the idea of collective rights is long accepted in international human rights law—particularly but not exclusively in human rights systems of the Global South. Considering that future generations can have identifiable basic interests as a collective of future human beings, they can also be conceived as appropriate collective right-holders for intergenerational rights.

Eventually, even the critics' common argument against human rights proliferation is not necessarily convincing if the limitations of intergenerational rights can be conceptually delineated.[19] Arguments against an unbearable expansion of human rights and the inclusion of new right-holders are reasonable to a certain degree, as they are concerned with an excessive reference to human rights law that could

---

[16] See *supra* in Sect. 5.2.1.

[17] See *supra* in Sect. 3.2.2 and *supra* note 9.

[18] See *supra* in Sect. 5.2.1.1.

[19] See *supra* in Sect. 5.2.1.2.

weaken the existing regime and rights. However, proliferation must not be overused to constrain any progressive new development of international human rights law, which is naturally a dynamic regime that must remain able to adapt to new societal challenges and threats. The scepticism about the proliferation and rhetorical devaluation of human rights should be understood as a helpful warning signal instead of an absolute counter-argument against new developments in human rights law. More specifically, the conceptualisation of planetary rights of future generations can also be understood as the temporal extension of existing human rights law to new right-holders due to the increasing challenges of intergenerational degradations of the environment. Overall, neither the non-existence argument, the individualistic perspective on human rights theory nor the general proliferation argument constitute convincing conceptional obstacles to the idea of future generations as holders of intergenerational rights.

Having resolved these conceptional and preliminary challenges, the second dimension of the discussion turns to the actual legal question—whether the operating system of public international law considers future generations to be right-holders.[20] This legal question depends on the positivist acknowledgement of such rights in international treaty or customary international law: Does the contemporary concept of intergenerational equity confer rights to future generations? The general manifestation does not require such rights as it is only based on the intergenerational obligation of States without corresponding right-holders. For this reason, the existing evidence of State practice and *opinio iuris* of intergenerational equity does not mention the *rights* of future generations, as already elaborated in Chap. 4.[21] In contrast, the specific doctrine of intergenerational equity is primarily based on the idea of future generations as corresponding right-holders. Some recent developments in international human rights law point to a possible future development that could include future generations as right-holders. These developments are often linked to the initiatives of a human right to a healthy environment, which could be considered a right of both present *and future* generations. In this sense, the specific doctrine of intergenerational equity would constitute a temporal extension of existing human rights law to future human beings in order to allow them to meet their needs in the future. As the development of a human right to a healthy environment in international law is still in its infancy, the few references to the *rights* of future generations do not suffice to change the legal framework in a way that establishes future generations as right-holders under current international law. Comparable to the normative differentiation between the legally binding general conception and the still emerging specific doctrine, the operative structures of intergenerational equity are equally limited to an obligation-based legal principle that does not introduce new right-holders. This does not hinder an according development of international law *de lege ferenda* in the future, as the conceptional objections have been refuted above.

[20] See *supra* in Sect. 5.2.2.

[21] See *supra* in Sect. 4.2.2.2.

*Returning to the thought experiment, the State representatives could object to the High Commissioner as far as she based her claims and accusations on the rights of her fellow future humans. Based on their own legal understanding, they could answer to her: "The members of your future generation do not have any legal rights under current international law. Our States might be obliged by intergenerational equity, but your generation is not entitled to raise any claims against them!"*

### 8.2.3 A Fragmented Institutional Framework of Representation

In the international legal discourse, the issue of rights of future generations is often directly linked to the issue of their representation, although the two discussions should be and have been addressed separately in this book. At least according to an interest theory of rights, the political or procedural invocation and enforcement of intergenerational equity is independent from the existence of rights of future generations. If a certain right exists, it is a different question who can demand the implementation of this right. If a certain right does *not* exist, the underlying interests can still be represented and claimed by an authorised entity. This representative entity would have to act on behalf of future generations in order to demand the compliance of States with intergenerational obligations. According to a deliberative democracy understanding of representation, it is not necessary that future generations as the represented entity have mandated their representative, but it is sufficient that the representative is recognised and accepted by the relevant audience—in this case States as the relevant duty-bearers of intergenerational obligations.[22] Consequently, there are no convincing conceptional arguments against the possibility of representation of future generations and their interests.

This representation would have to be accepted in international law and operationalised in the form of institutional frameworks of representation. Future generations could be represented on two levels—in policy-making before decisions that affect their interests; and on the procedural level of judicial proceedings in order to invoke violations of intergenerational equity. Chapter 5 examined both these dimensions in detail. Despite many differences, they generally have in common that the representation of future generations is inconsistent and fragmented in policy-making as well as on the judicial level.

With regard to the representation of future generations in policy-making, proposals on the establishment of a High Commissioner for Future Generations on the global level have shaped the discussion in international environmental law since the 1990s, particularly before the Rio Conference.[23] The attempts have been renewed in the context of the Rio+20 Conference in 2012. Due to the immense objections,

[22] See *supra* in Sect. 5.3.1.

[23] See *supra* in Sect. 5.3.2.2.

particularly raised by developed States, these proposals have never found their way into the respective outcome documents of the conferences. In its Report from 2013, the UNSG also suggested the establishment of either a High Commissioner or a special envoy, but none of these approaches were realised until today. Beside the continuation of existing institutions like the UNEP, the introduction of the HLPFSD was the only institutional concession at the Rio+20 conference. However, the task of the HLPFSD refers only to the surveillance of the sustainable development agenda without any explicit reference to future generations specifically. It cannot be considered to specifically represent the interests of future generations.

While the global level does not offer a representative institution for future generations, some States introduced comparable institutions in the last decades on the national level in order to strengthen the voice of future generations within national policy-making.[24] These commissioners, ombudspersons or advisory councils differ a lot from State to State, from legal system to legal system. Their functions, powers and influence range from mere advisory or consultative authority to stronger review and monitoring powers; some of them even had certain judicial functions. Yet, most of these institutions were equipped with rather soft advisory powers. Most importantly, these national forms of institutionalisation did not emanate from any international legal obligation or framework, but they were exclusively based on the domestic constitutional or legislative frameworks of the respective States. This voluntariness also allowed the dissolution or weakening of some of these institutions in recent years. Overall, the representation of future generations thus remains a voluntary option of national States without any binding institutional framework on the international nor on the national level.

The picture is even more fragmented with respect to the representation of future generations in judicial proceedings. There is an immense diversity of international and regional courts, tribunals and other judicial and quasi-judicial bodies that can be involved in questions of international environmental law. They are complemented by national courts that can decide on intergenerational equity and the representation of future generations. Chapter 5 thus structured the analysis of these complex judicial frameworks by distinguishing between the representation of future generations in inter-State proceedings, in individual complaints proceedings against States and in proceedings against private corporations. Parallel to the foregoing conclusion that private corporations do not constitute duty-bearers of intergenerational obligations *de lege lata*, proceedings against private corporations only offered two singular examples of explicit representation of future generations—the Dutch decision in *Milieudefensie v. Shell* and the Carbon Majors Report of the Philippines' Commission on Human Rights.[25]

In traditional international proceedings between States, future generations could be formally or informally represented by the judicial bodies themselves, by the

[24] See *supra* in Sect. 5.3.2.1.

[25] See *supra* in Sect. 5.3.3.4.

disputing States or by third actors within *amicus curiae* briefs.[26] For different reasons, none of these options have gained much support in the last decades and years. Although it would generally be possible to accept *amicus curiae* representation of future generations by independent entities within international organisations or from civil society, the practice of rendering *amicus curiae* briefs remained very scarce before inter-State courts and tribunals so far. In any case, States would constitute the most natural actors to claim a representative function for future generations anyway, as they are the main actors of inter-State proceedings. Further, the notion of obligations *erga omnes* and *erga omnes partes* would offer an adequate framework within the operating system of international law. Under the law of State responsibility, any State can invoke the observance of, at least, obligations *erga omnes partes* (i.e., obligations of a specific treaty regime owed to all State parties of that treaty). These obligations *erga omnes (partes)* envisage the achievement of legal goals beyond bilateral and reciprocal interests that benefit the interest of the whole international community, or of all treaty parties respectively. Norms of international environmental law, including intergenerational equity, typically aim at the fulfilment of such common interests of humanity. Regardless of the controversial classification of intergenerational equity as obligation *erga omnes (partes)*, the existing case law shows that no State has ever claimed to represent the interests of future generations of humankind and it is unlikely that this form of representation will be successful before international courts and tribunals anytime soon. This leaves the representation of future generations to the international courts and tribunals themselves, at least in an informal sense. While these bodies would not explicitly act on behalf of future generations, some individual opinions of judges have raised the idea of international courts being guardians for the interests of future generations. While it is not clear whether the courts will assume this role in the future, the issuance of advisory opinions would constitute a fitting procedural option to operationalise this representative function of the courts and tribunals. Again, there is no explicit example of this institutional framework, but the currently envisaged initiation of advisory proceeding before the ICJ on the responsibilities of States in the context of climate protection law could shed some light on this idea soon.

While the inter-State level does not offer any institutional framework of representation and only very few promising perspectives, the level of individual complaints proceedings of civil society actors against States is much more fruitful.[27] On the level of international and regional human rights bodies, the examples remained scarce and abstract with regard to future generations (e.g., in *Sacchi*, in *Billy et al.* and in *Duarte Agostinho*). The level of national human rights jurisprudence and climate change litigation offers more examples of explicit or implicit representation of the interests of future generations—notwithstanding the differences in procedural rules. As none of the cases were exclusively based on the representation of future generations, most courts abstained from deciding the question of representation. At

[26] See *supra* in Sect. 5.3.3.2.

[27] See *supra* in Sect. 5.3.3.3.

the same time, only few decisions explicitly *rejected* the idea of such representation. The analysis of the decided and pending cases is even more complicated as most complaints only implicitly raised a representative claim on behalf of future generations. Environmental NGOs and youth plaintiffs play the most important role in this context. The NGOs are often considered to represent not only their proper interests but also the general public interest of environmental protection, and children and youth are considered to also speak on behalf of future unborn generations. Indigenous communities increasingly also play a role in intergenerational litigation. The proceedings in *Oposa v. Factoran* in the Philippines, *Urgenda* in the Netherlands and *Future Generations* in Colombia constitute important examples of explicit invocation of future generations, while the latter's interests were also implicitly raised in some recent cases in the USA *(Juliana)* and Germany *(Neubauer et al.)*. However, many more cases are pending worldwide that have the potential of further shaping the institutional framework of representation for future generations. In a nutshell, the international, regional and national instances of individual complaints proceedings demonstrate a judicial framework of representation of future generations that is as fragmented and inconsistent as the judicial international legal system itself. Despite the many instances of explicit and implicit representation, there is no universal system that would integrate the different procedural possibilities of representation—let alone any kind of international legal obligation of States to implement intergenerational equity by establishing such representative frameworks.

*Returning to the thought experiment, the State representatives could not point the High Commissioner to one representative institution that would be able to bring together the different interests and claims of future generations. They would probably give a cacophony of answers as they would all refer to their different national and regional systems without any common basis on the global level. Some of them would offer complex national institutions and frameworks that could represent future generations' interests in policy-making and judicial complaints. Others would not be able to imagine any form of representation in their respective States or on the international level. After a sophisticated analysis of the current international legal system, the State representatives would tell the High Commissioner: "There is no competent and accepted institution under international law that could represent the interests of your generation today. No one universally speaks on their behalf!"*

## 8.3 Intertemporal Law—A Fitting Method to Assess Intergenerational Equity?

The findings of the first chapters offer a comprehensive overview of the *status quo* of intergenerational equity—both with regard to its substantive legal contents (Chaps. 2–4) and its structural foundations (Chap. 5). The *lex lata* of intergenerational equity is a general obligation of States to take into account the interests of future generations who do not hold a corresponding intergenerational right and whose interests are not represented in any binding institutional framework of international law. In contrast, a more specific manifestation of intergenerational equity could include detailed conservation duties of the present generation, potentially including corporations or individuals as duty-bearers. It would be based on the corresponding planetary rights of future generations who would be institutionally represented on the international level in policy-making as well as judicial proceedings. Yet, this specific doctrine only constitutes a potential future development of intergenerational equity *de lege ferenda*.

This analysis is based on the legal regime of the year 2025. It leaves out an intertemporal perspective on intergenerational equity that would preliminary answer which legal regime is actually applicable to the determination of the norm of intergenerational equity *de lege lata*. The fictional High Commissioner's counter-question on the point of view taken by the present generation is thus not only a hypothetical one, but it concerns the core of the so-called doctrine of intertemporal law and reflects the second main research question of this book. An intertemporal perspective on intergenerational equity requires a modified understanding of this doctrine of intertemporal law that allows temporally assessing the legal relationship between present and future generations (Sect. 8.3.1). This future-oriented modification of intertemporal law can be applied to the concept of intergenerational equity (Sect. 8.3.2).

### *8.3.1 Necessity to Modify the Doctrine of Intertemporal Law to the Particularities of Intergenerational Equity*

The doctrine of intertemporal law is a functional rule of general international law that assists in determining the temporally applicable legal regime in case that a substantive norm of international law has changed over time. Since it balances legal certainty and the flexibility for legal change, it consists of two complementary components: the principle of contemporaneity and evolutionary approaches to legal change. The principle of contemporaneity is the starting point for any intertemporal assessment. With regard to a legal norm that has changed from the moment of its creation in the past to the moment of its application within a dispute in the present, contemporaneity requires the legal regime at the time of the norm's creation to be relevant for the legal assessment of the respective dispute.[28] The principle of contemporaneity is easily applied to the concept of intergenerational equity. As shown in Chaps. 2 and 4, intergenerational equity has become part of binding customary international law between the 1990s and today. Its "time of creation" refers to this period of time. The temporally applicable legal regime of

[28] See *supra* in Sect. 6.1.

intergenerational equity would thus consist of the general manifestation of the concept as part of contemporary customary international law.

The second component of the doctrine of intertemporal law turns to evolutionary approaches for the determination of a norm's legal content. Under certain circumstances, a norm is not only to be assessed in light of the law contemporary to its creation, but also in light of the legal developments subsequent to this creation until the time of the norm's application in a dispute.[29] These evolutionary approaches have mainly developed in regard to treaty interpretation as independent approaches based either on the generic nature of a treaty term in light of the parties' intention or on the object and purpose of the treaty. Evolutionary interpretation is particularly relevant in the realm of human rights law. Furthermore, environmental obligations in a treaty can also trigger an evolutionary interpretation due to the integral nature of these obligations that often influences the object and purpose of the treaty.[30] This explains the evolutionary approaches the ICJ took, for instance, in its treaty interpretation in the *Gabčíkovo-Nagymaros Project* case or the *Whaling in the Antarctic* decision. As far as one of the conditions is met, the respective (treaty) norm must not only be assessed according to the legal regime at the time of its creation, but the interpreter must take into consideration the subsequent evolution of law.

The moment these evolutionary approaches are applied to the concept of intergenerational equity, the doctrine of intertemporal law reaches its limits. For several reasons, a direct application of the existing doctrine to intergenerational equity is inadequate; it needs to be modified to apply to the legal relationship between present and future generations. The first necessary modification results from the treaty-related character of the existing evolutionary approaches. As the holistic general conception of intergenerational equity is a norm of customary international law,[31] the treaty-related evolutionary interpretation rules cannot be directly applied to it. The conditions for evolutionary treaty interpretation (i.e., generic treaty terms and the object and purpose of a treaty) have to be modified accordingly to fit the framework of a customary norm. Chapter 7 adapted these conditions by assessing a correspondent "object and purpose" of the customary norm of intergenerational equity.[32]

Beyond this formal modification, the existing evolutionary approaches are also inadequate in substance to determine the temporally applicable legal regime of intergenerational equity. Normally, intertemporal law addresses the temporal delimitation between a legal regime in the past—at the time of a norm's creation—and a legal regime in the present—at the time of a dispute. This means that an unmodified application to intergenerational equity would require awaiting the emergence of an intergenerational dispute. At this point in the future, intertemporal law could assist in

[29] See *supra* in Sect. 6.2.

[30] See *supra* in Sect. 6.2.4.

[31] See *supra* in Sect. 4.2.2.1.

[32] See *supra* in Sect. 7.2.1 and Sect. 7.3.1.2.

determining whether the law of the (new) past or the law of the (new) present is applicable.

*In the image of the thought experiment, this would mean that the State representatives would address the High Commissioner's counter-question by telling her: "The law is as it is now. You should wait until the year 2100, when you are suffering from our alleged violations. Then, a court of law can tell you which legal regime is temporally applicable to the occurring dispute. Probably, the court will apply the new legal regime of this future according to the evolutionary component of intertemporal law."*

This is not convincing for two reasons: the irreversibility of most violations of intergenerational obligations and the inherently intertemporal nature of intergenerational equity. With regard to the irreversibility of intergenerational violations, it would be pointless for the potential right-holders in a future generation to wait for the effects of the violation to occur.[33] At that time in the future, they could claim these violations before a court or tribunal. The existing doctrine of intertemporal law might even assist them in applying a newly emerged, more specific manifestation of intergenerational equity vis-à-vis the responsible States in the future. But the harm to the environment will most likely be irreversibly done. This is particularly evident with regard to the effects of climate change and the exceedance of certain tipping points, such as the collapse of the Greenland ice sheet or the permafrost carbon release. Consequently, the retrospective application of the doctrine of intertemporal law in the future in order to determine the temporally applicable law is neither persuasive nor appropriate.

Beyond this irreversibility argument, the intertemporal nature of intergenerational equity also essentially differs from other constellations of intertemporal law.[34] Normally, intertemporal constellations, such as human rights disputes, are intertemporal with regard to the time that has passed between the creation of the norms and their later application. In the context of intergenerational equity, it is not only the temporal gap between different legal regimes that renders the concept intertemporal. More importantly, the legal relationship underlying the concept is inherently intertemporal as it links different generations across time. While the duty-bearer (a State) and the right-holder (an individual) in a traditional human rights dispute are contemporaries within the same generation, the duty-bearers and the potential right-holders within an intergenerational dispute are non-contemporaries who do not exist at the same time. Intergenerational equity is a legal norm that governs exactly this temporally extended relationship between different generations. This particularity shows that the existing doctrine of intertemporal law has not been elaborated in order to address the temporal extension of a legal relationship across time. Instead, the intertemporal nature of intergenerational equity is better reflected in *John Rawls'* hypothetical idea of an original position, in which representatives of all generations negotiate fair principles of (intergenerational) justice.

---

[33] See *supra* in Sect. 7.2.3.

[34] See *supra* in Sect. 7.2.2.

*Returning to the thought experiment, the State representatives would have to admit that their traditional perspective on intertemporal law is not sufficient to sweep aside the High Commissioner's objection. At this point, they would ask themselves and the High Commissioner: "But how do we then assess the temporally applicable legal regime of intergenerational equity? From which temporal point of view do we address our intergenerational obligations?"*

### 8.3.2 A Modified Doctrine of Intertemporal Law for the Assessment of Intergenerational Equity

As elaborated in Chap. 7, it is necessary to apply a modified doctrine of intertemporal law in order to determine the temporally applicable legal regime for the assessment of intergenerational equity today.[35] This modified doctrine is based on the existing two components of intertemporal law. However, the main modification is the necessary shift of perspective that results from the inherently intertemporal nature and the irreversibility argument. While the traditional intertemporal law doctrine relates the present to the past, a modification of intertemporal law to intergenerational equity must appropriately address the legal relationship between the present and the future. This requires changing the point of view from which to determine the temporally applicable legal regime. Intertemporal law must relate the legal regime in the present at the time of the creation of intergenerational equity to the legal regime in the future when the effects of intergenerational violations occur.

This prospective view on intergenerational equity refers to two different intertemporal legal regimes: the contemporaneous legal regime in the year 2025 and the evolutionary developments of law between today and a time in the future, e.g., the year 2100. The shift of perspective thus requires the present generation to anticipate and to take into consideration future developments of intergenerational equity when assessing its responsibilities towards future generations. At first sight, such a prospective approach seems unrealistic, illusionary and impossible as it requires predicting the future with certainty. However, this book offered two alternative or complementary means how to methodologically make certain assumptions on the future developments of intergenerational equity. The first approach again builds on the two manifestations of the concept that have been analysed in the foregoing chapters. While the general conception of intergenerational equity constitutes the current legal regime that would have to be applied under the principle of contemporaneity, the specific doctrine offers certain insights on the potential evolutionary development of intergenerational equity *de lege ferenda*. Therefore, it is not necessary to imagine an evolutionary future legal regime from scratch, but the detailed analysis in this book allows building upon specific intergenerational duties as well as structural perspectives on the issues of duty-bearers, right-holders and

[35] See *supra* in Sect. 7.3.

representation. It is also methodologically justified to rely on this emerging specific doctrine of intergenerational equity due to the transitional character of intergenerational equity as a customary norm. The concept of intergenerational equity can be considered in a period of transition between its currently binding general manifestation and an emerging specific manifestation that is already reflected in some instances of international documents, jurisprudence and scholarship. Consequently, it is possible to anticipate with a certain degree of probability the future developments of intergenerational equity. The evolutionary approaches of the modified doctrine of intertemporal law would thus point to the specific doctrine of intergenerational equity as it will probably develop until the year 2100.

Beyond this first proposal, Chap. 7 also offered a more sophisticated methodological framework to predict future change in international law. The works of *Paul Diehl* and *Charlotte Ku*[36] elaborate a framework of the international legal system that allows certain assumptions for the upcoming developments of intergenerational equity. Building on their distinction between the normative and the operating system of international law, the findings of this book on intergenerational equity can be easily translated into their system framework. This framework is based on the idea that the two sub-systems constantly interact with each other: the normative system can cause subsequent operating system change and the operating system offers the framework that can have impacts on subsequent developments in the normative system. The exact conditions for these system interactions have been elaborated by *Diehl* and *Ku*, and they further shape the methodological framework that allows making assumptions on future developments of international legal norms. While the detailed application of their conditions for system interaction goes beyond the scope of the present analysis, the introduction of this framework showed that it is methodologically possible to carefully predict future developments of intergenerational equity, at least with a certain likelihood.

Following from the two complementary suggestions, it is not impossible to anticipate the future evolutionary development of intergenerational equity. This means that the elaborated modified doctrine of intertemporal law offers a new and adequate perspective on the legal regime of intergenerational equity *de lege lata*. More specifically, legal developments of intergenerational equity that would normally be considered *lex ferenda* become relevant for present generations already today and must thus be considered *lex lata* from an intertemporal perspective.

[36]Diehl and Ku (2010).

## 8.4 And Now What?—An Intertemporal Outlook on Intergenerational Equity

The book has answered some open questions. It has demonstrated the distinction between two manifestations of intergenerational equity. It has assessed the legal nature of both these manifestations by analysing the international legal material that is concerned with future generations. Further, the book has offered a comprehensive analysis of the structural questions of intergenerational equity, including the duty-bearers, right-holders and frameworks of representation. Most importantly, it has elaborated a modified doctrine of intertemporal law that allows taking an appropriate intertemporal perspective on the concept of intergenerational equity. This new intertemporal perspective is not only limited to the contemporaneous regime *de lege lata*, but it illustrates how the evolutionary concept of intergenerational equity is situated in a period of transition between *lex lata*, the general conception, and *lex ferenda*, the specific doctrine. This transition of intergenerational equity must be considered from the prospective intertemporal perspective when determining the temporally applicable legal regime relevant for the assessment of intergenerational equity.

At the same time, the book left some questions open. How exactly do the normative and the operating system of intergenerational equity impact each other? Are the conditions for operating system change fulfilled? What does this mean for subsequent change of the normative system of intergenerational equity? Which assumptions on the future development of intergenerational equity result from a methodological application of this framework? The answers to these questions require further research that builds on the modified intertemporal perspective and on the framework of *Diehl* and *Ku*—or other appropriate frameworks to envisage future change of international law. Once these questions can be answered in more detail, it is possible to determine the exact contents of the legal concept of intergenerational equity today from an appropriately modified intertemporal perspective. For the time being, the present author is not able to give these exact answers. For instance, it is not clear in which direction the institutional framework of representation might development with regard to policy-making or judicial proceedings. Nonetheless, the following return to the introductory thought experiment of time travel outlines a possible future regime of intergenerational equity as well as the respective outcome of the suggested intertemporal assessment.

*After the intense and detailed exchange between the High Commissioner and the State representatives, the High Commissioner got an impression of the legal regime of intergenerational equity in the year 2025. She understood the general manifestation of intergenerational equity and the lack of effective structures to implement this general intergenerational obligation. Yet, the State representatives acknowledged eventually that this contemporaneous approach to their intergenerational obligations is not sufficient from a perspective of intertemporal law. They agreed on a modified intertemporal perspective that required them to also take into account the evolutionary developments of intergenerational equity between the year 2025 and the future legal regime in the year 2100.*

*"If we have to include the evolutionary developments of intergenerational equity into our intertemporal assessment, what does this future development look like?", the UNSG asks the High Commissioner.*

*The High Commissioner delineates this future legal regime of intergenerational equity in the year 2100: "We understand intergenerational equity as an intense and holistic framework that describes our relationship towards future generations of humanity. It consists of specific environmental duties to conserve the remaining planetary resources for future generations in a condition that is not worse than the condition we received them in. As we received the planetary resources already in a condition that does not allow us to meet all our basic needs, our own intergenerational obligations have become even stricter, so that we are obliged to do anything possible in order to build up again the natural resource base for our successors. Since the 2040s, these obligations have not only bound States, but in principle any member of our generation. Particularly, private corporations of all kinds are obliged under international law to comply with these intergenerational duties as they have contributed to a great part to the environmental degradation. The compliance with these obligations can be enforced against both States and corporations before international courts and tribunals. Furthermore, we value future generations as holders of intergenerational rights, so that our generation is directly bound by these rights. For some decades now, these intergenerational rights do not only appertain to future generations of humanity, but to future generations of all sentient species in general, as we consider the human species as equal to other sentient beings.*[37] *Ignoring our planetary duties would mean ignoring the rights of future sentient beings, which is considered a violation of pathocentric and humanitarian principles, such as dignity and equality of all sentient species. In order to guarantee the respect of these intergenerational rights, we have established adequate institutions in the course of the 21st century. First, we finally created the office of the High Commissioner for Future Generations in the mid-21st century, building upon the proposals of the Rio Conference and of your UNSG Report of 2013. This colleague of mine is authorised to represent future generations within every instance of international policy-making, he is capable of rendering advisory recommendations but also of reviewing new international legislation and preventing it if necessary. Further, he coordinates the work of national ombudspersons of future generations, as their establishment in domestic systems is prescribed by an international treaty of the mid-21st century. The interests of future generations can also be invoked on the judicial level after a subsequent reform of the system in the 2060s. Civil society actors can sue States and transnational corporations on behalf of future generations on the international level before the judicial branch of the High Commissioner for Future Generations. In a judicial proceeding, my colleague decides on the complaints and, in case of a breach of intergenerational equity, he*

[37] Cf. already *supra* in Sect. 5.2.1 [notes 183–184].

*subsequently reviews the decision's implementation by the respective respondents. Beyond this, the High Commissioner regularly reviews the implementation of intergenerational equity by States as well as transnational corporations. In case of repeated violation of intergenerational obligations, he is also authorised to invoke these violations before the successor of the ICJ."*

*The State representatives of the present generation are amazed and surprised by the progressive future developments of the international legal system with regard to intergenerational equity. "But are we bound by all of these future developments now?", they ask again.*

*"Not entirely, as your contemporaneous perspective remains relevant as well", the High Commissioner for Intergenerational Relations answers. "But you are obliged to take these evolutions into consideration instead of waiting for them to occur when it is too late. For instance, you should confer rights to future generations, to us, today already in order to strengthen their protection in your legal regime. And the existing attempts to hold transnational corporations accountable, why should they only be based on soft law instruments? You should begin negotiating legal agreements that establish the international legal responsibility of transnational corporations for environmental – and intergenerational – obligations. Finally, the proposals for institutional innovation have already existed for thirty years now. Stop preventing any stronger form of representation of future generations on the international level. You should reconsider the initiatives to establish a High Commissioner for Future Generations beginning now, not wait another three decades. The exact powers and functions of the new institutional framework, between policy-making and judicial functions, will develop in time. You can shape them according to your ideas, but they must be more effective for the implementation of intergenerational equity than your current institutional framework."*

*This reminds the UNSG of the 2013 Report of his predecessor, in which the latter built on John Rawls' idea of an obligation to maintain just institutions over time for future generations.*[38] *The UNSG agrees with the remarks of the High Commissioner for Intergenerational Relations and closes the discussion session with the following words: "Your descriptions of the future are startling and horrifying, your words and pleas are coherent and persuasive. In the end, any fair intergenerational justice principles and institutions must emanate from this intertemporal confrontation you put us in. We now better understand our intertemporal legal relationship with future generations. We thus have to assess the rules of this relationship from an intertemporal perspective that requires us to take into account both our own understanding of the law and your future perspective on the law. This 30th Conference of the Parties of the UNFCCC is the best occasion to start with this new intertemporal perspective!"*

Time travel is not possible. But that does not render the foregoing thought experiment preposterous. Indirectly, the book was even able to give an answer to the original provocative and rather moral question of the time traveller—*why* the

[38] United Nations Secretary-General (2013, para. 24). with reference to Rawls (1971/1999), p. 255.

present generation acts in explicit violation of its intergenerational responsibilities. The easy answer would be: because the policy-makers of the present generation took the wrong intertemporal perspective on these responsibilities. Now, that the correct intertemporal perspective is clear, the present generation is able to take at least a different mindset in its policy-making and judicial proceedings with regard to intergenerational equity. The present book suggests a first step in doing so.

> "Once the notion of time travel starts to come naturally to the human mind, it is supremely easy to assimilate it into our mode of thinking."—Maria Konnikova, 'How to Build a Time Machine', The New Yorker, 2016.

> "If someone says these proposals are impractical, or politically naive, then I would respond that we need impractical answers. [...] And if some of these answers seem radical or far-fetched today, then I say wait until tomorrow. Soon, it will be abundantly clear that it is business as usual that is utopian, whereas creating something very new and different is a practical necessity."—James G. Speth, 'The Bridge at the Edge of the World', 2008.

## References

Brown Weiss, E. (1989). *In fairness to future generations: International law, common patrimony, and intergenerational equity*. Transnational Publishers, Inc.

Diehl, P. F., & Ku, C. (2010). *The dynamics of international law*. Cambridge University Press. https://doi.org/10.1017/CBO9780511817328

Rawls, J. (1999). *A theory of justice*. (Revised edn). Harvard University Press. (Original work published 1971)

United Nations Secretary-General. (2013). *Intergenerational Solidarity and the Needs of Future Generations, Report of the Secretary-General* (15 August 2013). UN Doc. A/68/322.

World Commission on Environment and Development. (1987). *Report of the World Commission on Environment and Development: Our Common Future (Brundtland Report)* (1987). UN Doc. A/42/427 Annex.

# Table of Treaties

*1996 Protocol to the Convention on the Prevention of Marine Pollution by Dumping of Wastes and Other Matter, 1972* (London Protocol). Adopted 7 November 1996, entered into force 24 March 2006. 36 ILM 1.

*Additional Protocol to the American Convention on Human Rights in the Area of Economic, Social and Cultural Rights* (Protocol of San Salvador). Adopted 17 November 1988, entered into force 16 November 1999. OAS TS N°69.

*African Charter on Human and Peoples' Rights* (Banjul Charter). Adopted 17 June 1981, entered into force 21 October 1986. 1520 UNTS 217.

*African Convention on the Conservation of Nature and Natural Resources* (African Nature Convention). Adopted 15 September 1968, entered into force 16 June 1969. 1001 UNTS 3.

*Agreement Establishing the World Trade Organization* (WTO Agreement). Adopted 15 April 1994, entered into force 1 January 1995. 33 ILM 1125.

*Agreement Governing the Activities of States on the Moon and Other Celestial Bodies* (Moon Agreement). Adopted 5 December 1979, entered into force 11 July 1984. 1363 UNTS 3.

*Cartagena Protocol on Biosafety to the Convention on Biological Diversity* (Cartagena Protocol). Adopted 29 January 2000, entered into force 11 September 2003. 2226 UNTS 208.

*Charter of Fundamental Rights of the European Union* (EU Charter of Fundamental Rights). Adopted 7 December 2000, entered into force 1 December 2009. EU OJ C 326, 395.

*Charter of the United Nations* (UN Charter). Adopted 26 June 1945, entered into force 24 October 1945. 1 UNTS XVI.

*Convention Concerning the Protection of the World Cultural and Natural Heritage* (World Heritage Convention). Adopted 16 November 1972, entered into force 17 December 1975. 1037 UNTS 151.

*Convention for the Protection of Human Rights and Fundamental Freedoms* (ECHR). Adopted 4 November 1950, entered into force 3 September 1953. 213 UNTS 221.



A. Bustami, *The Legal Relationship between Present and Future Generations*,
https://doi.org/10.1007/978-3-032-03345-1

*Convention for the Protection of the Marine Environment of the North-East Atlantic* (OSPAR Convention). Adopted 22 September 1992, entered into force 25 March 1998. 2354 UNTS 67.

*Convention on Access to Information, Public Participation in Decision-making and Access to Justice in Environmental Matters* (Aarhus Convention). Adopted 25 June 1998, entered into force 30 October 2001. 2161 UNTS 447.

*Convention on Biological Diversity* (CBD). Adopted 5 June 1992, entered into force 29 December 1993. 1760 UNTS 79.

*Convention on Civil Liability for Damage Resulting from Activities Dangerous to the Environment* (Lugano Convention). Adopted 21 June 1993. 32 ILM 1228.

*Convention on International Trade in Endangered Species of Wild Fauna and Flora* (CITES). Adopted 3 March 1973, entered into force 1 July 1975. 993 UNTS 243.

*Convention on the Protection and Use of Transboundary Watercourses and International Lakes* (UNECE Water Convention). Adopted 17 March 1992, entered into force 6 October 1996. 1936 UNTS 269.

*Convention on the Rights of the Child* (Child Rights Convention). Adopted 20 November 1989, entered into force 2 September 1990. 1577 UNTS 3.

*Fourth ACP-EEC Convention* (1989 Lomé Convention). Adopted 15 December 1989, entered into force 1 September 1991. 1924 UNTS 4.

*International Convention for the Regulation of Whaling* (Whaling Convention). Adopted 2 December 1946, entered into force 10 November 1948. 161 UNTS 72.

*International Convention on Civil Liability for Oil Pollution Damage* (CLC). Adopted 29 November 1969, entered into force 19 June 1975. 973 UNTS 3.

*International Convention on Liability and Compensation for Damage in Connection with the Carriage of Hazardous and Noxious Substances by Sea, 2010* (2010 HNS Convention). Adopted 30 April 2010, entered into force not yet in force. Retrieved 3 January 2025, from https://www.hnsconvention.org/wp-content/uploads/2019/05/2010-HNS-Convention-English.pdf.

*International Covenant on Civil and Political Rights* (ICCPR). Adopted 16 December 1966, entered into force 23 March 1976. 999 UNTS 171.

*International Covenant on Economic, Social and Cultural Rights* (ICESCR). Adopted 16 December 1966, entered into force 3 January 1976. 999 UNTS 171.

*Kyoto Protocol to the United Nations Framework Convention on Climate Change* (Kyoto Protocol). Adopted 11 December 1997, entered into force 16 February 2005. 2303 UNTS 162.

*Montreal Protocol on Substances that Deplete the Ozone Layer* (Montreal Protocol). Adopted 16 September 1987, entered into force 1 January 1989. 1522 UNTS 3.

*Paris Agreement* (Paris Agreement). Adopted 12 December 2015, entered into force 4 November 2016. UN Doc. FCCC/CP/2015/L.9/Rev.1.

*Protocol of 1992 to Amend the International Convention on Civil Liability for Oil Pollution Damage, 1969* (1992 Protocol). Adopted 27 November 1992, entered into force 30 May 1996. 1956 UNTS 255.

*Protocol on Strategic Environmental Assessment to the Convention on Environmental Impact Assessment in a Transboundary Context* (Protocol to the Espoo

Convention). Adoptcd 21 May 2003, entered into force 11 July 2010. 2685 UNTS 140.

*Protocol to Amend the Vienna Convention on Civil Liability for Nuclear Damage* (1997 Vienna Protocol). Adopted 29 September 1997, entered into force 4 October 2003. 2241 UNTS 270.

*Regional Agreement on Access to Information, Public Participation and Justice in Environmental Matters in Latin America and the Caribbean* (Escazú Agreement). Adopted 4 March 2018, entered into force 22 April 2021. Retrieved 3 January 2025, from https://treaties.un.org/doc/Treaties/2018/03/20180312%2003-04%20PM/CTC-XXVII-18.pdf.

*Revised African Convention on the Conservation of Nature and Natural Resources* (Revised African Nature Convention). Adopted 11 July 2003, entered into force 23 July 2016. Retrieved 3 January 2025, from https://au.int/en/treaties/african-convention-conservation-nature-and-natural-resources-revised-version.

*Revised Arab Charter on Human Rights* (Revised Arab Charter). Adopted 22 May 2004, entered into force 15 March 2008. 12 International Human Rights Reports 893.

*Rome Statute of the International Criminal Court Rome, 17 July 1998* (Rome Statute). Adopted 17 July 1998, entered into force 1 July 2002. 2187 UNTS 3.

*Rotterdam Convention on the Prior Informed Consent Procedure for Certain Hazardous Chemicals and Pesticides in International Trade* (Rotterdam Convention). Adopted 10 September 1998, entered into force 24 February 2004. 2244 UNTS 337.

*Rules of Court of the International Court of Justice* (Rules of Court). Adopted 14 April 1978, entered into force 1 July 1978. Retrieved 3 January 2025, from https://www.icj-cij.org/en/rules.

*Statute of the International Court of Justice* (ICJ Statute). Adopted 26 June 1945, entered into force 24 October 1945. 1 UNTS XVI.

*Statute of the River Uruguay between the Government of the Eastern Republic of Uruguay and the Government of the Argentine Republic* (1975 Statute of the River Uruguay). Adopted 26 February 1975, entered into force 18 September 1976. 1295 UNTS 331.

*Treaty between the Hungarian People's Republic and the Czechoslovak Socialist Republic concerning the Construction and Operation of the Gabčíkovo-Nagymaros System of Locks* (1977 Treaty concerning the Gabčíkovo-Nagymaros System), entered into force 16 September 1977. 32 ILM 1247.

*Trusteeship Agreement for the Territory of Nauru* (Trusteeship Agreement). Adopted 21 October 1947, entered into force 1 Novemver 1947. 10 UNTS 3.

*UN Convention on the Law of Non-Navigational Uses of International Watercourses* (UN Watercourses Convention). Adopted 21 May 1997, entered into force 17 August 2014. 36 ILM 700.

*United Nations Convention on the Law of the Sea* (UNCLOS). Adopted 10 December 1982, entered into force 16 November 1994. 1833 UNTS 3.

*United Nations Convention to Combat Desertification in those Countries Experiencing Serious Drought and/or Desertification, Particularly in Africa* (UNCCD). Adopted 17 June 1994, entered into force 26 December 1996. 1954 UNTS 3.

*United Nations Convention to Combat Desertification in those Countries Experiencing Serious Drought and/or Desertification, Particularly in Africa* (UNCCD). Adopted 17 June 1994, entered into force 26 December 1996. 1954 UNTS 3.

*United Nations Framework Convention on Climate Change* (UNFCCC). Adopted 9 May 1992, entered into force 21 March 1994. 1771 UNTS 107.

*Vienna Convention on Civil Liability for Nuclear Damage* (Vienna Convention on Nuclear Damage). Adopted 21 May 1963, entered into force 12 November 1977. 1063 UNTS 265.

*Vienna Convention on the Law of Treaties* (VCLT). Adopted 23 May 1969, entered into force 27 January 1980. 1155 UNTS 331.

# Table of Legislation

European Communities, *Declaration of the Council of the European Communities and of the Representatives of the Governments of the Member States Meeting in the Council of 22 November 1973 on the Programme of Action of the European Communities on the Environment*. Adopted 22 November 1973. EU OJ C 112/1.

European Economic and Social Committee, *Opinion on the 'Communication from the Commission to the European Parliament, the Council, the European Economic and Social Committee and the Committee of the Regions: Rio+20: Towards the Green Economy and Better Governance' – The Contribution of European Organised Civil Society*. Adopted 22 September 2011. EU OJ C 376, 102–109, COM(2011) 363 final.

European Union, *Directive 2004/35/CE of the European Parliament and of the Council on environmental liability with regard to the prevention and remedying of environmental damage* (EU Environmental Liability Directive). Adopted 21 April 2004. EU OJ L 143, 56–75.

*German Climate Protection Law*. Adopted 12 December 2019, entered into force 18 December 2019. Bundesgesetzblatt I (2019), S. 2513.

*Basic Law for the Federal Republic of Germany* (Basic Law of Germany). Adopted 8 May 1949, entered into force 23 May 1949. Bundesgesetzblatt I (1949) S. 1.

*Constitution of the Federative Republic of Brazil* (DELETE). Adopted 5 October 1988, entered into force 5 October 1988. Retrieved 3 January 2025, from https://www.stf.jus.br/arquivo/cms/legislacaoConstituicao/anexo/brazil_federal_constitution.pdf.

*Constitution of the Kingdom of Norway* (Constitution of Norway). Adopted 16 May 1814, entered into force 17 May 1814. Retrieved 3 January 2025, from https://lovdata.no/dokument/NLE/lov/1814-05-17.

*Constitution of the Republic of Malawi*. Adopted 16 May 1994, entered into force 18 May 1995. Retrieved 3 January 2025, from https://www.constituteproject.org/constitution/Malawi_2017?lang=en.

*Déclaration des Droits de l'Homme et du Citoyen* (DDHC), entered into force 26 August 1789. Retrieved 3 January 2025, from https://www.conseil-



A. Bustami, *The Legal Relationship between Present and Future Generations*,
https://doi.org/10.1007/978-3-032-03345-1

constitutionnel.fr/le-bloc-de-constitutionnalite/declaration-des-droits-de-l-homme-et-du-citoyen-de-1789.

*Fundamental Law of Hungary*. Adopted 18 April 2011, entered into force 1 January 2012. Retrieved 3 January 2025, from https://www.constituteproject.org/constitution/Hungary_2011.pdf.

# Table of Cases

*The following list contains all case-related documents, including judicial and quasi-judicial decisions, but also respective complaints and petititions as well as amicus curiae briefs.*

## International Courts and Tribunals

Arbitral Tribunal. *Award regarding the Boundary between the Colony of British Guiana and the United States of Venezuela.* Arbitral Award. 3 October 1899. RIAA XXVIII (2007), 331.

Arbitral Tribunal. *Case concerning the delimitation of the maritime boundary between Guinea and Guinea-Bissau.* Ad Hoc Arbitration Tribunal Award. 14 February 1985. RIAA XIX (1985), 149.

Arbitral Tribunal. *Dispute between Texaco Overseas Petroleum Company / California Asiatic Oil Company and the Government of the Libyan Arab Republic (Compensation for Nationalized Property).* Arbitral Award on the Merits. 19 January 1977. (1978) 17 International Legal Materials 1.

Arbitral Tribunal. *Fur Seal Arbitration: Proceedings of the Tribunal of Arbitration, Convened at Paris, under the Treaty between the United States of America and Great Britain, concluded at Washington, February 29, 1892, for the Determination of Questions Between the Two Governments concerning the Jurisdictional Rights of the United States in the Waters of Bering Sea.* Memorial of the United States of America. Government Printing Office, 1895.

Arbitral Tribunal. *Pacific Fur Seal Arbitration (United States of America v. Great Britain).* Arbitral Award. 15 August 1893. RIAA XXVIII (1893), 263.

Arbitral Tribunal. *Revere Copper and Brass Inc. v. Overseas Private Investment Corporation.* Arbitral Award. 24 August 1978. (1978) 56 International Law Reports 258.



A. Bustami, *The Legal Relationship between Present and Future Generations*,
https://doi.org/10.1007/978-3-032-03345-1

Arbitral Tribunal. *RosInvestCo UK Ltd. v. The Russian Federation.* Award on Jurisdiction. 1 October 2007. Retrieved 3 January 2025, from https://www.italaw.com/sites/default/files/case-documents/ita0719.pdf.

Arbitral Tribunal. *Trail Smelter Arbitration.* Arbitral Award. 16 April 1938. RIAA III (1938), 1905.

Commission of Arbitration. *The Ambatielos Claim (Greece v. United Kingdom of Great Britain and Northern Ireland).* Arbitral Award. 6 March 1956. RIAA XII (1956), 83.

Committee on the Rights of the Child. *Sacchi et al. v. Argentina et al.* Petition. 23 September 2019. Retrieved 3 January 2025, from https://climatecasechart.com/non-us-case/sacchi-et-al-v-argentina-et-al/.

Committee on the Rights of the Child. *Sacchi et al. v. Argentina et al.* Amicus curiae briefs by UN Special Rapporteurs on human rights and the environment (David R. Boyd and John H. Knox). 1 September 2021. Retrieved 3 January 2025, from https://climatecasechart.com/non-us-case/sacchi-et-al-v-argentina-et-al/.

Committee on the Rights of the Child. *Sacchi et al. v. Argentina et al.* Decision. 22 September 2021. UN Doc. CRC/C/88/D/107/2019.

Eritrea-Ethiopia Boundary Commission. *Decision Regarding Delimitation of the Border between Eritrea and Ethiopia.* Arbitral Award. 13 April 2002. RIAA XXV (2002), 83.

Human Rights Committee. *Brun v. France.* Decision. 23 November 2006. UN Doc. CCPR/C/88/D/1453/2006.

Human Rights Committee. *Daniel Billy et al. v. Australia.* Complaint. 13 May 2019. Retrieved 3 January 2025, from https://climatecasechart.com/non-us-case/petition-of-torres-strait-islanders-to-the-united-nations-human-rights-committee-alleging-violations-stemming-from-australias-inaction-on-climate-change/.

Human Rights Committee. *Daniel Billy et al. v. Australia.* Decision. 22 September 2022. UN Doc. CCPR/C/135/D/3624/2019.

Human Rights Committee. *E.H.P. v. Canada.* Decision. 27 October 1982. UN Doc. CCPR/C/OP/1 at 20 (1984).

Human Rights Committee. *Ioane Teitiota v. New Zealand.* Decision. 24 October 2019. UN Doc. CCPR/C/127/D/2728/2016.

Human Rights Committee. *Portillo Cáceres v. Paraguay.* Decision. 25 July 2019. UN Doc. CCPR/C/126/D/2751/2016.

Human Rights Committee. *Roger Judge v. Canada.* Communication. 13 August 2003. UN Doc. CCPR/C/78/D/829/1998.

International Centre for Settlement of Investment Disputes. *Compañia de Aguas del Aconquijia S.A. and Vivendi Universal (formerly Compagnie Générale des Eaux v. Argentine Republic.* Decision on Annulment, Award. 3 July 2002. ICSID Case No. ARB/97/3.

International Centre for Settlement of Investment Disputes. *Corn Products International Inc. v. United Mexican States.* Decision on Responsibility, Award. 15 January 2008. ICSID Case No. ARB (AF)/04/01.

International Centre for Settlement of Investment Disputes. *Mondev International Ltd. v. United States of America.* Award. 11 October 2002. ICSID Case No. ARB (AF)/99/2 (NAFTA).

International Court of Justice. *Aegean Sea Continental Shelf Case (Greece v. Turkey).* Judgment. 19 December 1978. ICJ Reports 1978, 3.

International Court of Justice. *Application of the Convention on the Prevention and Punishment of the Crime of Genocide (Bosnia and Herzegovina v. Serbia and Montenegro).* Judgment. 26 February 2007. ICJ Reports 2007, 43.

International Court of Justice. *Application of the Convention on the Prevention and Punishment of the Crime of Genocide (Bosnia and Herzegovina v. Serbia and Montenegro).* Provisional Measures, Order. 8 April 1993. ICJ Reports 1993, 3.

International Court of Justice. *Application of the Convention on the Prevention and Punishment of the Crime of Genocide in the Gaza Strip (South Africa v. Israel).* Order. 26 January 2024. Retrieved 3 January 2025, from https://www.icj-cij.org/case/192/orders.

International Court of Justice. *Application of the Convention on the Prevention and Punishment of the Crime of Genocide (The Gambia v. Myanmar).* Preliminary Objections, Judgment. 22 July 2022. ICJ Reports 2022, 477.

International Court of Justice. *Application of the International Convention on the Elimination of All Forms of Racial Discrimination (Georgia v. Russian Federation).* Preliminary Objections, Judgment. 1 April 2011. ICJ Reports 2011, 70.

International Court of Justice. *Barcelona Traction, Light and Power Company, Limited (Belgium v. Spain), Second Phase.* Judgment. 5 February 1970. ICJ Reports 1970, 3.

International Court of Justice. *Barcelona Traction, Light and Power Company, Limited (Belgium v. Spain), Second Phase.* Separate Opinion of Judge Jessup. 5 February 1970. ICJ Reports 1970, 161.

International Court of Justice. *Case concerning Ahmadou Sadio Diallo (Republic of Guinea v. Democratic Republic of the Congo).* Preliminary Objections, Judgment. 24 May 2007. ICJ Reports 2007, 582.

International Court of Justice. *Case concerning Military and Paramilitary Activities in and against Nicaragua (Nicaragua v. United States of America).* Judgment (Merits). 27 June 1986. ICJ Reports 1986, 14.

International Court of Justice. *Case concerning the Continental Shelf (Tunisia v. Libyan Arab Jamahiriya).* Judgment (Merits). 24 February 1982. ICJ Reports 1982, 18.

International Court of Justice. *Certain Activities Carried Out by Nicaragua in the Border Area (Costa Rica v. Nicaragua) and Construction of a Road in Costa Rica along the San Juan River (Nicaragua v. Costa Rica).* Judgment. 16 December 2015. ICJ Reports 2015, 665.

International Court of Justice. *Certain Activities Carried Out by Nicaragua in the Border Area (Costa Rica v. Nicaragua), Compensation.* Judgment. 2 February 2018. ICJ Reports 2018, 15.

International Court of Justice. *Certain Activities Carried Out by Nicaragua in the Border Area (Costa Rica v. Nicaragua), Compensation.* Dissenting Opinion of Judge Ad Hoc Dugard. 2 February 2018. ICJ Reports 2018, 119.

International Court of Justice. *Certain Activities Carried Out by Nicaragua in the Border Area (Costa Rica v. Nicaragua), Compensation.* Separate Opinion of Judge Cançado Trindade. 2 February 2018. ICJ Reports 2018, 61.

International Court of Justice. *Certain Phosphate Lands in Nauru (Nauru v. Australia).* Judgment (Preliminary Objections). 26 June 1992. ICJ Reports 1992, 240.

International Court of Justice. *Corfu Channel Case (Merits).* Judgment. 9 April 1949. ICJ Reports 1949, 4.

International Court of Justice. *Dispute regarding Navigational and Related Rights (Costa Rica v. Nicaragua).* Judgment. 13 July 2009. ICJ Reports 2009, 213.

International Court of Justice. *Dispute regarding Navigational and Related Rights (Costa Rica v. Nicaragua).* Separate Opinion of Judge Sepúlveda-Amor. 13 July 2009. ICJ Reports 2009, 273.

International Court of Justice. *Dispute regarding Navigational and Related Rights (Costa Rica v. Nicaragua).* Separate Opinion of Judge Skotnikov. 13 July 2009. ICJ Reports 2009, 283.

International Court of Justice. *East Timor (Portugal v. Australia).* Judgment. 30 June 1995. ICJ Reports 1995, 90.

International Court of Justice. *Fisheries Jurisdiction (United Kingdom v. Iceland).* Merits, Judgment. 25 July 1974. ICJ Reports 1974, 3.

International Court of Justice. *Gabčíkovo-Nagymaros Project (Hungary v. Slovakia).* Judgment. 25 September 1997. ICJ Reports 1997, 7.

International Court of Justice. *Gabčíkovo-Nagymaros Project (Hungary v. Slovakia).* Separate Opinion of Vice-President Weeramantry. 25 September 1997. ICJ Reports 1997, 88.

International Court of Justice. *Gabčíkovo-Nagymaros Project (Hungary v. Slovakia).* Separate Opinion of Judge Bedjaoui. 25 September 1997. ICJ Reports 1997, 120.

International Court of Justice. *Kasikili/Sedudu Island (Botswana v. Namibia).* Judgment. 13 December 1999. ICJ Reports 1999, 1045.

International Court of Justice. *Kasikili/Sedudu Island (Botswana v. Namibia).* Declaration of Judge Higgins. 13 December 1999. ICJ Reports 1999, 1113.

International Court of Justice. *Land and Maritime Boundary between Cameroon and Nigeria (Cameroon v. Nigeria: Equatorial Guinea intervening).* Judgment. 10 October 2002. ICJ Reports 2002, 303.

International Court of Justice. *Land and Maritime Boundary between Cameroon and Nigeria (Cameroon v. Nigeria: Equatorial Guinea intervening).* Separate Opinion of Judge Al-Khasawneh. 10 October 2002. ICJ Reports 2002, 492.

International Court of Justice. *Legal Consequences Arising from the Policies and Practices of Israel in the Occupied Palestinian Territory, Including East Jerusalem.* Advisory Opinion. 19 July 2024. Retrieved 3 January 2025, from https://www.icj-cij.org/case/186/advisory-opinions.

International Court of Justice. *Legal Consequences for States of the Continued Presence of South Africa in Namibia (South West Africa) notwithstanding Security Council Resolution 276 (1970)*. Advisory Opinion. 21 June 1971. ICJ Reports 1971, 16.

International Court of Justice. *Legal Consequences for States of the Continued Presence of South Africa in Namibia (South West Africa) notwithstanding Security Council Resolution 276 (1970)*. Dissenting Opinion of Judge Gerald Fitzmaurice. 21 June 1971. ICJ Reports 1971, 220.

International Court of Justice. *Legal Consequences of the Construction of a Wall in the Occupied Palestinian Territory*. Advisory Opinion. 9 July 2004. ICJ Reports 2004, 136.

International Court of Justice. *Legal Consequences of the Separation of the Chagos Archipelago from Mauritius in 1965*. Written Statement by the Republic of Cyprus. 11 May 2018. Retrieved 3 January 2025, from https://www.icj-cij.org/public/files/case-related/169/169-20180511-WRI-01-00-EN.pdf.

International Court of Justice. *Legal Consequences of the Separation of the Chagos Archipelago from Mauritius in 1965*. Advisory Opinion. 25 February 2019. ICJ Reports 2019, 95.

International Court of Justice. *Legality of the Threat or Use of Nuclear Weapons*. Advisory Opinion. 8 July 1996. ICJ Reports 1996, 226.

International Court of Justice. *Legality of the Threat or Use of Nuclear Weapons*. Dissenting Opinion of Judge Weeramantry. 8 July 1996. ICJ Reports 1996, 429.

International Court of Justice. *Maritime Delimitation in the Area between Greenland and Jan Mayen (Denmark v. Norway)*. Separate Opinion of Judge Weeramantry. 14 June 1993. ICJ Reports 1993, 211.

International Court of Justice. *Minquiers and Ecrehos (France v. United Kingdom)*. Judgment. 17 November 1953. ICJ Reports 1953, 47.

International Court of Justice. *Minquiers and Ecrehos (France v. United Kingdom)*. Individual Opinion of Judge Levi Carneiro. 17 November 1953. ICJ Reports 1953, 85.

International Court of Justice. *North Sea Continental Shelf Cases (Germany v. Denmark; Germany v. Netherlands)*. Judgment (Merits). 20 February 1969. ICJ Reports 1969, 3.

International Court of Justice. *Obligations concerning Negotiations Relating to Cessation of the Nuclear Arms Race and to Nuclear Disarmament (Marshall Islands v. United Kingdom)*. Preliminary Objections, Judgment. 5 October 2016. ICJ Reports 2016, 833.

International Court of Justice. *Obligations concerning Negotiations Relating to Cessation of the Nuclear Arms Race and to Nuclear Disarmament (Marshall Islands v. United Kingdom)*. Dissenting Opinion of Judge Cançado Trindade. 5 October 2016. ICJ Reports 2016, 907.

International Court of Justice. *Obligations of States in Respect of Climate Change*. UNGA Request for Advisory Opinion. 29 March 2023. UN Doc. A/RES/77/276.

International Court of Justice. *Obligations of States in Respect of Climate Change*. Written Statement by the Center for International Environmental Law (CIEL),

Memorandum on the Rights of Future Generations. 20 March 2024. Retrieved 3 January 2025, from https://climatecasechart.com/non-us-case/request-for-an-advisory-opinion-on-the-obligations-of-states-with-respect-to-climate-change/.

International Court of Justice. *Obligations of States in Respect of Climate Change.* Written Statement by Greenpeace International. 21 March 2024. Retrieved 3 January 2025, from https://climatecasechart.com/non-us-case/request-for-an-advisory-opinion-on-the-obligations-of-states-with-respect-to-climate-change/.

International Court of Justice. *Obligations of States in Respect of Climate Change.* Written Statement by World's Youth for Climate Justice. 22 March 2024. Retrieved 3 January 2025, from https://climatecasechart.com/non-us-case/request-for-an-advisory-opinion-on-the-obligations-of-states-with-respect-to-climate-change/.

International Court of Justice. *Obligations of States in Respect of Climate Change.* Press Release. 12 April 2024. Retrieved 3 January 2025, from https://www.icj-cij.org/sites/default/files/case-related/187/187-20240412-pre-01-00-en.pdf.

International Court of Justice. *Obligations of States in Respect of Climate Change.* Verbatim Records. 2 December 2024. Retrieved 3 January 2025, from https://www.icj-cij.org/case/187/oral-proceedings.

International Court of Justice. *Pulp Mills on the River Uruguay (Argentina v. Uruguay).* Judgment. 20 April 2010. ICJ Reports 2010, 14.

International Court of Justice. *Pulp Mills on the River Uruguay (Argentina v. Uruguay).* Joint Dissenting Opinion of Judges Al-Khasawneh and Simma. 20 April 2010. ICJ Reports 2010, 108.

International Court of Justice. *Pulp Mills on the River Uruguay (Argentina v. Uruguay).* Separate Opinion of Judge Cançado Trindade. 20 April 2010. ICJ Reports 2010, 125.

International Court of Justice. *Questions relating to the Obligation to Prosecute or Extradite (Belgium v. Senegal).* Judgment. 20 July 2012. ICJ Reports 2012, 422.

International Court of Justice. *Request for an Examination of the Situation in Accordance with Paragraph 63 of the Court's Judgment of 20 December 1974 in the Nuclear Tests (New Zealand v. France) Case.* Dissenting Opinion of Judge Sir Geoffrey Palmer. 22 September 1995. ICJ Reports 1995, 381.

International Court of Justice. *Request for an Examination of the Situation in Accordance with Paragraph 63 of the Court's Judgment of 20 December 1974 in the Nuclear Tests (New Zealand v. France) Case.* Dissenting Opinion of Judge Weeramantry. 22 September 1995. ICJ Reports 1995, 317.

International Court of Justice. *Request for Interpretation of the Judgment of 15 June 1962 in the Case concerning the Temple of Preah Vihear (Cambodia v. Thailand) (Cambodia v. Thailand).* Separate opinion of Judge Cançado Trindade. 18 July 2011. ICJ Reports 2011, 566.

International Court of Justice. *Request for the Indication of Interim Measures of Protection, Nuclear Tests Case (Australia v. France).* Request submitted by the Government of Australia. 9 May 1973. Retrieved 3 January 2025, from https://www.icj-cij.org/public/files/case-related/58/10725.pdf.

International Court of Justice. *Request for the Indication of Interim Measures of Protection, Nuclear Tests Case (New Zealand v. France).* Order. 22 June 1973. ICJ Reports 1973,135.

International Court of Justice. *Right of Passage over Indian Territory Case (Portugal v. India).* Judgment (Merits). 12 April 1960. ICJ Reports 1960, 6.

International Court of Justice. *Rights of United States Nationals in Morocco Case (France v. United States of America).* Judgment. 27 August 1952. ICJ Reports 1952, 176.

International Court of Justice. *South West Africa, Second Phase (Ethiopia v. South Africa; Liberia v. South Africa).* Judgment. 18 July 1966. ICJ Reports 1966, 6.

International Court of Justice. *South West Africa, Second Phase (Ethiopia v. South Africa; Liberia v. South Africa).* Dissenting Opinion of Judge Tanaka. 18 July 1966. ICJ Reports 1966, 250.

International Court of Justice. *Temple of Preah Vihear (Cambodia v. Thailand).* Judgment. 15 June 1962. ICJ Reports 1962, 6.

International Court of Justice. *Western Sahara.* Advisory Opinion. 16 October 1975. ICJ Reports 1975, 12.

International Court of Justice. *Whaling in the Antarctic (Australia v. Japan: New Zealand intervening).* Judgment. 31 March 2014. ICJ Reports 2014, 226.

International Court of Justice. *Whaling in the Antarctic (Australia v. Japan: New Zealand intervening).* Separate Opinion of Judge Cançado Trindade. 31 March 2014. ICJ Reports 2014, 348.

International Criminal Tribunal for the former Yugoslavia. *Prosecutor v. Kupreškić et al.* Trial Judgment. 14 January 2000. Retrieved 3 January 2025, from https://casebook.icrc.org/case-study/icty-prosecutor-v-kupreskic-et-al.

International Tribunal for the Law of the Sea. *Request for an Advisory Opinion submitted by the Commission of Small Island States on Climate Change and International Law (COSIS).* Advisory Opinion. 21 May 2024. Retrieved 3 January 2025, from https://www.itlos.org/en/main/cases/list-of-cases/request-for-an-advisory-opinion-submitted-by-the-commission-of-small-island-states-on-climate-change-and-international-law-request-for-advisory-opinion-submitted-to-the-tribunal/.

International Tribunal for the Law of the Sea. *Responsibilities and obligations of States sponsoring persons and entities with respect to activities in the Area (Request for Advisory Opinion submitted to the Seabed Disputes Chamber).* Advisory Opinion. 1 February 2011. ITLOS Reports 2011, 10.

Permanent Court of Arbitration. *Award in the Arbitration regarding the Iron Rhine ("Ijzeren Rijn") Railway between the Kingdom of Belgium and the Kingdom of the Netherlands.* Arbitral Award. 24 May 2005. RIAA XXVII (2005), 35.

Permanent Court of Arbitration. *Dispute Concerning Access to Information Under Article 9 of the OSPAR Convention between Ireland and the United Kingdom of Great Britain and Northern Ireland.* Final Award. 2 July 2003. RIAA XXIII (2003), 59.

Permanent Court of Arbitration. *Gentini Case (of a general nature) (Italy v. Venezuela).* Arbitral Award. 13 February 1903. RIAA X (1903), 551.

Permanent Court of Arbitration. *Grisbådarna Case.* Arbitral Award. 23 October 1909. RIAA XI (1961), 147.

Permanent Court of Arbitration. *In the Matter of the Indus Waters Kishenganga Arbitration before the Court of Arbitration constituted in accordance with the Indus Waters Treaty 1960 between the Government of India and the Government of Pakistan signed on 19 September 1960 (Islamic Republic of Pakistan v. Republic of India).* Partial Award. 18 February 2013. Retrieved 3 January 2025, from https://pcacases.com/web/sendAttach/1681.

Permanent Court of Arbitration. *Island of Palmas Case (United States v. The Netherlands).* Arbitral Award. 4 April 1928. RIAA II (1928), 829.

Permanent Court of Arbitration. *North Atlantic Coast Fisheries Case (Great Britain v. United States).* Arbitral Award. 7 September 1910. RIAA XI (1910), 167.

Permanent Court of International Justice. *Case concerning the Factory at Chorzów (Germany v. Poland) (Claim for Indemnity).* Judgment (Merits). 13 September 1928. PCIJ Ser. A, No. 10.

World Trade Organization Appellate Body. *China – Measures Affecting Trading Rights and Distribution Services for Certain Publications and Audiovisual Entertainment Products.* Report of the Appellate Body. 21 December 2009. WTO Doc. WT/DS363/AB/R.

World Trade Organization Appellate Body. *United States – Import Prohibition of Certain Shrimp and Shrimp Products.* Report of the Appellate Body. 12 October 1998. WTO Doc. WT/DS58/AB/R.

## Regional Human Rights Bodies

African Commission on Human and Peoples' Rights. *Social and Economic Rights Action Center (SERAC) and Center for Economic and Social Rights (CESR) v. Nigeria (Ogoniland case).* Decision on Communication. 27 October 2001. Retrieved 3 January 2025, from http://hrlibrary.umn.edu/africa/comcases/155-96.html.

European Commission on Human Rights. *Noel Narvii Tauira and 18 others v. France.* Decision on the admissibility. 4 December 1995. Retrieved 3 January 2025, from https://hudoc.echr.coe.int/eng?i=001-87173.

European Court of Human Rights. *Case of Budayeva and others v. Russia.* Judgment. 20 March 2008. ECHR 2008-II 167.

European Court of Human Rights. *Case of Christine Goodwin v. the United Kingdom.* Judgment. 11 July 2002. ECHR 2002-VI 1.

European Court of Human Rights. *Case of Fadeyeva v. Russia.* Judgment. 9 June 2005. ECHR 2005-IV 255.

European Court of Human Rights. *Case of Golder v. the United Kingdom.* Judgment. 21 February 1975. ECHR Series A no. 18.

European Court of Human Rights. *Case of Hatton and others v. the United Kingdom.* Grand Chamber Judgment. 8 July 2003. ECHR 2003–VIII 189.

European Court of Human Rights. *Case of Loizidou v. Turkey (Preliminary Objections).* Judgment. 23 March 1995. ECHR Series A no. 310.

European Court of Human Rights. *Case of López Ostra v. Spain.* Judgment. 9 December 1994. ECHR Series A no. 303-C.

European Court of Human Rights. *Case of National Union of Belgian Police v. Belgium.* Separate Opinion of Judge Sir Gerald Fitzmaurice. 27 October 1975. Reports of Judgments and Decisions Series A no. 19.

European Court of Human Rights. *Case of Öneryildiz v. Turkey.* Judgment. 30 November 2004. ECHR 2004-XII 1-153.

European Court of Human Rights. *Case of Powell and Rayner v. the United Kingdom.* Judgment. 21 February 1990. ECHR Series A no. 172.

European Court of Human Rights. *Case of Tyrer v. The United Kingdom.* Judgment. 25 April 1978. ECHR Series A no. 26.

European Court of Human Rights. *Demir and Baykara v. Turkey.* Grand Chamber Judgment. 12 November 2008. ECHR 2008-V 333.

European Court of Human Rights. *Duarte Agostinho and others v. Portugal and 32 other States.* Complaint. 2 September 2020. Retrieved 3 January 2025, from https://climatecasechart.com/non-us-case/youth-for-climate-justice-v-austria-et-al/.

European Court of Human Rights. *Duarte Agostinho and others v. Portugal and 32 other States.* Amicus Brief by the European Commissioner for Human Rights. 5 May 2021. Retrieved 3 January 2025, from https://climatecasechart.com/non-us-case/youth-for-climate-justice-v-austria-et-al/.

European Court of Human Rights. *Duarte Agostinho and others v. Portugal and 32 other States.* Amicus Brief by UN Special Rapporteur on human rights and the environment (David R. Boyd) and UN Special Rapporteur on toxics and human rights (Marcos A. Orellana). 4 May 2021. Retrieved 3 January 2025, from https://climatecasechart.com/non-us-case/youth-for-climate-justice-v-austria-et-al/.

European Court of Human Rights. *Duarte Agostinho and others v. Portugal and 32 other States.* Judgment. 9 April 2024. Retrieved 3 January 2025, from https://hudoc.echr.coe.int/eng?i=001-233261.

European Court of Human Rights. *Greenpeace Nordic and Others v. Norway.* Complaint. 15 June 2021. Retrieved 3 January 2025, from https://climatecasechart.com/non-us-case/greenpeace-nordic-assn-v-ministry-of-petroleum-and-energy-ecthr/.

European Court of Human Rights. *Marckx v. Belgium.* Judgment. 13 June 1979. ECHR Series A no. 31.

European Court of Human Rights. *Plan B.Earth and Others v United Kingdom.* Application. 11 July 2022. Retrieved 3 January 2025, from https://climatecasechart.com/non-us-case/plan-bearth-and-others-v-united-kingdom/.

European Court of Human Rights. *Republic of Ireland v. the United Kingdom.* Judgment. 18 January 1978. Reports of Judgments and Decisions Series A no. 25.

European Court of Human Rights. *Verein Klimaseniorinnen Schweiz et al. v. Switzerland*. Judgment. 9 April 2024. Retrieved 3 January 2025, from https://hudoc.echr.coe.int/eng?i=001-233206.

Inter-American Commission on Human Rights. *Kuna Indigenous People of Madungandi and Embera Indigenous People of Bayano and their Members v. Panama*. Report. 30 November 2012. IAComHR Report N° 125/12, Case 12.354.

Inter-American Commission on Human Rights. *Petition to the Inter-American Commission on Human Rights Seeking Relief from Violations Resulting from Global Warming Caused by Acts and Omissions of the United States (Submitted by Sheila Watt-Cloutier, with the Support of the Inuit Circumpolar Conference, on Behalf of All Inuit of the Arctic Regions of the United States and Canada*. Petition. 7 December 2005. Retrieved 3 January 2025, from https://climatecasechart.com/non-us-case/petition-to-the-inter-american-commission-on-human-rights-seeking-relief-from-violations-resulting-from-global-warming-caused-by-acts-and-omissions-of-the-united-states/.

Inter-American Commission on Human Rights. *Petition to the Inter-American Commission on Human Rights Seeking Relief from Violations Resulting from Global Warming Caused by Acts and Omissions of the United States (Submitted by Sheila Watt-Cloutier, with the Support of the Inuit Circumpolar Conference, on Behalf of All Inuit of the Arctic Regions of the United States and Canada*. Decision on Inadmissibility. 16 November 2006. Retrieved 3 January 2025, from https://climatecasechart.com/non-us-case/petition-to-the-inter-american-commission-on-human-rights-seeking-relief-from-violations-resulting-from-global-warming-caused-by-acts-and-omissions-of-the-united-states/.

Inter-American Court of Human Rights. *Case of the Ituango Massacres v. Colombia (Preliminary Objections, Merits, Reparations and Costs)*. Judgment. 1 July 2006. Retrieved 3 January 2025, from https://www.corteidh.or.cr/docs/casos/articulos/seriec_148_ing.pdf.

Inter-American Court of Human Rights. *Climate Emergency and Human Rights*. Request for an Advisory Opinion. 9 January 2023. Retrieved 3 January 2025, from https://climatecasechart.com/non-us-case/request-for-an-advisory-opinion-on-the-scope-of-the-state-obligations-for-responding-to-the-climate-emergency/.

Inter-American Court of Human Rights. *Indigenous Communities of the Lhaka Honhat Association (Our Land) v. Argentina*. Judgment (Merits, Reparations and Costs). 6 February 2020. OEA Series C No. 400.

Inter-American Court of Human Rights. *Indigenous Communities of the Lhaka Honhat Association (Our Land) v. Argentina*. Partially Dissenting Opinion of Judge Pérez Manrique. 6 February 2020. OEA Series C No. 400.

Inter-American Court of Human Rights. *Indigenous Communities of the Lhaka Honhat Association (Our Land) v. Argentina*. Separate Opinion of Judge Mac-Gregor Poisot. 6 February 2020. OEA Series C No. 400.

Inter-American Court of Human Rights. *Inhabitants of La Oroya v. Peru (Preliminary Objections, Merits, Reparations and Costs)*. Judgment. 27 November 2023. OEA Series C No. 511.

Inter-American Court of Human Rights. *Juan Humberto Sánchez v. Honduras (Interpretation of the Judgment of Preliminary Objection, Merits, Reparations and Costs).* Judgment. 26 November 2003. OEA Series C No. 102.

Inter-American Court of Human Rights. *Mayagna (Sumo) Awas Tingni Community v. Nicaragua (Merits, Reparations and Costs).* Judgment. 31 August 2001. OEA Series C No. 79.

Inter-American Court of Human Rights. *Mayagna (Sumo) Awas Tingni Community v. Nicaragua (Merits, Reparations and Costs).* Joint Separate Opinion of Judges Cançado Trindade, Pacheco Gómez and Abreu Burelli. 31 August 2001. OEA Series C No. 79.

Inter-American Court of Human Rights. *Sawhoyamaxa Indigenous Community v. Paraguay (Merits, Reparations and Costs).* Separate Opinion of Judge Cançado Trindade. 29 March 2006. OEA Series C No. 125.

Inter-American Court of Human Rights. *The Effect of Reservations on the Entry into Force of the American Convention on Human Rights (Arts. 74 and 75) (Requested by the Inter-American Commission on Human Rights).* Advisory Opinion. 24 September 1982. OEA Series A No. 2.

Inter-American Court of Human Rights. *The Environment and Human Rights (Requested by the Republic of Colombia).* Advisory Opinion. 15 November 2017. Retrieved 3 January 2025, from https://www.corteidh.or.cr/docs/opiniones/seriea_23_ing.pdf.

Inter-American Court of Human Rights. *The Environment and Human Rights (Requested by the Republic of Colombia).* Concurring Opinion of Judge Sierra Porto. 15 November 2017. Retrieved 3 January 2025, from https://www.corteidh.or.cr/docs/opiniones/seriea_23_ing.pdf.

Inter-American Court of Human Rights. *The Environment and Human Rights (Requested by the Republic of Colombia).* Concurring Opinion of Judge Vio Grossi. 15 November 2017. Retrieved 3 January 2025, from https://www.corteidh.or.cr/docs/opiniones/seriea_23_ing.pdf.

Inter-American Court of Human Rights. *The Right to Information on Consular Assistance in the Framework of the Guarantees of the Due Process of Law (Requested by the United Mexican States).* Advisory Opinion. 1 October 1999. OEA Series A No. 16.

Inter-American Court of Human Rights. *Yakye Axa Indigenous Community v. Paraguay (Merits, Reparations and Costs).* Judgment. 17 June 2005. OEA Series C No. 125.

## European Union Courts

Court of First Instance of the European Communities. *Greenpeace and others v. Commission.* Order. 9 August 1995. European Case Law Identifier ECLI:EU:T:1995:147.

Court of Justice of the European Union, General Court. *Sabo and Others v Parliament and Council (EU Biomass Case).* Order. 6 May 2020. European Case Law Identifier ECLI:EU:T:2020:179.

Court of Justice of the European Union. *Carvalho and Others v Parliament and Council (People's Climate Case).* Judgment. 25 March 2021. European Case Law Identifier ECLI:EU:C:2021:252.

Court of Justice of the European Union. *Council of the European Union, European Parliament, European Commission v Vereniging Milieudefensie and Stichting Stop Luchtverontreiniging Utrecht.* Opinion of Advocate General Jääskinen. 8 May 2014. European Case Law Identifier ECLI:EU:C:2014:310.

Court of Justice of the European Union. *First Corporate Shipping.* Opinion of Advocate General Léger. 7 March 2000. European Case Law Identifier ECLI: EU:C:2000:108.

Court of Justice of the European Union. *Gemeinde Altrip, Gebrüder Hört GbR, Willi Schneider v Land Rheinland-Pfalz.* Opinion of Advocate General Cruz Villalón. 20 June 2013. European Case Law Identifier ECLI:EU:C:2013:422.

Court of Justice of the European Union. *Greenpeace and others v. Commission.* Judgment. 2 April 1998. European Case Law Identifier ECLI:EU:C:1998:153.

Court of Justice of the European Union. *Sabo and Others v Parliament and Council (EU Biomass Case).* Order. 14 January 2021. European Case Law Identifier ECLI:EU:C:2021:24.

Court of Justice of the European Union. *The Queen, on the application of David Edwards and Lilian Pallikaropoulos v Environment Agency and Others.* Opinion of Advocate General Kokott. 18 October 2012. European Case Law Identifier ECLI:EU:C:2012:645.

## Domestic Courts

Borgarting Court of Appeal. *Greenpeace Nordic Ass'n and Nature and Youth v. Ministry of Petroleum and Energy (People v. Arctic Oil).* Judgment. 23 January 2020. Retrieved 3 January 2025, from https://climatecasechart.com/non-us-case/greenpeace-nordic-assn-and-nature-youth-v-norway-ministry-of-petroleum-and-energy/.

Brussels Court of First Instance. *ASBL Klimaatzaak v. Belgian State et al.* Judgment. 17 June 2021. Retrieved 3 January 2025, from https://climatecasechart.com/non-us-case/vzw-klimaatzaak-v-kingdom-of-belgium-et-al/.

Calcutta High Court. *People United for Better Living v. State of West Bengal.* Order. 24 September 1992. 97 CWN 142.

Circuit Court of the First Circuit of the State of Hawai'i. *Navahine F. v. Hawai'i Department of Transportation.* Settlement Agreement. 17 May 2024. Retrieved 3 January 2025, from https://climatecasechart.com/case/navahine-f-v-hawaii-department-of-transportation/.

Commission on Human Rights of the Republic of the Philippines. *Requesting for Investigation of the Responsibility of the Carbon Majors for Human Rights Violations or Threats of Violations Resulting from the Impacts of Climate Change.* Petition. 12 May 2015. Retrieved 3 January 2025, from https://climatecasechart.com/non-us-case/in-re-greenpeace-southeast-asia-et-al/.

Commission on Human Rights of the Republic of the Philippines. *Requesting for Investigation of the Responsibility of the Carbon Majors for Human Rights Violations or Threats of Violations Resulting from the Impacts of Climate Change.* Memorandum. 19 September 2019. Retrieved 3 January 2025, from https://climatecasechart.com/non-us-case/in-re-greenpeace-southeast-asia-et-al/.

Commission on Human Rights of the Republic of the Philippines. *Requesting for Investigation of the Responsibility of the Carbon Majors for Human Rights Violations or Threats of Violations Resulting from the Impacts of Climate Change.* Final Report. 6 May 2022. Retrieved 3 January 2025, from https://climatecasechart.com/non-us-case/in-re-greenpeace-southeast-asia-et-al/.

Court of Appeal of Brussels. *Klimaatzaak et al. v. Belgian State et al.* Judgment. 30 November 2023. Retrieved 3 January 2025, from https://climatecasechart.com/non-us-case/vzw-klimaatzaak-v-kingdom-of-belgium-et-al/.

Federal Constitutional Court of Germany. *Climate Change (Neubauer et al.).* Complaint. 6 February 2020. Retrieved 3 January 2025, from https://climatecasechart.com/non-us-case/neubauer-et-al-v-germany/.

Federal Constitutional Court of Germany. *Climate Change (Neubauer et al.).* Order. 24 March 2021. 74 (2021) NJW 1723–1751.

Federal Court of Appeal of Canada. *La Rose et al. v. His Majesty the King of Canada et al.* Judgment. 13 December 2023. 2023 FCA 241.

Federal Court of Canada. *La Rose et al. v. Her Majesty the Queen of Canada et al.* Complaint. 25 October 2019. Retrieved 3 January 2025, from https://climatecasechart.com/non-us-case/la-rose-v-her-majesty-the-queen/.

Federal Court of Canada. *La Rose et al. v. Her Majesty the Queen of Canada et al.* Order. 27 October 2020. 2020 FC 1008.

Federal High Court of Nigeria in the Benin Judicial Division. *Gbemre v. Shell Petroleum Development Company Nigeria Ltd. et al.* Judgment. 14 November 2005. (2005) African Human Rights Law Reports 151.

Federal Regional Court of the 4th Region. *Institute of Amazonian Studies (IAS) v. Brazil.* Complaint. 8 October 2020. Retrieved 3 January 2025, from https://climatecasechart.com/non-us-case/institute-of-amazonian-studies-v-brazil/.

Federal Regional Court of the 4th Region. *Institute of Amazonian Studies (IAS) v. Brazil.* Order. 20 August 2021. Retrieved 3 January 2025, from https://climatecasechart.com/non-us-case/institute-of-amazonian-studies-v-brazil/.

Federal Supreme Court of Brazil. *Partido Socialista Brasileiro (PSB) et al. v. Brazil.* Application. 11 November 2020. Retrieved 3 January 2025, from https://climatecasechart.com/non-us-case/brazilian-socialist-party-and-others-v-brazil/.

French Constitutional Council. *In Re Climate Resilience Bill.* Amicus curiae brief by Notre Affaire à Tous Association. 15 October 2019. Retrieved 3 January 2025, from http://climatecasechart.com/non-us-case/external-contribution-to-the-french-constitutional-council/.

Hague Court of Appeal. *The State of the Netherlands v. Urgenda Foundation.* Judgment. 9 October 2018. European Case Law Identifier ECLI:NL:GHDHA:2018:2610.

Hague Court of Appeal. *Vereniging Milieudefensie et al. v. Royal Dutch Shell plc.* Statement of Defence on Appeal. 18 October 2022. Retrieved 3 January 2025, from https://climatecasechart.com/non-us-case/milieudefensie-et-al-v-royal-dutch-shell-plc/.

Hague Court of Appeal. *Vereniging Milieudefensie et al. v. Royal Dutch Shell plc.* Judgment. 12 November 2024. European Case Law Identifier ECLI:NL:GHDHA:2024:2100.

Hague District Court. *Urgenda Foundation v. The State of the Netherlands.* Judgment. 24 June 2015. European Case Law Identifier ECLI:NL:RBDHA:2015:7196.

Hague District Court. *Vereniging Milieudefensie et al. v. Royal Dutch Shell plc.* Summons. 5 April 2019. Retrieved 3 January 2025, from https://climatecasechart.com/non-us-case/milieudefensie-et-al-v-royal-dutch-shell-plc/.

Hague District Court. *Vereniging Milieudefensie et al. v. Royal Dutch Shell plc.* Judgment. 26 May 2021. European Case Law Identifier ECLI:NL:RBDHA:2021:5339.

High Court of Justice. *Plan B Earth and Others v. Prime Minister.* Complaint. 1 May 2021. Retrieved 3 January 2025, from https://climatecasechart.com/non-us-case/plan-b-earth-and-others-v-prime-minister/.

Higher Regional Court of Hamm. *Lliuya v. RWE.* Order. 30 November 2017. 2018 ZUR 118.

Lahore High Court, Lahore Judicial Department. *Asghar Leghari v. Federation of Pakistan.* Judgment. 25 January 2018. Retrieved 3 January 2025, from https://climatecasechart.com/non-us-case/ashgar-leghari-v-federation-of-pakistan/.

Lahore High Court, Lahore Judicial Department. *Maria Khan v. Federation of Pakistan.* Order. 15 February 2019. Retrieved 3 January 2025, from https://climatecasechart.com/non-us-case/maria-khan-et-al-v-federation-of-pakistan-et-al/.

Lahore High Court, Lahore Judicial Department. *Sheikh Asim Farooq v. Federation of Pakistan etc.* Judgment. 30 August 2019. Retrieved 3 January 2025, from https://climatecasechart.com/non-us-case/sheikh-asim-farooq-v-federation-of-pakistan-etc/.

National Green Tribunal at Principal Bench, New Delhi. *Ridhima Pandey v. India.* Petition. 25 March 2017. Retrieved 3 January 2025, from https://climatecasechart.com/non-us-case/pandey-v-india/.

Oslo District Court. *Greenpeace Nordic Ass'n and Nature and Youth v. Ministry of Petroleum and Energy (People v. Arctic Oil).* Plaintiff's Petition. 18 October 2016. Retrieved 3 January 2025, from https://climatecasechart.com/non-us-case/greenpeace-nordic-assn-and-nature-youth-v-norway-ministry-of-petroleum-and-energy/.

Oslo District Court. *Greenpeace Nordic Ass'n and Nature and Youth v. Ministry of Petroleum and Energy (People v. Arctic Oil).* Judgment. 4 January 2018. Retrieved 3 January 2025, from https://climatecasechart.com/non-us-case/greenpeace-nordic-assn-and-nature-youth-v-norway-ministry-of-petroleum-and-energy/.

Regional Court of Essen. *Lliuya v. RWE.* Judgment. 15 December 2016. 2017 ZUR 370.

Republic of Philippines Supreme Court. *Oposa v. Factoran.* Decision. 30 July 1993. 33 International Legal Materials 173–206.

Supreme Court of Argentina. *Asociación Civil por la Justicia Ambiental v. Province of Entre Ríos, et al. (Delta del Paraná).* Complaint. 2 July 2020. Retrieved 3 January 2025, from https://climatecasechart.com/non-us-case/asociacion-civil-por-la-justicia-ambiental-v-province-of-entre-rios-et-al/.

Supreme Court of Bangladesh. *Farooque vs. Government of Bangladesh.* Decision. 25 July 1996. 1 BLC (AD) (1996) 189.

Supreme Court of Colombia. *Future Generations v. Ministry of the Environment and Others.* Complaint. 29 January 2018. Retrieved 3 January 2025, from https://climatecasechart.com/non-us-case/future-generation-v-ministry-environment-others/.

Supreme Court of Colombia. *Future Generations v. Ministry of the Environment and Others.* Amicus Brief from Dr. James E. Hansen. 16 March 2018. Retrieved 3 January 2025, from https://climatecasechart.com/non-us-case/future-generation-v-ministry-environment-others/.

Supreme Court of Colombia. *Future Generations v. Ministry of the Environment and Others.* Decision. 5 April 2018. Retrieved 3 January 2025, from https://climatecasechart.com/non-us-case/future-generation-v-ministry-environment-others/.

Supreme Court of India. *Goa Foundation v. Union of India & Ors.* Judgment. 21 April 2014. 435 SCC 2012.

Supreme Court of India. *Vellore Citizens Welfare Forum vs Union Of India & Ors.* Judgment. 28 August 1996. 1996 5 SCR 241.

Supreme Court of Pakistan. *D. G. Khan Cement Company Ltd. v. Government of Punjab.* Judgment. 15 April 2021. Retrieved 3 January 2025, from https://climatecasechart.com/non-us-case/d-g-khan-cement-company-v-government-of-punjab/.

Supreme Court of Pakistan. *Rabab Ali v. Federation of Pakistan.* Petition. 1 April 2016. Retrieved 3 January 2025, from https://climatecasechart.com/non-us-case/ali-v-federation-of-pakistan-2/.

Supreme Court of Spain. *Greenpeace v. Spain.* Complaint. 15 December 2020. Retrieved 3 January 2025, from https://climatecasechart.com/non-us-case/greenpeace-v-spain/.

Supreme Court of Spain. *Greenpeace v. Spain.* Judgment. 20 June 2023. Retrieved 3 January 2025, from https://climatecasechart.com/non-us-case/greenpeace-v-spain/.

Supreme Court of the Netherlands. *The State of the Netherlands v. Urgenda Foundation.* Judgment. 20 December 2019. 59 International Legal Materials 4.

US Court of Appeals for the 9th Circuit. *Juliana v. United States.* Opinion. 17 January 2020. 947 F.3d 1159.

US Court of Appeals for the 9th Circuit. *Juliana v. United States.* Dissenting Opinion of Judge Staton. 17 January 2020. 947 F.3d 1175.

US Court of Appeals for the 9th Circuit. *Juliana v. United States.* Order, Rehearing en banc denied. 10 February 2021. 986 F.3d 1295.

US District Court for the District of New Jersey. *Cape May County Chapter, Inc., Izaak Walton League of America v. Tito Macchia et al.* Judgment. 16 June 1971. 329 F.Supp. 504.

US District Court for the District of Oregon, 9th Circuit. *Juliana v. United States.* Complaint. 12 August 2015. Retrieved 3 January 2025, from http://climatecasechart.com/case/juliana-v-united-states/.

US District Court for the District of Oregon, 9th Circuit. *Juliana v. United States.* Opinion and Order. 10 November 2016. 217 F. Supp. 3d 1224.

US District Court for the District of Oregon, 9th Circuit. *Juliana v. United States.* Expert Report of James E. Hansen. 28 June 2018. Retrieved 3 January 2025, from http://climatecasechart.com/case/juliana-v-united-states/.

US District Court for the Northern District of California, Oakland Division. *Native Village of Kivalina and City of Kivalina v. ExxonMobil Corporation et al.* Judgment. 30 September 2009. 663 F.Supp.2d 863.

US Supreme Court. *Sierra Club v. Morton.* Judgment. 19 April 1972. 405 U.S. 727.

Waitangi Tribunal, New Zealand. *Mataatua District Maori Council v. New Zealand.* Application. 4 July 2017. Retrieved 3 January 2025, from https://climatecasechart.com/non-us-case/mataatua-district-maori-council-v-new-zealand/.

MIX
Papier aus verantwortungsvollen Quellen
Paper from responsible sources
FSC® C105338

If you have any concerns about our products,
you can contact us on
**ProductSafety@springernature.com**

In case Publisher is established outside the EU,
the EU authorized representative is:
**Springer Nature Customer Service Center GmbH**
**Europaplatz 3, 69115 Heidelberg, Germany**

Printed by Libri Plureos GmbH
in Hamburg, Germany